What Works with Children, Adolescents, and Adults?

What Works with Children, Adolescents, and Adults? provides an up-to-date review of research on the effectiveness of psychotherapy and psychological interventions with children, adolescents, adults, people in later life, and people with intellectual and pervasive developmental disabilities.

Drawing on recent meta-analyses, systematic reviews and key research studies in psychotherapy, this volume presents evidence for:

- the overall effectiveness and cost-effectiveness of psychotherapy
- the contribution of common factors to the outcome of successful psychotherapy
- the effectiveness of specific psychotherapy protocols for particular problems.

This comprehensive, user-friendly guide will inform clinical practice, service development and policy. It will be invaluable to psychotherapists, service managers, policymakers, and researchers.

Alan Carr is Professor and Director of Clinical Psychology at University College Dublin, and Consultant Psychologist and Family Therapist at the Clanwilliam Institute Dublin.

What Works with Children, Adolescents, and Adults? offers a review of the evidence base for three handbooks published by Routledge: *The Handbook of Child and Adolescent Clinical Psychology* (Carr, 2006), *The Handbook of Adult Clinical Psychology* (Carr & McNulty, 2006), and *The Handbook of Intellectual Disability and Clinical Psychology Practice* (O'Reilly, Carr, Walsh, & McEvoy, 2007).

'*"What Works"* is an outstanding achievement. Professor Carr has effectively translated psychotherapy research findings into principles for clinical practice and public policy. This wide-ranging review is the first to examine treatment outcomes in children, adolescents, adults, the aged, and populations with special needs, providing conclusions with wisdom and reason. Must reading for students and professionals.'

Professor Michael Lambert
Department of Psychology
Brigham Young University, USA

'In recent years there has been increasing demand to move towards a clinical practice that is informed by sound research evidence and inevitably this has meant that there has also been a huge increase in the number of publications telling us what the research evidence actually says. To have a useful impact in such a crowded field is not easy but I have little doubt that *"What Works with Children, Adolescents, and Adults"* will be one of the books that people will really value reading. As in his previous publications Alan Carr draws on his impressive knowledge of the field and his ability to provide a very accessible and readable text. This is a book that will be useful both for the novice to this area providing a good overview and explanation of basic concepts as well as for the more expert reader for whom it will provide an excellent resource of up-to-date research evidence. An excellent book which I highly recommend.'

Ivan Eisler
Reader in Family Psychology and Family Therapy
Kings College, Institute of Psychiatry, London

This book offers a unique and comprehensive up-to-date review of the research into the effectiveness of psychotherapy and psychological interventions with children, adolescents, adults, people in later life, and people with intellectual and pervasive developmental disabilities. Thanks to Alan Carr who has done an admirable job. The book presents a helpful guide to mental health professionals who aim to provide evidence based interventions. I highly recommend this book as a valuable source of information for students, clinicians and researchers in clinical psychology and psychiatry.

Professor Anegen Trillingsgaard
Department of Psychology
University of Aarhus, Denmark

What Works with Children, Adolescents, and Adults?

A review of research on the effectiveness of psychotherapy

Alan Carr

Routledge
Taylor & Francis Group

LONDON AND NEW YORK

First published 2009 by Routledge
27 Church Road, Hove, East Sussex BN3 2FA

Simultaneously published in the USA and Canada
by Routledge
270 Madison Avenue, New York NY 10016

*Routledge is an imprint of the Taylor & Francis Group,
an Informa business*

© 2009 Alan Carr

Typeset in Times by RefineCatch Limited, Bungay, Suffolk
Printed and bound in Great Britain by
TJ International, Padstow, Cornwall
Paperback cover design by Sandra Heath

This publication has been produced with paper manufactured to
strict environmental standards and with pulp derived from
sustainable forests.

British Library Cataloguing in Publication Data
A catalogue record for this book is available from the British Library

Library of Congress Cataloging-in-Publication Data

Carr, Alan, Dr.
   What works with children, adolescents, and adults?: a review of
research on the effectiveness of psychotherapy / Alan Carr.
      p.; cm.
   Includes bibliographical references and index.
ISBN 978-0-415-45290-8 (hardback) – ISBN 978-0-415-45291-5 (pbk.)
1. Evidence-based psychiatry. 2. Psychotherapy–Evaluation. I. Title.
   [DNLM: 1. Psychotherapy–methods–Review. WM 420 C311w 2008]
   RC455.2.E94C37 2008
616.89'14–dc22   2008005410

ISBN: 978–0–415–45290–8 (hbk)
ISBN: 978–0–415–45291–5 (pbk)

Contents

List of figures

List of tables

Preface

'Brother, the greatest of all virtues is curiosity and the end of all desire is wisdom.'

'I might observe, not in order to combat your views but merely to continue an interesting conversation, that wisdom may not be the end of everything. Goodness and kindliness are, perhaps, beyond wisdom.'

James Stephens, *The Crock of Gold* (1912, pp. 11–12, Dublin: Gill & Macmillan)

This book provides an up-to-date review of research on the effectiveness of psychotherapy with children, adolescents, adults, people in later life, and people with intellectual and pervasive developmental disabilities. It has been written to inform clinical practice, policy concerning mental health service development, and psychotherapy research. It is my intention in this book to show that, when it comes to psychotherapy, both of the attributes valued by James Stephens's philosophers, in the quotation from *The Crock of Gold* which opens this Preface, are essential. Wisdom, drawn from a careful consideration of scientific evidence is important, but so too are goodness and kindliness, in the form of empathic, collaborative clinical practice.

What Works with Children, Adolescents, and Adults? provides a review of the evidence base for our three handbooks of clinical psychology: *The Handbook of Child and Adolescent Clinical Psychology* (Carr, 2006), *The Handbook of Adult Clinical Psychology* (Carr & McNulty, 2006), and *The Handbook of Intellectual Disability and Clinical Psychology Practice* (O'Reilly *et al.*, 2007).

I was inspired to write this book following the success of my previous volume *What Works with Children and Adolescents? A Critical Review of Psychological Interventions with Children, Adolescents and their Families*, published by Routledge in 2000. I received a great deal of positive feedback from readers on this book, and many suggestions about how to improve it. In a nutshell, these included covering research on the effectiveness of psychotherapy with adults and older adults, as well as research that focused on children and adolescents; covering research on common factors in psychotherapy, as well as research on the effectiveness of specific psycho-therapy protocols for specific problems; adopting a style that is less 'stat-istical', focusing more on authoritative narrative and quantitative reviews, and less on individual studies, with a strong focus on the clinical 'take-home message' about what works. The upshot of this feedback was to write a new book (not a second edition of *What Works with Children and Adolescents?*).

This book has the following structure. In Chapter 1, a definition of psycho-therapy is given and an outline of some of the more influential psychotherapy traditions. The way types of research evidence which support the effectiveness of psychotherapy may be organized into a hierarchy from the least to the most persuasive is also presented. The chapter closes with a discussion of various approaches that have been taken to translating evidence for the effectiveness of psychotherapy into procedures for routine clinical practice. Chapter 2 reviews results from major meta-analyses of child and adult psy-chotherapy trials which evaluate the overall effectiveness of psychotherapy with a range of problems. It also focuses on results of meta-analyses of the overall effectiveness of psychotherapy conducted within the context of four major psychotherapy traditions: psychodynamic, cognitive behavioural, humanistic, and systemic. In Chapter 3, empirical evidence for the role of factors common to all effective approaches to psychotherapy is considered. In Chapter 4, the focus is on evidence for the effectiveness of specific psycho-therapy protocols and psychological interventions for children and adoles-cents with specific types of problems. The effectiveness of psychological interventions for people with intellectual disabilities and pervasive develop-mental disorders is also considered. Chapter 5 addresses the effectiveness of psychotherapy with adults and people in later life with specific types of prob-lems. In Chapter 6 the effectiveness of additional interventions not con-sidered elsewhere in the book is discussed. In Chapter 7, conclusions on evidence for the effectiveness of psychotherapy are drawn, and the implica-tions of these for clinical practice, policy and future research are considered.

Acknowledgements

While I was working on an early draft of this book, the Irish Council for Psychotherapy (ICP) commissioned me to write a report on the effectiveness of psychotherapy. The ICP is the umbrella organization that incorporates professional associations for major psychotherapy associations in Ireland, including those representing psychoanalytic, systemic, humanistic, cognitive behavioural and constructivist traditions. I took time out from writing this book to complete the ICP report. While this book and the ICP report are distinctly different documents, the broad arguments in both are similar. I received much helpful feedback on early drafts of the report from colleagues within the ICP, for which I am extremely grateful. Both the report and this book have, no doubt, profited from this feedback.

I began writing this book while a visiting professor at the University of Aarhus in Denmark in 2005. I am grateful to Professors Anegen Trillingsgaard and Ask Elklit for their gracious invitation to Aarhus, for their hospitality during my visit, and for their generous funding. The book was concluded during a sabbatical in 2008, funded by a University College Dublin President's Research Fellowship. My thanks to UCD for this financial support.

I am grateful to the hundreds of colleagues from around the world who kindly sent me PDFs of their review papers and meta-analyses, without which the book could not have been written.

Special thanks go to colleagues from the UCD clinical psychology doctoral programme who offered support in various ways while I was writing this book, especially Muriel Keegan, Dr Barbara Dooley, Dr Eimear Farrell, Dr Gary O'Reilly, Dr Muireann McNulty, Dr Jessica Bramham, Dr Teresa Burke, Dr Michael Byrne, Dr Colleen Cormack, Dr Jennifer Hayes, Dr Suzanne Guerin, and Dr Eilis Hennessy.

The Society of Authors, as the Literary Representative of the Estate of James Stephens, kindly gave permission for the extract from *The Crock of Gold*.

Some of the more important insights into psychotherapy have arisen within the context of my family, and so to them I am particularly grateful.

Alan Carr
University College Dublin
March 2008

Chapter I

Psychotherapy, psychotherapy research, and translating science into practice

The central question addressed in this book is: In the field of psychotherapy, what works for children, adolescents, and adults? To answer this question, a wide-ranging review of scientific evidence concerning the effectiveness of psychotherapy is presented. The evidence reviewed shows, unequivocally, that psychotherapy and psychological interventions are effective in helping children, adolescents, adults, and people in later life, with a wide range of psychological difficulties. The review demonstrates that the evidence base for psychotherapy and psychological interventions is a large rigorous body of scientific work, which has clear implications for practice, policy and future research. The implications of the current psychotherapy evidence base for future research and policy is considered in Chapter 7. The main concern of this book, and a central theme of Chapters 2 to 6, is articulating the clinical practice implications of the results of research on psychotherapy and psychological interventions. As a preamble to addressing this central issue, some introductory comments will be offered in this chapter on psychotherapy, the process of conducting psychotherapy research, and ways in which research results can be used to inform practice. These comments are offered to answer such questions as: What is psychotherapy? What is psychotherapy research? How can the results of psychotherapy research be used to inform clinical practice?

This chapter opens with a cursory statement about the origins of psychotherapy and an outline of the psychodynamic, humanistic, cognitive behavioural, and systemic therapeutic traditions. A definition of psychotherapy follows. Then a hierarchy of types of evidence from the least to the most persuasive is presented. The hierarchy includes case studies, single group outcome studies, controlled group outcome studies, narrative literature reviews, and meta-analyses. In the remainder of this book, greatest weight will be given to meta-analyses and narrative reviews of controlled group outcome studies in presenting scientific evidence for the effectiveness of psychotherapy and psychological interventions. Finally, the chapter closes with a discussion of different approaches to translating scientific evidence into practice procedures; specific empirically supported treatments and general practice guidelines; and psychotherapy research programmes which focus on either common factors or specific techniques.

Origins of psychotherapy

Modern psychotherapy has a long past and a short history. Its origins date back thousands of years, but psychotherapy, as it is currently practised, is no more than a hundred years old. In the western world, the idea that skilled dialogue can alleviate distress may be traced to Socrates (469–399 BC) and the classical Greek philosophers. Sigmund Freud (1856–1939) in Austria, founder of psychoanalysis and the psychodynamic tradition, played a central role in the establishment of modern psychotherapy as a discipline and profession. Psychotherapy flourished first in North America and later in the UK, other parts of Europe and elsewhere. The humanistic, cognitive behavioural, and systemic psychotherapy traditions developed in the wake of the trail blazed by psychoanalysis and psychodynamic psychotherapy.

Psychotherapy traditions

There are over four hundred schools of psychotherapy and at least a dozen approaches that are widely practised in the English-speaking world (Corsini & Wedding, 2004). However, available research evidence – the central concern of this book – is usefully conceptualized as falling within the psychodynamic, humanistic, cognitive behavioural, and systemic psychotherapy traditions.

Psychodynamic psychotherapy

Psychodynamic (or psychoanalytic) psychotherapy is an approach to practice that has evolved from the seminal work of Sigmund Freud (Gabbard, 2004; Messer & Warren, 1998). Within this tradition, psychological disorders are assumed to arise from unresolved unconscious conflicts and the associated use of maladaptive (and unconscious) defence mechanisms. A defining feature of this approach is the use of free association and interpretation, particularly transference interpretation, to help clients become aware of how unconscious conflicts, motivations, emotions, memories, and defences underpin or maintain their current difficulties. Psychodynamic psychotherapists facilitate the working through of complex emotions arising from insights into unconscious material, and provide containment of clients' problematic internal states in this process. Psychodynamic therapy helps clients resolve unconscious conflicts and find more adaptive solutions to the problems they currently face in their lives. Within the psychodynamic tradition, the twin goals of therapy are character change and symptom alleviation. Character change involves clients transforming their habitual ways of managing internal conflictual states and important relationships in their lives.

Humanistic psychotherapy

Humanistic psychotherapy is an overarching term for a tradition that includes a variety of therapy models, for example, Carl Rogers' client-centred therapy, Fritz Perls' gestalt therapy and various experiential therapies (Cain & Seeman, 2001). Within this tradition, it is assumed that avoidance or denial of current feelings, emotions, and desires, and deliberate or inadvertent failure to take responsibility for these aspects of experience prevent personal growth and give rise to psychological symptoms. A defining feature of humanistic psychotherapy is the use of the therapeutic relationship between client and therapist as a resource in promoting personal growth. Within this relationship, the therapist is warm, empathic, and emotionally congruent. A second defining feature of the humanistic tradition is facilitating personal growth by helping clients become more fully aware of, and to take responsibility for, their immediate feelings, emotions, and wishes, which may be outside normal awareness. Within the humanistic tradition, personal growth is the main goal of therapy. Resolving presenting problems is often secondary to this superordinate goal.

Cognitive behavioural therapy

Cognitive behavioural therapy includes approaches that fall within the broad traditions of learning theory and cognitive science (Clark & Fairburn, 1997). John Watson in the USA (1878–1958) was a founding figure of behaviour therapy and Aaron T. Beck was the founder of cognitive therapy. Within this tradition it is assumed that psychological problems are inadvertently learned and maintained by cognitive and behavioural social learning processes, and these learning processes often operate outside awareness. A defining feature of cognitive behavioural therapy is the use of highly specific treatment procedures (grounded in social learning theory and cognitive science) for specific problems, such as cognitive procedures to change depressive thinking patterns or exposure to feared stimuli to overcome anxiety. A strong collaborative therapeutic relationship between clients and therapists is required to implement these highly specific treatment procedures. Resolving presenting problems is the primary goal of cognitive behavioural therapy. However, this may entail developing skills which enhance general well-being and interpersonal adjustment.

Systemic therapy

Systemic therapy includes approaches that involve working directly with couples, parents, families, and social networks (Carr, 2006). In the USA, the Englishman, Gregory Bateson (1904–1980), while not a clinician himself, inspired the development of systemic therapy and the family therapy movement. Within the systemic tradition it is assumed that psychological problems may arise for a variety of reasons, but once they occur problems may be inadvertently maintained by the way clients interact with members of their families and social systems, and the implicit or explicit belief systems and narratives that underpin these interaction patterns. Usually clients and family members are unaware of these problem-maintaining patterns of inter-action. It is also assumed that members of clients' families and social systems constitute an important resource for resolving psychological problems. A defining feature of systemic therapy is the conjoint involvement of the client and members of their family or social system in understanding and address-ing the presenting problems. Family therapy, parent training, couples therapy, sex therapy, and multisystemic therapy all fall into this category. Resolving presenting problems and enhancing relationships within the family and the client's social system are the main goals of systemic therapy.

Psychotherapy integration

In an informal way, many clinicians routinely draw on multiple psycho-therapeutic models depending upon their training experiences and prefer-ences, their clients' needs, and the therapeutic context. However, this informal eclecticism, which is part and parcel of routine clinical practice, is paralleled by formal attempts at theoretical integration. Psychotherapy integration is a growing movement within the broad field of psychotherapy (Norcross & Goldfried, 2003). At a conceptual level transtheoretical and integrative models that draw together constructs from different theories into more com-plex frameworks have been developed. These models provide coherent rationales for employing a variety of clinical techniques. They also focus attention on critical factors common to many forms of psychotherapy, such as the therapeutic alliance. For example in the UK, Anthony Ryle's (2003) cognitive analytic therapy reflects a synthesis of constructs and practices from both the psychodynamic and cognitive behavioural traditions. In the USA, Prochaska and DiClemente's (2003) transtheoretical approach provides a framework for integrating levels, stages, and processes of change associated with behavioural, cognitive, systemic, and psychodynamic psychotherapeutic models.

Psychotherapy modalities

Psychotherapy may be offered to individuals, groups, couples, families, and wider social networks. With individual therapy only a single therapist and client participate in therapy sessions (Lambert, 2004). With group therapy, one therapist, or sometimes two co-therapists, conduct therapy sessions with a group of up to ten clients (Fuhriman & Burlingame, 2001). Often group members share similar problems, such as anxiety, depression, addiction, low self-esteem, or relationship problems. Within group therapy clients benefit from support provided by other people with similar problems. They also benefit from observations and feedback of other group members and group problem solving. With couples and family therapy, one or more therapists convene sessions with a couple or family (Carr, 2006). In some instances, members of couples' or families' wider social systems may be involved. While this type of practice is centrally associated with the systemic tradition, psychodynamic, humanistic, and cognitive behavioural approaches to couples and family therapy are widely used. Multiple couples and family therapy, and parent training programmes are also widely used by psychotherapists. Within such programmes, one or more therapists convene sessions with groups of couples, families, or parents who share similar problems. As with group therapies, the benefits include the processes of group support, feedback, and problem solving. Combining individual, group, couple, and family therapy sessions, and sessions with clients' wider social system, is also widely practised. For example, in individual psychodynamic psychotherapy with depressed children, concurrent parent sessions may be conducted (Kennedy, 2004). Multisystemic therapy for delinquent adolescents involves concurrent family therapy, individual therapy, and wider systemic therapy sessions (Henggeler & Lee, 2003). Dialectical behaviour therapy for borderline personality disorder involves concurrent individual and group therapy (Robins & Chapman, 2004).

Definition of psychotherapy

All approaches to psychotherapy share a number of common features. Psychotherapy is a contractual process in which trained professionals with expert knowledge of their discipline interact with clients to help them resolve psychological problems and address mental health difficulties. Psychotherapy may be offered to children and adults on an individual, couple, family, or group basis. Psychotherapy has evolved as a way of addressing psychological problems and mental health difficulties. Common problems include depression, anxiety, conduct problems, drug and alcohol abuse, eating disorders, personality disorders, psychosis, somatic complaints of unclear origin, family conflict, psychosexual problems, relationship problems, identity problems, and adjustment difficulties arising from physical illness, violence, abuse, disabilities or life transitions. In this volume, the term psychological intervention is used to refer to specific psychotherapeutic practices, where the nuanced connotation of the former term seems more appropriate than the latter.

Psychotherapy contract

The psychotherapy process is a contractual arrangement in which therapists and clients (or patients) agree, explicitly or implicitly, to fulfil certain roles:

- *Therapist's role.* Therapists agree to offer clients a service in a professional and skilled manner and to adhere to ethical standards which safeguard clients' best interests.
- *Client's role.* Clients agree to co-operate, to the best of their ability, with treatment procedures, for example, by attending regular meetings; talking about their concerns; exploring factors related to the origin, maintenance, and resolution of their problems; taking steps to address factors that may lead to a resolution of their difficulties; and agreeing to address ambivalence about problem resolution when this occurs, as it invariably does.
- *Fees.* In private practice, the psychotherapy contract involves an agreed sessional fee paid by the client or a health insurance company. In public health services, the state covers this cost.

Psychotherapy training

To be able to offer a skilled and professional service to clients, psychotherapists typically have expert training in a particular approach to psychotherapy. In addition, many have training in another health profession such as psychology, social work, nursing, psychiatry, or occupational therapy. Some professionals in these disciplines develop psychotherapy skills as part of their basic professional training. Psychotherapy training usually involves coursework, self-reflection, supervised clinical practice, and a commitment to continuing professional development:

- *Coursework* covers material on how to conceptualize psychological problems and mental health difficulties; how to interpret relevant scientific research findings; and technical skills for conducting one or more specific types of psychotherapy for one or more specific types of problems.
- *Self-reflection* usually involves participation in personal psychotherapy to allow practitioners to develop an experiential appreciation of the psychotherapeutic process from the client's perspective.
- *Supervised clinical practice* involves working with clients under the guidance of a trained, skilled therapist for a specified number of hours and in some instances with a specified number and range of cases.
- *Continuing professional development* is central to good psychotherapy practice. This often involves supervision of cases by more experienced therapists or peer supervision with other senior colleagues. It also involves reading professional journals and books; attending professional conferences and training events; and taking part in professional committees.

Ethics

To facilitate ethical practice, psychotherapists are typically members of a professional psychotherapy association and adhere to the code of ethics of that association. Codes of ethics specify that therapists should practise within the limits of their competence, observe client confidentiality, practise in a way that prevents clients from harming themselves or others, and not taking advantage of their special relationship with their clients by, for example, avoiding having sexual or financial transactions with their clients.

Statutory registration

In many jurisdictions there is statutory registration of psychotherapists, and therapists must be licensed to practise their profession legally. Registration and licensing protects the public from charlatans, by ensuring an adequate standard of training and adherence to a code of ethics.

Psychotherapy and counselling

In some jurisdictions and services, psychotherapy is distinguished from counselling. While both counselling and psychotherapy involve engaging clients with psychological problems in a therapeutic relationship with a view to problem resolution, distinctions may be made between these professions along a number of dimensions. Psychotherapists usually have more extensive training. In Europe it takes seven years to train as a psychotherapist. It takes less to train as a counsellor. Counsellor training programmes usually focus on specific problems or client groups, for example, drug and alcohol abuse. In contrast, psychotherapy training programmes cover a broader range of problems and client groups, but usually focus on a specific therapeutic approach, for example, systemic, psychodynamic, humanistic, or cognitive behavioural therapy.

Psychotherapy and mental health professions

Distinctions may be made between the independent profession of psychotherapy on the one hand, and the mental health professions of psychology, social work, psychiatry, and psychiatric nursing on the other. The professional training of psychologists, social workers, psychiatrists, and psychiatric nurses entails an element of psychotherapy training. Some within these professions complete specialist psychotherapy training. Many within these professions offer a psychotherapy service. However, the remits of these professions cover a variety of other elements, besides psychotherapy. In contrast, in jurisdictions where an independent psychotherapy profession is recognized, practitioners within this profession usually confine their professional service predominantly to psychotherapy.

Psychotherapy in multimodal treatment programmes

In certain contexts clients may be offered psychotherapy as part of multi-modal programmes which may also include pharmacotherapy or other physical treatments. For example, a multidisciplinary adult mental health team may routinely offer a multimodal programme of psychotherapy combined with antidepressants for depression (APA, 2000b; NICE, 2004a). A multidisciplinary child and adolescent mental health team may routinely offer a multimodal programme for children with attention deficit hyper-activity disorder (ADHD) which includes parent training, school-based behavioural consultation, child-focused self-instructional training, and methylphenidate (American Academy of Child & Adolescent Psychiatry, 2007a; American Academy of Paediatrics, 2001).

Evidence-based practice

Evidence-based practice in the field of mental health and psychotherapy has evolved as part of the broader movement of evidence-based medicine (Sackett *et al.*, 1996, 2000). Evidence-based practice in medicine and psycho-therapy involves the judicious and compassionate use of the best available scientific evidence to make decisions about patient or client care. In psycho-therapy, it involves taking account of available scientific evidence about 'what works' on the one hand, and clients' unique problems, needs, rights, and preferences on the other, and making balanced compassionate judgements (APA Presidential Task Force on Evidence Based Practice, 2006; Norcross *et al.*, 2006).

Hierarchy of evidence

A central aim of this book is to present a summary of current scientific evidence for the effectiveness of psychotherapy. In this context, it is useful to organize categories of available scientific evidence into a hierarchy, from the least to the most persuasive, as illustrated in Figure 1.1. The hierarchy includes the following types of evidence:

- narrative accounts and qualitative analyses of therapy with individual cases
- single group outcome studies
- controlled comparative group outcome studies and controlled single case design studies
- narrative reviews of controlled outcome studies
- meta-analyses of controlled outcome studies.

Stronger
evidence

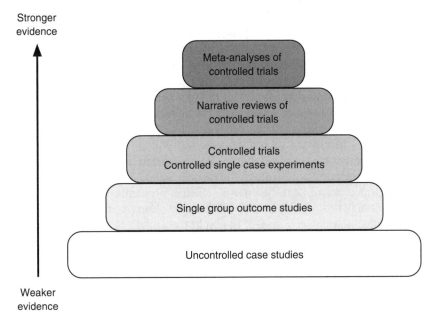

Weaker
evidence

Figure 1.1 Hierarchy of evidence.

A description of each category will be outlined below. In later chapters, evidence from higher levels in this hierarchy will be given priority. Highest priority will be given to results of meta-analyses which quantitatively summarize results of many controlled trials involving the treatment of many hundreds of clients.

Case studies

In narrative accounts and qualitative analyses of therapy with individual cases, descriptions and explanations are given of the way therapy was conducted and the impact of therapy on clients' problems or symptoms. Such studies offer important insights into the details of how specific types of psychotherapy may be conducted with specific cases. In all psychotherapy traditions pioneers began by reporting case studies. Case studies are useful for teaching the subtle skills of psychotherapy (Wedding & Corsini, 2005). The main limitation of much case study evidence is that any observed improvements in clients' problems may be due to idiosyncratic responses of individual cases, biased observation by the psychotherapist, invalid or unreliable assessment of clients' problems, or to the passage of time.

Single group outcome studies

Single group outcome studies provide more convincing evidence of the effectiveness of psychotherapy. In such studies, a group of cases with similar sorts of problems is assessed before and after treatment with a standard set of assessment instruments. Because data are collected on more than one case, single group outcome studies rule out the possibility that improvement is the idiosyncratic response of a single case. Where structured interviews are used to assess outcome, and where pre-therapy and post-therapy assessment interviews are conducted by different members of a research team, usually interviewers are unaware of whether a client has been treated or not, and this prevents interviewer bias from influencing results. Also, in these studies, well-developed scientific measures of clients' problems or symptoms are made, so it may be said with confidence that any observed improvements have been validly and reliably assessed. In psychotherapy studies, self-report questionnaires and structured clinical interviews are the most commonly used assessment measures. Measures of a wide range of problems – for example, anxiety, depression, drug abuse, and psychotic symptoms – have been developed. Typically an instrument yields one or more diagnoses or problem scale scores. For these sorts of instruments to be considered scientifically valid, they must have been shown (in instrument development studies) to measure what they purport to measure. So a valid measure of depression has been shown in development studies to measure depression, and not boredom or exhaustion. For assessment instruments to be considered reliable, they must yield the same score on two consecutive assessment occasions, within a brief time period (for example, two weeks). This is referred to as test–retest reliability. For interviews to be considered reliable, two raters should provide similar ratings for the same client. This is referred to as interrater reliability. The main shortcoming with evidence based on single group outcome studies is that they leave open the possibility that improvements in clients' functioning may be due to the passage of time.

Comparative group outcome studies

To rule out the possibility that observed improvements in clients' problems following psychotherapy are due to the passage of time, gains made by treated cases are compared with gains made by untreated cases in a control group. In psychotherapy studies, clients in control groups usually do not receive any treatment, or receive routine clinical management of their problems, but not the form of psychotherapy being evaluated in the study. An example of results from a comparative group outcome study is given in Figure 1.2. After therapy, the average score of the group that received couples therapy for chronic depression was lower than that before therapy, and this gain was maintained at follow-up a year later. Overall this pattern of

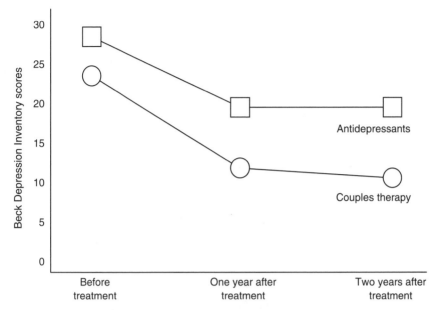

Figure 1.2 Improvement in mean symptom scores on the Beck Depression Inventory for adults with chronic depression receiving systemic couples therapy or anti-depressants before treatment, one year after treatment, and two years after treatment.

Adapted from: Leff *et al.* (2000). The London Depression Intervention Trial. Randomised controlled trial of antidepressants versus couple therapy in the treatment and maintenance of people with depression living with a partner: clinical outcomes and costs. *British Journal of Psychiatry*, 177, 95–100.

improvement was better than that for cases treated with antidepressants. In Figure 1.3, a second example shows that at six years follow-up, a higher proportion of adolescents who received family therapy for anorexia were recovered, compared with the control group who received individual therapy. In comparative group outcome studies the probability that differences in improvement shown by the treatment and control groups could have occurred due to chance is evaluated with statistical tests. In the psycho-therapy outcome research literature, by convention, a treatment is considered to be effective if the differences in improvement rates between treatment and control groups could only have occurred by chance in 5 cases out of 100. This probability level is referred to as $p < .05$. Thus, in a comparative group outcome study, if the treatment group improved more than the control group and this difference was statistically significant, we may conclude that psycho-therapy led to greater improvement than would have occurred due to the passage of time, and that the extent of this improvement was greater than could have occurred due to chance. There are many variations of the basic

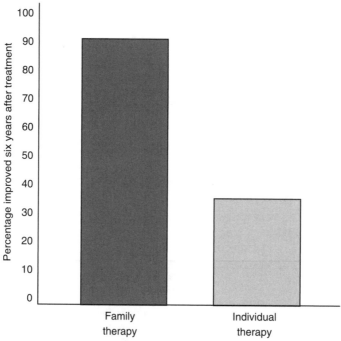

Figure 1.3 Improvement rates at six years follow-up for adolescents with anorexia who received family or individual therapy.

Adapted from: Eisler *et al.* (1997). Family and individual therapy in anorexia nervosa: a 5-year follow-up. *Archives of General Psychiatry*, 54, 1025–1030.

controlled treatment outcome study, but the gold standard is the randomized controlled trial.

Randomized controlled trials

In randomized controlled trials, cases are randomly assigned to treatment and control groups, to rule out the possibility that differences in improvement rates are due to responsive and unresponsive cases having been systematically assigned to treatment and control groups. Where randomization is not possible, cases in treatment and control groups may be matched on important variables such as problem type, severity, and chronicity; number of co-morbid problems; and demographic factors such as age, gender, socio-economic status, marital status, and so forth. In some randomized controlled trials the effectiveness of a new treatment is compared with 'treatment as usual'; with a placebo treatment; or two novel treatments are compared. There is a tradition in medical randomized controlled trials to use 'sugar pills' as placebos, so patients in the control group do not receive the medicine which is being evaluated, but believe that they are being helped since they are receiving what looks like an active treatment (the placebo sugar pill). In some psychotherapy treatment outcome studies, clients receive placebo therapy. This usually involves having as much contact with a therapist as those in the treatment group, but receiving some innocuous, though credible, placebo psychotherapy, for example, engaging in 'intellectual discussions' about plausible topics. When placebo control groups are included in randomized controlled trials, they rule out the possibility that treatment gains were due simply to therapist contact rather than psychotherapeutic techniques and processes.

Controlled single case designs

Just as the randomized controlled trial is the gold standard for group outcome studies of psychotherapy effectiveness, controlled single case studies are the gold standard for case studies of psychotherapy effectiveness. Such designs have been extensively used in investigating the impact of specific treatments in cases of intellectual and pervasive developmental disabilities such as autism. The multiple baseline across cases is a good example of such a design. In this type of study, frequent reliable and valid measurements of a central problem are made with a small number of cases (usually three to five) until all cases show a stable baseline. At this point, the first case, but not the others, commence psychotherapy. Once the first case shows significant and sustained improvement, then the next case begins psychotherapy. The same pattern is followed in initiating treatment with other cases in the study. A graph of the results from such a (hypothetical) study is given in Figure 1.4. From the graph it may be seen that at the start of the study all three cases had stable baselines and improvement in each case coincided with the onset of therapy. If only the first case had been treated, there would have been no way of knowing whether improvement was due to treatment or the passage of time. But the fact that the untreated cases showed no improvement until treatment began provides evidence for effectiveness of treatment.

Narrative reviews of outcome studies

While an individual treatment outcome study with positive results provides evidence that in one context a specific form of psychotherapy was effective for a group of clients with a specific type of problem, a narrative review of outcome studies synthesizes the results of many outcome studies. In a narrative review of group outcome studies of psychotherapy with specific problems, systematic computer-based and manual literature searches are conducted to identify treatment outcome studies. The reviewer then summarizes key findings of these studies and draws conclusions about the effectiveness of specific forms of psychotherapy with specific types of problems. Narrative reviews of treatment outcome studies provide more convincing evidence than the results

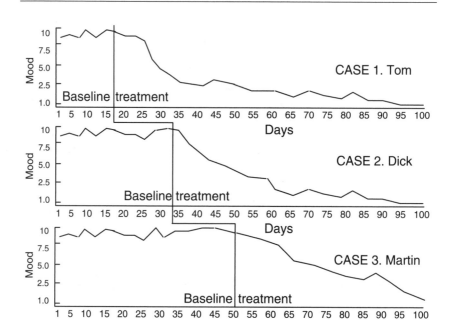

Figure 1.4 Graph of results of multiple baseline across cases in a psychotherapy outcome study.

of a single outcome study, because they show evidence that positive results have or have not been replicated. However, the conclusions drawn in narrative reviews of many treatment outcome studies are inevitably biased by the conscious and unconscious prejudices of the reviewer.

Meta-analyses of controlled outcome studies

Meta-analysis is a systematic and quantitative approach to reviewing evidence from multiple treatment outcome studies which aims to overcome the impact of reviewer bias on the review process. Meta-analyses provide a quantitative index of the effectiveness of psychotherapy, based on large numbers of controlled studies which include large numbers of cases. In a meta-analysis of group outcome studies, effect sizes are calculated for each study and then averaged across all studies. In later chapters, wherever possible, results of meta-analyses will be presented as evidence for the effectiveness of psychotherapy.

Effect sizes

Average effect sizes, calculated in meta-analyses, express quantitatively the degree to which treated groups improved more than the control groups. A graphic explanation of the calculation of an effect size is given in Figure 1.5 and a system for interpreting average effect sizes from meta-analyses is given in Table 1.1. Effect sizes of .8 and above are considered large. In later chapters, in most instances where average effect sizes from meta-analyses are reported, the approximate success rate associated with the effect size will be given, based on column 4 in Table 1.1. In some instances based on column 3 of Table 1.1, the percentage of untreated cases in the control group that the average treated case fares better than after treatment, will be given. In some instances, effect sizes are based on a comparison of pre-treatment and post-treatment means, rather than on post-treatment means of treatment and control groups. In subsequent chapters, where this occurs, it will be explicitly noted and such effect sizes will be referred to as pre–post-treatment effect sizes.

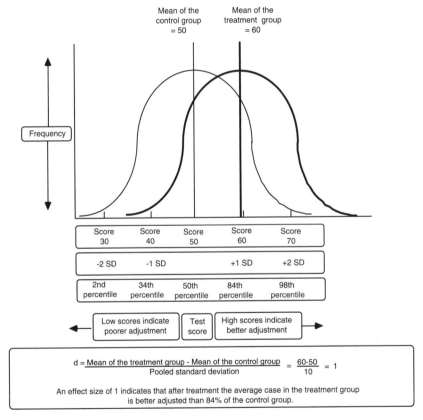

Figure 1.5 Graphic representation of an effect size of 1.

Table 1.1 Interpretation of effect sizes

Effect size d	Cohen's designation[1]	Percentage of untreated cases that the average treated case fares better than[2]	Success rate for treated group[3]	Success rate for untreated group[3]	Percentage of outcome variance accounted for by treatment[4]	Correlation with outcome[5]
1.0		84	72	28	20	.44
.9		82	71	29	17	.41
.8	Large	79	69	31	14	.37
.7		76	67	33	11	.33
.6		73	64	36	8	.29
.5	Medium	69	62	38	6	.24
.4		66	60	40	4	.20
.3		62	57	43	2	.15
.2	Small	58	55	45	1	.10
.1		54	53	47	0	.00

Note: This table is adapted from Wampold (2001, p. 53).
1. From Cohen (1988).
2. From Glass (1976).
3. From Rosenthal and Rubin's (1982) Binomial Effect Size Display, assuming overall success rate of .5, success rate for treated cases is .5 correlation with outcome/2, and success rate for untreated cases is .5-correlation with outcome/2.
4. From Rosenthal (1994, p. 239), percentage of variance = $d^2/(d^2 + 4)$.
5. From Wampold (2001, p. 53), correlation = $\sqrt{d^2/(d^2 + 4)}$.

Converting odds ratios to effect sizes

Where outcomes of controlled trials are reported dichotomously as treatment successes or failures the results of meta-analyses are often expressed as odds ratios. These can be converted to effect sizes by dividing the natural log of the odds ratio by 1.81 (Chinn, 2000). In later chapters, results of meta-analyses which have been reported as odds ratios will be converted to effect sizes, since these can be interpreted using Table 1.1 and understood using Figure 1.5.

Methodological factors that influence effect sizes

When interpreting the results of meta-analyses it is important to keep in mind that a number of methodological factors have been found to influence average effect sizes. These include the methodological rigour of the studies; the type of outcome measure used to calculate effect sizes; the use of weighting procedures in calculating average effect sizes; and researcher allegiance to specific forms of therapy. Each of these issues deserves comment.

Methodological quality of studies

In the first major meta-analysis of psychotherapy outcome studies, Mary Smith and Gene Glass's team (Smith & Glass, 1977; Smith *et al.*, 1980) found that the average effect size for high quality studies was .88, while that for moderate and low quality studies was .78. Thus, Smith and Glass concluded that the strongest evidence for the effectiveness of psychotherapy comes from meta-analysis of the most scientifically rigorous treatment outcome studies. In studies of high methodological quality, homogeneous cases with clearly defined problems were randomly assigned to groups and assessed with reliable and valid instruments before and after treatment. Poor quality studies had some or all of the following methodological problems: lack of case homogeneity, vague problem specification, poor reliability and validity of assessment instruments, and lack of randomization.

Reactivity of measures

In routine clinical practice, and in treatment outcome studies, psychotherapy leads to greater changes on 'reactive' measures of specific problems the therapy was designed to address than on broad measures of overall adjustment. Therefore, it is not surprising that the results of meta-analyses are affected by the types of outcome measures used to calculate effect sizes. For example, Shadish *et al.* (2000) in a meta-analysis of 90 studies found larger average effect sizes for measures of specific problems, compared with measures of general adjustment.

Weighting effect sizes by sample size

Hedges and Olkin (1985) have argued that it is more valid to weight effect sizes for each study, based on the number of participants, with greater weight being given to studies involving more participants. When this statistical refinement is used to compute overall effect sizes in meta-analyses, smaller effect sizes are obtained. For example, Shadish *et al.* (1997) in a reanalysis of data from a number of previous meta-analyses (including Smith *et al.*'s 1980 seminal study) found that effect sizes based on unweighted procedures were in the .7–.8 range, whereas when weighting procedures were used, effect sizes between .4 and .6 were obtained. It is important to keep this in mind, since prior to the mid-1990s weighted effect sizes were rarely reported. In later chapters, it is noted where unweighted effect sizes have been used.

Researcher allegiance

Smith *et al.* (1980), in their seminal meta-analysis, found average effects of .95 and .66 for types of psychotherapies favoured and not favoured by researchers, respectively. The difference between these two effect sizes of .29 is a rough estimate of allegiance effects. Thus, therapy approaches favoured by researchers were evaluated more positively. Gaffan *et al.* (1995) in a meta-analysis of studies of cognitive therapy for depression found that allegiance effects decreased from the 1970s to the 1990s. This is partly due to researchers giving non-favoured therapies a 'fair trial' by, for example, having such therapies delivered by skilled therapists following a well-defined protocol for the alternative therapy.

Efficacy and effectiveness treatment outcome studies

A useful distinction is made between efficacy and effectiveness in comparative group outcome studies (Cochrane, 1972). In efficacy studies clients with a specific type of problem (and no co-morbid difficulties) are randomly assigned to treatment and control groups. The treatment group receives a pure and potent form of a very specific type of psychotherapy from specialist psychotherapists in practice centres of excellence. Efficacy studies are typically conducted at university affiliated centres, with carefully selected clients who meet stringent inclusion and exclusion criteria. For example, often patients with co-morbid substance abuse and personality disorders or self-harming behaviour are excluded in efficacy studies of treatments for depression. Therapists are highly trained, intensively supervised, have small caseloads, and the fidelity with which they offer treatment is scientifically checked by rating the degree to which recordings of therapy sessions conform to treatment protocols specified in therapy manuals. Effectiveness studies, in contrast, are conducted in routine clinical settings, rather than centres of excellence, with typical therapists carrying normal caseloads, offering treatment to clients who are representative of typical referrals, and while therapy manuals and supervision are often employed, there is a greater degree of flexibility about their use than in efficacy studies. Efficacy studies tell us how well treatments work under ideal conditions. Information about the impact of treatments under routine conditions is provided by effectiveness studies. Effectiveness studies tell us how well manualized therapies work when flexibly implemented by regular psychotherapists with a normal level of supervision, with clients who have a main presenting problem, along with additional complex co-morbid difficulties. It is useful to think of effectiveness and efficacy studies as representing the extremes of a continuum along which a variety of treatment outcome study designs fall.

Evidence-based practice and practice-based evidence

The distinction between efficacy and effectiveness studies is paralleled by the distinction between evidence-based practice and practice-based evidence

(Barkham & Mellor-Clark, 2003). Efficacy studies are one source of scientific information for evidence-based practice. They indicate how well treatments work under ideal conditions. Practice-based evidence is a second source of information that can scientifically inform practice. Practice-based evidence indicates how well treatments work under routine conditions. With practice-based evidence, for all clients attending routine psychotherapy services, a standard assessment is completed before treatment and after treatment (or at regular intervals). These data are periodically analysed to give information on improvement rates in groups or subgroups of psychotherapy clients under normal health service conditions. In the UK, the 34-item Clinical Outcome Routine Evaluation (CORE) is a free brief but comprehensive assessment instrument widely used to collect data in practice research networks, i.e. groups of routine psychotherapy services linked to a university-based research team (Audin et al., 2001; Barkham et al., 1998; CORE System Group, 1999; Evans et al., 2000, 2002; Mellor-Clark & Barkham, 2006). In North America the Outcome Questionnaire (OQ-45; Lambert et al., 2004) and the Outcome Rating Scale (ORS; Miller et al., 2003) have been used for similar purposes.

Translating scientific evidence into clinical practice

There is no single correct process for translating scientific evidence into practice procedures for routine clinical use with clients. However, a number of solutions have been proposed, some examples of which are presented in Table 1.2. At one extreme there are those who favour the identification of specific empirically supported treatment protocols using stringent criteria which take into account highly specific types of evidence, notably randomized controlled trials (Chambless & Ollendick, 2001). At the other extreme there are those who support the use of multiple sources of evidence to inform the development of general practice guidelines with differing 'strengths' of implication for practice (Wolpert et al., 2006). In North America this has evolved into a dialogue between those within the cognitive behavioural tradition who champion empirically supported treatment (EST) protocols as the way forward, and psychotherapists from other traditions who propose more flexible alternatives (Goodheart et al., 2006; Norcross et al., 2006).

Empirically supported treatments

Within the American Psychological Association, the division of clinical psychology has championed the development of empirically supported treatments (ESTs). Chambless et al. (1998) have drawn up a list of such treatments using what have come to be known as the Chambless criteria. These are set out in Table 1.2. The Chambless criteria have been used to

Table 1.2 Translating scientific evidence into clinical practice

Chambless et al.'s (1998) APA Division 12 task force criteria for Empirically Established Treatments (ESTs)
Also used for treatments for older adults (Gatz et al., 1998) and treatments for chronic pain (Wilson & Gil, 1996)

Well-established treatment	I. At least two good between group studies show the treatment is efficacious by A, B or both
	  A. Superior to pill or psychotherapy placebo or other treatment
	  B. Equivalent to established treatment (in study with adequate sample size)
	or
	II. A large series of single-case design experiments show the treatment is efficacious by
	  A. Using good experimental design and
	  B. Comparison with another treatment
	and
	III. Treatment is clearly described or a manual is used
	and
	IV. Sample characteristics are specified
	and
	V. At least two research teams find the treatment is efficacious

Probably efficacious treatments	I. Two studies show treatment outcome is superior to that of waiting-list control groups or II. One or more studies meet criteria IA or IB, III, IV, but not V for well-established treatment or III. A small series of single-case design experiments show the treatment is efficacious
Experimental treatments	Treatments not yet tested in studies that meet criteria for well-established or probably efficacious treatments
Translation rule:	**Translate research evidence into practice, by using treatment protocols for well-established treatments first, and if that is not possible, using those for treatments that are probably efficacious.**

Journal of Paediatric Psychology's criteria for Empirically Established Treatments (Spirito, 1999)

Well-established treatment	Same as APA Division 12 task force criteria
Probably efficacious treatments	Same as APA Division 12 task force criteria

Promising interventions	I. At least one well-controlled between group study and one less well-controlled group study by different investigators shows the treatment is efficacious
	or
	II. A small series of single-case design experiments meet criteria for well-established treatments
	or
	III. At least two or more well-controlled between group studies by the same investigator show the treatment is efficacious
Experimental treatments	Same as APA Division 12 task force criteria
	Translate research evidence into practice, by using treatment protocols for clearly effective treatments first, and then those for promising treatments or those with limited support
Translation rule:	**Translate research evidence into practice, by using treatment protocols for well-established treatments first, and if that is not possible, using those for treatments that are probably efficacious, or promising interventions.**

Roth and Fonagy's (2005) criteria for effective and promising treatments from *What Works for Whom?*

Clearly effective treatments	I. At least two between group studies show the treatment is superior to a control or other treatment condition
	or
	II. A single high quality randomized controlled trial shows the treatment is effective and in this trial
	A. Therapists follow a manual or clearly described therapeutic method in which other therapists could be trained
	B. The patient group is clearly described
Promising, limited support treatments	I. Treatment must be innovative and a promising line of intervention
	or
	II. Treatment is widely practised and with only limited support for effectiveness
Translation rule:	**Translate research evidence into practice, by using treatment protocols for clearly effective treatments first, and if that is not possible, using those for promising treatments or those for treatments with limited support.**

Nathan and Gorman's (2002) six categories of evidence from *A Guide to Treatments that Work*

| Type 1 studies | Randomized prospective clinical trials with random assignment, blind assessment, inclusion and exclusion criteria, state-of-the-art diagnostic methods, adequate sample size for statistical power, and clearly described statistics |

(Continued overleaf)

Table 1.2 continued

Type 2 studies	Like Type 1 studies but with some methodological flaws
Type 3 studies	Open uncontrolled treatment evaluation trials, retrospective case control trials
Type 4 studies	Meta-analyses
Type 5 studies	Narrative reviews
Type 6 studies	Case studies, essays, and opinion papers
Translation rule:	**Translate research evidence into practice, by using treatment protocols from Type 1 studies first, and if that is not possible, sequentially using those from lower levels in the evidence hierarchy.**

Wolpert *et al.*'s (2006) six categories of evidence and four levels of strength of practice implications from *Drawing on the Evidence*

Evidence category 1a	Evidence from meta-analyses of randomized controlled trials
Evidence category 1b	Evidence from at least one randomized controlled trial
Evidence category 2a	Evidence from at least one controlled study without randomization
Evidence category 2b	Evidence from at least one quasi-experimental study
Evidence category 3	Evidence from descriptive studies such as comparative studies, corelational studies, and case-control studies
Evidence category 4	Evidence from expert committee reports, opinion papers, or clinical papers
Practice implication strength A	Directly based on category 1 evidence
Practice implication strength B	Directly based on category 2 evidence or extrapolated from category 1 evidence
Practice implication strength C	Directly based on category 3 evidence or extrapolated from category 2 evidence
Practice implication strength D	Directly based on category 4 evidence or extrapolated from category 3 evidence
Translation rule:	**Translate research evidence into practice, by using protocols with practice implication strength A first, and if that is not possible, sequentially using those from lower levels in the practice implication strength hierarchy.**

Note: Chambless *et al.* (1998). Update on empirically validated therapies, II. *The Clinical Psychologist*, 51, 3–16.

Gatz *et al.* (1998). Empirically validated psychological treatments for older adults. *Journal of Mental Health & Aging*, 4, 9–46.

Wilson, J. J. & Gil, K. M. (1996). The efficacy of psychological and pharmacological interventions for the treatment of chronic disease-related and non-disease-related pain. *Clinical Psychology Review*, 16, 573–597.

Spirito, A. (1999). Empirically supported treatments in pediatric psychology [Special Issue]. *Journal of Pediatric Psychology*, 24, 87–174.

Roth, T. & Fonagy, P. (2005). *What Works for Whom? A Critical Review of Psychotherapy Research* (Second Edition). New York: Guilford Press.

Nathan, P. & Gorman, J. (2002). *A Guide to Treatments that Work* (Second Edition). New York: Oxford University Press.

Wolpert *et al.* (2006). *Drawing on the Evidence: Advice for Mental Health Professionals Working with Children and Adolescents*. London: CAMHS.

evaluate psychological treatments based on the weight of empirical support from efficacy studies. A distinction is made between treatments which are well established, and those which are probably efficacious. The benefits of well-established treatments have been shown in independent controlled studies of homogeneous client groups in which treatment manuals were used, to exceed those of another treatment or a placebo condition which controls for the amount of therapist contact and expectancy of improvement. In contrast, treatments classified as probably efficacious have been shown in controlled studies to produce benefits greater than those which occur for a waiting list control group. Treatments that do not meet either of these criteria are classified as experimental.

Are ESTs suitable for routine practice?

ESTs have been criticized for being brief, manualized interventions, based on efficacy studies with monosymptomatic clients, unsuited to the multiple needs of routine clients who present with complex co-morbid problems and issues of diversity (Sue, 2003; Westen *et al.*, 2004). However, there is a small but growing literature which shows that ESTs can be transported into routine clinical settings, and that in these settings they have positive impacts, but less positive than in randomized controlled efficacy trials (Chambless & Ollendick, 2001). It has also been found that they are slightly more effective than treatments which do not meet the Chambless criteria for being empirically supported (Weisz *et al.*, 2006).

Why so few psychodynamic, systemic, and humanistic ESTs?

Most psychotherapy protocols for children and adults classified as ESTs, fall within the cognitive behavioural therapy tradition (Chambless & Ollendick, 2001). The poor representation of psychodynamic, humanistic, and systemic therapies on the list of ESTs reflects the fact that fewer placebo controlled or comparative treatment outcome research trials have been conducted within these other therapeutic traditions. Many from within these traditions have argued that the criteria for ESTs are restrictive and could disenfranchise therapies which fall outside the cognitive behavioural tradition (e.g. Bohart *et al.*, 1998). Evidence from less stringently controlled studies and meta-analyses supports the effectiveness of systemic, psychodynamic, and humanistic therapies. Some of this evidence will be reviewed in later chapters. The dearth of randomized placebo controlled or comparative trials of systemic, psychodynamic, and humanistic psychotherapy justifies prioritizing these sorts of studies in a future research agenda.

Empirically supported principles of change

The criteria for listing ESTs are open to abuse by groups that wish to aggressively market a trademarked treatment protocol that is simply well-established treatment procedures repackaged and supported with the results of two controlled efficacy trials. To avoid this 'old wine in new bottles' problem, it is probably more useful for both scientists and clinicians to identify empirically supported principles of change that can be incorporated into individually tailored formulation-based treatment programmes, rather than EST packages (Castonguay & Beutler, 2006; Rosen & Davison, 2003). These empirically supported principles of change will probably involve using treatment procedures that aim to reduce problem-maintaining factors or enhance protective factors that have been identified in basic research on the problem in question.

Statistical error in specifying ESTs

Lists of ESTs in Chambless et al.'s (1998) paper are based on studies in which the outcome of treatment and comparison groups were compared by conducting statistical tests on assessment instrument scores. In all of these statistical tests, the aim was to determine if the differences between treatment and control groups were statistically significant, or could have occurred due to chance. A central assumption of these statistical tests is that the scores of all individuals are independent. If the scores are not independent, then it increases the chance of detecting spurious treatment-specific intergroup differences (Type 1 error). For example, if there is good cohesion in a psychotherapy group and all members support each other, give each other honest interpersonal feedback, and practise new skills together, the better outcome of the group may be due to this, rather than the treatment protocol. Similarly, if one member of a treatment group skips sessions or gives dishonest interpersonal feedback, others may follow suit, and the poorer scores of the group may be due to this process, rather than to the therapy described in the treatment manual. These dependencies associated with group-administered treatments, when not properly accounted for, can increase Type I errors dramatically. Thirty-three of the 101 studies on Chambless et al.'s (1998) EST list involved group-administered treatments. None of these 33 included appropriate data analyses. After making corrections for these improper analyses, Baldwin et al. (2005) found that only 12.4% to 68.2% of tests that were originally reported as significant remained statistically significant, depending on what assumptions were made about how large the dependencies among observations really were. Of the 33 studies, 6 to 19 studies no longer had any statistically significant results after correction. Thus, a number of ESTs lack empirical support.

A final word on ESTs

ESTs have been useful in highlighting the fact that there are quite a number of psychotherapy protocols which are efficacious for specific problems. They have also underlined the need for studies evaluating the efficacy of psychotherapy protocols from the psychodynamic, systemic, and humanistic traditions. However, ESTs have been problematic in suggesting to policymakers and funders that psychotherapy protocols which do not meet EST criteria are ineffective. A large body of practice-based evidence, effectiveness studies, and meta-analyses (reviewed in later chapters) supports the effectiveness of systemic, psychodynamic, and humanistic approaches to therapy. Chambless *et al.*'s (1998) list of ESTs, and the criteria that define them, make it more likely that policymakers and funders will not take account of this evidence. From a scientific perspective, ESTs do not help us find the 'active ingredients' of effective protocols. It may therefore be more fruitful in the future to develop criteria for specifying empirically supported principles of change for specific problems, and to develop general guidelines for incorporating these into routine psychotherapy practice. Of course such a project focusing on the role of specific principles of change for specific problems must be complemented by a focus on factors common to all forms of psychotherapy.

Broad treatment guidelines

The organization of evidence into a hierarchy based on the methodological rigour and scale of the research and the use of evidence from all levels of the hierarchy to inform practice guidelines with different strengths is an alternative to identifying empirically supported treatment protocols. Guideline development allows evidence from both efficacy and effectiveness studies to be used to inform practice. It also allows practice-based evidence and results of effectiveness studies to be given consideration in making treatment decisions. This is the approach taken by a UK-based group in *Drawing on the Evidence* (Wolpert *et al.*, 2006), and others (e.g. Castonguay & Beutler, 2006). It is also the approach favoured in this book. Widely cited evidence-based clinical practice guidelines from the USA and UK are given in Table 1.3.

Common factors and specific therapeutic techniques

There has been an ongoing debate among psychotherapy researchers between those who point to the critical role of common factors (especially the therapeutic alliance) in contributing to the efficacy of psychotherapy (Norcross, 2002), and those who point to the importance of specific techniques (Chambless & Ollendick, 2001). Research on common factors (reviewed in Chapter 3) provides evidence for important client and therapist characteristics and

Table 1.3. Sources for evidence-based clinical practice guidelines

National Institute for Clinical Excellence (NICE)	*http://www.nice.org.uk/*. Includes guidelines for depression in adults and children, bipolar disorder, anxiety, OCD, PTSD, eating disorders, schizophrenia, self-harm, violence, dementia, ADHD, drug abuse, personality disorders, child abuse, alcohol use, smoking cessation.
British Psychological Society Centre for Outcomes Research and Effectiveness in association with: UK Council For Psychotherapy; Royal College of Psychiatrists; British Confederation of Psychiatrists; Royal College of General Practitioners; Mind; Depression Alliance; UK Advocacy Network	Department of Health (2001). *Treatment Choice in Psychological Therapies and Counselling.* London: Department of Health Publications. *http://www.nelmh.org/downloads/other_info/treatment_ choice_psychological_therapies.pdf*. Includes guidelines for adult depression, panic disorder with agoraphobia, social phobia, generalized anxiety disorder, PTSD, OCD, eating disorders, somatic disorders, personality disorders, deliberate self-harm.
American Psychological Association	Chambless *et al.* (1998). Update on empirically validated therapies, II. *The Clinical Psychologist*, 51, 3–16. Includes references to ESTs for adult depression, anxiety, headache, bulimia, smoking cessation, marital discord, childhood enuresis, oppositional defiant disorder. Norcross, J. C. (Ed.) (2002). *Psychotherapy Relationships that Work: Therapist Contributions and Responsiveness to Patient Needs.* New York: Oxford University Press.
American Psychiatric Association Practice Guidelines	*http://www.psych.org/psych_pract/treatg/pg/prac_ guide.cfm*. Includes guidelines for various disorders in adults, including depression, bipolar disorder, anxiety, OCD, PTSD, eating disorders, schizophrenia, suicidal behaviour, dementia, delirium, HIV/ AIDS, personality disorders.
American Academy of Child & Adolescent Psychiatry Practice Parameters	*http://www.aacap.org/page.ww?section=Practice+ Parameters&name=Practice+Parameters*. Includes guidelines for various disorders in children and adolescents including reactive attachment disorder, enuresis, specific learning and language disabilities, intellectual disability, ADHD, oppositional defiant disorder, conduct disorders, depression, bipolar disorder, anxiety, OCD, PTSD, schizophrenia, suicidal behaviour.

aspects of the therapeutic context that influence recovery. Research on the impact of specific treatment protocols for particular problems (reviewed in Chapters 4 and 5) provides evidence for how to maximize the chances of common factors operating with certain problems. Common factors such as the therapeutic alliance can only operate when therapists and clients engage in specific interactions. So specific treatment protocols are vehicles through which common factors may have a positive impact on clients' well-being.

Conclusions

In this chapter three main questions have been addressed. These concerned the definition of psychotherapy, the nature of psychotherapy research, and the translation of research findings into procedures for clinical practice. The answers to these questions will be briefly recapped below.

What is psychotherapy?

Modern psychotherapy has developed over the past one hundred years. Psychotherapy is a contractual process in which trained professionals interact with clients to help them resolve psychological problems. Psychotherapy and psychological interventions may be offered to children, adults, older adults, and people with intellectual and pervasive developmental disabilities on an individual, couple, family, or group basis to effectively alleviate a wide variety of difficulties. In addressing the scientific evidence base for the effectiveness of psychotherapy, it is useful to distinguish between therapy conducted within the psychodynamic, humanistic, cognitive behavioural, and systemic traditions.

What is psychotherapy research?

Psychotherapy research is the systematic inquiry into the process and outcome of interventions conducted to alleviate psychological problems. Research on the effectiveness of psychotherapy may be organized into a hierarchy from uncontrolled case studies which provide the least persuasive evidence for the effectiveness of psychotherapy, through uncontrolled and controlled trials, to meta-analyses which provide the most persuasive evidence of psychotherapy's effectiveness. In later chapters, greatest weight will be given to meta-analyses of controlled trials.

How can the results of psychotherapy research be used to inform clinical practice?

There is no single correct process for translating results of psychotherapy research into clinical practice procedures. Some favour the use of efficacy studies to identify specific empirically supported treatments. Others favour the use of multiple sources of evidence to inform the development of general practice guidelines.

Research on psychotherapy has focused on both common factors and specific techniques. Research on common factors provides evidence for important general aspects of the therapeutic context that influence recovery. This research will be reviewed in Chapter 3. Research on specific treatment protocols provides evidence for how to maximize the chances of common factors operating when engaging in psychotherapy with clients who have certain specific types of problems. This research will be reviewed in Chapters 4 and 5. However, a critical question, particularly for policymakers and service funders, concerns evidence for the overall effectiveness of psychotherapy. This issue – the overall effectiveness of psychotherapy – is the central focus of the next chapter.

Further reading

Kaslow, F. (2002). *Comprehensive Handbook of Psychotherapy* (Vols 1–4). New York: John Wiley.

Chapter 2

The overall effectiveness and cost-effectiveness of psychotherapy

This chapter is concerned with the questions: Does psychotherapy work? and: Is psychotherapy cost-effective? Currently, evidence for the effectiveness of psychotherapy is overwhelming. Major meta-analyses of hundreds of treatment trials involving thousands of child, adolescent, and adult clients with a wide range of problems show unequivocally that psychotherapy works. There is also a large body of evidence which shows that patients who receive psychotherapy use less other medical services, and that this leads to significant overall cost offset. In this chapter some of this evidence will be reviewed.

Questions about the effectivness of psychotherapy

In a seminal paper Hans Eysenck (1952) concluded from a review of 24 uncontrolled studies and data from untreated cases that the evidence available at the time did not support the effectiveness of psychotherapy. However, he also remarked that the evidence base was weak and recommended that well-designed studies be conducted to rigorously evaluate the effectiveness of psychotherapy. Levitt (1957) published a similar paper on the effectiveness of psychotherapy for children and adolescents in which he reached similar conclusions to those of Eysenck.

Since the 1950s a central question addressed by many psychotherapy researchers has been 'Does psychotherapy work?' Broad-based treatment outcome studies of heterogeneous groups of clients receiving broadly defined therapy approaches and reviews of such studies have been conducted to answer this very general question.

More refined questions about the effectiveness of psychotherapy have also emerged, the most widely known of which is that posed by Gordon Paul: 'What treatment, by whom, is most effective for this individual with that specific problem, under which set of circumstances?' (Paul, 1967, p. 111). This question has inspired narrower studies of the effects of specific treatment protocols on specific client groups with particular types of problems and careful reviews and meta-analyses of such treatment outcome studies. In

Chapters 4 and 5 this evidence will be addressed. However, in this chapter our main concern is with the broader question about the overall effectiveness of psychotherapy.

Meta-analysis and overall effectivness

Twenty-five years after Eysenck's seminal paper, Mary Smith and Gene Glass (1977) published the first major meta-analysis of psychotherapy outcome studies in the *American Psychologist* and followed it up with a book on the topic in 1980 (Smith *et al.*, 1980). The main contribution of Smith and Glass was to show that the results of many treatment outcome studies could be systematically, quantitatively synthesized to reach a valid and useful conclusion. On the basis of their 1977 quantitative review of 375 controlled evaluations of psychotherapy, they concluded that the typical therapy client is better off than 75% of untreated individuals. This conclusion rested on the observation that the average effect size was .68, and was interpreted using the system given in Table 1.1 (p. 16).

Since 1977 many meta-analyses have been conducted which have confirmed the efficacy of psychotherapy (Lambert & Ogle, 2004; Wampold, 2001; Weisz, 2004). In a synthesis of 68 separate meta-analyses of psychotherapy with children, adolescents, and adults with a wide range of different psychological problems, Grissom (1996) found an aggregate effect size of .75, indicating that the average treated case fared better than 77% of untreated controls. This effect size may also be interpreted as showing that approximately 68% of treated cases improved, compared with 32% of untreated cases in control groups.

Consumer Reports survey of effectiveness of psychotherapy

The results of a large USA Consumer Reports survey of 4100 adult psychotherapy clients with a wide range of problems, which has received much attention from psychotherapy researchers, are consistent with the results of the meta-analyses cited above (Seligman, 1995). While consumer survey results have more limited scientific validity than the results of meta-analyses of controlled treatment outcome studies, the results of the Consumer Reports survey is of interest because of its scale, the fact that the results are consistent with the results of meta-analyses, because they have direct bearing on the funding of psychotherapy through managed care programmes in the USA, and because Martin Seligman, a past president of the American Psychological Association, was a consultant to the survey and championed the presentation of the results to the scientific community. From the results of the survey Martin Seligman concluded that psychotherapy clients benefited very substantially from psychotherapy. He also concluded that those who received long-term treatment did considerably better than those who received short-term treatment, and that less improvement occurred when managed care or the client's health insurance company constrained their choice of therapist and the duration of therapy. A number of factors had no significant impact on improvement following psychotherapy, including the additional use of psychotropic medication such as antidepressants, the type of theoretical ordination of the psychotherapist, and the profession of the psychotherapist. Clients who received medication and those who did not had similar outcomes. Clients treated with different types of therapy reported similar improvement rates. Similar improvement rates occurred regardless of whether clients were treated by therapists whose basic professional training was in psychology, psychiatry, or social work. While these results are those of a biased sample of undiagnosed consumers, involving outcome measures of unknown clinical reliability and validity, they are remarkably consistent with the results of meta-analyses reviewed in this and other chapters.

Effects of psychotherapy with adults

While Smith and Glass's meta-analyses (Smith & Glass, 1977; Smith *et al.*, 1980), mentioned above, included mainly studies of psychotherapy with adults, they also included many studies of therapy with children. With a view to determining the effects of psychotherapy for adults with psychological problems, Shapiro and Shapiro (1982) conducted a meta-analysis of 143 studies of psychotherapy exclusively involving adult populations. They found an overall effect size of 1.03, indicating that after treatment the average adult who participated in psychotherapy fared better than 84% of untreated control group cases. Two further meta-analyses deserve mention in this section because they offer support for the effectiveness of psychotherapy with adults. Andrews and Harvey (1981) in a meta-analysis of 81 studies including only clinically distressed adults obtained an overall effect size of .72, indicating that the average treated case fared better than 77% of untreated controls. Landman and Dawes (1982) in a meta-analysis of 42 studies, marked by a high level of methodological rigour, obtained an overall effect size of .9, indicating that the average treated case fared better than 82% of untreated controls. The studies included in the meta-analyses by Andrews and Harvey (1981) and Landman and Dawes (1982) were subsets of those included in Smith and Glass's original 1977 meta-analysis. These later meta-analyses are particularly important because they show that Smith and Glass's original meta-analytic findings were not an artefact of including either studies of unrepresentative, non-distressed clients or studies lacking in methodological rigour in their meta-analysis.

Effectiveness of psychotherapy with children and adolescents

The results of four broad meta-analyses of studies involving children and adolescents with a diverse range of psychological problems receiving a variety of different forms of psychotherapy provide evidence for the overall effectiveness of psychotherapy with children. These meta-analyses include more than 350 treatment outcome studies. Casey and Berman (1985), in a meta-analysis of 75 studies conducted between 1952 and 1983 on psychotherapy with children under 13, obtained an overall effect size of .71, averaging across multiple outcome measures. This indicates that, after treatment, the average treated case fared better than 76% of untreated control group cases. Weisz *et al.* (1987), in a meta-analysis of 106 studies conducted between 1952 and 1983 of psychotherapy with 4–18-year-old children and adolescents, found an overall effect size of .79. This indicates that, after treatment, the average treated case fared better than 79% of untreated control group cases. Kazdin *et al.* (1990), in a meta-analysis of 223 studies conducted between 1970 and 1988 of psychotherapy with 4–18-year-old children and adolescents, found an overall effect size of .88 for treatment versus waiting list control comparisons. This indicates that, after treatment, the average treated case fared better than 81% of untreated control group cases. Kazdin *et al.* (1990) obtained an effect size of .77 for treatment versus placebo comparisons, showing that, after treatment, the average treated case fared better than 78% of cases that received a placebo treatment. In this context, placebo treatments involved contact with a therapist and engagement in plausible, though theoretically ineffective, activities such as participation in discussion groups or engagement in recreational activities with a therapist. Weisz *et al.* (1995), in a meta-analysis of 150 studies conducted between 1967 and 1993 of psychotherapy with 2–18-year-old children and adolescents, found an overall effect size of .71. This indicates that, after treatment, the average treated case fared better than 76% of untreated control group cases. In both of the analyses conducted by John Weisz's team, effect sizes following treatment and those obtained at about six months follow-up were very similar (Weisz *et al.*, 1987, 1995). This indicates that not only is psychotherapy for children effective, but also that these effects are maintained up to six months after treatment has ended.

Meta-analyses of clinically representative therapy trials

It was noted earlier that one of the criticisms of broad meta-analyses is that many of the studies included in them involved clients who were not representative of those who attend typical services. That is, they contained many efficacy studies in which clients had less chronic or complex problems than those routinely referred for therapy, were solicited by a researcher rather than referred for treatment, and the therapy was not conducted by typical therapists with routine caseloads and normal clinical service working conditions. To address this criticism, meta-analyses have been conducted of studies selected because they contained clients representative of those who attend regular outpatient clinics. For example, Shadish *et al.* (1997) conducted a secondary analysis of 56 studies of clinically representative psychotherapy of children, adolescents and adults from 15 previous meta-analyses. The studies were conducted in non-university, community settings; included patients referred for treatment, not solicited by the researcher; and involved experienced professional therapists with normal caseloads. The average effect size from these 56 clinically representative studies was .68, and was not significantly different from the average effect size from the 15 original meta-analyses, which was .59. The results of this meta-analysis show that psychotherapy is effective when conducted under clinically representative conditions.

Meta-analyses of studies of main types of therapy

Within each of the four main psychotherapeutic traditions outlined in Chapter 1, broad meta-analyses of controlled outcome studies have been conducted to determine the overall effectiveness of particular approaches to psychotherapy with a range of psychological problems. What follows is a summary of such meta-analyses, and conclusions from important narrative reviews for the psychodynamic, humanistic, cognitive behavioural, and systemic traditions.

Psychodynamic psychotherapy

Within the psychodynamic tradition, a distinction is made between short-term psychodynamic psychotherapy and intensive long-term psychoanalysis. The former involves weekly sessions for periods of 6 to 12 months, while the latter involves two or more sessions per week, usually for periods longer than a year. Controlled studies and meta-analyses have been conducted for psychodynamic psychotherapy but not psychoanalysis.

Three meta-analyses provide evidence for the effectiveness of psychodynamic psychotherapy for a broad range of problems in adults, notably anxiety, mood, and personality disorders (Crits-Christoph, 1992; Anderson & Lambert, 1995; Leichsenring *et al.*, 2004). In the earliest of these, Crits-Christoph (1992) reviewed 11 well-controlled studies, and found an overall success rate of 86% for brief psychodynamic therapy. This rate was greater than that of waiting list controls and about equal to those of other psychotherapies and medication. Anderson and Lambert (1995), in a later meta-analysis of 26 studies conducted between 1974 and 1994, found that short-term psychodynamic psychotherapy had an effect size of .71 relative to no treatment and .34 relative to minimal treatments. They also found that the outcomes for psychodynamic psychotherapy and alternative treatments including cognitive behavioural therapy were similar. In a third meta-analysis of 17 studies conducted between 1970 and 2004, Leichsenring *et al.* (2004) found that short-term psychodynamic psychotherapy yielded significant and large pre-treatment–post-treatment effect sizes for target problems (effect size = 1.39), general psychiatric symptoms (effect size = .9), and social functioning (effect size = .8). These effect sizes were stable and increased at follow-up to 1.57, .95, and 1.19 respectively. The between group effect size based on five studies that included waiting list or minimal treatment control groups was .7 for general psychiatric symptoms. This indicates that after treatment the average treated case fared better than 76% of controls. In this meta-analysis, the outcome for psychodynamic psychotherapy did not differ from that of other forms of psychotherapy in the 14 studies where such comparisons were made. The results of these three meta-analyses clearly support the effectiveness of short-term psychodynamic psychotherapy for common psychological problems in adults.

A number of narrative reviews of psychodynamic psychotherapy deserve mention because of their scope and impact. In an exhaustive review of empirical studies of the effectiveness of psychodynamic therapy, Fonagy *et al.* (2005) found that the evidence base for psychodynamic psychotherapy is smaller than that for other forms of therapy (notably, cognitive behavioural therapy), but in most areas where systematic research has been conducted such as depression, and some of the anxiety and personality disorders, psychodynamic therapy has been found to be at least as effective as other forms of psychotherapy.

On behalf of the German Association for Psychodynamic Psychotherapy, Richter *et al.* (2002) and Loew *et al.* (2002) conducted very thorough narrative reviews of the evidence for the effectiveness of psychodynamic psychotherapy with adults and children. Richter *et al.* (2002) identified 28 controlled diagnosis-specific studies which evaluated the effectiveness of psychoanalytic psychotherapy. These studies covered the following specific problems: mood disorders, anxiety disorders, stress disorders, dissociative, conversion and somatoform disorders, eating disorders, adjustment disorders, personality disorders, behavioural deviations, drug dependency and abuse, schizophrenia, and psychotic disorders. They also reviewed nine controlled studies covering a range of problem types. Loew *et al.* (2002) reviewed 64 uncontrolled studies evaluating the effectiveness of psychodynamic psychotherapy which were not included in Richter *et al.*'s (2002) review. Taken together the results of these reviews provided evidence for the effectiveness of psychodynamic psychotherapy with a range of psychological problems in children and adults.

In the UK, Kennedy (2004) reviewed the evidence base for the effectiveness of psychodynamic psychotherapy with children and adolescents and identified 37 reports on 32 different studies. She concluded that the results of these studies provided support for the overall effectiveness of psychodynamic psychotherapy for a range of child and adolescent problems including depression, emotional disorders, disruptive behaviour disorders, anorexia, poorly controlled diabetes, and problems arising from child abuse. The review also indicated that a number of factors influenced the effectiveness of psychodynamic psychotherapy. For young people, psychodynamic psychotherapy is more effective with emotional disorders than conduct disorders; with children who have less (rather than more) severe problems; and with younger children (rather than with older children or adolescents). More intensive therapy is more effective than less intensive therapy, particularly for youngsters with severe problems. Concurrent intervention with parents enhances the effectiveness of individual psychodynamic psychotherapy, particularly with younger children.

Unfortunately, controlled studies of the outcome of long-term psychoanalysis have not been conducted. However, a number of important uncontrolled evaluations deserve mention. Fonagy et al. (2002) in an open door review which included a series of mainly retrospective outcome studies of long-term psychoanalysis involving over 300 cases found long-term beneficial effects for a majority of children and adults with a wide range of difficulties including anxiety, depression, and personality disorders. Also, more intensive therapy was more effective. Sandell et al. (1999) in a comparative study of 700 Swedish psychoanalysis and psychotherapy cases found that the majority of clients who participated in psychoanalysis showed improvement in symptoms and social adjustment. Because these studies did not include an untreated control group of cases with similar problems to treated cases, there is the possibility that the improvements observed could have been due to the passage of time. However, Fonagy and Sandell's results are encouraging and show that controlled studies in this area would be worthwhile.

Humanistic psychotherapy

Elliott et al. (2004) conducted a thorough review of treatment outcome studies that fall broadly within the humanistic psychotherapy tradition. They included studies of client-centred therapy, experiential therapy, gestalt therapy, and emotionally focused therapy in the review. It included 112 uncontrolled studies in which pre–post-treatment effect sizes were computed; 37 controlled studies in which effect sizes based on comparisons with waiting list controls were made; and 55 studies in which humanistic therapy was compared with other forms of treatment. Clients in these studies had a wide variety of psychological problems including anxiety disorders, mood disorders, eating disorders, personality disorders, and relationship distress. Across all studies the average duration of treatment was 22 sessions. The average unweighted pre–post-treatment effect size was .99. The unweighted effect size based on comparison with untreated controls was .89. The more

conservative weighted effect sizes were .86 for pre–post-treatment comparisons and .78 for treatment-control comparisons. These results indicate that
the average treated case after therapy fared better than 80–84% of cases
before therapy and 78–81% of untreated cases. The outcome for humanistic
experiential therapies and other forms of psychotherapy including cognitive
behavioural therapy were similar. The results of this comprehensive review
indicate that humanistic psychotherapy is a highly effective form of treatment
for a range of common psychological problems in adulthood.

Cognitive behavioural therapy

In a review of 16 meta-analyses that included 332 studies of the effectiveness
of cognitive behavioural therapy (CBT) with 16 different disorders or populations, Butler *et al.* (2006) obtained a large mean weighted effect size of .95 for
depression and a range of anxiety disorders in children, adolescents, and
adults. Thus, the average treated case with anxiety and depression fared better
than 83% of untreated controls. For bulimia the mean pre–post-treatment
effect size of 1.27 was also large, indicating that the average treated case fared
better than 89% of cases before treatment. For marital distress, anger control,
and chronic pain in adults, and childhood somatic disorders, effect sizes were
moderate with a mean of .62. Thus, the average treated case with these problems fared better than 73% of untreated controls. For sexual offending the
average effect size of .35 was relatively small. However, it was the most effective form of psychotherapy for reducing recidivism in this population. Thus,
the average treated sex offender fared better than 64% of untreated controls.
There was significant evidence for the long-term effectiveness of cognitive
behavioural therapy for depression and anxiety disorders. Averaging across
the four mean effect sizes, the overall average effect size from this review
of 16 meta-analyses was .79, indicating that the average treated case fared
better than 79% of untreated controls at follow-up at least six months after
therapy. Major narrative reviews of the extensive literature of the efficacy
and effectiveness of behavioural and cognitive behavioural therapies with a
wide range of child, adolescent, and adult disorders are consistent with the
findings of this review of 16 meta-analyses (Emmelkamp, 2004; Hollon &
Beck, 2004).

Rational emotive therapy

Rational emotive therapy, developed by Albert Ellis, shares much in common
with cognitive therapy and so is mentioned here. In rational emotive therapy,
clients develop a facility for challenging irrational beliefs which underpin
problematic emotional and behavioural patterns (Ellis & Greiger, 1986). In a
meta-analysis of 70 rational emotive therapy outcome studies Lyons and
Woods (1991) found an effect size of 1.02. The average treated case fared

better than 84% of untreated waiting list control group cases. Client who spent longer in therapy with more experienced therapists had better outcomes. In a meta-analysis of 19 studies of rational emotive therapy with children, Galloway *et al.* (2004) concluded that rational emotive therapy was effective in alleviating a range of problems in children and adolescents including anxiety, disruptive behaviours, irrationality, poor self-concept, and underachievement.

Personal construct psychotherapy

Constructivist psychotherapy, or personal construct psychotherapy, developed by George Kelly (1955), shares in common with cognitive therapy a focus on resolving psychological problems by changing belief systems, and so is mentioned here. In a meta-analysis of 20 controlled studies of personal construct psychotherapy with clients suffering from a wide range of psychological difficulties, Metcalfe *et al.* (2007) found a post-treatment effect size of .34 for studies of clients with clinical problems and 1.04 for clients with subclinical problems. At 2–12 months follow-up the effect size for studies of clients with clinical problems was .30. Thus, for clinical problems the average treated case fared better than 63% of untreated controls after treatment and 62% at follow-up. For subclinical problems the average treated case fared better than 84% of untreated controls after treatment. Individual and group therapy formats were equally effective. In those studies where personal construct psychotherapy was compared with cognitive behavioural or psychodynamic psychotherapy, no significant differences were found between different types of psychotherapies. In the 13 studies of clinical problems, clients included parents of children with behaviour problems or disabilities; children and adolescents with psychological problems; adults experiencing distress associated with physical illness; and older adults with psychological problems. In the seven studies of subclinical problems, clients included student volunteers with social anxiety or phobias; adults with compliance difficulties attending an exercise programme; older adults with adjustment problems; and stressed staff working with older adults. In all of these studies, waiting list or standard care control groups were used. These results were consistent with the conclusions of previous meta-analyses and narrative reviews of the outcome literature for constructivist psychotherapy and support its effectiveness (Viney *et al.*, 2005; Winter, 2003).

Acceptance and commitment therapy

Acceptance and commitment therapy which has evolved within the cognitive behavioural tradition also deserves mention because of its growing importance within the field of psychotherapy (Hayes *et al.*, 2003). It includes the following core components: acceptance (rather than avoidance); changing relationship to negative thoughts (rather than attempting to change the frequency or content of such thoughts); enhancing ongoing non-judgemental experience of the world; mindfulness exercises to foster a sense of self as context; choosing values; and engaging in committed action to achieve goals consistent with these values. In a meta-analysis of 21 controlled studies of acceptance and commitment therapy involving clients with a range of problems including depression, anxiety disorders, personality disorders, psychosis, and other problems, Hayes *et al.* (2006) obtained a weighted effect size after treatment and at five months follow-up of .66. This indicates that the average participant in acceptance and commitment therapy fared better than 74% of those who received no treatment, or treatment as usual.

Taken together the results of these meta-analyses, reviews of meta-analyses, and narrative reviews offer strong support for the effectiveness of therapies that fall broadly within the cognitive behavioural therapy tradition for a wide range of common psychological problems in children, adolescents, and adults.

Systemic therapy

Shadish and Baldwin (2003) reviewed 20 meta-analyses of marital and family interventions for a wide range of child and adult focused problems. These included: child and adolescent conduct and emotional disorders; drug and alcohol abuse in adolescents and adults; adult anxiety, depression, and psychosis; and marital distress. Of the 20 meta-analyses 16 were of therapy studies and four included marital and family enrichment studies. Of the 17 therapy meta-analyses, four were of both marital and family therapy studies; six were of marital therapy studies; and seven were of family therapy studies. For marital and family therapy the average effect size across all therapy meta-analyses was .65 after therapy and .52 at follow-up six months to a year later. These results show that, overall, the average treated couple or family with clinically significant problems fared better after treatment than 75% of untreated controls, and at follow-up fared better than about 71% of cases in control groups. After therapy the average effect of marital therapy was .84, and this was higher than that for family therapy where the effect size was .58. These results show that for cases with clinically significant problems, the average treated couple fared better after treatment than about 80% of untreated controls, but the average treated family fared better than 72% of control group cases. For marital and family enrichment, the effect sizes after therapy and at follow-up were .48 and .32 respectively. These results show that, overall, the average treated couple or family without clinically significant problems fared better after enrichment programmes than 68% of untreated controls, and at follow-up fared better than about 63% of cases in control groups. Shadish and Baldwin's (2003) synthesis of the results of 20 meta-analyses supports the efficacy of systemic therapy for couples and families with a wide range of clinically significant problems and for couples and families without clinical problems but who want to develop family strengths such as communication and problem-solving skills and greater emotional cohesion.

Group therapy

In a meta-analysis of 111 trials of adult outpatient group therapy, Burlingame *et al.* (2003) found an average effect size of .58 which indicated that the average participant in group treatment fared better than 72% of untreated controls. In a meta-analysis of 24 controlled and 46 uncontrolled trials of inpatient adult group therapy, Kosters *et al.* (2006) found effect sizes of .31 for controlled studies based on treatment–control group effect sizes, and .59 for uncontrolled studies based on pre–post-treatment effect sizes. These effect sizes show that the average treated case fared better than 62% of untreated cases and 72% of cases before treatment. Inpatients with mood disorders showed greater improvement compared with those who had psychosomatic complaints, post-traumatic stress disorder, and psychosis. The results of these two meta-analyses show that both inpatients and outpatients benefit from group therapy, but the benefits for outpatients are probably greater. In a further meta-analysis of 23 outcome studies that directly compared group and individual psychotherapy, McRoberts *et al.* (1998) found a negligible effect size, indicating that the outcomes for individual and group therapies were similar. In a major narrative review of past studies and previous meta-analyses of group therapy, Burlingame *et al.* (2004) concluded that, overall, group and individual therapy were equally effective for many disorders in adults and specific group protocols were particularly effective for depression, anxiety disorders, adjustment to cancer, and schizophrenia when included as part of a multimodal programme where patients also received antipsychotic medication. However, the benefits of group therapy are not confined to adults. In a meta-analysis of 56 outcome studies of group therapy with children and adolescents, Hoag and Burlingame (1997) found an average effect size of .61 which indicated that the average group therapy client fared better than 73% of untreated controls. Thus, there is good evidence for the effectiveness of group therapy with children and adolescents. Alongside this evidence for the effectiveness of group therapy for young people, there is continuing controversy over possible contagion effects when antisocial children or adolescents are treated in group settings. Dishion and Dodge (2005) have presented considerable evidence to show that aggregating aggressive youngsters in treatment settings can lead to increased antisocial behaviour. In contrast, Kaminer (2005) has reviewed a series of controlled trials which show that group-based cognitive behaviour therapy reduces adolescent drug abuse. Further research is required to identify the circumstances under which contagion effects associated with antisocial youngsters in group therapy occurs.

Effects of psychotherapy and medical procedures

To place the evidence on the overall effectiveness of psychotherapy in a broader context, it is useful to ask: Are the moderate to large effect sizes associated with psychotherapy very different from those associated with the medical and surgical treatment of physical illnesses, diseases, and medical conditions? In Figure 2.1 it may be seen that the overall effect size for psychotherapy and medical and surgical procedures are both in the moderate range between .5 and .8. The effect size for psychotherapy of .75 is from Grissom's (1996) synthesis of 68 meta-analyses mentioned earlier, and the effect size of .5 for medical and surgical procedures is from Caspi's (2004) synthesis of 91 meta-analyses of various medical and surgical treatments for a range of medical conditions. From the data in Figure 2.1, it may be concluded that the moderate to large effect sizes associated with psychotherapy are similar to or slightly better than those associated with the treatment of medical conditions.

Deterioration and drop-out

A consistent finding within the psychotherapy research literature is that up to 10% of clients deteriorate following treatment (Lambert & Ogles, 2004; Lilienfeld, 2007). In a review of 46 studies on negative outcome in adult psychotherapy, Mohr (1995) found that deterioration was associated with particular client and therapist characteristics and particular features of psychotherapy. Deterioration was more common among clients with borderline

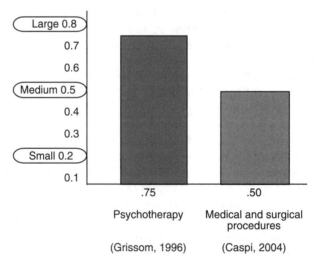

Figure 2.1 Mean effect sizes from meta-analyses of psychotherapy and medical and surgical procedures.

personality disorder, obsessive-compulsive disorder, or severe interpersonal difficulties. Lack of motivation and the expectation of benefiting from psychotherapy without personal effort were also associated with deterioration. Deterioration was more common when unskilled therapists lacked empathy and did not collaborate with clients in pursuing agreed goals. Failure to appropriately manage countertransference, and frequent transference interpretations, were also associated with deterioration. In a review of research on deterioration in psychotherapy, Lilienfeld (2007) has proposed a preliminary list of potentially harmful therapies (PHTs). The list specifies therapeutic approaches which have been shown in treatment trials to lead to deterioration for a significant minority of clients. Examples of PHTs include boot camps, scared straight programmes, and group therapy for adolescent conduct disorder; facilitated communication for people with intellectual and pervasive developmental disabilities; critical incident stress debriefing for unscreened survivors of traumatic events; and grief counselling for normal bereavement. (Evidence supporting these conclusions is given in the relevant sections of Chapters 4 and 5.)

Dropping out of psychotherapy is a relatively common event. In a meta-analysis of 125 studies, Wierzbicki and Pekarik (1993) found a mean drop-out rate of 47%. Dropout rates were higher for minority ethnic groups, less-educated clients, and those with lower incomes.

From this review it is clear that about one in ten clients deteriorate following therapy and that marginalized clients with particularly troublesome disorders and negative attitudes to psychotherapy are vulnerable to dropping out of psychotherapy and deterioration. On the other hand, adopting an empathic, collaborative, and supportive approach to engaging these vulnerable clients in therapy may lessen the risk of drop-out and deterioration.

Waiting time and engagement in therapy

There is growing evidence that the amount of time clients spend on a waiting list has an impact on their willingness to engage in psychotherapy. Reitzel *et al.* (2006) in a study of over 300 adults referred for psychotherapy in the USA found that those who had spent longer on waiting lists were less likely to attend therapy, but no more likely to prematurely terminate therapy. Strang *et al.* (2005), in a randomized trial of the effects of time on a waiting list on clinical outcomes in opiate addicts awaiting outpatient treatment in London, found that shorter waiting times were associated with more clients engaging in treatment. Bell and Newns (2004) in a study of 125 clients attending an eating disorder programme found that waiting time (but not diagnosis, age, or gender) was associated with attending a first appointment. Hicks and Hickman (1994) in a study of 60 couples referred for marital therapy in the UK found that longer waiting times (greater than two weeks) were associated with reduced likelihood of attending intake interviews. From these studies it may be concluded that early access to psychotherapy services can facilitate therapeutic engagement.

Quality control in psychotherapy

High quality psychotherapy is more effective than lower quality therapy. In this context, high quality involves a reasonable caseload, initial skills training in the specific model of therapy, ongoing regular supervision, and conducting psychotherapy according to the principles of practice specified for the model with sufficient flexibility to take account of each client's unique characteristics. This conclusion has been borne out by the effectiveness of model programmes such as Scott Henggeler's multisystemic therapy for adolescents with conduct disorder (Henggeler & Lee, 2003). Henggeler has developed a quality assurance system which includes manualized treatment and supervision and shown that client recovery is directly related to adherence to these protocols.

Medical cost-offset

The evidence reviewed so far shows that psychotherapy is effective. However, an important concern is the financial implications of providing such a psychotherapy service. In this context, two questions are of interest. First, do clients who avail of psychotherapy services use less medical services and so incur reduced medical costs? This saving is referred to as the medical cost-offset. Second, is the medical cost-offset associated with psychotherapy greater than the cost of providing psychotherapy? If so, we can conclude that psychotherapy has a total cost-offset. Findings of meta-analyses and narrative reviews of the cost-offset literature throw light on both of these questions.

In a meta-analysis of 91 studies conducted between 1967 and 1997, Chiles *et al.* (1999) found that psychotherapy and psychological interventions led to significant medical cost-offsets. Participants in reviewed studies included surgery inpatients, high health-service users, and people with psychological and substance use disorders who received psychotherapy or psychological interventions alone or as part of multimodal programmes. Chiles and his team concluded that medical cost-offsets occurred in 90% of studies and ranged from 20–30%. In 93% of studies where data were provided, cost-offsets exceeded the cost of providing psychotherapy. Greater cost-offsets occurred for older inpatients who required surgery, oncology, and cardiac rehabilitation than for outpatients who required care for minor injuries and illnesses. Structured psychological interventions, tailored to patient needs associated with their medical conditions, led to greater medical cost-offsets than traditional psychotherapy. In an earlier set of meta-analytic studies involving Blue Cross and Blue Shield US Federal Employees Plan claim files and

58 controlled studies, Mumford *et al.* (1984) found that in 85% of studies medical cost-offsets for psychotherapy occurred. These were due to shorter periods of hospitalization for surgery, cancer, heart disease, and diabetes, particularly in patients over 55.

In a review of psychological interventions for people with a variety of health-related difficulties, Groth-Marnat and Edkins (1996) found that medical cost-offsets occurred when such interventions targeted patients preparing for surgery and patients with difficulty adhering to medical regimens. Medical cost-offset also occurred for smoking cessation programmes, rehabilitation programmes, and programmes for patients with chronic pain disorders, cardiovascular disorders, and psychosomatic complaints.

Two other important reviews of the medical cost-offset literature which focused largely on primary mental health problems in adults, rather than adjustment to physical illness, deserve mention. In a review of 30 studies of psychotherapy for psychological disorders and drug and alcohol abuse, Jones and Vischi (1979) found that medical cost-offsets occurred in most cases. In a review of 18 studies of psychotherapy for psychological disorders, Gabbard *et al.* (1997) found that in more than 80% of studies medical cost-offsets exceeded the cost of providing psychotherapy. Particularly significant cost-offsets occurred for complex problems, notably in studies of psychoeducational family therapy for schizophrenia and dialectical behaviour therapy for personality disorders by reducing the need for inpatient care and improving occupational adjustment.

From the evidence reviewed here, it is clear that psychotherapeutic interventions have a significant medical cost-offset. Those who participate in psychotherapy use less other medical services at primary, secondary, and tertiary levels and are hospitalized less than those who do not receive psychotherapy.

Psychotherapy and reduced use of emergency services

There is some evidence to indicate that in certain circumstances psychotherapy can lead to a reduction in the use of accident and emergency services, especially among frequent users of such services with chronic psychological difficulties. Studies of dialectical behaviour therapy with clients with borderline personality disorder, and a history of frequent emergency psychiatric admissions associated with deliberate self-harm and suicidality, show that this form of psychotherapy reduces the frequency of visits to accident and emergency departments (Robins & Chapman, 2004). For example, Linehan *et al.* (2006) in a randomized controlled trial involving 100 clients with borderline personality disorder found that those who participated in a programme of dialectical behaviour made significantly less use of emergency services during a two-year follow-up period than a control group who received routine community-based treatment.

Summary and conclusion

This chapter was concerned with questions about the overall effectiveness of psychotherapy, and its cost-effectiveness.

Does psychotherapy work?

The evidence for the effectiveness of psychotherapy reviewed in this chapter is overwhelming. Major meta-analyses of hundreds of treatment trials involving thousands of clients show unequivocally that psychotherapy works. A summary of the results of broad meta-analyses of psychotherapy outcome studies referred to in this chapter is given in Figure 2.2 and Table 2.1. The effect sizes summarized in Figure 2.2 which range from .65 to 1.02 are medium to large, according to Cohen's (1988) system for interpreting effect sizes. Collectively the summary data in Figure 2.2 indicate that the average child or adult case treated with psychodynamic, humanistic, cognitive behavioural, or systemic therapy fared better than 74–84% of untreated cases. These effect sizes also indicate that the average success rate for treated cases ranged from 65–72%. In contrast, the average success rate for untreated control groups

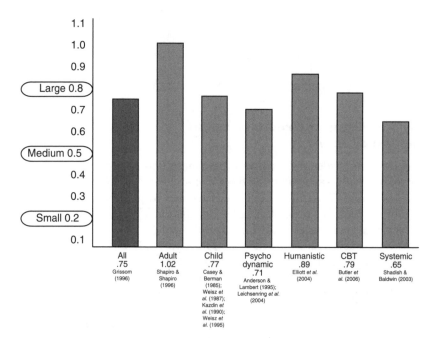

Figure 2.2 Mean effect sizes from meta-analyses of psychotherapy with adults and children, and therapy from different traditions.

Table 2.1 Summary of results of broad meta-analyses

Main focus of meta-analysis	Author	Date	Number of studies	Population	Type of studies	Effect size for treatment vs. waiting list control	% of untreated cases that the average treated case fares better than	% of outcome variance accounted for by treatment	% success for treated group	% success for control group
Adults and children	Grissom	1996	68 meta-analyses	Adults & children	All meta-analyses	.75	77	12	68	32
Adults	Smith & Glass	1977	375	Mainly adults	All published & unpublished studies up to mid-1970s	.68	75	10	66	34
	Smith et al.	1980	475	Mainly adults	All published & unpublished studies up to late 1970s	.85	80	15	70	30
	Shapiro & Shapiro	1982	143	Adults	Studies of adults up to 1979	1.03	84	20	72	28
	Andrews & Harvey	1981	81	Mainly adults	Studies of clinically distressed clients from Smith & Glass (1977)	.72	77	11	67	33
	Landman & Dawes	1982	42	Mainly adults	Methodologically rigorous studies	.90	82	17	70	30

(Continued overleaf)

Table 2.1 continued

Main focus of meta-analysis	Author	Date	Number of studies	Population	Type of studies	Effect size for treatment vs. waiting list control	% of untreated cases that the average treated case fares better than	% of outcome variance accounted for by treatment	% success for treated group	% success for control group
Children	Casey & Berman	1985	75	4–13 year olds	Studies conducted between 1952 and 1983	.71	76	10	66	34
	Weisz et al.	1987	106	4–18 year olds	Studies conducted between 1952 and 1983	.79	79	13	67	33
	Kazdin et al.	1990	223	4–18 year olds	Studies conducted between 1970 and 1988	.88	81	12	69	31
	Weisz et al.	1995	150	2–18 year olds	Studies conducted between 1967 and 1993	.71	76	10	66	34
Clinically representative samples	Shadish et al.	1997	56	Adults & children	Studies from other meta-analyses	.68	75	10	66	34
	Shadish et al.	2000	90	Adults & children	Studies from other meta-analyses	.41	66	4	60	40

		Year	Number	Population	Studies					
Psychodynamic	Crits-Christoph	1992	11	Adults	Studies before 1992	86%				
	Anderson & Lambert	1995	26	Adults	Studies conducted between 1974 and 1994	.71	76	10	66	34
	Leichsenring et al.	2004	17 (5)*	Adults	Studies conducted between 1970 and 2004	.70	76	10	66	34
Humanistic	Elliott et al.	2004	222 (37)*	Adults	Studies conducted between 1970 and 2002	.89	82	17	70	30
Cognitive behavioural	Butler et al.	2006	16 meta-analyses	Adults & children	All large meta-analyses	.79	79	13	67	33
Rational emotive therapy	Lyons & Woods	1991	70	Adults	All available studies	1.02	84	20	72	28
Acceptance and commitment therapy	Hayes	2006	21	Adults	All available studies	.66	74	9	65	35
Constructivist	Viney et al.	2005	15	Adults	All available studies	.55	71	7	63	37
Marital and family therapy	Shadish & Baldwin	2003	16 meta-analyses	Couples & families	All large meta-analyses	.65	74	9	65	35

* Only number in brackets studies were used to calculate the between group effect size.

range from 28–35%. The evidence reviewed in this chapter allows the following conclusions to be drawn:

- Psychotherapy is highly effective for a majority of cases with common psychological problems.
- Psychotherapy is effective for both adults and children.
- Psychotherapy conducted within psychodynamic, humanistic, cognitive behavioural, and systemic traditions is effective for many common psychological problems.
- The overall magnitude of the effects of psychotherapy in alleviating psychological disorders is similar to the overall magnitude of the effect of medical and surgical procedures in treating a wide variety of medical conditions.
- About one in ten clients deteriorate as a result of psychotherapy.
- Client recovery is dependent upon the delivery of a high quality psychotherapy service, which may be maintained through quality assurance systems.
- Early access to psychotherapy services can facilitate therapeutic engagement.

Is psychotherapy cost-effective?

The evidence reviewed in this chapter shows that psychotherapy is cost-effective. Patients who receive psychotherapy use less other medical services. This leads to reduced medical costs. The money saved in this way more than covers the cost of psychotherapy. That is, psychotherapy leads to a significant total cost-offset. For frequent emergency service users, psychotherapy can also lead to a reduction in the use of accident and emergency services.

A striking feature of the evidence for the overall effectiveness of psychotherapy presented in this chapter is the remarkable similarity in positive outcome rates of diverse approaches with a range of populations and problems. It seems plausible to propose that certain common therapeutic processes or factors underpin all effective psychotherapies which are tailored to meet clients' specific therapeutic needs. A discussion of such common factors provides a point of departure for Chapter 3.

Further reading

Lambert, M. (2004). *Bergin and Garfield's Handbook of Psychotherapy and Behaviour Change* (Fifth Edition). New York: John Wiley.

Common factors in psychotherapy

The evidence reviewed in Chapter 2 indicates that psychotherapy is effective in helping most people overcome psychological problems. A question arising from this conclusion is: What factors common to the wide variety of effective psychotherapies are responsible for their effectiveness? In this chapter the role of factors common to all forms of psychotherapy is the central focus. In Chapters 4 and 5 specific psychotherapy protocols that have been found to be particularly effective with a number of distinct problems will be considered.

Common factors and specific psychotherapies

A striking feature of the evidence reviewed in Chapter 2 in support of the overall effectiveness of psychotherapy is the similarity in outcomes of diverse approaches with a range of populations and problems. All approaches to psychotherapy when averaged across different populations, problems, and studies lead to moderate to large effect sizes, and benefits for two-thirds to three-quarters of treated cases. This finding has led to the hypothesis that a set of common factors may underpin all effective psychotherapies.

One possibility is that psychotherapy is no more than a placebo, a psychological sugar pill that gives clients hope and creates the expectation of improvement. It was mentioned in Chapter 1 that to evaluate this hypothesis researchers have conducted studies in which a specific form of psychotherapy is compared with a psychological or pharmacological placebo condition. Common psychological placebo conditions involve engaging in intellectual discussion groups, participating in recreational activities, or receiving an inert procedure that is described as providing subliminal treatment. Sugar pills are typically used as pharmacological placebos. In a quantitative review of 46 meta-analyses of psychotherapy with children and adults involving hundreds of studies and thousands of participants, Grissom (1996) compared the effects of groups receiving psychotherapy with placebos, and also conducted a number of other important comparisons. A summary of these, converted to average post-treatment, between-groups effect sizes is given in Figure 3.1. The effect size for psychotherapy compared with placebos was .58. Thus, the

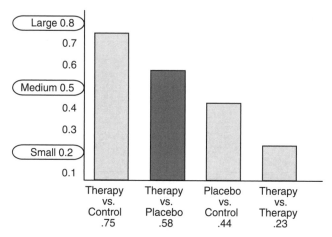

Figure 3.1 The effects of psychotherapy compared with placebo control groups.
Adapted from: Grissom (1996).

average treated case fared better than 72% of cases in control groups who received placebos. An effect size of .58 is also approximately equivalent to success rates of 63% for treated cases and 35% for cases receiving placebos. This shows that psychotherapy is not just a placebo that generates hope, but a set of procedures that actively influences the recovery process.

From Figure 3.1 it may also be seen that the effect size for therapy versus waiting list control groups (.75) is larger than the effect size of placebo versus waiting list control groups (.44). This shows that the effects of psychotherapy are nearly double those of placebos.

A third important conclusion may be drawn from the small average effect size (.23) arising from the comparison of different psychotherapy protocols and approaches in Figure 3.1. This effect size indicates that recovery rates for different forms of psychotherapy are very similar, and that specific psycho-therapeutic factors play a less important role in influencing recovery than common factors.

The results of two important analyses of the relative contribution of common and specific factors to psychotherapy outcome are summarized in Figure 3.2. In a non-quantitative narrative review of over a hundred psycho-therapy studies, Michael Lambert (1992; Lambert & Barley, 2002) estimated that common factors were about twice as important as specific factors in contributing to the outcome of psychotherapy. From the left-hand panel in Figure 3.2, it may be seen that Lambert estimated that about 30% of psycho-therapy outcome variance may be accounted for by common factors, and 15% by specific factors. Lambert estimated that 15% of the remainder of the variance in outcome was due to placebo effects or creating the expectation of recovery. The remaining 40% of variance in outcome, according to Lambert's

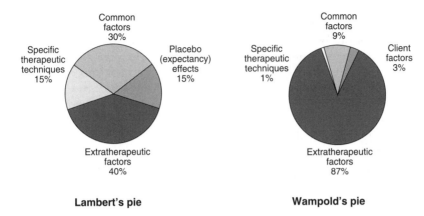

Figure 3.2 Factors that affect the outcome of psychotherapy.

Adapted from: Lambert & Barley (2002); Wampold (2001).

analysis, was accounted for by factors outside therapy such as social support from family and friends.

The results of an analysis conducted by Bruce Wampold (2001) are presented in the right-hand panel in Figure 3.2. Wampold, like Lambert, concluded that common factors are more important than specific factors in determining the outcome of psychotherapy, but the results of his rigorous analysis led to a far more extreme statement of this position than that made by Lambert. Wampold (2001) conducted a quantitative review of more than a dozen meta-analyses, and estimated that common factors are nine times more influential than specific factors in determining the outcome of psychotherapy. He reviewed broad meta-analyses, in which studies of the effects of therapy for a wide variety of populations and problems were synthesized. He also reviewed meta-analyses in which the focus was on the effectiveness of different forms of psychotherapy for a specific problem such as depression or anxiety. He concluded that only 13% of the variance of outcome for psychotherapy clients is due to psychotherapy (including common, specific, and other factors). This was based on his computation of an overall effect size for psychotherapy of between .7 and .8, and using the conversion system in the sixth column in Table 1.1 (p. 16), which is headed 'percentage of outcome variance accounted for by treatment'. A corollary of his first conclusion was that the remaining 87% of the variance of outcome for psychotherapy clients is due to extra-therapeutic factors. He also concluded that only 1% of the variability in outcome for psychotherapy clients was due to specific factors. This was based on the average between-treatment effect size of .2, similar to that reported earlier in Figure 3.1, and converted to a variance estimate using the sixth column in Table 1.1. He estimated that 3% of the variance in outcome was due to unexplained therapy factors, probably client characteristics.

The remaining 9% of the variance in outcome he concluded was accounted for by common factors.

Lambert's and Wampold's pies (as I have called them in Figure 3.2) represent extreme interpretations of the available data. However, they share one important conclusion. Common factors have a far greater impact than specific factors in determining whether or not clients benefit from psychotherapy. The major impact of common factors on the outcome of psychotherapy provides a possible explanation for the similarity in outcome of different psychotherapy approaches.

The Dodo bird verdict

The hypothesis that different psychotherapies may lead to similar improvement rates, was first referred to as the 'Dodo bird verdict' by Saul Rosenzweig in 1936. The reference is to a quotation from Lewis Carroll's *Alice's Adventures in Wonderland*: 'At last the Dodo said, "*Everybody* has won, and *all* must have prizes." ' The Dodo bird's remark was made after a caucus race in which competitors started at different points and ran in different directions for half an hour. In a series of papers starting in 1975, Lester Luborsky and his team concluded that there was strong empirical evidence to support the Dodo bird verdict (Luborsky *et al.*, 1975, 1993, 1999, 2002). For example, in a quantitative review of 17 meta-analyses of comparisons of a range of different treatments with each other, Luborsky *et al.* (2002) found an average effect size .20, which is small and non-significant. When such differences were corrected for the therapeutic allegiance of the researchers involved in comparing the different psychotherapies, these differences tended to become even further reduced in size and significance (Luborsky *et al.*, 1999). Researcher allegiance resulted in their preferred psychotherapies being delivered in a more sophisticated manner than non-preferred approaches. (The impact of researcher allegiance on effect size has already been referred to in Chapter 1, in the section outlining how meta-analyses of controlled outcome studies are conducted.)

However, not all reviewers agree with Rosenzweig and Luborsky's position. They have marshalled a body of evidence which casts doubt on the validity of the Dodo bird verdict (Hunsley & DiGiulio, 2002). For example, Reid (1997) reviewed results of 42 focused meta-analyses of studies of specific treatments for specific problems such as depression, panic disorder, bulimia, and so forth. He concluded that 74% of these meta-analyses showed evidence of differential treatment effects. Cognitive behavioural treatments led to better outcomes for many problems. A similar conclusion has been drawn in major broad meta-analyses of both child and adult problems. Weisz *et al.* (1995), in the meta-analysis of 150 child and adolescent psychotherapy outcome studies mentioned earlier, found that the mean effect size on non-reactive measures for cognitive behavioural treatments was .52, which was significantly greater than the mean effect size of .25 for client-centred and insight-oriented therapies. Weisz *et al.* (2006), in a further meta-analysis of 32 randomized controlled trials, largely involving youngsters with conduct problems and drug abuse, found that evidence-based cognitive behavioural and systemic treatments were more effective than usual care. The average adjusted effect size after treatment was .3 and at one-year follow-up was .38. These small to medium effect sizes indicate that the average client who received an evidence-based treatment fared better than 62% of those who received usual care after treatment and 65% at follow-up. Shadish *et al.* (2000) in a meta-analysis of 90 studies in which clients, treatments, and therapists were representative of typical clinical settings found that treatment effect sizes were larger for cognitive behavioural than traditional approaches to psychotherapy.

The conflicting findings of Luborsky *et al.* (2002) on the one hand, and Reid (1997), Weisz *et al.* (1995, 2006), and Shadish *et al.* (2000) on the other, have to some extent been reconciled by Wampold's (2001) analysis of the comparative psychotherapy outcome research mentioned in the last section. He agrees that in many instances statistically significant post-treatment differences between different therapies occur, but the average effect size of these difference is about .2, whereas the average effect size for most therapies is about .8. Common factors are therefore far more important than specific factors. However, therapists must engage in specific forms of therapy for common factors to have a medium through which to operate. For example, in family therapy the process of convening family meetings, helping family members view individual problems as part of a pattern of family interaction, and exploring alternative interaction patterns creates a context within which therapists develop good working alliances with clients (which is one of the most important common factors).

Categories of common factors

In considering common factors, it is useful to distinguish between client factors, therapist factors, and factors associated with the therapeutic context, including the dose of therapy received, the quality of the therapeutic alliance, and therapeutic procedures.

Client factors

Clarkin and Levy (2004) conducted a comprehensive narrative review of more than a hundred empirical studies and review papers on client characteristics that have been found to correlate with therapeutic outcome. They concluded that the following client characteristics have been associated with therapeutic outcome: personal distress; symptom severity; functional impairment; case complexity; readiness to change; early response to therapy; psychological mindedness; ego-strength; capacity to make and maintain relationships; the availability of social support; and socio-economic status

(SES). Clients with moderate to high personal distress were more motivated to engage and participate in therapy. When other factors were controlled for, and taken into account in analyses, clients experiencing lower levels of personal distress made less therapeutic progress. Clients with severe symptoms and considerable functional impairment, involving difficulties carrying out their normal social and occupational roles, made less therapeutic progress than those with less severe symptoms and functional impairment. In complex cases, where clients had multiple, co-morbid chronic problems, particularly personality disorders, slower therapeutic progress was made than in less complex cases. A positive therapy outcome occurred where clients were not resistant to therapy and showed a readiness to change. Readiness to change in this context refers to a client's status on Prochaska's stages of change: pre-contemplation, contemplation, action, preparation, and maintenance (Prochaska & Norcross, 2002). Clients who were psychologically minded and who had high ego-strength benefited more from therapy than those who lacked these attributes. Psychologically minded people understand their problems in intrapsychic terms, rather than blaming them on external factors. Ego-strength is the capacity to tolerate conflict and distress, while showing flexibility and persistence in pursuing valued goals. In the social domain, the capacity to make and maintain relationships, the availability of a social support network, and high SES were all associated with a better therapeutic response than the absence of these features.

In a review of a series of psychotherapy outcome studies of adolescent and adult depression, bulimia, and alcohol abuse, Lambert (2005) found that a sizeable minority of clients show a pronounced early response to psychotherapy and subsequently show a more rapid recovery. Incidentally, in pharmacological treatment studies, a 'premature response' to medication is predicative of a poor outcome, since it reflects a placebo effect rather than a pharmacological effect. However, in psychotherapy the common factors of engaging in treatment, forming a therapeutic alliance, and being offered a credible rationale for therapy, promotes recovery before specific factors such as those associated with cognitive behaviour therapy, psychodynamic or family therapy would be predicated to have taken effect.

From this review it is clear that highly distressed clients with focal problems from well-functioning families with low levels of life stress and high levels of social support respond well to therapy. Clients with multiple complex co-morbid problems from multiproblem families with high levels of life stress and low levels of social support respond less well to therapy. Clients who are psychologically minded, who are ready and motivated to engage in therapy, who actively participate in the therapy process, and who show early improvement benefit more from therapy than those who do not.

Therapy context factors

The dose–effect relationship

Within the therapeutic context, a particularly important factor to consider is the amount of therapy clients receive. Research on the psychotherapy dose–effect relationship aims to address this issue by asking the question: How many sessions of therapy are necessary for recovery? The seminal study in this area was conducted by Kenneth Howard *et al.* (1986). In a probit analysis of 15 data sets from research studies spanning 30 years, involving over 2400 psychotherapy clients, Howard and his team found that 14% improved before their first therapy session; 53% improved after eight weekly sessions; 75% were improved by 26 sessions; and after 52 sessions, 83% had improved. Since Howard's study, more stringent criteria for improvement have been adopted in dose–effect studies, notably Jacobson *et al.*'s (1984) criterion of clinically significant improvement. According to this criterion, to show clinically significant improvement cases must move from the clinical to the non-clinical range on a standardized scale by an amount that is statistically defined as reflecting reliable change. As a result of adopting this more conservative index of improvement, most studies that have been conducted since Howard's seminal paper have found his estimate of 8, as the minimum number of sessions required for 50% of cases to improve, to be too small (Hansen *et al.*, 2002). A summary of results of a number of dose–effect relationship studies is given in Table 3.1. From this table it is clear that aggregating results from more recent studies of the dose–effect relationship in psychotherapy, it may be concluded that, for most acute and chronic symptoms, up to 21 sessions of therapy are required for 50% of clients to recover, not eight sessions as originally suggested by Howard in 1986. Figure 3.3 contains data

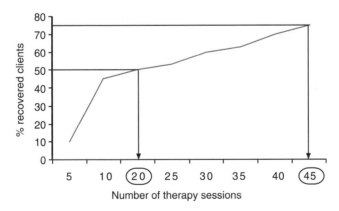

Figure 3.3 Psychotherapy dose–effect relationship.
Adapted from: Lambert *et al.* (2001).

Table 3.1 Results of dose–response studies

Author	Date	Sample size	Number of sessions for 50% of sample to show clinically significant recovery		Number of sessions for 75% of sample to show some improvement
Howard et al.	1986	2431	–		26
Kopta et al.	1994	854	5	(acute symptoms)	–
			14	(chronic symptoms)	
			104	(characterological symptoms)	
Maling et al.	1995	307	10	(control problems)	–
			38	(social detachment problems)	
Barkham et al.	1996	212	8	(depressive symptoms)	–
			16+	(interpersonal problems)	
Kadera et al.	1996	64	16		–
Anderson & Lambert	2001	140	13		50
Lambert, Hansen, & Finch	2001	6072	21		45
Hansen & Lambert	2003	4761	18		–

Adapted from: Hansen, Lambert, & Forman (2002). All samples include adult clients. Clinically significant recovery was evaluated using Jacobson et al.'s (1984) criterion.

from a large naturalistic study involving over 6000 clients, in which Lambert *et al.* (2001) showed that 21 sessions were required for clinically significant improvement in typical adult psychotherapy outpatients, but more than double this dose was required for 75% to make a clinically significant improvement. In Hansen *et al.*'s (2002) paper, in addition to reviewing all naturalistic effectiveness studies in which clients received differing doses of therapy, they also provided an overview of the dose–effect relationship in a sample of 28 methodologically robust psychotherapy efficacy studies, in which clients received predetermined fixed doses of therapy. These efficacy studies spanned a wide range of problem types and involved over 2000 clients. Hansen *et al.* (2002) concluded that in these efficacy studies 58–67% of clients improved within about 13 sessions. This suggests that slightly lower doses of psychotherapy may be required for recovery in clinical trials. This may reflect differences in the types of cases, types of therapy, or types of measures used in psychotherapy efficacy studies, compared with naturalistic dose–effect relationship studies. That is, compared with naturalistic studies, in efficacy studies less complex cases, more structured manualized therapy, and more reactive measures may be used which collectively lead to clients requiring less therapy to be classified as showing clinically significant improvement. However, the overall pattern of results from naturalistic studies and efficacy studies supports the conclusion that up to about 20 sessions of therapy is necessary for 50% of adult clients to recover from most acute and chronic symptoms of psychological distress.

The data summarized in Table 3.1 (p. 56) also show that different amounts of therapy are necessary for recovery from different types of problems, with more chronic or pervasive problems requiring more therapy sessions. In a probit analysis of clinically significant recovery in 854 patients, Kopta *et al.* (1994) found that symptoms of acute distress required five sessions; chronic symptoms required 14 sessions; and characterological symptoms required 104 sessions to achieve a 50% response rate. In a study of over 200 cases receiving 2, 8 or 16 sessions of either cognitive behavioural or psychodynamic therapy, Barkham *et al.* (1996) found that clinically significant recovery from interpersonal problems required higher doses of psychotherapy than did recovery from symptoms of depression or general distress. Only 40% showed recovery from interpersonal problems after 16 sessions. These results support the view that clients with pervasive characterological problems probably require more than 20 sessions of psychotherapy to make clinically significant progress.

Further support for the dose–effect relationship has come from major meta-analyses of outcome studies. For example, Shadish *et al.* (2000) in their meta-analysis of 90 studies of psychotherapy under clinically representative conditions found a correlation between therapy dose and effect size. No well-designed studies of the psychotherapy dose–effect relationship for children and adolescents have been conducted.

From this review it is clear that in adult psychotherapy there is a relationship between the dose of therapy received as indexed by the number of sessions, and the amount of improvement that occurs. More therapy leads to greater improvement, although the incremental benefit of each additional session diminishes as therapy progresses. Fifty per cent of clients can make a clinically significant recovery within about 20 sessions (or about six months of weekly sessions). However, for 75% of clients to show clinically significant recovery the dose must be doubled to about 40–50 sessions. In practical terms this amounts to weekly sessions over a period of about a year. The amount of therapy required to get optimal benefit varies depending upon client characteristics and diagnosis. For optimal benefit to be achieved, chronic characterological problems, like those associated with personality disorders, require more sessions than acute problems, like depression or anxiety.

The therapeutic alliance

Of all the common therapy context factors that contribute to the outcome of psychotherapy, the therapeutic alliance has received most attention. Research on this issue addresses the question: How important is the relationship between the therapist and the client for client recovery? In a meta-analysis of 79 trials of a range of different types of psychotherapy with a variety of adult psychotherapy populations, Martin *et al.* (2000) found a correlation of .22 between the therapeutic alliance and outcome. Shirk and Karver (2003) found precisely the same alliance–outcome correlation in a meta-analysis of 23 studies of a range of different types of psychotherapy with children and adolescents with a wide variety of psychological problems. Using the conversion system in Table 1.1 (p. 16), this correlation of .22 is equivalent to a moderate effect size of .45. It also indicates that the therapeutic alliance accounts for about 5% of the variance in outcome for psychotherapy clients. This is a very large contribution to the variance, in light of Wampold's (2001) estimate that overall psychotherapy accounts for 13% of the outcome for psychotherapy clients (as shown in Figure 3.2). When the effect of the alliance is expressed as a fraction of the overall effects of psychotherapy, it amounts to $\frac{5}{13}$, or 38%. Thus 38% of the effects of psychotherapy are due to the therapeutic alliance. Clearly, the therapeutic alliance is a major factor contributing to the outcome of all forms psychotherapy, and the most important common factor contributing to the effectiveness of psychotherapy.

The American Psychological Association Task Force on Empirically Supported Therapy Relationships, under the leadership of John Norcross (2002), conducted extensive literature reviews on all researched aspects of the therapeutic relationships and pinpointed ways in which strong therapeutic alliances may be fostered (Norcross, 2002). Their findings are remarkably consistent with those of David Orlinsky *et al.* (2004) who conducted a systematic wide-ranging narrative review of thousands of research studies on psycho-therapy process from 1950 to 2001. Both Norcross and Orlinsky confirmed the centrality of the therapeutic alliance to effective psychotherapy. They also concluded that a strong therapeutic alliance involves more than just good feelings or polite banter between therapists and clients. Rather, therapists and clients each contribute important elements which synergistically foster thera-peutic alliances. In effective therapy, clients engage in therapy in a co-operative way, initially availing of opportunities to prepare themselves for the client role, and then showing significant openness, expressiveness, and com-mitment to the therapy process, while therapists empathically collaborate with clients working towards consensually agreed therapeutic goals in a supportive and credible manner. In group therapy, therapists foster group cohesion. Within the therapy relationship, effective therapists show positive regard, genuineness, and provide clients with both relevant feedback and relevant self-disclosure information. Ruptures in the therapeutic alliance are common. These may be associated with client transference, therapist counter-transference or a mismatch between the client's needs on the one hand, and the therapist's way of conducting therapy on the other. Both Norcross and Orlinsky concluded that strong therapeutic alliances are maintained by managing such ruptures in therapeutic alliances and customizing therapeutic relationships to take account of clients' needs.

Common procedures

While an adequate number of sessions (20–45) and a good working alliance are important for effective psychotherapy, there is a range of procedures, common to most forms of therapy, that contributes to client recovery. These common procedures have been conceptualized in a variety of different ways. What follows is brief a synthesis of a number of the most influential and coherent of these common factor frameworks (Frank & Frank, 1991; Hubble et al., 1999; Karasu, 1986; Lambert & Ogles, 2004; Norcross & Goldfried, 2003; Sprenkle & Blow, 2004; Wampold, 2001). Effective therapy involves exploration and reconceptualization of both conscious and unconscious aspects of clients' problems; provision of a credible rationale for conducting therapy; generating hope and the expectation of improvement; and mobil-izing clients to engage in problem resolution. This mobilization process may involve helping clients develop more adaptive behaviour patterns and belief systems; more effective ways of regulating their emotions; and more support-ive emotional connections with themselves, their family members, and their therapists. There is also a developmental sequence common to most forms of psychotherapy in which interventions that support clients (such as reassur-ance and facilitating catharsis and emotional expression) precede interven-tions that promote learning to see problems in new ways (such as reframing and interpretation), and these in turn precede interventions that promote new forms of behaviour such as facing fears, regulating behaviour, interpersonal risk taking, and practising new skills.

Combining medication and therapy

For specific disorders, multimodal programmes in which psychotherapy and psychotropic medication are combined are more effective than either alone (Kazdin, 2004; Thase & Jindal, 2004). In children with attention deficit hyperactivity disorder, the effectiveness of psychotherapy, which includes parent-management training, school intervention, and self-instructional training for the child, can be greatly enhanced by combining this with stimulant therapy. In adults being treated with antipsychotic medication for schizophrenia, relapse rates may be reduced by offering psychoeducational family therapy to reduce family stress and cognitive behavioural therapy to improve symptom management. In adults being treated with mood stabilizing medication such as lithium for bipolar disorder, relapse rates can be reduced by offering cognitive behavioural therapy or psychoeducational family therapy. In adults the effectiveness of psychotherapy for depression, particularly severe depression, can be enhanced through the concurrent use of antidepressants. In both children and adults, the effectiveness of an exposure and response prevention, cognitive behavioural therapy protocol for obsessive-compulsive disorder can be enhanced through the use of antidepressants, notably clomipramine. For alcohol abuse in adults, disulfiram enhances the effectiveness of behavioural marital therapy, and psychotherapy improves the effectiveness of methadone maintenance for adult heroin addicts. A detailed review of evidence supporting the effectiveness of these multimodal programmes is given in Chapters 4 and 5. However, these research findings underline the value of combining psychotherapy and medication in specific circumstances, to facilitate adjustment and recovery.

Therapist factors

Bruce Wampold (2001) in a review of major meta-analyses, and reanalyses of data from large controlled psychotherapy outcome studies, concluded that 6–9% of the outcome variance is due to therapist effects. This is a large contribution to the outcome variance, in light of Wampold's (2001) estimate that overall, psychotherapy accounts for 13% of the outcome for psychotherapy clients (as shown in Figure 3.2). When the effect of the therapist is expressed as a fraction of the overall effects of psychotherapy, it amounts to $\frac{6}{13}-\frac{9}{13}$, or 46–69%. Thus, 46–69% of the effects of psychotherapy are due to the therapist (including therapist training, capacity to form an alliance, and specific therapeutic techniques). Clearly, the person of the therapist is a central factor contributing to the outcome of psychotherapy.

Lambert's (2007) research group have shown that there are considerable differences in the effectiveness of high and low functioning psychotherapists. In a series of studies involving 71 therapists, each of whom treated between 30 and 350 clients in routine outpatient psychotherapy, Lambert (2007) found large differences in the effectiveness of the top and bottom 10% of this group of therapists. Client improvement rates were 44% for the top 10% of therapists and 28% for the bottom 10%. Deterioration rates for the top and bottom 10% of therapists were 5% and 11% respectively. The allocation of therapists to these categories was based on their client recovery and deterioration rates as assessed by the Outcome Questionnaire 45 (Lambert *et al.*, 2004), which clients completed prior to each therapy session throughout the course of therapy.

Larry Beutler and his team (2004) conducted a comprehensive narrative review of more than a hundred empirical studies of therapist characteristics that have been found to correlate with therapeutic outcome. They concluded that the following therapist characteristics have been associated with therapeutic improvement: personal adjustment; therapeutic competence; matching therapeutic style to clients' needs; credibility; and problem-solving creativity. Effective therapists are well adjusted themselves. They are judged to be competent in offering therapy in a 'seamless' way. They match their style to clients' expectations and preferences. There is evidence for the effectiveness of three types of matching. For reflective, overcontrolled clients, an insight-oriented approach is particularly effective, whereas a symptom-focused, skills-building approach is more effective with impulsive, undercontrolled clients. For clients who are resistant to directives, a self-directed approach is most effective, whereas a directive approach is effective with non-resistant clients. For clients with a history of gratifying early relationships, confrontative insight-oriented approaches are effective, whereas supportive approaches are more effective for clients with histories of problematic early relationships. Beutler *et al.* (2004) also concluded that effective therapists creatively find new ways to formulate and reframe clients' problems, and offer clients credible rationales for learning and practising new adaptive skills for resolving problems.

Therapist training

A therapist factor of particular interest to psychotherapy trainers is the impact of therapist experience and training on therapeutic outcome. In a meta-analysis of the effects of psychotherapy training, Stein and Lambert (1995) found that for therapists with more training fewer clients dropped out of therapy, and their clients reported greater symptomatic improvement and greater satisfaction with therapy. The effect sizes for symptomatic improvement and satisfaction with therapy were .3 and .27 respectively. Using Table 1.1 (p. 16) for conversion, these effect sizes indicate that therapist training accounts for about 2% of the variance in outcome for psychotherapy clients. This is a moderate contribution to the variance, in light of Wampold's (2001) estimate that overall psychotherapy accounts for 13% of the outcome for psychotherapy clients (as shown in Figure 3.2). When the effect of therapist training is expressed as a fraction of the overall effects of psychotherapy, it amounts to $\frac{2}{13}$, or 15%. Thus, 15% of the effects of psychotherapy are due to therapist training. Clearly, therapist training is an important factor contributing to the outcome of psychotherapy.

This finding of a relationship between training experience and outcome is increasingly supported by well-conducted studies. For example, in a study conducted in a clinic for training therapists to use empirically validated treatments, Driscoll et al. (2003) found that client outcome was significantly related to therapists' total number of client contact hours. In a study on the effectiveness of three approaches to training in cognitive behavioural psychotherapy, Sholomskas (2005) found that therapists who attended a seminar and received supervision of their casework in the implementation of a manualized treatment protocol showed significantly better therapy skills as judged by independent observers than therapists who only reviewed the manual or completed a web-based training programme. The results of these two studies are examples from the growing body of evidence on the beneficial impact of training and experience on psychotherapy effectiveness. This evidence is in stark contrast to conclusions drawn from early studies in the area which suggested that there were no differences between the effectiveness of trained therapists and paraprofessionals with limited training (Atkins & Christensen, 2001).

Supervision and personal therapy

Supervision and engagement in personal therapy have a beneficial impact on therapist effectiveness. Lambert and Ogles (1997), in an extensive review of the effectiveness of psychotherapy supervision, concluded that supervision has a beneficial impact on both alliance formation and the use of technical skills. Milne and James (2000), in a systematic review of effective cognitive behavioural supervision, concluded that closely monitoring the supervisee, modelling competence, providing specific instructions, goal setting, and providing contingent feedback on performance have positive effects on therapist performance. Norcross (2005), in a synthesis of 25 years of research on the effects of personal therapy of mental health professionals, concluded that it has a positive impact on the quality of service psychotherapists offer to clients.

Flexible use of manuals

There is evidence that the flexible use of therapy manuals enhances therapy effectiveness for both children (Carr, 2000; Hibbs & Jensen, 2005; Kazdin & Weiss, 2003) and adults (Nathan & Gorman, 2007; Roth & Fonagy, 2005).

This is not surprising, since therapy manuals contain the blueprints for psychotherapy protocols that have been shown to lead to client recovery in efficacy studies. This in turn provides clinicians with clarity, and confidence that they are offering clients helpful and focused interventions based on credible rationales. Furthermore, the flexible rather than rigid use of manuals allows clinicians to match their therapy style to clients' needs. Finally, manuals probably help therapists avoid countertherapeutic practices such as drifting through therapy without a credible therapeutic focus and acting out destructive countertransference reactions evoked by clients with complex problems. From the foregoing, it is clear that the use of therapy manuals allows therapists not only to use specific techniques that are helpful with particular problems, but also to provide an avenue through which to offer their clients access to the 'common factors' characteristic of effective psychotherapy.

Therapy manuals evolved within the efficacy research tradition as a method for standardizing the way multiple therapists in a single study provided a particular psychotherapy protocol to a specific homogeneous group of clients with designated problems. Good therapy manuals provide a credible research-based rationale for treatment, broad principles or guidelines for conducting therapy, and detailed examples (with brief segments of therapy transcripts where appropriate) of how to use these guidelines in practice. For some types of therapy, such as psychodynamic or systemic therapy, this may be enough. For other types of therapy, for example, cognitive behavioural therapy, detailed session plans may be provided. To become proficient in using therapy manuals, therapists require ongoing supervision and periodic feedback on the extent to which they are adhering to the manualized therapy protocol. To facilitate this, good manuals include a briefing on supervision and integrity checklists for monitoring adherence. These contain a set of items used for rating therapy transcripts or tapes. The items specify what therapists who are using the manual accurately should and should not be doing in therapy sessions.

However, there is still much controversy over the widespread use of therapy manuals (Addis, 2002; Herschell et al., 2004). Those in favour of manuals point to their value in efficacy studies; positive instances where community-based clinicians have learned to use manualized therapy effectively; and the potential manuals have for enhancing initial psychotherapy training and ongoing continuing professional development. Those who question the value of manuals construe them as an inconvenient or ineffective imposition on clinical autonomy and judgement. They point to studies which show that in certain circumstances rigid adherence to manuals leads to worse therapy; in some efficacy studies there is little relationship between adherence to manualized protocols and client recovery; and in some instances manualized therapies lose their potency when moved from the university clinic to the community.

While the controversy continues, it is worth noting that there are numerous examples of manualized therapies that have been successfully moved from the university clinic to the community and which are highly acceptable to practising psychotherapists. Scott Henggeler's (Henggeler *et al.*, 1998) manual and related training and supervision system for multisystemic therapy for adolescent conduct problems and Marsha Linehan's (1993a, 1993b) manual and related training system for conducting dialectical behaviour therapy with adult borderline personality disorder are particularly good examples of therapy manuals that have built-in flexibility and can be used by community-based psychotherapists with these very difficult populations.

Receiving feedback

Providing therapists with feedback on client progress has been found to improve therapist effectiveness. In a meta-analytic review of three large-scale studies involving over 2600 clients and 100 therapists, Lambert *et al.* (2003) found that formally monitoring client progress before each session and giving this feedback to therapists had a significant impact on clients who showed a poor initial response to treatment. This feedback system reduced deterioration by 8% and increased positive outcomes by 13%. In all three studies in the meta-analysis, therapists were given clients' scores on the Outcome Questionnaire 45 before each session. The Outcome Questionnaire 45 gives an overall index of improvement or deterioration as well as scores for personal distress, interpersonal functioning, social role functioning, and quality of life (Lambert *et al.*, 2004). Where the Outcome Questionnaire 45 showed that clients were not making progress towards recovery or were deteriorating, this information was given to therapists along with suggestions that they consider taking corrective action by, for example, improving the therapeutic alliance, renegotiating the treatment contract, changing the treatment technique, intensifying treatment, or strengthening the client's social supports (Lambert, 2007).

In a study of 6424 clients with a wide range of problems such as anxiety, depression, and substance abuse from an international employee assistance programme, Miller *et al.* (2005) found that providing therapists with routine feedback on client outcome and the therapeutic alliance reduced drop-out and improved therapeutic effectiveness. The overall post-treatment effect size increased from .37 during a six-month baseline period when no feedback was available, to .79 more than a year after the feedback system was introduced. Thus the provision of feedback on outcome and alliance after each session almost doubled the effectiveness of therapy. In this research the Outcome Rating Scale (Miller *et al.*, 2003) and Session Rating Scale (Duncan *et al.*, 2004b) were used to assess outcome and the therapeutic alliance after each session. The Outcome Rating Scale, which is a short form of the Outcome Questionnaire 45 (Lambert *et al.*, 2004), inquires about general well-being, personal well-being, family relationships, and adjustment at work or school. The Session Rating Scale inquires about the therapeutic alliance, therapy goals, therapy methods, and the overall quality of the therapy session. Both of these four-item visual analogue scales, along with a computer administration, scoring and data management, and feedback system for use by individual practitioners or whole agencies called Partners for Change Outcome Management System (PCOMS) are available at http://www.talkingcure.com/. The system provides graphs of progress and suggestions for addressing deterioration when it occurs. These suggestions include talking with the client about the therapeutic alliance; exploring ways of aligning the therapeutic approach more closely with the client's theory of change; and engaging in consultation or supervision. Duncan and Miller's group have developed a 'common factors', client-directed, outcome-oriented approach to psychotherapy, partly arising from these findings. The approach rests on the assumption that a strong therapeutic alliance, shared therapeutic goals, and a consensus about how to achieve these, based largely on the client's theory of change, along with regular feedback on these issues and outcome are central to effective therapy (Duncan *et al.*, 2004b).

Conclusions

Factors common to the wide variety of effective psychotherapies are two to nine times more important than specific factors in determining whether or not clients benefit from psychotherapy. The central question addressed in this chapter was: What factors common to the wide variety of effective psychotherapies are responsible for their effectiveness? Common factors are not simply placebo effects because the effects of psychotherapy are nearly double those of placebos. Common factors include those associated with the client, the therapist, and the therapeutic process (see Table 3.2).

Client characteristics

Distressed clients with circumscribed problems from well-functioning families, with little life stress and much social support respond well to therapy. Those with multiple complex co-morbid problems from multiproblem families with much stress and little support respond less well to therapy. Psychologically minded clients with much ego-strength, who are motivated to engage in therapy, who actively participate in the therapy process, and who show early improvement benefit more from therapy than those who do not.

Therapist characteristics

About 46–69% of the effects of psychotherapy are due to the therapist (including therapist training, capacity to form an alliance, and specific

Table 3.2 Therapy, client, and therapist factors that affect positive psychotherapy outcome

Therapeutic context factors	Client factors	Therapist factors
Dose of 20–45 sessions	High personal distress	Personal adjustment
Positive therapeutic alliance	Low symptom severity	Therapeutic competence
• Empathy	Low functional impairment	Matching style to patient
• Collaboration and goal consensus	Low problem complexity / chronicity / co-morbidity	• Overcontrolled – insight
• Positive regard and genuineness	Readiness to change and lack of resistance	• Undercontrolled – symptom skills
• Relevant feedback and relevant self-disclosure	Early response to therapy	• Positive past relationships – insight
• Repair alliance ruptures	Psychological mindedness	• Negative past relationships – support
• Manage transference and countertransference	Ego-strength	• Compliant clients – directive
Common procedures	Capacity to make and maintain relationships	• Resistant clients – self-directed
Problem exploration	Social support	Credibility of rationales
Credible rationale	High socio-economic status	Problem-solving creativity
Mobilizing client		Specific training
Support and catharsis		Flexible manual use
Reconceptualizing problem		Supervision and personal therapy
Behavioural change		Feedback on client recovery
Combining psychotherapy and medication for specific problems		

therapeutic techniques). Effective therapists are technically competent, credible and creative in their approach to helping clients solve problems. They have engaged in personal therapy, are well adjusted, well trained, use therapy manuals flexibly, and use feedback on client progress to match their therapeutic style to clients' needs.

Therapeutic common factors

For 50–75% of psychotherapy clients to recover, 20–45 sessions of therapy are necessary. The therapeutic alliance is the single most important therapeutic common factor and accounts for about 38% of the effectiveness of psychotherapy. For a strong therapeutic alliance, the therapist must be empathic and collaborative, and the client must be co-operative and committed to recovery. The common procedures that characterize effective therapy include exploration and reconceptualization of conscious and unconscious aspects of problems; provision of a credible rationale for conducting therapy; generating hope and the expectation of improvement; and mobilizing clients to engage in problem resolution. These broad procedures may involve using therapeutic techniques such as providing support and encouraging emotional expression; facilitating new ways of viewing problems; and helping clients to develop new ways of behaving adaptively. For certain disorders, multimodal programmes in which psychotherapy and pharmacotherapy are combined are more effective than either alone.

Further reading

Lambert, M. (2004). *Bergin and Garfield's Handbook of Psychotherapy and Behaviour Change* (Fifth Edition). New York: Wiley.
Wampold, B. E. (2001). *The Great Psychotherapy Debate: Models, Methods, and Findings*. Mahwah, NJ: Lawrence Erlbaum Associates, Inc.

Effectiveness of psychotherapy and psychological interventions with specific problems in children, adolescents, and people with intellectual disabilities and pervasive developmental disorders

The central question addressed in this chapter is: What specific psychotherapy protocols and psychological interventions have been found to be effective for children, adolescents, and people with intellectual and pervasive developmental disabilities with a range of psychological problems? Or, put more succinctly: What works for children, adolescents, and people with disabilities?

In this chapter, evidenced-based conclusions will be presented about the effectiveness of specific psychotherapy protocols and psychological practices with specific problems in children, adolescents, and people with intellectual and pervasive developmental disabilities. Traditional psychiatric categories (such as attention deficit hyperactivity disorder, conduct disorder, anorexia nervosa, etc.) have been used to organize some of the evidence reviewed in this and the next chapter. Such categories are described in the American Psychiatric Association's *Diagnostic and Statistical Manual* (*DSM-IV-TR*, 2000a) and the World Health Organization's *International Classification of Diseases* (*ICD-10*, 1992). This categorical approach, premised on a medical model of psychological difficulties, may be ideologically unacceptable to service users and psychotherapists who adopt psychodynamic, humanistic, cognitive behavioural, and systemic frameworks. Many psychotherapists and service users view psychiatric diagnoses as being on a continuum with normal development and functioning, or as a reflection of systemic rather than individual shortcomings. However, the organization, administration, and funding of clinical services and research programmes are framed predominantly in terms of the ICD and DSM systems and so diagnostic categories from these systems have been used to organize the material in this chapter and the next.

To draw conclusions about the effectiveness of psychotherapy protocols and psychological interventions, extensive computer and manual literature searches for relevant evidence were conducted. The terms used in these searches included names of disorders and problems that may be treated with psychotherapy, for example, anxiety, depression, and so forth, along with terms reflecting the type of evidence being sought, such as meta-analysis, critical review, randomized controlled trial, treatment outcome study, and so forth. A range of databases such as PsycINFO and Medline were searched, along with the tables of contents of major academic journals in the fields of psychotherapy, counselling, psychology, psychiatry, social work, nursing, and related fields. In addition, a search was conducted of key textbooks, or volumes of authoritative edited chapters in the area (e.g. Barrett & Ollendick, 2004; Fonagy *et al.*, 2002; Hibbs & Jensen, 2005; Kazdin & Weisz, 2003). These intensive literature searches focused mainly on the ten-year period from 1997 to 2007. Earlier literature was searched less intensively. For each of the main problem areas, such as anxiety, depression, and so forth, the most recent and most authoritative meta-analyses and narrative literature reviews of the effectiveness of psychotherapy or psychological interventions were selected for inclusion. Where meta-analyses and narrative literature reviews could not be found, randomized controlled trials were selected for inclusion.

In this chapter, for each specific type of problem, results of selected meta-analyses, reviews, and outcome studies will briefly summarized. Then, implications for clinical practice will be presented. For comparative purposes, and where appropriate, reference will be made to the effectiveness of pharmacological and other physical interventions, although these are not the main focus of this volume. The research reviewed in this and other chapters has many implications for future research and policy development. A consideration of these issues will be reserved for the final chapter of this book.

The literature search described in this chapter yielded evidence to show that psychotherapeutic interventions alone, or as one element of multimodal programmes involving pharmacotherapy or other physical interventions, are effective for the following specific problems in childhood and adolescence:

- sleep problems
- toileting problems (enuresis and encopresis)
- attachment problems
- attention deficit hyperactivity disorder (ADHD)
- pre-adolescent oppositional defiant disorder
- adolescent conduct disorder
- adolescent drug abuse
- juvenile sex offending
- child and adolescent depression
- bipolar disorder
- attempted suicide and self-harm
- child and adolescent anxiety disorders (phobias, separation anxiety and generalized anxiety, selective mutism, obsessive-compulsive disorder, and post-traumatic stress disorder)

- eating disorders (feeding problems, anorexia nervosa, bulimia, obesity)
- Tourette's disorder
- paediatric pain problems (headaches, recurrent abdominal pain, painful medical procedures)
- adjustment to chronic medical conditions (asthma and diabetes)
- adjustment problems following major life transitions and stresses (parental separation, bereavement, child abuse and neglect)
- adjustment problems associated with intellectual disability
- adjustment problems associated with autism spectrum disorders.

What follows is a summary of the evidence for the effectiveness of specific psychotherapy protocols and psychological interventions for each of these types of problems.

Sleep problems

A systematic review of 41 studies of psychological interventions for sleep problems in young children by Mindell (1999) and of nine randomized controlled trials, five of psychological and pharmacological interventions by Ramchandani et al. (2000), indicate that both psychological and pharmacological interventions are effective in the short term, but only psychological interventions have positive long-term effects on children's sleep problems. Both reviews showed that effective treatment for settling and night waking problems in young children involves parental psychoeducation and support in behavioural management of sleep problems. In behavioural management programmes, parents are coached in reducing or eliminating children's daytime naps, developing positive bedtime routines, reducing parent–child contact at bedtime or during episodes of night waking, and introducing scheduled waking where children are awoken 15 to 60 minutes before the child's spontaneous waking time and then resettled. Trimeprazine is as effective as behavioural treatment in the short term, but its effects cease when medication is withdrawn.

Practice implications for sleep problems

Psychological interventions are the treatment of choice for childhood sleep problems.

Toileting problems

For childhood enuresis (wetting) and encopresis (soiling), the highly structured psychological interventions outlined below are effective in alleviating these difficulties in most cases.

Enuresis

In a systematic review and meta-analysis of 53 randomized controlled trials, Glazener *et al.* (2003) found that urine alarm programmes were an effective treatment for childhood nocturnal enuresis (bedwetting). These programmes involve coaching the child and family to use an enuresis alarm which alerts the child as soon as micturition begins. Urine alarm programmes, if used over 12–16 weeks, are effective in about 60–90% of cases (Houts, 2003). The urine wets a pad which closes a circuit, and sets off the urine alarm, which wakes the child, who gradually learns by this conditioning process to awake before voiding the bladder. In some instances, children learn to defer micturition till morning. For treatment to be effective parents must be centrally involved, so it is essential that they be helped to appreciate the amount of time and level of involvement required for successful treatment. Relapses may be prevented through overlearning, i.e. giving the child extra fluids at bedtime after successfully becoming dry after using the alarm. More sophisticated programmes involving urine alarms and additional behavioural components such as dry bed training and full spectrum home training have also been identified in major narrative reviews to be particularly effective (Mellon & McGrath, 2000). *Dry bed training* aims to condense many trials of rehearsal, retention and control training, awakening to the enuresis alarm, and cleanliness training into a very brief period of time (Azrin *et al.*, 1974). *Full spectrum home training* involves education; cleanliness training and using reward systems; retention control training; and overlearning (Houts & Liebert, 1984). There is also some evidence that modifications of the pad and bell apparatus are effective. For example, using an ultrasonic monitor to indicate when the bladder is nearly full instead of waiting for the child to wet the pad (Pretlow, 1999), or providing the child with biofeedback (Hoek *et al.*, 1998) are promising alternatives to the traditional urine alarm, and these newer interventions should be a focus for future research. Children with secondary enuresis, those with additional behavioural problems, and those who are experiencing stressful family circumstances are less responsive to treatment and more likely to relapse (Mikkelsen, 2001). Drug treatment such as desmopressin acetate (DDAVP) may be as effective as urine alarm programmes in the short term, but children relapse as soon as medication is stopped (Glazener *et al.*, 2003).

Encopresis

In a narrative review of 42 studies McGrath *et al.* (2000) found that for childhood encopresis (soiling) multimodal programmes involving medical assessment and intervention followed by behavioural intervention or biofeedback were particularly effective. Initially a paediatric medical assessment is conducted, and if a faecal mass has developed this is cleared with an enema. A balanced diet containing an appropriate level of roughage and regular laxative use are arranged. Effective therapy involves psychoeducation about encopresis coupled with a reward programme to reinforce appropriate daily toileting routines. Neither behavioural treatment alone nor dietary intervention and laxative use alone are as effective as both together, which in combination have success rates of 43–75%. Biofeedback to improve control of the external anal sphincter combined with medical assessment and intervention as described above is also effective. However, the use of biofeedback does not contribute to the effectiveness of a combined medical and behavioural programme (Brazzelli & Griffiths, 2001). Ritterband *et al.* (2003) have recently shown that psychoeducation and coaching in behavioural management of encopresis provided on the internet enhances the effectiveness of routine treatment in primary care settings.

Practice implications for enuresis and encopresis

Enuresis alarm programmes should be used for nocturnal enuresis and multimodal programmes involving medical assessment and intervention followed by behavioural intervention should be used for encopresis.

Attachment problems

Insecure attachment in infancy is a risk factor for psychological disorders in later life (Cassidy & Shaver, 1999). Attachment theory proposes that where parents are insufficiently sensitive to their offsprings' moment-to-moment needs, infants fail to develop secure attachments to their parents, whom they do not experience as a reliable source of security (Bowlby, 1988). This hypothesis has inspired the development of psychological intervention programmes to enhance parental sensitivity to infants, and the security of infant–mother attachment (Berlin & Ziv, 2005). In a meta-analysis of 70 studies evaluating a variety of interventions to enhance parental sensitivity and mother–infant attachment, Bakermans-Kranenburg *et al.* (2003) concluded that brief, highly focused behavioural interventions that specifically aimed to enhance maternal sensitivity to their infants were particularly effective in modifying insensitive parenting (effect size = .33) and reducing infant attachment insecurity (effect size = .20). These effect sizes are equivalent to success rates of 55–57%. Interventions had a greater effect on maternal sensitivity than infant attachment security. Programmes that were more effective in enhancing parental sensitivity were also more effective in enhancing attachment security, which supports the notion of a causal role of sensitivity in shaping attachment. The most effective interventions were under 15 sessions in duration; focused on helping mothers develop sensitivity to their infants' cues; involved fathers as well as mothers; and began after children were six months (rather than prenatally or during early infancy). In these programmes mothers learned to carry infants close to their chest, in their arms, or in special baby-carriers, for extended time periods. They also learned to recognize, interpret, and respond to infants' signals to pre-empt and minimize distress. Programmes used a variety of methods including workbooks, video modelling, video feedback, and direct coaching to achieve these aims. Such programmes were as effective for families with, as well as without, multiple problems. Broader programmes that aimed to address many psychosocial family issues over longer time periods were less effective than brief, behavioural, sensitivity focused programmes. However, there is evidence from a randomized controlled trial that psychoanalytic therapy which spans about a year is effective in reducing attachment insecurity in toddlers of mothers with a history of depression (Toth *et al.*, 2006). In a trial involving 130 mothers with a history of depression and their 1–2-year-old toddlers, Toth *et al.* (2006) found that, compared with a control group, mother–toddler dyads who engaged in toddler–parent psychotherapy showed a reduced rate of insecure attachments immediately after treatment and a year later when the children were about three years of age. The intervention involved about 45 conjoint mother–child sessions over a period of about a year. Therapists provided a containing relationship for mother–infant dyads; a context within which mothers and infants could develop positive internal working models of self and others; and opportunities to replace transactions typical of insecure attachment with secure attachment transactions. The intervention was based on Fraiberg *et al.*'s (1975) psychoanalytic approach to impaired infant–mother relationships.

Practice implications for attachment problems

For childhood attachment problems, in the first instance, brief 15-session psychological interventions, focused on enhancing mother's sensitivity to infant's signals and extending periods of mother–infant physical contact, are the treatment of choice. Where such programmes are ineffective, particularly where mothers have mental health problems, extended mother–infant psychodynamic therapy should be considered.

Attention deficit hyperactivity disorder

Attention deficit hyperactivity disorder (ADHD) is a syndrome of predominantly genetic aetiology, characterized by inattention, overactivity, and impulsivity (American Psychiatric Association, 2000a). Multimodal programmes, pharmacotherapy, and dietary interventions are widely used for ADHD and evidence for their effectiveness is reviewed below.

Multimodal programmes for ADHD

Hinshaw *et al.* (2007) conducted a systematic review of 14 methodologically robust randomized controlled studies of the effects of long-term treatment of ADHD, along with controlled single case studies and previous reviews. They concluded that effective psychological intervention for ADHD in preschool and school-aged children and adolescents is best offered as one element of a multimodal programme involving stimulant medication and behaviourally oriented family, school, and child-focused psychological interventions. About 70% of children with ADHD benefit from such multimodal programmes. In the short term, within such programmes, medication makes by far the most significant contribution to helping children regulate their activity levels and attention.

However, psychological interventions do not always increase the benefit of stimulant treatment. In two of the largest and most intensive trials, psychological interventions added no significant benefit to that conferred by stimulant medication. These trials were the MTA Co-operative Group (2004) study of 579 children, and Abikoff and colleagues' (2004) study of 103 children. In both studies multiple sites were involved; children had *DSM-IV* ADHD; children were 7–9 years old; stimulant medication was carefully titrated; clients participated in intensive psychological interventions for more than a year; and outcome was assessed by multiple informants. In both trials, cases were randomized to a number of trial arms, including stimulant medication and stimulant medication combined with intensive psychosocial intervention. In both trials there was no significant difference between these two conditions one and two years after starting treatment, and cases in both of these conditions fared significantly better than those that received psychosocial intervention only.

However, in the MTA study, at three years follow-up, there was no difference in the outcome of cases that received stimulant treatment alone, psychological intervention alone, or a multimodal programme involving both interventions (Jensen *et al.*, 2007). This finding may reflect the fact that at three years follow-up 45% of cases who had originally received the psychological intervention alone had started stimulant treatment, while only 71% of those in the multimodal programme continue on medication. It may also reflect the delayed impact of psychological intervention, when offered alone.

In their review of 14 randomized trials, Hinshaw *et al.* (2007) also concluded that where psychological interventions have an impact, they do so by enhancing parenting skills and the quality of interactions between children with ADHD, their families, teachers, and peers. Once psychological interventions are well established, it may be possible for children to remain asymptomatic on lower doses of medication, or for medication to be discontinued. Also, where co-morbid anxiety disorders are present, psychosocial interventions have a more pronounced effect on children's adjustment, than when ADHD occurs without such co-morbid problems. Similar conclusions have been reached in other systematic reviews (Anastopoulos *et al.*, 2005; Friemoth, 2005; Jadad *et al.*, 1999; Klassen *et al.*, 1999; Purdie *et al.*, 2002; Schachar *et al.*, 2002).

Effective psychological intervention for ADHD has three principal elements: parent management training; school-based behavioural management; and child-focused skills training (Hinshaw *et al.*, 2007). Parent management training focuses on promoting rule following at home while school interventions focus on the management of learning difficulties and conduct problems within the classroom. Both types of programmes are based on behavioural procedures where specific positive and negative behaviours are targeted. Reinforcement and extinction procedures are used to increase the frequency of positive target behaviours and reduce the frequency of negative target behaviours. There is growing evidence for the effectiveness of Barkley's (1997, 2000, 2005) Defiant Children programme which is a good example of how to conduct parent training in families with children with ADHD. There is also good evidence for the effectiveness of Pelham *et al.*'s (2005) Summer Treatment Programme and many procedures used in this programme may be adapted for regular classroom settings. In multimodal programmes, child-focused therapy aims to help children develop social and self-regulation skills, particularly anger management. Hinshaw's (2005) child-focused programme for children with ADHD has a growing evidence base. A promising innovation in the child-focused psychological treatment of ADHD is the use of computer-based programmes to train children to enhance the functioning of working memory, which in turn has a positive impact on inattention, impulsivity, and hyperactivity. One controlled study has provided support for the effectiveness of this treatment approach (Klingberg *et al.*, 2005) and future evaluations of this innovative intervention should be a research priority. Psychological interventions collectively contribute to normalizing ADHD behaviour, largely by improving parenting practices, and enhancing the way children with ADHD interact with their families and social networks. Studies on how and when these processes occur are required to inform decisions on reduction in medication dosage.

Pharmacotherapy of ADHD

The main effects of medication in ADHD are to improve attention and reduce activity levels. Methylphenidate, a stimulant, is the most widely used medication for ADHD. It is available in a form which is taken twice or three times a day, or as a slow release preparation taken only once a day. Both forms are equally effective, and reduce ADHD symptoms in children with a single diagnosis or with co-morbid conditions such as conduct disorder or pervasive developmental disorder. About 70% of children respond to methylphenidate and 13% to placebo (Paykina *et al.*, 2007). However, methylphenidate and other stimulants such as dextroamphetamine and pemoline may adversely affect growth and cardiovascular functioning; and lead to a variety of somatic complaints including loss of appetite, headaches, insomnia, and tics which occur in 5–12% of cases (Paykina *et al.*, 2007; Rapport & Moffitt, 2002). Currently, little is known about the long-term effects in adulthood of stimulant therapy throughout childhood and adolescence. This has provided an impetus for identifying other medications for treating ADHD. In wide-ranging reviews Paykina *et al.* (2007), Spencer *et al.* (2002) and Fonagy *et al.* (2002, Chapter 6) concluded that ADHD symptoms may be alleviated to some degree by a range of medications including atomoxetine, clonidine, tricyclic antidepressants, monoamine oxidaise inhibitors, selective serotonin reuptake inhibitors, and carbamezapine.

Diet and ADHD

Concerns about the side effects of medications generally have inspired exploration of dietary and complementary or alternative treatments for ADHD. In a review of 23 controlled studies of dietary interventions for ADHD, Jacobson and Schardt (1999) found that in 17 studies there was evidence that some children with ADHD who test positive for specific food allergies benefited from individually tailored exclusion diets. However, there is currently no evidence to support the use of complementary and alternative therapies in the treatment of ADHD (Brue & Oakland, 2002).

Practice implications for ADHD

Multimodal programmes involving stimulant medication and behaviourally oriented family, school and individually oriented psychological interventions should be offered to children with ADHD. These conclusions are consistent with international best practice guidelines (American Academy of Child & Adolescent Psychiatry, 2007a; American Academy of Paediatrics, 2001; Consensus Development Panel, 2000; Kutcher *et al.*, 2004).

Pre-adolescent oppositional defiant disorder

Oppositional defiant disorder refers to serious defiant, oppositional, non-compliant, rule-breaking behaviour; and to hostility and tantrums within the home or family context, but not within the wider community (American Psychiatric Association, 2000a; World Health Organization, 1992). These behaviour problems are maintained by both personal attributes (such as temperamental characteristics, self-regulation problems, and skills deficits) on the one hand and contextual factors (such as problematic parenting practices) on the other (Burke *et al.*, 2002). For pre-adolescent behaviour problems, behavioural parent training is the most strongly supported evidence-based intervention.

Parent training vs. child-focused interventions

In a meta-analysis of 30 behavioural parenting programmes and 41 child-focused skills training programmes, McCart *et al.* (2006) found that for children under 12 parent training programmes (effect size = .45) were significantly more effective than child-focused programmes (effect size = .23). The superiority (albeit modest) of parent training over child-focused programmes is borne out by two previous meta-analyses. In a meta-analysis of 30 studies of child-focused skills training programmes, Bennett and Gibbons (2000) found an effect size of .23, while Serketich and Dumas (1996), in a meta-analysis of 26 studies of the effectiveness of behavioural parent training for families of pre-adolescents, found an effect size of .86 for children's behaviour problems. Numerous other meta-analyses and systematic reviews concur that behavioural parent training is a particularly effective form of psychological intervention for pre-adolescent conduct problems (e.g. Barlow *et al.*, 2002; Behan & Carr, 2000; Brestan & Eyberg, 1998; Burke *et al.*, 2002; Coren *et al.*, 2002; Farrington & Welsh, 2003; Kazdin, 1997, 2003; Nixon, 2002; Nock, 2003). Collectively these reviews cover an evidence base of over 100 studies. They show that about 60–70% of pre-adolescents benefit from behavioural parent training programmes of 10 to 20 sessions. Gains are maintained at one-year follow-up. Maintenance of gains is enhanced by periodic booster sessions during the follow-up period. Behavioural parent training also has a positive impact on the high rate of parental adjustment problems, such as parental depression and marital distress, among parents of children with oppositional defiant disorder. For example, in their meta-analyses of parent training studies Serketich and Dumas (1996) found an effect size of .44 and McCart *et al.* (2006) found an effect size of .33 for parental adjustment. These effect sizes correspond to success rates of 58–61% for parental adjustment.

Behavioural parent training protocols for pre-adolescent oppositional defiant disorder

One of the most widely researched behavioural parent training programmes is based on Patterson's (1976) manual *Living With Children*. Programmes based on this approach include psychoeducation about the role of child characteristics and parenting practices in the development and maintenance of childhood behaviour problems. Such programmes also involve helping parents develop skills for pinpointing and monitoring antisocial and prosocial behavioural targets. A critical element of behavioural parent training is helping parents develop behavioural skills for increasing the frequency of children's prosocial behaviour (through attending, reinforcement, and engaging in child-directed interactions) and reducing the frequency of antisocial behaviour (through ignoring, time out, contingency contracts, and engaging in parent-directed interactions).

In the wake of Patterson's programme, a number of others have been developed. Those with strong evidence bases are *Parent–Child Interaction Therapy* (Brinkmeyer & Eyberg, 2003); the *Triple P* suite of programmes (Sanders *et al.*, 1998a, 1998b); the *Incredible Years* suite of programmes (Webster-Stratton & Reid, 2003); and Alan Kazdin's *Parent Management Training* (Kazdin, 2003).

Meta-analyses are now beginning to appear which focus on the efficacy of specific programmes. For example, Thomas and Zimmer-Gembeck (2007) conducted a meta-analysis of 13 studies of Parent–Child Interaction Therapy and 11 studies of the Triple P parenting programme. They found post-treatment effect sizes for parent-reported child behaviour problems of 1.45 for the standard ten-session Parent–Child Interaction Therapy and .69 for the standard 12-session Triple P parenting programme. These results suggest that Parent–Child Interaction Therapy may be more effective than the Triple P programme, possibly because the former involves giving immediate feedback to parents on how to interact with children, using a 'bug in the ear' device.

Feedback and behavioural parent training for pre-adolescent oppositional defiant disorder

Immediate feedback, video feedback, and video modelling have been used in effective behavioural parent training programmes. With video feedback approaches, parents learn child management skills by watching videotaped episodes of themselves using parenting skills with their own children. With immediate feedback, parents are directly coached in child management skills through a 'bug in the ear' while the therapist observes their interaction with their children from behind a one-way mirror. Eyberg's *Parent–Child Interaction Therapy* for parents of preschoolers is a good example of this approach (Brinkmeyer & Eyberg, 2003). With video-modelling-based approaches, parents learn child management skills through viewing video clips of actors illustrating successful and unsuccessful parenting skills. Webster-Stratton's *Incredible Years* programme is a good example of this type of approach and its effectiveness is supported by a strong evidence base (Webster-Stratton & Reid, 2003). One advantage of this type of approach is that it allows parent training to occur in a group format.

Child-focused skills training for pre-adolescent oppositional defiant disorder

The effectiveness of behavioural parent training programmes may be enhanced by concurrently engaging children in therapy which aims to remediate deficits in social and problem-solving skills. In this regard, there are growing evidence bases for Webster-Stratton's *Child Dinosaur Programme* (Webster-Stratton & Reid, 2003) and Kazdin's (2003) *Social Problem-Solving Skills Training* programme. Webster-Stratton's video-modelling-assisted, child-focused pro-gramme includes sessions on empathy, problem solving, anger control, friendship skills, communication skills, and managing school. Kazdin's child-focused, social problem-solving skills training involves coaching children to address conflict and complex interpersonal situations by breaking big unmanageable problems into smaller manageable problems; brainstorming solutions; evaluating the pros and cons of these; selecting the best option; implementing this; evaluating progress; modifying the solution if it is ineffect-ive; and celebrating success. Lochman's *Anger Coping Programme*, for which there is some evidence of effectiveness, may also be usefully combined with behavioural parent training to address youngsters' self-regulation deficits (Lochman *et al.*, 2003).

Parental stress and support interventions for pre-adolescent oppositional defiant disorder

In a meta-analysis of 31 studies, Reyno and McGrath (2006) found that pov-erty (effect size = .52), maternal mental health (effect size = .39), and single parent status (effect size = .20) predicted poor response to behavioural parent training. Clearly, high levels of parental stress and low levels of social support reduce the effectiveness of behavioural parent training. To address these bar-riers to effective behavioural parent training, adjunctive interventions which enhance parental support and stress management skills have been added to traditional behavioural parent training with positive incremental benefits. For example, in the meta-analysis mentioned above, Thomas and Zimmer-Gembeck (2007) found that the post-treatment effect sizes for parent-reported child behaviour problems were 2.16 for an enhanced version of the Parent–Child Interaction Therapy (compared with 1.45 for the standard version) and .96 for an enhanced version of the Triple P parenting programme (compared with .69 for the standard version). In the enhanced Parent–Child Interaction Therapy programme, in addition to the standard 12-session programme, there were six preliminary sessions which aimed to enhance parents' motivation to engage in treatment, and additional individual counselling to address parental difficulties such as depression, substance abuse, and marital difficulties. In the enhanced Triple P programme, in addition to the standard ten-session pro-gramme, there were sessions on troubleshooting obstacles to implementing new parenting strategies, coping skills training for managing anxiety and depression, and interventions to promote partner support.

Pre-adolescent children with callous unemotional traits and oppositional defiant disorder

Children with severe conduct problems coupled with callous unemotional traits are particularly unresponsive to behavioural parent training (Hawes &

Dadds, 2005). Callous unemotional traits are thought to be the precursors of psychopathy in children and are strongly genetically determined. They include lack of empathy, lack of remorse, and constricted affect. In an evaluation of behavioural parent training with 56 families, Hawes and Dadds (2005) found that families of children with callous unemotional traits showed a poorer response after treatment and at six months follow-up. Boys with high callous unemotional traits were less responsive to discipline with time out than boys without such traits and reacted to this discipline with less affect. The modification of parent training programmes to meet the unique needs of families of children with callous unemotional traits is an important priority for future research in this area.

The therapeutic alliance in parent training for pre-adolescent oppositional defiant disorder

The therapeutic alliance is as vital to effective parent training as to success with other forms of psychotherapy. In a study of 185 families engaged in concurrent behavioural parent training and child-focused social problem-solving skills training, Kazdin *et al.* (2005) found that stronger parent–therapist and child–therapist alliances led to better therapeutic outcomes. Research on the therapeutic alliance may be an important focus for enhancing behavioural parent training programmes to meet the needs of the 30–40% of families who cannot benefit from routine treatment. Using the therapeutic alliance to engage at-risk families in treatment, enhance adherence to home-work assignments, and prevent drop-out are some of the main challenges to be addressed in further developing behavioural parent training.

Practice implications for pre-adolescent oppositional defiant disorder

For pre-adolescent behaviour problems, behavioural parent training is the intervention of choice. This may be offered on a single family or group basis. Video modelling may be incorporated into group programmes. Immediate or video-based feedback may be used during parent training. Concurrent child-focused interventions may be added to enhance children's social skills and anger management. Where parents have high levels of life stress and little social support, additional interventions may be offered to address these issues. These conclusions are consistent with international best practice guidelines (American Academy of Child & Adolescent Psychiatry, 2007b).

Conduct disorder

Conduct disorder refers to a pattern of persistent, serious, aggressive, and destructive rule-breaking behaviour at home and within the wider community

(American Psychiatric Association, 2000a; World Health Organization, 1992). For adolescents with conduct disorder, their antisocial behaviour may be maintained by personal attributes on the one hand and contextual factors on the other (Burke *et al.*, 2002). Problematic temperamental characteristics, self-regulation routines, attributional styles, and social and academic skills deficits are among some of the more notable personal factors that maintain conduct disorders. Conduct problem-maintaining contextual factors include problematic relationships with parents, school staff, and professionals within health, social and juvenile justice services, as well as membership of deviant peer groups.

In a meta-analysis of eight family-based treatment studies of adolescent conduct disorder, Woolfenden *et al.* (2002) found that family-based treatments including functional family therapy, multisystemic therapy, and treatment foster care were more effective than routine treatment. Compared with treatment-as-usual, family-based treatments significantly reduced time spent in institutions; the risk of rearrest; and the recidivism rate for one to three years following treatment. These effective family-based psychosocial interventions for adolescent conduct disorder fall on a continuum of care which extends from functional family therapy, through more intensive multisystemic therapy, to very intensive treatment foster care (Brosnan & Carr, 2000; Kazdin, 2007; Nock, 2003).

Functional family therapy for adolescent conduct disorder

Functional family therapy is an evidence-based, manualized model for conducting systemic family therapy in cases where adolescents have conduct disorders or have become involved in juvenile offending (Sexton & Alexander, 2003). Functional family therapy involves distinct stages of engagement, where the emphasis is on forming a therapeutic alliance with family members; behaviour change, where the focus is on facilitating competent family problem-solving; and generalization, where families learn to use new skills in a range of situations and to deal with setbacks. Whole family sessions are conducted on a weekly basis. Treatment spans 8–30 sessions over three to six months. A comprehensive system for transporting functional family therapy to community settings, training and supervising therapists, and for maintaining treatment fidelity in these settings, has also been developed. In a systematic review of 13 clinical trials of functional family therapy, Alexander *et al.* (2000) concluded that this approach to therapy is effective in reducing recidivism by 26–73% in adolescent offenders with conduct disorders from a variety of ethnic groups over follow-up periods of up to five years, compared with those receiving routine services. It also leads to a reduction in conduct problems in siblings of offenders. In a review of a series of large-scale effectiveness studies, Sexton and Alexander (2003) found that functional family therapy was $5000–12,000 less expensive per case than juvenile detention or residential treatment and led to crime and victim cost savings of over $13,000 per case. The same review concluded that in a large-scale effectiveness study, the drop-out rate for functional family therapy was about 10% compared to the usual drop-out rates of 50–70% in routine community treatment of adolescent offenders. This is in part due to the fact that during the initial engagement and motivation phase of functional family therapy, therapists use supportive techniques to reduce negative family interactions, and low rates of negative family interaction have been found to reduce drop-out from functional family therapy.

Multisystemic therapy for adolescent conduct disorder

For adolescents unresponsive to functional family therapy, with more severe conduct problems, multisystemic therapy is appropriate. Multisystemic therapy is an evidence-based manualized approach to treatment which combines intensive family therapy with individual skills training for the adolescent, and intervention in the wider school and interagency network (Henggeler & Lee, 2003). Multisystemic therapy involves helping adolescents, families, and involved professionals understand how adolescent conduct problems are maintained by recursive sequences of interaction within the youngsters' family and social network; using individual and family strengths to develop and implement action plans and new skills to disrupt these problem-maintaining patterns; supporting families to follow through on action plans; helping families use new insights and skills to handle new problem situations; and monitoring progress in a systematic way. Multisystemic therapy involves regular, frequent home-based family and individual therapy sessions with additional sessions in the school or community settings over three to five months. Therapists carry low caseloads of no more than five cases and provide 24-hour, seven-day availability for crisis management. A comprehensive system for transporting multisystemic therapy to community settings, training and supervising therapists, and for maintaining treatment fidelity in these settings has also been developed. In a meta-analysis of 11 studies evaluating the effectiveness of multisystemic therapy, Borduin *et al.* (2004) found a post-treatment effect size of .55, equivalent to a success rate of 63% and positive effects were maintained up to four years after treatment. Multisystemic therapy had a greater impact on improving family relations than on improving individual adjustment or peer relations. In a systematic review of eight studies, Henggeler and Lee (2003) concluded that compared with treatment-as-usual, multisystemic therapy led to significant improvements in individual and family adjustment which contributed to significant reductions in out-of-home placement, recidivism, behaviour problems, substance abuse, and school absence. Multisystemic therapy led to a 25–70% decrease in rearrests and a 47–64% decrease in rates of out-of-home placement over one to four years. These outcomes entailed cost savings of over $60,000 per case in placement, juvenile justice, and crime victim costs.

Multidimensional treatment foster care for adolescent conduct disorder

For adolescents who cannot be treated within their own families, multidimensional treatment foster care is a viable alternative. This combines procedures similar to multisystemic therapy with specialist foster placement, in which foster parents use behavioural principles to help adolescents modify their conduct problems (Chamberlain & Smith, 2003, 2005). Treatment foster care parents are carefully selected, and before an adolescent is placed with them they undergo intensive training. This focuses on the use of behavioural parenting skills for managing antisocial behaviour and developing positive relationships with antisocial adolescents. They also receive ongoing support and consultancy throughout placements which last six to nine months. Concurrently, the biological family and young person engage in weekly family therapy with a focus on parents developing behavioural parenting practices, and families developing communication and problem-solving skills. Adolescents also engage in individual therapy, and wider systems consultations are carried out with youngsters' schoolteachers, probation officers, and other involved professionals, to ensure all relevant members of youngsters' social systems are co-operating in ways that promote youngsters' improvement. About 85% of adolescents return to their parents' home after treatment foster care. In a review of two studies of treatment foster care for delinquent male and female adolescents, Chamberlain and Smith (2003) found that compared with care in a group home for delinquents, multidimensional treatment foster care significantly reduced running away from placement, rearrest rate, and self-reported violent behaviour. The benefits of multidimensional treatment foster care were due to the improvement in parents' skills for managing adolescents in a consistent, fair, non-violent way and reductions in adolescents' involvement with deviant peers. These positive outcomes of multidimensional treatment foster care entailed cost savings of over $40,000 per case in juvenile justice and crime victim costs.

Negative contagion effects associated with group programmes for adolescent conduct disorder

Traditionally, adolescents with conduct problems have been treated in residential group settings. There is now strong evidence to show that the benefits of the apparent initial cost savings of group treatment are outweighed by the negative contagion effects. That is, a significant proportion of youngsters with conduct disorder treated in residential group settings deteriorate over the course of treatment and develop more significant conduct problems by interacting with deviant peers (Dishion & Dodge, 2005). Meta-analyses have shown that 'scared straight' programmes (Petrosino et al., 2003) and boot camps (MacKenzie et al., 2001) increase antisocial behaviour and recidivism. There is little doubt that some group programmes, such as adventure- or wilderness-based therapy, in which groups of delinquents are engaged in challenging adventure activities, increase self-esteem but meta-analyses show that these programmes have little effect on antisocial behaviour (Bedard *et al.*, 2003; Neill, 2003).

Practice implications for adolescent conduct disorder

For adolescents with conduct disorder, family-based interventions may be offered on a continuum of care which extends from functional family therapy, through more intensive multisystemic therapy, to very intensive treatment foster care.

Adolescent drug abuse

Adolescent drug abuse refers to a continuous pattern of drug use leading to significant impairment in functioning (Liddle, 2005). In a systematic narrative review of 53 studies of the treatment of adolescent drug abusers, Williams and Chang (2000) concluded that the average rate of sustained abstinence after psychological intervention was 38% with a range from 30 to 55% at six months, and 32% with a range from 14 to 47% at one year. Adolescents who benefited most from treatment had less severe drug abuse before treatment; strong support from their families and peer groups to stop abusing drugs; and did not drop out of treatment before programme completion. Williams and Chang's (2000) review covered therapeutic community programmes, outward bound programmes, 12-step Minnesota model programmes, outpatient individual therapy, and outpatient family therapy. They concluded that comparative studies consistently showed family therapy to be more effective than other types of treatment for adolescent drug abuse.

Family therapy for adolescent drug abuse

In a meta-analysis of seven studies of the effectiveness of family therapy compared to alternative therapies for adolescent drug abuse, Stanton and Shadish (1997) found an effect size of .39 for reduced drug use at follow-up, which is equivalent to a success rate of 60%. In three wide-ranging reviews of 13 controlled trials of family therapy for adolescent drug abuse, along with many therapy process studies, Liddle and his team (Liddle, 2004; Ozechowski & Liddle, 2000; Rowe & Liddle, 2003) concluded that for a significant proportion of youngsters family therapy was more effective than routine individual or group psychotherapies in engaging and retaining youngsters in therapy, reducing drug use, and improving psychological, educational, and family adjustment. These gains were maintained a year or more after treatment. The engagement rate for family therapy was typically over 80% whereas with individual therapy it was about 60%. Liddle's team also concluded that family therapy was more cost-effective than residential treatment.

Effective family therapy for adolescent drug abuse involves regular family session over a three- to six-month period, as well as direct work with young-sters and other involved professionals, with the intensity of therapy matched to the severity of the youngster's difficulties (Cormack & Carr, 2000; Liddle, 2004; Liddle *et al.*, 2005; Muck *et al.*, 2001; Ozechowski & Liddle, 2000; Rowe & Liddle, 2003; Santiseban *et al.*, 2006; Szapocznik & Williams, 2000; Williams & Chang, 2000). Family therapy for adolescent drug abuse involves distinct phases of engaging youngsters and their families in treatment; help-ing families organize for youngsters to become drug free; helping families create a context for the youngster to maintain a drug-free lifestyle; helping youngsters acquire skills to remain drug free; family reorganization; co-operation with other community services and professionals; relapse preven-tion training for youngsters and their families; and disengagement. In some instances youngsters may require such therapy to be offered as part of a multimodal programme involving medical assessment, detoxification, and methadone maintenance, if youngsters are addicted to heroin and unready to become completely drug free. Two manualized models of family treat-ment which have particularly strong evidence bases are Liddle's *Multidimen-sional Family Therapy* (Liddle, 2005) and Szapocznik's *Brief Strategic Family Therapy* (Szapocznik *et al.*, 2002).

Cognitive behavioural therapy for adolescent drug abuse

There is also evidence for the effectiveness of cognitive behavioural therapy for adolescent drug abuse. In three narrative reviews of controlled trials and uncontrolled studies, Waldron and Kaminer (Kaminer, 2005; Kaminer & Waldron, 2006; Waldron & Kaminer, 2004) concluded that while family ther-apy leads to more rapid improvement in adolescent drug abusers, after 6 to 12 months individual or group-based cognitive behavioural therapy is as effective as family therapy. Furthermore, contagion effects common in group treatment of antisocial youngsters (Dishion & Dodge, 2005) have not been found in cognitive behavioural group treatment studies of adolescent drug abusers. Waldron and Kaminer, in their reviews, concluded that older males with mood disorders derive most benefit from cognitive behavioural therapy for substance abuse, and youngsters with co-morbid conduct disorder show least improvement. Cognitive behavioural therapy protocols for substance abuse in adolescence include motivational interviewing to facilitate engage-ment in treatment; self-monitoring, contingency contracting, and substance refusal skills training to help youngsters reduce or cease substance use; coping, communication, and problem-solving skills training to help youngsters man-age life difficulties and negative mood states associated with substance abuse; and relapse prevention to promote long-term improvement.

Motivational interviewing for adolescent drug abuse

Motivational interviewing and related non-confrontational interventions designed to help people with drug problems weigh up the pros and cons of drug abuse, and so become more motivated to enter treatment, have been found to have positive effects in adults (Hettema *et al.*, 2005). In a review of the small but growing literature on motivational enhancement interventions for adolescent cigarette smoking and alcohol use, Tevyaw and Monti (2004) concluded that these approaches led to decreases in smoking and drinking, and alcohol-related life difficulties, and increased treatment engagement. Motivational enhancement interventions are most effective with less-motivated adolescents.

Practice implications for adolescent drug abuse

Family therapy is the treatment of choice for adolescent drug abuse. Where families cannot be engaged in therapy, individual or group-based cognitive behavioural therapy may be offered, with the caution that group treatment entails the risk of contagion effects, and may be most appropriate for older adolescents with co-morbid mood disorders.

Juvenile sex offending

Juvenile sex offending includes a range of deviant sexual behaviours, ranging from non-contact offences such as exposure, through contact offences such as masturbation, to oral, anal, and vaginal penetrative sex, and these offences may be perpetrated against other juveniles or adults (O'Reilly *et al.*, 2005).

In a meta-analysis of nine treatment trials for juvenile sex offenders involving 2986 cases, Reitzel and Carbonell (2006) found that treated juvenile sex offenders showed 12 percentage points or 63% less sexual recidivism than controls after an average follow-up period of about five years. The sexual offending recidivism rate was 7% for treated cases and 19% for untreated cases. These results are consistent with those of a previous meta-analysis (Walker *et al.*, 2004).

In Reitzel and Carbonell's (2006) meta-analysis, the mean age of participants was 14.6 years and 41% were from ethnic minorities. The nine studies in their meta-analysis evaluated a range of community-based and residential programmes, with an average duration of 13 months. Most programmes incorporated a combination of individual, group, and family-based sessions. Of the various programmes evaluated in the nine studies, multisystemic and cognitive behavioural programmes were particularly well developed. In multisystemic programmes, skills training interventions with juvenile offenders were combined with family therapy and network meetings with involved professionals, in light of a coherent systemic formulation of factors maintaining sexual deviance, to achieve clearly defined goals. This approach is described in *Multisystemic Treatment with Juvenile Sexual Offenders and their Families* (Borduin *et al.*, in press). Cognitive behavioural programmes focus on helping juvenile offenders accept responsibility for sexual offending and understanding personal and situational factors that increase the risk of offending; modifying justificatory cognitive distortions and developing victim empathy; developing social skills for forming intimate relationships; developing skills for coping with negative mood states; and forming a relapse prevention plan. This approach is described in *Handbook of Clinical Intervention with Young People who Sexually Abuse* (O'Reilly *et al.*, 2005).

Practice implications for juvenile sex offenders

Treatment for juvenile sex offenders should be guided by a broad-based multisystemic and developmental framework, and take account of youngsters' strengths as well as sexual deviance. Treatment should involve sessions with youngsters and their families and wider professional networks. Multisystemic and cognitive behavioural programmes are particularly well developed, and should be prioritized. While treatment can be effective for a proportion of juvenile sex offenders, it is only one element of effective overall management of juvenile sex offenders and community protection. Monitoring and support by correctional agencies and juvenile offenders' families are other key elements of a wider community protection strategy. These conclusions are broadly consistent with international best practice and policy guidelines (American Academy of Child & Adolescent Psychiatry, 1999; Association for the Treatment of Sexual Abusers, http://www.atsa.com/; Miner *et al.*, 2006; National Organization for the Treatment of Abusers, http://www.nota.co.uk/).

Child and adolescent depression

Major depression in children and adolescents is an episodic disorder characterized by low or irritable mood, loss of interest in normal activities, and most of the following symptoms: psychomotor agitation or retardation, fatigue, low self-esteem, pessimism, inappropriate excessive guilt, suicidal ideation, impaired concentration, and sleep and appetite disturbance (American Psychiatric Association, 2000a; World Health Organization, 1992). Typical episodes last for four months, and recur periodically with inter-episode intervals varying from a few months to a number of years. In contrast to this episodic disorder, dysthymia is a persistent disorder characterized by low mood and at least two of the other symptoms of major depression.

In the most comprehensive available meta-analysis of 35 randomized controlled studies of psychotherapy for child and adolescent depression, Weisz *et al.* (2006) obtained an effect size of .34. This indicates that the average treated case fared better than 63% of untreated cases and is equivalent to a success rate of about 58%. This modest effect size is more valid than the larger effect size of .72 found by Michael and Crowley (2002) in an earlier, smaller, and less methodologically robust meta-analysis of 14 trials of psychotherapy for child and adolescent depression. Weisz *et al.* (2006) also found that there were no significant differences in outcome between cognitive behavioural treatments and other treatments, or between treatments conducted under optimal or routine clinical conditions, a conclusion also reached by Spielmans *et al.* (2007) in a meta-analysis of treatments for both depression and anxiety in children and adolescents. Weisz *et al.* (2006) found that treatment gains were maintained at six months follow-up, but not at one year follow-up. This is not surprising given the episodic and recurrent nature of major depression. A summary of results of reviews and key studies of psychotherapy conducted within particular therapeutic traditions will now be offered.

Cognitive behavioural therapy for child and adolescent depression

There is evidence from a number of reviews for the effectiveness of cognitive behavioural therapy in the treatment of child and adolescent depression. In a systematic review of six studies of cognitive behavioural therapy for major depression in children and adolescents, Harrington *et al.* (1998) found a remission rate of 62% for treated cases and 36% for untreated cases. In a meta-analysis of studies of cognitive behavioural therapy for depression in adolescence, Lewinsohn and Clarke (1999) found a post-treatment effect size of 1.27. They also found that 63% of patients showed clinically significant improvement. In a meta-analysis of six studies of cognitive behavioural therapy for depression in adolescence, Reinecke *et al.* (1998) obtained a post-treatment effect size of 1.02 and a follow-up effect size at 6–12 months of .61. Collectively these results indicate that between just over 60% to just over 70% of young people diagnosed with a depressive disorder benefit from cognitive behavioural therapy.

In an important comparative trial (summarized in Weersing & Brent, 2003), Brent and his team found that immediately after treatment more youngsters who received cognitive behavioural therapy (60%) were in remission compared with those who received family therapy (38%) or supportive therapy (39%). However, at two years follow-up there were no significant differences between the outcomes of the three groups. Recovery rates were 94% for cognitive behavioural therapy, 77% for family therapy, and 74% for supportive therapy. In all three groups, a negative family environment characterized by maternal depression and family conflict on the one hand, and severe cognitive distortions and depressive symptomatology on the other, were associated with poorer outcome. The positive effects of cognitive behavioural therapy arose predominantly from changes in depressive cognitive distortions. Positive changes in family functioning accounted for improvements in the family therapy group. In all three groups a rapid improvement during the first couple of sessions occurred in just over a third of cases, and was predictive of a positive outcome. Therapeutic factors common to all three types of therapy, such as the quality of the therapeutic alliance, probably accounted for this rapid improvement. All participants in this study received 12–16 sessions. During the follow-up period, 62% used other services for depression, 33% for family problems, and 31% for conduct problems. The results of the study suggest it may be worthwhile combining individually oriented cognitive behavioural therapy and family therapy to address both intrapsychic and interpersonal depression-maintaining factors, and to extend therapy beyond 16 sessions so that additional services are not required.

Cognitive behavioural therapy for depression rests on the hypothesis that low mood is maintained by a depressive thinking style and a constricted lifestyle that entails low rates of response-contingent positive reinforcement. Cognitive behavioural therapy programmes for adolescents evaluated in treatment trials have two main components which target these two maintaining factors: behavioural activation and challenging depressive thinking (Compton *et al.*, 2004). In challenging depressive thinking, youngsters learn mood monitoring, and how to identify and challenge depressive negative automatic thoughts and cognitive distortions that accompany decreases in mood. With behavioural activation youngsters reorganize their daily routines so they involve more pleasant events, physical exercise, and social interaction. They also develop skills to support this process including social skills, relaxation skills, communication and problem-solving skills, and relapse prevention skills. Some cognitive behavioural programmes for depression in young people include concurrent intervention with parents, which helps them understand factors that maintain depression and support youngsters in following through on the behavioural activation and cognitive components of the child-focused part of the programme. Cognitive behavioural therapy usually spans 10–20 child-focused sessions and may be offered on an individual or group basis. Where concurrent parent sessions occur, usually about 5–10 of these are offered. Lewinsohn's group-based programme (Clarke *et al.*, 2003; Rohde *et al.*, 2005) and Brent's (Weersing & Brent, 2003) and Weisz's (Weisz *et al.*, 2003) individual cognitive behavioural therapy programmes are good examples of well-developed evidence-based approaches in this area.

Psychodynamic therapy for child and adolescent depression

Two trials provide evidence for the effectiveness of psychodynamic psychotherapy with children and adolescents with depression (Muratori *et al.*, 2003; Trowell *et al.*, 2007). In a randomized controlled study of 72 youngsters aged 9–15 assigned to psychodynamic or family therapy, Trowell *et al.* (2007)

found that about 75% of cases in both groups were fully recovered after therapy. One hundred per cent of those who received psychodynamic therapy and 81% of those who received family therapy were fully recovered at six months follow-up (but this group difference was not significant). Psychodynamic and family therapy also led to a significant reduction of double depression (major depression with co-morbid dysthymia) and rates of other co-morbid conditions. In this study psychodynamic therapy involved an average of 25 individual sessions and 12 concurrent parent sessions spanning nine months, following a manual based on Malan and Osimo (1992) and Davenloo's (1978) model of brief psychodynamic psychotherapy. In this model the focus is on interpreting the links between defences, anxiety, and unconscious feelings and impulses, within the context of the transference relationship with the therapist, the relationship with significant people in the child's current life, and early relationships with parents or caregivers. Family therapy involved an average of 11 sessions spanning nine months based on Byng-Hall (1995) and Will and Wrate's (1985) integrative model of family therapy.

In a non-randomized controlled study of 58 children aged 6–10 years, most of whom had dysthymia, assigned to psychodynamic therapy or community-based treatment as usual, Muratori *et al.* (2003) found that at two years follow-up 66% of those who received psychodynamic psychotherapy were recovered compared with 38% in the control group. Also, those who received psychodynamic therapy used fewer other services (30 vs. 34%). In this study, psychodynamic therapy involved 11 conjoint parent–child sessions and several additional individual sessions for children only, based on Camer and Palacio Espasa's (1993) model. Within this model in the first phase, parent-focused work occurs where parent–child interactions are interpreted in terms of their defensive functions. Play-based, child-focused work occurs in the second phase, with the aim of helping the child understand and articulate links between feelings, wishes, and symptoms. In the final phase, the core-conflictual theme that links the parent's defensive style to the child's symptoms is explored.

Taken together, the results of these two trials provide evidence for the effectiveness of psychodynamic therapy with children and adolescents for two-thirds of children and virtually all adolescents with depression. The exceptionally positive outcome of psychodynamic psychotherapy in Trowell *et al.*'s (2007) study is very impressive and requires replication.

Interpersonal therapy for child and adolescent depression

There is evidence from three controlled efficacy studies, a controlled effectiveness study, and a single group outcome study (summarized in Mufson & Dorter, 2003; Mufson *et al.*, 2005; Rossello & Bernal, 2005) that interpersonal psychotherapy is an effective treatment for adolescent depression which leads to recovery in more than 75% of cases. In two comparative studies, inter-personal therapy was found to be as effective as cognitive behavioural therapy for adolescent depression (Rossello & Bernal, 2005). Interpersonal therapy for adolescent depression targets five interpersonal difficulties which are assumed to be of particular importance in maintaining depression: (1) grief associated with the loss of a loved one; (2) role disputes involving family members and friends; (3) role transitions such as starting or ending relation-ships within family, school or peer group contexts, moving houses, gradu-ation, or diagnosis of an illness; (4) interpersonal deficits, particularly poor social skills for making and maintaining relationships; and (5) relationship difficulties associated with living in a single parent family. In interpersonal therapy, the specific focal interpersonal factors that maintain the youngster's depressive symptoms are addressed within a series of child-focused and conjoint family sessions.

Family therapy for child and adolescent depression

There is evidence from five studies for the effectiveness of family therapy for child and adolescent depression, two of which have already been mentioned (Trowell et al., 2007; Weersing & Brent, 2003). In a comparative study, Trowell et al. (2007) found that 11 sessions of family therapy were as effective as a programme which included 25 sessions of psychodynamic therapy coupled with 12 adjunctive parent sessions; 75% of cases no longer met the criteria for depression after treatment; and 81% were recovered at six months follow-up. Byng-Hall (1995) and Will and Wrate's (1985) integrative model of family therapy were used in this trial. Therapy involved techniques from many schools of family therapy and helped families understand the links between the youngster's depression, problematic family scripts, and insecure family attachment patterns. It also helped family members develop more secure attachments to each other and re-edit problematic family scripts to form a more coherent narrative about how to manage stress and life-cycle transitions.

In a controlled study of attachment-based family therapy for depression with 32 adolescents, Diamond et al. (2002) found that after treatment 81% of treated cases no longer met the criteria for depression, whereas 47% of the waiting list control group did. At six months follow-up 87% of cases were not depressed. Attachment-based family therapy involves the following sequence of interventions which have been shown in process studies to underpin effect-ive treatment: relational reframing; building alliances with the adolescent first and then with the parents; repairing parent–adolescent attachment; and building family competency (Diamond, 2005).

In another comparative study, Brent's team (Weersing & Brent, 2003) found that only 38% of depressed adolescents were recovered immediately after family therapy, but at two years follow-up 77% no longer met the criteria for depression. Family therapy was less effective in the short term, but as effective in the long term as cognitive behavioural therapy. Improvements in family functioning accounted for youngsters' recovery. A behavioural systems approach to family therapy was used in this trial. This involved using family-based behavioural interventions such as problem monitoring, communication and problem-solving skills training, contingency contracting, and relapse prevention to reduce family conflict, enhance family relationships, and promote better mood management.

In a controlled trial involving the families of 31 adolescents, Sanford *et al.* (2006) evaluated the incremental benefit of adding psychoeducational family therapy to a routine treatment programme involving predominantly supportive counselling and antidepressant medication. Three months after treatment 75% of the family therapy group and 47% of controls no longer met the criteria for depression, and parent–adolescent relationships in the family therapy group were significantly better than in the control group. A 13-session, home-based adaptation of Falloon *et al.*'s (1984) family therapy model was used in this study. Treatment included psychoeducation about depression, communication and problem-solving skills training, and relapse prevention.

In a single group outcome study for adolescents with co-morbid depression and substance abuse, Curry *et al.* (2003) found that after a combined programme of cognitive behavioural therapy and family therapy, 50% of cases recovered from depression and 66% from substance abuse. The programme spanned ten weeks, with weekly family therapy sessions and twice weekly cognitive behavioural therapy group sessions. Robin and Foster's (1989) model of family therapy for negotiating parent–adolescent conflict was used in this programme.

Collectively these studies lend support for attachment-based, psychoeducationally oriented, and behavioural systems approaches to family therapy as effective treatments for depressed adolescents.

Pharmacotherapy for child and adolescent depression

In a meta-analysis of 13 studies of the effectiveness of tricyclic antidepressants for depression in young people, Hazell *et al.* (2002) concluded that tricyclic antidepressants are ineffective with children and only have a small impact on adolescent depression. In contrast, there is growing evidence that selective serotonin reuptake inhibitors may have a role in the treatment of depression in young people. In reviews of controlled trials of serotonin reuptake inhibitors for child and adolescent depression, Cheung *et al.* (2005) and Vasa *et al.* (2006) found a number of serotonin reuptake inhibitors, notably fluoxetine, alleviated the symptoms of depression in about two-thirds of children and adolescents and led to complete remission in about a third of cases. However, because serotonin reuptake inhibitors may lead to increased suicidal ideation and behaviour, considerable caution is required in using them in the treatment of children and adolescents with mood disorders (Fortune & Hawton, 2005; Hall, 2006; Healy, 2003).

Results of the large multisite Treatment for Adolescent Depression Study (TADS Team, 2004), which involved 439 depressed adolescents, showed that cognitive behavioural therapy combined with fluoxetine led to a significantly higher improvement rate (71.0%) than medication alone (60.6%), which in turn led to a significantly higher improvement rate than cognitive behavioural therapy alone (43.2%). Cognitive behavioural therapy combined with serotonin reuptake inhibitors also led to the greatest reduction in suicidal thinking, compared with the other two conditions. This provides a rationale for combining serotonin reuptake inhibitors with cognitive behavioural therapy in moderate depression. In an analysis of factors related to outcome in the TADS study, Curry et al. (2006) found that cognitive behavioural therapy combined with serotonin reuptake inhibitors was more effective than antidepressants alone for mild to moderate depression and for depression with high levels of cognitive distortion, but not for severe depression or depression with low levels of cognitive distortion.

In contrast to the results of the TADS study, Goodyer et al. (2007) in the UK multicentre Adolescent Depression Antidepressant and Psychotherapy Trial (ADAPT) involving 208 adolescents with severe depression who had not responded to an initial brief trial of psychotherapy, found that there was no significant benefit in terms of recovery from depression or reduction in suicidal ideation associated with adding 19 sessions of cognitive behavioural therapy to routine outpatient consultations at a specialist clinic and serotonin reuptake inhibitors. By 28 weeks 57% of trial participants showed clinically significant improvement including reduced suicidality. The sample in this study included cases of severe depression that would have been excluded from the TADS study because of suicidality, depressive psychosis, or co-morbid conduct disorder. Thus for severe adolescent depression, of the type typically referred to UK specialist services, the addition of cognitive behavioural therapy to routine specialist care and antidepressant treatment confers no additional benefit. Two additional US studies have yielded similar results. In a randomized trial involving 152 depressed adolescents, Clarke et al. (2005) found that the addition of cognitive behavioural therapy to routine treatment with serotonin reuptake inhibitors had a negligible impact on the course of depressive symptoms. In a randomized multisite trial involving 73 moderately depressed adolescents, Melvin et al. (2006) found that treatment with antidepressants (sertraline), cognitive behavioural therapy, and both combined had similar outcomes six months after treatment.

The results of the studies reviewed in this section support the use of serotonin reuptake inhibitors in severe depression in young people, when they do not respond to a brief trial of psychotherapy. However, because there is some evidence that treatment with serotonin reuptake inhibitors may be associated with increased suicide risk in adolescents, regular monitoring of this is essential (Fortune & Hawton, 2005; Hall, 2006; Healy, 2003).

Electroconvulsive therapy for child and adolescent depression

There are currently no data from controlled trials to support the use of electroconvulsive therapy with adolescents (Findling *et al.*, 2004; Walter *et al.*, 1999).

Practice implications for child and adolescent depression

From this review it may be concluded that effective psychotherapy for child and adolescent depression should optimally include both individual and family components. Effective protocols have been developed within the cognitive behavioural, interpersonal, psychodynamic, and family therapy traditions. The family-based component of effective psychotherapy for child and adolescent depression includes family psychoeducation; facilitating family understanding and support of the depressed youngster; and organizing home–school liaison to help the youngster re-establish normal home and school routines. The individual psychotherapy component involves exploration of contributing factors; facilitating mood monitoring; increasing physical exercise, social activity, and pleasant events; modification of depressive thinking styles, depression-maintaining defence mechanisms, and depression-maintaining patterns of social interaction; the development and use of social problem-solving skills; and the development of relapse prevention skills. Particularly effective psychotherapy programmes for child and adolescent depression involve about a dozen family sessions and twice as many individual sessions. Psychotherapy may be offered as part of a multimodal programme of which antidepressants are one element. However, caution is warranted in using serotonin reuptake inhibitors with youngsters, since they may increase suicide risk. The central role of psychotherapy in the treatment of child and adolescent depression is acknowledged in international best practice guidelines (American Academy of Child & Adolescent Psychiatry, 1998a; NICE, 2004a).

Bipolar disorder

Bipolar disorder is a recurrent episodic mood disorder, with a predominantly genetic basis, characterized by episodes of mania or hypomania, depression, and mixed mood states (American Psychiatric Association, 2000a; World Health Organization, 1992). The course of bipolar disorder is significantly affected by stressful life events and family circumstances on the one hand, and family support on the other. The primary treatment for bipolar disorder is pharmacological, and involves the initial treatment of acute manic, hypomanic, depressive, or mixed episode, and the subsequent prevention of further episodes with mood stabilizing medication such as lithium. Preliminary evidence from three studies suggests that psychoeducational family therapy may be helpful in adolescent bipolar disorder. Psychoeducational family therapy aims to reduce family stress and enhance family support for youngsters with bipolar disorder who are concurrently taking mood stabilizing medication such as lithium carbonate or carbamezapine (Miklowitz & Goldstein, 1997). In a single group outcome study of 20 bipolar adolescents, Miklowitz et al. (2004) found that a 21-session, family-focused treatment programme involving psychoeducation, and communication and problem-solving skills training led to improvements in depressive and manic symptoms and behaviour problems. In another single group outcome study of 34 bipolar adolescents, Pavuluri et al. (2004) found that a 12-session, family-focused treatment programme involving psychoeducation, communication and problem-solving skills training, and cognitive behavioural therapy for bipolar adolescents led to improvements in depressive and manic symptoms and global functioning. In a controlled trial involving the families of 35 youngsters with bipolar disorder or major depression, Fristad et al. (2003) found that the addition of an eight-session, multifamily group psychoeducation to routine treatment with medication and counselling, led to significant gains in knowledge and enhanced family relationships.

Practice implications for bipolar disorder in children and adolescents

Multimodal programmes which include mood stabilizing medication and family therapy are the current treatment of choice for bipolar disorder in adolescence. The important role of psychotherapy in the treatment of bipolar disorder in young people is acknowledged in international best practice guidelines (American Academy of Child & Adolescent Psychiatry, 2007c; Kowatch et al., 2005).

Suicide in adolescence

Psychotherapeutic interventions from the systemic tradition, notably multisystemic therapy, and the cognitive behavioural tradition show particular promise in improving the adjustment of adolescents who have attempted suicide (Bridge et al., 2006; Donaldson et al., 2003; Gould, 2003; Klomek & Stanley, 2007). Psychological interventions can also enhance engagement in psychotherapy. Evidence to support these assertions is reviewed below.

Engaging suicidal adolescents in psychotherapy

Attempted suicide is a risk factor for later suicide attempts, so engaging adolescents who have attempted suicide in psychotherapy is an important step in preventing subsequent self-harm (Bridge *et al.*, 2006). Because this process can be challenging, procedures to enhance engagement in psychotherapy have been developed, and evidence from two trials supports their effectiveness. Donaldson *et al.* (1997) compared the rates of missed psychotherapy appointments and suicidal attempts of 78 adolescents who received standard psychiatric evaluation in a hospital emergency department following attempted suicide with that of 23 adolescents who, in addition to standard care, received an intervention to enhance engagement in psychotherapy. This intervention involved a verbal agreement between adolescents and their parents or guardians to attend at least four psychotherapy sessions and then three phone interviews over an eight-week period focusing on reducing suicidal ideation and engaging in psychotherapy. The intervention to enhance engagement in psychotherapy led to significantly fewer missed psychotherapy appointments and fewer suicide attempts. None of the participants in the intervention designed to enhance engagement in psychotherapy reattempted suicide, compared to 9% in the standard treatment group. In a later randomized controlled trial of 63 adolescents who had attempted suicide, Spirito *et al.* (2002) found that at three months follow-up, after taking account of barriers to receiving services in the community, adolescents who received an intervention to enhance engagement in psychotherapy attended significantly more treatment sessions than those who received standard care.

Multisystemic therapy

Multisystemic therapy is an evidence-based manualized approach to treatment, originally developed for adolescent conduct disorder as was noted above, but which has been adapted for use with adolescents who have severe mental health problems including attempted suicide. The application of multisystemic therapy to such problems is described in *Multisystemic Treatment of Children and Adolescents with Serious Emotional Disturbance* (Henggeler *et al.*, 2002). Multisystemic therapy combines intensive family therapy with individual skills training for the adolescent, and intervention in the wider school and interagency network. It involves regular, frequent home-based family and individual therapy sessions with additional sessions in the school or community settings over three to five months. Huey *et al.* (2004) evaluated the effectiveness of multisystemic therapy for suicidal adolescents in a randomized controlled study of 156 African American adolescents at risk for suicide referred for emergency psychiatric hospitalization. Most of these youngsters were depressed, but also had multiple other co-morbid difficulties.

Compared with emergency hospitalization and treatment by a multi-disciplinary psychiatric team, Huey *et al.* found that multisystemic therapy was significantly more effective in decreasing rates of attempted suicide at one year follow-up.

Dialectical behaviour therapy for suicidal adolescents

Dialectical behaviour therapy was originally developed as a comprehensive evidence-based approach for treating adults with borderline personality disorder and a history of repeated self-harm. This literature will be considered in Chapter 5. An adaptation of the approach for use with adolescents who have attempted suicide is described in Miller *et al.*'s (2007) *Dialectical Behaviour Therapy with Suicidal Adolescents*. The approach involves individual therapy for adolescents combined with multifamily psychoeducational therapy. Individual behavioural assessment and therapy focuses on the use of change-directed techniques (such as problem solving) and acceptance techniques (such as validation) to achieve personal goals. Multifamily psychoeducational therapy helps family members understand self-harming behaviour and develop skills for protecting and supporting suicidal youngsters. Dialectical behaviour therapy for suicidal adolescents includes modules on mindfulness, distress tolerance, emotion regulation, and interpersonal effectiveness skills to address problems in the areas of identity, impulsivity, emotional liability, and relationship problems respectively. In a study of 27 suicidal adolescents who participated in dialectical behaviour therapy, Miller *et al.* (2000) found that it led, as predicted, to significant reductions in identity confusion, impulsivity, emotional instability, and interpersonal problems. Adolescents rated distress tolerance and mindfulness as the most important skills acquired in dialectical behaviour therapy.

Evidence from two controlled outcome studies supports the effectiveness of dialectical behaviour therapy with adolescents who have attempted suicide. In a study of suicidal adolescents with borderline personality features, Rathus and Miller (2002) compared the outcome for 29 cases who received dialectical behaviour therapy plus psychoeducational multifamily therapy, and 82 cases who received psychodynamic therapy plus family therapy. In each programme, participants attended therapy twice weekly. Both programmes led to reductions in suicidal ideation. Significantly more cases completed the dialectical behaviour therapy programme, and significantly fewer were hospitalized during treatment. In a further study of 62 suicidal adolescent inpatients, Katz *et al.* (2004) found that both dialectical behaviour therapy and routine inpatient care led to significant reductions in parasuicidal behaviour, depressive symptoms, and suicidal ideation, but dialectical behaviour therapy led to significantly greater reductions in behaviour problems.

Youth Nominated Support Team

Youth Nominated Support Team is a manualized systemic intervention for adolescents who have attempted suicide, in which adolescents nominate a parent or guardian and three other people from their family, peer group, school, or community to be members of their support team (King *et al.*, 2000). For each case, support team members receive psychoeducation explaining how the adolescent's psychological difficulties led to the suicide attempt, the treatment plan, and the role that support team members can play in helping the adolescent towards recovery and managing situations where there is a risk of further self-harm. Support team members are encouraged to maintain weekly contact with the adolescent and are contacted regularly by the treatment team to facilitate this process. King *et al.* (2006) evaluated the Youth Nominated Support Team programme in a randomized controlled trial of 197 girls and 82 boys who had attempted suicide and been hospitalized. They found that, compared with routine treatment with psychotherapy and antidepressant medication, the Youth Nominated Support Team programme led to decreased suicidal ideation and mood-related functional impairment in girls at six months follow-up, but had no significant impact on boys.

Family therapy for adolescent suicide

Two studies have evaluated the impact of specialized family therapy interventions for suicidal adolescents. In a study of 140 Hispanic adolescent girls who had attempted suicide, Rotheram-Borus *et al.* (2000) evaluated a programme in which suicidal girls and their mothers, during their initial attendance at a hospital emergency department, were engaged in a family therapy session after watching a video drama focused on suicidality. Hospital emergency staff were also trained in inducting these families into the programme. Compared with standard care, the emergency department family therapy programme led to a significant reduction in adolescent depression over an 18-month follow-up period. Also, in families of girls with greatest psychological difficulties, it led to significant reduction in maternal distress.

In a randomized trial of 162 adolescents who had attempted suicide, Harrington *et al.* (1998) compared cases who received a specialist assessment followed by four sessions of home-based, problem-solving family therapy along with routine medical care, with a control group who received routine medical care only. Parents in the family therapy group were more satisfied with treatment, but family therapy only led to a significantly greater reduction in suicidal ideation for adolescents without major depression. Both treatments were equally cost-effective (Byford *et al.*, 1999).

Individual cognitive behavioural and client-centred therapy for suicidal adolescents

There is evidence from one study that cognitive behavioural and client-centred supportive individual therapy are equally effective as adjuncts to routine medical care of adolescent attempted suicide. In a randomized comparative study of 39 adolescents who had attempted suicide, Donaldson *et al.* (2005) found that both cognitive-behavioural, skills-based, and client-centred supportive therapy protocols led to similar and significant decreases in suicidal ideation and depressed mood at three and six month follow-ups. Sixty per cent of participants completed the treatment protocol and there were six reattempts during the follow-up period.

Group therapy for self-harming and suicidal adolescents

There is evidence from two studies that group therapy may have a beneficial impact on self-harming or suicidal adolescents. In a randomized controlled trial of 63 adolescents who had deliberately harmed themselves on at least two occasions within the preceding year, Wood *et al.* (2001) found that six months after treatment adolescents who had engaged in group therapy were less likely to have repeated deliberate self-harm on two or more further occasions than adolescents who received standard care (6% vs. 31%). They also used fewer medical services, had better school attendance, and a lower rate of behavioural problems than adolescents who received standard care.

In a single group outcome study of 250 suicidal adolescents who attended an inpatient psychoeducational suicide prevention group therapy programme, Esposito-Smythers *et al.* (2006) found that all adolescents reported that they had learned something helpful in the group that would keep them from attempting suicide in the future. Participants found the construction of a Reasons To Live List as the most helpful therapeutic activity, while the creation of a Safety List was the least helpful.

Antidepressant medication and suicide in adolescence

There is currently controversy about suicide risks associated with treating adolescent suicidality and depression with selective serotonin uptake inhibitors, with some reports showing increased risk and others showing reduced risk (Dubicka *et al.*, 2006; Fortune & Hawton, 2005; Olfson *et al.*, 2003).

Practice implications for attempted suicide in adolescence

The available evidence suggests that the engagement of adolescents who have attempted suicide in psychotherapy may be enhanced by facilitating verbal agreements between the adolescents and their parents or guardians to attend psychotherapy sessions and conducting follow-up phone interviews with adolescents over two months with a focus on reducing suicidal ideation and psychotherapy attendance. A number of psychotherapy protocols, particularly those which include individual therapy for adolescents combined with systemic therapy for members of their family and social support networks, may be more effective than routine care and so should be considered when treating adolescents who have attempted suicide. Multi-systemic therapy for adolescents with severe mental health problems, dialectical behaviour therapy for suicidal adolescents, and nominated support network therapy are well-developed protocols which show particular promise. With adolescents who have attempted suicide, antidepressant medication should only be used with extreme caution, regular monitoring and within the context of a multimodal programme that includes psychotherapy, because it may increase the risk of further suicide attempts. The importance of psychological interventions in treating young people who have attempted suicide is acknowledged in international best practice guidelines (Shaffer & Pfeffer, 2001).

Child and adolescent anxiety disorders

Anxiety disorders in children and adolescents include selective mutism (fear of speaking in school); separation anxiety (fear of leaving parents and going to school); simple phobias (fear of specific animals, natural disasters, or other stimuli); social phobia (fear of novel social situations); generalized anxiety disorder (anxiety about multiple stimuli and situations and fear of loss of control of worrying process); obsessive-compulsive disorder (repetitive rituals are conducted to reduce anxiety associated with cues such as dirt or lack of symmetry); and post-traumatic stress disorder (avoidance strategies are used to reduce anxiety associated with intrusive traumatic memories) (American Psychiatric Association, 2000a; World Health Organization, 1992). Typically, the treatment of post-traumatic stress disorder and obsessive-compulsive disorder have been investigated separately from other childhood anxiety disorders, and this convention will be followed in reviewing the literature on childhood anxiety disorders below. Literature relevant to these two disorders will be considered after first reviewing evidence for the effectiveness of psychotherapy in the treatment of other anxiety disorders in children and adolescents.

In a meta-analysis of studies of psychological treatments for anxiety and depression in children and adolescents, Spielmans et al. (2007) concluded that psychological interventions were effective, but aggregating across studies there was no evidence of the significant superiority of any one form of treatment.

Cognitive behavioural therapy for anxiety disorders in children and adolescents

In a meta-analysis of 20 studies of cognitive behavioural therapy for anxiety disorders in children and adolescents aged 4–17 years, Ishikawa *et al.* (2007) found an overall effect size for cognitive behavioural therapy versus no treatment control groups of .61, indicating that the average treated case fared better than 73% of untreated controls, and this is equivalent to a success rate of about 64%. Treatment gains were maintained at up to 24 months follow-up. Individual, group, and family-based cognitive behavioural therapy programmes led to similar improvement rates, and extending treatment beyond ten sessions did not significantly enhance treatment outcome. However, the outcome for cases treated at university clinics (ES = .77) was better than that of cases studies treated in routine clinical settings (ES = .37). In this meta-analysis trials included children with the full range of anxiety disorders. The most frequently evaluated programme for childhood anxiety disorders was Kendall's *Coping Cat* programme (Kendall *et al.*, 2005) or variations of it such as the *Coping Koala* programme or the *FRIENDS* programme (Barrett *et al.*, 2000). The Coping Cat programme involves 16 sessions and includes psychoeducation, self-monitoring, relaxation and cognitive coping skills training, creation of a hierarchy of anxiety-provoking situations, and gradual imaginal and in-vivo exposure to feared situations in the anxiety hierarchy.

The results of Ishikawa and colleagues' (2007) meta-analysis are consistent with another conducted by In-Albon and Schneider (2007). In their meta-analysis of 24 studies of cognitive behavioural treatment of childhood anxiety disorders involving 1275 cases, In-Albon and Schneider found an effect size, based on a comparison of treatment and control groups at post-treatment, of .66. They found within group effect sizes of .86 after treatment (based on 24 studies), 1.6 at an average follow-up period of ten months (based on 16 studies), and long-term outcome effect sizes between .61 and 1.54 based on three studies that reported three to seven year follow-up data. Sixty-nine per cent of cases that completed treatment were classified as recovered after treatment and 72% were classified as recovered at ten months follow-up. Individual, group, and family-based programmes had similar outcomes.

The results of Ishikawa *et al.*'s (2007) and In-Albon and Schneider's (2007) meta-analyses are slightly more positive than those arising from an earlier systematic review of ten randomized controlled trials of cognitive behavioural therapy for anxiety disorders in 6–18-year-olds, in which Cartwright-Hatton *et al.* (2004) found a remission rate of 57% after treatment and 64% at follow-up. Trials which only included cases with simple phobias, OCD, and PTSD were excluded from this review, and most cases had generalized anxiety disorder, separation anxiety disorder, or social phobia. In this review, as in the more recent meta-analysis, the most widely evaluated programme for childhood anxiety was Kendall's Coping Cat programme (Kendall *et al.*, 2005).

Historically, selective mutism has not been classified with the anxiety disorders, but in recent years there has been a growing acceptance that it is best conceptualized in this way (Morris & March, 2004). In a systematic review of 23 case studies and uncontrolled single group outcome studies, Cohan *et al.* (2006) found tentative support for the effectiveness of cognitive behaviour therapy for selective mutism. Successful treatments involved anxiety management training; gradual exposure to anxiety-provoking social situations which involved speaking in school; and concurrent shaping and reinforcement of successive approximations to appropriate speaking behaviour in classroom situations. Controlled trials of this treatment approach are required.

Family therapy for anxiety disorders in children and adolescents

Family-based treatments for childhood anxiety disorders cover programmes in which parents and children are seen conjointly or separately. Reviews of the effectiveness of family-based treatment for anxiety disorders show that it is at least as effective as individual therapy, and probably more effective where parents have anxiety disorders (Barmish & Kendall, 2005; Diamond & Josephson, 2005). Some studies show that targeting parents as well as children adds little to the effectiveness of cognitive behavioural anxiety management programmes for a range of anxiety disorders (e.g. Mendlowitz *et al.*, 1999; Silverman *et al.*, 1999; Siqueland *et al.*, 2005; Spence *et al.*, 2000). However, others point to the additional value of a family-based approach in treating childhood anxiety disorders.

In a comparison of a family-based treatment with individual cognitive behavioural therapy, Barrett *et al.* (1996) found that after treatment (84% vs. 57%), at six months (84% vs. 71%) and one year (96% vs. 70%) follow-up, family-based treatment was more effective than individually oriented treatment in reducing the percentage of children with anxiety disorders, although this difference was not significant. Barrett's family-based programme is called *FRIENDS* (Barrett & Shortt, 2003). The child-focused element of the programme is similar to Kendall's Coping Cat programme. In the family-based component of FRIENDS, parents learn to reward their children's coping behaviour, ignore anxious behaviour, manage their own anxiety, and develop communication and problem-solving skills. A number of other studies support the effectiveness of family-based treatment of childhood anxiety disorders. In an evaluation of a group-based version of the FRIENDS programme, Barrett (1998) found that it was more effective than a child-focused treatment in improving the quality of family functioning, reducing internalizing and externalizing behaviour problems, but both treatments were equally effective in reducing the percentage of children with anxiety disorders. In a comparison of child-focused cognitive behavioural therapy alone and child-focused therapy combined with parental anxiety management training, Cobham *et al.* (1998) found that children whose parents did not have anxiety did equally well in both programmes (82% vs. 80%). However, where parents had anxiety disorders, the combined programme was far more effective (77 vs. 39%) in reducing the percentage of children with anxiety disorders. Improvement was maintained six months and one year after treatment. Thus, family-based treatment of childhood anxiety disorders may be most appropriate where parents also have anxiety disorders.

In the treatment of school refusal a systems-based cognitive behavioural approach has been found to be particularly effective in all major narrative reviews (Elliott, 1999; Heyne & King, 2004; King & Bernstein, 2001; King *et al.*, 2000) and four controlled trials (Blagg & Yule, 1984; Heyne *et al.*, 2002; King *et al.*, 1998; Last *et al.*, 1998), leading to recovery in more than two-thirds of cases. Effective intervention involves working directly with children, parents, and teachers. Children learn relaxation, coping, and social skills and plan to use this in a return to school programme. Parents and teachers are helped to support the child in the process of returning to regular school attendance and in using anxiety management and social skills to deal with the anxiety and social challenges this evokes.

Psychodynamic therapy for anxiety disorders in children and adolescents

Only a single controlled study of psychodynamic psychotherapy for childhood anxiety disorders could be located. In a non-randomized controlled study of 58 children aged 6–10 years, some of whom had anxiety disorders assigned to psychodynamic therapy or community-based treatment as usual, Muratori *et al.* (2003) found that at two years follow-up, 66% of those who received psychodynamic psychotherapy were recovered compared with 38% in the control group. (Details of the type of therapy offered are described in the section above on psychodynamic psychotherapy for mood disorders.)

Pharmacotherapy for anxiety disorders in children and adolescents

There is some evidence from a couple of controlled trials for the effectiveness of selective serotonin reuptake inhibitors with selective mutism, generalized anxiety disorder, separation anxiety disorder, and social phobia (Garland, 2002; Stein & Seedat, 2004). However, because selective serotonin reuptake inhibitors may increase suicide risk, they should be used very cautiously, and only with frequent clinical monitoring in children and adolescents (Hall, 2006; Healy, 2003).

Practice implications for anxiety disorders in children and adolescents

In children and adolescents, psychotherapy is an effective treatment, and the treatment of choice, for separation anxiety, selective mutism, simple phobias, social phobia, and generalized anxiety disorder. Effective psychotherapy in children may be individual or family based. It involves psychoeducation, helping children and families monitor anxiety and avoidance behaviour, facilitating the development of relaxation, coping, and social skills, and the use of these skills during gradual exposure to feared stimuli and situations. Parents may be helped to implement reward programmes to reinforce successful completion of exposure exercises and to avoid inadvertent reinforcement of avoidant behaviour. In cases of school refusal and selective mutism, home–school liaison is also required. The important role of psychotherapy in the treatment of anxiety disorders is acknowledged in international best practice guidelines (American Academy of Child & Adolescent Psychiatry, 2007d).

Child and adolescent obsessive-compulsive disorder

With obsessive-compulsive disorder (OCD) repetitive rituals are conducted to reduce anxiety associated with cues such as dirt or lack of symmetry (American Psychiatric Association, 2000a; World Health Organization, 1992). In a meta-analysis of 18 studies of the treatment of paediatric OCD, Abramowitz *et al.* (2005) found an effect size of 1.98 for psychotherapy where exposure and response prevention was the main intervention (based on ten comparisons) and 1.13 for selective serotonin reuptake inhibitors (based on 11 comparisons) for OCD symptoms. This finding of the effectiveness of exposure and response prevention programmes is consistent with the results of other narrative reviews (Barrett *et al.*, 2004; March *et al.*, 2005; Rapoport & Inoff-Germain, 2000). With exposure and response prevention, children are exposed to cues (such as dirt) that elicit anxiety-provoking obsessions (such as ideas about contamination), while not engaging in compulsive rituals (such as hand washing), until habituation occurs. Exposure and response prevention may be conducted in an individual, group, or family therapy context, coupled with family therapy focusing on psychoeducation, externalizing the problem, monitoring symptoms, and helping parents and siblings support and reward the child for completing exposure and response prevention homework exercises (Barrett *et al.*, 2004; Storch *et al.*, 2007). Family therapy also helps parents and siblings avoid inadvertent reinforcement of children's compulsive rituals. While available evidence shows that psychotherapy is more effective than selective serotonin reuptake inhibitors, a case may be made for multimodal treatment in which psychotherapy and antidepressants are combined in the treatment of OCD in children and adolescents, although controlled studies of combined treatments have not been conducted (Beer *et al.*, 2002). Also, because they may be associated with increased suicide risk in adolescents, selective serotonin reuptake inhibitors should be used cautiously and with frequent clinical monitoring (Hall, 2006; Healy, 2003).

Practice implications for OCD in children and adolescents

For OCD in children and adolescents, family-based cognitive behavioural psychotherapy in which exposure and response prevention is the central component is the current treatment of choice. For children who do not respond to this intervention, a multimodal programme involving such psychotherapy and selective serotonin reuptake inhibitors may be considered, provided suicidal risk, associated with selective serotonin reuptake inhibitors, is adequately monitored. The value of psychological intervention in the treatment of OCD in young people is acknowledged in international best practice guidelines (American Academy of Child & Adolescent Psychiatry, 1998b; March *et al.*, 1997; NICE, 2005a).

Child and adolescent post-traumatic stress disorder

Post-traumatic stress disorder (PTSD) involves anxiety-provoking intrusive memories and images of traumatic events, the use of various coping strategies to avoid these intrusive experiences or cues that elicit them, and hyperarousal (American Psychiatric Association, 2000a; World Health Organization, 1992).

Trauma-focused cognitive behavioural therapy for PTSD in young people

In a meta-analysis of six studies of trauma-focused cognitive behavioural therapy for children who had experienced sexual abuse, Macdonald *et al.* (2006) obtained an effect size of .43 which is equivalent to a success rate of about 60%, and concluded that trauma-focused cognitive behavioural therapy was an effective intervention for PTSD in young people who had been sexually abused. This conclusion is consistent with those of narrative reviews (e.g. Carr, 2004; Cohen, 2003; Dyregrov & Yule, 2006; Enright & Carr, 2002; Saigh *et al.*, 2004; Taylor & Chemtob, 2004). Trauma-focused cognitive behavioural therapy involves creating a therapeutic context within which children are exposed to anxiety-provoking trauma-related memories until habituation occurs. To help clients cope with exposure to traumatic memories, relaxation and cognitive coping skills are developed. Where children have been sexually abused or assaulted, treatment may also involve training in self-protective skills. These child-focused interventions may be conducted as part of a broader systemic intervention programme conducted on a family or group therapy basis, that maximizes family, school, and peer group support. Within such programmes families are offered psychoeducation, invited to monitor symptoms, and regularize the child's daily routines.

Eye movement desensitization reprocessing for PTSD in adolescence

For sexually abused adolescent girls, Jaberghaderi *et al.* (2004) found that eye movement desensitization reprocessing (EMDR) was as effective but quicker in alleviating trauma symptoms as trauma-focused cognitive behavioural therapy. In EMDR, the client is asked to hold in mind the disturbing images, thoughts, and bodily sensations associated with their memory of traumatic events, while tracking the clinician's moving finger with their eyes. This procedure is repeated until distressing aspects of the traumatic memory are reduced (Shapiro, 1995).

Psychodynamic therapy for PTSD in young people

For sexually abused girls, Trowell *et al.* (2002), in a randomized controlled trial, found that 30 sessions of individual focal psychoanalytic psychotherapy (Malan & Osimo, 1992) were more effective than 18 sessions of psychoeducational group therapy in the treatment of PTSD, but the two treatments were equally effective for major depression and other anxiety disorders. In both treatments concurrent parent support was provided.

Systemic therapy for PTSD in children following domestic violence

In a controlled trial of the effectiveness of conjoint child–parent psychotherapy for children exposed to domestic violence, Lieberman and Van Horn (2005) found that preschool children who engaged in this type of therapy showed better adjustment than controls. The protocol in this study was a manualized trauma-focused treatment which spanned 2–50 sessions. Trauma-focused play sessions between parent and child were used to facilitate the construction of a joint coherent trauma narrative (Lieberman & Van Horn, 2005).

Practice implications for PTSD with children and adolescents

There is currently replicated evidence for the effectiveness of trauma-focused cognitive behavioural therapy for PTSD, so this may be the treatment of choice. However, there is also evidence from single trials for the effectiveness of psychoanalytic psychotherapy, systemic family interventions, and EMDR in the treatment of PTSD in children and adolescents, so these treatments may also be considered. All of these protocols share the basic procedure of creating a safe and supportive context within which the young person is exposed to truama-related cues and memories until habituation and processing of traumatic memories occurs. The central role of psychotherapy in the treatment of PTSD in young people is acknowledged in international best practice guidelines (American Academy of Child & Adolescent Psychiatry, 1998c; NICE, 2005b).

Child and adolescent eating disorders

Psychotherapy can be effective in helping to address infant feeding problems, child and adolescent anorexia and bulimia nervosa, and obesity in young people. Evidence relevant to this assertion is considered below.

Infant feeding problems

Severe feeding problems in infancy and childhood include food refusal, lack of self-feeding, swallowing problems, and frequent vomiting. Such problems are often associated with failure to thrive (Iwaniec, 2004). In a systematic review of 29 controlled single case and group studies, Kerwin (1999) identified a number of behavioural programmes that are effective in ameliorating severe feeding problems and improving weight gain in infants and children with developmental disabilities. These programmes involved prompting, shaping, and reinforcing appropriate feeding behaviour and ignoring inappropriate feeding responses. Effective treatments were either offered directly to infants or children, or parents were trained in delivering the treatment programmes. More large-scale controlled trials of such programmes are required.

Practice implications for infant feeding problems

For infant feeding problems, behavioural programmes which include prompting, shaping, and reinforcing appropriate feeding behaviour and ignoring inappropriate feeding responses is the treatment of choice.

Anorexia and bulimia nervosa in adolescence

An excessive concern with the control of body weight and shape along with an inadequate and unhealthy pattern of eating are the central features of eating disorders in young people. A distinction has been made between anorexia nervosa and bulimia nervosa with the former being characterized primarily by weight loss and the latter by a cyclical pattern of bingeing and purging (American Psychiatric Association, 2000a; World Health Organization, 1992).

Family therapy for anorexia in adolescence

Most treatment outcome studies of adolescents with eating disorders have focused primarily on anorexia. In a systematic narrative review of six uncontrolled and five randomized treatment trials of family therapy for adolescent anorexia, Eisler (2005) concluded that after treatment between a half and two-thirds achieve a healthy weight. At six months to six year follow-up, 60–90% have fully recovered and no more than 10–15% are seriously ill. Eisler also noted that the negligible relapse rate following family therapy is superior to the moderate outcomes for individually oriented therapies. It is also far superior to the high relapse rate following inpatient treatment, which is 25–30% following first admission, and 55–75% for second and further admissions. These conclusions are consistent with those of previous narrative reviews (le Grange & Lock, 2005; Mitchell & Carr, 2000; Wilson & Fairburn, 2007). Family therapy for adolescent anorexia involves helping parents work together to refeed their youngster, or refeeding the youngster as an inpatient. This is followed by helping the family support the youngster in developing an autonomous, healthy eating pattern, and an age-appropriate lifestyle.

Family therapy for bulimia nervosa in adolescence

Two trials of family therapy for bulimia in adolescence show that it is more effective than supportive therapy (le Grange *et al.*, 2007), and as effective as cognitive behavioural therapy (Schmidt *et al.*, 2007), which is considered to be the treatment of choice for bulimia in adults, due its strong empirical support (Wilson & Fairburn, 2007). In both trials, at six months follow-up, over 70% of cases treated with family therapy showed partial or complete recovery. Family therapy for adolescent bulimia involves helping parents work together to supervise the young person during mealtimes and afterwards, to break the binge–purge cycle. As with anorexia, this is followed by helping families support their youngsters in developing autonomous, healthy eating patterns, and age-appropriate lifestyles.

Practice implications for anorexia and bulimia nervosa in young people

For young people with anorexia nervosa and bulimia nervosa, family therapy is the treatment of choice. Useful treatment manuals for these two eating disorders are: *Treatment Manual for Anorexia Nervosa: A Family Based Approach* (Lock *et al.*, 2001) and *Treating Bulimia in Adolescents: A Family Based Approach* (le Grange & Lock, 2007). These conclusions on psychotherapy for anorexia and bulimia nervosa in children and adolescents are consistent with international best practice guidelines (American Psychiatric Association, 2000a; NICE, 2004d; RANZCP Clinical Practice Guidelines Team for Anorexia Nervosa, 2004).

Child and adolescent obesity

Childhood obesity occurs where there is a body mass index above the ninety-fifth percentile with reference to age- and sex-specific growth charts (Lissau *et al.*, 2004). Childhood obesity is of particular concern because it is a risk factor for cardiovascular, pulmonary, endocrine, and orthopaedic diseases (Jelalian *et al.*, 2007). Childhood obesity is due predominantly to lifestyle factors including poor diet and lack of exercise, and so psychological treatment programmes focus on lifestyle change. In a meta-analysis of 16 studies of treatments for childhood obesity, Young *et al.* (2007) found pre–post-treatment effect sizes of .89 for behavioural family therapy, .52 for other interventions, and .18 for waiting list control groups. The pre-treatment to follow-up effect size was .84 for behavioural family therapy, so gains made during treatment were maintained at follow-up. In a systematic narrative review of 42 randomized controlled trials of treatments for obesity in children, Jelalian and Saelens (1999) concluded that family-based behavioural weight reduction programmes were more effective than dietary education and other routine interventions. They led to a 5–20% reduction in per cent of youngsters overweight after treatment and at ten-year follow-up 30% were no longer obese. These results are consistent with those of other narrative reviews, (Epstein, 2003; Jelalian *et al.*, 2007; Zametkin *et al.*, 2004). Where obesity occurs with other co-morbid psychological disorders, individual, familial, and contextual variables specific to weight should be assessed. These include motivation and existing support to change current eating and physical activity patterns, extent of weight-related conflict within the family, and the impact of weight on current functioning, because information about these issues may inform prioritization of treatment objectives (Jelalian *et al.*, 2007).

Practice implications for obesity in young people

Effective family-based behavioural weight reduction programmes are typically of about 12 sessions duration and involve helping parents and children to monitor dietary habits, physical exercise, and weight, and to make small permanent reductions in children's caloric intake and increases in activity level. For children to achieve these goals, parents are coached in using prompting and reward programmes in the home setting to promote changes in diet and exercise. Cues and opportunities for eating outside set mealtimes within the home are reduced. Effective programmes are of long duration with frequent sessions. Early sessions focus on goal setting and contracting. Later sessions involve developing relapse prevention skills for managing high risk situations. Because obesity is a chronic problem, infrequent follow-up sessions are required to maintain treatment gains. Where appropriate, interventions to address peer teasing and poor body image may be incorporated into treatment. Programmes that concurrently target parent weight loss as well as child weight loss are particularly effective. These conclusions are consistent with international guidelines for best practice (Barlow & Dietz, 1998).

Tourette's syndrome

Tourette's syndrome is characterized by chronic motor and vocal tics that interfere substantially with social or occupational functioning (American Psychiatric Association, 2000a; World Health Organization, 1992). Pharmacological treatment with haloperidol, pimozide, risperidone, and clonidine reduces the frequency of tics, and these are often considered the treatments of choice (Leckman et al., 1991; Sallee et al., 1997; Scahill et al., 2003; Shapiro et al., 1989). However, some patients find medication unacceptable because it is either ineffective or leads to unwanted side effects. Evidence from five controlled trials (which included both children and adults) indicates that habit reversal therapy, a behavioural treatment specifically for tics, is moderately effective in reducing tic frequency for a proportion of Tourette's syndrome patients. It also leads to improvements in life satisfaction and psychosocial functioning (Azrin & Peterson, 1990; Deckersbach et al., 2006; O'Connor et al., 2001; Verdellen et al., 2004; Wilhelm et al., 2003). Habit reversal programmes involve self-monitoring of sensations that precede tics and then developing and practising competing responses that are incompatible with tics when these sensations occur (Azrin & Nunn, 1973). In addition, patients learn diaphragmatic breathing and relaxation techniques to reduce arousal which often exacerbates tics. They also set goals for tic reduction and positively reinforce themselves for achieving these goals. Self-monitoring, competing responses, breathing, and relaxation techniques are learned and practised in therapy sessions and at home between sessions.

Practice implications for Tourette's syndrome

For young people with Tourette's syndrome who do not wish to take medication, habit reversal is the treatment of choice.

Paediatric pain problems

For children with persistent headaches, recurrent abdominal pain, or distress associated with painful medical procedures, psychological interventions are effective in reducing pain and distress.

Headaches in young people

A distinction may be made between tension and migraine headaches, with the former being associated with muscular tension and the latter with vasodilatation and constriction (Connelly, 2003). In a systematic narrative review of

31 studies, Holden *et al.* (1999) concluded that for both tension and migraine headaches, relaxation training is a central component of effective psychotherapy. For migraine, thermal biofeedback alone or combined with training in relaxation and cognitive coping strategies is also an effective treatment. These results are consistent with those of other systematic reviews (e.g. Connelly, 2003; Eccleston *et al.*, 2002; Holroyd, 2002; Spirito & Kazak, 2006).

Practice implications for headaches in young people

For headaches in young people relaxation training is an effective psychological intervention. For migraine in young people thermal biofeedback may also be considered.

Recurrent abdominal pain in children

In recurrent abdominal pain, repeated stomach aches for which no biomedical cause can be identified is the central complaint (Banez & Cunningham, 2003). The condition leads to school absence and disruption of the child's life. There are significant overlaps between the symptoms shown by children and adolescents with the conditions currently referred to as recurrent abdominal pain, separation anxiety, and school refusal, and future research may show that the amalgamation of the three categories is appropriate. Results of four trials have shown that family-based cognitive behavioural therapy is effective in alleviating recurrent abdominal pain for which no biomedical cause is evident (Finney *et al.*, 1989; Robins *et al.*, 2005; Sanders *et al.*, 1989, 1994). Such programmes involve family psychoeducation, relaxation, and coping skills training to help children manage pain, and contingency management implemented by parents to motivate children to engage in normal daily routines. This conclusion is consistent with those of other systematic narrative reviews (Janicke & Finney, 1999; Murphy & Carr, 2000; Spirito & Kazak, 2006; Weydert *et al.*, 2003).

Practice implications for recurrent abdominal pain in young people

For recurrent abdominal pain, family-based cognitive behavioural therapy which includes psychoeducation, relaxation, and coping skills training, and contingency management to motivate children to engage in normal daily routines is the treatment of choice.

Procedure-related pain in young people

Psychological interventions have been developed to help children cope with painful, and potentially distressing, paediatric medical procedures such as injections, dental treatments, bone marrow aspirations, lumbar puncture, burn debridement, and surgery. In a systematic narrative review of 13 treatment outcome studies, Powers (1999) concluded that cognitive behavioural therapy was an effective treatment for paediatric procedure-related pain. This conclusion is consistent with the results of other systematic narrative reviews (Murphy & Carr, 2000; Spirito & Kazak, 2006). In a systematic review of 27 studies of psychological and pharmacological interventions for procedure-related pain, Kuppenheimer and Brown (2002) found that both were effective, and at present there is little evidence to suggest that either is more efficacious, but both types of procedures combined may be more effective than either alone.

Practice implications for procedure-related pain in young people

Effective psychological interventions for procedure-related pain involve preparing children for these procedures and supporting them during the procedures. Preparation includes providing procedural and sensory preparatory information, showing the child a videotaped model coping with the procedure, relaxation skills training, visualization and cognitive coping skills training, behavioural rehearsal, enacting the procedure in play therapy, and providing incentives to cope with the painful procedures. During painful procedures effective therapy involves distraction with pleasant stimuli such as an age-appropriate multisensory toy or imagery-based distraction enhanced through hypnosis.

Adjustment of children to chronic medical conditions

In children and adolescents with chronic medical conditions where non-adherence to complex medical regimes seriously compromises physical health and leads to frequent hospitalization, psychological intervention improves illness management (Kibby *et al.*, 1998; Lemanek *et al.*, 2001).

Adjustment of children and adolescents to asthma

Asthma is a chronic respiratory disease characterized by reversible airway obstruction, airway inflammation, and airway hyperresponsiveness to a variety of stimuli (Lehrer *et al.*, 2002). Asthma attacks are characterized by breathing distress. The frequency and duration of such attacks is determined by the interaction between abnormal respiratory system physiological processes to which some youngsters have a predisposition; physical environmental triggers (such as allergens and viral infections of the respiratory system); and psychological processes, particularly stress. Asthma affects all areas of a child's life and can lead to sleep disturbances, restrictions in daily activity, repeated hospitalization, hypoxia, seizures, brain damage and, if left untreated, asthma is potentially fatal. Psychological interventions for asthma aim to help young people and their families manage factors that exacerbate their condition more effectively. In a meta-analysis of 32 trials of psychological and educational interventions for children and adolescents with asthma, Guevara *et al.* (2003) found effect sizes of .50 for improved lung function; .36 for self-efficacy; .29 for number of days of restricted activity; and .21 for number of visits to an emergency department. These effect sizes correspond to success rates of 55–62%. Thus, psychological interventions are moderately effective in improving the functioning of children with asthma. These results are consistent with those of systematic narrative reviews (Brinkley *et al.*, 2002; Lemanek *et al.*, 2001; McQuaid & Nassau, 1999).

Practice implications for asthma in young people

Effective psychological interventions for children with asthma and their families aim to help them understand the condition; adhere to medication regimes; reduce exposure to environmental triggers; and manage stress.

Adjustment of children and adolescents to diabetes

Type 1 diabetes is an endocrine disorder typically diagnosed in childhood, characterized by complete pancreatic failure (Cox & Gonder-Frederick, 1992). The condition is treated with a medical self-management regime which involves regular testing of blood-sugar levels, self-injection with insulin, following a low sugar and regular meals diet plan, and regulating levels of physical exercise and stress which affect blood-sugar levels. Poor adherence to this regime can lead to serious acute complications notably hyper- or hypoglycaemic crises which can result in coma. The long-term complications of poorly controlled diabetes include retinopathy, renal failure, and heart disease. Psychological interventions for poorly controlled diabetes aim to help youngsters, with support from their parents, adhere to their medical regime. In a meta-analysis of 18 randomized and non-randomized trials of psychological interventions for diabetic adolescents, Hampson *et al.* (2000) obtained effect sizes of .37 for psychosocial adjustment and .33 for metabolic control. In a later and more restrictive meta-analysis of 10 randomized trials of diabetic children and adolescents, Winkley *et al.* (2006) obtained effect sizes of .46 for psychological adjustment and .35 for metabolic control. The effect sizes from these two meta-analyses correspond to success rates of 57–61%. Together the results of these meta-analyses show that psychological interventions have a moderate effect on psychological adjustment and metabolic control in young people with diabetes. The results of these meta-analyses are consistent with those of systematic narrative reviews (e.g. Farrell *et al.*, 2002). For brittle diabetes where frequent medical crises occur, there is evidence from one trial that family crisis intervention and intensive inpatient psychoanalytic psychotherapy may be effective (Fonagy & Moran, 1990).

Practice implications for diabetes in young people

The most frequently validated interventions for poorly controlled diabetes in young people are cognitive-behavioural family systems oriented programmes that include child-focused and family-based components. The child-focused component helps youngsters develop illness management and self-regulation skills by providing psychoeducation about the diabetic medical regime and offering relaxation training and coping skills training. The family-based component equips parents and youngsters with the skills to manage conflict and create a supportive context within which youngsters learn to take responsibility for managing their diabetes. Family interventions include psychoeducation, communication and problem-solving skills training, and contingency management for parents. These conclusions on psychological intervention for children and adolescents with Type 1 diabetes are consistent with international best practice guidelines (NICE, 2004e).

Adjustment problems following major life stresses

Psychological interventions are effective in helping children and families adjust to major life stresses and transitions including parental separation, death of a parent, and maltreatment. A summary of supportive evidence follows below.

Parental separation and divorce

Parental separation and divorce are associated with significant adjustment problems in many children (Amato, 2001). Three systematic reviews of trials of psychological intervention programmes for children of divorce, indicate that such programmes may be effective in helping children cope with the stress entailed by this family life cycle transition (Haine *et al.*, 2003; O'Halloran & Carr, 2000; Pedro-Carroll & Jones, 2005). In a review of six studies which evaluated child-focused programmes, four studies which evaluated parent-focused interventions, and three studies which evaluated combined child- and parent-focused programmes, Haine *et al.* (2003) concluded that all three types of interventions have beneficial effects on the adjustment of children following parental separation or divorce. The child-focused programmes helped youngsters develop coping skills within a supportive group context. Parenting skills training occurred in the parent-focused programmes. Combined programmes included both of these elements. In a review of nine studies which evaluated six child-focused and three parent- and child-focused intervention programmes, O'Halloran and Carr (2000) found an overall effect size of .37 for child adjustment. An effect size of .78 was found in Pedro-Carroll and Jones' (2005) systematic review of eight studies evaluating the *Children of Divorce Intervention Programme*, a well-developed and widely disseminated, child-focused programme.

All three reviews concluded that psychological treatment programmes are effective in helping children and young teenagers cope with the sequelae of parental separation and divorce and that these programmes have a positive impact on negative mood states, divorce-related beliefs, self-esteem, home-based behaviour problems, school-based behaviour problems, and relationships with family members and peers. The benefits of these programmes occur because they help children develop effective coping skills, and help their parents strengthen their parenting skills.

Practice implications for young people following parental separation or divorce

For children whose parents have separated or divorced, psychological intervention programmes that focus on the child, the parents or both may be offered to improve psychological adjustment to this life transition. Child-focused programmes may be conducted on a group basis in schools or out-patient settings and include catharsis, psychoeducation, problem-solving, and stress management training to help children grieve the loss of an intact family structure and develop skills required to manage the psychological and social challenges they face as a result of their parents' separation. Parent-focused programmes facilitate the development of listening and discipline skills to enhance the quality of the parent–child relationship. They also help parents reduce the exposure of children to stressful parental conflict. Programmes that combine parent- and child-focused elements also create a context within which parents may help their children to transfer skills learned in treatment sessions into their day-to-day lives.

Death of a parent

A small number of single group outcome studies and controlled trials have shown that psychotherapy leads to improved adjustment in children following loss of a parent (Black & Urbanowicz, 1987; Cohen *et al.*, 2002, 2006a; Cohen & Mannarino, 2004; Kissane & Bloch, 2002; Rotherham-Borus *et al.*, 2001, 2003, 2004; Sandler *et al.*, 1992, 2003). Effective psychotherapy for youngsters with complicated or traumatic grief following parental bereavement involves both family and individual interventions. Family intervention involves engaging families in treatment, facilitating family grieving, facilitating family support, decreasing parent–child trauma, and helping the family to reorganize so as to cope with the demands of daily living in the absence of the deceased parent. The individual component of treatment involves exposure of the child to traumatic grief-related memories and images until a degree of habituation occurs, in a manner similar to the treatment of post-traumatic stress disorder. This may be facilitated by viewing photos, audio and video recordings of the deceased, developing a coherent narrative with the child about their past life with the deceased, and a way to preserve a positive relationship with the memory of the deceased parent in the present.

The Teens and Adults Learning to Communicate (TALC) programme developed by Rotheram-Borus and her team (2001, 2003, 2004) deserves particular mention because of the evidence for its long-term benefits and the scale of the trial in which it was evaluated. The TALC programme is an intensive family-based intervention for adolescents whose parents have AIDS. Rotherham-Borus and her team (2001, 2003, 2004, 2006a, 2006b) evaluated this programme within the context of a randomized controlled trial involving 307 parents with AIDS and their 412 adolescent children. At two, four, and six years follow-up, adolescents in the TALC programme showed better adjustment than the control group who received routine services. Specifically, the adolescents showed less distress, fewer behaviour problems, less drug abuse, fewer teenage pregnancies, and better occupational adjustment.

The TALC programme aimed to help parents and adolescents manage the process of parental decline and death, and also helped adolescents and their new carers manage the grief process and the formation of a new family structure. The programme included 16 group sessions for parents; eight group sessions for teenagers; eight conjoint parent and teenager group sessions; and a further 16 sessions for young people and their new carers. Parent sessions covered managing emotions (fear, anger, and sadness) associated with AIDS, disclosing the diagnosis to the family, and planning the future. The young person sessions covered helping youngsters make sense of their parent's diagnosis, and managing the emotions, particularly sadness, anger, and fear, associated with this. Conjoint parent–adolescent sessions dealt with communication, conflict management, managing drug abuse, encouraging young people to have safe sex, and planning custody of the young person after the parent's death. In the later stages of the parent's illness or following parental death, the programme included 16 further sessions for young people and 16 concurrent sessions for their new carers. These focused on grieving and coping with loss. They also addressed how the young person and the new carer would communicate, develop a positive relationship, resolve conflicts, and address adolescent discipline issues. There were sessions devoted to anger management, safe sex, pregnancy and parenthood, and drug use.

Practice implications for bereaved young people

Where young people have suffered bereavement, the treatment of choice is combined child- and family-focused interventions which facilitate the grieving process and promote adjustment to a new family structure. *Family Focused Grief Therapy: A Model of Family-centred Care during Palliative Care and Bereavement* (Kissane & Bloch, 2002) and *Treating Trauma and Traumatic Grief in Children and Adolescents* (Cohen *et al.*, 2006a) are evidence-based treatment manuals for guiding treatment with bereaved young people. For young people whose parents are at risk of death from AIDS, the following is an evidence-based guide to treatment: *Intervention Manuals for Project TALC (Teens and Adults Learning to Communicate) Parents Living with AIDS* (Rotheram-Borus, 1998).

Child abuse and neglect

Physical and sexual abuse and neglect have a negative impact on child development and adjustment (Myers *et al.*, 2002). Fortunately, there is evidence that psychotherapy can help children resolve these difficulties. In a broad meta-analysis of 21 controlled trials of psychotherapy for child maltreatment (including neglect and both physical and sexual abuse), Skowron and Reinemann (2005) found an average weighted effect size of .54, which is equivalent to a 62% success rate, and indicates that the average treated case fared better than 71% of cases that received routine community case management or no treatment.

Child sexual abuse

It was noted above in the section on the treatment of PTSD that there is good evidence for the effectiveness of trauma-focused cognitive behavioural therapy for survivors of child sexual abuse. In a meta-analysis of six studies of trauma-focused cognitive behavioural therapy, Macdonald *et al.* (2006) found an effect size of .43, which is equivalent to a success rate of 60%. It was also noted that single controlled trials showed that eye movement desensitization reprocessing (EMDR; Jaberghaderi *et al.*, 2004) and focal psychoanalytic psychotherapy (Trowell *et al.*, 2002) led to improvement in PTSD symptoms in survivors of child sexual abuse. These findings are consistent with the results of previous narrative reviews (Chaffin & Friedrich, 2004; Cohen *et al.*, 2006b; Putnam, 2003; Ramchandani & Jones, 2003; Reeker *et al.*, 1997; Stevenson, 1999).

Practice implications for survivors of child sexual abuse

For child sexual abuse, effective treatment involves concurrent treatment of abused children and their non-abusing parents, in group or individual sessions, with periodic conjoint parent–child sessions. Where intrafamilial sexual abuse has occurred, it is essential that the offender live separately from the victim until they have completed a treatment programme and been assessed as being at low risk for reoffending. Effective child-focused therapy involves catharsis and identification of multiple complex emotions associated with abusive experiences. Through repeated exposure to abuse-related memories by recounting their experiences, children process and habituate to intense negative feelings evoked by traumatic memories. Effective treatment for sexually abused children also includes relaxation and coping skills training; learning assertiveness and safety skills; and addressing victimization, sexual development, and identity issues. Concurrent and conjoint work with non-abusing parents and abused children focuses on helping parents develop supportive and protective relationships with their children, and develop support networks for themselves. *Treating Sexually Abused Children and their Non-offending Parents: A Cognitive Behavioural Approach* (Deblinger & Heflinger, 1996) is a useful treatment manual for child sexual abuse.

Physical abuse

Systematic narrative reviews concur that for physical child abuse, effective psychotherapy is family based and addresses specific problems in relevant subsystems including children's post-traumatic adjustment problems; parenting skills deficits; and the overall supportiveness of the family and social network (Chaffin & Friedrich, 2004; Edgeworth & Carr, 2000; MacLeod & Nelson, 2000; Skowron & Reinemann, 2005; Tolan *et al.*, 2005).

Kolko's (1996; Kolko & Swenson, 2002) cognitive behavioural family therapy and Eyeberg's parent–child interaction therapy (Chaffin *et al.*, 2004; Hembree-Kigin & McNeil, 1995; Timmer *et al.*, 2005) are manualized approaches to family-based treatment which have been shown in randomized controlled trials to reduce the risk of further child abuse. Results from parent–child interaction therapy have been particularly impressive. In a controlled trial of parent–child interaction therapy, Chaffin *et al.* (2004) found that at two years follow-up only 19% of parents who participated in parent–child interaction therapy had a re-report for physical abuse compared with 49% of parents assigned to standard treatment. Parent–child interaction therapy involved a preliminary six-session motivational enhancement module in which parents were helped to evaluate the pros and cons of parent training, and develop motivation to actively engage in therapy. Thereafter, seven sessions were devoted to live coaching of parents and children in positive child-directed interactions; and a further seven sessions were devoted to live coaching of parents and children in behavioural management of discipline issues using time out and related procedures.

Practice implications for families in which physical child abuse has occurred

Where parents have very poorly developed self-regulation and child-management skills, the child may initially be placed in a residential unit or therapeutic day care centre, which provides the child with a protective, supportive, and intellectually stimulating context within which positive parent–child interaction may be fostered. Effective parent-focused interventions for physical abuse include behavioural parent training which equips parents with child-management skills and individual therapy which helps parents develop the skills required for regulating negative emotional states, notably anger, anxiety, and depression. *Parent–Child Interaction Therapy* (Hembree-Kigin & McNeil, 1995) is a useful evidence-based manual for behavioural parent training. Effective interventions for the family and wider system within which physical child abuse occurs entail co-ordinated intervention with problematic subsystems based on a clear assessment of interaction patterns that may contribute to abuse or neglect. The aim of such intervention is to restructure relationships within the child's social system so that interaction patterns that may contribute to abuse will not recur. Here therapy may focus on enhancing the quality of the marital relationship; the supportiveness of the extended family; and co-ordination of other inputs to the family from educational, social, and health services. *Assessing and Treating Physically Abused Children and their Families: A Cognitive Behavioural Approach* (Kolko & Swenson, 2002) is a useful evidence-based manual for family therapy in cases of physical child abuse.

Neglect

In a systematic review of 14 investigations, Allin *et al.* (2005) concluded that most studies in the evidence base for the effectiveness of psychotherapy in the treatment of child neglect were poorly conducted, so only limited confidence may be placed in their results. With this caveat, there was evidence for the effectiveness of play therapy and systemic family-based therapy.

Practice implications for families in which child neglect occurs

Effective play therapy interventions for neglected children should provide a context for intellectual stimulation and developing play skills, as well as an opportunity for catharsis of complex emotions within a safe environment. Effective play therapy protocols may include resilient peers (as buddies) within play therapy, and are conducted within the context of a day programme. Effective family-based interventions focus on enhancing the quality of parent–child relationships, supporting vulnerable parents directly, and co-ordinating the services they receive from community agencies.

Intellectual disability

Intellectual disability (or mental retardation) involves significant deficits in intellectual functioning as shown by an IQ below 70 and significant deficits in adaptive behaviour (Carr *et al.*, 2007). For people with intellectual disabilities, there is evidence for the effectiveness of behavioural interventions conducted within the context of an applied behaviour analysis approach for managing challenging behaviour; for behavioural parent training to help families of children with an intellectual disability manage their behaviour problems; and for cognitive behavioural therapy to help adults with intellectual disability manage aggression. There is also tentative preliminary support for the effectiveness of cognitive behavioural psychotherapy with anxiety, depression, social skills deficits, and weight control problems in people with intellectual disability. There is some evidence that group-based cognitive behavioural therapy may reduce stress in parents of children with intellectual disability. Finally, there is some evidence to support the use of atypical antipsychotic medication (notably risperidone) to reduce challenging behaviour. This evidence is summarized below.

Behavioural interventions for challenging behaviour in intellectual disability

Evidence for the effectiveness of behavioural interventions conducted within the context of an applied behaviour analysis framework comes from three systematic reviews and meta-analyses of experimental single case design studies (Carr *et al.*, 1999; Didden *et al.*, 1997, 2006). In a systematic review and meta-analysis of 109 experimental single case design studies published between 1985 and 1996 involving 230 people with intellectual disabilities, Carr *et al.* (1999) found that positive behaviour support interventions based on applied behaviour analysis were effective in reducing self-injury, aggression, property destruction, and tantrums. Participants were predominantly children or adolescents with severe or profound intellectual disabilities. Just over two-thirds of cases (68%) showed an 80% reduction in problem behaviour, which is an index of clinically significant improvement. The most successful interventions were based on a functional analysis of the problem behaviour and involved a change in the behaviour of members of the client's social system. Effective positive behaviour support interventions included both those which altered antecedent stimulus situations that precipitated challenging behaviour, as well as those that altered the consequences or reinforcement contingencies that followed challenging behaviour.

In a meta-analysis of 482 experimental single case studies carried out between 1968 and 1994 on the treatment of problem behaviours of individuals with intellectual disabilities, Didden *et al.* (1997) found that response-contingent behavioural interventions based on a functional analysis of challenging behaviour were effective in significantly reducing the level of problem behaviour, and more effective than non-contingent or pharmacological interventions, or those that focused on altering antecedent stimulus situations. Most of the cases in Didden's meta-analysis were young children with moderate or severe intellectual disabilities presenting with high frequency self-injurious or aggressive behaviour in segregated settings.

While the preceding two reviews show that behavioural interventions are effective for people with moderate, severe, and profound intellectual disabilities, there is also evidence for the effectiveness of behavioural interventions for people with mild intellectual disabilities. In a meta-analysis of 80 studies of the effectiveness of behavioural treatments for challenging behaviours in individuals with mild intellectual disability, Didden *et al.* (2006) found that these interventions were highly effective. In these 80 studies there were 75% non-overlapping data points between baseline and treatment phases and 35% of zero data for treatment phases. The most effective behavioural interventions were based on functional analysis, were consistently delivered, and the target problem behaviour was reliably assessed.

Taken together the results of these three reviews indicate that for people with intellectual disabilities with challenging behaviour, behavioural interventions, developed within an applied behaviour analysis framework, are the treatment of choice. Such interventions should be based on a functional assessment of the antecedents and consequences of the challenging behaviour and involve the reliable and ongoing assessment of the target behaviour along with its antecedents and consequences. Antecedent interventions should remove or reduce the intensity of aversive stimuli or situations that precipitate challenging behaviour; replace such aversive stimuli or situations with those that match the individual's needs and preferences; or equip the individual with prosocial skills for communicating their needs in aversive situations so they do not have to revert to challenging behaviour. Interventions that alter the consequences of challenging behaviour include extinction and differential reinforcement of prosocial competing behaviours. These conclusions are consistent with those of narrative reviews (Emerson, 2001; Grey & Hastings, 2005) and expert consensus guidelines (Rush & Frances, 2000).

Parent training programmes for families of children with intellectual disability

In a systematic review of nine controlled evaluation studies and a description of one new controlled trial, Quinn *et al.* (2007) concluded that group-based behavioural parent training was effective in reducing behaviour problems in children with intellectual disabilities. These programmes involved training parents to foster children's adaptive behaviour and skills on the one hand, and manage children's oppositional or challenging behaviour on the other, using principles from behavioural psychology and social learning theory.

Training was offered to parents in groups of 5–10 participants over periods of 4–20 weeks in sessions of 1–2 hours duration. The incorporation of parent training programmes into overall care plans for children and adolescents with intellectual disabilities and behaviour problems is consistent with international guidelines for best practice (Szymanski & King, 1999).

Cognitive behavioural anger control interventions for adults with intellectual disability

In a narrative review of six controlled studies and 13 case series and case reports, Taylor and Novaco (2005) found that cognitive behavioural anger management training was effective for adults with mild intellectual disability. Effective programmes include detailed assessment and formulation of anger problems; self-monitoring; cognitive restructuring to address anger escalating cognitions; slow breathing and relaxation training for arousal reduction; social skills and assertiveness training for managing anger-provoking interpersonal situations; and desensitization to a hierarchy of anger-provoking situations. Thus, for adults with mild intellectual disability and anger control problems, particularly those living in the community (where it may not be feasible to use behavioural interventions within the context of an applied behaviour analysis framework), cognitive behavioural therapy is the treatment of choice.

Psychotherapy and intellectual disability

The evidence base for the routine use of psychotherapy in the treatment of common clinical problems such as anxiety and depression in people with intellectual disability is not well developed. In a broad-ranging systematic narrative review of 92 studies published between 1968 and 1998 and a meta-analysis of nine of these which included treatment and control groups, Prout and Nowak-Drabik (2003) concluded that overall, psychotherapy was moderately effective for a range of psychological difficulties in people with intellectual disabilities, but that the quality of studies limited the confidence that could be placed in this conclusion. Similar conclusions have been reached by other reviewers (Willner, 2005). In Prout and Nowak-Drabik's (2003) review the focus was predominantly on face-to-face interventions from cognitive behavioural, psychodynamic, and eclectic traditions.

Behavioural interventions conducted within an applied behavioural analysis framework by teachers or residential staff were omitted from this review. The nine studies in Prout and Nowak-Drabik's (2003) meta-analysis included four which evaluated social skills training, two which evaluated anxiety management training, and two which evaluated weight loss programmes. The effect size from the meta-analysis was 1.01. This indicates that for people with intellectual disabilities with social skills deficits, anxiety problems, or weight difficulties, the average treated case fared better than 84% of untreated cases.

Since the publication of this major review, some controlled trials of psychotherapy for common problems such as depression in people with intellectual disability have appeared. For example, McCabe *et al.* (2006) compared the effectiveness of group-based cognitive behavioural therapy for depression in 34 adults with mild or moderate intellectual disability with a control group of 15 similar cases who received routine treatment. After treatment and at three months follow-up, compared to the control group, the treatment group showed a significant improvement in depression, negative automatic thoughts, and positive feelings about the self.

Taken together the evidence reviewed in this section provides tentative preliminary support for the effectiveness of cognitive behavioural psychotherapy with anxiety, depression, social skills deficits, and weight control problems in people with intellectual disability.

Interventions to reduce stress in parents of children with intellectual disability

In a systematic review of psychological interventions which aim to reduce parental stress in families containing a child with an intellectual disability, Hastings and Beck (2004) concluded that the strongest evidence base was for group-based cognitive behavioural interventions. There was also some evidence that parent-led support networks (e.g. Santelli *et al.*, 2001; Singer *et al.*, 1999), respite care (Chan & Sigafoos, 2001), routine keyworker-based case management (Liabo *et al.*, 2001), and family therapy (Pelchat *et al.*, 1999) reduce parental stress. Hastings and Beck (2004) reviewed six trials of cognitive behavioural therapy in detail. Most of these group programmes helped parents develop skills for self-monitoring thoughts and feelings, cognitive restructuring, and problem solving. These relatively brief programmes led to significant reductions in anxiety and depression for most parents.

Pharmacotherapy for challenging behaviour in intellectual disability

In an exhaustive ten-year review of over 100 studies of pharmacotherapy in intellectual disability, Matson *et al.* (2000) concluded that most studies conducted between 1990 and 1999 had significant methodological flaws. These prevented sound conclusions from being drawn about the effectiveness of most forms of pharmacotherapy for psychological problems or challenging behaviour in people with intellectual disabilities. Despite this lack of evidence, they found that the use of a wide range psychotropic medications was highly prevalent, especially for challenging behaviour and dual diagnosis. Broadly speaking, attempts have been made to show that the effects of antidepressants, anxiolytics, and antipsychotic medications have similar effects in people with intellectual disability as in people with normal ability level. To some limited extent this conclusion has been supported, but the uncontrolled nature of most studies offers suggestive rather than definitive evidence.

In a systematic review of the use of pharmacotherapy in children and adolescents with intellectual disabilities, Handen and Gilchrist (2006) also concluded that the methodological quality of studies was poor, and most were case reports, single group outcome studies, or very small controlled trials. The available data, with all its limitations, suggests that young people with intellectual disability respond to various psychotropic medications in ways similar to youngsters of normal ability. Thus, psychostimulants may be useful for treating hyperactivity; antipsychotics for treating psychosis; antidepressants for treating low mood; and mood stabilizers for treating bipolar disorder. However, psychotropic medication is less effective with youngsters with intellectual disability than with those of normal ability, and the side effects are more frequent. Because of this and the weak evidence base, psychotropic medication should be used very cautiously to treat psychological disorders in children and adolescents with intellectual disability.

In an exhaustive review of 195 studies of the effectiveness of typical and atypical antipsychotic medication in people with intellectual disabilities, LaMalfa *et al.* (2006) concluded that atypical antipsychotics, specifically risperidone and olanzapine, were the treatment of choice for schizophrenia and psychotic states, with clozapine being the most appropriate option for non-responders to these two interventions. However, they also highlighted the paucity of methodologically sound studies, and acknowledged that their conclusions were based on results of a few small controlled trials.

For challenging behaviour in intellectual disability, risperidone has been gaining considerable popularity (Grey & Hastings, 2005). In a review of six controlled trials of risperidone, Singh *et al.* (2005) concluded that it may be effective in reducing behaviour problems in some people with intellectual disabilities or pervasive developmental disorders.

From this cursory review it may be concluded that despite their widespread use, the evidence base for the use of pharmacotherapy to treat challenging behaviour and psychological disorders in children and adolescents with intellectual disabilities is very limited, and so should be used cautiously. These conclusions are consistent with international best practice guidelines (Rush & Frances, 2000).

Practice implications for intellectual disability

For challenging behaviour, applied behaviour analysis interventions are the treatment of choice. Where such interventions are not practical, behavioural parent training may be used for young children, anger management training with adults, and risperidone may also be used with both children and adults. Cognitive behavioural therapy may be considered for anxiety, depression, social skills deficits, and weight control problems in people with intellectual disability. Group-based cognitive behavioural therapy may be used to reduce stress in parents of children with intellectual disability.

Autism spectrum disorders

Children who show extremely marked abnormalities in their capacity for reciprocal social interaction, in communication and language development, in the development of symbolic play, and in addition display restricted, repetitive patterns of activities and interests from infancy are diagnosed as having pervasive developmental disorders or autism spectrum disorders (Zager, 2005). These include autism, Asperger's syndrome, Rett's disorder, disintegrative disorder, and pervasive developmental disorder not otherwise specified (PDDNOS).

Early intervention

In a thorough systematic narrative review of controlled and uncontrolled single case design and group design studies of early intervention programmes for children with autism, the National Research Council in the USA (2001) drew the following broad conclusions about effective early intervention for children with autism. Intervention should be initiated early (e.g. before three years of age) and involve at least 25 hours a week 52 weeks a year, with a low pupil–teacher ratio. Programmes should have individualized goals that take account of the child's strengths, deficits, and needs so as to facilitate the development of language, social skills, and the regulation of problem behaviour. Children's families should be centrally involved in goal setting, programme planning, and implementation. Programmes should be delivered and evaluated by interdisciplinary professional teams with appropriate specialist knowledge and skills in the area of evidence-based practice for autism spectrum disorders. These conclusions are consistent with those of other systematic and selective reviews (Harris et al., 2005; Jordan & Jones, 1999; Mastergeorge et al., 2003; Scott & Baldwin, 2005; Simpson et al., 2005).

Within the context of these broad conclusions, applied behavioural analysis interventions (including trainer-led, discrete trial training, and child-led naturalistic approaches), structured teaching, communication-focused programmes, and programmes to promote social interaction have greatest empirical support (Mastergeorge et al., 2003). Effective pharmacological treatments for autism spectrum disorders include atypical antipsychotic medications for aggression and self-injurious behaviour; selective serotonin reuptake inhibitors for repetitive behaviour; and stimulants for hyperactivity and inattention (des Portes *et al.*, 2003; McDougle *et al.*, 2006; Scahill & Martin, 2005). What follows is a review of each of these areas.

Applied behaviour analysis

Applied behaviour analysis (ABA) involves the design, implementation, and evaluation of environmental interventions to help people reduce problem behaviour and develop skills. It includes the functional analysis of the relations between environment and behaviour, and then introducing specific antecedents and consequences, based on the functional assessment, to produce practical changes in target skills and behaviours. Comprehensive reviews of hundreds of experimental single case design research studies show that applied behaviour analysis is effective in teaching language and social skills (Goldstein, 2002; McConnell, 2002; Odom *et al.*, 2003) and reducing problem behaviour (Horner *et al.*, 2002).

Within the broad field of applied behaviour analysis, a distinction may be made between trainer-led, discrete trial training and child-led, naturalistic or milieu approaches (Mastergeorge *et al.*, 2003). With discrete trial training, complex skills are taught in one-to-one training sessions by breaking them down into multiple simpler components. Prompting, shaping, chaining, and reinforcement processes are used to facilitate skill acquisition. With naturalistic approaches, parents and teachers reinforce spontaneous self-initiated responses in normal home and school settings. In a review of ten controlled single case design studies, Delprato (2001) found that when children with autism learned language and communication skills through naturalistic approaches, they generalized skills use to many situations, whereas with discrete trial training less generalization beyond the training situation occurred. However, discrete trial training may be particularly appropriate where self-initiated behaviour rarely occurs.

Lovaas' applied behaviour analysis programme

Ivar Lovaas' University of California Los Angeles Young Autism Programme is based on trainer-led, discrete trial training, where each learning situation is set up by an adult, who prompts the child to perform a particular response and reinforces it. Lovaas showed that 47% of autistic preschool children who participated in a 40-hour per week applied behaviour analysis programme for three years made clinically significant improvements, achieving a normal IQ and mainstream school placement (Lovaas, 1987). Only 2% of the comparison group who received treatment-as-usual achieved these goals. The gains of the children who participated in Lovaas' programme were maintained into early adolescence (McEachin *et al.*, 1993). A cost-benefit analysis has shown that intensive early intervention with applied behaviour analysis for children with autism can lead to considerable cost savings

(Jacobson *et al.*, 1998). In systematic reviews of controlled group outcome studies of applied behaviour analysis for preschool children with autism spectrum disorders, Smith (1999), Finnegan and Carr (2002), Lovaas and Smith (2003), and Sallows and Graupner (2005) concluded that intensive applied behavioural analysis is effective in improving functioning in preschool children with autism. These reviews show that in all there have been a couple of replications of Lovaas' original study, and over a dozen studies of variations on it, most involving less intensive programmes with less than 40 hours per week for three years, more group teaching and less one-to-one teaching, less intensive therapist training and supervision, and less use of aversive procedures to control challenging behaviour. There is a consensus that less frequent use of aversive procedures does not reduce programme effectiveness. The degree to which decreasing programme intensity reduces its effectiveness is still unclear. Therefore at a policy level there is little consensus on whether the incremental gains associated with very intensive programmes of 40 hours per week are justified, if this reduces the availability of less intensive treatment programmes of 20–30 hours per week to more children. There is a consensus from extant research that certain children respond better than others to applied behaviour analysis early intervention programmes. Better outcome occurs for younger children with higher IQs; with less severe autism symptoms; and with more language, imitation, and joint attention skills (Sallows & Graupner, 2005).

Lovaas' applied behaviour analysis programme is described in *Teaching Children with Developmental Delays: Basic Intervention Techniques* (Lovaas, 2002). It is designed for preschoolers from two to six years of age and is of about three years duration. A typical programme involves 40 hours of one-to-one treatment per week, and parental continuation of the treatment programme outside of these hours in the home setting. The curriculum covers language skills, peer group social skills, skills required for integration into mainstream educational settings, and the reduction in challenging and socially inappropriate behaviour. The programme begins with discrete trial training involving short clear instructions, prompts to maximize success, and fading of prompts as learning occurs, along with immediate reinforcement for correct responses. Once a child has acquired basic communication skills in the one-to-one therapy context, there is a progression to incidental teaching in dyads, small groups, and regular classes. This progression is essential to help children generalize the use of skill from the therapeutic situation to other social contexts.

Pivotal response training

Children with autism have difficulty generalizing responses learned in one-to-one discrete trial training situations to routine peer group, classroom and family social contexts. It is this observation that has informed the development of child-led, naturalistic, or milieu approaches where spontaneously initiated communicative or social responses are selectively reinforced in the child's normal social environment. Pivotal response training (Koegel *et al.*, 2003) is a particularly well-developed naturalistic, applied behavioural analysis approach. In pivotal response training, children are taught to increase the competence and frequency with which they produce self-initiated responses. Training is conducted by parents and teachers or key workers using natural stimuli in routine home or school situations, rather than in one-to-one situations with artificial stimuli such as flash cards. Important pivotal responses in autism spectrum disorder include behaviours which indicate that the child is motivated to communicate or interact with others, and self-initiated positive communicative or interactive behaviours. In pivotal response training, the frequency of pivotal responses is increased by providing children with choices or making a range of activities available to them, reinforcing pivotal responses or attempts at producing them using natural and direct reinforcers, and interspersing the learning of new responses with opportunities to be reinforced for producing previously learned responses. Pivotal response training procedures are manualized for parents and professionals (Koegel *et al.*, 1989; Koegel & Koegel, 2006).

In a review of ten experimental single case design studies and comparative group outcome studies, Koegel *et al.* (2003) concluded that pivotal response training helps children with autism learn to imitate social interactions and use language more competently and more frequently in home, school, and peer-group settings.

Structured teaching

TEACCH is the acronym for a structured approach to teaching children with autism spectrum disorders and stands for Treatment and Education of Autistic and related Communication Handicapped Children (Mesibov *et al.*, 2005). While it is widely used, this programme is supported by only two small controlled trials (Ozonoff & Cathcart, 1998; Panerai *et al.*, 2002) and uncontrolled single group outcome studies (e.g. Panerai *et al.*, 1998). The TEACCH approach aims to make the world intelligible to the autistic child by acknowledging deficits (such as communication problems and difficulties in social cognition) and structuring learning activities so that they capitalize upon their strengths (such as visual processing abilities, good rote memories, and unique special interests). The child follows a curriculum of structured learning activities, capitalizing upon their interests, in designated teaching areas within the school, following visual work schedules, with an appropriate degree of autonomy or support as required. Concurrently parents are trained to continue school-based work programmes at home. The system is described in a series of manuals and the book *The TEACCH Approach to Autism Spectrum Disorders* (Mesibov *et al.*, 2005).

Communication and language

In a systematic review of 60 studies (most of which were experimental single case designs), Goldstein (2002) found evidence for the effectiveness of a range of behavioural interventions in enhancing communication in children with autism spectrum disorders. There was evidence for the effectiveness of both trainer-led discrete trial training and child-led naturalistic milieu teaching (which includes pivotal response training mentioned above) in which parents and class teachers reinforce language use in natural settings. There was some evidence that the latter leads to greater generalization, a finding consistent with Delprato's (2001) review mentioned above. Similar conclusions have been reached in other systematic narrative reviews (e.g. Paul & Sutherland, 2005; Prizant & Wetherby, 2005; Rogers, 2006).

A second conclusion was that functional communication training reduces challenging behaviour. In functional communication training, the communicative function of a challenging behaviour (such as aggression or self-injury) is established through careful functional assessment, and then the individual is taught language or other communicative skills to serve the same communicative function as the challenging behaviour (Durand & Merges, 2001). In a systematic review of eight experimental single case design studies involving 22 participants who had a diagnosis of autism, Mancil (2006) found that functional communication training was effective in improving communication and reducing challenging behaviour. In these studies, the most common functions of challenging behaviour were gaining attention or escaping from situations which individuals found aversive. However, the reviewed studies provided limited information on the long-term maintenance of treatment gains, and the generalization of these to multiple social contexts.

A third conclusion drawn by Goldstein (2002) was that behavioural interventions which included sign language are effective in enhancing communication in those with limited communication abilities. However, the use of signing has declined in recent years as other augmentative or alternative communication systems have become more popular. A popular example of such a system is the Picture Exchange Communication System (PECS). The system was developed by Frost and Bondy (2002) and involves teaching children to exchange a picture for a desired item and eventually learn to construct complex picture-based sentences to make requests. PECS is theoretically based on the principles of applied behaviour analysis and practices from within the field of augmentative and alternative communication. Controlled single case design and comparative group outcome studies support the effectiveness of PECS for enhancing communication in children with autism spectrum disorder (Charlop-Christy *et al.*, 2002; Koita *et al.*, 2003; Kravits *et al.*, 2002; Tincani, 2004; Yoder & Stone, 2006).

Social interaction-promoting interventions

In a systematic review of 55 studies, McConnell (2002) found evidence for positive impacts of four categories of intervention to facilitate social interaction in young children with autism spectrum disorders. These included ecological interventions, collateral skills interventions, child-specific interventions, and peer-based interventions. Ecological interventions such as providing children with preferred structured activities, following periods of low stimulation, in peer groups that include developmentally normal children, had positive but modest effects on social interaction. Interventions that facilitated the development of play skills also had positive but modest effects. Similar modest increases in social interaction occurred following social skills training, provided the use of social skills was prompted and reinforced following initial training. Large increases in social interaction occurred in response to peer-mediated interventions, where normally developing peers were trained and reinforced for interacting with children with autism. These findings suggest that social interaction in preschool children with autism may be facilitated by training them and normally developing peers in social and play skills, and then prompting and reinforcing them for using these skills in school and home settings. These conclusions are consistent with those of other systematic reviews (e.g. Rogers, 2000).

Social stories are an increasingly popular intervention for promoting social skills in children with autism. A social story is an individualized narrative to help a person with autism understand and manage a confusing or challenging social situation (Gray, 2000). Social stories aim to address the deficits people with autism have with perspective taking, a vulnerability which hampers their development of social skills. Social stories contain (1) descriptive sentences which objectively outline the situation and who is involved; (2) perspective sentences which specify internal states of relevant people; (3) directive sentences which indicate what is expected of the person with autism in the situation; (4) affirmative statements which express relevant cultural norms; (5) co-operative statements about who will provide help; and (6) control sentences which help the person with autism remember the story in the relevant situation and prepare their response (Sansosti et al., 2004). In a systematic review of ten controlled single case design studies and a further ten case studies and uncontrolled group studies, Nichols et al. (2005) found that social story interventions were effective in a proportion of cases in increasing daily living skills and social skills, and decreasing problem behaviour in children with autism spectrum disorders. A similar conclusion was reached by Sansosti et al. (2004) in an earlier review of a subset of the studies reviewed by Nichols et al.

Behavioural interventions for challenging behaviour in autism

Horner *et al.* (2002) reviewed five previous systematic reviews and meta-analyses of behavioural interventions for people with developmental disabilities involving a large number of studies, and nine controlled studies involving 24 children under eight with autism spectrum disorders. They concluded that for aggression, tantrums, self-injury, and stereotypy, behavioural interventions were effective in leading to a 90% reduction in problem behaviours in 60% of cases. Effective interventions were based on a functional assessment of problem behaviours and included skills training interventions to provide alternatives to challenging behaviours (i.e. functional communication training mentioned above), antecedent interventions to pre-empt challenging behaviour, and reactive behavioural interventions to extinguish challenging behaviours or reinforce alternative competing prosocial behaviours.

Pharmacological interventions

In autism spectrum disorders, pharmacological treatments have been identified to address specific target symptoms. These include antipsychotic medications for aggression and self-injurious behaviour; selective serotonin reuptake inhibitors for stereotypical, repetitive behaviour; and stimulants for hyperactivity and inattention (des Portes, 2003; McDougle *et al.*, 2006; Scahill & Martin, 2005). For aggression and self-injurious behaviour there is strong evidence from systematic reviews of controlled trials (e.g. Dinca & Spencer, 2005) to support the use of risperidone (an atypical antipsychotic). Risperidone has largely replaced the use of typical antipsychotics (such as haloperidol) because it has fewer side effects. In a review of the use of selective serotonin reuptake inhibitors to reduce repetitive behaviour in autism, Kolevzon *et al.* (2006) identified three controlled trials and ten open trials. They concluded that there was tentative support for the use of selective serotonin reuptake inhibitors in the treatment of anxiety and repetitive behaviours in autism spectrum disorders. Evidence from one large trial and ten smaller trials supports the effectiveness of methylphenidate for hyperactivity and inattention in autism (Scahill & Martin, 2005; Research Units on Paediatric Psychopharmacology Autism Network, 2005).

A range of other pharmacological treatments are under investigation, including naltrexone, mood stabilizers, and drugs that affect glutamate function, but currently there is insufficient evidence to support their routine use in clinical practice (McDougle *et al.*, 2006; Scahill & Martin, 2005).

Popular ineffective interventions

A variety of psychological and biological interventions have become popular, but have either been shown to be ineffective or are inadequately researched. Some of these are mentioned below.

Auditory integration training

This involves listening to individually tailored, electronically modified music programmes for specified time periods, with the aim of ameliorating unique auditory processing deficits and improving concentration in children with autism (who typically show variations in auditory sensitivity). Berard's method, the Tomatis method, and Samonas sound therapy are three versions of auditory integration training. In a systematic review of six controlled trials, Sinha *et al.* (2006) found no support for the effectiveness of auditory integration training in alleviating the core symptoms of autism, and limited evidence for its impact on challenging behaviour. They concluded that auditory integration training was not an effective treatment for autism, a view which is consistent with the American Academy of Paediatrics (1998) committee on children with disabilities.

Sensory integration therapy

This involves the use of carefully planned and controlled sensory experiences including vestibular, proprioceptive, and somatorsensory activities such as swinging, deep pressure touch, and tactile stimulation (Dawson & Watling, 2000). It aims to improve the functioning of people with autism by addressing their sensory and motor abnormalities. In a systematic review of four studies, Dawson and Watling (2000) found limited evidence for the effectiveness of sensory integration training in improving the functioning of individuals with autism spectrum disorders. The studies were poorly designed, including few cases and no control groups. These results are consistent with those of previous reviews (e.g. Vargas & Camilli, 1999).

Facilitated communication

This rests on the assumption that people with autism have unimpaired cognitive, language comprehension, and reading abilities, but significant speech or language production deficits. Facilitated communication involves the therapists holding autistic people's hands, wrists, or arms to help them spell messages on a keyboard or a board with printed letters. In a systematic review of five previous review papers and 29 studies published between 1995 and 2000, Mostert (2001) concluded that there was no evidence to support the effectiveness of facilitated communication in treating communication problems in people with autism spectrum disorders. This position was consistent with that taken by the American Academy of Paediatrics (1998) committee on children with disabilities and the American Psychological Association (1994).

Novel or untested psychological interventions

In a wide-ranging review of novel or untested treatments (as well as effective or promising treatments) for autism spectrum disorders, Simpson *et al.* (2005) concluded that the evidence base for the following is too weak to warrant their routine use in clinical practice: holding therapy, gentle teaching, the Son-Rise programme, developmental individual difference relationship based model of intervention (floor time or DIR), pet/animal therapy, relationship development intervention, vanDijk curricular approach, FAST ForWord, power cards, Irlen lenses, art therapy, and music therapy.

Secretin

Despite its popularity and high media profile, available evidence does not support the use of secretin for autism. In a review of 15 methodologically robust double-blind trials of secretin, Sturmey (2005) found that collectively the trial results offered no support for the effectiveness of secretin in the treatment of autism spectrum disorders.

Dietary interventions

There is only very limited evidence for the effectiveness of dietary interventions for autism. In an extensive literature search, Millward *et al.* (2004) identified only one randomized controlled trial of gluten and/or casein free diet in people with autism. The trial included only ten participants in the treatment group and ten in the control group. Results indicated that a combined gluten and casein free diet may reduce some autistic traits.

Novel biological treatments

In a wide-ranging review of novel biological treatments for autism spectrum disorders, Levy and Hyman (2005) concluded that the evidence base for these is too weak to warrant their routine use in clinical practice. The reviewed treatments included: intravenous immunoglobulins, antiviral agents, chelation, digestive enzymes, antifungal agents, specific antibiotics (vancomycine and d-cycloserine), vitamin B6, vitamin B12 and magnesium, vitamin C, folic acid, dymethylglycine, trytophan, tyrosine, cyproheptadine, carnosine, oxytocin, and various fatty acids.

Implications for practice

For children with autism, individualized, structured, evidence-based programmes should be initiated early and involve at least 25 hours a week,
52 weeks a year, with a low pupil–teacher ratio, and parent involvement. Such
programmes should include both trainer-led, discrete trial training and child-
led naturalistic behaviourally-based approaches to facilitate the development
of communication and to promote social interaction. Signing and picture-
based systems may be used, as appropriate, to facilitate the development of
communication. Interventions to promote social interaction should be medi-
ated by normally developing peers, where normally developing peers are
trained and reinforced for interacting with children with autism. Interventions for challenging behaviour should be based on a functional assessment
and include skills training interventions to provide alternatives to challenging
behaviour, antecedent interventions to pre-empt challenging behaviour, and
reactive behavioural interventions to extinguish challenging behaviour or
reinforce alternative competing prosocial behaviour. With regard to medication, risperidone may be used for aggression and self-injury; selective serotonin reuptake inhibitors for stereotypies; and stimulants for hyperactivity
and inattention.

Danger of oversimplificaiton

There is a danger that in summarizing a very large body of evidence within
the constraints of a single chapter, the complexity of the psychotherapy process and the high level of skill required to facilitate this process may not be
fully conveyed. For example, in earlier sections of this chapter reference is
made to key elements of effective psychotherapy programmes such as psychoeducation, changing negative or maladaptive thinking styles, replacing maladaptive with adaptive coping strategies, changing daily routines, making
lifestyle changes, social skills training, facilitating the development of supportive relationships with family and peers, developing better problem-
solving skills, facilitating exposure to feared situations, and so forth. There is
a danger that such key elements may be misconstrued as simple procedures
which could be offered by technicians. To pre-empt this misconstrual, it is
important to emphasize the complexity of the process of psychotherapy.
Clients with psychological disorders engage in a variety of maladaptive coping strategies, use a variety of subtle defence mechanisms, and engage in
subtle counterproductive thinking patterns. Most of these maladaptive coping strategies, defence mechanisms, and thinking patterns occur outside
clients' awareness. That is, these are often unconscious processes. Furthermore, many of these processes involve problematic relationships or interaction patterns, underpinned by problematic belief systems and narratives
within the family, peer group, school, or workplace.

Helping clients to become aware of these processes and relationship patterns, to understand that they are counterproductive, and to evolve more adaptive coping strategies, defence mechanisms, thinking styles, and relationships, is a highly skilled process. This is partly because of clients' resistance to change. It is one of the extraordinary paradoxes of psychotherapy, that clients come to therapy to resolve psychological problems by changing how they live their lives, and yet a significant portion of their time in therapy is spent dealing with their resistance to and ambivalence about changing how they live their lives. Effective psychotherapy with individuals, families, and groups always involves addressing resistance. The complexity of psychotherapy is mentioned here because the description of the key elements of effective evidence-based psychotherapy with specific disorders set out above in this chapter, and indeed in the chapter that follows, often makes the process sound simple and uncomplicated. From the foregoing, it is clear that conducting psychotherapy is a highly skilled process.

Conclusion

The central question addressed in this chapter was: What works for children, adolescents, and people with disabilities? Extensive computer and manual literature searches yielded a wealth of empirical evidence supporting the benefits of psychotherapy and psychological interventions for a wide range of problems in children, adolescents, and people with developmental disabilities, including:

- sleep problems
- toileting problems (enuresis and encopresis)
- attachment problems
- attention deficit hyperactivity disorder
- pre-adolescent oppositional defiant disorder
- adolescent conduct disorder
- adolescent drug abuse
- juvenile sex offending
- child and adolescent depression
- bipolar disorder
- attempted suicide and self-harm
- child and adolescent anxiety disorders (phobias, separation anxiety and generalized anxiety, selective mutism, obsessive-compulsive disorder, post-traumatic stress disorder)
- eating disorders (feeding problems, anorexia nervosa, bulimia, obesity)
- Tourette's disorder
- paediatric pain problems (headaches, recurrent abdominal pain, painful medical procedures)
- adjustment to chronic medical conditions (asthma and diabetes)

- adjustment problems following major life transitions and stresses (parental separation, bereavement, child abuse and neglect)
- adjustment problems associated with intellectual disability
- adjustment problems associated with autism spectrum disorders.

Specific practices and protocols identified in this chapter may usefully be incorporated into routine clinical practice with clients who present with the problems itemized above. A list of therapy manuals and resources and self-help material for clients is given below, which therapists may find useful, if used flexibly, in translating the results of this research review into clinical practice.

Further reading

The items in this reading list are predominantly evidence based, and most are sufficiently detailed to inform clinical practice.

Children's sleep problems

For professionals

Mindell, J. & Owens, J. (2003). *A Clinical Guide to Paediatric Sleep: Diagnosis and Management of Sleep Problems*. Philadelphia: Lippincott Williams & Wilkins.
Stores, G. (2001). *A Clinical Guide to Sleep Disorders in Children and Adolescents*. Oxford: Oxford University Press.
Stores, G. & Wiggs, L. (2001). *Sleep Disturbance in Children and Adolescence with Disorders of Development: Its Significance and Management*. London: MacKeith Press.

For clients

Daymond, K. (2001). *The ParentTalk Guide to Sleep*. London: Hodder and Stoughton.
Douglas, J. & Richman, N. (1984). *My Child Won't Sleep*. Harmondsworth: Penguin,
Durand, V. (1998). *Sleep Better: A Guide to Improving Sleep for Children with Special Needs*. Baltimore, MD: Paul H Brookes.
Ferber, R. (1985). *Solve Your Child's Sleep Problems*. London: Dorling Kindersley.
Lansky, V. (1991). *Getting Your Child to Sleep. . . . and Back to Sleep*. Deephaven: Book Peddlers.
Quine, L. (1997). *Solving Children's Sleep Problems: A Step by Step Guide for Parents*. Huntingdon: Beckett Karlson.

Children's toileting problems

For professionals

Buchanan, A. (1992). *Children Who Soil: Assessment and Treatment*. Chichester: John Wiley.

Herbert, M. (1996). *Toilet Training, Bedwetting and Soiling*. Leicester: British Psychological Society.

For clients

Azrin, N. & Besalel, V. (1979). *A Parent's Guide to Bedwetting Control*. New York: Simon & Schuster.

Galvin, M. & Ferrero, S. (1991). *Clouds and Clocks: A Story for Children Who Soil*. Washington, DC: Magination Press.

Houts, A. & Liebert, R. (1985). *Bedwetting: A Guide for Parents and Children*. Springfield, IL: Charles C Thomas.

Attachment problems

Berlin, L. & Ziv, Y. (2005). *Enhancing Early Attachments: Theory, Research, Intervention and Policy*. New York: Guilford Press.

Attention deficit hyperactivity disorder in children

For professionals

Barkley, R. (1997). *Defiant Children: A Clinician's Manual for Parent Training* (Second Edition). New York: Guilford Press.

Barkley, R. (2005). *Attention Deficit Hyperactivity Disorder: A Handbook for Diagnosis and Treatment* (Third Edition). New York: Guilford Press.

DuPaul, G. & Stoner, G. (1994). *ADHD in Schools: Assessment and Intervention Strategies*. New York: Guilford Press.

For clients

Barkley, R. (2000). *Taking Charge of ADHD: The Complete Authoritative Guide for Parents*. New York: Guilford Press.

Nadeau, K., Dixon, E. & Rose, J. (1998). *Learning to Slow Down and Pay Attention: A Book for Kids About ADD*. Washington, DC: Magination Press.

Quinn, P., Stern, J. & Russell, N. (1998). *The 'Putting on the Brakes' Activity Book for Young People with ADHD*. Washington, DC: Magination Press.

Quinn, P., Stern, J. & Russell, N. (2001). *Putting on the Brakes: Young People's Guide to Understanding Attention Deficit Hyperactivity Disorder*. Washington, DC: Magination Press.

Pre-adolescent oppositional defiant disorder

For professionals

Dadds, M. & Hawes, D. (2006). *Integrated Family Intervention for Child Conduct Problems*. Brisbane: Australian Academic Press.

Hembree-Kigin, T. L. & McNeil, C. B. (1995). *Parent–Child Interaction Therapy*. New York: Plenum Press.

Herbert, M. (1987). *Behavioural Treatment of Children With Problems*. London: Academic Press.

Incredible Years Programme webpage. http://www.incredibleyears.com/.

Kazdin, A. (2005). *Parent Management Training*. Oxford: Oxford University Press.

Larson, J. & Lochman, J. (2002). *Helping School Children Cope with Anger: A Cognitive Behavioural Intervention*. New York: Guilford Press.

McMahon, R. & Forehand, R. (2003). *Helping the Non-Compliant Child* (Second Edition). New York: Guilford Press.

Parent Child Interaction Therapy webpage. http://pcit.phhp.ufl.edu/.

Parents Plus Programme webpage. http://www.parentsplus.ie/.

Patterson, G. (1976). *Living with Children*. Champaign, IL: Research Press.

Sanders, M. & Dadds, M. (1993). *Behavioural Family Intervention*. Needham Heights, MA: Allyn & Bacon.

Shure, M. (1992). *I Can Problem Solve (CPS): An Interpersonal Cognitive Problem Solving Program*. Champaign, IL: Research Press.

Triple P webpage. http://www.triplep.net/.

For clients

Barkley, R. (1998). *Your Defiant Child: Eight Steps to Better Behaviour*. New York: Guilford Press.

Forehand, R. & Long, N. (1996). *Parenting the Strong-Willed Child: The Clinically Proven Five Week Programme for Parents of Two to Six Year Olds*. Chicago: Contemporary Books.

Webster-Stratton, C. (1992). *Incredible Years: Trouble-Shooting Guide for Parents of Children Aged 3–8*. Toronto: Umbrella Press.

Adolescent conduct disorder

For professionals

Alexander, J., Barton, C., Gordon, D., Grotpeter, J., Hansson, K., Harrison, R., Mears, S., Mihalic, S., Parsons, B., Pugh, C., Schulman, S., Waldron, H. & Sexton, T. (1998). *Blueprints for Violence Prevention, Book Three: Functional Family Therapy (FFT)*. Boulder, CO: Centre for the Study and Prevention of Violence (http://www.colorado.edu/cspv/publications/blueprints.html).

Alexander, J. & Parsons, B. (1982). *Functional Family Therapy*. Monterey, CA: Brooks Cole.

Chamberlain, P. (1994). *Family Connections: A Treatment Foster Care Model for Adolescents With Delinquency*. Eugene, OR: Northwest Media (http://www.northwestmedia.com/foster/connect.html).

Chamberlain, P. (2003). *Treating Chronic Juvenile Offenders: Advances Made Through the Oregon Multidimensional Treatment Foster Care Model*. Washington, DC: American Psychological Association.

Henggeler, S., Mihalic, S., Rone, L., Thomas, C. & Timmons-Mitchell, J. (1998).

Blueprints for Violence Prevention, Book Six: Multisystemic Therapy (MST). Boulder, CO: Centre for the Study and Prevention of Violence (http://www.colorado.edu/cspv/publications/blueprints.html).

Henggeler, S., Schoenwald, S., Bordin, C., Rowland, M. & Cunningham, P. (1998). *Multisystemic Treatment of Antisocial Behaviour in Children and Adolescents.* New York: Guilford Press.

Sexton, T. L. & Alexander, J. F. (1999). *Functional Family Therapy: Principles of Clinical Intervention, Assessment, and Implementation.* Henderson, NV: RCH Enterprises.

For clients

Fogatch, M. & Patterson, G. (1989). *Parents & Adolescent Living Together. Part 1. The Basics.* Eugene, OR: Castalia.

Fogatch, M. & Patterson, G. (1989). *Parents & Adolescent Living Together. Part 2. Family Problem Solving.* Eugene, OR: Castalia.

Sharry, J. (2002). *Parent Power: Bringing Up Responsible Children and Teenagers.* Chichester: John Wiley.

Adolescent drug abuse

For professionals

Liddle, H. A. (2005). *Multidimensional Family Therapy for Adolescent Substance Abuse.* New York: Norton (www.chestnut.org/LI/cyt/products/MDFT_CYT_v5.pdf).

Szapocznik, J., Hervis, O. & Schwartz, S. (2002). *Brief Strategic Family Therapy for Adolescent Drug Abuse.* Rockville, MD: National Institute for Drug Abuse (http://www.drugabuse.gov/TXManuals/bsft/BSFTIndex.html).

Szapocznik, J. & Kurtines, W. (1989). *Breakthroughs in Family Therapy with Drug Abusing Problem Youth.* New York: Springer.

Juvenile sex offenders

For professionals

Borduin, C. M., Letourneau, E. J. & Henggeler, S. H. (in press). *Multisystemic Treatment with Juvenile Sexual Offenders and their Families.* New York: Guilford Press.

Burton, J. & Rasmussen, L. (1997). *Treating Children with Sexually Abusive Behaviour Problems: Guidelines for Child and Parent Intervention.* New York: Haworth.

Hunter, J. (2008). *Juvenile Sex Offenders: A Cognitive Behavioural Treatment Programme. Therapist Guide.* Oxford: Oxford University Press.

Lundrigan, P. (2001). *Treating Youth Who Sexually Abuse: An Integrated Multi-Component Approach.* New York: Haworth.

O'Reilly, G., Marshall, W., Carr, A. & Beckett, R. (2005). *Handbook of Clinical Intervention with Young People who Sexually Abuse.* London: Routledge.

Page, J., Murphy, W. and Way, I. (2007). *Manual for Structured Group Treatment With Adolescent Sexual Offenders.* New York: Wood N Barnes.

Print, B., Griffin, H., Beech, A., Quayle, J., Bradshaw, H., Hennker, J. & Morrisson, T. (2007). *AIM2, An Initial Assessment Model for Young People Who Display Sexually Harmful Behaviour*. Salford: GMAP (rita@aimproject.org.uk).

Rich, P. (2003). *Understanding Juvenile Sexual Offenders: Assessment, Treatment, and Rehabilitation*. Chichester: John Wiley.

Ryan, G. & Lane, S. (1997). *Juvenile Sexual Offending: Causes, Consequences, and Correction*. New York: Jossey Bass.

Steen, C. (1999). *The Relapse Prevention Workbook for Youth in Treatment*. Brandon, VT: Safer Society Press.

For clients

Allred, T. (1997). *Stop! Just for Kids: For Kids with Sexual Touching Problems by Kids with Sexual Touching Problems*. Brandon, VT: Safer Society Press.

Hunter, J. (2008). *Juvenile Sex Offenders: A Cognitive Behavioural Treatment Programme. Workbook*. Oxford: Oxford University Press.

Pithers, W. (1993). *From Trauma to Understanding: A Guide for Parents of Children with Sexual Behaviour Problems*. Brandon, VT: Safer Society Press.

Child and adolescent depression

For professionals

Brent, D. Therapy manuals. www.wpic.pitt.edu/research/star/ or BrentDA@upmc.edu.

Byng-Hall, J. (1995). *Rewriting Family Scripts: Improvisation and Change*. New York: Guilford Press. A family therapy approach that may be used for child and adolescent depression.

Langelier, C. (2001). *Mood Management Leader's Manual: A Cognitive-Behavioural Skills-Building Program for Adolescents*. Thousand Oaks, CA: Sage.

Malan, D. (1995). *Individual Psychotherapy and the Science of Psychodynamics* (Second Edition). London: Butterworth-Heinemann. A psychodynamic approach that may be used for adolescent depression.

Manual for Lewinsohn's Coping with Depression Course. www.kpchr.org/public/acwd/acwd.html.

Mufson, L., Dorta, K., Moreau, D. and Weissman, M. (2004). *Interpersonal Psychotherapy for Depressed Adolescents* (Second Edition). New York: Guilford Press.

Stallard, P. (2002). *Think Good – Feel Good: A Cognitive Behaviour Therapy Workbook for Children and Young People*. Chichester: John Wiley.

Stallard, P. (2005). *A Clinicians Guide to Think Good Feel Good: The Use of CBT with Children and Young People*. Chichester: John Wiley.

Weisz, J. therapy manuals. weisz@psych.ucla.edu.

For clients

Fitzpatrick, C. (2004). *Coping with Depression in Young People: A Guide for Parents*. Chichester: John Wiley.

Langelier, C. (2001). *Mood Management: A Cognitive-Behavioural Skills-Building Program for Adolescents. Skills Workbook*. Thousand Oaks, CA: Sage.

Juvenile bipolar disorder

For professionals

Miklowitz, D. J. & Goldstein, M. J. (1997). *Bipolar Disorder: A Family-Focused Treatment Approach*. New York: Guilford Press.

For clients

Miklowitz, D. J. & George, E. L. (2007). *The Bipolar Teen: What You Can Do to Help Your Child and Your Family*. New York: Guilford Press.

Suicide in adolescence

For professionals

Berman, A., Jobes, D. & Silverman, M. (2006). *Adolescent Suicide: Assessment and Intervention* (Second Edition). Washington, DC: American Psychological Association.

Henggeler, S. W., Schoenwald, S. K., Rowland, M. D. & Cunningham, P. B. (2002). *Multisystemic Treatment of Children and Adolescents with Serious Emotional Disturbance*. New York: Guilford Press.

King, C. A., Kramer, A. & Preuss, L. (2000). *Youth-Nominated Support Team Intervention Manual*. Ann Arbor, MI: University of Michigan, Department of Psychiatry.

Miller, A., Rathus, J. & Linehan, M. (2007). *Dialectical Behaviour Therapy with Suicidal Adolescents*. New York: Guilford Press.

For clients

Cobain, B. & Larch, J. (2006). *Dying To Be Free: A Healing Guide for Families After a Suicide*. Centre City, MN: Hazelden.

Anxiety in children and adolescents

For professionals

Albano, A. & Marten Dibartolo, P. (2007). *Cognitive Behavioural Therapy for Social Phobia in Adolescents: Stand up, Speak Out. Therapist Guide*. Oxford: Oxford University Press.

Chorpita, B. (2006). *Modular Cognitive-Behaviour Therapy for Childhood Anxiety Disorders*. New York: Guilford Press.

Cohen, J., Mannarino, A. & Deblinger, E. (2006). *Treating Trauma and Traumatic Grief in Children and Adolescents*. New York: Guilford Press.

Eisen, A. & Schaefer, C. (2007). *Separation Anxiety in Children and Adolescents: An Individualized Approach to Assessment and Treatment*. New York: Guilford Press.

FRIENDS anxiety management programme website. http://www.friendsinfo.net/.

Heyne, D. & Rollings, S. (2002). *School Refusal*. Oxford: Blackwell.

Kearney, C. & Albano, A. (2007). *When Children Refuse School: Therapist Guide* (Second Edition). Oxford: Oxford University Press.

Kendall, P. C. (2000). *Cognitive-Behavioural Therapy for Anxious Children: Therapist Manual* (Second Edition). Ardmore, PA: Workbook Publishing.

Kendall, P., Choudhurry, M., Hudson, J. & Webb, A. (2002). *The CAT Project Therapist Manual*. Ardmore, PA: Workbook Publishing (www.workbookpublishing.com).

March, J. & Mulle, K. (1998). *OCD in Children and Adolescents: A Cognitive-Behavioural Treatment Manual*. New York: Guilford Press.

Ollendick, T. & March, J. (2003). *Phobic and Anxiety Disorders in Children and Adolescents: A Clinical Guide to Effective Psychosocial and Pharmacological Interventions*. Oxford: Oxford University Press.

Piacentini, J., Langley, A. & Roblek, T. (2007). *Cognitive Behavioural Treatment of Childhood OCD: It's Only A False Alarm. Therapist Guide*. Oxford: Oxford University Press.

Sage, R. & Sluckin, A. (2004). *Silent Children: Approaches to Selective Mutism*. Leicester: University of Leicester. (Video & book available from Mrs Lindsay Whittington, Sec of SMIRA, +44-116-212-7411 smiraleicester@hotmail.com.)

For clients

Albano, A. & Marten Dibartolo, P. (2007). *Stand Up, Speak Out, Workbook*. Oxford: Oxford University Press (adolescent social phobia treatment programme).

Chrestman, K., Gilboa-Schechtman, E. & Foa, E. (2007). *Reclaiming Your Life From PTSD: Teen Workbook*. Oxford: Oxford University Press.

Johnson, M. & Wintgens, A. (2001). *The Selective Mutism Resource Manual*. Milton Keynes: Speechmark.

Kearney, C. & Albano, A. (2007). *When Children Refuse School: Parent Workbook*. (Second Edition). Oxford: Oxford University Press.

Last, C. (2006). *Help for Worried Kids*. New York: Guilford Press.

March, J. & Benton, C. (2007). *Talking Back to OCD*. New York: Guilford Press.

Piacentini, J., Langley, A. & Roblek, T. (2007). *It's Only A False Alarm: A Cognitive Behavioural Treatment Programme. Workbook*. Oxford: Oxford University Press.

Rapee, R., Spense, S., Cobham, V. & Wignal, A. (2000). *Helping Your Anxious Child: A Step-By-Step Guide for Parents*. San Francisco: New Harbinger

Rapoport, J. (1991). *The Boy Who Couldn't Stop Washing*. New York: Penguin.

Eating disorders in young people

For professionals

Fairburn, C. & Wilson, G. (1993). *Binge Eating: Nature, Assessment & Treatment*. New York: Guilford Press (contains a treatment manual for bulimia).

Garner, D. & Garfinkel, P. (1997). *Handbook of Treatment for Eating Disorders* (Second Edition). New York: Guilford Press.

le Grange, D. & Lock, J. (2007). *Treating Bulimia in Adolescents: A Family-Based Approach*. New York: Guilford Press.

Lock, J., le Grange, D., Agras, W. & Dare, C. (2001). *Treatment Manual for Anorexia Nervosa: A Family Based Approach*. New York: Guilford Press.

Treasure, J. & Schmidt, U. (1993). *Clinician's Guide to Getting Better Bit(e) by Bit(e)*. Hove, UK: Psychology Press.

For clients

Bryant-Waugh, R. & Lask, B. (1999). *Eating Disorders: A Parent's Guide*. London: Penguin.

Cooper, P. (1995). *Bulimia Nervosa: A Guide to Recovery*. London: Robinson.

Crisp, A., Joughin, N., Halek, C. & Bower, C. (1996). *Anorexia Nervosa: The Wish to Change. Self-Help and Discovery, The Thirty Steps* (Second Edition). Hove, UK: Psychology Press.

Fairburn, C. (1995). *Overcoming Binge Eating*. New York: Guilford Press.

Fox, C. & Joughin, C. (2002). *Eating Problems in Children: Information for Parents*. London: Gaskell.

Lock, J. J. & le Grange, D. (2004). *Help Your Teenager Beat an Eating Disorder*. London: Routledge.

Treasure, J. (1997). *Anorexia Nervosa: A Survival Guide for Families, Friends and Sufferers*. Hove, UK: Psychology Press.

Treasure, J. & Schmidt, U. (1993). *Getting Better Bit(e) by Bit(e): A Survival Kit for Sufferers of Bulimia Nervosa and Binge Eating*. Hove, UK: Psychology Press.

Tourette's syndrome in young people

For professionals

Azrin, N. & Nunn, R. (1973). Habit reversal: a method of eliminating nervous habits and tics. *Behaviour Research and Therapy*, 11, 619–628.

Chowdhury, U. (2004). *Tics and Tourette Syndrome*. London: Jessica Kingsley Publishers.

Leckman, J. & Cohen, D. (1998). *Tourette Syndrome, Tics Obsessions, Compulsions: Developmental Psychopathology and Clinical Care*. New York: John Wiley.

For clients

Carroll, A. & Robertson, M. (2000). *Tourette Syndrome: A Practical Guide for Teachers, Parents and Carers*. London: David Fulton.

Pain in children and adolescents

For professionals

Blanchard, E. & Andrasik, F. (1985). *Management of Chronic Headache: A Psychological Approach*. New York: Pergamon Press.

McGrath, P. (1990). *Pain in Children: Nature, Assessment and Treatment*. New York: Guilford Press.

For clients

Davis, M., Robbins-Eshelman, E. & McKay, M. (2000). *The Relaxation and Stress Reduction Workbook* (Fifth Edition). Oakland, CA: New Harbinger.

McGrath, P., McGrath, P. J., Cunningham, S., Lascelles, M. & Humphries, P. (1990). *Help Yourself: A Treatment for Migraine Headaches*. Ottawa: University of Ottawa Press.

Asthma in young people

For professionals

Bender, B. (2000). *Childhood Asthma Video*. Washington, DC: American Psychological Association (http://www.apa.org/videos/4310592.html).

For clients

Asthma and children webpage. http://www.asthmaandchildren.com/.

Parcel, G. (1979). *Teaching Myself About Asthma*. St Louis, MO: CV Mosby.

Diabetes in young people

For professionals

American Diabetes Association (1990). *Diabetes Support Group for Young Adults: Facilitators Manual*. Alexandria, VA: American Diabetes Association.

McNabb, W. (2000). *In Control: A Behaviour-Orientated Diabetes Self-Management Education Program*. Chicago, IL: Centre for Research in Medical Education and Health Care, Department of Medicine, University of Chicago.

For parents

Pirner, C. & Westcott, N. (1994). *Even Little Kids Get Diabetes*. New York: Albert Whitman.

Physical abuse

For professionals

Hembree-Kigin, T. & McNeil, C. (1995). *Parent–Child Interaction Therapy*. New York: Plenum.

Kolko, D. J. & Swenson, C. C. (2002). *Assessing and Treating Physically Abused Children and their Families: A Cognitive Behavioural Approach*. Thousand Oaks, CA: Sage.

MacDonald, G. (2001). *Effective Interventions for Child Abuse and Neglect: An Evidence-Based Approach to Planning and Evaluating Interventions*. Chichester: John Wiley.

Child sexual abuse

For professionals

Deblinger, A. & Heflinger, A. (1996). *Treating Sexually Abused Children and their Non-Offending Parents: A Cognitive Behavioural Approach*. Thousand Oaks, CA: Sage.

Trepper, T. & Barrett, M. (1989). *Systemic Treatment of Incest: A Therapeutic Handbook*. New York: Brunner-Mazel.

Young people's adjustment to divorce

For professionals

Dowling, E. & Gorell-Barnes, G. (1999). *Working with Children and Parents Through Separation and Divorce: The Changing Lives of Children*. Basingstoke: Macmillan Press.

Herbert, M. (1996). *Separation and Divorce: Helping Children Cope*. Leicester: British Psychological Society.

Pedro-Carroll, J. (2006). *Children of Divorce Intervention Programme*. Available from Dr. JoAnne Pedro-Carroll, The Children's Institute, 274 North Goodman, Suite D103, Rochester, NY 14607. Phone: (585) 295–1000, ext 264. Email: jpcarroll@childrensinstitute.net.

Stolberg, A., Zacharias, M. & Complair, C. W. (1991). *Children of Divorce: Leaders' Guide, Kids' Book and Parents' Book*. Circle Pines, MN: American Guidance Service.

For clients

Hetherington, E. & Kelly, J. (2002). *For Better or For Worse: Divorce Reconsidered*. New York: Norton.

Sharry, J., Reid, P. & Donohoe, E. (2001). *When Parents Separate: Helping Your Children Cope*. Dublin: Veritas.

Grief and bereavement in young people

For professionals

Cohen, J., Mannarino, A. & Deblinger, E. (2006). *Treating Trauma and Traumatic Grief in Children and Adolescents*. New York: Guilford Press.

Kissane, D. & Bloch, S. (2002). *Family Focused Grief Therapy: A Model of Family-Centred Care during Palliative Care and Bereavement*. Maidenhead: Open University Press.

Rotheram-Borus, M. (1998). *Intervention Manuals for Project TALC (Teens and Adults Learning to Communicate) Parents Living with AIDS*. Los Angeles, CA: UCLA Semel Institute Centre for Community Health (http://chipts.ucla.edu/interventions/manuals/intervhra1.html).

For clients

Krementz, J. (1981). *How It Feels When A Parent Dies*. New York: Knopf.

Mallon, B. (1998). *Helping Children to Manage Loss: Positive Strategies for Renewal and Growth*. London: Jessica Kingsley Publishers.

Rando, T. (1991). *How To Go On Living When Someone You Love Dies*. New York: Bantam.

Schaefer, D. & Lyons, C. (1986). *How Do We Tell the Children*. New York: Newmarket.

Turner, M. (1998). *Talking with Children and Young People about Death and Dying: A Workbook*. London: Jessica Kingsley Publishers.

Ward, B. (1995). *Good Grief: Exploring Feelings, Loss and Death* (Second Edition). London: Jessica Kingsley Publishers. Vol. 1, with under elevens. Vol. 2, with over elevens and adults.

Intellectual disability

For professionals

Carr, A., O'Reilly, G., Walsh, P. & McEvoy, J. (2007). *Handbook of Intellectual Disability and Clinical Psychology Practice*. London: Routledge.

Emerson, E. (2001). *Challenging Behaviour. Analysis and Intervention in People with Severe Intellectual Disabilities* (Second Edition). Cambridge: Cambridge University Press.

Taylor, J. L. & Novaco, R. W. (2005). *Anger Treatment for People with Developmental Disabilities: A Theory, Evidence and Manual Based Approach*. Chichester: Wiley.

Zager, D. (2005). *Autism Spectrum Disorders: Identification, Education and Treatment* (Third Edition). Mahwah, NJ: Lawrence Erlbaum Associates, Inc.

Autism

For professionals

Frost, L. & Bondy, A. (2002). *PECS: The Picture Exchange Communication System Training Manual* (Second Edition). Cherry Hill, NJ: Pyramid Educational Consultants.

Gray, C. (2000). *The New Social Story Book*. Arlington, TX: Future Horizons.

Koegel, R. & Koegel, L. (2006). *Pivotal Response Treatments for Autism: Communication, Social, and Academic Development*. Baltimore, MD: Paul H Brookes.

LOVAAS website. http://www.lovaas.com/.

Lovaas, O. (2002). *Teaching Children with Developmental Delays: Basic Intervention Techniques*. Austin, TX: Pro-Ed.

Mesibov, G., Shea, V. & Schopler, E. (2005). *The TEACCH Approach to Autism Spectrum Disorders*. New York: Springer.

TEACCH website. http://www.teacch.com/welcome.html.

Volkmar, F., Paul, R., Klin, A. & Cohen, D. (2005). *Handbook of Autism and Pervasive Developmental Disorders* (Third Edition, Vols 1 and 2). New York: Wiley.

Wall, K. (2004). *Autism and Early Years Practice: A Guide for Early Years Professionals, Teachers and Parents*. London: Paul Chapman.

For parents

Attwood, T. (1998). *Asperger's Syndrome*. London: Jessica Kingsley Publishers.

Gillbrg, C. (2002). *A Guide to Asperger Syndrome*. Cambridge: Cambridge University Press.

Harris, S. (1994). *Siblings of Children with Autism: A Guide for Families*. Bethesda, MD: Woodbine House.

Howlin, P. (1998). *Children with Autism and Asperger's Syndrome: A Guide for Practitioner's and Carers*. Chichester: John Wiley.

Jordon, R. & Powell, S. (1995). *Understanding and Teaching Children with Autism*. New York: Wiley.

National Autistic Society (1993). *Approaches to Autism* (Second Edition). London: National Autistic Society.

Vermeulen, P. (2000). *I Am Special: Introducing Children and Young People to the Autistic Spectrum Disorder*. London: Jessica Kingsley Publishers.

Wing, L. (1996). *The Autistic Spectrum: A Guide for Parents and Professionals*. Constable: London.

Effectiveness of psychotherapy and psychological interventions with specific problems in adulthood and later life

The central question addressed in this chapter is: What specific psychotherapy protocols and psychological interventions have been found to be effective for adults and older adults with a range of psychological problems? Or, put more succinctly: What works for adults? In this chapter, evidence for the effectiveness of specific psychotherapy protocols and psychological interventions with specific psychological problems in adulthood and later life will be reviewed. Traditional psychiatric categories (such as mood disorders, anxiety disorders, eating disorders, etc.) have been used to organize material in this chapter. As was noted in the opening of Chapter 4, these categories may be ideologically unacceptable to service users and psychotherapists, many of whom view psychiatric diagnoses as being on a continuum with normal development and functioning, or as a reflection of systemic rather than individual constraints. However, the organization, administration, and funding of clinical services and research programmes are framed predominantly in terms of such categories, and so these have been used to organize the material in this chapter. For each problem area, extensive computer and manual literature searches for relevant evidence were conducted using the same methodology as described in Chapter 4. For computer searches PsychInfo, Medline and other databases were used. For manual literature searches, bibliographies of authoritative texts in the area were consulted (e.g. Castonguay & Beutler, 2006; Nathan & Gorman, 2007; Roth & Fonagy, 2005).

In this chapter, for each specific type of problem, results of selected meta-analyses, reviews, and outcome studies will be briefly summarized. Then implications for clinical practice will be outlined. For comparative purposes, and where appropriate, reference will be made to the effectiveness of pharmacotherapy and other physical interventions, although these are not the main focus of this volume. The research reviewed in this and other chapters has many implications for future research and policy development. These issues will be addressed in the final chapter of this book.

The literature search yielded evidence to show that psychotherapeutic interventions alone, or as elements of multimodal programmes involving pharmacotherapy or other physical interventions, are effective for the following specific problems in adulthood:

- mood disorder and related problems, specifically major depression, bipolar disorder, suicide, and self-harm
- anxiety disorders, including generalized anxiety disorder, panic disorder, specific phobias, social phobia or social anxiety disorder, obsessive-compulsive disorder, post-traumatic stress disorder
- somatoform disorders and difficulties, including medically unexplained symptoms, hypochondriasis, body dysmorphic disorder
- adjustment to illness including preparation for surgery, adjustment to conditions with high mortality rates such as cancer and heart disease, and adjustment to chronic medical conditions involving adherence to complex regimes such as diabetes, asthma, hypertension
- facilitating coping with conditions involving pain and fatigue such as chronic pain, low back pain, fibromyalgia, chronic fatigue syndrome, headaches, arthritis, irritable bowel syndrome
- eating disorders, including obesity, bulimia, anorexia, binge eating disorder
- insomnia
- substance abuse and addiction, including alcohol and drug abuse, nicotine addiction, compulsive gambling
- schizophrenia
- personality disorders
- anger and aggression
- sexual offending
- relationship problems, including marital distress, psychosexual problems, domestic violence
- psychological problems associated with older adulthood, including dementia, late life depression, anxiety, and insomnia.

What follows is a summary of the evidence for the effectiveness of psychotherapy or psychological interventions for each of these types of problems.

Mood disorders in adults

Psychotherapy alone and in combination with pharmacotherapy has been shown to be effective in the management of mood disorders and related difficulties, particularly depression, bipolar disorder, suicidality, and self-harm.

Depression in adults

Major depression is an episodic disorder characterized by low mood, loss of interest in normal activities, and most of the following symptoms:

psychomotor agitation or retardation, fatigue, low self-esteem, pessimism, inappropriate excessive guilt, suicidal ideation, impaired concentration, and sleep and appetite disturbance (American Psychiatric Association, 2000a; World Health Organization, 1992). Eighty-five per cent of clients experience recurrent episodes of depression and on average people with major depression have four episodes of 20 weeks each over the course of their lifetimes. As the condition progresses the frequency and duration of depressive episodes increases. In contrast to this episodic disorder, dysthymia is a persistent disorder characterized by low mood and at least two of the other symptoms of major depression. Most patients with dysthymia develop major depression.

Cognitive behavioural therapy for depression in adults

In a systematic review of 13 studies, Craighead *et al.* (2007) concluded that 50–70% of outpatients recovered from depression after a course of about 16 weeks of cognitive behavioural therapy. Cognitive behavioural therapy was as effective as antidepressants in the short term and led to fewer relapses in the long term. Similar results were reported by Westen and Morrison (2001) in a review of 12 studies of cognitive behavioural therapy for depression. They found a post-therapy improvement rate of 54%.

Cognitive behavioural therapy includes two main components: behavioural activation in which clients are helped to increase their rates of pleasant activities, and cognitive restructuring in which the focus is on accessing and challenging depression-maintaining cognitions. Beck *et al.*'s (1979) *Cognitive Therapy of Depression* and Persons *et al.*'s (2001) *Essential Components of Cognitive Behaviour Therapy for Depression* are useful treatment manuals.

There is growing evidence that cognitive behavioural therapy during depression and following recovery reduces relapse rates to a greater degree than antidepressant medication. In a meta-analysis of 28 studies, Vittengl *et al.* (2007) found that average relapse rates following a course of cognitive behavioural therapy were 29% within one year and 54% within two years. Similar relapse rates occurred for other brief psychotherapies and combined cognitive behavioural therapy and antidepressant medication. However, relapse rates after antidepressant medication were found to be significantly higher, averaging 65% within one year. Thus, cognitive behavioural therapy was more effective than antidepressant medication in reducing relapse in depression. Continuing cognitive behavioural therapy following recovery reduced relapse rates to 42% after 114 weeks. It was significantly more effective than maintenance antidepressant medication where the average relapse rate during the same period was 61%.

Of the maintenance cognitive behavioural therapy approaches, protocols which include mindfulness as a central component show most promise. Mindfulness-based cognitive therapy for people who have recovered from three or more episodes of depression has been shown in two trials to delay further relapses (Baer, 2003). This meditation-based therapy helps clients develop skills for breaking the link between depressive thinking and mood, by adopting a 'being' rather than a 'doing' mind state, and is well described in Segal *et al.*'s (2002) *Mindfulness-Based Cognitive Therapy for Depression*.

In a thorough review, Craighead *et al.* (2007) found that a favourable response to cognitive behavioural therapy was associated with high learned resourcefulness; higher levels of social functioning and an intact marriage; the absence of chronic depression and social phobia; and low pre-treatment levels of depressive symptoms and cognitions.

All of the evidence reviewed in this section so far concerns the impact of cognitive behavioural therapy on outpatients. There is some evidence for the effectiveness of cognitive behavioural therapy with inpatients, who typically present with more severe symptoms. Stuart and Bowers (1995) in a review of eight trials found that with inpatients cognitive behavioural therapy alone and in combination with antidepressants was effective for a proportion of cases.

Behaviour therapy for depression in adults

Behavioural activation, problem-solving therapy and Lewinsohn *et al.*'s (1984) *Coping with Depression* course are distinctly behavioural approaches to the treatment of mood disorders. Results of meta-analyses reported below support the effectiveness of these behavioural interventions for depression. With behavioural activation, clients increase the frequency of pleasant activities and positive social interactions, and monitor both their mood and daily activities. In a meta-analysis of 16 studies evaluating the effectiveness of behavioural activation for depression, Cuijpers *et al.* (2007a) found a post-treatment effect size of .87, which is equivalent to a success rate of 70%, and the benefits of treatment were maintained at follow-up. In ten studies behavioural activation and cognitive behavioural therapy were compared and found to be equally effective after treatment and at follow-up.

In problem-solving therapy clients learn to define large apparently insoluble problems as a set of smaller more manageable difficulties, and then to systematically solve each of these by exploring and evaluating options, implementing the best option and evaluating its impact on the target problem. In a meta-analysis of 13 controlled trials of problem-solving therapy for unipolar mood disorders, Cuijpers *et al.* (2007b) found an effect size of 0.34, which is equivalent to a success rate of 58%, and lower effects occurred in studies of clients with major depression (as opposed to dysthymia, or subclinical depressive symptoms).

Lewinsohn's *et al.*'s *Coping with Depression* course (1984) is a behavioural activation and psychoeducational mood-management programme which may be administered as bibliotherapy or as a programme for recruited target groups, such as people at risk for depression, or those recovering from depression. In a meta-analysis of 20 studies of the *Coping with Depression* course, Cuijpers (1998) found that it was effective in alleviating depressive symptoms, with effect sizes that were comparable to those of other treatment modalities for depression. However, the samples studied were media recruited rather than referred cases, and while all had depressive symptoms, not all may have been suffering from a current mood disorder.

These three meta-analyses show that behavioural activation can be an effective treatment for depressive symptoms, and in some cases for clinical depression. This conclusion is consistent with Craighead *et al.*'s (2007) narrative review of eight studies of behavioural therapy for major depressive disorder.

Interpersonal therapy for depression in adults

In a meta-analysis of 13 studies of interpersonal psychotherapy for depression, de Mello *et al.* (2005) found that it was significantly superior to placebo interventions and cognitive behavioural therapy in reducing depressive symptoms. Reductions in depressive symptoms were expressed as weighted mean differences. A weighted mean difference lower than 0 indicates that interpersonal therapy was superior to the comparison group. The weighted mean difference based on nine studies for comparisons with placebo control groups was −3.57, and the weighted mean difference based on three studies for a comparison with groups that received cognitive behavioural therapy was −2.16. Remission rates were 68% and 49% for interpersonal therapy and placebo respectively; and 56% and 47% for interpersonal therapy and cognitive behavioural therapy respectively, and these differences in remission rates were not significant. The combination of interpersonal therapy and medication did not show an additive effect compared to medication alone for acute treatment, for maintenance treatment, or for prophylactic treatment.

In a narrative review, Craighead *et al.* (2007) found that the following factors were predictive of a positive treatment response to interpersonal therapy for depression: high pre-treatment level of social functioning; the absence of co-morbid personality disorder, cognitive dysfunction, and panic disorder with agoraphobia; low depression severity; and a low level of trait neuroticism.

Interpersonal therapy is described in Weissman *et al.*'s (2000) *Comprehensive Guide to Interpersonal Psychotherapy* and Klerman *et al.*'s (1984) *Interpersonal Psychotherapy of Depression*. In this type of therapy the link between four categories of interpersonal difficulties and depression are assessed and relevant interpersonal difficulties addressed in therapy over about 16 sessions. The four categories of interpersonal difficulties are: (1) grief associated with the loss of a loved one; (2) role disputes involving family members, friends, or colleagues; (3) role transitions such as starting or ending relationships within the family or work context, moving jobs or houses, graduation, promotion, retirement, or diagnosis of an illness; (4) interpersonal deficits, particularly poor social skills for making and maintaining relationships.

Psychodynamic psychotherapy for depression in adults

In a meta-analysis of six studies of the comparative effectiveness of brief psychodynamic psychotherapy and cognitive behavioural therapy, Leichsenring (2001) found no significant difference between treatments in depressive symptoms, general psychiatric symptomatology, and social functioning after therapy. For psychodynamic therapy, improvement rates across studies and functional domains ranged from 45–70% after treatment and 26–83% at follow-up. The improvement rates ranged from 51–87% after treatment, and 30–86% at follow-up for cognitive behavioural therapy. In two trials, psychodynamic psychotherapy combined with antidepressant medication has been found to lead to better outcomes than medication alone (Burnand *et al.*, 2002; de Jonghe *et al.*, 2001). In psychodynamic psychotherapy, the focus is on interpreting the links between defences, anxiety, and unconscious feelings and impulses, within the context of the transference relationship with the therapist, the relationship with significant people in the client's current life, and early relationships with parents or caregivers. Useful treatment manuals which have been used in research trials are McCullough-Vaillant's (1997) *Changing Character: Short-Term Anxiety Regulating Psychotherapy for Restructuring Defences, Affects and Attachments*; Malan's (1995) *Individual Psychotherapy and the Science of Psychodynamics*, and Luborsky's (1984) *Principles of Psychoanalytic Psychotherapy: A Manual for Supportive-Expressive Treatment*.

Couples therapy for depression in adults

In narrative reviews of controlled trials of couples therapy for depression, Gupta *et al.* (2003) and Beach (2003) found evidence for the effectiveness of behavioural marital therapy, cognitive marital therapy, conjoint interpersonal therapy, and systemic couples therapy in the treatment of depressed marital partners. There is also evidence from a recent trial for the effectiveness of emotionally focused couples therapy in the treatment of depression (Dessaulles *et al.*, 2003). All of these approaches to couples therapy require about 20 conjoint therapy sessions and focus on both relationship enhancement and mood management. What follows is a review of the eight available studies on couples therapy for depression.

In three trials behavioural marital therapy was as effective as individual cognitive behaviour therapy in alleviating depressive symptoms and more effective than individual therapy in alleviating co-morbid marital distress (Beach & O'Leary, 1992; Emanuels-Zuurveen & Emmelkamp, 1996; Jacobson *et al.*, 1991). In one of these trials, Beach and O'Leary (1992) also showed that behavioural couples therapy improved the quality of the marital relationship, which in turn accounted for the alleviation of depressive symptomatology. Behavioural marital therapy involves communication and problem-solving skills training and behavioural exchange procedures. The application of this approach to depression is described in Beach *et al.*'s (1990) *Depression in Marriage: A Model for Aetiology and Treatment*.

Two trials of cognitive marital therapy have been conducted. Teichman *et al.* (1995) found that cognitive marital therapy was more effective than standard individual cognitive therapy for depressive symptoms and Emanuels-Zuurveen and Emmelkamp (1997) found that spouse-assisted cognitive therapy and standard cognitive therapy were equally effective. A central process in cognitive marital therapy is using guided discovery, Socratic questioning, and behavioural experiments to identify and modify cognitive factors that maintain dysphoria and relationship distress. A good description of these approaches is contained in Epstein and Baucom's (2002) *Enhanced Cognitive-Behavioural Therapy for Couples*.

In a controlled trial, Foley *et al.* (1989) found that conjoint interpersonal couples therapy was as effective as standard individually administered interpersonal therapy in improving both depression and interpersonal functioning. Both versions of interpersonal therapy were based on Klerman *et al.*'s (1984) *Interpersonal Psychotherapy of Depression*.

In two trials, couples therapy was found to be as effective or more effective than antidepressant medication. Leff *et al.* (2000) found that systemic couples therapy was more effective than antidepressants in reducing depressive symptoms after treatment and at two years follow-up. Dessaulles *et al.* (2003) found that emotionally focused couples therapy was as effective as antidepressants in alleviating depression. The therapeutic approach used in Leff's study is described in Jones and Asen's (2002) *Systemic Couple Therapy and Depression*. It involved enactment of couples issues in therapy sessions, disruption of problematic behavioural cycles, and setting tasks to develop less problematic ways of interacting. The approach used in Dessaulles' study is given in Johnson's (2004) *The Practice of Emotionally Focused Couple Therapy*. This involves helping couples use non-problematic ways to express and meet each other's attachment needs.

Psychotherapy contexts and depression in adults

The evidence reviewed so far in this section has focused predominantly on the provision of psychotherapy in specialist service settings to moderately depressed outpatients on a single case basis. There is some evidence for the positive impact of psychotherapeutic interventions for depression in other contexts, notably, bibliotherapy, computer-assisted therapy, therapy offered in primary care settings, and psychotherapy offered within a group (rather than on a single case basis).

Bibliotherapy

In a narrative review of 29 studies and a meta-analysis of 17 of these, Gregory *et al.* (2004) found an effect size of 0.77 for bibliotherapy of depressive symptoms, which is equivalent to a success rate of 70%. In most studies, participants were recruited through media announcements rather than referred for treatment, and so probably represented less severe cases of depression. Also, in most studies there was some degree of therapist contact and support.

Computer-assisted therapy

In a meta-analysis of 12 randomized controlled trials of internet-based interventions for anxiety and depression, Spek *et al.* (2007) found an effect size of .27 for depression and .96 for anxiety, which are equivalent to success rates of 56% and 71% respectively. Interventions with therapist support had greater impact than those without therapist support.

Primary care

In a review of 12 controlled trials, Schulberg *et al.* (2002) concluded that when used to treat major depression a depression-specific psychotherapy (including cognitive behavioural therapy, interpersonal therapy, or client-centred therapy) produces better clinical outcomes than a primary care physician's usual approach. For minor depression or dysthymia, evidence for the effectiveness of psychotherapy compared with usual care is equivocal.

Group therapy

In a meta-analysis of 15 studies of group therapy for depression, McDermut *et al.* (2001) found an effect size of 1.03, which is equivalent to a success rate of 72%. Cognitive behavioural and psychodynamic forms of group therapy were included in these studies. Where comparisons were made between individual and group therapy in nine studies, both had equivalent outcomes.

Psychotherapy factors and depression in adults

Extensive narrative reviews show that specific client attributes, therapist characteristics, alliance factors, and therapeutic techniques are associated with a positive outcome in the treatment of dysphoric clients (Beutler *et al.*, 2006; Castonguay *et al.*, 2006; Follette & Greenberg, 2006). What follows is a summary of key findings from these reviews.

Client and therapist characteristics

In a narrative review, Beutler *et al.* (2006) concluded that certain client and therapist characteristics influence the outcome of psychotherapy with dysphoric clients. Positive outcome is more probable where clients have a strong social support network; where clients and therapists are from the same racial or ethnic group; and where clients and therapists have secure attachment styles. Negative outcome is associated with depression severity and chronicity; high functional impairment; co-morbid personality disorder; being from an ethnic minority; and being older. A positive therapeutic outcome is associated with the match between therapists' styles and clients' characteristics. In this regard, positive outcomes have been found to occur if therapists offer highly impaired clients intensive long-term treatment (rather than time-limited treatment); use less directive techniques with resistant clients; show religious tolerance and offer religiously oriented therapy where that is the client's preference; focus on the development of social and symptom-management skills (rather than insight) with impulsive clients; and focus on insight and self-understanding (rather than self-regulation skills) with indecisive, non-impulsive clients.

Therapeutic alliance

In a narrative review, Castonguay *et al.* (2006) concluded that a positive outcome when working with dysphoric clients is associated with a good therapeutic alliance in individual therapy, and group cohesiveness within group therapy. Strong therapeutic alliances in individual therapy, and cohesiveness in group therapy are characterized by active engagement, empathy, caring, warmth, acceptance, authenticity, the provision of feedback to clients, appropriate supportive self-disclosure, a willingness to repair ruptures in the therapeutic alliance in a non-defensive way, the management of countertransference, and the sparing use of accurate relational interpretations.

Therapeutic techniques

In a narrative review, Follette and Greenberg (2006) concluded that a positive outcome when working with dysphoric clients is associated with a number of general therapeutic techniques. These include structuring therapy to achieve goals; challenging depressive thinking and behaviour with new experiences; increasing clients' access to rewarding experiences; reducing gains associated with avoidant and depressive behaviour; enhancing social functioning and support; and enhancing emotional awareness, regulation, and expression.

Physical treatments for depression in adults

While the evidence reviewed so far supports the effectiveness of psycho-therapy in the treatment of depression, there is also evidence for the effective-ness of physical (or non-psychological) interventions for depression. These include antidepressant medication, St John's Wort, light therapy, and electro-convulsive therapy. What follows is a brief summary of some of this evidence.

Antidepressant medication

In a systematic review and meta-analysis of 315 trials of a range of newer antidepressants published between 1980 and 1998, Williams *et al.* (2000) con-cluded that newer antidepressants were more effective than placebo for major depression and dysthymia in adults and older adults in primary care and specialist settings. There was no difference between newer antidepressants and older tricyclic antidepressants, but the former had fewer undesirable side effects. The newer antidepressants considered in this paper were selective serotonin reuptake inhibitors (SSRI), serotonin and noradrenaline reuptake inhibitor (SNRI), reversible inhibitors of monoamine oxidase (RIMA), 5-hydroxy-tryptophan (HT)-2 receptor antagonists, aminobutyric acid (GABA) mimetics, 5-HT-1a receptor agonists, and dopamine reuptake inhibi-tors. These results are consistent with those from Nemeroff and Schatzberg's (2007) extensive narrative review, and this reflected the international con-sensus about the efficacy of antidepressants until early in 2008. In two meta-analyses published early in 2008 which include newly released US Food and Drug Administration antidepressant trials, smaller effect sizes of SSRIs were found than previously was the case, ranging from .31 to .32, and the evidence suggested that they were most effective with severe but not mild or moderate depression (Kirsch *et al.*, 2008; Turner *et al.*, 2008). There is evidence that the long-term use of antidepressants may prevent relapse. On the basis of pooled results of 31 randomized trials that included 4410 patients, Geddes *et al.* (2003) found that continuing treatment with a range of different antidepres-sants reduced the odds of depressive relapse by around two-thirds, which is approximately equivalent to a halving of the absolute risk. The pooled odds ratio for relapse was 3.0 which is equal to an effect size of .6, or an approxi-mate success rate of 64%.

St John's Wort

Williams *et al.* (2000) conducted a meta-analysis of 14 trials of St John's Wort (hypericum) and concluded that it was more effective than placebo and as effective as tricyclic antidepressants. These results are consistent with those of Linde *et al.* (2005) who found, in a meta-analysis of 37 double-blind random-ized trials, that St John's Wort and antidepressants were equally effective.

Light therapy

Light therapy has been developed as a treatment for seasonal affective disorder, or winter depression as it is colloquially known. Light therapy was developed on the premise that the reduced exposure to sunlight in winter precipitates and maintains episodes of this type of depression. In a meta-analyses of 21 studies, Golden *et al.* (2005) found an effect size of .84 for light therapy for depression (eight studies) and .73 for dawn simulation for seasonal affective disorder (five studies). These effect sizes are equivalent to success rates of 70% and 67% respectively.

Electroconvulsive therapy

In a meta-analysis of electroconvulsive therapy (ECT) for severe depression, Carney *et al.* (2003) found that ECT was more effective than simulated ECT (6 trials, effect size = .91) and antidepressants (18 trials, effect size = .8). Bilateral ECT was more effective than unilateral (22 trials, effect size = .32), and high dose ECT was more effective than low dose (effect size = .57). The main negative side effects of ECT are temporary anterograde and retrograde amnesia. Carney *et al.* (2003) found that bilateral ECT led to greater memory impairment than unilateral ECT. Treatment three times a week led to more memory impairment than treatment twice a week; and high dose ECT produced more memory impairment than did low dose. These results are consistent with those of other meta-analyses (e.g. Kho *et al.*, 2003). Despite its negative impact on memory, ECT may be the treatment of choice for severe depression that does not respond to antidepressants and psychotherapy. In deciding on frequency, dosage, and unilateral or bilateral administration, the benefits in terms of effectiveness must be balanced against the costs in terms of memory impairment.

Psychotherapy and medication for depression in adults

Psychotherapy and antidepressant medication are equally effective in alleviating depression, and combined multimodal programmes involving both treatments may be appropriate in some cases, as the evidence reviewed below shows. In a quantitative review of six studies comparing the effectiveness of tricyclic antidepressants and cognitive or interpersonal psychotherapy, Casacalenda *et al.* (2002) found remission rates for antidepressants, psychotherapy, and control conditions of 46.4%, 46.3%, and 24.4%, respectively. Treatment duration ranged from 10–34 weeks. In a meta-analysis and narrative review of the multimodal treatment of depression, Friedman *et al.* (2004) examined the effects of psychotherapy combined with antidepressants, compared with either component alone. The 22 studies included cognitive, interpersonal, and psychodynamic treatments. For multimodal treatment versus antidepressants, Friedman *et al.* found average effect sizes ranging from .18–.68 for improvement, recovery, and relapse. For multimodal treatment versus psychotherapy, on the same outcome indices, they found average effect sizes ranging from .1–.89. They also concluded that multimodal programmes in which psychotherapy and antidepressants are combined may be particularly effective for chronic or severely depressed patients, and in relapse prevention, especially among clients who discontinue antidepressants. Similar conclusions were reached by Aaronson *et al.* (2007), Hollon *et al.* (2006) and Otto *et al.* (2005) in systematic narrative reviews.

Practice implications for depression in adults

From this review it may be concluded that a range of different types of psychotherapy is effective in alleviating moderate levels of depression in outpatients. These include behaviour therapy and cognitive behavioural therapy; psychodynamic and interpersonal psychotherapy; and couples therapy. These various forms of therapy help clients understand factors that have contributed to the development and maintenance of their depression; develop healthier, active daily routines; stop depressive thinking styles from dominating their mood; develop supportive relationships with family members and others; and address complex interpersonal and relationship issues. About 20 sessions probably constitutes a fair trial for most clients, although more sessions may be required for more severe depression. In severe depression, initial treatment response to psychotherapy may be enhanced and the interval between episodes of depression can be lengthened if psychotherapy is offered as one element of a multimodal programme involving antidepressant medication and psychotherapy. Mindfulness-based cognitive therapy may be offered to clients who have recovered from three or more episodes of depression to delay further relapses. Where severe depression does not respond to such multimodal programmes, ECT may be considered. In the first instance, when clients first present with depression, bibliotherapy or computer-assisted therapy may be offered with therapist support, as the first stage in a stepped care approach to the management of mood disorders. St John's Wort may be considered as an alternative to antidepressants in some cases, and light therapy may be considered for seasonal affective disorder. International professional guidelines highlight the importance of including psychotherapy in the routine treatment of depression (American Psychiatric Association, 2000b; NICE, 2004a; Schulberg *et al.*, 1998; Segal *et al.*, 2001).

Bipolar disorder in adults

Bipolar disorder is a recurrent episodic mood disorder characterized by episodes of mania or hypomania, depression, and mixed mood states (American

Psychiatric Association, 2000a; World Health Organization, 1992). Genetic factors play a central role in the aetiology of bipolar disorder, but its course is affected by exposure to intra- and extra-familial stress, individual and family coping strategies, and medication adherence (Lam & Jones, 2006). The primary treatment for bipolar disorder is pharmacological, and involves the initial treatment of acute manic, hypomanic, depressive, or mixed episodes, and the subsequent prevention of further episodes with mood stabilizing medication such as lithium (Geddes *et al.*, 2004; Keck & McElroy, 2007). The primary aim of adjunctive psychological interventions is to reduce relapse and rehospitalization rates, and increase quality of life by improving medication adherence and enhancing the way individuals with bipolar disorder and their families manage stress and vulnerability to relapse. In a meta-analysis of eight controlled studies, Scott *et al.* (2007) found that psychological intervention led to a 40% reduction in relapse rates compared to standard pharmacological treatment. Therapies were most effective in preventing relapses in clients who were euthymic, and least effective in those with many previous episodes. Gutierrez and Scott (2004), Jones *et al.* (2005), Mansell *et al.* (2005), Miklowitz and Craighead (2007), and Sajatovic *et al.* (2004) in narrative reviews of over ten controlled studies concluded that psychoeducational therapy, cognitive behavioural therapy, interpersonal social rhythm therapy, and family therapy are particularly effective in multimodal programmes for bipolar disorder. Evidence from one large trial suggests that intensive forms of psychotherapy are more effective than brief psychoeducation in reducing relapse in bipolar patients on maintenance medication. In a large randomized controlled trial comparing three sessions of brief psychoeducation with 30 sessions over nine months of cognitive behavioural therapy, interpersonal and social rhythm therapy, and family-focused therapy for patients receiving maintenance pharmacological therapy for bipolar disorder, Miklowitz *et al.* (2007) found that the three intensive psychotherapies led to greater recovery rates after a year (64.4 vs. 51.5%) and shorter times to recovery than brief psychoeducation.

Psychoeducational therapy for bipolar disorder in adults

Results from six controlled trials show that psychoeducation increased knowledge about bipolar disorder and its treatment, adherence to medication regimes, and in some instances reduced relapse rates in people with bipolar disorder, with manualized and more intensive programmes having greater positive impact (Colom *et al.*, 2003; Harvey & Peet, 1991; Peet & Harvey, 1991; Perry *et al.*, 1999; Seltzer *et al.*, 1980; Simon *et al.*, 2005, 2006; van Gent & Zwart, 1991). In these studies psychoeducation involved providing information to clients and family members about factors affecting the aetiology and course of bipolar disorder; the rationale for treatment during the acute phase; the importance of medication adherence for relapse prevention; and recognizing and managing prodromes. Bauer and McBride's (1996) *Life Goals Program* is a useful resource for psychoeducational treatment of bipolar disorder.

Cognitive behavioural therapy for bipolar disorder in adults

Results of five trials show that cognitive behavioural therapy was effective in improving mood regulation, preventing relapse, and reducing rehospitalization in people with bipolar disorder (Cochran, 1984; Lam *et al.*, 2000, 2003, 2005; Scott *et al.*, 2001; Miklowitz *et al.*, 2007). Results from one trial showed that this positive effect only occurred for those with fewer than 12 previous episodes (Scott *et al.*, 2006). Cognitive behavioural therapy in these trials included self-monitoring of activity and mood states; cognitive restructuring to modify thinking patterns associated with depressive or manic mood states; and behavioural interventions such as problem solving, relaxation, and behavioural activation to facilitate regular daily routines, and regulation of high and low mood states. Lam *et al.*'s (1999) *Cognitive Therapy for Bipolar Disorder* is a useful therapy manual for this approach.

Interpersonal social rhythm therapy for bipolar disorder in adults

Results from two trials (Frank *et al.*, 2005; Miklowitz *et al.*, 2007) show that interpersonal social rhythm therapy helped patients achieve more stable social rhythms, enhanced recovery from depressive episodes, and reduced relapse rate. This type of therapy aims to help clients develop regular sleep–waking cycles, since dysregulation of circadian rhythms may precipitate relapses. It also aims to help clients address stressful social factors which may affect the course of bipolar disorder. There is a particular focus on grief, role disputes, role transitions, and social skills deficits. Frank's (2005) *Treating Bipolar Disorder: A Clinician's Guide to Interpersonal and Social Rhythm Therapy* is a useful treatment manual for this therapeutic approach.

Family therapy for bipolar disorder in adults

Results from five trials show that family therapy alone or in combination with interpersonal social rhythm therapy was effective in reducing relapse and, in some instances, rehospitalization in patients with bipolar disorder on maintenance mood-stabilizing medication (Miklowitz & Goldstein, 1990; Miklowitz *et al.*, 2003b, 2004, 2007; Rea *et al.*, 2003). In these trials family therapy was conducted over 21 sessions and included family-based psycho-education, relapse prevention, communication, and problem-solving skills training. The approach is described in Miklowitz and Goldstein's (1997) *Bipolar Disorder: A Family-Focused Treatment Approach*. In three trials, other less-intensive family-based interventions have not yielded these positive effects (Clarkin *et al.*, 1990, 1998; Miller *et al.*, 2004).

Practice implications for bipolar disorder in adults

Psychoeducational therapy, cognitive behaviour therapy, interpersonal social rhythm therapy, and family therapy are particularly effective in multimodal programmes for bipolar disorder, which include mood-stabilizing medication. For psychotherapy to be effective in reducing relapse in patients with bipolar disorder on maintenance mood-stabilizing medication, it must be intensive (20–30 sessions) and help individuals understand factors that contribute to the aetiology of bipolar disorder and the relapse process; adhere to medication regimes; avoid drug and alcohol abuse; develop stable daily routines for social activities and sleeping; manage stress; identify and cope with prodromes when they occur; stop manic or depressive thinking styles from dominating their mood states; and develop supportive relationships with family members and others. International professional guidelines highlight the importance of including psychotherapy in the routine treatment of bipolar disorder (American Psychiatric Association, 2002; Goodwin, 2003; Grunze *et al.*, 2002, 2003; NICE, 2006).

Suicide and self-harm in adults

Available evidence suggests that for people who attempt suicide or engage in deliberate self-harm, psychological interventions (following emergency care) do not usually affect overall suicide rates in the year following intervention (Crawford *et al.*, 2007), but certain psychological interventions reduce rates of repeated self-harm, and levels of depression, hopelessness, and life problems (Brown *et al.*, 2005; Hawton *et al.*, 1999; Hepp *et al.*, 2004; Linehan *et al.*, 2006; Townsend *et al.*, 2001). In a meta-analysis of 18 studies of the effectiveness of psychotherapy following self-harm for preventing suicide, Crawford *et al.* (2007) found there was no significant difference in suicide rates between treatment and control cases. Average rates of suicide in treatment and control groups over the year following intervention were similar to those found in studies of self-harming patients. Psychotherapy in these studies was offered on an individual basis; ranged from 2–50 sessions; and included cognitive behavioural therapy, interpersonal therapy, and dialectical behaviour therapy.

In a review and meta-analysis of 23 controlled trials, Hawton *et al.* (1999) found a trend for problem-solving therapy, dialectical behaviour therapy, provision of a card to allow emergency contact with services, and depot flupenthixol (for people with psychosis) to reduce the frequency of deliberate self-harm in self-harming patients, compared with routine treatment. Similar conclusions were reached by Hepp *et al.* (2004) in a systematic narrative review of 25 trials of psychological intervention to reduce repeated self-harm. They found that, compared with treatment as usual, psychological interventions had a significant impact on reducing repetition of self-harm in only five trials. Effective interventions included problem-solving therapy, dialectical behaviour therapy, psychodynamic therapy, and community outreach.

Further support for problem-solving therapy and dialectical behaviour therapy comes from two other reviews. In a meta-analysis of six trials of problem-solving therapy, Townsend *et al.* (2001) found that compared with treatment as usual, problem-solving therapy led to significantly greater improvements in depression, hopelessness, and life problems. In a review of seven trials of dialectical behaviour therapy, Linehan *et al.* (2006) concluded that this programme led to significant reductions in the frequency of deliberate self-harm and suicide attempts in female clients with borderline personality disorder.

Evidence from a single large trial supports the effectiveness of cognitive therapy for suicidal people. In a study of 120 adults who had attempted suicide, Brown *et al.* (2005) found that patients who received ten sessions of cognitive therapy were 50% less likely to make a repeat suicide attempt during the 18-month follow-up period than those who received standard care, and they also were significantly less depressed and hopeless during this period.

From this review of the evidence it is clear that problem-solving therapy, dialectical behaviour therapy, and cognitive therapy are the manualized psychotherapeutic interventions that have the strongest support for reducing self-harm. These are described in Linehan's (1993a, 1993b) *Cognitive-Behavioural Treatment of Borderline Personality Disorder* and *Skills Training Manual for Treating Borderline Personality Disorder*, D'Zurilla and Nezu's (2006) *Problem Solving Therapy*, and Brown and colleagues' (2002) *Cognitive Therapy Treatment Manual for Suicide Attempters*. Problem-solving therapy and cognitive therapy are brief interventions (ten sessions). In contrast, dialectical behaviour therapy is an intensive intervention which may span up to a year and involves individual therapy and group skills training. Dialectical behaviour therapy will be considered in more detail in the section on personality disorders later in this chapter. In problem-solving therapy clients are helped to define large complex problems as smaller solvable problems, generate alternative solutions, examine the pros and cons of these, develop a solution plan, and then implement and evaluate it. The cognitive therapy programme evaluated in Brown and colleagues' (2005) trial involved cognitive restructuring of beliefs about hopelessness and suicide ideation; problem solving to address factors that triggered the recent suicide attempt; increasing social support; and increasing adherence to adjunctive treatments including antidepressant medication, substance abuse programmes, and other psychological interventions.

Practice implications for suicide and self-harm in adults

For self-harm, problem-solving therapy, cognitive therapy, or dialectical behaviour therapy may be offered, following the acute management of self-harm and attempted suicide. They should be provided within the context of an outreach service, and be delivered after the acute self-harm or suicide attempt has been managed following best practice guidelines (American Psychiatric Association, 2003; NICE, 2004b).

Anxiety disorders in adults

Anxiety disorders in adults include generalized anxiety disorder, panic disorder, simple phobias, social phobia, obsessive-compulsive disorder, and post-traumatic stress disorder (American Psychiatric Association, 2000a; World Health Organization, 1992). In the first instance, evidence for the effectiveness of psychotherapy for anxiety disorders as a whole will be presented, followed by evidence specific to each anxiety disorder.

Compared to other forms of psychotherapy, cognitive behavioural therapy has the largest evidence base for the treatment of anxiety disorders (Barlow & Allen, 2004; Deacon & Abramowitz, 2004; Norton & Price, 2007). In a meta-analysis of 108 studies of cognitive behavioural therapy involving all types of anxiety disorders, Norton and Price (2007) found that cognitive restructuring and exposure therapy alone, in combination or combined with relaxation training, were all equally effective treatments for anxiety disorders and yielded a large pre–post-treatment effect size of 1.58, which did not diminish significantly at follow-up. This very large effect size is approximately equivalent to a success rate of 83%. Clients receiving cognitive behavioural treatments showed significantly greater improvements than those in waiting list or placebo control groups. Clients with generalized anxiety disorder and PTSD had significantly more positive outcomes than those with social anxiety disorder. These results are consistent with Deacon and Abramowitz's (2004) narrative review of ten years of meta-analytic findings. They are also consistent with Hollon et al.'s (2006) systematic narrative review which concluded that the effects of cognitive behavioural therapy are enduring, unlike those of pharmacotherapy. Another important benefit of psychotherapy is that it does not involve the problems of dependence associated with some anxiolytics such as the benzodiazepines.

Common psychotherapeutic factors in the treatment of anxiety disorders in adults

Systematic narrative reviews show that a number of client characteristics, alliance factors, and therapeutic techniques influence the outcome of psychotherapy for all forms of anxiety disorders (Newman et al., 2006a, 2006b;

Stiles & Wolfe, 2006; Woody & Ollendick, 2006). What follows is a summary of key findings from these reviews.

Client characteristics

In extensive narrative reviews, Newman and colleagues concluded that a number of factors were associated with a poorer outcome for clients with anxiety disorders (Newman *et al.*, 2006a, 2006b). Non-compliance with homework, especially tasks involving exposure to anxiety-provoking stimuli, is associated with a poorer outcome, since this is essential for habituation to anxiety-provoking stimuli to occur. A poorer outcome is also associated with the following factors which may underpin functional impairment: symptom severity, chronicity and distress; and the presence of co-morbid depression, substance use, interpersonal problems, and personality disorders. Beliefs associated with a poorer outcome include low expectations of therapeutic success, an external locus of control, and negative self-attributions. Important contextual risk factors for poor therapeutic outcome include a history of problematic relationships with parents and low socio-economic status.

Therapeutic alliance

In an extensive narrative review, Stiles and Wolfe (2006) concluded that therapy for anxiety disorders is more likely to be effective where there is cohesiveness in group therapy or a strong therapeutic alliance in individual therapy. Within such alliances therapists adopt an empathic, positive, and congruent position, and collaborate with clients in setting goals. They skilfully mange their negative countertransference reactions to clients; repair alliance ruptures promptly and non-defensively; use an optimum level of self-disclosure; strive for moderation and accuracy when offering transference interpretations; and give accurate feedback on progress.

Therapeutic techniques

In an extensive narrative review, Woody and Ollendick (2006) concluded that effective psychotherapy for anxiety disorders involves challenging clients' misconceptions about feared situations through discussion and behavioural experiments, and repeated exposure to these anxiety-provoking situations to reduce fear and avoidance. They also concluded that effective therapy enhanced skills for managing feared situations. These include cognitive, relaxation, problem-solving, and social skills. Finally, they concluded that effective therapy is structured and directive; focused on behavioural change; brief but intensive with sessions spaced close together; and emotionally evocative, since fear arousal is essential for habituation to occur.

Computer-based self-help for anxiety disorders in adults

In a review of 16 studies, 11 of which involved computer-based cognitive behavioural therapy programmes for anxiety symptoms, Kaltenthaler *et al.* (2004) found that computer-based cognitive behavioural therapy was better than treatment as usual and at least as effective as regular cognitive behavioural therapy. In a meta-analysis of seven randomized controlled trials of internet-based interventions for anxiety, Spek *et al.* (2007) found an effect size of .96. Four studies were of panic disorder, one of social phobia, one of subclinical PTSD and one for the prevention of anxiety. Interventions with therapist support had the largest effect. The computer-based programmes included in these studies were White's (1997) *Stresspac, Fear Fighter*, and *Beating the Blues*.

Practice implications for anxiety disorders in adults

From this review of evidence about the treatment of the full range of anxiety disorders, it may be concluded that psychotherapy is particularly effective. Exposure to feared stimuli within the context of a strong therapeutic alliance, and the development of skills to cope with exposure and process negative affect until habituation occurs, are central to effective psychotherapy. Within a stepped care model, minimal contact computer-based interventions may be offered as an initial intervention. Medication is effective in the short term, but its effects are not as enduring as those of psychotherapy, and clients need to have this information to make an informed choice about their preferred treatment.

Generalized anxiety disorder in adults

In generalized anxiety disorder (GAD), there is anxiety about multiple stimuli and situations, and also a fear of loss of control over the worrying process (American Psychiatric Association, 2000a; World Health Organization, 1992).

Cognitive behavioural therapy for GAD in adults

In a meta-analysis of studies of cognitive behaviour therapy for GAD with anxiety as the dependent variable, Mitte (2005a) obtained effect sizes of .82 and .57 for comparisons with waiting list and placebo controls respectively. In a systematic narrative review of 17 trials of cognitive behavioural therapy for GAD, Barlow *et al.* (2007) concluded that at 6 to 24 months follow-up, clinically significant improvement rates ranged from 42–62%. Cognitive behavioural therapy for GAD involves psychoeducation, relaxation training, exposure to both stimuli that elicit anxiety and to the process of worrying (which is perceived as uncontrollable and anxiety provoking), and cognitive restructuring of threat-oriented beliefs. There is some evidence that components of this larger treatment package may have similar effects. In a meta-analysis comparing the effects of relaxation training and cognitive therapy, Siev and Chambless (2007) found both were equally effective.

Psychodynamic therapy for GAD in adults

In a single group outcome study of clients with generalized anxiety disorder, Crits-Christoph *et al.* (1996) found that 16 sessions of short-term psychodynamic psychotherapy led to remission in 79% a year after treatment. In a controlled trial, Durham *et al.* (1999) found that a year after therapy only 14% of cases treated with psychodynamic psychotherapy showed clinically significant change compared with 60% of cases who received cognitive behavioural therapy, but at ten years follow-up the outcomes for both therapies were similar (Durham *et al.*, 2003).

Pharmacotherapy for GAD in adults

Evidence from meta-analyses show that cognitive behavioural therapy is more effective than traditional benzodiazepine medication for GAD. In a meta-analysis of six studies where cognitive behavioural therapy and pharmacotherapy with benzodiazepines were compared, Mitte (2005b) obtained an effect size favouring cognitive behavioural therapy of .33. In another meta-analysis of 48 studies of pharmacotherapy with benzodiazepines or buspirone for GAD, Mitte *et al.* (2005) obtained an effect size for anxiety symptoms of .31 for comparisons with placebo control groups. In a systematic narrative review of more recent studies Roy-Byrne and Cowley (2007) concluded that for GAD the most effective pharmacotherapies with the least side effects were selective serotonin reuptake inhibitors and buspirone. However, relapse following discontinuation is common (Hollon *et al.*, 2006).

Practice implications for GAD in adults

For GAD, cognitive behavioural therapy is the treatment of choice. The importance of psychotherapy in the treatment of GAD is recognized in international guidelines (NICE, 2007a).

Panic disorder in adults

Recurrent unexpected panic attacks are the central feature of panic disorder (American Psychiatric Association, 2000a; World Health Organization, 1992). Normal fluctuations in autonomic arousal are misperceived as signals for the inevitable onset of panic attacks, and so these fluctuations in arousal are anxiety provoking. Secondary agoraphobia often develops, where there is an avoidance of public places in which panic attacks are expected to occur.

Cognitive behavioural therapy for panic disorder in adults

In a meta-analysis of 124 studies of psychological and pharmacological interventions for panic disorder with and without agoraphobia, Mitte (2005b) drew the following conclusions. Patients who received cognitive behavioural therapy had better outcomes than waiting list or placebo controls with weighted effect sizes for anxiety symptoms of .87 and .51 respectively. These effect sizes are equivalent to approximate success rates of 70% and 62% respectively. Outcomes for predominantly behavioural treatment protocols compared with cognitive behavioural protocols were similar for anxiety symptoms, but cognitive behavioural programmes led to a significantly better outcome for depressive symptoms. Compared with placebo controls, pharmacotherapy led to an effect size of .38 for anxiety. Outcomes for benzodiazepines, tricyclic antidepressants, and selective serotonin reuptake inhibitors were similar. Outcomes for cognitive behavioural therapy, pharmacological therapy, and multimodal programmes including both psychotherapy and medication were similar. In a systematic narrative review of 16 studies, Barlow *et al.* (2007) concluded that exposure to feared internal and external stimuli is central to effective cognitive behavioural therapy for panic disorder with and without agoraphobia, and the role of other treatment components is probably less central for effective therapy. For panic disorder, exposure to interoceptive cues which are misinterpreted as unrealistically dangerous is the central component of treatment. For agoraphobia the central component of treatment is exposure to feared life situations associated with the onset of panic attacks. Typically treatment begins with psychoeducation outlining the rationale for exposure therapy, and clients may also be offered training in relaxation, breathing exercises to reduce hyperventilation, and cognitive therapy to address problematic beliefs associated with panic attacks and avoidant behaviour. Relaxation, breathing, and cognitive skills are then used to tolerate exposure to interoceptive and environmental anxiety-eliciting cues until habituation occurs. Craske and Barlow's (2006) *Master Your Anxiety and Panic: Therapist Guide* describes this type of treatment which typically spans 10–15 sessions.

Couples therapy for panic disorder in adults

In a review of 12 studies of couples-based treatment for panic disorder for agoraphobia, Byrne *et al.* (2004a) concluded that partner-assisted cognitive behavioural exposure therapy provided on a per case or group basis led to clinically significant improvement in agoraphobia and panic symptoms for 54–86% of cases. This type of couples therapy was as effective as individually based treatment. Treatment gains were maintained at follow-up. In some studies couples-based interventions had a positive impact on co-morbid relationship distress, although this has also been found in studies of individually based exposure therapy. The most effective couples programmes combined communication training with partner-assisted exposure and cognitive therapy to address problematic beliefs which underpinned avoidant behaviour.

Psychodynamic psychotherapy for panic disorder in adults

Two trials support the effectiveness of brief psychodynamic psychotherapy for panic disorder. In an uncontrolled trial, Milrod et al. (2000) found a remission rate of 90% following brief psychodynamic psychotherapy for panic disorder. In a comparative trial, Wiborg and Dahl (1996) found relapse rates nine months after medication discontinuation of 77% for clomipramine alone and 20% for clomipramine combined with brief psychodynamic psychotherapy. In these trials, psychodynamic psychotherapy focused on exploring the conscious and unconscious meaning of panic symptoms which were typically associated with fears about separation, anger expression, and sexuality. Defences associated with conflicts over these issues were interpreted in the transference relationship and worked through. A description of this type of treatment is given in Milrod et al.'s (1997) *Manual of Panic-Focused Psychodynamic Psychotherapy*.

Pharmacotherapy for panic disorder in adults

In a meta-analysis of 43 studies, Bakker et al. (2002) found that while tricyclic antidepressants and selective serotonin reuptake inhibitors were equally effective in the treatment of panic disorder, the drop-out rates from studies were 31% for tricyclic antidepressants and only 18% for selective serotonin reuptake inhibitors, suggesting that the latter are tolerated better. These results are consistent with Roy-Byrne and Cowley's (2007) extensive narrative review in which they concluded that selective serotonin reuptake inhibitors were the most effective and best tolerated medication for panic disorder. However, relapse following discontinuation is common (Hollon et al., 2006).

Self-help for panic disorder in adults

In her meta-analysis of 124 studies of interventions for panic disorder, Mitte (2005b) conducted a subanalysis of eight studies of bibliotherapy and obtained a weighted effect size of .8 for comparisons with waiting list controls. In most of these studies, Culm's (1990) *Coping with Panic* was the cognitive behavioural self-help book.

Practice implications for panic disorder in adults

For panic disorder with agoraphobia, exposure-based cognitive behavioural therapy or spouse-assisted exposure therapy are the treatments of choice with the largest evidence base. Psychodynamic therapy is also effective but rests on a smaller evidence base. Selective serotonin reuptake inhibitors may be considered, but relapse following discontinuation is common. Self-help bibliotherapy with therapist support may be offered initially within a stepped care model of service provision. The role of psychotherapy in the treatment of panic disorder is recognized in international best practice guidelines (American Psychiatric Association, 1998; Australian and New Zealand Clinical Practice Guidelines for the Treatment of Panic Disorder and Agoraphobia, 2003; NICE, 2007a; Swinson, 2006).

Specific phobias in adults

In an extensive systematic review of empirical studies, Anthony and Barlow (2002) concluded that cognitive behavioural exposure-based treatment was the most effective available treatment for specific phobias, including fears of animals, choking, heights, flying, dental procedures, and injections. The most effective treatment for specific phobias involves exposure to feared stimuli in vivo (rather than imaginal exposure) for extended time periods lasting two or more hours spaced close together over a few days, rather than over weeks. Where it is not practical to conduct in vivo exposure, simulated exposures using virtual reality technology have been shown to be effective. In a systematic review of case studies and a small number of controlled trials, Krijn *et al.* (2004) concluded that virtual reality exposure therapy was an effective treatment for fear of heights and of flying. In this type of therapy, after psychoeducation in which the rationale for therapy is explained, clients enter anxiety-provoking virtual reality situations and remain there for prolonged periods until habituation and fear reduction occurs. Clients may be trained in relaxation and cognitive coping skills to help them tolerate exposure to anxiety-eliciting stimuli. Where clients have injection or blood injury phobia and are apt to faint at the sight of blood, they may be trained in applied tension (tensing all muscles for 15 seconds and then releasing tension for 15 seconds) before and during exposure to prevent fainting (Hellstrom *et al.*, 1996).

Practice implications for specific phobias

For specific phobias the treatment of choice is in vivo exposure, or where this is impractical virtual reality exposure. This should be conducted for sessions lasting two or more hours spaced close together over a few days. Exposure should be preceded by psychoeducation and training in anxiety-management skills, or applied tension in the case of blood phobia, for use during exposure sessions.

Social phobia in adults

Social phobia is characterized by extreme fear and avoidance of social situations such as speaking, writing, or eating in public, due to the belief that the inept performance of these actions will result in embarrassment and rejection by others (American Psychiatric Association, 2000a; World Health Organization, 1992).

Cognitive behavioural therapy for social phobia in adults

In a review of five previous meta-analyses of psychological treatments for social phobia, Rodebaugh *et al.* (2004) found moderate to large effect sizes for a variety of cognitive behavioural therapy protocols, both after treatment and at 6 to 12 months follow-up. Individual and group treatment formats were equally effective. Treatment protocols included exposure to anxiety-provoking situations alone; cognitive restructuring alone; combined exposure and cognitive restructuring; social skills training; and applied relaxation. Treatment protocols which included exposure to anxiety-provoking social situations were the most effective, with large effect sizes of .8 or greater. In a systematic narrative review, Barlow *et al.* (2007) concluded that currently exposure-based treatment coupled with cognitive therapy aimed at reducing fear of negative evaluation and use of safety behaviours (avoidant coping strategies) is the cognitive behavioural treatment of choice and leads to clinically significant improvement rates of 61–86%. In an extensive narrative review, Rodebaugh *et al.* (2004) concluded that an expectation of improvement and completion of homework assignments involving exposure to anxiety-provoking situations were associated with a better response to treatment for people with social phobia. They also found that a poorer response to treatment was associated with co-morbid avoidant personality disorder.

Pharmacotherapy for social phobia in adults

In a review of five previous meta-analyses of pharmacological treatments for social phobia, Rodebaugh *et al.* (2004) found moderate to large effect sizes for a number of medications, notably selective serotonin reuptake inhibitors which have limited side effects, unlike monoamine oxidase inhibitors and benzodiazepines which are also effective but have serious side effects. However, Rodebaugh *et al.* (2004), in a narrative review of comparative studies, concluded that while cognitive behavioural treatments and medication are equally effective in the short term, higher relapse rates at follow-up occur for both medication and medication combined with cognitive behaviour therapy.

Psychodynamic therapy for social phobia in adults

Leichsenring *et al.* (2007) have developed a treatment manual for psychodynamic psychotherapy for social phobia, and a trial evaluating its effectiveness
is underway.

Practice implications for social phobia in adults

For social phobia, cognitive behavioural therapy involving exposure-based
treatment and cognitive restructuring is currently the psychological treatment
of choice. Selective serotonin reuptake inhibitors are the medications of choice,
although their effects following discontinuation may not be as enduring as
those of psychotherapy.

Obsessive-compulsive disorder in adults

Obsessive-compulsive disorder (OCD) is characterized by obsessive thoughts
elicited by specific cues (such as dirt) and compulsive anxiety-reducing rituals
(such as hand washing) (American Psychiatric Association, 2000a; World
Health Organization, 1992).

Cognitive behavioural therapy of OCD in adults

In a meta-analysis of 15 studies of cognitive behavioural therapy for OCD,
Eddy *et al.* (2004) found a treatment–control group effect size of 1.12 and a
pre–post effect size of 1.53. For treatment completers, the average improvement rate was 64%, and the average recovery rate was 38%. Psychotherapy
spanned 12–20 sessions and exposure and response prevention was slightly
more effective than cognitive therapy. These results are consistent with those
of other meta-analyses and narrative reviews (Abramowitz *et al.*, 2002;
Fisher & Wells, 2005; Franklin & Foa, 2007). With exposure and response
prevention, clients are exposed to cues (such as dirt) that elicit anxiety-
provoking obsessions (such as ideas about contamination), while not engaging in compulsive rituals (such as hand washing), until habituation occurs.
With cognitive therapy, the focus is on challenging problematic beliefs sub-
serving OCD symptoms. Such beliefs include the idea that we should control all of our thoughts; thinking of an action is equivalent to carrying it
out; and failing to prevent harm is morally equivalent to causing harm.
Abramowitz's (2006) *Understanding and Treating Obsessive-Compulsive Disorder: A Cognitive-Behavioural Approach* is a useful therapy manual.

Systemic therapy for OCD in adults

Five trials of systemic couples or family-based approaches to the treatment of OCD, reviewed by Renshaw *et al.* (2005), have shown that such approaches are as effective or in some instances more effective than individually based cognitive behavioural therapy for adults with OCD (Emmelkamp *et al.*, 1990; Emmelkamp & DeLange, 1983; Grunes *et al.*, 2001; Mehta, 1990; Van Noppen *et al.*, 1997). Effective systemic treatment protocols have involved providing family members with psychoeducation about OCD and its treatment in conjoint or separate sessions, or in multiple family sessions. The aim of this is to prevent family members from over-accommodating or antagonistically responding to the person with OCD. This has been combined with exposure and response prevention in which family members have played a supportive role.

Pharmacotherapy for OCD in adults

In a meta-analysis of 32 trials of medication for OCD, Eddy *et al.* (2004) found a treatment–control group mean effect size of .83 and a pre–post effect size of 1.18. The average improvement rate was 64% for treatment completers. Serotonin reuptake inhibitors, notably colmipramine, were the most effective form of pharmacotherapy; a conclusion consistent with results of other meta-analyses and narrative reviews (Ackerman & Greenland, 2002; Dougherty *et al.*, 2007). Eddy *et al.* (2004) also found that multimodal programmes involving psychotherapy and medication were more effective than medication alone. The pre–post effect sizes were 1.72 for multimodal programmes, 1.52 for psychotherapy alone, and 1.18 for medication alone.

Practice implications for OCD in adults

Exposure and response prevention conducted on a family or individual basis is the psychotherapeutic treatment of choice for OCD. In cases that do not respond to psychotherapy, a multimodal programme involving psychotherapy and serotonin reuptake inhibitors (especially clomipramine) is appropriate. These conclusions are consistent with best practice guidelines (American Psychiatric Association, 2007a; NICE, 2005a).

Post-traumatic stress disorder in adults

Post-traumatic stress disorder (PTSD) occurs following a major trauma and is characterized by intrusive anxiety-provoking traumatic memories, the use of avoidant coping strategies to deal with these, and hyperarousal (American Psychiatric Association, 2000a; World Health Organization, 1992).

Psychological interventions for PTSD in adults

In a meta-analysis of 38 randomized controlled trials of treatments for chronic PTSD, Bisson et al. (2007) found that two individually delivered treatment protocols – trauma-focused cognitive behavioural therapy and eye movement desensitization – were equally effective, and both were the most effective treatments for PTSD of all approaches covered in the review. Psychodynamic and supportive psychotherapy were the least effective. Stress management training and group-based cognitive behavioural therapy were moderately effective. For trauma-focused cognitive behavioural therapy and eye movement desensitization and reprocessing, weighted effect sizes based on clinician and self-rated PTSD symptoms ranged from 1.1 to 1.7. These effect sizes are equivalent to approximate success rates of 72–82%. Effect sizes for stress management and group cognitive behavioural therapy ranged from .33 to 1.1. These effect sizes are equivalent to approximate success rates of 57–72%. For psychodynamic and supportive therapy effect sizes ranged from .43 to .61. These effect sizes are equivalent to approximate success rates of 60–64%. These results are consistent with those of other meta-analyses and systematic narrative reviews (Bradley et al., 2005; Najavitis, 2007). Both trauma-focused cognitive behavioural therapy and eye movement desensitization and reprocessing involve prolonged exposure to traumatic memories within the context of supportive therapeutic relationships. This is coupled with strategies (such as controlled breathing, revising problematic trauma-related beliefs, or engaging in eye movements) which facilitate tolerating the anxiety associated with exposure to traumatic memories. Useful treatment manuals are Taylor's (2006) *Clinician's Guide to PTSD* and Shapiro's (2001) *Eye Movement Desensitization and Reprocessing: Basis Principles, Protocols and Procedures*.

Pharmacotherapy for PTSD in adults

In a systematic narrative review of 75 studies of the impact of a range of medications on chronic PTSD, Gollier et al. (2007) concluded that three classes of antidepressants – selective serotonin reuptake inhibitors, tricyclic antidepressants, and monoamine oxidase inhibitors – are effective in reducing PTSD symptoms in a proportion of chronic PTSD patients. Improvement rates ranged from 2–79% with selective serotonin reuptake inhibitors being preferred because they have the fewest side effects.

Adult survivors of childhood sexual abuse

For adult survivors of child sexual abuse (some of whom have PTSD), group psychotherapy can alleviate distress. In a review of 12 controlled studies of psychotherapy for adult survivors of child sexual abuse (some of whom had PTSD), Peleikis and Dahl (2005) found a weighted mean effect size of .63. This effect size is equivalent to an approximate success rate of 64%. Most studies involved short-term group therapy of up to 20 sessions, which was conducted within cognitive behavioural, psychodynamic, or humanistic traditions.

Single session early interventions for PTSD in adults

Despite its popularity, the weight of evidence shows that single session interventions following traumatic events are not effective in preventing the onset of PTSD symptomatology. In a review of 13 randomized controlled trials of single session psychological debriefing interventions following traumatic events, Bisson (2003) concluded that these types of interventions had no significant impact. In only three of the 11 studies the treated group fared significantly better than the control group at follow-up.

Practice implications for PTSD in adults

For PTSD, trauma-focused cognitive behavioural therapy and eye movement desensitization and reprocessing are the psychotherapy interventions of choice. Selective serotonin reuptake inhibitors are the most effective medications with the fewest side effects, but relapse may occur following discontinuation. For adult survivors of child sexual abuse, brief 20-session group therapy may be effective. Single session post-trauma debriefing interventions are ineffective in preventing PTSD. Best practice guidelines recommend a central place for psychotherapy in the treatment of PTSD (American Psychiatric Association, 2004a; Ballenger et al., 2004; Foa et al., 2000; NICE, 2005b).

Somatoform disorders in adults

For a proportion of cases psychotherapy has been shown to be effective in addressing somatoform disorders and difficulties including medically unexplained symptoms, health anxiety, and body dysmorphic disorder.

Medically unexplained symptoms in adults

Three diagnostic categories involve medically unexplained symptoms. Where clients present with medically unexplained sensory or motor impairment, this is referred to as conversion disorder. With somatization disorder, clients experience multiple unexplained physical symptoms; and where fewer unexplained symptoms occur, this is referred to as undifferentiated somatoform disorder (American Psychiatric Association, 2000a; World Health Organization, 1992). In a systematic narrative review Looper and Kirmayer (2002) identified four uncontrolled and one controlled trial of treatments for conversion disorder; four controlled trials of treatments for somatization disorder; and five controlled trials of treatments for undifferentiated somatoform disorder. They concluded that in a proportion of cases psychological interventions, particularly cognitive behavioural therapy, were effective for these conditions and reduced symptom severity and use of medical services. These results are consistent with those of previous reviews (Allen *et al.*, 2002; Kroenke & Swindle, 2000; Simon, 2002).

Practice implications for medically unexplained symptoms in adults

Effective psychotherapy for medically unexplained symptoms involves coordination of patient care by a single designated professional; psychoeducation; relaxation and coping skills training; graded exercise and promotion of engagement in previously avoided routine activities of daily living; and regularization of care giving and receiving family relationships. Co-ordination of care by a single professional helps clients manage uncertainty and anxiety associated with multiple conflicting messages from multiple professionals. Psychoeducation helps clients develop more adaptive understanding of the role of psychological and interpersonal factors in maintaining and potentially alleviating their symptoms. Relaxation and coping skills training empower clients to regulate physiological arousal and symptom-related distress. Through graded exercise and engagement in activities of daily living, clients normalize their lives and overcome entrenched patterns of avoidance. Often marital or family therapy sessions are necessary to facilitate this process, since this may involve changes in symptom-maintaining patterns of care giving and care receiving behaviour. Woolfolk and Allen's (2007) *Treating Somatization: A Cognitive-Behavioural Approach* is a useful treatment manual.

Hypochondriasis – health anxiety in adults

The central feature of hypochondriasis is fear of having a serious disease, and this anxiety is based upon misinterpretation of bodily sensations. In hypochondriasis, health anxiety is accompanied by avoidance of disease-related stimuli, frequent bodily checking, and medical reassurance seeking (American Psychiatric Association, 2000a; World Health Organization, 1992). In a meta-analysis of 25 trials of a variety of treatments for hypochondriasis, Taylor *et al.* (2005) concluded that cognitive behavioural therapy was a particularly effective treatment in the short and long term, with pre–post-treatment and pre-treatment follow-up effect sizes of 2.05 and 1.74 respectively. These effect sizes are equivalent to approximate success rates of 85% and 82% respectively. Effect sizes for psychoeducation, cognitive therapy, exposure and response prevention, and stress management ranged from .83 to 1.59. These effect sizes are equivalent to approximate success rates of 69 to 81%. No trials of psychodynamic, humanistic, or systemic therapy have been conducted. Pre–post-treatment effect sizes for antidepressants (mainly selective serotonin reuptake inhibitors) ranged from 1.07 to 1.92, and the most effective was fluoxetine. These effect sizes are equivalent to approximate success rates of 72% to 84%. However, there are no follow-up data to show that these effects are enduring.

Practice implications for hypochondriasis in adults

Effective psychotherapy for hypochondriasis (or health anxiety) involves psychoeducation about how health anxiety is maintained by misinterpretation of bodily sensations; self-monitoring of bodily sensations, emotions, and health-related beliefs; re-evaluating health-related beliefs; engaging in exposure to situations that elicit health anxiety (including stopping habitual health checking routines) until habituation occurs; relaxation and anxiety management training; and developing satisfying daily routines and long-term plans. A better response to treatment occurs in cases where there is acute onset of mild symptoms of short duration; the absence of co-morbid personality disorders or serious medical conditions; low life stress; and the absence of reinforcement for illness behaviour. Taylor and Asmundson's (2004) *Treating Health Anxiety: A Cognitive Behavioural Approach* is a useful treatment manual.

Body dysmorphic disorder in adults

With body dysmorphic disorder (BDD), there is a preoccupation with a perceived defect in appearance, or an excessive concern over a slight physical abnormality (American Psychiatric Association, 2000a; World Health Organization, 1992). In a meta-analysis of 15 studies of a range of treatments for body dysmorphic disorder, Williams *et al.* (2006) found effect sizes of 1.63 for cognitive behavioural therapy and .92 for antidepressant medication. These are equivalent to approximate success rates of 83% and 71% respectively. They concluded that psychotherapy was more effective than medication in the treatment of body dysmorphic disorder.

Practice implications for BDD in adults

Effective psychotherapy for body dysmorphic disorder involves helping clients enter situations in which they experience anxiety associated with others having opportunities to evaluate aspects of their bodies they misperceive as defective, until habituation occurs. To facilitate habituation, patients do not conceal aspects of their bodies they misperceive as defective in these situations and refrain from frequent grooming, mirror checking, and reassurance seeking. Thus, this is an exposure and response prevention therapy model. Effective psychotherapy also helps clients develop more adaptive beliefs about their bodies. Phillips's (2005) *The Broken Mirror: Understanding and Treating Body Dysmorphic Disorder* is a useful treatment resource.

Adjustment to illness in adults

Psychotherapeutic interventions have been shown to be effective in helping patients adjust to illness and illness-related procedures, notably preparation for surgery; life-threatening illness such as cancer and heart disease; and chronic medical conditions such as asthma, diabetes, and hypertension.

Preparation for surgery in adults

Psychotherapeutic procedures may be used to help patients prepare for anxiety-provoking surgical procedures, and to adjust to the aftermath of major surgical procedures. In a meta-analysis of 38 studies, Johnston and Vogele (1993) found that psychological preparation of adult patients for surgery led to benefits in eight areas: reducing negative affect, pain reduction, reducing pain medication usage, shortening duration of hospitalization, improving behavioural indices of recovery, improving physiological indices of recovery, increasing patient satisfaction, and reducing overall medical costs. Across these eight areas, providing procedural information, behavioural instructions, and relaxation training led to greatest improvement. These findings are consistent with those of systematic narrative reviews (Block *et al.*, 2003; Vogele, 2004).

Practice implications for surgery preparation in adults

Psychological preparation for surgery involves psychoeducation in which patients receive information about surgical procedures and typical sensory responses to these procedures; training in post-operative self-care skills which will speed recovery; and training in relaxation and cognitive coping skills to manage pre-operative anxiety and facilitate adjustment to post-operative pain and discomfort. Effective programmes involve a supportive therapeutic relationship, the provision of information using multimedia (oral, written, video modelling), the involvement of family members in the programme, and opportunities to rehearse and practise coping skills.

Adjustment to life-threatening illnesses in adults

Life-threatening illnesses such as cancer and heart disease evoke psychological distress. Furthermore, the secondary prevention of conditions such as cancer and heart disease entails significant lifestyle changes. In a systematic review of 35 meta-analyses and narrative reviews, Rodgers *et al.* (2005)

concluded that psychotherapy from psychodynamic, humanistic, systemic, cognitive behavioural, and other traditions alleviates illness-related distress and facilitates positive lifestyle changes in patients with cancer and heart disease.

Adjustment to cancer in adults

There is still considerable debate over the extent and clinical significance of the positive effects of psychological interventions for cancer patients. Optimistic reviewers have underlined the preponderance of positive outcomes from treatment trials, while pessimistic reviewers have expressed particular concerns over the methodological rigour of trials (Stefanek *et al.*, 2006). With this in mind, the results of a recent meta-analysis of 15 high quality randomized controlled trials of the effects of cognitive behavioural therapy and patient education on depression, anxiety, and quality of life in adult cancer survivors deserve mention. In this meta-analysis, Osborn *et al.* (2006) found that cognitive behavioural therapy led to an effect size of 1.2 for depression, 1.99 for anxiety, and .91 for quality of life, and gains in quality of life were maintained at follow-up. These effect sizes are equivalent to approximate success rates of 75%, 85%, and 71% respectively. In contrast, patient education had no significant impact on adjustment to cancer. In a meta-analysis of cognitive behavioural therapy for distress and pain in breast cancer, Tatrow and Montgomery (2006) found effect sizes of $d = 0.31$ for distress and .49 for pain. These effect sizes are equivalent to approximate success rates of 57% and 62% respectively. Individually based treatment was more effective than group therapy. While this evidence shows that psychotherapy has an impact on adjustment to cancer, there is no credible evidence that it lengthens survival. In an extensive systematic narrative review, Coyne *et al.* (2007) concluded that, to date, no adequately designed studies have been conducted to determine the impact of psychological interventions on survival of cancer patients.

Adjustment to heart disease in adults

In a meta-analysis of 36 trials of psychological interventions for patients with heart disease, Rees *et al.* (2004) found that such interventions led to small but significant reductions in anxiety and depression, but had no impact in preventing further heart attacks or mortality. This is a less optimistic conclusion than that reached in previous meta-analyses which included less methodologically robust studies (e.g. Dusseldorp *et al.*, 1999). However, there is evidence that exercise-based programmes have a positive impact on patients recovering from heart disease. In a meta-analysis of 48 trials of exercise-based cardiac rehabilitation in patients with coronary heart disease, Taylor *et al.* (2004) found that compared with usual care, cardiac rehabilitation was associated with reduced overall mortality (odds ratio = 0.80 or effect size = .12) and reduced cardiac mortality (odds ratio = 0.74 or effect size = .17). Exercise-based cardiac rehabilitation also led to reductions in cholesterol and triglyceride levels, systolic blood pressure, and cigarette smoking.

Practice implications for adjustment to life-threatening illness in adults

Effective psychological interventions for enhancing psychological adjustment to serious medical conditions such as cancer and heart disease involve providing support, facilitating expression of illness-related emotional reactions, psychoeducation about factors associated with psychological adjustment to illness, facilitating the development of stress management skills, especially relaxation, meditation and cognitive coping skills, enhancing family support, and promoting healthier lifestyles, particularly through engaging in regular exercise in the case of patients with heart disease and reducing behavioural risk factors such as smoking, overweight, and a high cholesterol diet. These conclusions are consistent with those of international best practice guidelines (Cooper *et al.*, 2007; DeBacker *et al.*, 2004; Leon *et al.*, 2005; National Breast Cancer Centre & National Cancer Control Initiative, 2003; National Comprehensive Cancer Network, 1999; New Zealand Guidelines Group, 2002; NICE, 2004c; Scottish Intercollegiate Guidelines Network, 2002).

Adjustment to chronic medical conditions in adults

Psychotherapy facilitates adjustment to chronic illnesses such as asthma, diabetes, and hypertension – illnesses requiring adherence to complex illness and lifestyle management regimes, and sometimes entailing considerable psychological distress.

Asthma in adults

Asthma is a chronic respiratory disease characterized by reversible airway obstruction, inflammation, and hyperresponsiveness to a variety of environmental triggers such as allergens and viral infections of the respiratory system. The frequency and duration of asthma attacks is determined by the interaction between abnormal respiratory system physiological processes; environmental triggers; and psychological stress. People with asthma have to consistently reduce exposure to physical and psychological stimuli that trigger or exacerbate asthma attacks, and routinely take a range of oral and inhaler medications to control their condition. Failure to do so can lead to distress, medical complications, hospitalization and in some instances asthma attacks can be fatal. Asthma self-management programmes help patients control their environment and adhere to their medical regimes so as to reduce the negative impact of asthma on their health and well-being (Kotses & Harver, 1998). In a meta-analysis of 31 studies of the effects of psychoeducational self-management programmes for adults with asthma, Devine (1996) found that such programmes led to significant improvements in occurrence of asthmatic attacks, dynamic respiratory volume, peak expiratory flow rate, functional status, adherence to treatment regime, use of health services, use of medication, knowledge of inhaler use, and psychological well-being. Effective programmes included psychoeducation; skills training in adherence; training in trigger avoidance; stress management; and symptom monitoring using a peak flow meter. In systematic reviews Ritz and colleagues concluded that evidence for the effectiveness of relaxation training (Ritz, 2001) and biofeedback (Ritz *et al.*, 2004) for adults with asthma is inconclusive at present, with only some studies showing positive effects, and in most cases these are not clinically significant. These conclusions are consistent with those of other systematic reviews (e.g. Lehrer *et al.*, 2002).

Diabetes in adults

Type 1 and Type 2 diabetes are medical conditions characterized by high blood sugar levels. In Type 1 diabetes, which most commonly has its onset in childhood, high blood sugar is due to a deficit in insulin secretion. In Type 2 diabetes, which typically occurs in adulthood and is associated with obesity, high blood sugar is due to reduced insulin production, or to the body becoming resistant to the effects of insulin. People with Type 1 and Type 2 diabetes have to routinely complete self-management tasks to achieve optimum glycaemia control. These include self-monitoring of blood sugar levels, administration of insulin orally or by injection, maintaining a strict dietary and exercise regime, weight control (in the case of Type 2 diabetes), and management of psychological distress and interpersonal difficulties associated with diabetes. Poor adherence to this regime can lead to serious acute complications notably hyperglycaemic or hypoglycaemic crises which can result in coma. The long-term complications of poorly controlled diabetes include retinopathy, renal failure, and heart disease. Psychological interventions for poorly controlled diabetes aim to facilitate adherence to self-management regimes (Snoek & Skinner, 2005). In a meta-analysis of controlled trials of counselling, cognitive behavioural therapy, family systems therapy, and psychodynamic therapy for improving glycaemia control in Type 1 diabetes, Winkley *et al.* (2006) included 11 studies of adults and 10 studies of children and adolescents. They found that psychological interventions improved glycaemic control in young people with Type 1 diabetes but had no effect in adults. In a meta-analysis of 25 controlled trials of counselling, cognitive behavioural therapy, and psychodynamic therapy for improving glycaemic control in Type 2 diabetes, Ismail *et al.* (2004) found that psychological therapies led to improvements in long-term glycaemic control and psychological distress but not in weight control or blood glucose concentration. For adults with Type 2 diabetes, psychosocial intervention programmes that improve illness management and psychological adjustment include psychoeducation; skills training in adherence to diabetic medical regimes; weight loss programmes; and interventions to address personal distress and improve social support (Gonder-Frederick *et al.*, 2002).

Hypertension in adults

Hypertension is characterized by a systolic blood pressure of greater than 140mmHg and a diastolic blood pressure greater than 90mmHg. A distinction is made between secondary hypertension, which is due to an identifiable cause such as kidney disease, and primary or essential hypertension which occurs in the absence of an identifiable medical problem. In a review of previous systematic reviews and meta-analyses covering over a hundred randomized controlled trials, Linden and Moseley (2006) concluded that for people with essential hypertension, behavioural treatments reduced blood pressure compared with waiting list controls, and that greater reductions occurred where initial levels were high. Multicomponent psychological treatments were more effective than single component treatments. Among biofeedback treatments, thermal feedback and electrodermal activity feedback were more effective than EMG or blood pressure feedback. For hypertension, effective psychological intervention involves relaxation training or biofeedback, and a lifestyle change programme that facilitates weight reduction, physical exercise, reduced sodium and alcohol intake, and potassium supplements (Blumenthal *et al.*, 2002; Linden & Chambers, 2004).

Practice implications for adjustment to chronic medical conditions in adults

For chronic medical conditions effective psychological interventions involve psychoeducation, skills training in specific practices essential for appropriate lifestyle change and self-management of the chronic condition, and psychotherapeutic interventions to address clients' ambivalence about making relevant lifestyle changes, self-managing their chronic conditions, and adhering to medical regimes.

Coping with pain and fatigue in adults

When psychotherapy is included as one element of a multimodal, multidisciplinary programme it is effective in helping adult clients manage chronic pain, low back pain, fibromyalgia, chronic fatigue syndrome, headaches, arthritis, and irritable bowel syndrome.

Chronic pain in adults

In a meta-analysis of 25 trials of interventions for chronic pain, Morley *et al.* (1999) found that psychological treatments (cognitive behavioural therapy and biofeedback) compared with waiting list controls led to a median effect size of .5 across a range of domains including pain, mood, activity level, coping, and social functioning. This effect size is approximately equivalent to a success rate of 62%. Compared with alternative active treatments, cognitive behavioural therapy produced significantly greater changes in pain experience and expression and cognitive coping. Effective psychological interventions involve psychoeducation; relaxation and coping skills training; graded exercise planning; reinforcement for engaging in adaptive behaviour inconsistent with the illness role; and building social support, especially within the family.

Effective psychological intervention for chronic pain is offered as one element of an intensive multidisciplinary programme involving physiotherapy, occupational therapy, and medical management, and is usually offered within a group therapy context (Turk, 2002; Turk & Burwinkle, 2005).

Low back pain in adults

In a meta-analysis of 22 studies of psychological and multidisciplinary interventions for chronic low back pain, Hoffman *et al.* (2007) found post-treatment effect sizes of .41 for pain intensity, .23 for pain interference, and .41 for quality of life. These effect sizes are approximately equivalent to success rates of 55–60%. For all psychological interventions (as opposed to multidisciplinary interventions), the pain intensity effect size was .48. For relaxation training or biofeedback the pain intensity effect size was .75 and for cognitive behaviour therapy it was .62. These effect sizes are approximately equivalent to success rates of 64–68%. These results highlight the particular value of relaxation training, biofeedback, and cognitive behavioural therapy in the treatment of low back pain.

Fibromyalgia in adults

Fibromyalgia is a chronic debilitating illness characterized by widespread musculoskeletal pain and fatigue. In a meta-analysis of 49 studies of the efficacy of psychological and pharmacological treatments for fibromyalgia, Rossy *et al.* (1999) found that psychological approaches and antidepressants both alleviated symptoms of fibromyalgia. In a systematic narrative review of psychological treatments for fibromyalgia, Adams and Sim (2005) concluded that there is evidence for the effectiveness of aerobic exercise and cognitive behavioural therapy. Effective psychotherapy for fibromyalgia is offered as part of a multidisciplinary programme involving medical pain management, physiotherapy, occupational therapy, and graded exercise. Psychotherapy includes psychoeducation; relaxation, coping skills, assertiveness, and sleep management training; usually in a group context with other fibromyalgia patients (Adams & Sim, 2005; Busch *et al.*, 2002; Rossy *et al.*, 1999; Sim & Adams, 2002).

Chronic fatigue syndrome in adults

Chronic fatigue syndrome is a debilitating condition characterized primarily by chronic physical and mental fatigue, which may be accompanied by sleep disruption, low mood, headaches, and pain symptoms. The condition is also referred to as myalgic encephalomyelitis and postviral fatigue syndrome. In a systematic review of 44 trials, Whiting *et al.* (2001) concluded that there was evidence that graded exercise assignment and cognitive behavioural therapy both had beneficial effects on the primary symptoms of chronic fatigue syndrome. Thus, effective psychotherapy for chronic fatigue syndrome involves graded exercise and learning cognitive coping skills within the context of a supportive psychotherapeutic relationship.

Recurrent headaches in adults

A distinction is made between tension-type headaches and migraine, both of which involve recurrent head pain, but which are subserved by different physiological mechanisms (Holroyd, 2002). In a systematic review of six previous meta-analyses of treatments of migraine and six previous meta-analyses of treatments for tension headaches, Rains *et al.* (2005) concluded that relaxation training, biofeedback, and cognitive behavioural therapy led to reductions of 35–55% in migraine and tension headaches and improvements were maintained at long-term follow-up. They also concluded that for migraine these treatments were as effective as widely used medications such as propranolol and flunarizine. These conclusions are consistent with those of other reviews and meta-analyses (Holroyd, 2002; Nestoriuc & Martin, 2007; Stewart, 2004). For both migraine and tension headaches, effective psychotherapy involves psychoeducation and progressive muscle relaxation training. The effectiveness of this can be enhanced with biofeedback and cognitive behavioural coping skills training for managing stresses that contribute to headaches. Electromyograph (muscle tension) biofeedback is effective for both tension and migraine headaches, and thermal biofeedback has a positive effect on migraine. These conclusions are consistent with international best practice guidelines (Campbell *et al.*, 2000; Silberstein & Rosenberg, 2000).

Arthritis in adults

With arthritis, people experience chronic pain, and associated disability and negative mood states. In a meta-analysis of 27 randomized controlled trials of psychosocial interventions for managing pain and disability in people with osteoarthritis or rheumatoid arthritis, Dixon *et al.* (2007) obtained an effect size of 0.17 for pain ratings; .15 for disability; .34 for joint swelling; .28 for anxiety; .20 for depression; and .70 for active coping. These effect sizes are approximately equivalent to success rates between 54% and 67%. Effective programmes were predominantly cognitive behavioural in orientation and included psychoeducation, training in relaxation and cognitive coping skills, and involvement of marital partners or family members in therapy to enhance social support. These findings are consistent with those of past reviews (Keefe *et al.*, 2002).

Irritable bowel syndrome in adults

Irritable bowel syndrome (IBS) is characterized by abdominal pain, increased bowel frequency, constipation, bloating, the sensation of incomplete evacuation, and psychological distress associated with these symptoms. Standard treatment is a symptom-directed approach with drugs aimed at pain, constipation, and diarrhoea (Farthing, 2005). Psychological treatments may also be used. In a systematic review of 32 studies of such treatments, and a meta-analysis of 17 of these, Lackner *et al.* (2004) concluded that psychological interventions were effective in alleviating the symptoms of irritable bowel syndrome. The effect sizes were .26 for abdominal pain, .57 for bowel dysfunction, .54 for depression, and .39 for anxiety. These effect sizes are approximately equivalent to success rates of 56% to 63%. Psychotherapeutic interventions evaluated in the meta-analysis included psychoeducation; relaxation training, hypnotherapy, and biofeedback; cognitive behavioural therapy, and brief psychodynamic therapy. The effectiveness of these approaches is also supported by other systematic reviews (e.g. Blanchard, 2005; Blanchard & Scharff, 2002; Whitehead, 2006). All of these forms of therapy provide clients with a new and coherent way of understanding their condition within the context of a supportive psychotherapeutic relationship. Relaxation training, hypnotherapy, and biofeedback enhance clients' capacity to regulate physiological arousal and discomfort associated with their symptoms. Psychodynamic therapy, and assertiveness training (which is included in some cognitive behavioural programmes), empower clients to break vicious cycles of social interaction through which symptoms are maintained. These forms of therapy also help clients develop more supportive social networks. Blanchard's (2001) *Irritable Bowel Syndrome: Psychosocial Assessment and Treatment* is a particularly useful treatment resource for this condition.

Practice implications for pain management in adults

Effective psychological interventions for various pain conditions involve psychoeducation; relaxation skills training; developing specific skills necessary for managing the particular pain condition; graded exercise planning; reinforcement for engaging in adaptive behaviour inconsistent with the illness role; and building social support, especially within the family. Effective psychological intervention for pain conditions is optimally offered as one element of a multidisciplinary multimodal programme.

Eating disorders in adults

Psychotherapy has been shown to be effective for a proportion of cases with a range of eating disorders including obesity, anorexia, bulimia, and binge eating disorder.

Obesity in adults

Obesity is defined as having a body mass index of 30 or greater, and this is calculated by dividing an individual's weight in kilograms by their height in meters squared (World Health Organization, 1998). Morbid obesity occurs when body mass index exceeds 40.

Cognitive behavioural programmes for obesity in adults

Cognitive behavioural therapy for obesity involves using cognitive and behavioural procedures, and family involvement to help clients achieve goals associated with maintaining a low calorie diet and regular daily exercise. It is usually provided on a group basis for 10–30 sessions. In a systematic review of 42 randomized controlled trials of cognitive behavioural therapy for obesity, Wadden *et al.* (2005) concluded that cognitive behavioural programmes of 30 weeks duration led to 10% weight loss, while programmes of under ten sessions led to under 5% weight loss. Weight loss in these programmes occurred at the rate of about .5 kg a week. 35% of initial weight loss was regained in the following year. Five years after treatment 50% of clients had returned to their original weight. However, clients who had attended weekly programmes for 30 weeks maintained their weight loss if they subsequently attended fortnightly maintenance sessions for a year. About 50% dropped out after a year, and monthly rather than fortnightly sessions were found to be ineffective in preventing weight gain. However, phone- and internet-based maintenance programmes prevented some degree of weight gain. Programmes that involved replacing some snacks and meals with liquid supplements or that specified the size of portions led to more rapid weight loss. Long-term outcomes for programmes that used low calorie (1500–1800 kcal per day) and very low calorie (800 kcal per day) diets were similar, because weight gain was greater in the year following completion of very low calorie diets.

Pharmacotherapy for obesity in adults

In a systematic review of 11 randomized controlled double-blind trials for olistat, and three for sibutramine, Padwal *et al.* (2003) found that compared with a placebo control group orlistat-treated patients displayed a 2.7 kg or 2.9% greater reduction in weight and patients on sibutramine displayed a 4.3 kg or 4.6% greater weight reduction at one year follow-up. Thus, orlistat and sibutramine appear modestly effective in promoting weight loss. This conclusion is consistent with that of other reviews of pharmacological interventions for obesity (e.g. Bray, 2005). In two systematic reviews involving 84 randomized controlled trials of obesity treatment programmes, Avenell's team concluded that programmes which included orlistat or sibutramine, cognitive behavioural therapy, regular exercise, and low calorie diets were more effective than dietary interventions alone in leading to weight reduction and improved risk factors for cardiovascular disorders and Type 2 diabetes (Avenell *et al.*, 2004a, 2004b).

Surgery for obesity in adults

In a systematic review and meta-analysis of 136 studies, Buchwald *et al.* (2004) found that effective weight loss was achieved in morbidly obese patients with an average body mass index of 46.9 after undergoing bariatric surgery. The mean percentage of excess weight loss was 61% for all patients; 47.5% for patients who underwent gastric banding; 61.6% for gastric bypass; 68.2% for gastroplasty; and 70.1% for biliopancreatic diversion or duodenal switch. A substantial majority of patients with diabetes, hyperlipidemia, hypertension, and obstructive sleep apnoea experienced complete resolution or improvement.

Self-help and commercial programmes for obesity in adults

Self-help programmes are alternatives to clinically based interventions. In a systematic review of popular US obesity self-help programmes, Tsai *et al.* (2005) concluded that randomized controlled trials provided support for the effectiveness of Weight Watchers, with participants losing about 5% of body weight in the first year and about 3% in the second year. This programme includes a low calorie diet, physical exercise programme, the use of behavioural weight control methods, peer support provided by weekly group meetings, and credible facilitation by a successful lifetime member of Weight Watchers. No studies have been conducted to assess the effectiveness of self-help groups such as Overeaters Anonymous.

Practice implications for obesity in adults

In a stepped care approach to obesity, self-help groups such as Weight Watchers are a useful first line intervention. Where limited progress is made, professional intervention may be considered. Effective psychotherapy for obesity in adults involves goal setting; daily monitoring of eating and exercise; weekly monitoring of weight; a low calorie diet of about 1500 kcal per day which should produce weight loss of .5 kg per week; about an hour's daily physical exercise; organization of environmental cues, reinforcement, and significant relationships to support lifestyle changes in eating and exercise; the development of coping skills to address beliefs and urges that interfere with lifestyle change and weight loss; and relapse prevention planning (Wadden *et al.*, 2005). Effective programmes are of long duration (30 weeks) with frequent sessions. Partner or group support for weight loss is provided by using marital or group therapy formats. In the psychotherapy of obesity, early sessions focus on goal setting and contracting. Later sessions address the development of relapse prevention skills. Because obesity is a chronic problem, fortnightly follow-up sessions, telephone or internet maintenance sessions are required to retain treatment gains. Cooper *et al.*'s (2003) *Cognitive-Behavioural Treatment of Obesity – A Clinician's Guide* is a useful therapy manual. Multimodal treatment with psychotherapy and medication (orlistat or sibutramine) enhances treatment effectiveness. For morbid obesity surgery is effective but must be combined with the lifestyle change (such as that outlined above) if weight loss is to be maintained. Apple *et al.*'s (2006) *Preparing for Weight Loss Surgery: Therapist Guide* is a useful clinical resource.

Anorexia nervosa in adults

Anorexia nervosa is characterized by severe restricted food intake; weight loss with a body mass index below 17.5 kilograms per meter of height squared; an overvaluing of thinness; an intense fear of becoming fat despite emaciation; and amenorrhea (American Psychiatric Association, 2000a; World Health Organization, 1992).

Cognitive behavioural therapy for anorexia nervosa in adults

Six trials of cognitive behavioural therapy have been carried out with adult anorexics (Ball & Mitchell, 2004; Channon *et al.*, 1989; Halmi *et al.*, 2005; Mcintosh *et al.*, 2005; Pike *et al.*, 2003; Serfaty *et al.*, 1999). These studies have shown that brief cognitive behavioural therapy of about 20 sessions is as effective as behavioural therapy, behavioural family therapy, and interpersonal therapy in preventing relapse after weight restoration; and is more acceptable to patients than nutritional counselling and antidepressant medication alone, because these two treatments had very high drop-out rates (over

70%). Across these six trials only a small minority of participants who received brief cognitive behavioural therapy were in remission after treatment. Wilson *et al.* (2007) has argued that in most of these trials an inadequate therapy dosage was used, given that the best available cognitive behavioural treatment programmes span one to two years and involve 50–100 sessions (Fairburn *et al.*, 2003; Garner *et al.*, 1997). In these trials, the development of a collaborative alliance with clients was the central focus of the initial sessions, and in later sessions cognitive therapy was used to help clients address dysfunctional beliefs underpinning their self-starvation, while behavioural techniques were used to promote the development of more normal eating patterns, and broader cognitive behavioural strategies were also used to help clients manage negative mood states, and interpersonal problems.

Psychodynamic, cognitive analytic, and family therapy for anorexia nervosa in adults

There have been five trials of psychodynamic therapy, cognitive analytic therapy, and family therapy for adults with anorexia (Ball & Mitchell, 2004; Dare *et al.*, 2001; Eisler *et al.*, 1997; Hall & Crisp, 1987; Treasure *et al.*, 1995). The results of these trials have shown that, for a proportion of patients, each of these treatments can be helpful, but the results were too inconsistent to draw valid conclusions concerning which treatments were most effective. Individual psychodynamic therapy was found to be more effective than family therapy in one study (Eisler *et al.*, 1997), and as effective as family therapy in another (Dare *et al.*, 2001). Cognitive analytic therapy was found to be no more effective than routine behavioural treatment in one study (Treasure *et al.*, 1995) and less effective than psychodynamic and family therapy in another (Dare *et al.*, 2001). Family therapy has been found to be as effective as cognitive behavioural therapy in one study (Ball & Mitchell, 2004), as effective as psychodynamic therapy in another study (Dare *et al.*, 2001), and less effective than psychodynamic therapy in a third study (Eisler *et al.*, 1997). In these studies the following therapeutic procedures were used. In psychodynamic psychotherapy, therapists saw patients in individual sessions, gave no advice about eating behaviour, but addressed the conscious and unconscious meanings of the symptom, the impact of the symptom on patients' current relationships and their transference relationships with the therapist (Dare, 1995; Malan, 1995). In cognitive analytic therapy, which involved individual and family sessions, a diagram was developed of the place of anorexia in patients' experience of themselves and their early and current family relationships and their transference relationships with therapists, and this diagrammatic formulation was used as the basis for therapy (Ryle, 1990). Family therapy involved conjoint family sessions and aimed at the elimination of the controlling role of the eating disorder in determining the relationship between patients and members of their families (Dare, 1991).

Pharmacotherapy for anorexia nervosa in adults

In a systematic review of 14 trials investigating a range of psychopharmacological treatments, Mitchell (2001) concluded that selective serotonin reuptake inhibitors may prevent relapse in recovered people with anorexia, but there is no consistent evidence at present for the effectiveness of medication in the treatment of anorexia. However, Walsh *et al.* (2006) in a recent large randomized placebo controlled trial found that serotonin reuptake inhibitors added no significant benefit to cognitive behavioural therapy.

Practice implications for anorexia nervosa in adults

The evidence base for informing psychotherapy with anorexia is far weaker than that for bulimia. Effective psychotherapy for adults with anorexia probably involves addressing developmental and interpersonal difficulties associated with self-starvation on the one hand and helping clients develop and maintain regular and appropriate eating patterns on the other. There is some evidence for the effectiveness of individual therapy with adult anorexia conducted from psychodynamic, cognitive behavioural, and cognitive analytic perspectives. Probably family therapy is less useful with adults, but is the treatment of choice for anorexic adolescents as outlined in the previous chapter. Psychotherapy for adults with anorexia should be offered as part of a multimodal, multidisciplinary programme that involves weight restoration and management of medical complications of anorexia nervosa. These evidence-based conclusions are consistent with international guidelines for best practice and results of recent systematic reviews (American Psychiatric Association, 2006a; NICE, 2004d; RANZCP Clinical Practice Guidelines Team for Anorexia Nervosa, 2004).

Bulimia nervosa in adults

Bulimia nervosa is an eating disorder characterized by overvaluing a slim idealized body shape; a cyclical pattern of restrained eating, uncontrolled bingeing and purging by, for example, vomiting or misusing laxative; and personal distress (American Psychiatric Association, 2000a; World Health Organization, 1992).

Psychotherapy for bulimia nervosa in adults

Thompson-Brenner *et al.* (2003) conducted a meta-analysis of 26 studies involving 51 treatment conditions, of which 36 were cognitive behavioural or behavioural and 15 were some other form of therapy. Post-treatment effect sizes for all treatments compared with waiting list controls were .88 for binge eating episodes and 1.01 for episodes of purging. These gains were maintained a year after treatment where effect sizes were 1.63 and 1.01 for episodes of bingeing and purging respectively. Across all treatments, the recovery rate after treatment was 40%, and the recovery rate of 45.6% for individual therapy was higher than that of 26.7% for group therapy. A year after treatment, 43.7% of cases were recovered. In this meta-analysis there were no significant differences in outcome between therapies, but more studies of cognitive behavioural therapy had been conducted than any other form of therapy, so it is the best validated. Cognitive behavioural therapy aims to disrupt the binge–purge cycle by helping clients use meal planning and stimulus control techniques to develop a normal eating routine. It also aims to modify beliefs and values concerning shape, weight, and self-worth that underpin the binge–purge cycle, and to equip clients with strategies for managing potential relapse situations (Fairburn *et al.*, 1993, 2003). Of the other forms of therapy that have been investigated, interpersonal therapy has been shown to be as effective as cognitive behavioural therapy at one year follow-up, but not immediately after treatment (Wilson & Fairburn, 2007). With interpersonal therapy the focus is on helping clients resolve interpersonal difficulties associated with their eating disorder (Weissman *et al.*, 2000).

Pharmacotherapy for bulimia nervosa in adults

In a meta-analysis of 31 studies of pharmacotherapy alone and in combination with psychotherapy, Nakash-Eisikovits *et al.* (2002) found that there was evidence for the short-term efficacy of a range of antidepressants in the treatment of bulimia. These included selective serotonin reuptake inhibitors, tricyclic antidepressants, mono-amine oxidaise inhibitors, and atypical antidepressants. The overall post-treatment effect size was .6 for episodes of both bingeing and purging, and the overall post-treatment recovery rate was about 25%. In the only study where follow-up data were available, 30% of cases were recovered a year after antidepressant treatment. When these outcomes are compared with those for psychotherapy found in Thompson-Brenner and colleagues' (2003) meta-analysis summarized above, it may be concluded that psychotherapy is more effective than pharmacotherapy in alleviating bingeing and purging in bulimia. In their meta-analysis of the very small number of trials of multimodal treatment programmes, Nakash-Eisikovits *et al.* (2002) found that programmes in which psychotherapy and antidepressants were combined were more effective in alleviating bingeing and purging than medication alone (effect size = .35) and psychotherapy alone (effect size = .3).

Self-help for bulimia nervosa in adults

Reviews of trials of self-help interventions for bulimia concur that guided self-help involving bibliotherapy and either individual or group psychoeducational support with a health professional can alleviate the symptoms of bulimia in a proportion of cases (Shapiro *et al.*, 2007; Wilson *et al.*, 2000; Wilson & Fairburn, 2007).

Practice implications for bulimia nervosa in adults

Both cognitive behavioural therapy and interpersonal therapy may be used in treating bulimia nervosa, and the effects of such programmes may probably be enhanced with antidepressant medication. With cognitive behavioural therapy, clients learn effective methods for symptom control by developing a regular and flexible pattern of eating that includes previously avoided foods; reducing concern with body shape and weight; and coping with high-risk situations for binge eating and purging to prevent relapse. Fairburn and colleagues' (1993) *Cognitive Behaviour Therapy for Binge Eating and Bulimia Nervosa: A Comprehensive Treatment Manual* is a useful resource for this type of therapy.

With interpersonal therapy clients address interpersonal difficulties associated with their eating disorder, specifically those associated with loss, lifecycle transitions, role disputes, and social skills deficits. For this approach Weissman and colleagues' (2000) *Comprehensive Guide to Interpersonal Psychotherapy* is a useful resource. Psychotherapy for bulimia may be offered within the context of a stepped care model, where guided self-help is initially available on the understanding that only some clients will respond to this minimal contact approach. Fairburn's (1995) *Overcoming Binge Eating* is the self-help book that has been used in a number of successful guided self-help trials. These conclusions are consistent with those in international best practice guidelines (American Psychiatric Association, 2006a; NICE, 2004d).

Binge eating disorder in adults

Binge eating disorder is characterized by recurrent binge eating in the absence of the compensatory behaviours that occur in bulimia.

Psychotherapy for binge eating disorder in adults

In a narrative review of controlled trials of various psychological interventions for binge eating disorder, Wilson and Fairburn (2007) concluded that cognitive behavioural therapy (Fairburn *et al.*, 1993, 2003), interpersonal therapy (Weissman *et al.*, 2000), dialectical behaviour therapy (Telch *et al.*, 2001), and behavioural weight loss (Cooper *et al.*, 2003) treatments led to significant reductions in bingeing, and behavioural weight loss programmes also led to short-term weight loss for people with binge eating disorder.

Pharmacotherapy for binge eating disorder in adults

In a systematic review of nine trials of pharmacotherapy, and three trials of pharmacotherapy combined with psychotherapy for binge eating disorder, Brownley *et al.* (2007) concluded that antidepressants (notably selective serotonin reuptake inhibitors) were effective in leading to short-term reductions in bingeing. Both sibutramine and topiramate had a significant short-term impact on weight reduction. However, cognitive behaviour therapy (with or without antidepressants) was more effective than antidepressants alone in reducing bingeing.

Self-help for binge eating disorder in adults

In a review of four trials of guided self-help or psychoeducational group treatment, Wilson and Fairburn (2007) concluded that self-help using books or videotapes in conjunction with minimal contact with a health professional to support clients in following the programme in the book or video reduced bingeing in a proportion of clients with binge eating disorder.

Practice implications for binge eating disorder in adults

For binge eating disorder, cognitive behavioural therapy, behavioural weight loss therapy, interpersonal therapy, and dialectical behaviour therapy may all be considered because there is some evidence that each is effective with a proportion of clients. Psychotherapy for binge eating disorder may be offered within the context of a stepped care model, where guided self-help is initially offered on the understanding that only some clients will respond to this minimal contact approach. Fairburn's (1995) *Overcoming Binge Eating* is the self-help book that has been used in a number of successful guided self-help trials. These conclusions are consistent with those in international best practice guidelines (NICE, 2004d).

Insomnia in adults

Insomnia involves complaints of difficulty falling or staying asleep, and is associated with significant distress and impaired daytime functioning (American Psychiatric Association, 2000a; World Health Organization, 1992).

Psychotherapy for insomnia in adults

In a systematic review of 37 controlled and uncontrolled studies of psychological treatments for primary insomnia, Morin *et al.* (2006) concluded that stimulus control therapy, relaxation training, paradoxical intention, sleep restriction, and cognitive behavioural therapy were effective interventions for insomnia. These psychological interventions were effective in both primary insomnia and insomnia secondary to physical and psychological disorders such as chronic pain, cancer, or alcohol dependence, and also among chronic users of hypnotic medication. Sleep improvements after treatment were sustained in the longer term, from one to 36 months. Individual and group-based delivery of interventions were equally effective. In studies where psychological and pharmacological interventions were compared, both were equally effective in the short term. However, the effectiveness of hypnotics typically ceases once they are discontinued. In a meta-analysis of 23 randomized controlled trials of psychological interventions for insomnia, Irwin *et al.* (2006) found overall effect sizes of .64 for waking after sleep onset; .76 for sleep quality; and .52 for both sleep onset latency and sleep efficiency, which are equivalent to approximate success rates of 62–68%. Multicomponent cognitive behavioural interventions, relaxation training, and behavioural programmes that involved stimulus control, sleep compression, and paradoxical interventions were all equally effective for adults under and over 55 years. These conclusions are consistent with those of other systematic reviews (Edinger & Means, 2005; Pallesen *et al.*, 1998; Smith *et al.*, 2002, 2005; Wang *et al.*, 2005; Wilson & Nutt, 2007).

Pharmacotherapy for insomnia in adults

In a systematic review of pharmacological interventions for insomnia, Wilson and Nutt (2007) concluded that benzodiazepines and Z-drugs (e.g. zolpidem and zopiclone) are first-line pharmacological interventions for insomnia, although chronic benzodiazepine use can lead to dependence. Certain anti-depressants (e.g. trazodone and mirtazapine) have sedative effects and so may be used to treat insomnia secondary to depression. There is also some evidence for the effectiveness of synthetic melatonin (ramelteon) in the treatment of insomnia.

Practice implications for insomnia in adults

Effective psychotherapy for insomnia involves psychoeducation about sleep, and the rationale for using cognitive and behavioural strategies; cognitive therapy to address beliefs and misconceptions that maintain insomnia; stimulus control where clients learn to associate the bedroom with sleep and establish a consistent sleep–wake cycle; relaxation training to reduce bedtime arousal and rumination; sleep restriction to curtail time spent in bed to actual sleep time; and paradoxical intention where clients attempt to remain awake (rather than worrying about falling asleep). These conclusions are consistent with international best practice guidelines (Morgenthaler *et al.*, 2006). Morin and Espie's (2003) *Insomnia: Psychological Assessment and Management* is a useful treatment manual for insomnia.

Alcohol and drug abuse in adults

In reviewing the literature on psychotherapy for substance abuse, a useful distinction may be made between studies of treatments for alcohol abuse, and studies of treatment for illicit drug abuse. In the following sections, studies of treatments for alcohol abuse will be reviewed first, and those concerned with illicit drug abuse will be addressed later. Having said that, the distinction between alcohol and illicit drug abuse is not always clearly made in the research literature. For example, participants in many treatment outcome studies abuse both alcohol and illicit drugs, and in some meta-analyses studies of treatments for both alcohol and illicit drug abuse are combined. Below, it will be noted where this occurs. The review of literature on treatments for substance abuse will close with a consideration of psychotherapeutic processes common to effective treatment of both alcohol and illicit drug abuse.

There is a very large body of evidence to show that psychological interventions are effective in helping people recover from alcohol abuse. For example, to determine the overall effectiveness of treatment programmes for people with alcohol abuse, Miller *et al.* (2001) combined the results of seven large multisite studies involving thousands of North American participants and found that about one-third of clients remained abstinent during the year following treatment, and the remaining two-thirds showed large and significant decreases in drinking and related problems.

Because many treatments have been shown to be effective for alcohol problems, an important concern is which interventions are most effective. In a systematic quantitative review of 381 clinical trials involving over 75,000 clients and 99 different treatment modalities, Miller *et al.* (2003) rank ordered interventions in terms of the evidence base for their overall effectiveness. The most effective, clearly defined psychological treatments in rank order were motivational enhancement therapy (Miller *et al.*, 1994), community reinforcement (Meyers & Smith, 1995), cognitive behavioural skills training (Kadden *et al.*, 1994), and behavioural marital therapy (O'Farrell & Fals-Stewart, 2006). The most effective pharmacological interventions were acomprosate and naltrexone (which reduce craving), and to a lesser extent disulfiram (which induces illness if alcohol is taken). Interventions designed to educate, confront, shock, or foster insight regarding the nature and causes of substance use problems were the least effective. These conclusions about the most effective psychological and pharmacological therapies are consistent with those of other systematic reviews (Finney *et al.*, 2007; McCrady & Nathan, 2006; O'Brien & McKay, 2007).

The effective psychological treatments for alcohol problems identified by Miller *et al.* (2003) were all brief outpatient therapies, and there was no evidence that inpatient treatment or intensive long-term outpatient care was more effective than these brief psychological therapies. (In contrast to this finding for alcohol abuse, with chronic illicit drug abuse, as will be shown below in the section on therapeutic communities for drug abuse, duration of treatment is strongly associated with outcome.) Two major multisite controlled trials of manualized brief interventions for alcohol abuse deserve particular mention, because of their scale, the rigour with which they were conducted, the fact that they evaluated some of the highly effective treatments identified by Miller *et al.* (2003), and the support their findings provide for the effectiveness of brief psychological interventions for alcohol problems. Project MATCH, which involved 1726 people in North America, showed that four sessions of motivational enhancement therapy, 12 sessions of 12-step facilitation, and 12 sessions of cognitive behavioural therapy were equally effective in ameliorating alcohol-related problems (Project MATCH Research Group, 1998). After three years almost 30% of participants were abstinent, and those who were drinking when assessed had been abstinent for about two-thirds of the time during the three-year follow-up period. The United Kingdom Alcohol Treatment Trial (UKATT) which involved 742 people showed that three sessions of motivational enhancement therapy and eight sessions of social behaviour and network therapy led to significant and similar reductions in alcohol consumption and alcohol-related problems over 12 months (UKATT Research Team, 2005). Alcohol consumption reduced by 45% and alcohol-related problems reduced by 50%. Brief descriptions of the effective treatments identified in these two large studies are presented below, along with further evidence for their effectiveness.

Motivational enhancement therapy for alcohol abuse in adults

Motivational enhancement therapy, which falls within the client-centred humanistic tradition, helps clients change their alcohol use behaviour by inducing cognitive dissonance. This is achieved by facilitating their evaluation of the pros and cons of continuing drinking (Miller & Rollnick, 2002). The following FRAMES formulation is used by therapists conducting this type of therapy:

F: Provide Feedback on behaviour.
R: Reinforce the patient's Responsibility for changing behaviour.
A: State your Advice about changing behaviour.
M: Discuss a Menu of options to change behaviour.
E: Express Empathy for the patient.
S: Support the patient's Self-efficacy.

This approach is described in the MATCH project treatment manual *Motivational Enhancement Therapy Manual* (Miller *et al.*, 1994). In a meta-analysis of motivational enhancement therapy studies for alcohol and drug abuse, Hettema *et al.* (2005) found effect sizes for alcohol abuse of .41 after treatment and .26 at follow-up, based on 32 trials. These effect sizes are approximately equivalent to success rates of 60% and 56% respectively. The effect sizes for drug abuse were .51 after treatment and .29 at follow-up based on 13 trials. These effect sizes are approximately equivalent to success rates of 62% and 57% respectively.

Twelve-step facilitation and Alcoholics Anonymous for alcohol abuse in adults

Twelve-step facilitation, which was evaluated in the MATCH project, is a structured intervention to enhance engagement with Alcoholics Anonymous (AA) (Nowinski *et al.*, 1994). This therapy is based on the concept of alcoholism as a spiritual and medical disease, which can only be controlled through acceptance of divine support. While 12-step facilitation was shown in the MATCH project to be as effective as motivational enhancement therapy and cognitive coping skills training, there is little evidence for the effectiveness of AA. Meta-analyses of 74 evaluations of AA by Tonigan *et al.* (1996) and 21 studies by Kownacki and Shadish (1999) have not provided strong support for the effectiveness of AA, possibly because many studies are poorly designed and the better designed studies involve participants who were coerced into treatment.

Cognitive behavioural therapy for alcohol abuse in adults

This approach is based on the relapse prevention model which points to a range of factors which contribute to relapse including trigger situations, perceived reinforcing effects of substance use, the abstinence violation effect, coping skills, affective states, self-efficacy, outcome expectancies, craving, motivation, and distal risk factors such as family history, social support, and drug dependence (Witkiewitz & Marlatt, 2004). Cognitive behavioural coping skills training for relapse prevention involves a range of intervention to address these factors including identifying specific high-risk situations, enhancing skills for coping with those situations, increasing self-efficacy, and restructuring perceptions of the relapse process. Other strategies include developing a balanced lifestyle, developing positive addictions, employing stimulus control techniques and urge management, and developing relapse prevention plans. These procedures are described in *Overcoming Your Alcohol or Drug Problem* (Daley & Marlatt, 2006) and in the MATCH project treatment manual *Cognitive-Behavioural Coping Skills Therapy Manual* (Kadden *et al.*, 1994). In a meta-analysis of ten studies of relapse prevention, Irvin *et al.* (1999) found that cognitive behavioural relapse prevention treatment for alcohol misuse was moderately effective yielding an effect size of .37 after treatment, and adjunctive use of medication increased its effectiveness for alcohol problems (to an effect size of .48). These effect sizes are approximately equivalent to success rates of 58% and 61%.

Community reinforcement for alcohol abuse in adults

The Community Reinforcement Approach is a behavioural programme for treating substance abuse problems based on the premise that contingencies in a client's social system encourage or discourage alcohol and drug abuse. Social, recreational, familial, and vocational reinforcers are identified during assessment. These are then used to help clients recover and to make a sober lifestyle more rewarding than drug or alcohol abuse. The community reinforcement approach, which includes coping skills training, family or couples therapy, and jobs club attendance, is described in *Clinical Guide to Alcohol Treatment: The Community Reinforcement Approach* (Meyers & Smith, 1995). In a systematic review of 11 randomized controlled trials, Roozen *et al.* (2004) found that, compared with usual care, the community reinforcement approach led to significant reductions in the number of drinking days, particularly when combined with disulfiram (a medication which induces illness when alcohol is taken). They also concluded that the community reinforcement approach led to significantly greater abstinence rates for cocaine and opioid users.

Systemic interventions for alcohol abuse in adults

In a systematic narrative review of 38 controlled studies of systemic marital and family interventions for the treatment of alcohol problems, O'Farrell and Fals-Stewart (2003) concluded that these approaches were effective in helping families promote the engagement of family members with alcohol problems in treatment, and helping people with alcohol problems recover.

For helping families promote the engagement of family members with alcohol problems, O'Farrell and Fals-Stewart (2003) concluded that Community Reinforcement and Family Training was more effective than all other family-based methods, leading to engagement rates above 60% in controlled studies. This approach helps sober family members improve communication, reduce the risk of physical abuse, encourages sobriety and treatment seeking in people with alcohol problems, and helps sober family members engage in activities outside the family to reduce dependence on the person with the alcohol problem. It is described in *Motivating Substance Abusers to Enter Treatment: Working with Family Members* (Smith & Meyers, 2004).

For helping people with alcohol problems recover, O'Farrell and Fals-Stewart (2003) concluded that behavioural couples therapy was more effective than other systemic and individual approaches. Compared with individual approaches, behavioural couples therapy produced greater abstinence, fewer alcohol-related problems, greater relationship satisfaction, and better adjustment in children of people with alcohol problems. It also showed greater reductions in domestic violence, and periods in jail and hospital, leading to very significant cost savings. The most effective forms of behavioural couples therapy incorporate either a disulfiram contract or a sobriety contract into a treatment programme which includes problem-solving and communication training and relationship enhancement procedures. The therapy aims to reduce alcohol abuse, enhance family support for efforts to change, and promote patterns of interaction conducive to long-term abstinence. It is described in *Behavioural Couples Therapy for Alcoholism and Substance Abuse* (O'Farrell & Fals-Stewart, 2006).

Social behavioural network therapy, which was found to be as effective as motivational enhancement therapy in the UKATT trial, helps clients address their alcohol problems by building supportive social networks and developing coping skills (Copello *et al.*, 2002). It combines elements of family-based interventions such as community reinforcement, and cognitive behavioural coping skills training and relapse prevention approaches to addictions. The approach is described in the *Social Behavioural Network Therapy Manual* (Copello *et al.*, 1999).

Controlled drinking interventions for alcohol abuse in adults

A proportion of clients with alcohol problems prefer controlled drinking to abstinence as a treatment goal. Behavioural self-control training is a cognitive behavioural approach that aims to help problem drinkers control their drinking. The programme includes self-monitoring of urges to drink; self-monitoring of the quantity and frequency of alcohol intake; setting specific goals or limits for drinking; drink refusal skills training; contracts involving rewards and consequences for drinking behaviour; and relapse prevention. In a meta-analysis of 17 randomized controlled trials of behavioural self-control training for problem drinkers, Walters (2000) found that this controlled drinking intervention was more effective than no treatment and as effective as abstinence-oriented interventions in reducing problem drinking. It is therefore appropriate to invite clients to choose controlled drinking or abstinence as treatment goals.

In a controlled trial of the effects of a computerized version of behavioural self-control training called *The Drinker's Check-up*, Hester *et al.* (2005) found that after a year participants reduced the quantity and frequency of drinking and alcohol-related problems by 50%.

There is also evidence for the effectiveness of bibliotherapy in promoting controlled drinking. In a meta-analysis of 22 studies evaluating the effectiveness of bibliotherapy for alcohol problems, Apodaca and Miller (2003) found that bibliotherapy reduced harmful drinking and was as effective as more intensive interventions in this regard.

Moderation-oriented cue exposure is a newer intervention designed to facilitate controlled drinking. In this treatment, clients begin by taking a small 'priming' drink of their favourite beverage, and subsequently are exposed to the sight, smell, and taste of this beverage until their ratings of the strength of their urges to drink return to baseline levels. A rationale for the approach, based on extinction of classically conditioned responses, is given at the outset. Between sessions planned episodes of controlled drinking occur, along with self-monitoring of urges to drink. Three trials have shown that this intervention is as effective as behavioural self-control training (Dawe *et al.*, 2002; Heather *et al.*, 2000; Sitharthan *et al.*, 1997).

Pharmacotherapy for alcohol abuse in adults

Medication has been used in the initial short-term detoxification of people with alcohol dependence, and as a long-term maintenance therapy to prevent relapse following detoxification. For detoxification, meta-analyses confirm that benzodiazepines are significantly more effective than placebos in preventing withdrawal symptoms, particularly delirium and seizures, and are currently the medication of choice (Holbrook *et al.*, 1999; Ntais *et al.*, 2005). They are typically administered in reducing dose over about seven days. Beta-Blockers, clonidine, carbamazepine, and neuroleptics may be used as adjunctive therapy but are not recommended as monotherapy (Mayo-Smith, 1997).

In their systematic quantitative review of 381 clinical trials involving over 75,000 clients, Miller *et al.* (2003) rank ordered acomprosate, naltrexone, and disulfiram as the three most effective pharmacological treatments for prevention of relapse in clients with alcohol problems. Acomprosate and naltrexone reduce craving and disulfiram induces illness if alcohol is taken, and so operates as a psychological threat to prevent alcohol use. Miller *et al.* found that evidence for the effectiveness of acomprosate and naltrexone was far more robust than that for disulfiram. Similar conclusions were drawn by Garbutt *et al.* (1999) in a meta-analysis of 41 studies of pharmacological treatments for alcohol dependence. They found that both acamprosate and naltrexone led to reductions in drinking frequency and higher rates of abstinence, but disulfiram had a less pronounced impact on reducing drinking frequency and no impact on abstinence rates. These conclusions are consistent with those of other meta-analyses and reviews (Mann *et al.*, 2004; Srisurapanont & Jarusuraisin, 2005; Suh *et al.*, 2006). However, as was mentioned earlier in the section on systemic marital and family interventions for alcohol problems, disulfiram may enhance the effectiveness of behavioural couples therapy, where a 'disulfiram contract' is monitored by the client's partner (O'Farrell & Fals-Stewart, 2003).

Illicit drug abuse in adults

In a meta-analysis of 78 studies of treatments for illicit drug abuse in which an active treatment group was compared with a minimal or no treatment control group, Prendergast *et al.* (2002) obtained an effect size of .3 for reduction in drug abuse, which is approximately equivalent to a success rate of 57%. The best outcomes occurred where programmes were well implemented and where researchers had a favourable allegiance to the treatment. They also found similar success rates for outpatient drug free programmes and inpatient therapeutic communities, although different client groups may have been involved in studies of these two modalities.

Systemic interventions for drug abuse in adults

In a meta-analysis of 15 studies of systemic couples and family therapy interventions for adolescent and adult drug abuse involving 1571 cases, Stanton and Shadish (1997) found an overall effect size for reduction in drug abuse of .43 which is approximately equivalent to a success rate of 60%. The effect size for adults was .48 and for adolescents was .43 and these did not differ significantly. In the 15 studies included in this meta-analysis, cases in comparison groups received alternative treatments including individual therapy, group therapy, and generic treatment as usual. There was considerable heterogeneity in the types of systemic interventions used in the 15 studies in this meta-analysis, but collectively they underline the importance of family involvement in the treatment of illicit drug abuse.

Contingency management for cocaine and opioid abuse in adults

Contingency management where clients are reinforced for abstinence with voucher-based or monetary-based incentives or prizes have been used to treat drug abuse, notably opioid and cocaine abuse. Three meta-analyses support the effectiveness of this approach. In a meta-analysis of 47 studies of contingency management for treatment of substance use, Prendergast *et al.* (2006) found effect sizes of .66 for cocaine use, .65 for opiate use, and .42 for polydrug abuse. These effect sizes are roughly equivalent to success rates between 60% and 65%. The average effect size was .42 and this declined over time. In a meta-analysis of 30 studies of the effects of contingency management interventions in outpatient methadone treatment settings on drug abuse as detected by urinalysis, Griffith *et al.* (2000) found an effect size of .25 which is approximately equivalent to a success rate of 56%. In a meta-analysis of 30 controlled studies of contingency management, Lussier *et al.* (2006) found an effect size for abstinence of .32 which is approximately equivalent to a success rate of 57%. Contingency management also improved clinic attendance and medication compliance. Both Griffith *et al.* and Lussier *et al.* found that promptly delivered vouchers and incentives with greater monetary value were more effective than less valuable vouchers delivered after a time delay. These results show that contingency management programmes using valuable and promptly delivered incentives improve abstinence, clinic attendance, and medication adherence of clients seeking treatment for cocaine, opioid, and polydrug abuse. In doing so, they facilitate clients' capacity to engage in other aspects of treatment focused on lifestyle change, such as community reinforcement. A description of how to combine contingency management with the community reinforcement approach is given in *A Community Reinforcement Plus Vouchers Approach: Treating Cocaine Addiction* (Budney & Higgins, 1998).

Therapeutic communities for drug abuse in adults

The treatment of chronic drug dependence in drug free therapeutic communities began with Synanon, Daytop, and Phoenix House in the USA. Therapeutic communities facilitate the development of drug free lifestyles through engagement in structured community living and therapeutic activities with ex-addicts who have successfully become drug free (DeLeon, 2003). In a systematic review of seven studies of the effects of therapeutic communities on drug abuse, Smith *et al.* (2006) concluded that the outcomes for different types of therapeutic communities and other forms of residential treatment were similar, but that in prison settings, therapeutic communities led to better outcomes than prison-based mental health programmes or imprisonment without treatment. Evidence for the effectiveness of therapeutic communities also comes from large naturalistic longitudinal cohort studies rather than randomized controlled trials.

In the national treatment outcome research study (NTORS), 496 clients with chronic drug problems from 54 UK centres who were treated in either inpatient therapeutic communities or outpatient methadone maintenance programmes were followed up five years after treatment (Gossop *et al.*, 2001). About half (47%) of clients from residential therapeutic community programmes were abstinent from opiates at five year follow-up, compared with about a third (35%) of those from methadone maintenance programmes.

In the drug abuse treatment outcome study (DATOS), 1396 drug abusers from 96 US centres were followed up one and five years after treatment in either long-term residential therapeutic communities or short-term inpatient settings, outpatient methadone maintenance programmes, or outpatient drug free programmes (Hubbard *et al.*, 2003). A greater reduction in drug abuse occurred where clients spent longer in treatment, and greater reductions in crime and unemployment occurred when clients spent at least six months in long-term residential therapeutic communities. Improvements evident a year after treatment were maintained at five year follow-up. In a second US multisite study of 88 residential treatment programmes involving 2376 drug abusers, Moos *et al.* (1999) found that clients who were treated in therapeutic communities, psychosocial rehabilitation, and 12-step programmes, had better outcomes a year after treatment than those treated in eclectic programmes. Clients who completed treatment, spent longer in treatment, and those who engaged in programmes with a more directed treatment orientation had the best outcomes.

In the Australian treatment outcome study (ATOS), 657 drug abusers from residential therapeutic communities, methadone/buprenorphine maintenance programmes, detoxification programmes, and an untreated control group were followed up after a year (Teesson *et al.*, 2006). Over half of participants in all three treatment programmes were heroin abstinent compared with a quarter of those in the untreated control group. There were also significant reductions in criminality, psychopathology, and injection-related health problems in all three treatment groups. Greatest improvement occurred in those who spent longer in treatment, and who had fewer treatment interruptions.

In a Danish national multisite study of residential treatment for drug abusers, Pedersen and Hesse (2007) found that therapeutic communities retained clients with complex problems in treatment for longer and had better outcomes than residential programmes based on 12-step principles or non-specific therapeutic models.

This review suggests that, for chronic drug abusers, treatment in therapeutic communities can reduce illicit drug abuse and drug-related problems. The effectiveness of such programmes is associated with treatment duration, stability, and coherence. Principles for clinical practice in therapeutic communities are described in *The Therapeutic Community: Theory, Model, and Method* (De Leon, 2000).

Vocational rehabilitation for drug abuse in adults

Narrative reviews by Magura *et al.* (2004) and Platt (1995) conclude that vocational rehabilitation and other vocational services for substance users are associated with improvements in drug abuse and drug-related adjustment problems.

Treatments for stimulant abuse in adults

In a systematic review of 53 trials of psychological interventions for stimulant dependence, Shearer (2006) concluded that there is some evidence for the effectiveness of motivational enhancement therapy, community reinforcement, and contingency management in the treatment of cocaine and amphetamine dependence. (Meta-analyses of studies of motivational enhancement therapy, community reinforcement, and contingency management have been reviewed above in the section on alcohol abuse, and will not be covered again here.) Shearer (2006) also concluded that for the treatment of stimulant abuse there was limited or mixed evidence for the effectiveness of routine psychotherapy, cognitive behavioural therapy, cue exposure, or 12-step programmes.

Because of their scale, two large North American multisite trials of psychological interventions for stimulant dependence deserve special mention.

These are the National Institute of Drug Abuse Collaborative Cocaine Treatment Study (Crits-Christoph *et al.*, 1999) and the Centre for Substance Abuse Treatment, Methamphetamine Treatment Project (Rawson *et al.*, 2004). In the National Institute on Drug Abuse Collaborative Cocaine Treatment Study which involved 487 cocaine-dependent clients, Crits-Christoph *et al.* (1999) compared group drug counselling alone with individual drug counselling, cognitive behavioural therapy, and supportive-expressive psychodynamic therapy, each of which was combined with group drug counselling. Weekly treatment spanned six months, with less frequent sessions occurring over a further three months. The highest rates of abstinence and largest reduction in drug abuse a year after starting treatment were achieved by clients who engaged in combined individual and group drug counselling. Greatest retention in therapy was achieved by clients who engaged in cognitive behavioural therapy or supportive-expressive psychodynamic therapy. Similar outcomes occurred for all four treatments on measures of psychiatric symptoms, employment, medical, legal, family, social, interpersonal, or alcohol use problems (Crits-Christoph *et al.*, 2001). This trial underlines the unique effectiveness of a highly specific approach to drug counselling which is described in the treatment manual *Individual Drug Counselling* (Mercer & Woody, 1999).

In the Centre for Substance Abuse Treatment, Methamphetamine Treatment Project, which involved 978 methamphetamine-dependent clients at eight sites, Rawson *et al.* (2004) compared the effectiveness of the four-month Matrix Intensive Outpatient Program with treatment as usual. While both programmes led to similar significant improvements in drug abuse and adjustment at six months follow-up, clients who participated in the Matrix programme showed less drug abuse and higher abstinence rates during treatment, and greater retention in treatment. The programme is described in the *Matrix Intensive Outpatient Program Therapist Manual* (Rawson *et al.*, 1995). It involves intensive outpatient care three times a week for 16 weeks and includes regular urine testing, recovery and relapse prevention skills training, membership of a support group, family education, and involvement in 12-step self-help meetings.

From the foregoing review, it is clear that psychological interventions have an important role to play in the treatment of stimulant dependence. In contrast, there is little evidence for the effectiveness of pharmacological interventions in this area. In a systematic review of 45 randomized controlled trials of pharmacological treatments, De Lima *et al.* (2002) found no evidence supporting the efficacy of antidepressants, carbamazepine, dopamine agonists, disulfiram, mazindol, phenytoin, nimodipine, or lithium in the treatment of cocaine dependence.

Treatments for opiate abuse in adults

Medication has been used in the initial short-term detoxification of people with opioid dependence, and for long-term maintenance therapy. Systematic reviews have shown that detoxification with tapering doses of methadone (Amato *et al.*, 2002), buprenorphine (Gowing *et al.*, 2000), and alpha2 adrenergic agonists (Gowing *et al.*, 2001) significantly reduces withdrawal symptoms from heroin compared with placebos. However, without psychological intervention to maintain abstinence, most clients relapse.

For chronic heroin and opiate addiction, agonist-maintenance programmes are a widely used treatment. They are particularly appropriate where clients view the prospect of detoxification (and potential withdrawal symptoms) as too distressing. Agonist-maintanance programmes prevent withdrawal symptoms, reduce health risks (such as HIV or hepatitis infection), reduce time-consuming and dangerous illicit drug-seeking behaviour, and offer an opportunity to make lifestyle changes, which may be facilitated by psychological interventions. Currently, methadone, buprenorphine, and levo-acetylmethadol (LAAM) are the principal medications used in agonist-maintenance programmes (O'Brien & McKay, 2007).

In a synthesis of five meta-analyses of maintenance treatments for opioid dependence involving 52 studies and 12,075 participants, Amato *et al.* (2005) compared high and low dose methadone maintenance treatment with methadone detoxification treatment, and buprenorphine, heroin, and LAAM maintenance treatments. They concluded that high dose methadone maintenance, of at least 60 mg per day, was the most effective treatment for retaining clients in treatment and suppressing heroin use. Similar conclusions were reached by Farre *et al.* (2002) in a meta-analysis of 13 randomized controlled trials involving 1944 participants.

In a meta-analysis of 12 trials involving 981 heroin-dependent clients, Amato *et al.* (2004) found that adding any psychological intervention to methadone maintenance significantly reduced heroin abuse during treatment. A heterogeneous group of interventions was used in the 12 studies in this review. Treatments were drawn largely from the cognitive behavioural and psychodynamic traditions.

Psychotherapy factors associated with positive outcome for drug and alcohol abuse in adults

Characteristics of clients and therapists, features of the therapeutic alliance, and particular therapeutic techniques and processes have been shown in extensive narrative reviews of empirical studies to have an impact on the effectiveness of therapy for people with drug and alcohol problems (Haaga *et al.*, 2006; Lebow *et al.*, 2006; McCrady *et al.*, 2006; McCrady & Nathan, 2006).

Client and therapist characteristics

In extensive narrative reviews, Haaga *et al.* (2006) and McCrady *et al.* (2006) concluded that risk factors for poor outcome in the treatment of alcohol and drug abuse include chronic, severe, polydrug abuse, and co-morbid psychological problems or antisocial personality disorder. They also concluded that good outcome is associated with being employed, readiness to change, and high self-efficacy for maintaining abstinence. Finally, they concluded that therapists with and without personal histories of alcohol and drug abuse are equally effective in treating substance use disorders; and that mental health or addiction specialists are more effective than primary care workers.

Therapeutic alliance

In an extensive narrative review, Lebow *et al.* (2006) concluded that a strong therapeutic alliance characterized by empathy, congruence and positive regard, and supportive group programmes which foster cohesiveness help clients engage and remain in treatment, and are associated with reductions in drug and alcohol use during and after treatment. The availability of social support from non-drug-using family members, peers, and sponsors is associated with better outcome. The involvement of family members, supportive peers, or sponsors in therapy and relapse prevention can help clients engage and remain in treatment, reduce drug and alcohol abuse, and reduce relapse rate.

Therapeutic techniques

In extensive narrative reviews, McCrady and Nathan (2006) and McCrady *et al.* (2006) concluded that effective treatment for drug and alcohol abuse is based on a formulation which takes account of personal and contextual factors associated with clients' drug and alcohol abuse; is structured and problem focused; includes individual, group, and family interventions as appropriate to address specific therapy tasks; includes intensive time-limited initial intervention and less intensive long-term relapse prevention arrangements; matches the intensity of treatment to client needs; and provides clients with access to services for treating their co-morbid psychological and medical problems.

Practice implications for alcohol and drug abuse in adults

To engage clients with alcohol and drug problems in therapy, the community reinforcement and family training approach may be used with clients' families, if clients themselves are reluctant to contact services, and where clients do contact services themselves, motivational enhancement therapy is an appropriate first intervention. For clients who have become physiologically dependent on alcohol or opiates, detoxification may be necessary. For alcohol problems, brief outpatient interventions may be as effective in some cases as more intensive inpatient interventions. However, for chronic drug abuse, interventions that retain clients in treatment for longer are more effective. Also, for more chronic heroin abusers, residential therapeutic community treatment may be appropriate. For clients with both drug and alcohol problems, following detoxification clients may be helped to develop skills for coping with situations where they are at risk of alcohol or substance abuse through cognitive behavioural skills training. Clients may be motivated to use these skills and supported in doing so through their spouses' or families' involvement in behavioural couples therapy or the community reinforcement approach.

For stimulant dependence, contingency management programmes involving financial incentives for clear urine tests may be used to motivate clients to remain drug free and to remain in therapy. In some instances, for alcohol problems, controlled drinking interventions such as self-control training or cue exposure may be considered, where controlled drinking rather than abstinence is the client's preferred treatment goal. Twelve-step facilitation may be used to help clients engage with Alcoholics Anonymous (AA) and other 12-step self-help groups. These psychosocial interventions may be offered in conjunction with pharmacological interventions. For alcohol abuse, medications which reduce craving (naltrexone and acamprosate) or induce illness if alcohol is taken (disulfiram) may be considered. For heroin addiction, replacement drugs such as methadone may be appropriate. Interventions designed to educate, confront, shock, or foster insight regarding the nature and causes of substance use problems are ineffective and should not be used. The centrality of psychological interventions to the effective treatment of drug and alcohol problems is consistent with international best practice guidelines (American Psychiatric Association, 2006b; Lingford-Hughes *et al.*, 2004; NICE, 2007b).

Smoking cessation in adults

There is evidence for the effectiveness of psychological interventions and pharmacotherapy in the treatment of nicotine addiction and the promotion of smoking cessation.

Psychological interventions for smoking cessation in adults

Results of meta-analyses reviewed below show that individual, group, and telephone-based counselling are effective in promoting smoking cessation, with individual and group counselling being more effective than telephone-based counselling. The impact of counselling is enhanced if it is combined with pharmacological interventions. In a systematic review of 21 studies involving over 7000 participants, Lancaster and Stead (2005) found that individual counselling was more effective than self-help or minimal interventions for smoking cessation. They obtained an odds ratio equivalent to an effect size of .25 which approximates a success rate of 55%. In a systematic review of 55 trials involving over 5000 participants, Stead and Lancaster (2005) concluded that group counselling for smoking cessation was more effective than self-help or minimal interventions. They obtained an odds ratio equivalent to an effect size of .39 which approximates a success rate of 60%. There was no evidence that group therapy was more effective than individual counselling. In a systematic review of 48 trials of telephone counselling for smoking cessation involving over 35,000 participants, Stead *et al.* (2006) concluded that smokers who received multiple sessions of call-back counselling fared better than those who received fewer telephone sessions, engaged in self-help only, or who received pharmacological therapy only. The odds ratio obtained for counselling initiated by a call to a helpline was equivalent to an effect size of .19 and approximated a success rate of 55%. Telephone counselling not initiated by calls to helplines also increased smoking cessation rates, and an odds ratio equivalent to an effect size of .16 was obtained which approximates a success rate of 54%. In a meta-analysis of nine studies, Park *et al.* (2004) found that interventions which enhanced support of cohabiting partners for smoking cessation (and reduced criticism) increased rates of smoking cessation. In a meta-analysis, Mojica *et al.* (2004) found that smoking cessation counselling by psychologists, physicians, and nurses were all equally effective, but multimodal programmes involving nicotine replacement therapy and counselling were almost twice as effective as counselling alone. In a systematic review to identify best practices, Manske *et al.* (2004) concluded that effective smoking cessation programmes involved four or more sessions of 60 to 90 minutes duration, and included providing information about smoking, multicomponent cognitive behavioural therapy, self-monitoring, and obtaining social support from family or peers. In these effective protocols, multicomponent cognitive behavioural therapy includes becoming motivated to stop smoking by considering risks of continued smoking, setting a quit date, getting ready to quit, preparing for relapse management, managing withdrawal, and managing potential weight gain (Cofta-Woerpel *et al.*, 2007; Irvin Vidrine *et al.*, 2006; Perkins *et al.*, 2007).

Pharmacological interventions for smoking cessation in adults

In a systematic review of meta-analyses of pharmacotherapy for smoking cessation, Aveyard and West (2007) concluded that nicotine replacement therapy (with patch, gum, lozenge, inhaler, or nasal spray), the antidepressant bupropion, and varenicline, a partial agonist acting on nicotinic receptors, are reasonable first line interventions, with nortriptyline being an appropriate second line intervention. In a meta-analysis of pharmacological interventions for smoking cessation, Wu *et al.* (2006) found that varenicline was superior to bupropion, which in turn was superior to nicotine replacement therapy in facilitating smoking cessation.

Ineffective interventions for smoking cessation

While individual, group and telephone counselling, and varenicline, bupropion, and nicotine replacement therapy, are effective in facilitating smoking cessation, evidence for the effectiveness of a number of other approaches is inconclusive. Systematic reviews of 40 studies of skills-based relapse prevention interventions to help abstinent smokers cope with situations where there is a high risk of relapse (Hajek *et al.*, 2005), 14 studies of hypnotherapy (Abbot *et al.*, 1998), and 24 studies of acupuncture (White *et al.*, 1997) found no evidence for their effectiveness in facilitating smoking cessation. These conclusions are consistent with those of other previous systematic reviews and meta-analyses (Cofta-Woerpel *et al.*, 2006, 2007; Irvin Vidrine *et al.*, 2006; Lancaster *et al.*, 2000).

Practice implications for smoking cessation in adults

Multimodal programmes which combine psychological and pharmacological interventions are particularly effective for smoking cessation. Individual, group, and telephone-based counselling may be combined with varenicline, bupropion, and nicotine replacement therapy, depending upon clients' needs and preferences. An evidence-based approach to practice in this area is given in *The Tobacco Dependence Treatment Handbook: A Guide to Best Practices* (Abrams *et al.*, 2003). These conclusions are consistent with those of international guidelines (American Psychiatric Association, 2006b; Fiore *et al.*, 2000; Lingford-Hughes *et al.*, 2004; NICE, 2002a).

Compulsive gambling in adults

In a meta-analysis of 22 studies of cognitive behavioural therapy for compulsive gambling involving 1434 participants, Pallesen *et al.* (2005) found very large effect sizes of 2.01 after treatment and 1.59 at 17 months follow-up. These effect sizes are equivalent to approximate success rates of 85% and 81%. In a narrative review of 11 studies, Toneatto and Ladouceur (2003) found that cognitive behavioural treatments of problem gambling were particularly effective. In a meta-analysis of 16 studies of pharmacotherapy for pathological gambling, Pallesen *et al.* (2007) found an effect size of .78 after treatment. Similar outcomes occurred for antidepressants, opiate antagonists, and mood stabilizers, which were the three main classes of pharmacotherapy evaluated in studies included in Pallesen and colleagues' meta-analysis. The post-treatment effect size for pharmacotherapy was large by psychotherapy standards, and approximated a success rate of 68%, but was considerably smaller than that for cognitive behavioural therapy cited above.

Practice implications for compulsive gambling in adults

Cognitive behavioural therapy is the treatment of choice for problem gambling. This involves addressing erroneous beliefs about gambling, problem-solving skills training, and trigger recognition and avoidance. A description of this approach is given in *Overcoming Pathological Gambling: Therapist Guide* (Ladouceur & Lachance, 2006).

Schizophrenia in adults

Schizophrenia is currently conceptualized as a recurrent episodic psychotic disorder characterized by positive and negative symptoms and disorganization (American Psychiatric Association, 2000a; World Health Organization, 1992). Delusions and hallucinations are the main positive symptoms of schizophrenia. Negative symptoms include poverty of speech, flat affect, and passivity. While genetic and neurodevelopmental factors associated with prenatal and perinatal adversity play a central role in the aetiology of schizophrenia, its course is affected by exposure to intrafamilial and extrafamilial stress, individual and family coping strategies, and medication adherence (Kuipers *et al.*, 2006; Walker *et al.*, 2004). The primary treatment for schizophrenia is pharmacological. It involves the initial treatment of acute psychotic episodes, and the subsequent prevention of further episodes with antipsychotic medication which targets the dopamine system – a system which is thought to be dysregulated in people with schizophrenia (Sharif *et al.*, 2007). A distinction is made between older typical antipsychotic medications, such as chlorpromazine, which mainly alleviate positive symptoms, and newer atypical antipsychotic drugs, such as clozapine, which are now the treatments of choice because they have fewer side effects than typical antipsychotics and alleviate negative as well as positive symptoms. The primary aim of adjunctive psychological interventions in schizophrenia is to reduce relapse and rehospitalization rates and improve psychological functioning and quality of life.

In a large meta-analysis of 106 studies of interventions for schizophrenia, Mojtabai *et al.* (1998) found that, compared with medication alone, multi-modal programmes which included both psychological and pharmacological interventions yielded an effect size of .39, which is approximately equivalent to a comparative success rate of 60%. They also found that, after an average of 17 months, the relapse rate for service users with schizophrenia who received psychological therapy plus medication was 20% lower than that of those who received medication only. The relapse rate for medication only was 52% and that for medication combined with psychotherapy was 32%.

Pfammatter *et al.* (2006) conducted an extensive review of 21 meta-analyses of psychological therapies for schizophrenia, and conducted further meta-analyses of the most methodologically robust randomized controlled trials for four distinct types of psychological interventions: psychoeducational family therapy, cognitive behavioural therapy, social skills training, and cognitive rehabilitation. They found that each of the four classes of interventions had a positive impact on specific aspects of adjustment. What follows is a summary of key findings from Pfammatter *et al.*'s (2006) review.

Psychoeducational family therapy for schizophrenia in adults

About half of medicated clients with schizophrenia relapse, and relapse rates are higher in unsupportive or stressful family environments, characterized by high levels of criticism, hostility, or overinvolvement (Kuipers, 2006). The aim of psychoeducational family therapy is to reduce family stress and enhance family support so as to delay or prevent relapse and rehospitalization. In their review of three meta-analyses of psychoeducational family therapy (Pharoah *et al.*, 2006; Pilling *et al.*, 2002a; Pitschel-Walz *et al.*, 2001) and a new meta-analysis of 31 randomized controlled trials involving over 3500 clients, Pfammatter *et al.* (2006) found that, compared with medication alone, a multimodal programme including psychoeducational family therapy and medication led to lower relapse and rehospitalization rates, and improved medication adherence. One to two years after treatment, the average effect sizes across these four meta-analyses for relapse and rehospitalization rates were .32 and .48 which are equivalent to approximate success rates of 57% and 61%. The effect size for medication adherence was .30 which is equivalent to an approximate success rate of 57%. In a review of 18 studies containing over 1400 cases, the authors of the UK NICE guidelines for schizophrenia concluded that, to be effective, psychoeducational family therapy must span at least six months and include at least ten sessions (NICE, 2003). In a meta-analysis of 18 studies, Lincon *et al.* (2007) concluded that psychoeducation directed at service users without family involvement has no significant impact on relapse rate or adherence,

Psychoeducational family therapy may take a number of formats including therapy sessions with single families; therapy sessions with multiple families; group therapy sessions for relatives; or parallel group therapy sessions for relative and patient groups. Therapy involves psychoeducation based on the stress vulnerability or biopsychosocial models of schizophrenia with a view to helping families understand and manage the condition, the medication, related stresses, and early warning signs of relapse. Psychoeducational family therapy also helps families develop communication and problem-solving skills. Useful treatment manuals for this approach include *Family Work for Schizophrenia* (Kuipers *et al.*, 2002), *Managing Stress in Families* (Falloon *et al.*, 1993), and *Multifamily Groups in the Treatment of Severe Psychiatric Disorders* (McFarlane, 2004).

Cognitive behavioural therapy for schizophrenia in adults

Positive symptoms, notably delusions and hallucinations, persist for about a quarter to a half of medicated service users with schizophrenia (Fowler *et al.*, 1995). The aim of cognitive behavioural therapy is to help service users manage these residual positive symptoms. In their review of four meta-analyses of cognitive behavioural therapy (Gould *et al.*, 2001; Rector & Beck, 2001; Tarrier, 2005; Tarrier & Wykes, 2004; Zimmermann *et al.*, 2005) and a new meta-analysis of 17 randomized controlled trials involving over 480 clients, Pfammatter *et al.* (2006) found that, compared with medication alone, a multimodal programme including cognitive behavioural therapy and medication led to a significant reduction in positive symptoms in clients with schizophrenia. For positive symptoms, the average effect sizes across these five meta-analyses were .54 after treatment and .64 at follow-up. These effect sizes are equivalent to approximate success rates of 62% and 65%.

Cognitive behavioural therapy may be offered on an individual or group basis. It involves a collaborative therapeutic alliance within which service users develop self-monitoring and stress management skills. They are also helped to develop strategies for managing positive symptoms, particularly re-evaluating problematic perceptions and beliefs associated with delusions and hallucinations. Useful treatment manuals for this approach include *Cognitive Therapy for Delusions, Voices and Paranoia* (Chadwick *et al.*, 1996) and *Cognitive Therapy of Schizophrenia* (Kingdon & Turkington, 2005).

Social skills training for schizophrenia in adults

People with schizophrenia typically show deficits in social competence, which in turn render them vulnerable to engaging in stressful social interactions, and to social isolation (Walker *et al.*, 2004). The aim of social skills training is to enhance social competence, and so prevent social isolation or inter-personal stress. In their review of two meta-analyses of social skills training (Benton & Schroeder, 1990; Corrigan, 1991) and a new meta-analysis of 19 randomized controlled trials involving over 680 clients, Pfammatter *et al.* (2006) found that, compared with medication alone, a multimodal pro-gramme including social skills training and medication led to significant improvements in social skills in service users with schizophrenia. For social skills, the average effect sizes across these four meta-analyses was .99 after treatment and 1.02 at follow-up. These effect sizes are equivalent to an approximate success rate of 72%. In contrast to these positive effects on the acquisition of social skills, Pilling *et al.* (2002b) in a meta-analysis of nine randomized controlled trials found that social skills training had no significant impact on relapse rates, global adjustment, or quality of life.

Social skills training is usually offered within a group therapy context, and involves the development of communication, conversation, assertiveness, medication management, and social problem-solving skills. Modelling, rehearsal, shaping, and reinforcement are used during the training process. Useful treatment manuals for this approach include *Social Skills Training for Schizophrenia: A Step-by-Step Guide* (Bellack *et al.*, 2004) and *Social Skills Training for Psychiatric Patients* (Liberman *et al.*, 1989).

Cognitive remediation for schizophrenia in adults

Cognitive impairment is common in schizophrenia and may involve deficits in executive functioning, social cognition, attention, and memory (Kurtz & Nichols, 2007). These deficits compromise the capacity of clients to benefit from other psychological interventions and rehabilitation programmes. The aim of cognitive remediation is to improve cognitive functioning and help clients develop strategies to compensate for their cognitive deficits. In their review of four meta-analyses of social skills training (Krabbendam & Aleman, 2003; Kurtz *et al.*, 2001; Pilling *et al.*, 2002b; Twamley *et al.*, 2003) and a new meta-analysis of 19 randomized controlled trials involving over 700 clients, Pfammatter *et al.* (2006) found that compared with medication alone, a multimodal programme including cognitive remediation training and medication led to significant improvements in cognitive functioning for service users with schizophrenia. Across a range of measures of cognitive functioning including general cognitive functioning, social cognition, executive functioning, attention, general memory, visual memory, and verbal memory, the average effect size from these five meta-analyses was .37. This is equivalent to an approximate success rate of 59%. However, not all meta-analyses found significant effects (e.g. Pilling *et al.*, 2002b).

Cognitive remediation is a highly structured set of interventions which involves service users engaging in repetitive paper and pencil or computerized exercises which help them improve their attention, memory, executive functioning, or social cognition. A useful treatment manual is *Cognitive Remediation Therapy for Schizophrenia: Theory and Practice* (Wykes & Reeder, 2005).

Brenner *et al.*'s (1994) *Integrated Psychological Therapy for Schizophrenic Patients* describes a programme that combines preliminary cognitive remediation with later social skills training in a staged group training model. In a meta-analysis of 21 studies involving over 900 service users with schizophrenia, Roder *et al.* (2006) found that typical treatment involved an average of 44 sessions over 17 weeks, at a rate of about three sessions per week. In comparing integrated psychological therapy with control conditions on overall functioning, Roder *et al.* (2006) found weighted effect sizes of .36 after treatment and .45 at eight months follow-up, These effect sizes are approximately equivalent to success rates of 58% and 61%. In specific domains, the post-treatment effect sizes were .41 for cognitive functioning and .31 for social functioning, which shows the cognitive remediation and social skills components of the programme had desired effects in the domains they targeted.

Promoting medication adherence in schizophrenia in adults

Relapse in schizophrenia is often associated with non-adherence to medication regimes. A variety of interventions have been developed to address this problem. In a systematic review of 39 studies, Zygmunt *et al.* (2002) found that only 13 of the interventions evaluated significantly improved adherence. Effective interventions specifically targeted adherence; offered motivational interviewing to address service users' ambivalence about taking medication; provided service users with behavioural problem-solving skills training to address difficulties in taking medication; and involved family members in promoting adherence. Broad-based programmes and programmes that involved service user psychoeducation only, but which did not include service users' families, were ineffective.

Vocational rehabilitation for schizophrenia in adults

Unemployment is a highly prevalent problem in schizophrenia, which vocational interventions aim to address (Cook & Razzano, 2005). In a systematic review of 11 randomized controlled trials of vocational rehabilitation for people with severe psychological disorders, Twamley *et al.* (2003) found that individual placement and support and supported employment were both effective in promoting engagement in work. The weighted mean effect size for days at work was .66, which is approximately equivalent to a success rate of 65%. In the five studies that compared individual placement and support or supported employment with conventional vocational rehabilitation services, 51% of the service users in individual placement and support or supported employment worked competitively compared with 18% of those in the comparison groups. The weighted mean effect size was .79. In a review of four studies of the conversion of day treatment to supported employment, and nine randomized controlled trials comparing supported employment to alternative approaches, Bond (2004) found that between 40% and 60% of service users in supported employment obtained competitive employment compared with less than 20% of controls. Employed service users showed improved self-esteem and better symptom control. Effective vocational rehabilitation involves assessment, rapid placement in competitive employment (rather than a sheltered workshop), and the provision of individualized vocational support and training while service users are in employment rather than beforehand (Cook & Razzano, 2005).

Assertive community treatment of schizophrenia in adults

People with chronic relapsing schizophrenia have difficulty maintaining contact with community services, and so may either become disconnected from such services or become chronically hospitalized. With assertive community treatment, service users receive intensive, continuous individualized treatment, rehabilitation, and support services from a community-based multidisciplinary team in which team members carry small caseloads (Allness & Knoedler, 1998; Burns & Fim, 2002). In a meta-analysis of six randomized controlled trials, Coldwell and Bender (2007) found that assertive community treatment led to a 37% reduction in homelessness and a 26% improvement in psychiatric symptom severity compared with standard case management. In a systematic review of 25 randomized controlled trials, Bond *et al.* (2001) concluded that assertive community treatment substantially reduces psychiatric hospital use, increases housing stability, and moderately improves symptoms and subjective quality of life. It is highly successful in engaging service users in treatment. Bond *et al.* (2001) found that the more closely case management programmes followed assertive community treatment principles, the better the outcomes. While assertive community treatment services are costly, these costs are offset by a reduction in hospital use by service users with a history of extensive hospital use. In a meta-analysis of 44 studies involving over 6000 service users, Ziguras and Stuart (2000) found that assertive community treatment was more effective than treatment as usual in reducing care costs and family burden, and in improving family satisfaction with services.

Practice implications for schizophrenia in adults

Clients with schizophrenia should be offered multimodal treatment programmes which integrate pharmacological and psychological interventions. Pharmacological interventions include initial treatment of acute psychotic episodes, and later maintenance therapy with atypical antipsychotic medication. Psychological interventions include psychoeducational family therapy to promote family support, medication adherence, and prevent relapse; cognitive behavioural therapy to help clients manage residual positive symptoms; social skills training to enhance social competence and reduce social isolation; cognitive rehabilitation to help clients overcome or compensate for cognitive deficits; and individual placement and support or supported employment to promote vocational adjustment. Where service users have difficulty retaining contact with routine outpatient services, treatment should be offered by an assertive community treatment team. These conclusions are broadly consistent with international guidelines for best practice (American Psychiatric Association, 2004b; Lehman *et al.*, 2004; McEvoy *et al.*, 1999; NICE, 2003).

Personality disorders in adults

Personality disorders are enduring, inflexible, and pervasive patterns of experience and behaviour that deviate markedly from cultural norms and cause significant distress or impairment in functioning (American Psychiatric Association, 2000a; World Health Organization, 1992). For a *DSM* diagnosis of personality disorder, significant difficulties must occur in at least two of the following areas: cognition, affectivity, impulsivity, and interpersonal functioning. In *DSM-IV-TR* (American Psychiatric Association, 2000a) ten specific personality disorders are classified into three clusters. The first cluster, characterized by odd or eccentric behaviour, includes the paranoid, schizoid, and schizotypal personality disorders. The second cluster, characterized by dramatic behaviour, includes the antisocial, borderline, histrionic, and narcissistic personality disorders. The third cluster includes the avoidant, dependent, and obsessive-compulsive personality disorders all of which are characterized by anxiety and fearfulness. In *ICD-10* (WHO, 1992) personality disorders are conceptualized in the same way as in *DSM*, but schizotypal syndrome is listed as a psychotic condition and narcissistic personality disorder is omitted.

Psychodynamic and cognitive behavioural therapy for personality disorders in adults

In a meta-analysis of 15 studies of psychotherapy for personality disorders, Perry *et al.* (1999) found pre–post-treatment unweighted effect sizes of 1.1 for self-report measures and 1.3 for observer ratings. These large pre–post effect sizes suggest that on average clients made large gains over the course of treatment. In the three studies that included control groups, a between group effect size of .8 occurred, which is approximately equivalent to a 69% success rate. In the four studies where data were available, 52% of cases were assessed as recovered after 1.3 years of treatment. Most types of personality disorders were included in the studies, with few trials using homogeneous groups with a single personality disorder. Treatments were predominantly psychodynamic or cognitive behavioural and involved an average of 54 sessions over 35 weeks.

In a later meta-analysis of 14 studies of psychodynamic psychotherapy and 11 studies of cognitive behavioural psychotherapy, Leichsenring and Leibing (2003) found pre–post-treatment unweighted effect sizes of 1.46 for psychodynamic psychotherapy and 1.00 for cognitive behavioural therapy. These large pre–post effect sizes suggest that on average clients made large gains over the course of treatment. Eleven studies included comparison groups. Most types of personality disorders were included in the studies, with few trials using homogeneous groups with a single personality disorder, although there was a predominance of borderline personality disorders across all studies. For psychodynamic therapy the average duration of treatment was 23 sessions over 37 weeks, and for cognitive behavioural therapy it was 13 sessions over 16 weeks. For psychodynamic therapy, longer treatment was associated with better outcome.

Borderline personality disorder in adults

There is evidence from controlled trials for the effectiveness of dialectical behavioural therapy, cognitive behaviour therapy, and a psychodynamic partial hospitalization programme in the treatment of borderline personality disorder.

Dialectical behaviour therapy for borderline personality disorder

In a review of seven randomized controlled trials and six non-randomized trials of dialectical behaviour therapy for borderline personality disorder, Lieb *et al.* (2004) concluded that it led to significant reductions in the frequency of deliberate self-harm, rehospitalization, attendance at accident and emergency departments, drug abuse, and psychological adjustment. These conclusions are consistent with those of other reviews (Martens, 2005; Robins & Chapman, 2004). Dialectical behaviour therapy is described in Linehan's (1993a, 1993b) *Cognitive-Behavioural Treatment of Borderline Personality Disorder* and *Skills Training Manual for Treating Borderline Personality Disorder*. Dialectical behaviour therapy is based on the assumption that people with borderline personality disorder lack well-developed interpersonal, self-regulation, and distress tolerance skills, and that personal and contextual factors inhibit the use of such skills or reinforce dysfunctional behaviour. Dialectical behaviour therapy is a comprehensive treatment programme which includes group-based skills training, detailed behavioural assessment of problem behaviours, individual cognitive behavioural therapy, telephone contact, co-ordination of the treatment network, and intensive supervision for therapists. Group-based skills training enhances interpersonal, self-regulation, and distress tolerance skills. Individual behavioural assessment and therapy focuses on the use of change-directed techniques (such as problem solving) and acceptance techniques (such as validation) to achieve personal goals. Telephone contact and treatment network co-ordination reinforce clients' use of new skills on a daily basis.

Cognitive behavioural therapy for borderline personality disorder

In a UK-based randomized controlled trial, Davidson *et al.* (2006) found that cases with borderline personality disorder fared better after 16 sessions of cognitive behavioural therapy over a period of a year than those who received treatment as usual. Two years after commencing treatment, compared with the control group, those who received cognitive behavioural therapy had fewer negative outcomes (suicidal acts, rehospitalization, or accident and emergency contact). The approach used is described in Davidson's (2000) *Cognitive Therapy for Personality Disorders: A Guide for Clinicians*. Treatment is guided by individualized case formulations, and includes both cognitive restructuring and behavioural techniques.

Psychodynamic therapy for borderline personality disorder

Bateman and Fonagy (1999, 2001) found that an 18-month psychodynamic partial hospitalization programme for borderline personality disorder led to fewer days in hospital and improvements in depressive symptoms, self-harm, and interpersonal functioning. Gains occurred after six months of treatment and were maintained at 18 months follow-up. The programme is described in Bateman and Fonagy's (2004) *Mentalization-Based Treatment for Borderline Personality Disorder*. It includes group and individual psychodynamic psychotherapy which aims to increase the capacity for mentalization. Mentalization is the capacity to think about mental states of the self and others as separate from yet potentially causing actions.

Cluster C personality disorders in adults

There is evidence from three controlled trials for the effectiveness of both psychodynamic psychotherapy and cognitive behavioural therapy in the treatment of cluster C personality disorders.

Psychodynamic psychotherapy for cluster C personality disorders

In a randomized controlled trial involving 40 weekly therapy sessions for clients with cluster C personality disorders, Svartberg *et al.* (2004) found that two years after treatment 54% of the short-term dynamic psychotherapy patients and 42% of the cognitive therapy patients had recovered symptomatically. The psychodynamic therapy manual was McCullough-Vaillant's (1997) *Changing Character* and the cognitive therapy protocol was Beck and Freeman's (1990) *Cognitive Therapy of Personality Disorders*.

Cognitive behavioural therapy for cluster C personality disorders

Two controlled trials showed that cognitive behavioural therapy was particularly effective with avoidant personality disorder. Alden (1989) found that clients who participated in ten weeks of behavioural group therapy involving combinations of graded exposure, social skills training, and intimacy-focused social skills training showed significant improvement but not remission compared to untreated controls. In a randomized controlled trial in which treatment involved 20 sessions over six months, Emmelkamp *et al.* (2006) found that clients who received cognitive behavioural therapy showed significantly greater improvement than those who participated in brief dynamic psychotherapy, who in turn showed greater improvement than an untreated control group. At six months follow-up, 91% of the cognitive behavioural therapy group and 64% of the brief dynamic psychotherapy group no longer met the criteria for avoidant personality disorder. The cognitive behavioural protocol was based on Beck and Freeman's (1990) *Cognitive Therapy of Personality Disorders* and Emmelkamp *et al.*'s (1992) *Anxiety Disorders*. The psychodynamic protocol was based on Malan's (1995) *Individual Psychotherapy and the Science of Psychodynamics* and Luborsky's (1984) *Principles of Psychoanalytic Psychotherapy*.

Therapeutic communities for personality disorders in adults

Therapeutic communities for people with personality disorders may be run in prisons, hospitals, or day hospitals. In these communities there are usually daily meetings of service users and staff, and a predominance of group activities. The hallmark of therapeutic communities is their democratic, participative approach to decision making. This creates a context within which service users significantly influence the way their therapeutic communities are run. Complex participative community processes are the central therapeutic factors of therapeutic communities (Jones, 1952). In a systematic review of 52 outcome studies of the effects of therapeutic communities on people with personality disorders and a meta-analysis of 29 of these, Lees *et al.* (1999) found that a significant positive effect occurred in 19 of the 29 studies in their meta-analysis. Participants in these trials were young offenders or psychiatric service users with a range of personality disorders. In their narrative review, Lees *et al.* (1999) concluded that for people with personality disorder, long-term treatment in therapeutic communities may lead to improvements in mental health and interpersonal functioning, and that the longer a service user stays in treatment, the better the outcome. They also found that secure therapeutic communities were effective in managing difficult prisoners, and significantly reducing serious prison discipline incidents including fire setting, violence, self-harm, and absconding.

Psychotherapy factors and personality disorder in adults

Extensive narrative reviews show that specific client and therapist character-istics, therapeutic alliance factors, programme design factors, and therapeutic techniques are associated with a positive outcome in the treatment of person-ality disorders (Bateman & Fonagy, 2000; Fernandez-Alderez *et al.*, 2006; Linehan *et al.*, 2006; Smith *et al.*, 2006). What follows is a summary of key findings from these reviews.

Client and therapist characteristics

In an extensive narrative review, Fernandez-Alderez *et al.* (2006) concluded that certain client and therapist characteristics influence the outcome of psy-chotherapy with clients who have personality disorders. Positive outcomes are more probable where clients have the ability to engage in treatment and some history of positive relationships in their lives. Positive outcomes are more probable where therapists are patient, flexible, and creative in their approach to therapy; are comfortable with long-term, intense therapeutic relationships; are tolerant of their own negative feelings about patients and the therapy process; and have specific training in treating a specific personality disorder.

Therapeutic alliance

In an extensive narrative review, Smith *et al.* (2006) concluded that when working with clients who have personality disorders a positive outcome is associated with a good therapeutic alliance in individual therapy, and group cohesiveness within group therapy. Within such alliances, therapists take an active role in structuring treatment and indicating clearly what types of behaviours are unacceptable. They also make accurate relational interpret-ations that focus on clients' central interpersonal issues, and do so at a fre-quency that matches clients' readiness to assimilate them. Therapists create strong therapeutic alliances by using treatment manuals flexibly, fostering a sense of ease in their interactions with clients, focusing on clients' core issues in therapy sessions, and skilfully repairing ruptures in the therapeutic alliance by avoiding the expression of negative countertransference.

Programme design and therapeutic techniques

In extensive narrative reviews of the design and delivery of psychotherapy programmes for service users with personality disorders, Bateman and Fon-agy (2000) and Linehan *et al.* (2006) concluded that effective programmes share a number of common features. They are theoretically coherent (not eclectic), offering an explanation for problematic behaviours and interpersonal styles, and for the role of psychotherapy in offering a solution to these problems. They are well structured and of long duration, usually extending beyond a year. They include procedures for helping clients engage in treatment, maintain therapeutic contact, and adhere to therapeutic regimes. Effective psychotherapy programmes may include sequential or concurrent individual, group, and family sessions, following a pre-established coherent pattern. Effective outpatient psychotherapy programmes are offered within the context of broader multimodal, multidisciplinary services in which there are clear policies and practices for inpatient care, use of medication, and crisis management where high-risk behaviour including self-harming, aggression, or other crises occur. Effective programmes have a clear focus on key problem areas such as self-harm, aggression, and difficult interpersonal relationships. Effective therapeutic techniques strike a balance between a focus on acceptance of clients' constrains and limitations on the one hand, and a focus on behavioural change and developing less problematic ways of living on the other. Psychotherapists offering effective treatment programmes for personality disorders receive sustained intensive supervision, in which intense countertransference reactions elicited by psychotherapy with these clients are addressed.

Pharmacotherapy for personality disorders in adults

There is some evidence that pharmacotherapy may be helpful in managing certain specific symptoms associated with personality disorders. In a narrative review, Koenigsberg et al. (2007) concluded that antipsychotic medication may have a positive impact on psychotic-like symptoms in patients with schizotypal and borderline personality disorder; atypical antipsychotic medication (notably olazapine) and mood stabilizers reduce impulsivity and irritability in patients with borderline personality disorder; and antidepressants have a significant positive impact on mood and irritability in borderline personality disorder.

Practice implications for personality disorders in adults

For borderline personality disorder dialectical behaviour therapy is the treatment of choice. Cognitive behavioural therapy and psychodynamically oriented partial hospitalization are also effective treatments for borderline personality disorder. For other personality disorders, either psychodynamic or cognitive behavioural therapy of at least a year's duration, or therapeutic community-based treatment may be effective in a proportion of cases. Adjunctive psychopharmacological interventions for symptom management may be integrated into psychological treatment programmes for personality disorders. The central role of psychotherapy in the treatment of personality disorders is consistent with international guidelines for best practice (Alwin *et al.*, 2006; American Psychiatric Association, 2001; National Institute of Mental Health in England, 2003).

Anger and aggression in adults

Anger control, aggression, and violence constitute significant clinical problems. Three meta-analyses throw light on the effectiveness of psychological interventions for anger. In a meta-analysis of 50 trials of cognitive behavioural therapy involving 1640 cases, Beck and Fernandez (1998) found a weighted effect size of .7 for anger. This is equivalent to an approximate success rate of 67%. In a later meta-analysis of 57 studies of anger treatment programmes involving 1841 clients, DiGiuseppe and Tafrate (2003) found effect sizes of .71 for anger; 1.16 for aggression; and .83 for positive behaviours. These are equivalent to approximate success rates of 67%, 72%, and 69% respectively. DiGiuseppe and Tafrate (2003) also found that at four and a half months follow-up, treatment gains were maintained, as indexed by an average effect size of .59 which is equivalent to an approximate success rate of 64%. In these meta-analyses, studies of adults, adolescents, and children were included. Cognitive behavioural therapy, the principal intervention evaluated, involved cognitive interventions such as cognitive restructuring, and reappraisal of anger-provoking situations, and behavioural interventions such as relaxation training, problem solving, and conflict management skills training. Treatment was delivered in individual and group contexts. Del Vecchio and O'Leary (2004) conducted a meta-analytic review of 23 studies evaluating the treatment of anger in non-institutionalized adults. They found an effect size of .82 (equivalent to an approximate success rate of 69%) for programmes characterized predominantly by cognitive interventions; an effect size of .92 (equivalent to an approximate success rate of 71%) for programmes characterized predominantly by relaxation training; and an effect size of .68 (equivalent to an approximate success rate of 67%) for combined cognitive behavioural programmes. They also found that cognitive therapy was particularly effective for suppressed anger. In contrast, for clients in a current state of anger, relaxation training was found to be most effective.

Practice implications for treatment of anger in adults

Currently cognitive behavioural interventions are the treatment of choice for anger management problems in adults. A useful therapist manual is *Anger Management: The Complete Treatment Guidebook for Practitioners* (Kassinove & Tafrate, 2002).

Sexual offending in adults

Sexual offending includes a range of deviant sexual behaviours ranging from non-contact offences such as exposure, through contact offences such as masturbation, to oral, anal, and vaginal penetrative sex, and these offences may be perpetrated against juveniles or adults (Marshall *et al.*, 2006).

In a meta-analysis of 69 studies published in five languages involving 22,181 participants, Losel and Schmucker (2005) found that treated offenders showed six percentage points, or 37% less sexual recidivism than controls after an average follow-up period of about five years. The average rate of recidivism in treated groups was 11.1% and in control groups was 17.5%. The overall treatment effect size was .29 and falls within the typical range found in meta-analyses of offender treatment programmes (Marshall & McGuire, 2003). In about 70% of studies in this meta-analysis, participants had committed contact (rather than non-contact) offences, so the results concern quite severe and serious sexual offending.

Losel and Schmucker (2005) found that four categories of treatment led to significant reductions in recidivism. In rank order of effectiveness these were: surgical castration which was the most effective treatment; anti-androgen medication; behaviour therapy; and cognitive behavioural therapy. The odds ratio for surgical castration, based on eight studies, was 15.34, which is equivalent to an effect size of 1.5 and an approximate success rate of greater than 72%. The odds ratio for anti-androgen medication, based on six studies, was 3.08, which is equivalent to an effect size of .62 and an approximate success rate of 64%. The odds ratio for behaviour therapy, based on seven studies, was 2.19, which is equivalent to an effect size of .43 and an approximate success rate of 60%. The odds ratio for cognitive behavioural therapy based on 35 studies was 1.45, which is equivalent to an effect size of .21 and an approximate success rate of 55%. Insight-oriented programmes and therapeutic communities did not lead to significant effect sizes.

From the effect sizes of the four effective treatment types, it is clear that biological interventions have greater impact than psychological interventions. However, surgical castration is not widely practised for ethical reasons in most jurisdictions, and when it is, for example, in Germany, it occurs only with informed consent and the recommendation of an expert committee. The two main anti-androgen medications for treating sex offenders are medroxy-progesterone acetate (MDA or depo-Provera) which is mainly used in the USA and cyproterone acetate (CPA or Androcur) which is mainly used in Europe. They are typically administered as long-acting depo injections. Both greatly reduce sexual offending by reducing levels of sexual arousal. A proportion of offenders drop out of treatment due to side effects, which include headaches, cramps, blood clots, and weight gain. The effectiveness of anti-androgen medication ceases once it is withdrawn, so it is best practice to offer it as part of a multimodal programme involving cognitive behavioural intervention also (Maletzky, 2002).

Behavioural and cognitive behavioural programmes are the psychological interventions which have been shown significantly to reduce sex offenders' recidivism. Behavioural programmes use conditioning procedures which specifically aim to reduce sexual arousal to deviant sexual stimuli and increase sexual arousal to non-deviant sexual stimuli. Many involve aversive conditioning or covert sensitization where auditorally presented deviant sexual scenarios are paired with foul odours (such as ammonia or rotting tissue). Cognitive behavioural programmes may involve these techniques, but also incorporate a broad range of other interventions. These include helping sexual offenders accept responsibility for sexual offending and understanding personal and situational factors that increase the risk of offending; modifying justificatory cognitive distortions and developing victim empathy; developing social skills for forming intimate relationships; developing skills for coping with negative mood states; and forming a relapse prevention plan. Most effective programmes for sexual offending are structured and involved intensive group therapy over a period of about a year, and in some instances include adjunctive individual sessions and sessions with significant members of the offender's social network which are probably important for relapse prevention.

Specific contextual and process factors are associated with more effective treatment programmes for sex offenders. In their meta-analysis Losel and Schmucker (2005) found that voluntary outpatient programmes were more effective than prison-based mandatory treatment. In a review of factors that influence the effectiveness of sexual offender treatment, Harkins and Beech (2007) concluded that for group-based treatment more cohesive groups facilitated by therapists who showed warmth, empathy, and a rewarding, directive, yet non-confrontational style were associated with treatment gains.

Practice implications for the treatment of adult sex offenders

Currently, comprehensive cognitive behavioural programmes are the psychological treatment of choice for adult sex offenders. *Treating Sexual Offenders: An Integrated Approach* (Marshall *et al.*, 2006) is a useful evidence-based manual for sex offender treatment. While treatment can be effective for a proportion of sex offenders, it is only one element of effective overall management of sexual offenders and community protection. Monitoring and support by probation services, other correctional agencies, offenders' families, and offenders' social support systems are other key elements of a wider community protection strategy. These conclusions are broadly consistent with international best practice and policy guidelines (Association for the Treatment of Sexual Abusers, http://www.atsa.com/; National Organization for the Treatment of Abusers, http://www.nota.co.uk/).

Relationship problems in adulthood

Marital or relationship distress, psychosexual problems, and domestic violence constitute three important types of relationship problems for which psychological interventions have been shown to be effective.

Relationship distress in adulthood

In a systematic review of 20 meta-analyses of marital and family therapy, Shadish and Baldwin (2003) identified six meta-analyses of studies which evaluated the effectiveness of marital therapy. For these, the average effect size was .84, which is equivalent to an approximate success rate of 70%. The studies in these meta-analyses evaluated a range of different types of couples therapy including emotionally focused, behavioural, and insight-oriented approaches. However, most trials have been conducted with behavioural or emotionally focused approaches.

Emotionally focused vs. behavioural couples therapy

There is growing evidence that emotionally focused couples therapy may be more effective than behavioural couples therapy. In a meta-analysis of 23 studies of couples therapy for relationship distress, Wood et al. (2005) found that for mildly distressed couples, behavioural, emotionally focused, and other systemic approaches to couples therapy were equally effective. However, with moderately distressed couples, emotionally focused couples therapy was more effective than behavioural marital therapy. These conclusions are consistent with those of other meta-analyses (Johnson et al., 1999; Shadish & Baldwin, 2005; Wright et al., 2007). In a meta-analysis of four controlled trials, Johnson et al. (1999) obtained an effect size of 1.3 for emotionally focused couples therapy, which is equivalent to an approximate success rate of 75%. In comparison, Shadish and Baldwin (2005) found an effect size of .58 in a meta-analysis of 30 controlled trials of behavioural marital therapy, which is equivalent to an approximate success rate of 64%. In both of these meta-analyses weighted effect sizes were computed based on differences between post-therapy means of treatment and control groups. Wood et al. (2005) computed effect sizes based on differences between pre- and post-therapy mean scores, and found that the within group effect size for emotionally focused couples therapy, which was 1.37 (based on five trials), was significantly greater than that for behavioural marital therapy, which was 1.09 (based on 29 trials).

Emotionally focused couples therapy

This approach rests on the premise that an insecure attachment bond underpins relationship distress and related conflict. Partners are anxious that their attachment needs will not be met within their relationship, and this anxiety fuels chronic relationship conflict. The aim of emotionally focused couples therapy is to help partners understand this, and develop ways to meet each other's attachment needs, so they experience attachment security within their relationship. The manualized approach, which involves up to 20 sessions, is described in *The Practice of Emotionally Focused Couple Therapy: Creating Connection* (Johnson, 2004). The best predictors of a good outcome in emotionally focused couples therapy are the strength of the therapeutic alliance and the female partner's belief that her male partner still cares about her (Johnson *et al.*, 1999; Johnson, 2003). Emotionally focused couples therapy is effective for couples with low income and low educational levels, and is effective with young and old couples and couples with traditional and non-traditional values.

Behavioural couples therapy

This approach rests on the premise that an unfair relationship bargain underpins relationship distress and related conflict. Partners fail to negotiate a fair exchange of pleasing responses to each other, and this sense of injustice fuels chronic relationship conflict. The aim of behavioural marital therapy is to help partners develop communication and problem-solving skills and behavioural exchange procedures so they can negotiate a fairer relationship. Cognitive components have been added to this basic model to help couples challenge destructive beliefs and expectations which contribute to relationship distress and replace these with more benign alternatives. In a review of comparative studies, Byrne *et al.* (2004b) concluded that these cognitive innovations add little to the effectiveness of behavioural couples therapy. Integrative behavioural couples therapy, a recent refined version of behavioural marital therapy, includes a strong emphasis on building tolerance for partners' negative behaviours, acceptance of irresolvable differences, and empathic joining around such problems. A single trial has shown that this approach does not enhance the overall effectiveness of traditional behavioural marital therapy, but may lead to more rapid and sustained improvement in couples who stay together (Christensen *et al.*, 2006). Integrative behavioural couples therapy is described in *Acceptance and Change in Couple Therapy: A Therapist's Guide to Transforming Relationships* (Jacobson & Christensen, 1998). Jacobson and Addis (1993) have identified predictors of outcome in behavioural couples therapy. The best predictors of a successful outcome are initial levels of couple distress, with more distressed couples having a poorer outcome. Couples who benefit most from behavioural marital therapy are more emotionally engaged with each other and do not opt for premature closure in their attempts at relationship-based problem solving. Younger couples and couples with non-traditional values benefit most from behavioural marital therapy, which is less effective with older traditional couples who engage in distancer–pursuer interaction patterns.

Insight-oriented marital therapy

In a comparative trial, Snyder *et al.* (1991) found that four years after treatment only 3% of cases who had completed insight-oriented marital therapy were divorced compared with 38% of those in behavioural marital therapy, so insight-oriented marital therapy holds considerable promise as a particularly effective approach to couples therapy. Insight-oriented marital therapy rests on the premise that the inadvertent use of unconscious defences and relational patterns, which evolved within partners' families of origin or previous relationships, underpin relationship distress and conflict. The aim of therapy is to help partners understand how family-of-origin experiences or experiences in previous relationships compel them to inadvertently engage in destructive interaction patterns, and then to replace these with more constructive alternatives (Snyder & Schneider, 2002).

Cost-effectiveness of couples therapy

Caldwell *et al.* (2007) estimated that the free provision of emotionally focused and behavioural marital therapy would lead to considerable and significant cost savings for government, because it would prevent a range of legal and health care costs arising from divorce and divorce-related health problems.

Practice implications for relationship distress in adulthood

For moderate relationship distress, emotionally focused couples therapy is the treatment of choice. Behavioural couples therapy and insight-oriented couples therapy are second line alternatives.

Psychosexual problems in adulthood

The treatment of female hypoactive sexual desire, orgasmic disorder (the absence of orgasm during intercourse), dysparunia (painful intercourse), and vaginismus (involuntary spasm of the vagina when intercourse is attempted); and male erectile disorder (absence of erection when intercourse is attempted) and premature ejaculation will be considered in this section.

Hypoactive sexual desire

In a narrative review of trials of interventions for female hypoactive sexual desire, Duterte *et al.* (2007) concluded that 50–70% of cases made modest gains following cognitive behavioural therapy, but in some cases these gains were not sustained at long-term follow-up. They also concluded that there was some evidence from controlled trials and case series for the effectiveness of androgen therapies for hypoactive sexual desire, particularly in postmenopausal women. Masters and Johnson's (1970) sensate focus exercise is the main behavioural intervention included in effective cognitive behavioural programmes for hypoactive sexual desire. This begins with psychoeducation about the human sexual response. Couples are advised to refrain from sexual intercourse and sexual contact except as outlined in prescribed homework exercises. These involve giving and receiving pleasurable caresses along a graded sequence progressing over a number of weeks from non-sexual to increasingly sexual areas of the body, culminating in full intercourse. Cognitive interventions focus on challenging beliefs, attitudes, and expectations that diminish sexual desire and psychological intimacy.

Female orgasmic disorder

In a narrative review of 29 psychological treatment outcome studies for female orgasmic disorder, involving over 500 participants, Meston (2006) concluded that directed masturbation combined with sensate focus exercises were effective in most cases. The intervention involves a graded programme which begins with psychoeducation and is followed by a series of exercises that are practised over a number of weeks. These involve visual and tactile total body exploration; masturbation using sexual fantasy and imagery; optional use of a vibrator; masturbating to orgasm in the presence of one's partner; and later explaining sexual techniques that are effective for achieving orgasm to one's partners and practising these. Meston (2006) concluded that this intervention was more effective than systematic desensitization and sensate focus. For secondary orgasmic disorder, the outcome for this intervention was less favourable, and better results may be achieved when it is combined with couples therapy focusing on relationship issues, although this remains to be tested in controlled trials.

Female sexual pain disorders

Female dysparunia and vaginismus are most commonly associated with vulvar vestibulitis syndrome. In this syndrome burning pain occurs in response to touch or pressure due to erythema of the tissues surrounding the vagina and eurethra openings. In a narrative review, Meston and Bradford (2007) concluded that cognitive behavioural, biofeedback, and surgical interventions were effective for reducing dysparunia and vaginismus in women with vulvar vestibulitis syndrome. Effective cognitive behavioural programmes included psychoeducation; cognitive therapy to challenge beliefs and expectations underpinning anxiety about painful sex; and systematic desensitization. Systematic desensitization involves initially abstaining from attempts at intercourse; learning progressive muscle relaxation; and then pairing relaxation with the gradual insertion of a series of dilators of increasing diameter into the vagina, until this can be achieved without discomfort; and finally progressing through sensate focus exercises to intercourse. Effective biofeedback programmes involve weekly electromyographic feedback sessions and daily pelvic floor muscle exercises to reduce hypertonicity and increase the strength and stability of the pelvic floor muscles. Vestibulectomy, the effective surgical procedure for vulvar vestibulitis syndrome, involves removal of sensitive tissue. Meston and Bradford (2007) argue that this should only be considered when less invasive psychological interventions have been ineffective.

Male erectile disorder

Prior to 1998 and the marketing of sildenafil (Viagra), psychological intervention based on Masters and Johnson's (1970) sensate focus sex therapy was the main treatment for male erectile problems and was shown to be effective in up to 60% of cases. However, with the introduction of sildenafil and other phosphodiesterase Type 5 (PDE-5) inhibitors (notably vardenafil and tadalafil), PDE-5 inhibitors have come to be first line interventions for erectile disorder. In a meta-analysis of 123 randomized controlled trials of PDE-5 inhibitors, Bekkering *et al.* (2007) found that significantly more treated cases improved compared with placebo controls. However, not all cases respond to PDE-5 inhibitors, and there is an emerging practice of using multimodal programmes involving PDE-5 inhibitors combined with psychological interventions in such cases (McCarthy & Fucito, 2005). In a study of 53 cases of acquired erectile disorder, Banner and Anderson (2007) found that those who received sildenafil and cognitive behavioural sex therapy had a 48% success rate for erectile function and 65.5% for satisfaction. In contrast, those who received sildenafil alone had a 29% erection success rate and a 37.5% satisfaction rate.

Premature ejaculation

For premature ejaculation, Masters and Johnson (1970) developed the stop–start and squeeze techniques where the couple cease intercourse and the base of the penis is squeezed each time ejaculation is imminent. In a narrative review of mainly uncontrolled trials, Duterte *et al.* (2007) concluded that success rates with this method may be initially as high as 80% but may dwindle in the long term to 25% at follow-up. In an extensive review of controlled trials and meta-analyses, Hellstrom (2006) concluded that fluoxetine, sertraline, paroxetine, and clomipramine are all effective in alleviating premature ejaculation, but currently dapoxetine hydrochloride (DPX), a serotonin transport inhibitor, is the treatment of choice, because of its rapid onset of action and profile of minimal side effects compared with antidepressants. Hellstrom (2006) also concluded that there is evidence from a number of trials to show that topical formulations which contain aesthetic agents can increase ejaculatory latency times.

Prognostic factors in the treatment of psychosexual problems

Hawton (1995) in an extensive review concluded that motivation for treatment (particularly the male partner's motivation); early compliance with treatment; the quality of the relationship (particularly as assessed by the female partner); the physical attraction between partners; and the absence of serious psychological problems are predictive of a positive response to treatment for psychosexual difficulties.

Practice implications for treating psychosexual problems in adulthood

For female orgasmic disorder, a directed masturbation programme is the treatment of choice. Systematic desensitization and electromyographic biofeedback are effective for reducing dysparunia and vaginismus in women with vulvar vestibulitis syndrome. Only where these interventions are ineffective should surgical intervention be considered. For hypoactive sexual desire, programmes that combine sensate focus exercises with interventions that challenge beliefs that diminish sexual desire are appropriate, and androgen therapy may be considered in post-menopausal women. For male erectile dysfunction, multimodal programmes involving PDE-5 inhibitors combined with psychological interventions are the treatments of choice. For premature ejaculation, programmes that include the stop–start and squeeze technique are the psychological treatments of choice and where these are ineffective, antidepressants or dapoxetine hydrochloride may be considered. Psychosexual disorders typically occur within the context of relationships, and so focal psychosexual interventions are probably best offered within the context of couples therapy (Althof et al., 2005). *Principles and Practice of Sex Therapy* (Leiblum, 2006) and *Sexual Dysfunction: A Guide for Assessment and Treatment* (Wincze & Carey, 2001) are useful treatment guides. The importance of psychological interventions in the treatment of psychosexual problems is acknowledged in international best practice guidelines (Basson et al., 2000; Lue et al., 2004).

Domestic violence

In a meta-analysis of 22 studies for the treatment of domestically violent males, Babcock et al. (2004) found a small overall effect size of .18 for both partner and police reports of recidivism. This is a very small effect size. Babcock *et al.* (2004) included studies that evaluated feminist psychoeducational programmes based on the Duluth model and cognitive behavioural programmes in this meta-analysis, and found that both types of group-based programmes for perpetrators had similar impacts on recidivism. In psychoeducational programmes, perpetrators' patriarchal authoritarian beliefs that males have the right to dominate females are challenged, and an alternative egalitarian ideology is offered. In cognitive behavioural programmes, perpetrators learn anger management, communication, and assertiveness skills, which they can use to prevent further violence. Feder and Wilson (2005) also found small or negligible effect sizes in a meta-analysis of studies of court-mandated treatment for domestically violent males. Both of these meta-analyses also showed that there was considerable variability in perpetrators' response to treatment. Thus, domestically violent males constitute a very heterogeneous group that differs widely in its responsiveness to treatment (Stuart, 2005). Some but not all domestically violent males are amenable to treatment, and so assessment for treatment suitability is essential. For couples who wish to stay together and in which the male can agree to a no-harm contract, Stith and Rosen (2003) in a narrative review of six studies found that couples therapy was effective in reducing domestic violence. In a later study, Stith *et al.* (2004) found that a multicouple treatment programme was more effective than a single couple programme in reducing domestic violence and related marital distress. Male violence recidivism rates were 25% for the multicouple group and 43% for the individual couple group. Key elements of treatment include the perpetrator taking responsibility for the violence; solution-focused practices, challenging beliefs and cognitive distortions which justify violence; anger management training; communication and problem-solving skills training; and relapse prevention. Anger management training focuses on teaching couples to recognize anger cues; to take time out when such cues are recognized; to use relaxation and self-instructional methods to reduce anger-related arousal; to resume interactions in a non-violent way; and to use communication and problem-solving skills more effectively for conflict resolution.

Practice implications for domestic violence

In cases of domestic violence referred for treatment, assessment for treatment suitability is essential. Some but not all domestically violent males are amenable to treatment. Psychoeducational and cognitive behavioural group treatment programmes for aggressive males lead to small or negligible improvements. For couples who wish to stay together and in which the male can agree to a no-harm contract, couples therapy, particularly group-based couples therapy with a specific focus on violence reduction, is effective in reducing domestic violence.

Grief and bereavement in adulthood

In major narrative reviews of previous meta-analyses, systematic reviews, and treatment outcome studies for grief counselling, Regehr and Sussman (2004) and Stroebe *et al.* (2005) concluded that individuals with normal grieving patterns do not benefit from psychotherapy, but those with complicated grief reactions characterized by sustained high levels of distress benefit significantly from psychological interventions. Clients who had ambivalent relationships with the deceased have been found to benefit from psychotherapy that addresses 'unfinished business' in their relationships with the deceased. Clients who are less psychologically minded benefit more from supportive, problem-solving oriented therapy. These conclusions are consistent with those of some previous reviews. For example, Schut *et al.* (2001) in a previous narrative review found that grief counselling had greatest impact on more complicated grief processes, and on measures of social well-being rather than satisfaction. The most pronounced effects occurred in seven studies of people who showed complicated grief reactions a considerable time after bereavement. Modest effects occurred in seven studies which targeted people at high risk of complicated grief, as indexed by such features as traumatic death, loss of a child, or high levels of distress. Predominantly negative findings arose from their review of 17 studies which targeted unscreened bereaved people. In a previous meta-analysis of 35 studies involving 2284 cases, Allumbaugh and Hoyt (1999) found an overall effect size of .43, and the largest effect sizes (between 1.17 and 3.05) occurred for self-selected clients who had more complicated grief reactions, whereas those recruited by investigators for treatment studies showed the smallest effect sizes. In contrast to these findings, negligible effect sizes were found in two earlier, and frequently cited, meta-analyses of the effects of grief counselling. In a meta-analysis of 11 controlled studies of grief counselling, Kato and Mann (1999) found a small overall effect size of .11 and Fortner (1999), in a meta-analysis of 23 studies, found an overall effect size of .13. There were methodological difficulties with these very widely cited meta-analyses that reduce confidence in the validity of their small effect sizes and in the claim by Fortner (1999) that grief counselling leads to deterioration in many cases (Larson & Hoyt, 2007).

Practice implications for grief and bereavement in adulthood

Grief counselling may be appropriately offered to people suffering from complicated bereavement characterized by sustained high levels of distress. Worden's (2001) *Grief Counselling and Grief Therapy: A Handbook for the Mental Health Professional* is a useful practice manual.

Psychological problems in later life

In this section, evidence supporting the effectiveness of psychological inter-ventions either alone, or as part of multimodal intervention programmes involving pharmacotherapy, for late life psychological problems is reviewed. There will be a particular focus on the treatment of dementia and late life depression, anxiety, and insomnia.

Dementia

There is evidence for the effectiveness of a variety of psychological and pharmacological interventions for cognitive decline and challenging behav-iour associated with dementia. What follows is a review of this material.

Psychological interventions for dementia

Effective psychological interventions for cognitive decline in dementia include reminiscence therapy, reality orientation, and cognitive stimulation (Spector *et al.*, 2000, 2003; Woods *et al.*, 2005). Ineffective interventions include cognitive training, cognitive rehabilitation, and validation therapy (Clare & Woods, 2004; Neal & Barton-Wright, 2003). Behavioural and environmental interventions are effective in managing challenging behaviour associated with dementia (Logsdon *et al.*, 2007). Caregiver support programmes may have a range of positive effects for people caring for an older relative with dementia (Pinquart & Sorensen, 2006).

Reminiscence therapy for cognitive decline in dementia

Reminiscence therapy involves the discussion of past activities, events, and experiences. Aids such as audio and video recordings, pictures, archives, life story books, and outings to memorable places may be used to facilitate this process. Reminiscence therapy is typically offered in weekly group meetings over 5–20 sessions. Family caregivers may be included. While reminiscence therapy was developed to improve mood, it has been used in the treatment of dementia (Norris, 1986). In this context, the aim is to facilitate the recall of autobiographical memories and the communication of these within a group setting. This builds on the capacity of people with dementia to easily recall remote but not recent memories, and in doing so contributes to the mainten-ance of a clear sense of personal identity (Woods *et al.*, 2005). In a meta-analysis of four trials of reminiscence therapy for dementia, involving 144 participants, Woods *et al.* (2005) found that it led to significant improvements in functional behaviour immediately following intervention, and to signifi-cant improvements in cognition and mood four to six weeks later. When caregivers participated in reminiscence therapy sessions, this led a significant decrease in caregiver strain.

Reality orientation for cognitive decline in dementia

With reality orientation clients are repeatedly presented with orientation information about time, place, people, activities, and schedules to help them maintain an accurate understanding of their moment-to-moment situation. Reality orientation can be offered as a continuous intervention by residential care staff who involve older adults in reality-based communication throughout the day, or in a therapeutic group format, focused on orientation-related activities (Holden & Woods, 1995). In a meta-analysis of six randomized controlled trials of reality orientation for dementia, involving 125 cases, Spector *et al.* (2000) found significant effect sizes for both cognition and behaviour. In these studies reality orientation was offered as a group-based intervention three to five times a week over 4–20 weeks, with reality orientation group discussion, group activities, and a reality orientation board as central features of the intervention. This board displayed information such as the day, date, weather, name of next meal, and other orientation details. There is some evidence that reality orientation may enhance pharmacological interventions for dementia. In a randomized controlled trial involving 156 older adults with Alzheimer's disease, Onder *et al.* (2005) found that when the cholinesterase inhibitor donepezil was combined with reality orientation, this multimodal programme led to significantly greater improvement in cognitive functioning than medication alone. Caregivers of the treated group were trained to offer the reality orientation programme at home three days a week, for 30 minutes per day, for 25 consecutive weeks, and were invited to involve patients in regular reality orientation-based communication.

Cognitive stimulation for cognitive decline in dementia

Cognitive stimulation therapy is a recently developed refinement of reality orientation. With this approach, clients are helped through regular structured multisensory group exercises, and through reminiscence exercises, matched to their level of cognitive functioning, to develop strategies for managing memory deficits. In a randomized controlled trial of 201 older people with dementia, Spector *et al.* (2003) found that participants who engaged in twice weekly sessions of cognitive stimulation over a seven-week period showed significant improvement in cognitive functioning and quality of life. In a follow-up pilot study of 35 cases, eight of whom received once-weekly maintenance cognitive stimulation therapy for four months, Orrell *et al.* (2005) found that cognitive gains made during the initial seven-week programme were maintained. In contrast, gains in cognitive functioning were not maintained by those who did not receive maintenance cognitive stimulation therapy. An economic analysis based on service use costs of treatment and control group cases before and after the initial seven-week trial showed that cognitive stimulation therapy is cost-effective (Knapp *et al.*, 2006).

Cognitive training, cognitive rehabilitation, and validation therapy for cognitive decline in dementia

Cognitive training aims to improve memory functioning through regular guided practice on memory tasks in a training context, on the assumption that the effects of regular practice will generalize to the daily living environment. In contrast cognitive rehabilitation involves helping people with dementia develop strategies for making the most of remaining memory abilities and finding ways of compensating for memory deficits. In a systematic narrative review, Clare and Woods (2004) found six controlled trials of cognitive training which provided no support for the effectiveness of this intervention in improving cognitive functioning in people with dementia, and no controlled trials of cognitive rehabilitation. Validation therapy is based on the acceptance of the reality and personal truth of another's experience. In a systematic review of three trials of validation therapy, Neal and Barton-Wright (2003) found no support for the effectiveness of validation therapy in improving cognitive functioning in people with dementia.

Behavioural interventions for challenging behaviour in dementia

In a systematic review of 14 randomized controlled trials of psychological interventions for challenging behaviour in dementia, Logsdon *et al.* (2007) found evidence for the effectiveness of two types of interventions. The first were behavioural therapies that aimed to identify and modify antecedents and consequences of problem behaviours and increase pleasant events (Teri, 1990; Teri *et al.*, 2005). The second were individualized interventions based on progressively lowered stress threshold models that include environmental modifications to support the older person's cognitive limitations, and the incorporation of pleasant activities into a structured daily routine (Smith *et al.*, 2004). Most interventions spanned 8–20 hours of treatment, and involved training families or care staff to implement the intervention programme. These findings are consistent with those of an earlier systematic review by Cohen-Mansfield (2001) who concluded that effective psychosocial interventions for challenging behaviour shown by older adults with dementia involve assessing the context and function of the challenging behaviour and then using one or more of the following components to modify it: avoiding situations that precipitate it; reinforcing alternative responses to challenging behaviour; providing pleasant sensory intervention (e.g. music, viewing visual multimedia stimuli, or massage); arranging pleasant motor activities (e.g. walking, dancing); and facilitating pleasant social interaction with family friends or staff.

Caregiver support in dementia

Pinquart and Sorensen (2006) conducted a meta-analysis of 127 studies of interventions for caregivers of older adults with dementia. In this meta-analysis, caregivers were predominantly wives or daughters of the older adult with dementia, who were in their sixties, and had been in the caretaker role for over 3.5 years. Care receivers were in their mid-seventies. Pinquart and Sorensen (2006) found statistically significant effect sizes for caregiver relevant knowledge, depression, and burden after treatment and at an average of 11 months follow-up. Effect sizes for knowledge were .46 after treatment and .42 at follow-up, which are equivalent to approximate success rates of 61% and 60%. Effect sizes for depression were .24 after treatment and .17 at follow-up, which are equivalent to approximate success rates of 56% and 54%. Effect sizes for burden were .12 after treatment and .14 at follow-up, which are equivalent to an approximate success rate of 54% on both occasions.

Different programmes resulted in significant, if modest, benefits in different sets of domains, with skills training psychoeducational programmes affecting multiple domains, and structured multicomponent programmes being the only programme type to delay institutionalization of older adults with dementia. Skills training psychoeducational programmes led to significant improvements in relevant knowledge (effect size = .55), depression (effect size = .36), subjective well-being (effect size = .21), and burden (effect size = .20). Cognitive behavioural therapy with a focus on mood regulation led to significant improvements in depression (effect size = .70) and burden (effect size = .36). Respite care programmes led to improvements in subjective well-being (effect size = .27), burden (effect size = .26), and depression (effect size = .12). Counselling and case management led to significant improvement in caregiver burden (effect size = .36). Support groups led to significant improvement in subjective well-being (effect size = 2.03). Structured multi-component programmes, which included combinations of the interventions mentioned above along with environmental alterations as required, led to significantly greater delay in the institutionalization of older adults with dementia (effect size = .51). Compared with shorter programmes, longer more intensive programmes led to greater improvements in caregiver depression and greater delays in the institutionalization of older adults with dementia. Individual and group-based interventions were equally effective. Pinquart and Sorensen's (2006) meta-analysis is the most comprehensive to date. However, its findings are controversial because it demonstrated that psychological interventions for caregivers led to small but significant reductions in caregiver burden, and two previous but far less comprehensive meta-analyses have concluded that such interventions have no significant impact on caregiver burden (Acton & Kang, 2001; Brodaty et al., 2003). The positive effects of psychological interventions on other domains of caregiver functioning found by Pinquart and Sorensen (2006) are consistent with the results of a number of previous less comprehensive meta-analyses (Brodaty *et al.*, 2003; Sorensen *et al.*, 2002; Yin *et al.*, 2002) and systematic narrative reviews (Cooke *et al.*, 2001; Gallagher-Thompson & Coon, 2007; Pusey & Richards, 2001; Schulz *et al.*, 2002, 2005).

Pharmacotherapy for dementia

Pharmacological interventions have been developed to address cognitive decline and challenging behaviour associated with dementia.

Pharmacotherapy for cognitive decline in dementia

Systematic reviews of trials and meta-analyses of pharmacotherapy consistently show that cholinesterase inhibitors (donepezil, rivastigmine, and galantamine) and mementine have a significant impact on cognitive decline in dementia associated with Alzheimer's disease, Lewey Bodies, and Parkinson's disease (Burns & O'Brien, 2006; Tune, 2007). There is some evidence that gingko biloba and vitamin E may have small but significant effects on cognitive decline in dementia also (Burns & O'Brien, 2006).

Pharmacotherapy for challenging behaviour in dementia

In a systematic review of meta-analyses and controlled trials of pharmacotherapy for challenging behaviour in dementia, Madhusoodanan *et al.* (2007) concluded that atypical antipsychotics are the most effective drugs currently available, although their effects are limited, confined to a proportion of cases, and they entail significant side effects. In a meta-analysis of 15 trials, Schneider *et al.* (2006) found that aripiprazole and risperidone were the most effective atypical antipsychotic drugs for reducing challenging behaviour of people with dementia. These conclusions are consistent with those of previous systematic reviews (Bartels *et al.*, 2003).

Practice implications for dementia

For cognitive decline in dementia, cognitive stimulation, reminiscence therapy, and reality orientation may be offered either alone or in combination with cholinesterase inhibitors or mementine. For challenging behaviour, behavioural and environmental interventions may be offered either alone or in combination with atypical antipsychotic medication. Carers of older adults with dementia should be offered psychological intervention programmes, which address their unique profile of needs and which include some or all of the following components: skills-based psychoeducation, provision of support, psychotherapy for mood regulation, environmental modifications, and respite care. Effective psychological interventions for carers of older adults with dementia should be offered as part of multimodal case management packages that include multidisciplinary assessment of the older adult and family support network. The importance of psychological interventions for people with dementia and their carers is acknowledged in international guidelines for best practice (American Psychiatric Association, 2007b; American Psychological Association, 2004; Burns & O'Brien, 2006; Doody *et al.*, 2001; NICE, 2007c).

Late life depression

Psychotherapy is effective in alleviating depression in older adults. In systematic reviews Scogin *et al.* (2005) and Mackin and Areán (2005) concluded that for depression in older adults cognitive behavioural therapies, brief psychodynamic therapy, interpersonal therapy, and reminiscence therapy were all effective. These conclusions are consistent with previous systematic reviews which have been summarized by Bartels *et al.* (2003). In a meta-analysis of 25 randomized controlled trials of a range of different types of psychotherapy for depression in older adults, Cuijpers *et al.* (2006) found an effect size of .72 which is approximately equivalent to a success rate of 67%. There was no difference in the effectiveness of different types of psychological treatment of late life depression.

Psychotherapy vs. pharmacotherapy for late life depression

Psychotherapy is as effective as antidepressant medication in alleviating depression in older adults. In a meta-analysis of 89 trials of pharmacotherapy and psychotherapy for mood disorders in older adults involving 5328 older adults, Pinquart *et al.* (2006) found larger effect sizes for psychotherapy than for medication, although this may have been due to the use of more credible placebos in studies of antidepressant medication. Effect sizes for clinician-rated depression were 1.09 for psychotherapy and .69 for antidepressants. These are equivalent to approximate success rates of 72% and 67% respectively. For self-rated depression, effect sizes were .83 for psychotherapy and .62 for medication. These are equivalent to approximate success rates of 69% and 65% respectively.

Combined psychotherapy and pharmacotherapy for late life depression

In a systematic narrative review Mackin and Areán (2005) could find only two studies in which the effectiveness of multimodal programmes including psychotherapy and pharmacotherapy were compared to either alone. They concluded that as a long-term maintenance therapy for recurring depression, interpersonal therapy combined with antidepressants was more effective than monotherapy (Reynolds *et al.*, 1999); but that cognitive behavioural therapy combined with antidepressants was no more effective than cognitive behavioural therapy alone, but more effective than antidepressant medication alone (Thompson *et al.*, 2001).

Treatment of late life depression with co-morbid dementia

Psychological interventions are effective in alleviating depression in older adults with co-morbid dementia. In a systematic narrative review of 11 trials of psychological interventions for older adults with both dementia and depression, Teri *et al.* (2005) concluded that effective programmes fell into three broad categories: those which trained carers in communication skills and used a problem-solving approach to enhance the quality of life of the older person with dementia and depression; those which increased older people's social interaction; and those which modified environmental stimulation by either increasing or decreasing it to suit the older person's requirements.

Electroconvulsive therapy for late life depression

In a systematic review, Van der Wurff *et al.* (2003) concluded that there is currently insufficient evidence on the effectiveness and safety of electro-convulsive therapy with older adults to warrant its use for late life depression.

Practice implications for late life depression

In older adults who present with depression, either alone or with dementia, psychotherapy is optimally offered as the main intervention, or as one elem-ent of a multimodal programme that includes antidepressant medication. Effective forms of psychotherapy include cognitive behavioural therapies, brief psychodynamic therapy, interpersonal therapy, and reminiscence ther-apy. These various forms of therapy help clients understand factors that have contributed to the development and maintenance of their depression; develop healthier, active daily routines; stop depressive thinking styles from dominating their mood; recollect pleasant and meaningful aspects of their lives and put their overall life story in a positive perspective; and develop supportive relationships with family members and others. Useful treatment manuals include *Cognitive Behaviour Therapy with Older People* (Laidlaw *et al.*, 2003), *Interpersonal Psychotherapy for Depressed Older Adults* (Hin-richsen & Clougherty, 2006), and *The Past in the Present: Using Reminiscence in Health and Social Care* (Gibson, 2004). In older adults who have both dementia and depression, effective psychotherapy involves coaching carers in problem-solving skills and helping them use these to enhance the quality of care they offer to the depressed older adult by, for example, improving com-munication and scheduling regular pleasant events. Effective psychotherapy also involves scheduling regular daily opportunities for pleasant social inter-action and pleasant sensory experiences and motor activities. The importance of psychotherapy in the treatment of late life depression is acknowledged in international best practice guidelines (American Psychological Association, 2004; Lebowitz *et al.*, 1997; NICE, 2004a).

Late life anxiety disorders

Psychotherapy is an effective treatment for anxiety disorders in older adults, and as effective as pharmacological interventions.

Psychotherapy vs. pharmacotherapy for late life anxiety disorders

In a meta-analysis of 32 studies of psychotherapy and medication for anxiety disorders in older adults involving 2484 participants, Pinquart and Duberstein (2007) found an effect size of .80 for psychotherapy and .83 for medication, when effect sizes were computed controlling for non-specific change in con-trol groups. These effect sizes are approximately equivalent to success rates of 69%. Drop-out rates were similar for both interventions, and they led to similar reductions in depressive symptoms. In this meta-analysis, cognitive behavioural therapy was the predominant psychological intervention, and the predominant pharmacological interventions were benzodiazepines and selective serotonin reuptake inhibitors. These conclusions are consistent with those of previous meta-analyses. For example, in a meta-analysis of 15 trials of psychological interventions for anxiety disorders for older adults, involv-ing 495 participants, Nordhus and Pallesen (2003) found an effect size of .55 on self-rated and clinician-rated measures of anxiety, which is equivalent to an approximate success rate of 63%. Participants in most studies in this meta-analysis were older adults with generalized anxiety disorder, or clinical levels of trait anxiety. The studies mostly evaluated individual or group cognitive behavioural therapy spanning 4–20 sessions. Typical cognitive behavioural programmes included psychoeducation about anxiety, self-monitoring, relax-ation training, exposure to anxiety-provoking thoughts and situations using systematic desensitization, and cognitive restructuring focusing on modifying danger-related thoughts. Some programmes also included problem-solving skills training, behavioural activation, sleep hygiene, reflective listening, life review, and memory aids.

Simple and complex psychotherapeutic interventions for late life anxiety

Narrative reviews have concluded that simple interventions such as support-ive therapy and relaxation training are as effective as more elaborate cognitive behavioural therapy programmes. In a systematic review of 17 studies of psychotherapy for anxiety disorders in older adults, Ayers *et al.* (2007) found evidence for the effectiveness of supportive therapy, relaxation training alone, cognitive therapy alone (without relaxation training), and multicomponent cognitive behavioural therapy.

Practice implications for late life anxiety

Within a stepped care approach, supportive therapy, relaxation training, and multicomponent cognitive behavioural therapy may be offered to older people with anxiety disorders who require an alternative to pharmacotherapy.

Late life insomnia

There is evidence for the effectiveness of both psychological and pharmacological interventions for insomnia in older adults.

Psychological treatment of late life insomnia

In a systematic narrative review, McCurry *et al.* (2007) concluded that cognitive behavioural therapy, sleep restriction, and sleep compression were effective interventions for insomnia in older adults. Sleep restriction involves the abrupt reduction in the number of hours spent in bed per night. With sleep compression the time spent in bed per night is gradually reduced. Cognitive behavioural therapy programmes for insomnia may include sleep restriction or compression, along with other elements including psychoeducation, stimulus control, relaxation training, and helping patients address unhelpful beliefs about the sleep–waking process. In this context, stimulus control involves leaving the bedroom if sleep does not occur within 15 minutes of going to bed.

In a systematic narrative review, Nau *et al.* (2005) concluded that psychological interventions, such as those mentioned above, are also effective for insomnia secondary to co-morbid psychological disorders (e.g. depression); medical conditions (e.g. chronic pain); and dependency on sleeping medication if combined with a tapered reduction in medication use.

In a meta-analysis of 23 trials of interventions for insomnia, Irwin *et al.* (2006) included eight studies where participants were older adults. In these eight trials they found effect sizes of .73 for waking after sleep onset; .60 for sleep quality; .51 for sleep onset latency; and .38 for sleep efficiency. These effect sizes are equivalent to approximate success rates of 60–67%. In this meta-analysis, multicomponent cognitive behavioural interventions and more circumscribed behaviour programmes that included, for example, only sleep restriction or compression were equally effective.

Pharmacotherapy for late life insomnia

The outcome of psychological treatment for late life insomnia compares favourably with that found in trials of pharmacotherapy. In a meta-analysis of 24 trials of hypnotics, involving 2417 older adults with insomnia, Glass *et al.* (2005) found effect sizes of .63 for waking after sleep onset and .14 for sleep quality. These effect sizes are equivalent to approximate success rates of 54–65%. However, problematic side effects, such as falls and daytime fatigue, were more common with sedatives than with placebos. Also, frequent usage of hypnotics such as the benzodiazepines leads to dependence and rebound insomnia if discontinued.

Practice implications for late life insomnia

In older adults, psychological interventions are the initial treatment of choice because of their demonstrated efficacy and lack of side effects. Where psychological treatments are ineffective, pharmacotherapy may be considered. These conclusions are consistent with those of previous reviews (Montgomery & Dennis, 2004; Pallesen *et al.*, 1998).

Danger of oversimplification

There is a danger that in summarizing a very large body of evidence within the constraints of a single chapter the complexity and skilled nature of psychotherapy may not be fully conveyed. This point was made at the end of Chapter 4 in some detail, but because of its importance it is essential to make it again, if only briefly. In earlier sections of this chapter, reference was made to key elements of effective psychotherapy programmes such as changing maladaptive thinking styles or facilitating the development of supportive relationships with others. There is a danger that such key elements may be misconstrued as simple procedures which could be offered by technicians. This is not the case. Psychotherapy is a complex process. Clients with psychological disorders use a variety of subtle maladaptive coping strategies, defence mechanisms, counterproductive thinking patterns, and problematic relationship transactions, most of which occur outside clients' awareness. Helping clients to become aware of these processes and to evolve more adaptive alternatives is a highly skilled process. This is partly because of clients' resistance to change. Effective psychotherapy always involves addressing resistance, which is a complex process. The complexity of psychotherapy is mentioned here because the description of the key elements of effective evidence-based psychotherapy with specific disorders set out above in this chapter often makes the process sound simple and uncomplicated. It is not. Psychotherapy is a highly skilled process.

Conclusion

The central question addressed in this chapter was: What works for adults? Extensive computer and manual literature searches yielded a wealth of empirical evidence supporting the benefits of psychotherapy and psychological interventions for a wide range of problems in adulthood and later life including:

- mood disorders and related problems, specifically major depression, bipolar disorder, suicide, self-harm
- anxiety disorders including generalized anxiety disorder, panic disorder, specific phobias, social phobia or social anxiety disorder, obsessive-compulsive disorder, post-traumatic stress disorder
- somatoform disorders and difficulties including medically unexplained symptoms, hypochondriasis, body dysmorphic disorder
- adjustment to illness including preparation for surgery, adjustment to conditions with high mortality rates such as cancer and heart disease, and adjustment to chronic medical conditions involving adherence to complex regimes such as diabetes, asthma, hypertension
- facilitating coping with conditions involving pain and fatigue such as chronic pain, low back pain, fibromyalgia, chronic fatigue syndrome, headaches, arthritis, irritable bowel syndrome
- eating disorders including obesity, bulimia, anorexia, binge eating disorder
- insomnia
- substance abuse and addiction including alcohol and drug abuse, nicotine addiction, compulsive gambling
- schizophrenia
- personality disorders
- anger and aggression
- sexual offending
- relationship problems including marital distress, psychosexual problems, domestic violence
- psychological problems associated with older adulthood including dementia, late life depression, anxiety, insomnia.

Specific practices and protocols identified in this chapter may usefully be incorporated into routine clinical practice with clients who present with the problems listed above. A list of therapy manuals and resources and self-help material for clients is given below, which therapists may find helpful if used flexibly in translating the results of this research review into clinical practice.

Further reading

The items in this reading list are predominantly evidence based and are sufficiently detailed to inform clinical practice.

Depression in adults

For professionals – cognitive behaviour therapy manuals for depression

Beck, A., Rush, A., Shaw, B. & Emery, G. (1979). *Cognitive Therapy of Depression.* New York: Guilford Press.
Emery, G. (1999). *Overcoming Depression: Therapist Protocol.* Oakland, CA: New Harbinger.
Persons, J., Davidson, J. & Tomkins, M. (2001). *Essential Components of Cognitive Behaviour Therapy for Depression.* Washington, DC: American Psychological Association. Video series of five tapes. 1. Individualised case formulation and treatment planning. 2. Activity scheduling. 3. Using the thought record. 4. Schema change methods. 5. Structure of the therapy session.
Segal, Z., Williams, M. & Teasdale, J. (2002). *Mindfulness-Based Cognitive Therapy for Depression.* New York: Guilford Press.

For professionals – behaviour therapy manual for depression

Lewinsohn, P. M., Antonuccio, D. O., Steinmetz, J. L. & Teri, L. (1984). *The Coping with Depression Course: A Psychoeducational Intervention for Unipolar Depression.* Eugene, OR: Castalia Press.

For professionals – interpersonal therapy manuals for depression

Klerman, G., Weissman, M. & Rounsaville, B. (1984). *Interpersonal Psychotherapy of Depression.* New York: Basic Books.
Weissman, M., Markowitz, J. & Klerman, G. (2000). *Comprehensive Guide to Interpersonal Psychotherapy.* New York: Basic Books.

For professionals – psychodynamic therapy manuals for depression

Luborsky, L. (1984). *Principles of Psychoanalytic Psychotherapy: A Manual for Supportive-Expressive Treatment.* New York: Basic Books.
Malan, D. (1995). *Individual Psychotherapy and the Science of Psychodynamics* (Second Edition). London: Butterworth-Heinemann.
McCullough-Vaillant, L. (1997). *Changing Character: Short-Term Anxiety Regulating Psychotherapy for Restructuring Defences, Affects and Attachments.* New York: Basic Books.

For professionals – couples therapy manuals for depression

Beach, S. R. H., Sandeen, E. E. & O'Leary, K. D. (1990). *Depression in Marriage: A Model for Etiology and Treatment.* New York: Guilford Press.

Jones, E. & Asen, E. (1999). *Systemic Couples Therapy for Depression*. London: Karnac.

For clients – self-help books on depression

Burns, D. (1999). *Feeling Good: The New Mood Therapy*. New York: Avon.
Burns, D. (1999). *The Feeling Good Handbook*. New York: Plume.
Emery, G. (2000). *Overcoming Depression: Client Manual*. Oakland, CA: New Harbinger.
Gilbert, P. (2000). *Overcoming Depression: A Self-Help Guide Using Cognitive Behavioural Techniques*. London: Robinson.
Gilson, M. & Freeman, A. (2004). *Overcoming Depression: A Cognitive Therapy Approach for Taming the Depression BEAST. Client Workbook*. Oxford: Oxford University Press.
Greenberger, D. & Padesky, C. (1995). *Mind Over Mood: Changing How You Feel by Changing the Way You Think*. New York: Guilford Press.
Kabat Zinn, J. (1995). *Wherever You Go, There You Are. Mindfulness Meditation in Everyday Life*. New York: Hyperion (http://www.stressreductiontapes.com/).
Lewinsohn, P., Munoz, R., Youngren, M. & Zeiss, A. (1996). *Control Your Depression*. Englewood Cliffs, NJ: Prentice Hall.
McCullough, J. (2002). *Patient's Manual for CBASP*. New York: Guilford Press.
Rosenthal, N. (2005). *Winter Blues: Everything You Need to Know to Beat Seasonal Affective Disorder*. New York: Guilford Press.
Weissman, M. (1995). *Mastering Depression: A Patient's Guide to Interpersonal Psychotherapy*. San Antonio, TX: Psychological Corporation.
Williams, M., Teasdale, J., Segal, Z. & Kabat-Zinn, J. (2007). *The Mindful Way Through Depression: Freeing Yourself from Chronic Unhappiness*. New York: Guilford Press.

Bipolar disorder in adults

For professionals – psychoeducational manuals for bipolar disorder

Bauer, M. & McBride, L. (1996). *Structured Group Psychotherapy for Bipolar Disorder: The Life Goals Program*. New York: Springer.
Colm, F., Vieta, E. & Scott, J. (2006). *Psychoeducation Manual for Bipolar Disorder*. Cambridge: Cambridge University Press.

For professionals – cognitive behaviour therapy manuals for bipolar disorder

Lam, D., Hayward, P., Bright, J. & Jones, S. (1999). *Cognitive Therapy for Bipolar Disorder*. Chichester: John Wiley.
Newman, C., Leahy, R., Beck, A., Reilly-Harrington, N. & Gyulai, L. (2002). *Bipolar Disorder: A Cognitive Therapy Approach*. Washington, DC: American Psychological Association.

Otto, M., Reilly-Harrington, N., Kogan, J., *et al.* (1999). *Cognitive Behaviour Therapy for Bipolar Disorder: Treatment Manual.* Boston: Massachusetts General Hospital.

Ramirez Basco, M. & Rush, A. (2007). *Cognitive Behavioural Therapy for Bipolar Disorder* (Second Edition). New York: Guilford Press.

For professionals – interpersonal therapy manual for bipolar disorder

Frank, E. (2005). *Treating Bipolar Disorder: A Clinician's Guide to Interpersonal and Social Rhythm Therapy.* New York: Guilford Press.

For professionals – family therapy manual for bipolar disorder

Milkowitz, D. & Goldstein, M. (1997). *Bipolar Disorder: A Family-Focused Treatment Approach.* New York: Guilford Press.

For clients – self-help books on bipolar disorder

Jones, S. H., Hayward, P. & Lam, D. H. (2003). *Coping with Bipolar Disorder* (Second Edition). Oxford: Oneworld.

Miklowitz, D. J. (2002). *The Bipolar Disorder Survival Guide: What You and Your Family Need to Know.* New York: Guilford Press.

Ramirez Basco, M. (2006). *The Bipolar Workbook: Tools for Controlling Your Mood Swings.* New York: Guilford Press.

Scott, J. (2001). *Overcoming Mood Swings.* London: Constable Robinson.

Attempted suicide and self-harm in adults

For professionals – treatment manuals for attempted suicide

Bongar, B. (2002). *The Suicidal Patient: Clinical and Legal Standards of Care* (Second Edition). Washington, DC: American Psychological Association.

Brown, G., Henriques, G., Ratto, C. & Beck, A. (2002). *Cognitive Therapy Treatment Manual for Suicide Attempters.* Philadelphia: University of Pennsylvania.

D'Zurilla, T. & Nezu, A. (2006). *Problem Solving Therapy* (Third Edition). New York: Springer Verlag.

Hawton, K. & Catalan, J. (1987). *Attempted Suicide: A Practical Guide to its Nature and Management* (Second Edition). Oxford: Oxford Medical Publications.

Jacobs, D. (1999). *The Harvard Medical School Guide to Suicide Assessment and Intervention.* San Francisco: Jossey Bass.

Rudd, M., Joiner, T. & Rajab, M. (2001). *Treating Suicidal Behaviour: An Effective Time-Limited Approach.* New York: Guilford Press.

For clients – self-help books on suicide and self-harm

Ellis, T. & Newman, C. (1996). *Choosing to Live: How to Defeat Suicide Through Cognitive Therapy.* New York: New Harbinger.

Nezu, A., Maquth-Nezu, C. & D'Zurilla, T. (2006). *Solving Life's Problems: A 5-Step Guide to Enhanced Well-Being*. New York: Springer Verlag.

Schmidt, U. & Davidson, K. (2004). *Life After Self-Harm*. London: Routledge.

Anxiety disorders in adults

For professionals – treatment manuals for a range of anxiety disorders

Andrews, G., Creamer, M., Crino, R., Hunt, C., Lampe, L. & Page, A. (2003). *The Treatment of Anxiety Disorders: Clinician's Guides and Patient Manuals* (Second Edition). Cambridge: Cambridge University Press.

Barlow, D. (2002). *Anxiety and its Disorders: The Nature and Treatment of Anxiety and Panic* (Second Edition). New York: Guilford Press.

McLean, P. & Woody, S. (2001). *Anxiety Disorders in Adults: An Evidence Based Approach to Psychological Treatment*. Oxford: Oxford University Press.

For clients – self-help books relevant to a range of anxiety disorders

Davis, M., McKay, M. & Robbins Eshelman, E. (2000). *The Relaxation and Stress Reduction Workbook* (Fifth Edition). Oakland, CA: New Harbinger.

Otto, M. W., Pollack, M. H. & Barlow, D. H. (1996). *Stopping Anxiety Medication: Panic Control Therapy for Benzodiazepine Discontinuation*. Boulder, CO: Graywind.

Generalized anxiety disorder (GAD) in adults

For professionals – therapy manuals for GAD

Dugas, M. & Robichaud, M. (2006). *Cognitive Behavioural Treatment for Generalized Anxiety Disorder*. New York: Routledge.

Wells, A. (1997). *Cognitive Therapy for Anxiety Disorders: A Practice Manual and Conceptual Guide*. Chichester: John Wiley.

White, J. (1999). *Overcoming Generalized Anxiety Disorder: Therapist Protocol*. Oakland, CA: New Harbinger.

Zinbarg, R., Craske, M. & Barlow, D. (2006). *Mastery of Your Anxiety and Worry: Therapist Guide* (Second Edition). Oxford: Oxford University Press.

For clients – self-help books for GAD

Barlow, D. & Rapee, R. (1991). *Mastering Stress: A Lifestyle Approach*. Dallas, TX: American Health Publishing.

Bourne, E. (1995). *The Anxiety and Phobia Workbook*. Oakland, CA: New Harbinger.

Craske, M. & Barlow, D. (2006). *Mastery of Your Anxiety and Worry Workbook* (Second Edition). Oxford: Oxford University Press.

Leahy, R. (2005). *The Worry Cure: Seven Steps to Stop Worry from Stopping You*. New York: Harmony.

White, J. (1999). *Overcoming Generalized Anxiety Disorder: Client Manual*. Oakland, CA: New Harbinger.

Panic disorder in adults

For professionals – cognitive behaviour therapy manuals for panic disorder

Craske, M. G. & Barlow, D. H. (2006). *Master Your Anxiety and Panic: Therapist Guide* (Fourth Edition). Oxford: Oxford University Press.

Taylor, S. (2000). *Understanding and Treating Panic Disorder: Cognitive-Behavioural Approaches*. Chichester: John Wiley.

Wells, A. (1997). *Cognitive Therapy for Anxiety Disorders: A Practice Manual and Conceptual Guide*. Chichester: John Wiley.

Zuercher-White, E. (1997). *Treating Panic Disorder and Agoraphobia: A Step By Step Clinical Guide*. Oakland, CA: New Harbinger.

Zuercher-White, E. (1999). *Overcoming Panic Disorder and Agoraphobia: Therapist Protocol*. Oakland, CA: New Harbinger.

For professionals – psychodynamic therapy manual for panic disorder

Milrod, B. L., Busch, F. N., Cooper, A. M. & Shapiro, T. (1997). *Manual of Panic-Focused Psychodynamic Psychotherapy*. Washington, DC: American Psychiatric Association.

For clients – self-help books for panic disorder

Antony, M. & McCabe, R. (2004). *10 Simple Solutions to Panic: How to Overcome Panic Attacks, Calm Physical Symptoms, & Reclaim Your Life*. Oakland, CA: New Harbinger.

Barlow, D. H. (2006). *Master Your Anxiety and Panic: Workbook* (Fourth Edition). Oxford: Oxford University Press.

Carbonell, D. (2004). *Panic Attacks Workbook: A Guided Program for Beating the Panic Trick*. New York: Ulysses Press.

Culm, G. (1990). *Coping With Panic*. Pacific Grove, CA: Brooks Cole.

Kennerly, H. (1997). *Overcoming Anxiety: A Self-Help Guide Using Cognitive-Behavioural Techniques*. London: Robinson.

Pollard, C. A. & Zuercher-White, E. (2003). *The Agoraphobia Workbook: A Comprehensive Program to End Your Fear of Symptom Attacks*. Oakland, CA: New Harbinger.

Silove, D. & Manicavasagar, V. (2001). *Overcoming Panic: A Self-Help Guide Using Cognitive Behavioural Techniques*. London: Robinson.

Wilson, R. R. (1996). *Don't Panic: Taking Control of Anxiety Attacks*. New York: Harper Perennial.

Zuercher-White, E. (1998). *An End to Panic* (Second Edition). Oakland, CA: New Harbinger.

Zuercher-White, E. (1999). *Overcoming Panic Disorder and Agoraphobia: Client Manual*. Oakland, CA: New Harbinger.

Phobias in adults

For professionals – therapy manuals for phobias

Antony, M. M. & Swinson, R. P. (2000). *Phobic Disorders and Panic in Adults: A Guide to Assessment and Treatment*. Washington, DC: American Psychological Association.

Bourne, E. J. (1998). *Overcoming Specific Phobia: A Hierarchy and Exposure-Based Protocol for the Treatment of All Specific Phobias. Therapist Protocol*. Oakland, CA: New Harbinger.

Craske, M., Antony, M. & Barlow, D. (2006). *Mastering Your Fears and Phobias: Therapist Guide* (Second Edition). Oxford: Oxford University Press.

For clients – self-help books for phobias

Antony, M., Craske, M. & Barlow, D. (2006). *Mastering Your Fears and Phobias: Workbook* (Second Edition). Oxford: Oxford University Press.

Bourne, E. J. (1998). *Overcoming Specific Phobias: A Hierarchy and Exposure-Based Protocol for the Treatment of All Specific Phobias. Client Manual*. Oakland, CA: New Harbinger.

Brown, D. (1996). *Flying Without Fear*. Oakland, CA: New Harbinger.

Hartman, C. & Huffaker, J. S. (1995). *The Fearless Flyer: How to Fly in Comfort and Without Trepidation*. Portland, OR: Eighth Mountain Press.

Social phobia in adults

For professionals – therapy manuals for social phobia

Antony, M. M. & Swinson, R. P. (2000). *Phobic Disorders and Panic in Adults: A Guide to Assessment and Treatment*. Washington, DC: American Psychological Association.

Beidel, D. C. & Turner, S. M. (1998). *Shy Children, Phobic Adults: Nature and Treatment of Social Phobia*. Washington, DC: American Psychological Association.

Heimberg, R. G. & Becker, R. E. (2002). *Cognitive-Behavioural Group Therapy for Social Phobia: Basic Mechanisms and Clinical Strategies*. New York: Guilford Press.

Hofmann, S. & Otto, M. (2008). *Cognitive Behaviour Therapy for Social Phobia*. New York: Routledge.

Hope, D., Heimberg, R. & Rurk, C. (2006). *Managing Social Anxiety: A Cognitive Behavioural Therapy Approach. Therapist Guide*. Oxford: Oxford University Press.

Leichsenring, F., Beutel, M. & Leibing, E. (2007). Psychodynamic psychotherapy for social phobia: a treatment manual based on supportive-expressive therapy. *Bulletin of the Menninger Clinic*, 71(1), 56–83.

Rapee, R. M. & Sanderson, W. C. (1998). *Social Phobia: Clinical Application of Evidence-Based Psychotherapy*. Northvale, NJ: Jason Aronson.

For clients – self-help books for social phobia

Anthony, M. (2004). *10 Simple Solutions to Shyness: How to Overcome Shyness, Social Anxiety & Fear of Public Speaking*. Oakland, CA: New Harbinger.

Antony, M. & Swinson, R. (2000). *The Shyness and Social Anxiety Workbook: Proven, Step-By-Step Techniques for Overcoming Your Fear*. Oakland, CA: New Harbinger.

Butler, G. (1999). *Overcoming Social Anxiety and Shyness: A Self-Help Guide Using Cognitive Behavioural Techniques*. London: Robinson.

Desberg, P. (1996). *No More Butterflies: Overcoming Shyness, Stage Fright, Interview Anxiety, and Fear of Public Speaking*. Oakland, CA: New Harbinger.

Hope, D., Heimberg, R. & Rurk, C. (2006). *Managing Social Anxiety: A Cognitive Behavioural Therapy Approach. Workbook*. Oxford: Oxford University Press.

Markway, B. G., Carmin, C. N., Pollard, C. A. & Flynn, T. (1992). *Dying of Embarrassment: Help for Social Anxiety and Phobia*. Oakland, CA: New Harbinger.

Rapee, R.M. (1998). *Overcoming Shyness and Social Phobia: A Step-By-Step Guide*. Northvale, NJ: Jason Aronson.

Schneier, F. & Welkowitz, L. (1996). *The Hidden Face of Shyness: Understanding and Overcoming Social Anxiety*. New York: Avon Books.

Soifer, S., Zgourides, G. D., Himle, J. & Pickering, N. L. (2001). *Shy Bladder Syndrome: Your Step-By-Step Guide to Overcoming Paruresis*. Oakland, CA: New Harbinger.

Stein, M. B. & Walker, J. R. (2001). *Triumph Over Shyness: Conquering Shyness and Social Anxiety*. New York: McGraw-Hill.

Zimbardo, P. (1987). *Shyness*. Reading, MA: Addison Wesley.

Obsessive-compulsive disorder (OCD) in adults

For professionals – treatment manuals for OCD

Abramowitz, J. (2006). *Understanding and Treating Obsessive-Compulsive Disorder: A Cognitive-Behavioural Approach*. Mahwah, NJ: Lawrence Erlbaum Associates, Inc.

Clark, D. (2004). *Cognitive Behavioural Therapy for OCD*. New York: Guilford Press.

Kozak, M. J. & Foa, E. B. (1997). *Mastery of Your Obsessive Compulsive Disorder: Therapist Guide*. New York: Oxford University Press.

Rachman, S. (2003). *The Treatment of Obsessions*. Oxford: Oxford University Press.

Steketee, G. (1998). *Overcoming Obsessive-Compulsive Disorder: Therapist Protocol*. Oakland, CA: New Harbinger.

Steketee, G. S. (1999). *Overcoming Obsessive-Compulsive Disorder: Therapist Protocol*. Oakland, CA: New Harbinger.

Steketee, G. & Frost, R. (2006). *Compulsive Hoarding and Acquiring: Therapist Guide*. Oxford: Oxford University Press.

Swinson, R. P., Antony, M. M., Rachman, S. & Richter, M. A. (1998). *Obsessive-Compulsive Disorder: Theory, Research, and Treatment*. New York: Guilford Press.

For clients – self-help books for OCD

Baer, L. (2000). *Getting Control: Overcoming Your Obsessions and Compulsions*. New York: Plume.

de Silva, P. & Rachman, S. (1998). *Obsessive-Compulsive Disorder: The Facts* (Second Edition). Oxford: Oxford: University Press.

Foa, E. & Kozak, M. (1997). *Mastery of Your Obsessive Compulsive Disorder: Client Workbook*. New York: Oxford University Press.

Foa, E. B. & Wilson, R. (2001). *Stop Obsessing! How to Overcome Your Obsessions and Compulsions*. New York: Bantam Books.

Grayson, J. (2003). *Freedom from Obsessive-Compulsive Disorder: A Personalized Recovery Program for Living with Uncertainty*. New York: Jeremy P. Tarcher/ Penguin.

Hill, F. (2000) *Understanding Obsessive-Compulsive Disorder*. London: Mind.

Hyman, B. M. & Pedrick, C. (1999). *The OCD Workbook: Your Guide to Breaking Free from Obsessive-Compulsive Disorder*. Oakland, CA: New Harbinger.

Neziroglu, F., Bubrick, J. & Yaryura-Tobias, J. A. (2004). *Overcoming Compulsive Hoarding*. Oakland, CA: New Harbinger.

Penzel, F. (2000). *Obsessive-Compulsive Disorders: A Complete Guide to Getting Well and Staying Well*. New York: Oxford University Press.

Purdon, C. A. & Clark, D. A. (2005). *Overcoming Obsessive Thoughts*. Oakland, CA: New Harbinger.

Schwartz, J. M. (1996). *Brainlock: Free Yourself from Obsessive-Compulsive Behaviour*. New York: ReganBooks.

Steketee, G. S. (1999). *Overcoming Obsessive-Compulsive Disorder: Client Manual*. Oakland, CA: New Harbinger.

Steketee, G. & Frost, R. (2006). *Compulsive Hoarding and Acquiring: Workbook*. Oxford: Oxford University Press.

Steketee, G. & White, K. (1991). *When Once Is Not Enough: Help for Obsessive-Compulsives*. Oakland, CA: New Harbinger.

Toates, F. & Coschug-Toates, O. (2002). *Obsessive-Compulsive Disorder* (Second Edition). London: Class Publishing.

Post-traumatic stress disorder (PTSD) in adults

For professionals – cognitive behaviour therapy manuals for PTSD

Foa, E., Hembree, E. & Rothbaum, B. (2007). *Prolonged Exposure Therapy for PTSD: Emotional Processing of Traumatic Experience. Therapist Guide*. Oxford: Oxford University Press.

Foa, E. & Rothbaum, B. (1998). *Treating the Trauma of Rape: Cognitive Behavioural Therapy for PTSD*. New York: Guilford Press.

Follette, C. (2001). *Cognitive-Behavioural Therapies for Trauma*. New York: Guilford Press.

Hickling, E. & Blanchard, E. (2006). *Overcoming the Trauma of Your Motor Vehicle Accident: A Cognitive-Behavioural Treatment Programme. Therapist Guide*. Oxford: Oxford University Press.

Smyth, L. (1999). *Overcoming Post-Traumatic Stress Disorder: Therapist Protocol*. Oakland, CA: New Harbinger.

Taylor, S. (2006). *Clinician's Guide to PTSD: A Cognitive Behavioural Approach*. New York: Guilford Press.

For professionals – EMDR treatment manual for PTSD

Shapiro, F. (2001). *Eye Movement Desensitization and Reprocessing: Basic Principles, Protocols and Procedures* (Second Edition). New York: Guilford Press.

For professionals – psychodynamic treatment manual for PTSD

Horowitz, M. (2001). *Stress Response Syndromes: Personality Styles and Interventions* (Fourth Edition). New York: Jason Aronson.

For clients – self-help books for PTSD

Herbert, C. & Wetmore, A. (1999). *Overcoming Traumatic Stress: A Self-Help Guide Using Cognitive Behavioural Techniques*. London: Robinson.
Hickling, E. & Blanchard, E. (2006). *Overcoming the Trauma of Your Motor Vehicle Accident: A Cognitive-Behavioural Treatment Programme. Workbook*. Oxford: Oxford University Press.
Kennerley, H. (2000). *Overcoming Childhood Trauma*. New York: NYU Press.
Matsakis, A. (1996). *I Can't Get Over It: A Handbook for Trauma Survivors* (Second Edition). Oakland, CA: New Harbinger.
Rosenbloom, D., Williams, M. & Watkins, B. (1999). *Life After Trauma: A Workbook for Healing*. New York: Guilford Press.
Rothbaum, B. (2007). *Reclaiming Your Life from a Traumatic Experience: A Prolonged Exposure Treatment Programme Workbook*. Oxford: Oxford University Press.
Scott, M. (2007). *Moving On After PTSD*. London: Routledge.
Shapiro, F. & Silk Forest, M. (2004). *EMDR: The Breakthrough 'Eye Movement' Therapy for Overcoming Anxiety, Stress, and Trauma*. New York: Basic Books.
Smyth, L. (1999). *Overcoming Post-Traumatic Stress Disorder: Client Manual*. Oakland, CA: New Harbinger.

Hypochondriasis – health anxiety in adults

For professionals – treatment manuals for health anxiety

Taylor, S. & Asmundson, G. (2004). *Treating Health Anxiety: A Cognitive Behavioural Approach*. New York: Guilford Press.
Woolfolk, R. & Allen, L. (2007). *Treating Somatization: A Cognitive-Behavioural Approach*. New York: Guilford Press.

For clients – self-help books for health anxiety

Asmundson, G. & Taylor, S. (2005). *It's Not All In Your Head: How Worrying About Your Health Could Be Making You Sick – And What You Can Do About It*. New York: Guilford Press.

Body dysmorphic disorder (BDD) in adults

For professionals – treatment manual for BDD

Phillips, K. (2005). *The Broken Mirror: Understanding and Treating Body Dysmorphic Disorder*. New York: Oxford University Press.

For clients – self-help books for BDD

Claiborn, J. & Pedirick, C. (2002). *The BDD Workbook: Overcome Body Dysmorphic Disorder and End Body Image Obsessions*. Oakland, CA: Harbinger.
Wilhelm, S. (2006). *Feeling Good About the Way You Look*. New York: Guilford Press.

Stressful medical conditions in adults

For clients – self-help stress management workbook

Davis, M., McKay, M. & Robbins Eshelman, E. (2000). *The Relaxation and Stress Reduction Workbook* (Fifth Edition). Oakland, CA: New Harbinger.

Cancer in adults

For professionals – treatment manuals for adjustment to cancer

Antoni, M. (2003). *Stress Management Intervention for Women with Breast Cancer*. Washington, DC: American Psychological Association.
Baum, A. & Ndersen, B. (2001). *Psychosocial Interventions for Cancer*. Washington, DC: American Psychological Association.
Moorey, S. & Greer, S. (2002). *Cognitive Behaviour Therapy for People with Cancer*. Oxford: Oxford University Press.
White, C. (2001). *Cognitive Behaviour Therapy for Chronic Medical Problems*. Chichester: John Wiley.

For clients – self-help books for adjustment to cancer

Antoni, M. (2003). *Stress Management Intervention for Women with Breast Cancer: Participants' Workbook*. Washington, DC: American Psychological Association.
Gersh, W. D., Golden, W. L. & Robbins, D. M. (1997). *Mind Over Malignancy: Living with Cancer*. Oakland, CA: New Harbinger.

Heart disease in adults

For professionals – a guidebook on adjustment to heart disease

Sotile, W. (1996). *Psychosocial Interventions for Cardiopulmonary Patients: A Guide for Health Professionals*. Champaign, IL: Human Kinetics Press.

For clients – self-help books on adjustment to heart disease

American Heart Association (1998). *American Heart Association Guide to Heart Attack Treatment, Recovery, and Prevention*. New York: Clarkson Potter.

Klingfield, P. (2006). *The Cardiac Recovery Handbook*. New York: Hatherleigh.
Maximin, A. & Stevic-Rust, L. (1997). *Heart Therapy: Regaining Your Cardiac Health*. Oakland, CA: New Harbinger.
Sotile, W. (2003). *Thriving with Heart Disease*. New York: Free Press.

Asthma in adults

For professionals – a treatment manual on adjustment to asthma

Kotses, H. & Harver, A. (1998). *Self-Management of Asthma*. New York: Informa Healthcare.

For clients – self-help books on adjustment to asthma

Adams, F. (2007). *The Asthma Sourcebook* (Third Edition). New York: McGraw-Hill.
Fanta, C., Cristiano, L., Haver, K. & Waring, N. (2003). *The Harvard Medical School Guide to Taking Control Of Asthma*. New York: Free Press.

Diabetes in adults

For professionals – a guidebook on adjustment to diabetes

Snoek, F. & Skinner, T. (2005). *Psychology in Diabetes Care* (Second Edition). Chichester: John Wiley.

For clients – self-help books on adjustment to diabetes

American Diabetes Association (2006). *American Diabetes Association Complete Guide to Diabetes* (Fourth Edition). New York: Bantam.
Rubin, R., Biermann, J. & Toohey, B. (1999). *Psyching Out Diabetes: A Positive Approach to Your Negative Emotions* (Third Edition). Los Angeles: Lowell House.
Saudek, C., Rubin, R. & Shump, C. (1997). *The Johns Hopkins Guide to Diabetes: For Today and Tomorrow*. Baltimore, MD: The Johns Hopkins University Press.

Pain in adults

For professionals – treatment manuals and videos on pain

Gatchel, R. (2006). *Pain Management Video*. Washington, DC: American Psychological Association (www.apa.org).
Otis, J. (2007). *Managing Chronic Pain: A Cognitive-Behavioural Therapy Approach. Therapist Guide*. Oxford: Oxford University Press.
Turk, D. & Gatchel, R. (2002). *Psychological Approaches to Pain Management: A Practitioner's Handbook* (Second Edition). New York: Guilford Press.

For clients – self-help books on pain

Catalano, E. M. & Hardin, K. N. (1996). *The Chronic Pain Control Workbook: A Step-By-Step Guide for Coping with and Overcoming Pain*. Oakland, CA: New Harbinger.

Caudill, M. A. (2001). *Managing Pain Before It Manages You*. New York: Guilford Press.

Otis, J. (2007). *Managing Chronic Pain: A Cognitive-Behavioural Therapy Approach. Workbook*. Oxford: Oxford University Press.

Turk, D. & Winter, F. (2006). *The Pain Survival Guide: How to Reclaim Your Life*. Washington, DC: American Psychological Association.

Fibromyalgia in adults

For professionals and clients – a guidebook on fibromyalgia

Wallace, D. & Brock Wallace, J. (1999). *Making Sense of Fibromyalgia*. New York: Oxford University Press.

Chronic fatigue syndrome (CFS) in adults

For professionals – treatment manual for CFS

Kinsella, P. (2007). *Cognitive Behavioural Therapy for Chronic Fatigue Syndrome*. London: Routledge.

For clients – self-help books on CFS

Friedberg, F. (1995). *Coping with Chronic Fatigue Syndrome: Nine Things You Can Do*. Oakland, CA: New Harbinger.

Teitelbaum, J. (2007). *From Fatigued to Fantastic* (Third Edition). Vonore, TN: Avery.

Headaches in adults

For professionals – treatment manual for headaches

Blanchard, E. & Andraisk, F. (1985). *Management of Chronic Headache: A Psychological Approach*. New York: Pergamon.

Borkum, J. (2007). *Chronic Headaches: Biology, Psychology and Behavioural Treatment*. New York: Routledge.

Martin, P. (1993). *Psychological Management of Chronic Headaches*. New York: Guilford Press.

Arthritis in adults

For professionals and clients – guidebooks

Fries, J. (1999). *Arthritis: A Take Care of Yourself Health Guide for Understanding Your Arthritis*. New York: Perseus.

Lorig, K., Fries, J. & Gecht, M. (2000). *The Arthritis Helpbook: A Tested Self-Management Program for Coping with Arthritis and Fibromyalgia* (Fifth Edition). New York: HarperCollins.

Irritable bowel syndrome in adults

For professionals – treatment manuals

Blanchard, E. (2000). *Irritable Bowel Syndrome: Psychosocial Assessment and Treatment*. Washington, DC: American Psychological Association.

Toner, B., Segal, Z., Emmott, S. & Myran, D. (2000). *Cognitive-Behavioural Treatment of Irritable Bowel Syndrome: The Brain–Gut Connection*. New York: Guilford Press.

Obesity in adults

For professionals – treatment manuals for obesity

Apple, R., Lock, J. & Preebles, R. (2006). *Preparing for Weight Loss Surgery: Therapist Guide*. Oxford: Oxford University Press.

Brownell, K. (2000). *The LEARN Programme for Weight Management 2000* (Tenth Edition). Dallas, TX: American Health Publishing Company.

Cooper, Z., Fairburn, C. & Hawker, D. (2003). *Cognitive-Behavioural Treatment of Obesity – A Clinician's Guide*. New York: Guilford Press.

For clients – self-help for obesity

Beck, J. S. (2007). *Beck Diet Solution Weight Loss Workbook: The 6-Week Plan to Train Your Brain to Think Like a Thin Person*. Des Moines: Oxmoor House.

Beck, J. S. (2007). *The Beck Diet Solution: Train Your Brain to Think Like a Thin Person*. Des Moines: Oxmoor House.

Woodward, B. G. (2001). *A Complete Guide to Obesity Surgery: Everything You Need to Know About Weight Loss Surgery and How to Succeed*. New Bern, NC: Trafford Publishing.

Anorexia, bulimia, and binge eating disorder in adults

For professionals – treatment manuals

Agras, W. & Apple, R. (2007). *Overcoming Your Eating Disorder: A Cognitive-Behavioural Approach for Bulimia Nervosa and Binge-Eating Disorder. Therapist Guide* (Second Edition). Oxford: Oxford University Press.

Crisp, A., McClelland, L., Joughin, N., Halek, C. & Bower, C. (1996). *Anorexia Nervosa: Clinician's Pack* (three book set). London: Routledge.

Fairburn, C., Marcus, M. & Wilson, G. (1993). Cognitive behaviour therapy for binge eating and bulimia nervosa: a comprehensive treatment manual. In C. G. Fairburn

& G. T. Wilson (Eds.), *Binge Eating: Nature, Assessment, and Treatment* (pp. 361–404). New York: Guilford Press.

Garner, D. & Garfinkel, P. (1997). *Handbook of Treatment for Eating Disorders* (Second Edition). New York: Guilford Press.

Palmer, B. (2000). *Helping People with Eating Disorders*. Chichester: John Wiley

Schmidt, U. & Treasure, J. (1997). *Clinician's Guide to Getting Better Bit(e) by Bit(e)*. Hove, UK: Psychology Press.

Weissman, M., Markowitz, J. & Klerman, G. (2000). *Comprehensive Guide to Interpersonal Psychotherapy*. New York: Basic Books.

For clients – self-help for anorexia nervosa, bulimia, and binge eating disorder

Agras, W. & Apple, R. (2007). *Overcoming Your Eating Disorder: A Cognitive-Behavioural Approach for Bulimia Nervosa and Binge-Eating Disorder. Guided Self-Help Workbook* (Second Edition). Oxford: Oxford University Press.

Cooper, M., Todd, G. & Wells, A. (2000). *Bulimia Nervosa – A Cognitive Therapy Programme for Clients*. London: Jessica Kingsley Publishers.

Cooper, P. J. (1995). *Bulimia Nervosa: A Guide to Recovery*. London: Robinson.

Crisp, A., Joughin, N., Halek, C. & Bower, C. (1996). *Anorexia Nervosa: The Wish to Change. Self-Help and Discovery, The Thirty Steps* (Second Edition). Hove, UK: Psychology Press.

Fairburn, C. (1995). *Overcoming Binge Eating*. New York: Guilford Press.

Freeman, C. (2001). *Overcoming Anorexia Nervosa*. London: Constable Robinson.

Schmidt, U. & Treasure, J. (1993). *Getting Better Bit(e) by Bit(e)*. Hove, UK: Psychology Press.

Treasure, J. (1997). *Anorexia Nervosa: A Survival Guide for Families, Friends and Sufferers*. Hove, UK: Psychology Press.

Treasure, J., Smith, G. & Crane, A. (2007). *Skills-Based Learning for Caring for a Loved One with an Eating Disorder*. London: Routledge.

Williams, C., Schmidt, U. & Aubin, S. (2005). *Overcoming Anorexia: A Self-Help CBT CD-ROM*. University of Leeds Media Innovations Ltd, 3 Gemini Business Park, Sheepscar Way, Leeds LS7 3JB. Tel: +44-113-262-1600; website: http://www.calipso.co.uk.

Williams, C., Schmidt, U. & Aubin, S. (2005). *Overcoming Bulimia: A Self-Help CBT CD-ROM*. University of Leeds Media Innovations Ltd, 3 Gemini Business Park, Sheepscar Way, Leeds LS7 3JB. Tel: +44-113-262-1600; website: http://www.calipso.co.uk.

Insomnia in adults

For professionals – treatment manuals for insomnia

Morin, C. & Espie, C. (2003). *Insomnia: Psychological Assessment and Management*. New York: Plenum (comes with CD).

For clients – self-help books for insomnia

Coates, T. & Thoresen, C. (1977). *How To Sleep Better*. Englewood Cliffs, NJ: Prentice Hall.

Espie, C. (2006). *Overcoming Insomnia and Sleep Problems*. London: Constable & Robinson.

Glovinsky, P. & Spielman, A. (2006). *The Insomnia Answer: A Personalized Program for Identifying and Overcoming the Three Types of Insomnia*. New York: Perigee Trade.

Alcohol and drug abuse in adults

For professionals – motivational interviewing treatment manuals for alcohol and drug abuse

Miller, W. R. & Rollnick. S. (2002). *Motivational Interviewing: Preparing People for Change* (Second Edition). New York: Guilford Press.

Miller, W. R., Zweben, A., DiClemente, C. C. & Rychtarik, R. G. (1994). *Motivational Enhancement Therapy Manual: A Clinical Research Guide for Therapists Treating Individuals with Alcohol Abuse and Dependence*. Rockville, MD: NIAAA (http://pubs.niaaa.nih.gov/publications/match.htm).

For professionals – systemic therapy manuals for alcohol and drug abuse

Budney, A. & Higgins, S. (1998). *A Community Reinforcement Plus Vouchers Approach: Treating Cocaine Addiction*. National Institute for Drug Abuse (http://www.nida.nih.gov/pdf/CRA.pdf).

Copello, A., Orford, J., Hodgson, R. & Tober, G. (2002). *Social Behaviour and Network Therapy Manual*. Birmingham: University of Birmingham and the UKATT (available from Gary.Slegg@new-tr.wales.nhs.uk).

Meyers, R. & Smith, J. (1995). *Clinical Guide to Alcohol Treatment: The Community Reinforcement Approach*. New York: Guilford Press.

O'Farrell, T. & Fals-Stewart, W. (2006). *Behavioural Couples Therapy for Alcoholism and Substance Abuse*. New York: Guilford Press (variations on this basic treatment manual are available at http://www.addictionandfamily.org/htm_pages/manuals.htm).

Smith, J. & Meyers, R. (2004). *Motivating Substance Abusers to Enter Treatment: Working with Family Members*. New York: Guilford Press.

For professionals – cognitive behaviour therapy manuals for alcohol and drug abuse

Carroll, K. (1998). *A Cognitive Behavioural Approach: Treating Cocaine Addiction*. National Institute for Drug Abuse (http://www.nida.nih.gov/pdf/CBT.pdf).

Daley, D. & Marlatt, A. (2006). *Overcoming Your Alcohol or Drug Problem: Effective Recovery Strategies. Therapist Guide* (Second Edition). Oxford: Oxford University Press.

Kadden, R., Carroll, K. M., Donovan, D., Cooney, N., Monti, P., Abrams, D., Litt, M. & Hester, R. (1994). *Cognitive-Behavioural Coping Skills Therapy Manual: A Clinical Research Guide For Therapists Treating Individuals with Alcohol Abuse and Dependence.* Rockville, MD: NIAAA (http://pubs.niaaa.nih.gov/publications/MATCHSeries3/Project%20MATCH%20Vol_3.pdf).
Kouimtsidis, C., Davis, P., Reynolds, M., Drummond, C. & Tarrier, N. (2007). *Cognitive-Behavioural Therapy in the Treatment of Addiction: A Treatment Planner for Clinicians.* Chichester: John Wiley.
Monti, P. M., Kadden, R. M., Rohsenow, D. J., Cooney, N. L. & Abrams, D. B. (2002). *Treating Alcohol Dependence: A Coping Skills Training Guide* (Second Edition). New York: Guilford Press.

For professionals – 12-step facilitation treatment guides for alcohol and drug abuse

Nowinski, J. (1999). *Family Recovery And Substance Abuse: A Twelve-Step Guide For Treatment.* Thousand Oaks, CA: Sage.
Nowinski, J., Baker, S. & Carroll, K. M. (1994). *Twelve-Step Facilitation Therapy Manual: A Clinical Research Guide for Therapists Treating Individuals with Alcohol Abuse and Dependence.* Rockville, MD: NIAAA (http://pubs.niaaa.nih.gov/publications/match.htm).

For professionals – various other treatment manuals for alcohol and drug abuse

De Leon, G. (2000). *The Therapeutic Community: Theory, Model, and Method.* New York: Springer.
Denning, P. (2004). *Practicing Harm Reduction Psychotherapy: An Alternative Approach to Addictions.* New York: Guilford Press.
Fletcher, A. (2001). *Sober for Good: New Solutions for Drinking Problems: Advice from Those Who Have Succeeded.* New York: Houghton Mifflin.
Mercer, D. & Woody, G. (1999). *Individual Drug Counselling.* National Institute for Drug Abuse (http://www.nida.nih.gov/PDF/Manual3.pdf).
Rawson, R. A., Obert, J. L. & McCann, M. J. (1995). *The Matrix Intensive Outpatient Program Therapist Manual.* Los Angeles: The Matrix Centre (http://www.matrixinstitute.org/).
Washton, A. & Zweben, J. (2006). *Treating Alcohol and Drug Problems in Psychotherapy Practice.* New York: Guilford Press.

For clients – self-help books on alcohol and drug abuse

Alcoholics Anonymous (1976). *Alcoholics Anonymous* (Third Edition). Malo, WA: Anonymous Press.
Colclough, B. (1993). *Tomorrow I'll Be Different: The Effective Way to Stop Drinking.* London: Viking.

Daley, D. & Marlatt, A. (2006). *Overcoming Your Alcohol or Drug Problem: Effective Recovery Strategies. Workbook* (Second Edition). Oxford: Oxford University Press.

Denning, P., Little, J. & Glickman, A. (2003). *Over the Influence: The Harm Reduction Guide for Managing Drugs and Alcohol.* New York: Guilford Press.

Ellis, A. & Velton, E. (1992). *When AA Doesn't Work for You.* Fort Lee, NJ: Barricade Books.

Meyers, R. & Wolfe, B. (2004). *Get Your Loved One Sober: Alternatives to Nagging, Pleading and Threatening.* New York: Haleden.

Miller, W. & Munzo, R. (2005) *Controlling Your Drinking: Tools to Make Moderation Work for You.* New York: Guilford Press.

Trickett, S. (1986). *Coming Off Tranquilizers.* New York: Thorsons.

Tyrer, P. (1986). *How to Stop Taking Tranquilizers.* London: Sheldon Press.

Smoking cessation in adults

For professionals – treatment guides for smoking cessation

Abrams, D., Niaura, R., Brown, R., Emmons, K., Goldstein, M. & Monti, P. M. (2003). *The Tobacco Dependence Treatment Handbook: A Guide to Best Practices.* New York: Guilford Press.

Perkins, K., Conklin, C. & Levine, M. (2007). *Cognitive Behaviour Therapy for Smoking Cessation: A Practical Guidebook to the Most Effective Treatments.* London: Routledge.

Spring, B. (2008). *Smoking Cessation with Weight Gain Control: Therapist Guide*: Oxford: Oxford University Press.

For clients – self-help for smoking cessation

Spring, B. (2008). *Smoking Cessation with Weight Gain Control: Workbook.* Oxford: Oxford University Press.

Compulsive gambling in adults

For professionals – treatment manuals for gambling

Grant, J. & Potenza, M. (2004). *Pathological Gambling: A Clinical Guide to Treatment.* Washington, DC: American Psychiatric Publishing.

Ladouceur, R. & Lachance, S. (2006). *Overcoming Pathological Gambling: Therapist Guide.* Oxford: Oxford University Press.

Ladouceur, R., Sylvain, C., Boutin, C. & Doucet, C. (2002). *Understanding and Treating the Pathological Gambler.* Chichester: John Wiley.

Petry, N. (2005). *Pathological Gambling: Aetiology, Comorbidity, and Treatment.* Washington, DC: American Psychological Association.

Petry, N. (2006). *Problem Gambling.* Videotape. Washington, DC: American Psychological Association.

For clients – self-help books for gambling

Blaszczynski, A. (1998). *Overcoming Compulsive Gambling*. London: Robinson.
Ladouceur, R. & Lachance, S. (2006). *Overcoming Pathological Gambling: Workbook*. Oxford: Oxford University Press.

Schizophrenia in adults

For professionals – psychoeducational family therapy manuals for schizophrenia

Bloch Thorsen, G., Gronnestad, T. & Oxnevad, A. (2006). *Family and Multi-Family Work with Psychosis*. London: Routledge.
Falloon, I., Laporta, M., Fadden, G. & Graham-Hole, V. (1993). *Managing Stress in Families*. London: Routledge.
Kuipers, E., Leff, J. & Lam, D. (2002). *Family Work for Schizophrenia* (Second Edition). London: Gaskell.
McFarlane, W. (2004). *Multifamily Groups in the Treatment of Severe Psychiatric Disorders*. New York: Guilford Press.
Smith, G., Gregory, K. & Higgs, A. (2007). *An Integrated Approach to Family Work for Psychosis: A Manual for Family Workers*. London: Jessica Kingsley Publishers.
Tarrier, N. & Barrowclough, C. (1997). *Families of Schizophrenic Patients: Cognitive Behavioural Intervention*. London: Nelson Thornes.

For professionals – cognitive behaviour therapy manuals for schizophrenia

Birchwood, M. & Tarrier, N. (1994) *Psychological Management of Schizophrenia*. Chichester: John Wiley.
Chadwick, P., Birchwood, M. & Trower, P. (1996). *Cognitive Therapy for Delusions, Voices and Paranoia*. Chichester: John Wiley.
Fowler, D., Garety, P. & Kuipers, L. (1995). *Cognitive Behavioural Therapy for Psychosis: Theory and Practice*. Chichester: John Wiley.
Gumley, A. & Schwannauer, M. (2006). *Staying Well After Psychosis: A Cognitive Interpersonal Approach to Recovery and Relapse Prevention*. Chichester: John Wiley.
Haddock, G. & Slade, P. (1996). *Cognitive-Behavioural Interventions with Psychotic Disorders*. London: Routledge.
Hogarty, G. (2002). *Personal Therapy for Schizophrenia and Related Disorders*. New York: Guilford Press.
Kingdom, D. & Turkington, D. (2005). *Cognitive Therapy of Schizophrenia*. New York: Guilford Press.
Morrison, A. (2003). *Cognitive Therapy for Psychosis: A Formulation-Based Approach*. London: Routledge.

For professionals – social skills training manuals for schizophrenia

Bellack, A., Mueser, K., Gingerich, S. & Agresta, J. (2004). *Social Skills Training for Schizophrenia: A Step-By-Step Guide* (Second Edition). New York: Guilford Press.

Liberman, R., DeRisi, W. & Mueser, K. (1989). *Social Skills Training for Psychiatric Patients*. New York: Pergamon.

For professionals – cognitive remediation guides for schizophrenia

Brenner, H., Roder, V., Hodel, B., Kienzle, N., Reed, D. & Liberman, R. (1994). *Integrated Psychological Therapy for Schizophrenic Patients*. Toronto: Hogrefe & Huber.

Wykes, T. & Reeder, C. (2005). *Cognitive Remediation Therapy for Schizophrenia: Theory and Practice*. London: Routledge.

For professionals – assertive community treatment manuals

Allness, D. & Knoedler, W. (1998). *The PACT Model of Community-Based Treatment for Persons with Severe and Persistent Mental Illness: A Manual for PACT Start-up*. Arlington, VA: National Alliance for the Mentally Ill.

Burns, T. & Fim, M. (2002). *Assertive Outreach in Mental Health: A Manual for Practitioners*. Oxford: Oxford University Press.

For clients – self-help for schizophrenia

Bernheim, K., Lewine, R. & Beale, C. (1982). *The Caring Family: Living with Mental Illness*. New York: Random House.

Freeman, D. (2006). *Overcoming Paranoid and Suspicious Thoughts*. London: Robinson.

Healy, C. (2007). *Understanding Your Schizophrenia Illness: A Workbook*. Chichester: John Wiley.

Keefe, R. & Harvey, P. (1994). *Understanding Schizophrenia: A Guide to the New Research on Causes and Treatment*. New York: Free Press.

Kuipers, E. & Bebbington, P. E. (2005) *Living with Mental Illness* (Third Edition). London: Souvenir Press.

Marsh, D. & Dickens, R. (1998). *How to Cope with Mental Illness in Your Family: A Self-Care Guide for Siblings, Offspring and Parents*. New York: Tarcher/Putnam.

Mueser, K. & Gingerich, S. (2006). *The Complete Family Guide to Schizophrenia*. New York: Guilford Press.

Sheehan, S. (1982). *Is There No Place On Earth For Me?* Boston, MA: Houghton Mifflin.

Torrey, E. F. (1995). *Surviving Schizophrenia: A Manual for Families, Consumers and Providers*. New York: Harper Perrenial.

Vine, P. (1982). *Families in Pain*. New York: Pantheon.

Wasow, M. (1982). *Coping with Schizophrenia*. Palo Alto, CA: Science and Behaviour Books.

Personality disorders in adults

For professionals – psychodynamic treatment manuals for personality disorders

Bateman, A. & Fonagy, P. (2006). *Mentalization-Based Treatment for Borderline Personality Disorder: A Practical Guide.* Oxford: Oxford University Press.

Luborsky, L. (1984). *Principles of Psychoanalytic Psychotherapy: A Manual for Supportive-Expressive Treatment.* New York: Basic Books.

Malan, D. (1995). *Individual Psychotherapy and the Science of Psychodynamics* (Second Edition). London: Butterworth-Heinemann.

McCullough, L., Kuhn, N., Andrews, S., Kaplan, A., Wolfe, J. & Lanza, C. (2003). *Treating Affect Phobia: A Therapist Manual for Short-Term Dynamic Psychotherapy.* New York: Guilford Press.

For professionals – cognitive behaviour therapy manuals and videos for personality disorders

Beck, A. & Freeman, A. (1990) *Cognitive Therapy for Personality Disorders.* New York: Guilford Press.

Davidson, K. (2000). *Cognitive Therapy for Personality Disorders: A Guide For Clinicians.* London: Arnold.

Freeman, A. & Fusco, G. (2003). *Borderline Personality Disorder: A Therapist's Guide to Taking Control.* New York: Norton.

Gunderson, J. (2001). *Borderline Personality Disorder: A Clinical Guide.* Washington, DC: American Psychiatric Press.

Linehan, M. (1993). *Cognitive-Behavioural Treatment of Borderline Personality Disorder.* New York: Guilford Press.

Linehan, M. (1993). *Skills Training Manual for Treating Borderline Personality Disorder.* New York: Guilford Press.

Linehan, M. M. (1995). *Treating Borderline Personality Disorder: The Dialectical Approach.* Video. New York: Guilford Press.

Linehan, M. M. (1995). *Understanding Borderline Personality Disorder: The Dialectical Approach.* Video. New York: Guilford Press.

Linehan, M. & Dimeff, A. (1997). *Dialectical Behaviour Therapy Manual of Treatment Interventions for Drug Abusers with Borderline Personality Disorder.* Seattle: University of Washington Press.

Linehan, M. M., Dimeff, L., Waltz, J. & Koerner, K. (2000). *DBT Skills Training Video: Opposite Action.* Seattle: Behavioural Technology Transfer Group.

Young, J. (1999). *Cognitive Therapy for Personality Disorders: A Schema Focused Approach* (Third Edition). Saratosa, FL: Professional Resource Press.

For clients – self-help for personality disorders

Fusco, G. & Freeman, A. (2004). *Borderline Personality Disorder: A Patient's Guide to Taking Control.* New York: Norton.

Kreger, R. & Shirley, J. (2002). *The Stop Walking on Eggshells Workbook: Practical Strategies for Living with Someone who has Borderline Personality Disorder*. Oakland, CA: New Harbinger.

Mason, P. T. & Kreger, R. (1998). *Stop Walking on Eggshells: Taking your Life Back When Someone you Care about has Borderline Personality Disorder*. Oakland, CA: New Harbinger.

Anger management in adults

For professionals – treatment manuals for anger management

Deffenbacker, J. & McKay, M. (1999). *Overcoming Situational and General Anger: Therapist Protocol*. Oakland, CA: New Harbinger.

Kassinove, H. & Tafrate, R. (2002). *Anger Management: The Complete Treatment Guidebook for Practitioners*. Atascadero, CA: Impact.

Novaco, R. (1975). *Anger Control: The Development and Evaluation of an Experimental Treatment*. Lexington, MA: Heath.

O'Neill, H. (2006). *Managing Anger* (Second Edition). Chichester: John Wiley.

Potter-Efron, R. (2005). *Handbook of Anger Management: Group, Individual, Couple and Family Approaches*. New York: Haworth Press.

For clients – self-help books for anger management

Beck, A. (2000). *Prisoners of Hate: The Cognitive Basis of Anger, Hostility, and Violence*. New York: HarperCollins.

Bilodeau, L. (1992). *The Anger Workbook*. Minneapolis, MN: Compcare.

Deffenbacker, J. & McKay, M. (1999). *Overcoming Situational and General Anger: Client Manual*. Oakland, CA: New Harbinger.

Potter-Efron, R. & Potter-Efron, R. (1995). *The Ten Most Common Anger Styles and What to Do about Them*. Oakland, CA: New Harbinger.

Tavris, C. (1989). *Anger: The Misunderstood Emotion*. New York: Touchstone.

Sexual offending in adults

For professionals – treatment manual on sexual offending

Marshall, W., Marshall, L., Serran, G. and Fernandez, Y. (2006). *Treating Sexual Offenders: An Integrated Approach*. New York: Routledge.

Relationship distress in adulthood

For professionals – couples therapy manuals for relationship distress

Epstein, N. B. & Baucom, D. H. (2002). *Enhanced Cognitive-Behavioural Therapy for Couples: A Contextual Approach*. Washington, DC: American Psychological Association.

Gottman, J. (1999). *The Marriage Clinic: A Scientifically-Based Marital Therapy*. New York: Norton.

Gurman, A. & Jacobson, N. (2002). *Clinical Handbook of Couple Therapy* (Third Edition). New York: Guilford Press.

Jacobson, N. & Christensen, A. (1998). *Acceptance and Change in Couple Therapy: A Therapist's Guide to Transforming Relationships*. New York: Norton.

Johnson, S. (2004). *The Practice of Emotionally Focused Couple Therapy: Creating Connection* (Second Edition). New York: Guilford Press.

For clients – self-help books for relationship distress

Christensen, A. & Jacobson, N. (2002). *Reconcilable Differences*. New York: Guilford Press.

Gottman, J. & Silver, N. (1999). *The Seven Principles for Making Marriage Work*. London: Weidenfeld & Nicolson.

Markman, H., Stanley, S. & Blumberg, S. L. (1994). *Fighting for Your Marriage*. San Francisco, CA: Jossey Bass.

Sexual dysfunction

For professionals – treatment manuals for sexual dysfunction

Hawton, K. (1985). *Sex Therapy: A Practical Guide*. Oxford: Oxford University Press.

Leiblum, S. (2006). *Principles and Practice of Sex Therapy* (Fourth Edition). New York: Guilford Press.

McCarthy, B. & McCarthy, E. (2003). *Rekindling Desire: A Step-By-Step Program to Help Low-Sex and No-Sex Marriages*. New York: Routledge.

Wincze, J. & Carey, M. (2001). *Sexual Dysfunction: A Guide for Assessment and Treatment* (Second Edition). New York: Guilford Press.

For clients – self-help books for sexual dysfunction

Foley, S., Kope, S. & Sugrue, D. (2002). *Sex Matters for Women*. New York: Guilford Press.

Leiblum, S. & Sachs, J. (2002). *Getting the Sex You Want: A Woman's Guide to Becoming Proud, Passionate and Pleased in Bed*. New York: Crown.

McCarthy, B. & McCarthy, E. (2002). *Sexual Awareness: Couple Sexuality for the Twenty-First Century*. New York: Carroll & Graf.

Metz, M. E. & McCarthy, B. W. (2003). *Coping with Premature Ejaculation: Overcome PE, Please Your Partner, and Have Great Sex*. Oakland, CA: New Harbinger.

Metz, M. E. & McCarthy, B. W. (2004). *Coping with Erectile Dysfunction: How to Regain Confidence and Enjoy Great Sex*. Oakland, CA: New Harbinger.

Zilbergeld, B. (1999). *The New Male Sexuality*. New York: Bantam.

Grief and bereavement in adults

For professionals – grief therapy manual

Worden, J. (2001). *Grief Counselling and Grief Therapy: A Handbook for the Mental Health Professional* (Third Edition). New York: Springer.

For clients – self-help books for bereavement

Abrams, R. (1999). *When Parents Die: Learning to Live with the Loss of a Parent* (Second Edition). London: Routledge.

Allen, M. & Marks, S. (1993). *Miscarriage: Women Sharing from the Heart*. Chichester: John Wiley.

Colgrove, M., Bloomfield, H. & McWilliams, P. (1993). *How to Survive the Loss of Love* (Second Edition). Los Angeles: Prelude Press.

Hewett, J. (1983). *After Suicide*. London: Westminster Press.

James, J. & Friedman, R. (1998). *The Grief Recovery Handbook: The Action Programme for Moving Beyond Death, Divorce and Other Losses*. New York: Harper Row.

Kubler-Ross, E. & Kessler, D. (2005). *On Grief & Grieving*. New York: Simon & Schuster.

Rando, T. (1991). *How to Go on Living When Someone You Love Dies*. New York: Bantam.

Tatelbaum, J. (1984). *The Courage to Grieve – Creative Living, Recovery & Growth Through Grief*. New York: HarperPerennial.

Psychological problems in older adults

For professionals – general resources

Jacoby, R. & Oppenheimer, C. (2002). *Psychiatry in the Elderly* (Third Edition). Oxford: Oxford University Press.

Woods, R. & Clare, L. (2008). *Handbook of Clinical Psychology of Ageing* (Second Edition). Chichester: John Wiley.

For professionals – caregiver support in dementia

Smith, M., Gerdner, L., Hall, J. & Buckwalter, K. (2004) History, development, and future of the progressively lowered stress threshold: a conceptual model for dementia care. *Journal of the American Geriatrics Society*, 52(10), 1755–1760.

Teri, L. (1990). *Managing and Understanding Behaviour Problems in Alzheimer's Disease and Related Disorders*. Training programme with video and written manual. Washington, DC: University of Washington, Alzheimer's Disease Research Centre (http://depts.washington.edu/adrcweb/).

For professionals – treatment manuals for depression in older adults

Gibson, F. (2004). *The Past in the Present: Using Reminiscence in Health and Social Care*. Baltimore, MD: Health Professions Press.

Hinrichsen, G. & Clougherty, K. (2006). *Interpersonal Psychotherapy for Depressed Older Adults*. Washington, DC: American Psychological Association.

Laidlaw, K., Thompson, L., Dicksiskin, L. & Gallagher-Thompson, D. (2003). *Cognitive Behaviour Therapy with Older People*. Chichester: John Wiley.

For clients – self-help book for older adulthood

Rowe, J. W. & Kahn, R. L. (1998). *Successful Aging*. New York: Pantheon Books.

Chapter 6

Additional elements in the psychotherapy evidence base

In this chapter the focus will be on a number of loose ends in the psychotherapy evidence base that have not been fully addressed in previous chapters, although some have been mentioned briefly. The chapter addresses the question: What other types of interventions that have not been fully addressed in previous chapters can help psychological problems? For severe mental health problems, evidence for the benefits of user involvement in service delivery and evaluation; the use of home treatment and day hospitals as alternatives to inpatient care; and the use of supported employment to enhance occupational adjustment will be considered. For anxiety, depression, and other common difficulties, evidence will be summarized on the effectiveness of psychotherapy as an early intervention in primary care, student counselling services, and crisis intervention programmes. A summary will also be given of evidence for the psychotherapeutic benefits of interventions requiring minimal therapist contact, including bibliotherapy, computer-based therapy, the use of homework assignments between sessions, and expressive writing exercises. The evidence base for the effectiveness of psychotherapy involving play, art, music, dance, and drama will be considered. So too will evidence for the effectiveness of hypnosis, mindfulness-based meditation, physical exercise, and massage, since in some instances aspects of these practices have been incorporated into multidisciplinary psychotherapeutic programmes.

Services for people with severe psychological problems

Evidence summarized in Chapter 5 has shown that multimodal programmes in which medication and psychotherapy are combined are effective for a number of severe psychological problems. However, an important consideration is the optimal context within which to offer such programmes. Fortunately there is some evidence from systematic reviews to throw light on this question. Specifically there is evidence to support user involvement in service delivery and evaluation; the use of home treatment and day hospitals as alternatives to inpatient care; and the use of supported employment to enhance occupational adjustment. This evidence is briefly summarized below.

User involvement

In a review of 12 studies of service user involvement in the delivery or evaluation of mental health services, Simpson and House (2002) found that involving service users in service delivery led to clients having greater satisfaction with their personal circumstances and less hospitalization. Mental health professionals trained by service users developed more positive attitudes towards service users. Clients reported greater dissatisfaction with services when interviewed by service users in service-based research projects. Simpson and House (2002) concluded that service user involvement in service delivery and evaluation is feasible.

Home treatment for severe psychological problems

People with severe psychological problems often have difficulty engaging with routine outpatient health services and drop out of treatment. When this leads to a severe deterioration in functioning, often hospitalization occurs. Following discharge, the same pattern of disengagement, deterioration, crisis, and rehospitalization may occur. Home treatment was developed to prevent this pattern from recurring, and to help clients recover from severe psychological problems while living in their normal residence. A variety of models of home treatment have been developed including assertive community treatment, intensive case management, and training in community living. (Assertive community treatment for schizophrenia has been briefly reviewed in Chapter 5.) All home treatment models involve well-co-ordinated, seven-day per week, multidisciplinary, multimodal home-based treatment with psychotropic medication and psychosocial interventions, often including family support (Burns et al., 2001). Within such programmes staff carry small caseloads (under 25 cases) and work flexible hours. In a review of 91 studies of home treatment for severe psychological problems, Burns et al. (2001) found that clients who received home treatment were hospitalized less than those who received routine outpatient care. Where comparisons were made with inpatient treatment, home treatment led to a mean reduction in hospitalization of five days per patient, per month. Home-based treatment, therefore, in some cases is a viable way of reducing hospitalization in people with severe psychological problems, particularly psychosis.

Day hospital care for severe psychological problems

Acute episodes of severe symptoms and impairment of social functioning in people with incapacitating psychological disorders may be treated on an inpatient basis or in certain instances in acute day hospitals. In a review of nine randomized controlled trials of acute day hospital care as an alternative to inpatient care for people with severe psychological disorders, Marshall *et al.* (2001) concluded that day hospital treatment was feasible for 23–38% of clients. People treated in day hospitals showed a significantly more rapid improvement in mental state, but not social functioning. Readmission rates were similar for clients who received both types of care, but day hospital care was cheaper than inpatient care and led to cost reductions of 21–37%. Thus, acute day hospital care is a viable alternative to inpatient care for a proportion of people with severe psychological disorders.

Day treatment programmes

Day treatment programmes offer intensive multimodal intervention for people with severe anxiety and mood disorders who do not respond to routine outpatient care. In a review of two controlled trials, Marshall *et al.* (2001) concluded that, compared with routine outpatient care, day treatment programmes led to greater improvement in psychological symptoms, but not to greater improvements in social functioning.

Supported employment

Prevocational training and supported employment are two approaches to improving occupational adjustment in people with severe psychological disorders. With prevocational training, a period of preparation for work occurs before entering employment. With supported employment, employment occurs without preparatory training, but training and support in managing occupational demands are offered once the person is working. In a review of 18 controlled trials, Marshall *et al.* (2001) concluded that supported employment led to more people joining and staying in the workforce than prevocational training (34% vs. 12%). Clients in supported employment worked more hours and earned more than those in prevocational training. Prevocational training was no more effective than routine community care in improving occupational adjustment. Thus, supported employment is currently the most effective way of helping people with severe psychological disorders return to work. This conclusion is consistent with the conclusions drawn in the section on vocational rehabilitation for schizophrenia in Chapter 5.

Early intervention

In this section evidence supporting the effectiveness of psychotherapy in community-based primary care, student counselling services, and crisis intervention programmes is reviewed. Each of these contexts represents an attempt to offer psychotherapy as an early intervention for psychological distress.

Primary care

In a meta-analysis of seven controlled trials of brief (1–14 sessions) humanistic psychotherapy for clients with anxiety and depression in primary care, Bower *et al.* (2003) found an effect size of .28 at one to six months follow-up and a negligible effect size after six months. Thus, at one to six months after treatment, the average client who had received psychotherapy in primary care fared better than 61% of cases who received routine general practice services. Just over a third of therapy clients showed reliable and clinically significant change at one to six months compared with just over a fifth of clients who received routine general practice services. One trial compared humanistic psychotherapy with cognitive behavioural therapy and another compared therapy with antidepressant medication. In both of these studies humanistic psychotherapy was as effective as the alternative treatments.

Psychotherapy with students

In a narrative literature review of psychotherapy with students in higher and further education, Connell *et al.* (2006) identified 13 effectiveness studies and 43 process studies. They drew the following very tentative conclusions. Brief psychodynamic psychotherapy and short-term eclectic humanistic psychotherapy are effective for common problems in student populations. Cognitive behavioural therapy is effective for test anxiety and addressing unresolved traumatic experiences in student populations. Crisis intervention is effective in preventing student drop-out. Connell *et al.* (2006) also concluded that the evidence base for psychotherapy with student populations was weak, with few controlled trials or meta-analyses, and that this is an area requiring significant further research. In the USA and the UK, the mean duration of therapy for students is about six sessions, and practice-based research focusing on therapy of this duration with routine student populations is required.

Crisis intervention

In a meta-analysis of 36 crisis intervention studies, Roberts and Everly (2006) found an overall effect size of 1.35 at an average follow-up period of a year. Thus the average treated case fared better after a year than 90% of untreated cases. Roberts and Everly classified the 36 studies into three groups: (a) 11 studies of 8–72 hours of family crisis intervention offered over a three-month period; (b) 19 studies of 4–12 hours of multisession crisis intervention or critical incident stress management (CISM) involving three sessions including pre-crisis training, individual or group crisis intervention right after the traumatic event, and post-event crisis counselling one month later; (c) six studies of single-session debriefing offered on an individual or group basis lasting up to two hours. Using Cohen's (1988) criteria, Roberts and Everly found that large effect sizes (greater than .8) occurred in 64% of the family crisis intervention studies; 48% of the multisession crisis intervention or CISM studies; and 17% of the single-session debriefing studies. They concluded that family crisis intervention is more effective than multisession individual or group-based crisis intervention, and both are more effective than single-session debriefing. This finding on the ineffectiveness of single-session post-trauma debriefing is consistent with the conclusion drawn about this intervention in the section on PTSD in Chapter 5 (p. 175).

Self-help and homework

Psychotherapy is a scarce resource. There is evidence that some of the benefits of psychotherapy may be reaped with limited therapist contact by engaging in self-help activities. In particular there is evidence that bibliotherapy, computer-based therapy, the use of homework assignments between sessions, and expressive writing exercises all have positive benefits. This evidence is summarized below.

Bibliotherapy and computer-based therapy

Bibliotherapy and computer-based psychotherapeutic interventions are among the more common types of professionally guided psychotherapeutic approaches to self-help, entailing minimal therapist contact. In a meta-analysis of 14 studies of cognitive behavioural bibliotherapy for adults with diagnoses of anxiety and depression, Den Boer *et al.* (2004) found effect sizes of .84 after treatment and .76 at follow-up. They concluded that the average person who engaged in bibliotherapy fared better than 80% of untreated controls after treatment and 77% of untreated controls at follow-up. The self-help books, all of which were based on empirically supported treatment programmes, included Isaac Mark's (1980) *Living with Fear*; David Burns's (1989) *Feeling Good*; and Peter Lewinsohn *et al.*'s (1986) *Control your Depression*. In most studies, in addition to following the programme set out in the cognitive behavioural therapy book, clients attended educational classes and self-help groups or received phone contact with therapists. Norcross *et al.*'s (2003) *Authoritative Guide to Self-Help Resources in Mental Health* is a good source of information on bibliotherapy for psychological problems. Also, lists of self-help books for clients have been included at the end of Chapters 4 and 5.

In a review of 16 studies including 11 controlled trials and five uncontrolled studies of computer-based cognitive behavioural therapy programmes for anxiety and depression, Kaltenthaler *et al.* (2004) found some support for the effectiveness of this type of self-help. Where comparisons were possible, most studies found computer-based cognitive behavioural therapy to be better than treatment as usual and at least as effective as regular cognitive behavioural therapy. In a meta-analysis of 12 randomized controlled trials of internet-based interventions for anxiety and depression, Spek *et al.* (2007) found an effect size of .27 for depression and .96 for anxiety. Interventions with therapist support had a large mean effect size, while interventions without therapist support had a small effect size of .24. The computer-based programmes included *Overcoming Depression, Beating the Blues, Stresspac,* and *Fear Fighter* and in most programmes, computer-based intervention was combined with some degree of therapist contact and in some cases with antidepressant medication. Guidance on the use of such programmes is available from NICE (2002b). Marks *et al.*'s (2007) *Hands-on Help: Computer Aided Psychotherapy* is an encyclopaedic review of about a hundred computer-based self-help programmes.

In the area of physical illness, there is some evidence for the effectiveness of computer-based psychoeducational interventions for chronic conditions. In a review of 21 psychoeducational outcome studies for child adolescent and adult patients with a range of disorders including diabetes and asthma, Lewis (1999) found that in most studies patients showed improved disease management and understanding of their conditions.

There is also some evidence that computer-based psychotherapeutic interventions can be effective with children. In a multicentre, randomized, controlled, double-blind trial involving 53 7–12-year-old children with ADHD, Klingberg *et al.* (2005) found that a computer program for training working memory led not only to significant improvements in this domain, but also in symptoms of inattention, hyperactivity, and impulsivity both after treatment and at follow-up.

These conclusions of the effectiveness of bibliotherapy and computer-based self-help are consistent with those drawn in Chapter 4 in the section on ADHD in children (p. 75), and in Chapter 5 in the sections on depression and anxiety in adults (p. 155 and p. 166).

Homework

In a meta-analysis of 27 studies, Kazantzis *et al.* (2000) found an effect size for homework assignments of .36 and an effect size for homework compliance of .22. This indicates that the average client invited to do homework fared better than 64% of those who did not receive such an invitation. Also, the average client who completed homework fared better than 60% of those who did not complete homework assignments.

Expressive writing

Writing in an emotionally expressive way about significant, stressful, or traumatic life events may sometimes be offered as a homework assignment to psychotherapy clients. There is considerable evidence that such assignments have multiple positive effects, although such evidence is from analogue rather than clinical studies. Nevertheless, the results of these studies have important implications for expressive writing as a potential homework assignment for psychotherapy clients. In a meta-analysis of 13 analogue studies of the health-enhancing effects of expressive writing, Smyth (1998) found an overall weighted effect size of .47, indicating that the average participant in studies of expressive writing fared better afterwards than 68% of controls who did not complete such exercises. The effect size for indices of physical health was .42; for indices of psychological well-being was .66; for indices of physiological functioning was .68; and for indices of general functioning was .33. Thus across these four domains the average participant in studies of expressive writing fared better afterwards than 62–75% of controls who did not complete such exercises. Expressive writing had no significant impact on health behaviour. A significant increase in distress immediately followed expressive writing, but this was unrelated to the four main positive outcomes. Writing about current rather than past traumas had a more positive effect on outcome. The number of weeks over which the writing tasks were spaced was related to outcome, but not the actual duration of the writing tasks. Thus the results of this meta-analysis suggest that expressive writing assignments spaced over at least four weeks in which clients are invited to write about current trauma or life stresses may be a useful homework assignment, where coping with current trauma or stress is a significant presenting problem.

Play-and art-based therapies

There is some evidence for the effectiveness of play- and art-based therapies. Psychotherapy in which play, art, music, dance, and drama feature as the central medium for therapeutic work has evolved predominantly within the psychodynamic and humanistic psychotherapy traditions, although aspects of these practices have been incorporated into a number of cognitive behavioural protocols and some approaches to systemic therapy. The evidence base for these play- and art-based therapy modalities is, broadly speaking, weaker than for talking therapy. However, the evidence summarized below indicates that further research on play- and art-based therapies is clearly warranted.

Play therapy

In play therapy, therapeutic goals for children with emotional problems are achieved through the medium of play (Reddy et al., 2005). Two major meta-analyses of play therapy have been conducted (Leblanc & Ritchie, 2001; Ray et al., 2001). In the first meta-analysis, Leblanc and Ritchie (2001) synthesized the results of 42 studies involving pre-adolescent children carried out between 1947 and 1997. They found an average treatment effect of .66. Treatment was more effective when parents were included in the process and when children received at least 30 treatment sessions. Play therapy was as effective as non-play therapies in treating children with emotional difficulties. In the second meta-analysis, Ray *et al.* (2001) synthesized the results of 94 studies conducted between 1940 and 2000 with children aged 3–16 years. (A slightly modified version of this meta-analysis was later published by Barton *et al.* in 2005.) They found an overall effect size of .83; an effect size of .93 for humanistic, non-directive play therapy; and an effect size of .73 for behavioural, directive play therapy. They also found that parental involvement was related to improvement. A significant number of studies evaluating filial therapy (Vanfleet *et al.*, 2005), a particularly well-developed model of play therapy with a high level of parental involvement, probably accounted for this finding. The results of these two meta-analyses indicate that the average child treated with play therapy fared better than 75–82% of untreated controls. Thus, there is considerable support for play therapy as a treatment for children experiencing emotional difficulties. In recent years empirically supported manualized play therapies have been developed for children who have experienced parental separation; domestic violence; trauma; chronic illness; hospitalization; and who have conduct or developmental disorders (Reddy *et al.*, 2005). The results of the meta-analyses reviewed in this section provide support for the effectiveness of play therapy for children with emotional problems.

Art therapy

In a review of 17 studies on the effectiveness of art therapy, Reynolds *et al.* (2000) concluded that art therapy may be effective. In a broader-ranging narrative review Gilroy (2006) reached similar conclusions. The evidence base for art therapy is currently quite small and few randomized controlled trials have been conducted. However, there is some evidence from a small number of controlled trials that it may be effective in helping children and adults deal with trauma and illness. In a comparative treatment outcome study, Chapman *et al.* (2001) found that paediatric trauma patients who participated in art therapy showed a greater reduction in acute stress symptoms than those who received routine hospital treatment. In a randomized controlled trial involving 111 female cancer patients, Monti *et al.* (2006) found that mindfulness-based art therapy led to a significant decrease in psychological distress and improvements in health-related quality of life compared with waiting list controls. In another randomized controlled trial involving 41 female breast cancer patients, Oster *et al.* (2006) found that art therapy led to improved coping two and six months after the start of radiotherapy.

Music therapy

In a meta-analysis of 11 controlled treatment outcome studies of music therapy for children with a range of psychological problems, Gold *et al.* (2004)

obtained a weighted effect size of .61. Thus, the average treated case fared better than 73% of untreated controls. Effects were greater for behavioural and developmental disorders than for emotional disorders; greater for eclectic, psychodynamic, and humanistic approaches than for behavioural models; and greater for behavioural and developmental outcomes than for social skills and self-concept. The results of this meta-analysis provide support for the role of music therapy in the treatment of some childhood psychological disorders.

Dance and movement therapy

In dance and movement therapy, therapeutic progress occurs through engagement in non-verbal dance and movement exercises (Cruz & Berrol, 2004). In a meta-analysis of 14 controlled studies and nine uncontrolled studies of dance and movement therapy with children, adults, and older adults with a range of problems including developmental disabilities, acquired disabilities associated with head injury, neurological disorders of older adulthood, anxiety disorders, and schizophrenia, Ritter and Graff-Low (1996) found an effect size of .3 for controlled studies and .38 for the uncontrolled studies across a range of dependent variables. The dependent variables included measures of body awareness; movement and co-ordination; and psychological adjustment. In 11 of the 14 studies where anxiety was the dependent variable, an effect size of .7 was obtained. These results suggest that the effects of dance and movement therapy are particularly significant for anxiety where the average treated case fared better than up to 76% of untreated controls. The strong impact of dance and movement therapy on anxiety may arise from the relaxation-inducing aspect of the intervention. The results of this meta-analysis provide support for the role of dance and movement therapy in the treatment of anxiety in some clinical populations.

Psychodrama

In psychodrama, clients are helped to resolve intrapsychic and interpersonal conflicts and address 'unfinished business' from their earlier life by dramatically enacting roles associated with these psychological difficulties. Psychodrama is typically offered in a group therapy format. Role reversal and doubling are two techniques central to psychodrama practice. With role reversal, a client enacts a conflict with a group member playing the part of the other person in the conflict. During the enactment, the client and other group member reverse roles. Through this process the client develops empathy for the other person involved in the conflict. With doubling a client enacts a problem-related scenario, and another group member takes part in this drama as the client's persona. Through this process the client gains immediate access to the conflict between self and persona. In a meta-analysis of

25 experimentally designed studies, Kipper and Ritchie (2003) found an over-all weighted effect size of .95 on self-report measures of a variety of aspects of psychological adjustment. The techniques of role reversal and doubling were the most effective interventions. The results of this meta-analysis are constrained by a number of limitations. Only a third of the 25 studies were conducted with clinical groups. Therapy duration ranged from 1–40 sessions, and duration of therapy was unrelated to effect size, probably because such a wide range of dependent measures of psychological adjustment was used in the 25 studies ranging from measures of empathy to measures of global psychopathology (MMPI). No follow-up data were available.

Other interventons

There is some evidence that hypnosis, mindfulness-based meditation, physical exercise, and massage may all have positive effects on psychological adjust-ment. In some instances aspects of these practices have been incorporated into multidisciplinary programmes or into psychotherapy protocols for a var-iety of psychological disorders. Also, in some instances, clients may ask their therapists about the possible benefits of these interventions as adjuncts to psychotherapy. It is with these concerns in mind that the following very curs-ory summary of evidence for the impact of these interventions on well-being is offered.

Hypnosis

In a meta-analysis of 57 randomized clinical studies of hypnosis, Flammer and Bongartz (2003) obtained a weighted effect size of .56. In the 32 studies where complaints were codable as *ICD-10* disorders an effect size of .63 was obtained. These results indicate that the average case treated with hypnosis fared better than 72–74% of untreated controls. In the six studies where the correlation between hypnotic suggestibility and treatment outcome was com-puted, the mean correlation was 0.44. This indicates that clients who were more suggestible derived greater benefit from hypnosis.

In a meta-analysis of 18 studies in which a cognitive behavioural therapy was compared with the same therapy supplemented by hypnosis, Kirsch *et al.* (1995) found that the addition of hypnosis enhanced treatment outcome, so that the average client receiving cognitive behavioural hypnotherapy showed greater improvement than 70% of clients receiving non-hypnotic treatment. Effects were particularly pronounced for obesity, especially at follow-up, indicating that hypnotized clients continued to lose weight after treatment ended.

In a narrative review of studies of paediatric clinical hypnosis, Gold *et al.* (2007) found preliminary evidence from a small number of case series and controlled trials for the effectiveness of hypnosis in the treatment of anxiety;

medical and dental procedural distress; headaches and pain; asthma and respiratory conditions; dermatological conditions; sleeping problem; enuresis and encopresis; nailbiting, thumb sucking, and habit problems. However, the evidence base is currently relatively small.

From these reviews it may be concluded that for some psychological problems in children and adults, hypnosis may be an effective treatment either alone or as an integral part of a cognitive behavioural treatment protocol.

Meditation, mindfulness, and yoga

Meditation has long been advocated as a practice for alleviating psychological distress and promoting well-being. A programme incorporating mindfulness-based meditation – mindfulness-based stress reduction – which aims to enhance awareness of moment-to-moment experience of perceptible psychological processes, has recently enjoyed considerable popularity as a way for managing stress, pain, and various psychological disorders. Mindfulness-based stress reduction involves ten weekly two-and-a-half hour sessions and a day-long intensive session. Between sessions, participants practise meditation exercises learned in treatment. In a meta-analysis of 20 studies of the effects of mindfulness-based stress reduction, Grosman *et al.* (2004) found an effect size of about .5 for indices of physical and psychological well-being. In a previous meta-analysis of 16 studies of mindfulness-based stress reduction, Baer (2003) found a very similar effect size of .59 after treatment and at follow-up. Taken together, the results of these two meta-analyses show that the average person who completed a mindfulness-based stress reduction programme fared better than 69–73% of those in control groups. Participants in the studies covered by these two meta-analyses included clients with pain, cancer, heart disease, depression, and anxiety, as well as stressed non-clinical groups. Thus, mindfulness-based stress reduction may help a broad range of individuals with clinical and subclinical difficulties in managing stress, pain, and negative mood states. These results are consistent with the conclusions about the effectiveness of mindfulness-based cognitive behavioural therapy as maintanance treatment to prevent relapse in chronic depression, described in the section on depression in Chapter 5 (pp. 150–151).

In a systematic narrative review of the impact of meditation on recovery for physical and psychological disorders, Arias *et al.* (2006) identified 20 randomized controlled trials. Strongest evidence for the efficacy of meditation in facilitating symptom reduction was found for epilepsy, premenstrual syndrome, menopausal symptoms, mood and anxiety disorders, autoimmune illness, and emotional distress in neoplastic disease.

In a systematic review, Pilkington *et al.* (2005) identified five randomized controlled trials of yoga as a treatment for depression and concluded that yoga may alleviate depressive symptoms. The major components of yoga are regulated breathing, moving through various postures, and meditation.

In a systematic review, Bower *et al.* (2005) identified nine studies of yoga for cancer patients, and concluded that yoga led to modest improvements in sleep quality, mood, stress, cancer-related distress, cancer-related symptoms, and overall quality of life.

Taken together, the results of these reviews provide preliminary evidence for the value of incorporating practices of meditation, mindfulness, and yoga into psychotherapy protocols and testing these in further controlled trials.

Exercise

In a narrative review of many meta-analyses and major cross-sectional and longitudinal studies, Salmon (2001) concluded that physical exercise pro-grammes have antidepressant and anxiolytic effects, and also help people become resilient to stress. In a meta-analysis of 37 studies of the effects of exercise on clinical depression, Craft and Landers (1998) found an overall mean effect size of .72, indicating that the average treated client fared better on measures of depression than 77% of untreated controls. In a meta-analysis of 70 studies, Puetz *et al.* (2006) found that exercise increased feelings of energy and lessened feelings of fatigue compared with control conditions by a mean weighted effect size of 0.37. Thus the average treated client fared better after treatment than 65% of untreated controls. Exercise programmes aver-aged 13 weeks, with three 45-minute sessions per week. Clients with anxiety and depression benefited most from treatment. The effect size for clients with anxiety and depression was .56; for clients in cardiac rehabilitation was .48; for cancer survivors was .36; and for fibromyalgia was .30. Greatest gains were made by older adults, and those who were particularly lacking in energy and fatigued before treatment. In a meta-analysis of 18 studies on the effects of exercise programmes for older adults, Colcombe and Kramer (2003) found an average weighted pre–post effect size of .48 for indices of improved cogni-tive functioning in treated groups, and .16 in control groups. Thus, gains in cognitive functioning made by older adults who exercised were three times greater than those made by those who did not. Greatest gains were associated with programmes over six months in duration. In a meta-analysis of 158 analogue studies of the effect of acute aerobic exercise on positive affect, Reed and Ones (2006) found a mean corrected effect size of .47, indicating that the average person who exercised had greater positive affect afterwards than 68% of non-exercising controls. Even low to moderate doses of low intensity exercise had positive effects, particularly where participants had low initial levels of positive affect.

Massage

Massage therapy, the manual manipulation of soft tissue to promote health and well-being, has been used for a wide variety of physical and psychological disorders, and is a very popular complementary and alternative medical therapy. There is growing evidence that it has a positive impact on pain, anxiety, and depression, and so is of interest to some clients with these problems. In a meta-analysis of 37 randomized controlled trials of the effects of massage therapy, Moyer *et al.* (2004) found that for multisession massage therapy the effect size for trait anxiety was .75, for depression was .62, and for pain was .31. In contrast, for single-session massage therapy the effect sizes were smaller and the only significant ones were heart rate (.41), state anxiety (.37), and blood pressure (.25). Single applications of massage therapy had no significant impact on negative mood or pain. Adults and children with a variety of physical and psychological disorders, including chronic pain, fibromyalgia, and hypertension, as well as healthy individuals participated in the 37 studies in this meta-analysis. The results of this meta-analysis show that the average person with these conditions, or indeed healthy people, after a course of multisession massage, reported less depression than 77% of untreated controls; less anxiety than 74% of untreated controls; and less pain than 62% of untreated controls. Thus, massage has positive effects on depression, anxiety, and pain. However, its impact on anxiety and mood disorders has not been evaluated.

Conclusion and practice implications

This chapter addressed the question: What other types of interventions that have not been fully addressed in previous chapters can help psychological problems? It tied up a number of loose ends which had not been considered or addressed fully in previous chapters, but which constitute important elements of the evidence base for psychotherapeutic interventions. A number of tentative conclusions may be drawn. For people with severe psychological problems, it is beneficial to involve service users in service delivery and evaluation; to offer multimodal programmes involving medication and psychotherapy within the context of home treatment and day hospitals as alternatives to inpatient care where appropriate; and to engage clients in supported employment programmes (rather than prevocational training programmes) to enhance occupational adjustment. For clients with anxiety, depression, and adjustment problems, brief psychotherapy in primary care, student counselling services, and crisis intervention programmes is effective in the short term. Within the context of a stepped care model of service delivery, bibliotherapy or computer-based cognitive therapy may be offered as a preliminary intervention since both have beneficial effects for anxiety and depression. Cognitive behavioural and expressive writing homework assignments may enhance the effectiveness of psychotherapy. Psychotherapy involving play, art, music, dance, and drama is effective in some contexts. Play and music therapy are particularly suited to children with emotional (but not conduct) problems. Art therapy may have a role in the treatment of trauma. Dance and movement therapy may have a role in the treatment of anxiety. Hypnosis, mindfulness-based meditation, physical exercise, and massage all have positive effects on psychological adjustment, and may be incorporated into multimodal multidisciplinary programmes, particularly for managing pain and negative mood states. Less confidence can be placed in these conclusions than those in previous chapters, because the evidence base for the issues covered in this chapter is less robust. Clearly, further research on these important issues is required.

Chapter 7

Conclusions

The central question addressed in this book was: In the field of psychotherapy, what works for children, adolescents, and adults? To answer this question, a wide-ranging review of scientific evidence concerning the effectiveness of psychotherapy was conducted. The large rigorous body of evidence reviewed showed, unequivocally, that psychotherapy and psychological interventions are effective in helping children, adolescents, adults, people in later life, and people with intellectual and pervasive developmental disabilities with a wide range of psychological difficulties.

Recap of answers to key questions

Each of the preceding chapters addressed a question, or set of questions, relevant to the central question of this book. The answers to these questions will be recapped in this chapter, before considering their implications for practice, policy, and future research.

What is psychotherapy?

Chapter 1 opened with a set of questions about the definition of psycho-therapy, the nature of psychotherapy research, and the translation of research findings into clinical practice procedures. It was noted in Chapter 1 that modern psychotherapy is only 100 years old. As currently practised it is a contractual process in which trained professionals work with clients to help them resolve psychological problems. Psychotherapy may be offered to child-ren, adults, older adults, and people with intellectual and pervasive devel-opmental disabilities on an individual, couple, family, or group basis to effectively alleviate a wide variety of difficulties. In addressing the scientific evidence base for the effectiveness of psychotherapy it is useful to distinguish between therapy conducted within the psychodynamic, humanistic, cognitive behavioural, and systemic traditions.

What is psychotherapy research?

In Chapter 1, psychotherapy research was described as the systematic inquiry into the process and outcome of interventions conducted to alleviate psychological problems. Research on the effectiveness of psychotherapy may be organized into a hierarchy from uncontrolled case studies which provide the least persuasive evidence for the effectiveness of psychotherapy, through uncontrolled and controlled trials, to meta-analyses which provide the most persuasive evidence of psychotherapy's effectiveness. Throughout this volume, greatest weight has been given to meta-analyses of controlled trials as evidence for the effectiveness of psychotherapy and psychological interventions.

How can the results of psychotherapy research be used to inform clinical practice?

Chapter 1 closed with the conclusion that there is no single correct process for translating results of psychotherapy research into clinical practice procedures. Some favour the use of efficacy studies to identify specific empirically supported treatments. Others favour the use of multiple sources of evidence to inform the development of general practice guidelines.

Does psychotherapy work?

Chapter 2 was concerned with evidence for the overall effectiveness, and cost-effectiveness, of psychotherapy. It was concluded that approximately two-thirds to three-quarters of people benefit from psychotherapy. In contrast, approximately only a quarter to a third of people recover from psychological problems without treatment. These conclusions are based on major meta-analyses of hundreds of treatment trials, involving thousands of children, adolescents, and adults treated with psychodynamic, humanistic, cognitive behavioural, and systemic therapy approaches to psychotherapy. The evidence reviewed in Chapter 2 also led to the following conclusions:

1   Psychotherapy is highly effective for a majority of cases with common psychological problems.
2   Psychotherapy is effective for both adults and children.
3   Psychotherapy conducted within psychodynamic, humanistic, cognitive behavioural, and systemic traditions is effective for many common psychological problems.
4   The overall magnitude of the effects of psychotherapy in alleviating psychological disorders is similar to the overall magnitude of the effect of medical and surgical procedures in treating a wide variety of medical conditions.

5   About one in ten clients deteriorate as a result of psychotherapy.
6   Client recovery is dependent upon the delivery of a high quality psycho-
    therapy service, which may be maintained through quality assurance
    systems.
7   Early access to psychotherapy services can facilitate therapeutic
    engagement.

Is psychotherapy cost-effective?

In Chapter 2, evidence for the cost-effectiveness of psychotherapy was
reviewed. It was concluded that patients who receive psychotherapy use less
other medical services. This leads to reduced medical costs. The money saved
in this way more than covers the cost of psychotherapy. That is, psychotherapy leads to a significant total cost-offset. For frequent emergency service
users, psychotherapy can also lead to a reduction in the use of accident and
emergency services.

How important are common factors?

A striking feature of the evidence for the overall effectiveness of psychotherapy presented in Chapter 2 was the remarkable similarity in positive outcome rates of diverse approaches with a range of populations and
problems. This observation inspired the questions addressed in Chapter 3
concerning the common factors underpinning all effective psychotherapeutic
interventions. Research reviewed in Chapter 3 showed that factors common
to the wide variety of effective psychotherapies are two to nine times more
important than specific factors in determining whether or not clients benefit
from psychotherapy.

Are common factors simply placebos?

Research reviewed in Chapter 3 showed that the effects of common factors
are not simply placebo effects, because the effects of psychotherapy are nearly
double those of placebos. Common factors may be conceptualized as those
associated with the client, the therapist, and the therapeutic process.

What common client characteristics affect therapy outcome?

In Chapter 3, evidence was reviewed which showed that specific client characteristics affect the outcome of psychotherapy. Distressed clients with circumscribed problems from well-functioning families, with little life stress and
much social support, respond well to therapy. Those with multiple, complex,
co-morbid problems from multiproblem families, with much stress and little

support, respond less well to therapy. Psychologically minded clients with much ego-strength, who are motivated to engage in therapy, who actively participate in the therapy process, and who show early improvement benefit more from therapy than those who do not.

What common therapist characteristics affect the outcome of psychotherapy?

In Chapter 3, evidence was reviewed which showed that specific therapist characteristics affect the outcome of psychotherapy. Effective therapists are technically competent, and both credible and creative in their approach to helping clients solve problems. They have engaged in personal therapy, are well adjusted, well trained, use therapy manuals flexibly, and use feedback on client progress to match their therapeutic style to clients' needs. About 46–69% of the effects of psychotherapy are due to therapist characteristics.

What process factors, common to the wide variety of effective psychotherapies, are responsible for their effectiveness?

In Chapter 3, evidence was reviewed which showed that certain factors, common to the practice of a wide variety of psychotherapy approaches, affect therapy outcome. For recovery in psychotherapy, an adequate 'dose' of therapy must be offered. For 50–75% of psychotherapy clients to recover, a dose of 20–45 sessions of therapy is necessary. The therapeutic alliance is the single most important common psychotherapeutic process factor, and accounts for about 38% of the effectiveness of psychotherapy. In a strong therapeutic alliance, the therapist is empathic and collaborative, and the client is co-operative and committed to recovery. The common procedures that characterize effective therapy include exploration and reconceptualization of conscious and unconscious aspects of problems; provision of a credible rationale for conducting therapy; generating hope and the expectation of improvement; and mobilizing clients to engage in problem resolution. These broad procedures may involve using therapeutic techniques such as providing support and encouraging emotional expression; facilitating new ways of viewing problems; and helping clients to develop new ways of behaving adaptively. For certain disorders, multimodal programmes in which psychotherapy and pharmacotherapy are combined are more effective than either alone.

What works with children and adolescents?

Chapter 4 was concerned with identifying specific psychotherapy protocols and psychological interventions that have been shown to be effective for particular problems in children, adolescents, and people with intellectual and pervasive developmental disabilities. Extensive computer and manual literature searches yielded a wealth of empirical evidence supporting the benefits of specific protocols with the list of disorders and problems contained in Table 7.1.

What works with adults?

Chapter 5 was concerned with identifying specific psychotherapy protocols and psychological interventions that have been shown to be effective for particular problems in adulthood and later life. Extensive computer and manual literature searches yielded a wealth of empirical evidence supporting the benefits of specific protocols with the list of disorders and problems contained in Table 7.2.

Table 7.1 Problems in childhood and adolescence for which psychotherapy and psychological interventions are effective

---

Sleep problems

Toileting problems
Enuresis and encopresis

Attachment problems

Attention deficit hyperactivity disorder (ADHD)

Pre-adolescent oppositional defiant disorder

Adolescent conduct disorder

Adolescent drug abuse

Juvenile sex offending

Child and adolescent depression

Bipolar disorder

Attempted suicide and self-harm

Child and adolescent anxiety disorders
Phobias, separation anxiety and generalized anxiety, selective mutism, obsessive-compulsive disorder, post-traumatic stress disorder

Eating disorders
Feeding problems, anorexia nervosa, bulimia, obesity

Tourette's syndrome

Paediatric pain problems
Headaches, recurrent abdominal pain, medical procedures

Adjustment to chronic medical conditions
Asthma and diabetes

Adjustment problems following major life transitions and stresses
Parental separation, bereavement, child abuse and neglect

Adjustment problems associated with intellectual disability

Adjustment problems associated with autism spectrum disorders

---

Table 7.2 Problems in adulthood for which psychotherapy and psychological interventions are effective

Mood disorders
Depression, bipolar disorder, suicide, self-harm

Anxiety disorders
Generalized anxiety disorder, panic disorder, phobias, social phobias, OCD, PTSD

Somatoform disorders
Medically unexplained symptoms, hypochondriasis, body dysmorphic disorder

Adjustment to illness
Preparation for surgery, life-threatening illness (cancer and heart disease), chronic medical conditions (asthma, diabetes, and hypertension)

Coping with pain and fatigue
Chronic pain, low back pain, fibromyalgia, chronic fatigue syndrome, headaches, arthritis, irritable bowel syndrome (IBS)

Eating disorders
Obesity, bulimia, anorexia, binge eating disorder

Insomnia

Substance abuse and addiction
Alcohol abuse, drug abuse, smoking, compulsive gambling

Schizophrenia

Personality disorders
Borderline personality disorders, cluster C personality disorders

Anger and aggression

Sexual offending

Relationship problems
Marital distress, psychosexual problems, domestic violence

Grief and bereavement

Psychological problems of older adulthood
Dementia, late life depression, late life anxiety, late life insomnia

What other types of interventions can help psychological problems?

In Chapter 6, evidence for the effectiveness of a number of disparate interventions for psychological problems, that had not been reviewed in previous chapters, were considered. The following conclusions were drawn. For people with severe psychological problems, it is beneficial to involve service users in service delivery and evaluation; to offer multimodal programmes involving medication and psychotherapy within the context of home treatment and day hospitals as alternatives to inpatient care where appropriate; and to engage clients in supported employment programmes (rather than prevocational training programmes) to enhance occupational adjustment.

For clients with anxiety, depression, and adjustment problems, brief psychotherapy in primary care, student counselling services, and crisis intervention programmes is effective in the short term. Within the context of a stepped care model of service delivery, bibliotherapy or computer-based cognitive therapy may be offered as a preliminary intervention since both have beneficial effects for anxiety and depression. Cognitive behavioural and expressive writing homework assignments may enhance the effectiveness of psychotherapy.

Psychotherapy involving play, art, music, dance, and drama is effective in some contexts. Play and music therapy are particularly suited to children with emotional (but not conduct) problems. Art therapy may have a role in the treatment of trauma. Dance and movement therapy may have a role in the treatment of anxiety.

Hypnosis, mindfulness-based meditation, physical exercise, and massage all have positive effects on psychological adjustment, and may be incorporated into multimodal multidisciplinary programmes, particularly for managing pain and negative mood states.

Practice implications

Detailed practice implications of psychotherapy research for specific disorders in specific populations have been given in Chapters 4 and 5. However, the research reviewed in previous chapters also has a number of more general practice implications. These include informing clients about the overall effectiveness of psychotherapy; offering clients feedback on positive client common factors that have implications for their prognosis; and maximizing therapist common factors. These implications are elaborated below.

Inform clients about the overall effectiveness of psychotherapy

When engaging clients in therapy and forming therapeutic contracts, it is good ethical practice to inform them about the overall effectiveness of psychotherapy; that is, to let them know that research shows that at best:

- a third to three-quarters of clients benefit from therapy
- about one in ten deteriorate as a result of therapy
- up to a third may recover without psychotherapy.

Provide feedback on positive client common factors

It is also ethical to let clients know, following assessment, if they have any of the client characteristics that are predictive of a good outcome, since this may generate hope and the expectation of improvement. These include:

- high motivation to engage in therapy
- active participation in the therapy process
- high psychological mindedness
- high ego-strength
- circumscribed problems
- high levels of distress
- low levels of incapacity
- low life stress
- high social support
- coming from a well-functioning family.

Maximize therapy process and therapist common factors

To become a more effective psychotherapist, it may be useful to try to maximize those common factors associated with the therapeutic process and the therapist as an individual which have been found to be associated with successful therapy. The following are some courses of action suggested by the research literature:

1   Make therapeutic contracts for an effective dose of therapy. For common adult problems this is 20–45 sessions, and for children and adolescents it may be 10–20 sessions, but with more complex problems more sessions may be required.
2   Engage clients in strong therapeutic alliances characterized by empathy and a collaboration.
3   Provide a credible rationale for conducting therapy.
4   Develop therapeutic credibility by becoming technically competent in one or more therapy protocols appropriate for the client group with whom you work.
5   Develop technical competence in flexibly using therapy protocols that have been found to be effective with the types of clients with whom you work (as outlined in Chapters 4 and 5), by engaging in continuing professional development, supervision, and practice.
6   If there is evidence for their effectiveness, offer psychotherapy as an element of multimodal programmes in which psychotherapy and pharmacotherapy are combined (as outlined in Chapters 4 and 5).
7   If you offer psychotherapy as an element of a multimodal programme, actively foster good collaborative multidisciplinary working relationships.
8   Develop therapeutic creativity by reading widely in many fields, engaging in continuing professional development, and engaging in psychotherapy supervision.
9   Routinely collect feedback on client progress and use this feedback to match your therapeutic style to the clients' needs, particularly where clients are not benefiting from therapy, using instruments such as the

Outcome Rating Scale (Miller *et al.*, 2003) and the Session Rating Scale (Duncan *et al.*, 2004) described in Chapter 3.

More detailed practice implications that may be useful with clients with particular problems have been given in Chapters 4 and 5.

Policy implications

It is appropriate to preface the policy implications of results of the work presented in this volume with a statement of the international scale of mental health problems. Mental health problems constitute a major international problem that is well documented on the World Health Organization's website (http://www.who.int/mental_health/en/index.html). Throughout the world, one in four people have significant mental health problems. Worldwide 450 million people are affected by psychological disorders. Mental health problems rank second in global burden of disease, following infectious disease. Psychological disorders entail staggering economic and social costs. People with psychological disorders have a poor quality of life and increased mortality. Worldwide about 873,000 people die by suicide every year. Within the European Union the economic costs of psychological disorders constitute 3–4% of the annual gross national product. Much of these costs are due to decreased productivity, absenteeism, and unemployment, and the remainder are due to service costs. Clearly, a cost-effective solution to this international problem is required. The research reviewed in this volume shows unequivocally that psychotherapy works. It is effective alone or in combination with pharmacotherapy for most mental health problems in adults and children. Furthermore, it is cost-effective.

The principal policy implication of the research reviewed in this book is to provide a psychotherapy service for all people with mental health problems. The provision of psychotherapy should be regulated to protect clients. Training and continuing professional development systems need to be developed, so that psychotherapists are trained in evidence-based psychotherapy practices. Psychotherapy should be provided within a stepped care model, so that the intensity of the service provided is matched to clients' needs. Evaluation systems should be built into the overall design of psychotherapy services. Service users should be involved in the refinement of psychotherapy services. Practice research partnerships involving service-based practice networks and university departments with expertise in psychotherapy research should be formed to spearhead research and development in the field of psychotherapy. Finally, funding systems need to be developed to support the provision of psychotherapy and its evaluation. In the following sections these policy implications will be elaborated.

Provide a psychotherapy service for people with mental health problems

The main policy implication arising from the research reviewed in this volume is the provision of a psychotherapy service for all people with mental health problems. That is, services which offer psychotherapy or psychological interventions should be developed for children, adolescents, adults, older adults, and people with intellectual and pervasive developmental disabilities with the range of problems listed in Tables 7.1 and 7.2. These services should be widely available and easily accessible.

Regulate the provision of psychotherapy

Because psychotherapy has the potential to cause significant harm in a small proportion of cases, it is essential that psychotherapy and psychological interventions be regulated, through statutory registration or some similar process, so that psychotherapy and psychological intervention can only be offered by appropriately trained and qualified professionals such as psychotherapists, psychologists, psychiatrists, social workers, and nurses. Regulation is essential to protect service users.

Provide training in evidence-based psychotherapy practice

Professionals who offer psychotherapy and psychological intervention should receive training in evidence-based psychotherapy practices and procedures. These include training in procedures common to all forms of psychotherapy such as those covered in Chapter 3, but also those that have been shown to be particularly effective for particular problems such as those described in Chapters 4 and 5. Evidence-based practices should be taught in initial pre-qualification training programmes and also in ongoing continuing professional development programmes.

Inform practice with evidence-based protocols

For specific client groups, the types of psychotherapy protocols and psychological interventions used should be broadly based on the types of protocols that have been shown to be effective, as outlined in Chapters 4 and 5. An important implication of this is that such services should not be exclusively based on cognitive behavioural therapy. This is mentioned because, in certain jurisdictions such as the USA and the UK, there is increasing discourse from many quarters, which quite inaccurately is championing cognitive behavioural therapy as the only effective form of psychotherapy. The evidence reviewed in Chapter 4 of this book shows that, with children and adolescents, there is strong evidence for the effectiveness of systemic family-based interventions for problems such as oppositional defiant disorder, conduct disorder, adolescent drug abuse and eating disorders. For adults, the material reviewed in Chapters 2 and 5 shows that there is strong evidence for the effectiveness of psychodynamic psychotherapy, humanistic psychotherapy, and systemic marital therapy for common problems of adulthood such as depression, alcohol problems, and illicit drug abuse.

Provide psychotherapy within a stepped care model

The evidence reviewed in this volume supports the policy of offering psychotherapy rapidly and within the context of a stepped care model, where the intensity of the service offered is matched to client need. Psychotherapeutic services should be offered as rapidly as possible, with short waiting times. This is because clients who do not access services rapidly are less likely to engage in therapy when it is offered, to deteriorate and later require more intensive services. Initially, within a primary care context, it is appropriate to offer low-contact, self-help psychotherapeutic interventions such as bibliotherapy or computer-assisted therapy with minimal therapist contact for a number of common problems such as anxiety and mood disorders. Where this is ineffective or inappropriate, then more intensive interventions may be offered as outlined in Chapters 4 and 5 in outpatient primary, secondary, and tertiary care services. Where service users have severe mental health problems, psychotherapy may be offered within the context of broad-based multimodal care plans that include pharmacotherapy, inpatient care, outreach services, and supported employment.

Build evaluation into psychotherapy service design

Evaluation practices, procedures, and systems should be built into the design and organization of psychotherapy services, so that services can be modified and refined in light of feedback on effectiveness. Within such systems, all clients should routinely complete very brief reliable and valid instruments before and after psychotherapy and at regular intervals. These data should be routinely computer processed, so that reports of individual client feedback may be made available to clients and therapists to fine-tune psychotherapy services to clients' needs; and aggregated reports of service performance may be used for service development and planning.

Involve service users

In addition to these quantitative approaches to service evaluation, periodic qualitative assessments of psychotherapy services should be conducted, with a central input from service users, so that they may contribute to service development (Warner et al., 2006).

Develop service–university practice research partnerships

Partnerships between psychotherapy services on the one hand and university departments with expertise in psychotherapy service evaluation on the other should be developed to facilitate service-based psychotherapy research and evaluation. There are good precedents for such practice research networks (Barkham *et al.*, 2008).

Develop funding systems

In jurisdictions where psychotherapy services are sparse or unavailable, systems for funding psychotherapy services require development. Such systems need to specify how psychotherapy services fit into broader health services; what the work contracts, salaries, and career structures for psychotherapists should be; how psychotherapy training, supervision, and continuing professional development will be managed and funded; and how psychotherapy research, especially research evaluating its effectiveness, will be funded.

Research implications

The literature reviewed in previous chapters has clear research implications. There is a need for more high quality efficacy and effectiveness research trials, as well as more practice-based research. There is a need for further studies on under-researched populations, problems, and approaches to psychotherapy. Research on enhanced treatment approaches for non-responders should be prioritized. Further research is required to evaluate the effectiveness of combinations of complementary psychotherapeutic interventions, and complementary psychotherapies and pharmacotherapies. The comparative effectiveness of different treatment protocols also needs to be investigated. Studies are required to evaluate the effects of the contexts within which psychotherapy is offered on its overall effectiveness. Part of this research programme will be translational research in which treatments shown to work in efficacy studies in specialist centres are evaluated in effectiveness studies in routine service contexts. There is a need for more research on both psychological and neurobiological change process in psychotherapy. The impact of client and therapist factors requires further investigations. Studies are needed on the effects of psychotherapy training on treatment outcome. Finally, there is a need for far more research on cost-effectiveness. In the following sections these research implications are elaborated.

Designing trials to evaluate the efficacy and effectiveness of psychotherapy

In future psychotherapy research, it is important that trials be adequately designed. Certain basic design features must be present to be able to draw valid conclusions. A preliminary power analysis should be conducted to determine the number of cases required to adequately test the effectiveness of the psychotherapy protocol being evaluated. Cases should be randomly assigned to trial arms. In efficacy trials, stringent inclusion and exclusion criteria should be used to define a treatment population with a clearly designated focal problem and few co-morbid difficulties. But in effectiveness studies or pragmatic trials, cases with a core problem and co-morbid difficulties, typical of cases attending routine mental health services, may be included. In such instances, it is valuable to assess co-morbid difficulties and client characteristics that may affect psychotherapy outcome. These include personal vulnerabilities and levels of stress and social support. If these are assessed prior to the trial, their impact on outcome may be determined during data analysis. There are arguments for and against the use of *DSM* and *ICD* diagnostic categories for defining psychological difficulties which are the targets for treatment in psychotherapy trials. However, realistically, for the foreseeable future, it is probable that only research that is framed in these terms will receive funding. Psychotherapy protocols evaluated in trials should be manualized, at a level of specificity that is appropriate to the psychotherapy approach being used. Some psychotherapy approaches require a high level of detail, while others do not. Therapists should be trained in flexibly implementing the psychotherapy protocol being evaluated in a trial, and offered ongoing supervision. Fidelity checklists should be used to ensure that therapists reliably implement the protocol. Ideally trials should not commence until therapists have demonstrated the capacity to implement the psychotherapy protocol with a high level of fidelity. Treatment fidelity should be monitored throughout the trial, to ensure that therapists are adhering to the psychotherapy protocol being evaluated. Therapist caseloads should also be monitored throughout the trial, especially in effectiveness studies, to give an indication as to the type of caseloads that may reasonably be carried by typical therapists providing the type of psychotherapy being evaluated. Also, the impact of both treatment fidelity and caseloads on outcome may be assessed during data analysis. Cases and controls should be assessed before and after treatment and at follow-up. Longer-term follow-up assessments are preferable since they allow meaningful relapse rates to be investigated, using survival analysis where appropriate. Where feasible, assessments should be carried out by research staff, not therapists, and ideally these staff should be 'blind' to the treatment clients received. Comprehensive assessment protocols should be used which include measures of specific treatment goals and core problems; general psychosocial functioning; and intrapsychic, interpersonal, and neurobiological theoretically based variables which the therapy protocol aims to change to alleviate symptoms. In addition to these assessments, it is valuable to use brief measures to assess the core problem, the therapeutic alliance, and therapy process variables thought to be critical to outcome periodically throughout treatment. Pattern of change in the core problem, the alliance and critical process variables over the course of therapy may be assessed during data analysis. If it is feasible, it is valuable to video or audio record all therapy sessions from the trial and create an archive which can be used as a resource for addressing a wide variety of therapy process research questions. Multiple analyses should be conducted on trial data. In comparing the outcomes of treatment and control group cases, analyses should be conducted of trial completers, but also of all cases that entered the trial (in intent-to-treat analyses). Differences between treatment and control group drop-out rates, recovery rates, and relapse rates should be analysed, using clinically meaningful definitions of recovery, and appropriate non-parametric inferential statistics (Jacobson *et al.*, 1999). Differences between treatment and control groups, before and after treatment and at follow-up, on continuous variables assessed with reliable and valid psychometric scales should be analysed with appropriate parametric inferential statistics. Appropriate multivariate statistics should be used to evaluate the effect of client baseline characteristics; therapist characteristics; and therapy process characteristics on outcome. Results of trials should be reported using CONSORT guidelines (Altman *et al.*, 2001; Moher *et al.*, 2001). The following is a useful guide for trial design: *Evidence-Based Outcome Research: A Practical Guide to Conducting Randomized Controlled Trials for Psychosocial Interventions* (Nezu & Nezu, 2007).

Practice-based research

Routine collection of standard data in large practice research networks facilitates the creation of practice-based data archives which may be used to answer a variety of important questions about the impact of therapist, client, or treatment factors on routine psychotherapy outcome in service networks. In these studies, outcome data are collected periodically, for example, after every session throughout therapy. From these outcome data, cases with different outcome responses to treatment may be identified, e.g. rapid responders, delayed responders, non-responders. Basic data on client characteristics (e.g. age, gender, diagnosis), therapist characteristics (e.g. age, gender, profession, caseload), and the therapy process (e.g. number of sessions attended) are also routinely collected. Practice research network data archives may be used to answer questions including those about dose–effect relationships; characteristics of rapid responders, delayed responders, non-responders; and the effects of providing therapists and clients with regular feedback on outcome. Preliminary research on these types of questions was reviewed in Chapter 3. In practice research networks a number of instruments are particularly useful. These include the CORE (Evans *et al.*, 2002), the Outcome Questionnaire 45 (OQ-45, Lambert *et al.*, 2004; Burlingame *et al.*, 2005), the Outcome Rating Scale (ORS, Miller *et al.*, 2003), and the

Session Rating Scale (SRS, Duncan *et al.*, 2004b), which assesses the thera-peutic alliance. A useful guide for practice-based research is: *A Core Approach to Delivering Practice-Based Evidence in Counselling and Psycho-logical Therapies* (Barkham *et al.*, 2008).

Under-researched populations

Most psychotherapy research has been conducted with adults. Less has been conducted with children and adolescents. Far less has been conducted with older adults and people with intellectual and developmental disabilities. These is a need for far more future research on these under-researched populations. There is also a dearth of research on the effectiveness of psycho-therapy with minority groups including gay and lesbian groups (Perez *et al.*, 1999) and ethnic minorities (Tseng & Streltzer, 2001).

Under-researched problems

We have limited evidence on the effectiveness of psychotherapy with some types of problems. For children and adolescents, externalizing behaviour problems and disruptive behaviour disorders have been well researched, but internalizing problems, mood disorders, self-harming, anxiety disorders, eat-ing disorders (particularly bulimia), psychotic disorders, and the whole area of child abuse and neglect have been less well researched, and are an import-ant focus for future research. With adults, mood, anxiety, psychotic, and substance use disorders have been well researched, but personality disorders, somatoform disorders, anorexia nervosa, psychosexual problems, and psy-chological problems in later life remain relatively under-researched. Future research should focus these areas.

Under-researched approaches to psychotherapy

We have limited evidence on the effectiveness of certain types of psycho-therapy. Broadly speaking, the evidence base for cognitive behavioural therapies for young people and adults is relatively well developed. The evidence base for psychodynamic and humanistic-experiential therapies is relatively poorly developed, and the evidence base for systemic marital and family therapies falls between these two extremes. There is a clear need for far more research on the effectiveness of psychodynamic and humanistic approaches. There is also a need for controlled research on widely used treatment modalities such as therapeutic communities for personality disorders and substance abuse; and self-help organizations such as Alcoholics Anonymous.

Treatment enhancement for non-responders

There is a need for research on enhanced treatment protocols specifically designed to meet the unique needs of non-responders. Protocols for non-responders may include special procedures for engaging clients in treatment; overcoming obstacles to fostering a strong collaborative therapeutic alliance; specific symptom-focused treatment techniques tailored to clients' unique needs and vulnerabilities; procedures for enhancing adherence to homework assignments; ways of addressing ruptures in the therapeutic alliance, resistance, and transference/countertransference issues; drop-out prevention strategies; and procedures for dealing with relapse prevention and the disengagement process in ways that take account of clients' profiles of strengths and shortcomings.

Multicomponent studies combining effective psychotherapies

There is limited evidence for the effectiveness of programmes in which two or more types of psychotherapy are combined. Where different types of psychotherapy can be coherently, concurrently, or sequentially combined, trials are required to evaluate the relative effectiveness of each therapy both alone and combined. It may be that some therapy protocols, when combined, have additive or synergistic effects. Alternatively, combined therapies may have antagonistic effects. For example, parent management training combined with child-focused problem-solving skills training for conduct problems is a promising area for future research. For anxiety disorders, depression, and eating disorders in children, trials are required on the optimal way of combining child-focused and family-focused interventions. For adults, ways of combining individual, group, and marital therapy for most disorders are required.

Multimodal programmes combining psychotherapy and pharmacotherapy

There are a number of areas in which trials of multimodal programmes involving psychotherapy combined with pharmacotherapy are required. It may be that for some disorders, when psychotherapy and pharmacotherapy are combined, they have additive or synergistic effects. Alternatively, combined therapies may have antagonistic effects. For example, this may be the case with some anxiety disorders. For children and young people, with the exception of ADHD, and a handful of trials involving mood disorders, there are very few studies of multimodal programmes involving pharmacotherapy combined with psychotherapy. Trials of multimodal programmes for depression, bipolar disorder, severe OCD, and psychosis in young people are urgently required. For challenging behaviour in people with intellectual or pervasive developmental disabilities, trials in which respirodone and psychological interventions based on applied behaviour analysis are combined are required, since each separately have been shown to be very effective. For adults, there is good evidence for the effectiveness of multimodal programmes involving pharmacotherapy and psychotherapy in the treatment of schizophrenia, mood disorders, and substance use disorders. However, there is a dearth of evidence on the effectiveness of such programmes for anxiety disorders, somatoform disorders, eating disorders, personality disorders, psychosexual disorders, and psychological problems in later life. Research on multimodal programmes for these problems should be a focus for future research.

Comparative effectiveness studies

Trials are required to compare the impact of different psychotherapy, pharmacotherapy, and mutimodal therapy protocols on symptoms and a range of change processes. It may be that for some problems, different therapy protocols have their beneficial effects through different processes, or alternatively apparently different therapy protocols facilitate positive changes through the same processes.

Studies of the impact of therapy context on effectiveness and translational research

Further trials are required to evaluate the effectiveness of treatments, which are known to work in one context, in other different contexts. In translational research, psychotherapy protocols that have been shown to work in efficacy studies conducted in specialist centres require testing in pragmatic effectiveness trials, in routine community-based primary and secondary care centres with typical patients and therapists. The effectiveness of individual psychotherapy protocols that work needs to be evaluated when offered in group, family-assisted, computer-assisted, or bibliotherapy contexts. The effectiveness of couple and family interventions that work need to be evaluated when offered on a multiple-family group basis.

Psychological change processes

The psychological processes by which specific psychotherapy protocols facilitate change for specific problems or the identification of 'active ingredients' of psychotherapy protocols require far greater attention in future trials. There is overwhelming evidence for the importance of the therapeutic alliance in facilitating change. However, the alliance occurs within the context of therapists and clients engaging in collaborative problem-solving activities which have specific aims such as exploring unconscious material in psychodynamic therapy, facilitating emotional experiences in humanistic therapy, modifying family transactions and beliefs in systemic therapy, challenging dysfunctional beliefs in cognitive therapy, and increasing skill and activity levels in behaviour therapy. These processes, by which therapy is proposed to work, should be routinely assessed in all trials, to determine if it is these factors that are in fact promoting therapeutic change.

Where therapy processes can be segmented into discrete components, such as cognitive restructuring and behavioural activation for depression, dismantling trials are required to determine the relative effectiveness of the entire treatment package and each of its constituent components. Cognitive behavioural protocols lend themselves readily to these type of studies. A challenge for researchers within humanistic, psychodynamic, and systemic traditions will be to design protocols that permit component analysis studies. The accumulation of research findings from dismantling studies carried out with the same sorts of problems but within different psychotherapy traditions may eventually throw light on important key therapeutic processes for specific problems shared by different approaches to therapy. These processes will come to be recognized as empirically supported treatment processes.

Neurobiological change processes

Very little research has been conducted on the neurobiological processes associated with effective psychotherapy. However, recent developments in neuroimaging technology have made the investigation of these processes feasible. For example, Linden (2006), in a review of research in this area, concluded that cognitive behavioural therapy for obsessive-compulsive disorder led to decreased metabolism in the right caudate nucleus, while cognitive behavioural therapy for phobias resulted in decreased activity in limbic and paralimbic areas. He also found that successful treatment of these conditions with serotonin reuptake inhibitors led to similar neurobiological changes. Where well-developed models of the neurobiology of specific psychological disorders or processes are available, and where efficacy studies provide evidence for strong positive effects of specific psychotherapy protocols, then neurobiological process studies involving these disorders and protocols should be prioritized to provide evidence for the neurobiological correlates of symptomatic improvement.

Participant factors

Further trials are required to evaluate the impact of therapist and client factors, and the interaction of these on treatment outcome, so that they may be used to enhance treatment effectiveness. For example, from research reviewed in Chapter 5 we know that impulsive patients make better gains with skills-focused symptom management approaches, and resistant clients fare better with self-direct therapy approaches. This information may be used to refine effective protocols for depression, anxiety, and other disorders, to involve self-directed skills acquisition for managing symptoms. Research findings on therapist attributes may also be used to affect service development policy. For example, we know that for many disorders socially disadvantaged clients from ethnic minorities have poor psychotherapy outcomes. We also know that where therapists and clients come from the same ethnic group, they have a better outcome. So, when developing psychotherapy services for ethnic minorities, ideally staff from these minorities should be given priority in the selection process.

Impact of training

There is a need for more research on effects of a variety of aspects of training on therapy outcome. These include studies of the effects of initial training, ongoing supervision, later continuing professional development, and personal psychotherapy on treatment outcome. In studies of the effects of initial training, investigations are required to determine the effects of various aspects of training such as academic tuition, clinical supervision, case studies, and research, on treatment outcome. In studies of the effects of supervision, there is a need to investigate the comparative effectiveness of various forms of supervision including live supervision, indirect supervision, and audio and video recording based supervision. In studies of continuing professional development, broad-based investigations of the overall impact of this type of ongoing training are required, along with studies of particular types of continuing professional development, such as learning manualized therapy protocols, attending conferences, attending journal clubs, and so forth. Studies of the effects of therapists engaging in personal psychotherapy on the treatment outcome of their clients are also required, to determine the optimal form such personal therapy should take.

Cost-effectiveness

Across all types of psychotherapy there is a need for far more research on long-term cost-effectiveness, and for cost-effectiveness data collection and analyses to be routinely built into trial research designs. For example, psychological treatments for anxiety disorders are brief and intensive, so cost a good deal in the short term, but their effects are more enduring than those of pharmacotherapy and over the long term are far more cost-effective. Research reviewed in Chapter 5 showed that with bipolar disorder intensive psychotherapy may reduce relapse and rehospitalization rates by 40%, which over 30 years may represent an enormous cost saving. Research to address these sorts of cost-effectiveness questions is urgently needed.

Closing comments

The research reviewed in this volume has shown conclusively that, when it comes to psychotherapy, both of the attributes valued by James Stephens' philosophers, in the quotation from *The Crock of Gold* which opened the Preface, are essential. Wisdom drawn from a careful consideration of scientific evidence is important, but so too are goodness and kindliness, in the form of empathic collaboration with our clients. In this closing chapter I have shown that, with regard to psychotherapy research, it is clearly a case of a lot done, but still a lot more to do.

Bibliography

Aaronson, C., Katzman, G. & Gorman, J. (2007). Combination pharmacotherapy and psychotherapy for the treatment of major depressive and anxiety disorders. In P. Nathan & J. Gorman (Ed.), *A Guide to Treatments that Work* (Third Edition, pp. 681–710). New York: Oxford University Press.

Abbot, N., Stead, L., White, A. & Barnes, J. (1998). Hypnotherapy for smoking cessation. *Cochrane Database of Systematic Reviews*, Issue 2. Art. No.: CD001008. DOI: 10.1002/14651858.CD001008.

Abikoff, H., Hechtman, L., Klein, R., Weiss, G., Fleiss, K., Etcovitch, J., Counsins, L., Greenfield, B., Martin, D. & Pollack, S. (2004). Symptomatic improvement in children with ADHD treated with long-term methylphenidate and multimodal psychosocial treatment. *Journal of the American Academy of Child and Adolescent Psychiatry*, 43, 802–811.

Abramowitz, J. (2006). *Understanding and Treating Obsessive-Compulsive Disorder: A Cognitive-Behavioural Approach*. Mahwah, NJ: Lawrence Erlbaum Associates, Inc.

Abramowitz, J., Franklin, M. & Foa. E. (2002). Empirical status of cognitive-behavioural therapy for obsessive-compulsive disorder: a meta-analytic review. *Romanian Journal of Cognitive Behavioural Psychotherapies*, 2(2), 89–104.

Abramowitz, J., Whiteside, S. & Deacon, B. (2005). The effectiveness of treatment for paediatric obsessive-compulsive disorder: a meta-analysis. *Behaviour Therapy*, 36(1), 55–63.

Abrams, D. B., Niaura, R., Brown, R. A., Emmons, K. M., Goldstein, M. G. & Monti, P. M. (2003). *The Tobacco Dependence Treatment Handbook: A Guide to Best Practices*. New York: Guilford Press.

Ackerman, D. & Greenland, S. (2002). Multivariate meta-analysis of controlled drug studies for obsessive-compulsive disorder. *Journal of Clinical Psychopharmacology*, 22(3), 309–317.

Acton, G. & Kang, J. (2001). Interventions to reduce the burden of care giving for an adult with dementia: a meta-analysis. *Research in Nursing and Health*, 24, 349–360.

Adams, N. & Sim, J. (2005). Rehabilitation approaches in fibromyalgia. *Disability and Rehabilitation: An International Multidisciplinary Journal*, 12, 711–723.

Addis, M. (2002). Methods for disseminating research products and increasing evidence-based practice: promises, obstacles, and future directions. *Clinical Psychology: Science and Practice*, 9, 367–378.

Alden, L. E. (1989). Short-term structured treatment for avoidant personality disorder. *Journal of Consulting & Clinical Psychology*, 57, 756–764.

Alexander, J. F., Pugh, C., Parsons, B. & Sexton, T. L. (2000). Functional family therapy. In D. Elliott (Ed.), *Blueprints for Violence Prevention* (Second Edition). Golden, CO: Venture.

Allen, L., Escobar, J., Lehrer, P., *et al.* (2002). Psychosocial treatments for multiple unexplained physical symptoms: a review of the literature. *Psychosomatic Medicine*, 64, 939–950.

Allin, H., Wathen, C. N. & MacMillan, H. (2005). Treatment of child neglect: a systematic review. *Canadian Journal of Psychiatry*, 50, 497–504.

Allness, D. & Knoedler, W. (1998). *The PACT Model of Community-Based Treatment for Persons with Severe and Persistent Mental Illness: A Manual for PACT Start-Up.* Arlington, VA: National Alliance for the Mentally Ill.

Allumbaugh, D. & Hoyt, W. (1999). Effectiveness of grief therapy: a meta-analysis. *Journal of Counselling Psychology*, 46, 370–380.

Althof, S. E., Leiblum, S. R., Chevret-Measson, M., Hartmann, U., Levine, S. B., McCabe, M., Plaut, M., Rodrigues, O. & Wylie, K. (2005). Psychological and interpersonal dimensions of sexual function and dysfunction. *Journal of Sexual Medicine*, 2, 793–800.

Altman, D., Schulz, K., Moher, D., Egger, M., Davidoff, R. & Elbourne, D. (2001). The revised CONSORT statement for reporting randomized trials: explanation and elaboration. *Annals of Internal Medicine*, 134, 663–694.

Alwin, N., Blackburn, R., Davidson, K., Hilton, M., Logan, C. & Shine, J. (2006). *Understanding Personality Disorder: A Report by the British Psychological Society.* Leicester: British Psychological Society.

Amato, L., Davoli, M., Ferri, M., Gowing, L. & Perucci, C. A. (2004). Effectiveness of interventions on opiate withdrawal treatment: an overview of systematic reviews. *Drug and Alcohol Dependence*, 73(3), 219–226.

Amato, L., Davoli, M., Minozzi, S., Ali, R. & Ferri, M. (2002). Methadone at tapered doses for the management of opioid withdrawal. *Cochrane Database of Systematic Reviews*, Issue 1. Art. No.: CD003409. DOI: 10.1002/14651858.CD003409.pub3.

Amato, L., Davoli, M., Perucci, C., Ferri, M., Faggiano, F. & Mattick, R. P. (2005). An overview of systematic reviews of the effectiveness of opiate maintenance therapies: available evidence to inform clinical practice and research. *Journal of Substance Abuse Treatment*, 28, 321–329.

Amato, P. R. (2001). Children of divorce in the 1990s: an update of the Amato and Keith (1991) meta-analysis. *Journal of Family Psychology*, 15, 355–370.

American Academy of Child & Adolescent Psychiatry (1998a). Practice parameters for the assessment and treatment of children and adolescents with depressive disorders. *Journal of the American Academy of Child and Adolescent Psychiatry*, 37, 63S–83S.

American Academy of Child & Adolescent Psychiatry (1998b). Practice parameters for the assessment and treatment of children and adolescents with obsessive compulsive disorder. *Journal of the American Academy of Child and Adolescent Psychiatry*, 37, 27S–45S.

American Academy of Child & Adolescent Psychiatry (1998c). Practice parameters for the assessment and treatment of children and adolescents with posttraumatic stress disorder. *Journal of the American Academy of Child and Adolescent Psychiatry*, 37, 4S–26S.

American Academy of Child & Adolescent Psychiatry (1999). Practice parameters for the assessment and treatment of children and adolescents who are sexually abusive to others. *Journal of the American Academy of Children and Adolescent Psychiatry*, 38, 55S–76S.

American Academy of Child & Adolescent Psychiatry (2007a). Practice parameters for the assessment and treatment of children, adolescents, and adults with Attention-Deficit/Hyperactivity Disorder. *Journal of the American Academy of Child and Adolescent Psychiatry*, 46, 894–921.

American Academy of Child & Adolescent Psychiatry (2007b). Practice parameter for the assessment and treatment of children and adolescents with oppositional defiant disorder. *Journal of the American Academy of Child and Adolescent Psychiatry*, 46, 126–141.

American Academy of Child & Adolescent Psychiatry (2007c). Practice parameter for the assessment and treatment of children and adolescents with bipolar disorder. *Journal of the American Academy of Child and Adolescent Psychiatry*, 46(1), 107–125.

American Academy of Child & Adolescent Psychiatry (2007d). Practice parameters for the assessment and treatment of children and adolescents with anxiety disorders. *Journal of the American Academy of Child and Adolescent Psychiatry*, 46(2), 267–283.

American Academy of Paediatrics (1998). Auditory integration training and facilitated communication for autism. *Paediatrics*, 102, 431–433.

American Academy of Paediatrics (2001). Clinical practice guideline: treatment of the school-aged child with attention-deficit/hyperactivity disorder. *Paediatrics*, 108(4), 1033–1104.

American Psychiatric Association (1998). *American Psychiatric Association Practice Guideline for the Treatment of Patients with Panic Disorder*. Washington, DC: APA.

American Psychiatric Association (2000a). *Diagnostic and Statistical Manual of the Mental Disorders* (Fourth Edition-Text Revision, DSM–IV-TR). Washington, DC: American Psychiatric Association.

American Psychiatric Association (2000b). *Practice Guideline for the Treatment of Patients with Major Depressive Disorder* (Second Edition). Washington, DC: American Psychiatric Association.

American Psychiatric Association (2001). *Practice Guideline for the Treatment of Patients with Borderline Personality Disorder*. Washington, DC: American Psychiatric Association.

American Psychiatric Association (2002). *American Psychiatric Association Practice Guideline for the Treatment of Patients with Bipolar Disorder*. Washington, DC: American Psychiatric Association.

American Psychiatric Association (2003). *Practice Guideline for the Assessment and Treatment of Patients with Suicidal Behaviours*. Washington, DC: American Psychiatric Association.

American Psychiatric Association (2004a). *American Psychiatric Association Practice Guideline for the Treatment of Patients with Acute Stress Disorder and Post-traumatic Stress Disorder*. Washington, DC: American Psychiatric Association.

American Psychiatric Association (2004b). *Practice Guideline for the Treatment of Patients with Schizophrenia* (Second Edition). Washington, DC: American Psychiatric Association.

American Psychiatric Association (2006a). *Practice Guideline for the Treatment of Patients with Eating Disorders* (Third Edition). Washington, DC: American Psychiatric Association.

American Psychiatric Association (2006b). *Treatment of Patients with Substance Use Disorders* (Second Edition). Washington, DC: American Psychiatric Association.

American Psychiatric Association (2007a). *Practice Guideline for the Treatment of Patients with Obsessive-Compulsive Disorder*. Washington, DC: American Psychiatric Association.

American Psychiatric Association (2007b). *Practice Guideline for the Treatment of Patients with Alzheimer's Disease and other Dementias* (Second Edition). Washington, DC: American Psychiatric Association.

American Psychological Association (1994). *Resolution on facilitated communication*. Retrieved from http://www.autism-watch.org/rx/fc(apa).shtml on 15.4.2007.

American Psychological Association (2004). Guidelines for psychological practice with older adults. *American Psychologist*, 59(4), 236–260.

American Psychological Association Presidential Task Force on Evidence Based Practice (2006). Evidence-based practice in psychology. *American Psychologist*, 61(4), 271–285.

Anastopoulos, A. D., Shelton, T. L. & Barkley, R. A. (2005). Family-based psychosocial treatments for children and adolescents with attention-deficit/ hyperactivity disorder. In E. Hibbs & P. Jensen (Eds.), *Psychosocial Treatments for Child and Adolescent Disorders: Empirically Based Strategies for Clinical Practice* (Second Edition, pp. 327–350). Washington, DC: American Psychological Association.

Anderson, E. & Lambert, M. (1995). Short-term dynamically oriented psychotherapy: a review and meta-analysis. *Clinical Psychology Review*, 15(6), 503–514.

Anderson, E. & Lambert, M. (2001). A survival analysis of clinically significant change in outpatient psychotherapy. *Journal of Clinical Psychology*, 57, 875–888.

Andrews, G. & Harvey, R. (1981). Does psychotherapy benefit neurotic patients? A reanalysis of the Smith, Glass, and Miller data. *Archives of General Psychiatry*, 38, 1203–1208.

Anthony, M. & Barlow, D. (2002). Specific phobias. In D. Barlow (Ed.), *Anxiety and its Disorders: The Nature and Treatment of Anxiety and Panic* (Second Edition, pp. 380–417). New York: Guilford Press.

Apodaca, T. & Miller, W. (2003). Meta-analysis of the effectiveness of bibliotherapy for alcohol problems. *Journal of Clinical Psychology*, 59, 289–304.

Apple, R., Lock, J. & Preebles, R. (2006). *Preparing for Weight Loss Surgery: Therapist Guide*. Oxford: Oxford University Press.

Arias, A., Steinberg, K., Banga, A. & Trestman, R. (2006). Systematic review of the efficacy of meditation techniques as treatments for medical illness. *Journal of Alternative and Complementary Medicine*, 12(8), 817–832.

Association for the Treatment of Sexual Abusers. http://www.atsa.com/.

Atkins, D. & Christensen, A. (2001). Is professional training worth the bother? *Australian Psychologist*, 36, 122–130.

Audin, K., Mellor-Clark, J., Barkham, M., Margison, F., McGrath, G., Lewis, S., Cann, L., Duffy, J. & Parry, G. (2001). Practice research networks for effective psychological therapies. *Journal of Mental Health*, 10, 241–251.

Australian and New Zealand Clinical Practice Guidelines for the Treatment of Panic

Disorder and Agoraphobia. (2003). *Australian and New Zealand Journal of Psychiatry*, 37(6), 641–656.

Avenell, A., Broom, J., Brown, T., Poobalan, A., Aucott, L., Stearns, S., Smith, W., Jung, R., Campbell, M. & Grant A. (2004a). Systematic review of the long-term effects and economic consequences of treatments for obesity and implications for health improvement. *Health Technology Assessment*, 8(21), 1–182.

Avenell, A., Brown, T. J., McGee, M. A., Campbell, M. K., Grant, A. M., Broom, J., Jung, R. & Smith, W. (2004b). What interventions should we add to weight reducing diets in adults with obesity? A systematic review of randomized controlled trials of adding drug therapy, exercise, behaviour therapy or combinations of these interventions. *Journal of Human Nutrition and Diet*, 17, 293–316.

Aveyard, P. & West, R. (2007). Managing smoking cessation. *British Medical Journal*, 335, 37–41.

Ayers, C., Sorrell, J., Thorp, S. & Wetherell, J. (2007). Evidence-based psychological treatments for late-life anxiety. *Psychology and Aging*, 22, 8–17.

Azrin, N. & Nunn R. (1973). Habit-reversal: a method of eliminating nervous habits and tics. *Behaviour Research and Therapy*, 11(4), 619–628.

Azrin, N. & Peterson, A. (1990). Treatment of Tourette syndrome by habit reversal: a waiting-list control group comparison. *Behaviour Therapy*, 21, 305–318.

Azrin, N., Sneed, T. & Fox, R. (1974). Dry bed training: rapid elimination of childhood enuresis. *Behaviour Research and Therapy*, 12, 147–156.

Babcock, J., Green, C. & Robie, C. (2004). Does batterers' treatment work? A meta-analytic review of domestic violence treatment. *Clinical Psychology Review*, 23, 1023–1053.

Baer, R. (2003). Mindfulness training as a clinical intervention: a conceptual and empirical review. *Clinical Psychology Science and Practice*, 10, 125–143.

Bakermans-Kranenburg, M. J., Van IJzendoorn, M. H. & Juffer, F. (2003). Less is more: meta-analyses of sensitivity and attachment interventions in early childhood. *Psychological Bulletin*, 129, 195–215.

Bakker, A., van Balkom, A. & Spinhoven, P. (2002). SSRIs vs. TCAs in the treatment of panic disorder: a meta-analysis. *Acta Psychiatrica Scandinavica*, 106(3), 163–167.

Baldwin, S., Murray, D. & Shadish, W. (2005). Empirically supported treatments or type I errors? Problems with the analysis of data from group-administered treatments. *Journal of Consulting and Clinical Psychology*, 73(5), 924–935.

Ball, J. & Mitchell, P. (2004). A randomized controlled study of cognitive behaviour therapy and behavioural family therapy for anorexia nervosa patients. *Eating Disorders: The Journal of Treatment & Prevention*, 12, 303–314.

Ballenger, J., Davidson, J. & Lecrubier, Y. (2004). Consensus statement update on posttraumatic stress disorder from the International Consensus Group on Depression and Anxiety. *Journal of Clinical Psychiatry*, 65, 55–62.

Banez, G. & Cunningham, C. (2003). Paediatric gastrointestinal disorders: recurrent abdominal pain, inflammatory bowel disease and rumination disorder/cyclic vomiting. In M. Roberts (Ed.), *Handbook of Paediatric Psychology* (Third Edition, pp. 462–480). New York: Guilford Press.

Banner, L. & Anderson, R. (2007). Integrated sildenafil and cognitive-behaviour sex therapy for psychogenic erectile dysfunction: a pilot study. *Journal of Sexual Medicine*, 4, 1117–1125.

Barkham, M., Evans, C., Margison, M., McGrath, G., Mellor-Clarke, J., Milne, D. &

Connel, J. (1998). The rationale for developing and implementing core outcome batteries for routine use in service settings and psychotherapy outcome research. *Journal of Mental Health*, 7(1), 35–47.

Barkham, M., Hardy, G. & Mellor-Clark, J. (2008) *A Core Approach to Delivering Practice-Based Evidence in Counselling and Psychological Therapies*. New York: John Wiley.

Barkham, M. & Mellor-Clark, J. (2003). Bridging evidence-based practice and practice-based evidence: developing a rigorous and relevant knowledge for the psychological therapies. *Clinical Psychology & Psychotherapy*, 10(6), 319–327.

Barkham, M., Rees, A., Stiles, W. B., Shapiro, D. A., Hardy, G. E. & Reynolds, S. (1996). Dose–effect relations in time-limited psychotherapy for depression. *Journal of Consulting & Clinical Psychology*, 64, 927–935.

Barkley, R. (1997). *Defiant Children: A Clinician's Manual for Parent Training* (Second Edition). New York: Guilford Press.

Barkley, R. (2000). *Taking Charge of ADHD: The Complete Authoritative Guide for Parents*. New York: Guilford Press.

Barkley, R. (2005). *Attention Deficit Hyperactivity Disorder: A Handbook for Diagnosis and Treatment* (Third Edition). New York: Guilford Press.

Barlow, D. & Allen, L. (2004). Scientific basis of psychological treatments for anxiety disorders: past, present, and future. In J. Gorman (Ed.), *Fear and Anxiety: The Benefits of Translational Research* (pp. 171–191). Washington, DC: American Psychiatric Publishing.

Barlow, D., Allen, L. & Basden, S. (2007). Psychosocial treatments for panic disorders, phobias, and generalized anxiety disorder. In P. Nathan & J. Gorman (Eds.), *A Guide to Treatments that Work* (Third Edition, pp. 351–394). New York: Oxford University Press.

Barlow, J., Parsons, J. & Stewart-Brown, S. (2002). *Systematic Review of the Effectiveness of Parenting Programmes in the Primary and Secondary Prevention of Mental Health Problems*. Oxford: Health Services Research Unit, University of Oxford.

Barlow, S. & Dietz, W. (1998). Obesity evaluation and treatment: expert committee recommendations. *Paediatrics*, 102. Available at: http://www.pediatrics.org/cgi/content/full/102/3 /e29.

Barmish, A. & Kendall, P. (2005). Should parents be co-clients in cognitive-behavioural therapy for anxious youth? *Journal of Clinical Child & Adolescent Psychology*, 34(3), 569–581.

Barrett, P. (1998), Evaluation of cognitive-behavioural group treatments for childhood anxiety disorders. *Journal of Clinical Child Psychology*, 27, 459–468.

Barrett, P., Dadds, M. & Rapee, R. (1996). Family treatment of childhood anxiety: a controlled trial. *Journal of Consulting and Clinical Psychology*, 64(2), 333–342.

Barrett, P., Healy-Farrell, L., Piacentini, J. & March, J. (2004). Obsessive-compulsive disorder in childhood and adolescence: description and treatment. In P. Barrett & T. Ollendick (Eds.), *Handbook of Interventions that Work with Children and Adolescents: Prevention and Treatment* (pp. 187–216). Chichester: John Wiley.

Barrett, P., Lowry-Webster, H. & Turner, C. (2000). *FRIENDS programme for Youth: Group Leader's Manual*. Brisbane: Australian Academic Press (www.friendsinfo.net).

Barrett, P. & Ollendick, T. (2004) *Handbook of Interventions that Work with Children and Adolescents: Prevention and Treatment*. Chichester: John Wiley.

Barrett, P. & Shortt, A. (2003). Parental involvement in the treatment of anxious children. In A. Kazdin & J. Weisz (Eds.), *Evidence Based Psychotherapies for Children and Adolescents* (pp. 101–119). New York: Guilford Press.

Bartels, S., Dums, A., Oxman, T., Schneider, L., Arean, P., Alexopoulos, G. & Jeste, D. (2003). Evidence-based practices in geriatric mental health care: an overview of systematic reviews and meta-analyses. *Psychiatric Clinics of North America*, 26(4), 971–990.

Barton, S., Rae, D., Rhine, T. & Jones, L. (2005). The efficacy of play therapy with children: a meta-analytic review of treatment outcomes. *Professional Psychology: Research and Practice*, 36(4), 376–390.

Basson, R., Berman, J., Burnett, A., Derogatis, L., Ferguson, D., Fourcroy, J., Goldstein, I., Graziotti, N., Heiman, J., Laan, E., Leiblum, S., Padua-Nathan, H., Rosen, R., Segraves, K., Segraves, R. T., Shabsigh, R., Sipski, M., Wagner, G. & Whipple, B. (2000). Report of the international consensus development conference on female sexual dysfunctions: definitions and classifications. *Journal of Urology*, 163, 888–893.

Bateman, A. & Fonagy, P. (1999). Effectiveness of partial hospitalization in the treatment of borderline personality disorder: a randomized controlled trial. *American Journal of Psychiatry*, 156, 1563–1569.

Bateman, A. & Fonagy, P. (2000). Effectiveness of psychotherapeutic treatment of personality disorder. *British Journal of Psychiatry*, 177, 138–143.

Bateman, A. & Fonagy, P. (2001). Treatment of borderline personality disorder with psychoanalytically oriented partial hospitalization: an 18-month follow-up. *American Journal of Psychiatry*, 158, 36–52.

Bateman, A. & Fonagy, P. (2004). *Mentalization-Based Treatment for Borderline Personality Disorder: A Practical Guide*. Oxford: Oxford University Press.

Bates, T. (2006). Social phobia. In A. Carr & M. McNulty (Eds.), *Handbook of Adult Clinical Psychology: An Evidence Based Practice Approach* (pp. 558–590). London: Routledge.

Bauer, M. & McBride, L. (1996). *Structured Group Psychotherapy for Bipolar Disorder. The Life Goals Program*. New York: Springer.

Beach, S. (2003). Affective disorders. *Journal of Marital and Family Therapy*, 29, 247–261.

Beach, S. & O'Leary, K. (1992). Treating depression in the context of marital discord: outcome and predictors of response for marital therapy versus cognitive therapy. *Behaviour Therapy*, 23, 507–258.

Beach, S., Sandeen, E. & O'Leary, K. (1990). *Depression in Marriage: A Model for Aetiology and Treatment*. New York: Guilford Press.

Beating the Blues. http://www.mentalhealth.org.uk/campaigns/depression-relief/.

Beck, A. (1976). *Cognitive Therapy and the Emotional Disorders*. New York: Meridian.

Beck, A. & Freeman, A. (1990). *Cognitive Therapy of Personality Disorders*. New York: Guilford Press.

Beck, A., Rush, A., Shaw, B. & Emery, G. (1979). *Cognitive Therapy of Depression*. New York: Guilford Press.

Beck, R. & Fernandez, E. (1998). Cognitive-behavioural therapy in the treatment of anger: a meta-analysis. *Cognitive Therapy & Research*, 22(1), 63–74.

Bedard, R., Rosen, L. & Vacha-Haase, T. (2003). Wilderness therapy programs for juvenile delinquents: a meta-analysis. *Journal of Therapeutic Wilderness Camping*, 3(1), 7–13.

Beer, D., Karitani, M., Leonard, H., March, J. & Swedo, S. (2002). Obsessive compulsive disorder. In S. Kutcher (Ed.), *Practical Child and Adolescent Psychopharmacology* (pp. 159–186). Cambridge: Cambridge University Press.

Behan, J. & Carr, A. (2000). Oppositional defiant disorder. In A. Carr (Ed.), *What Works with Children and Adolescents? A Critical Review of Psychological Interventions with Children, Adolescents and their Families* (pp. 102–130). London: Routledge.

Bekkering, G., Abou-Settaand, A. & Kleijnen, J. (2007). The application of quantitative methods for identifying and exploring the presence of bias in systematic reviews: PDE-5 inhibitors for erectile dysfunction. *International Journal of Impotence Research*. doi: 10.1038/sj.ijir.3901626. http://www.nature.com/ijir/journal/vaop/ncurrent/abs/3901626a.html.

Bell, L. & Newns, K. (2004). What factors influence failure to engage in a supervised self-help programme for bulimia nervosa and binge eating disorder? *European Eating Disorders Review*, 12(3), 178–183.

Bellack, A., Mueser, K., Gingerich, S. & Agresta, J. (2004). *Social Skill Training for Schizophrenia: A Step-by-Step Guide* (Second Edition). New York: Guilford Press.

Bennett, D. & Gibbons, T. (2000). Efficacy of child cognitive behavioural interventions for antisocial behaviour: a meta-analysis. *Child and Family Behaviour Therapy*, 22, 1–15.

Benton, M. & Schroeder, H. (1990). Social skills training with schizophrenics: a meta-analytic evaluation. *Journal of Consulting and Clinical Psychology*, 58, 741–747.

Berlin, L. & Ziv, Y. (2005). *Enhancing Early Attachments: Theory, Research, Intervention and Policy*. New York: Guilford Press.

Bernstein, D., Borkovek, T. & Hazlett-Stevens, H. (2000). *New Directions in Progressive Relaxation Training: A Guidebook for Helping Professionals*. Westport, CT: Praeger.

Beutler, L., Blatt, S., Alamohamed, S., Levy, K. & Angtuaco, L. (2006). Participant factors in treating dysphoric disorders. In L. Castonguay & L. Beutler (Eds.), *Principles of Therapeutic Change that Work* (pp. 13–64). Oxford: Oxford University Press.

Beutler, L., Castonguay, L. & Follette, W. (2006). Integration of therapeutic factors in dysphoric disorders. In L. Castonguay & L. Beutler (Eds.), *Principles of Therapeutic Change that Work* (pp. 111–120). Oxford: Oxford University Press.

Beutler, L., Malik, M., Alimohamed, S., Harwood, T., Talebi, H., Noble, S. & Wong, E. (2004). Therapist variables. In M. Lambert (Ed.), *Bergin and Garfield's Handbook of Psychotherapy and Behaviour Change* (Fifth Edition, pp. 227–306). New York: John Wiley.

Bisson, J. (2003). Single-session early psychological interventions following traumatic events. *Clinical Psychology Review*, 23, 481–499.

Bisson, J., Ehlers, A., Matthews, R., Pilling, S., Richards, D. & Turner, S. (2007). Psychological treatments for chronic post-traumatic stress disorder. *British Journal of Psychiatry*, 190, 97–104.

Black, D. & Urbanowicz, M. (1987). Family intervention with bereaved children. *Journal of Child Psychology and Psychiatry*, 28(3), 467–476.

Blagg, N. & Yule, W. (1984). The behavioural treatment of school refusal – a comparative study. *Behaviour Research and Therapy*, 22, 119–127.

Blanchard, E. (2001). *Irritable Bowel Syndrome: Psychosocial Assessment and Treatment*. Washington, DC: American Psychological Association.

Blanchard, E. (2005). A critical review of cognitive, behavioural, and cognitive-behavioural therapies for irritable bowel syndrome. *Journal of Cognitive Psychotherapy*, 19, 101–123.

Blanchard, E. & Scharff, L. (2002). Psychosocial aspects of assessment and treatment of irritable bowel syndrome in adults and recurrent abdominal pain in children. *Journal of Consulting and Clinical Psychology* [Special Issue]: *Behavioural Medicine and Clinical Health Psychology*, 70(3), 725–738.

Block, A., Gatchel, R., Deardorff, W. & Guyer, R. (2003). Conceptual models of surgery preparation. In A. Block, R. Gatchel, W. Deardorff & R. Guyer (Eds.), *The Psychology of Spine Surgery* (pp. 131–148). Washington, DC: American Psychological Association.

Blumenthal, J., Sherwood, A., Gullette, E., Georgiades, A. & Tweedy, D. (2002). Biobehavioural approaches to the treatment of essential hypertension. *Journal of Consulting and Clinical Psychology* [Special Issue]: *Behavioural Medicine and Clinical Health Psychology*, 70(3), 569–589.

Bohart, A., O'Hara, M. & Leitner, L. (1998). Empirically violated treatments: disenfranchisement of humanistic and other psychotherapies. *Psychotherapy Research*, 8(2), 141–157.

Bond, G. (2004). Supported employment: evidence for an evidence-based practice. *Psychiatric Rehabilitation Journal*, 27(4), 345–359.

Bond, G., Drake, R., Mueser, K. & Latimer, E. (2001). Assertive community treatment for people with severe mental illness: critical ingredients and impact on patients. *Disease Management & Health Outcomes*, 9(3), 141–159.

Borduin, C., Curtis, N. & Ronan, K. (2004). Multisystemic treatment: a meta-analysis of outcome studies. *Journal of Family Psychology*, 18(3), 411–419.

Borduin, C., Letourneau, E. & Henggeler, S. (in press). *Multisystemic Treatment with Juvenile Sexual Offenders and their Families*. New York: Guilford Press.

Bower, J., Woolery, A., Sternlieb, B. & Garet, D. (2005). Yoga for cancer patients and survivors. *Cancer Control*, 12(3), 165–171.

Bower, P., Rowland, N. & Hardy, R. (2003). The clinical effectiveness of counselling in primary care: a systematic review and meta-analysis. *Psychological Medicine*, 33, 203–215.

Bowlby, J. (1988). *A Secure Base: Clinical Applications of Attachment Theory*. London: Hogarth.

Bradley, R., Greene, J., Russ, E., Dutra, L. & Westen, D. (2005). A multidimensional meta-analysis of psychotherapy for PTSD. *American Journal of Psychiatry*, 162(2), 214–227.

Bray, G. (2005). Drug treatment of obesity. *Psychiatric Clinics of North America*, 28(1), 193–217.

Brazzelli, M. and Griffiths, P. (2001). Behavioural and cognitive interventions with or without other treatments for defecation disorders in children. *Cochrane Database of Systematic Reviews*, Issue 4. Art. No.: CD002240. DOI: 10.1002/14651858.CD002240.

Brenner, H., Roder, V., Hodel, B., Kienzle, N., Reed, D. & Liberman, R. (1994).

Integrated Psychological Therapy for Schizophrenic Patients. Toronto: Hogrefe & Huber.

Brestan, E. V. & Eyberg, S. M. (1998). Effective psychosocial treatments of conduct-disordered children and adolescents; 29 years, 82 studies, and 5,272 kids. *Journal of Clinical Psychology*, 27, 180–189.

Bridge, J., Goldstein, T. & Brent, D. (2006). Adolescent suicide and suicidal behaviour. *Journal of Child Psychology and Psychiatry*, 47, 372–394.

Brinkley, A., Cullen, R. & Carr, A. (2002). Prevention of adjustment problems in children with asthma. In A. Carr (Ed.), *Prevention: What Works with Children and Adolescents? A Critical Review of Psychological Prevention Programmes for Children, Adolescents and their Families* (pp. 222–248). London: Routledge.

Brinkmeyer, M. & Eyberg, S. (2003). Parent–child interaction therapy for oppositional children. In A. Kazdin & J. Weisz (Eds.), *Evidence Based Psychotherapies for Children and Adolescents* (pp. 204–223). New York: Guilford Press.

Brodaty, H., Green, A. & Koschera, A. (2003). Meta-analysis of psychosocial interventions for caregivers of people with dementia. *Journal of the American Geriatric Society*, 51, 657–664.

Brosnan, R. & Carr, A. (2000). Adolescent conduct problems. In A. Carr (Ed.), *What Works with Children and Adolescents? A Critical Review of Psychological Interventions with Children, Adolescents and their Families* (pp. 131–154). London: Routledge.

Brown, G., Henriques, G., Ratto, C. & Beck, A. (2002). *Cognitive Therapy Treatment Manual for Suicide Attempters.* Philadelphia: University of Pennsylvania.

Brown, G., Ten Have, T., Henriquez, G., Xie, S., Hollander, J. & Beck, A. (2005). Cognitive therapy for the prevention of suicide attempts. *Journal of the American Medical Association*, 294, 563–570.

Brownley, K., Berkman, N., Sedway, J., Lohr, K. & Bulik, C. (2007) Binge eating disorder treatment: a systematic review of randomized controlled trials. *International Journal of Eating Disorders*, 40, 337–348.

Brue, A. & Oakland T. (2002). Alternative treatments for attention-deficit/hyperactivity disorder: does evidence support their use? *Alternative Therapies*, 8(1): 68–74.

Buchwald, H., Avidor, Y., Braunwald, E., Jensen, M. & Pories, W. (2004). Bariatric surgery: a systematic review and meta-analysis. *Journal of the American Medical Association*, 292(14), 1724–1737.

Budney, A. & Higgins, S. (1998). *A Community Reinforcement Plus Vouchers Approach: Treating Cocaine Addiction.* Bethesda, MD: National Institute for Drug Abuse.

Burke, J., Loeber, R. & Birmaher, B. (2002). Oppositional defiant disorder and conduct disorder: a review of the past 10 years, part II. *Journal of the American Academy of Child & Adolescent Psychiatry*, 41(11), 1275–1293.

Burlingame, G., Fuhriman, A. & Mosier, J. (2003). The differential effectiveness of group psychotherapy: a meta-analytic perspective. *Group Dynamics: Theory, Research, and Practice*, 7, 3–12.

Burlingame, G., MacKenzie, K. & Strauss, B. (2004). Small group treatment: evidence for effectiveness and mechanisms of change. In M. Lambert (Ed.), *Bergin and Garfield's Handbook of Psychotherapy and Behaviour Change* (Fifth Edition, pp. 647–698). New York: John Wiley.

Burlingame, G., Wells, M., Lambert, M., Cox, J., Latkowski, M. & Justice, D.

(2005) *Administration and Scoring Manual for the Youth Outcome Questionnaire* (Y-OQ.2.2). Salt Lake City, UT: American Professional Credentialing Services.

Burnand, Y., Andreoli, A., Kolatte, E., Venturini, A. & Rosset, N. (2002). Psychodynamic psychotherapy and clomipramine in the treatment of major depression. *Psychiatric Services*, 53, 585–590.

Burns, A. & O'Brien, J. (2006). Clinical practice with anti-dementia drugs: a consensus statement from British Association for Psychopharmacology. *Journal of Psychopharmacology*, 20, 732–755.

Burns, D. (1989). *Feeling Good.* New York: Signet/New American Library.

Burns, T. & Fim, M. (2002). *Assertive Outreach in Mental Health: A Manual for Practitioners.* Oxford: Oxford University Press.

Burns, T., Knapp, M., Catty, J., Healey, A., Henderson, J., Watt, J. & Wright, C. (2001). Home treatment for mental health problems: a systematic review. *Health Technology Assessment* 5(15). http://www.ncchta.org.

Busch, A., Schachter, C., Peloso, P. & Bombardier, C. (2002). Exercise for treating fibromyalgia syndrome. *Cochrane Database of Systematic Reviews*, Issue 2. Art. No.: CD003786. DOI: 10.1002/14651858.CD003786.

Butler, A., Chapman, J., Forman, E. & Beck, A. (2006). The empirical status of cognitive-behavioural therapy: a review of meta-analyses. *Clinical Psychology Review.*

Byford, S., Harrington, R. & Torgerson, D. (1999). Cost-effectiveness analysis of a home-based social work intervention for children and adolescents who have deliberately poisoned themselves: results of a randomised controlled trial. *British Journal of Psychiatry*, 174, 56–62.

Byng-Hall, J. (1995). *Rewriting Family Scripts: Improvisation and Change.* New York: Guilford Press.

Byrne, M., Carr, A. & Clarke, M. (2004a). The efficacy of couples based interventions for panic disorder with agoraphobia. *Journal of Family Therapy*, 26(2), 105–125.

Byrne, M., Carr, A. & Clark, M. (2004b) The efficacy of behavioural couples therapy and emotionally focused therapy for couple distress. *Contemporary Family Therapy*, 26, 361–387.

Cain, D. & Seeman, J. (2001). *Humanistic Psychotherapies: Handbook of Research and Practice.* Washington, DC: American Psychological Association.

Caldwell, B., Woolley, S. & Cladwell, C. (2007). Preliminary estimates of cost-effectiveness for marital therapy. *Journal of Marital & Family Therapy*, 33(3), 392–405.

Camer, B. & Palacio Espasa, E. (1993). *La Pratique des Psychotherapies Mères-Bébés.* Paris: PUF.

Campbell, J., Penzien, D. & Wall, E. (2000). *Evidence-based guidelines for migraine headache: behavioural and physical treatments.* U.S. Headache Consortium. Retrieved September 2007, from http://www.aan.com/public/practiceguidelines/headache_gl.htm.

Carney, S., Cowen, P., Geddes, J., Goodwin, G., Rogers, R., Dearness, K., Tomlin, A., Eastaugh, J., Freemantle, N., Lester, H., Harvey, A. & Scott, A. (2003). Efficacy and safety of electroconvulsive therapy in depressive disorders: a systematic review and meta-analysis. *Lancet*, 361(9360), 799–808.

Carr, A. (2000). *What Works with Children and Adolescents?* London: Routledge.

Carr, A. (2004). Interventions for post-traumatic stress disorder in children and adolescents. *Paediatric Rehabilitation*, 7(4), 231–244.

Carr, A. (2006). *Family Therapy: Concepts, Process and Practice*. Chichester: Wiley.

Carr, A. & McNulty, M. (2006). Depression. In A. Carr & M. McNulty (Eds.), *Handbook of Adult Clinical Psychology* (pp. 291–345). London: Routledge.

Carr, A., O'Reilly, G., Walsh, P. & McEvoy, J. (2007). *Handbook of Intellectual Disability and Clinical Psychology Practice*. London: Routledge.

Carr, E., Horner, R., Turnbull, A., Marquis, J., McLaughlin, D. M., McAtee, M., Smith, C., Ryan, K., Ruef, M., Doolabh, A. & Braddock, D. (1999). *Positive Behaviour Support for People with Developmental Disabilities: A Research Synthesis*. Washington, DC: American Association on Mental Retardation.

Cartwright-Hatton, S., Roberts, C., Chitsabesan, P., Fothergill, C. & Harrington, R. (2004). Systematic review of the efficacy of cognitive behaviour therapies for childhood and adolescent anxiety disorders. *British Journal of Clinical Psychology*, 43, 421–436.

Casacalenda, N., Perry, J. & Looper, K. (2002). Remission in major depressive disorder: a comparison of pharmacotherapy, psychotherapy, and control conditions. *American Journal of Psychiatry*, 159, 1354–1360.

Casey, R. J. & Berman, J. S. (1985). The outcome of psychotherapy with children. *Psychological Bulletin*, 98, 388–400.

Caspi, O. (2004). How good are we? A meta-analytic study of effect sizes in medicine. *Dissertation Abstracts International: Section B: The Sciences and Engineering*, 65(5-B), 2607.

Cassidy, J. & Shaver, P. (1999). *Handbook of Attachment*. New York: Guilford Press.

Castonguay, L. & Beutler, L. (2006). *Principles of Therapeutic Change that Work*. Oxford: Oxford University Press.

Castonguay, L., Grosse Holtforth, M., Coombs, M., Beberman, R., Kakouros, A., Boswell, J., Reid, J. & Jones, E. (2006). Relationship factors in treating dysphoric disorders. In L. Castonguay & L. Beutler (Eds.), *Principles of Therapeutic Change that Work* (pp. 65–82). Oxford: Oxford University Press.

Chadwick, P., Birchwood, M. & Trower, P. (1996). *Cognitive Therapy for Delusions, Voices and Paranoia*. Chichester: Wiley.

Chaffin, M. & Friedrich, B. (2004). Evidence-based treatments in child abuse and neglect. *Children and Youth Services Review*, 26, 1097–1113.

Chaffin, M., Silovsky, J., Funderburk, B., Valle, L., Brestan, E. & Balachova, T. (2004). Parent–child interaction therapy with physically abusive parents: efficacy for reducing future abuse reports. *Journal of Consulting and Clinical Psychology*, 72, 500–510.

Chamberlain, P. & Smith, D. (2003). Antisocial behaviour in children and adolescents: the Oregon multidimensional treatment foster care model. In A. Kazdin & J. Weisz (Eds.), *Evidence Based Psychotherapies for Children and Adolescents* (pp. 281–300). New York: Guilford Press.

Chamberlain, P. & Smith, D. (2005). Multidimensional treatment foster care: a community solution for boys and girls referred from juvenile justice. In E. Hibbs & P. Jensen (Eds.), *Psychosocial Treatments for Child and Adolescent Disorders: Empirically Based Strategies for Clinical Practice* (Second Edition, pp. 557–574). Washington, DC: American Psychological Association.

Chambless, D., Baker, M., Baucom, D., Beutler, L., Calhoun, K. & Crits-Christoph,

P. (1998). Update on empirically validated therapies, II. *Clinical Psychologist*, 51, 3–16.

Chambless, D. & Ollendick, T. (2001). Empirically supported psychological interventions: controversies and evidence. *Annual Review of Psychology*, 52, 685–716.

Chan, J. & Sigafoos, J. (2001). Does respite care reduce parental stress in families with developmentally disabled children. *Child and Youth Care Forum*, 30, 253–263.

Channon, S., Hemsley, D., de Silva, P. & Perkins, R. (1989). A controlled trial of cognitive-behaviour and behavioural treatment of anorexia nervosa. *Behavioural Research on Therapy*, 27, 529–535.

Chapman, L. M., Morabito, D., Ladakakos, C., Schreier, H. & Knudson, M. M. (2001). The effectiveness of art therapy interventions in reducing post traumatic stress disorder (PTSD) symptoms in paediatric trauma patients. *Art Therapy: Journal of the American Therapy Association*, 18, 100–104.

Charlop-Christy, M., Carpenter, M., Le, L., LeBlanc, L. & Keller, K. (2002). Using the Picture Exchange Communication System (PECS) with children with autism: assessment of PECS acquisition, speech, social-communicative behaviour, and problem behaviour. *Journal of Applied Behaviour Analysis*, 35, 213–231.

Cheung, A., Emslie, G. & Mayes, T. (2005). Review of the efficacy and safety of antidepressants in youth depression. *Journal of Child Psychology & Psychiatry*, 46(7), 735–754.

Chiles, J., Lambert, M. & Hatch, A. (1999). The impact of psychological interventions on medical cost offset: a meta-analytic review. *Clinical Psychology: Science and Practice*, 6, 204–220.

Chinn, S. (2000). A simple method for converting an odds ratio to effect size for use in meta-analysis. *Statistics in Medicine*, 19, 3127–3131

Chowdhury, U. (2004). *Tics and Tourette Syndrome: A Handbook for Parents and Professionals*. London: Jessica Kingsley Publishers.

Christensen, A., Atkinson, D., Yi, J., Baucom, D. & George, W. (2006). Couple and individual adjustment for two years following a randomized clinical trial comparing traditional versus integrative behavioural couple therapy. *Journal of Consulting and Clinical Psychology*, 74(6), 1180–1191.

Cicchetti, D. & Toth, S. (1998). The development of depression in children and adolescents. *American Psychologist*, 53, 221–241.

Clare, L. & Woods, R. (2004). Cognitive training and cognitive rehabilitation for people with early-stage Alzheimer's disease: a review. *Neuropsychological Rehabilitation*, 14, 385–401.

Clark, D. & Fairburn, C. (1997). *Science and Practice of Cognitive Behaviour Therapy*. Oxford: Oxford University Press.

Clarke, G., Debar, L. & Lewinsohn, P. (2003). Cognitive behavioural group treatment for adolescent depression. In A. Kazdin & J. Weisz (Eds.), *Evidence-Based Psychotherapies for Children and Adolescents* (pp. 120–134). New York: Guilford Press.

Clarke, G., Debar, L., Lynch, F., Powell, J., Gale, J., O'Connor, E., Ludman, E., Bush, T., Lin, E., von Korff, M. & Herbert, S. (2005). A randomized effectiveness trial of brief cognitive-behaviour therapy for depressed adolescents receiving antidepressant medication. *Journal of the American Academy of Child and Adolescent Psychiatry*, 44(9), 888–898.

Clarkin, J., Carpenter, D., Hull, J., Wilner, P. & Glick, I. (1998). Effects of psychoeducational intervention for married patients with bipolar disorder and their spouses. *Psychiatry Services*, 49, 531–533.

Clarkin, J., Glick, I., Haas, G., Spencer, J., Lewis, A., Peyser, J., Demane, N., Good-Ellis, M., Harris, E. & Lestelle, V. (1990). A randomized clinical trial of inpatient family intervention, V: results for affective disorders. *Journal of Affective Disorders*, 18, 17–28.

Clarkin, J. & Levy, K. (2004). The influence of client variables on psychotherapy. In M. Lambert (Ed.), *Bergin and Garfield's Handbook of Psychotherapy and Behaviour Change* (Fifth Edition, pp. 194–226). New York: Wiley.

Cobham, V., Dadds, M. & Spence, S. (1998). The role of parental anxiety in the treatment of childhood anxiety. *Journal of Consulting and Clinical Psychology*, 66, 893–905.

Cochran, S. (1984). Preventing medical non-compliance in the outpatient treatment of bipolar affective disorders. *Journal of Consulting and Clinical Psychology*, 52, 873–878.

Cochrane, A. (1972). *Effectiveness and Efficiency: Random Reflections on Health Services*. London: Nuffield Provincial Hospitals Trust.

Cofta-Woerpel, L., Wright, K. & Wetter, D. (2006). Smoking cessation 1: pharmacological treatment. *Behavioural Medicine*, 32(2), 47–56.

Cofta-Woerpel, L., Wright, K. & Wetter, D. (2007). Smoking cessation 3: multicomponent interventions. *Behavioural Medicine*, 32, 135–149.

Cohan, S., Chavira, D. & Stein, M. (2006). Practitioner review: psychosocial interventions for children with selective mutism: a critical evaluation of the literature from 1990–2005. *Journal of Child Psychology and Psychiatry*, 47(11), 1085–1097.

Cohen, J. (1988). *Statistical Power Analysis for the Behavioural Sciences* (Second Edition). Mahwah, NJ: Lawrence Erlbaum Associates, Inc.

Cohen, J. (2003). Treating acute posttraumatic reactions in children and adolescents. *Biological Psychiatry*, 53, 827–833.

Cohen, J. & Mannarino, A. (2004). Treatment of childhood traumatic grief. *Journal of Clinical Child and Adolescent Psychology*, 33(4), 819–831.

Cohen, J., Mannarino, A. & Deblinger, E. (2006a). *Treating Trauma and Traumatic Grief in Children and Adolescents*. New York: Guilford Press.

Cohen, J., Mannarino, A., Greenberg, T., Padlo, S. & Shipley, C. (2002). Childhood traumatic grief: concepts and controversies. *Trauma, Violence, & Abuse*, 3(4), 307–327.

Cohen, J., Mannarino, A., Murray, L. & Igelman, R. (2006b). Psychosocial interventions for maltreated and violence-exposed children. *Journal of Social Issues*, 62(4), 737–766.

Cohen-Mansfield, J. (2001). Nonpharmacologic interventions for inappropriate behaviours in dementia: a review, summary, and critique. *American Journal of Geriatric Psychiatry*, 9, 361–381.

Colcombe, S. & Kramer, A. F. (2003). Fitness effects on the cognitive function of older adults: a meta-analytic study. *Psychological Science*, 14, 125–130.

Coldwell, C. & Bender, W. (2007). The effectiveness of assertive community treatment for homeless populations with severe mental illness: a meta-analysis. *American Journal of Psychiatry*, 164(3), 393–399.

Colom, F., Vleta, E., Martinez-Aran, A., Reinares, M., Goikolea, J. M., Benabarre, A.,

Torrent, C., Comes, M., Corbella, B., Parramon, G. & Corominas, J. (2003). A randomized trial on the efficacy of group psychoeducation in the prophylaxis of recurrences in bipolar patients whose disease is in remission. *Archives of General Psychiatry*, 60, 402–407.

Compton, S., March, J., Brent, D., Albano, A., Weersing, V. & Curry, J. (2004). Cognitive-behavioural psychotherapy for anxiety and depressive disorders in children and adolescents: an evidence-based medicine review. *Journal of the American Academy of Child & Adolescent Psychiatry*, 43, 930–959.

Connell, J., Cahill, J., Barkham, M., Gilbody, S. & Madill, A. (2006). *A Systematic Scoping Study of Research on Counselling in Higher and Further Education.* Rugby: British Association for Counselling and Psychotherapy (www.nacp.co.uk).

Connelly, M. (2003). Recurrent paediatric headache: a comprehensive review. *Children's Health Care*, 32, 153–189.

Consensus Development Panel (2000). National Institutes of Health Consensus Development Conference statement: diagnosis and treatment of attention-deficit/ hyperactivity disorder (ADHD). *Journal of the American Academy of Child and Adolescent Psychiatry*, 39(2), 182–193.

Cook, J. & Razzano, L. (2005). Evidence-based practices in supported employment. In C. Stout & R. Hayes (Eds.), *The Evidence-Based Practice: Methods, Models, and Tools for Mental Health Professionals* (pp. 10–30). Hoboken, NJ: Wiley.

Cooke, D., McNally, L., Mulligan, K., Harrison, M. & Newman, S. (2001). Psychosocial interventions for caregivers of people with dementia: a systematic review. *Aging and Mental Health*, 5, 120–135.

Cooper, A., Skinner, J., Nherera, L., Feder, G., Ritchie, G., Kathoria, M., Tumbull, N., Shaw, G., McDermott, K., Minhas, R., Packham, C., Squires, H., Thompson, D., Timmis, A., Walsh, J., Williams, H. & White, A. (2007). *Clinical Guidelines and Evidence Review for Post-Myocardial Infarction: Secondary Prevention in Primary and Secondary Care for Patients following a Myocardial Infarction.* London: National Collaboration Centre for Primary Care and Royal College of general Practitioners. Available at: http://guidance.nice.org.uk/CG48/guidance/pdf/English.

Cooper, Z., Fairburn, C. & Hawker, D. (2003). *Cognitive-Behavioural Treatment of Obesity : A Clinician's Guide.* New York: Guilford Press.

Copello, A., Orford, J., Hodgson, R. & Tober, G. (2002). *Social Behaviour and Network Therapy Manual.* Birmingham: University of Birmingham and the UKATT.

Copello, A., Orford, J., Hodgson, R., Tober, G. & Barrett, C. on behalf of the UKATT Research Team (2002). Social behaviour and network therapy: basic principles and early experiences. *Addictive Behaviour*, 27, 345–366.

CORE System Group (1999). *CORE System User Manual.* Leeds: CSG. http:// www.coreims.co.uk/index.php?name=EZCMS&page_id=6&.

Coren, E., Barlow, J. & Stewart-Brown, S. (2002). Systematic review of the effectiveness of parenting programmes for teenage parents. *Journal of Adolescence*, 26(1), 79–103.

Cormack, C. & Carr, A. (2000). Drug abuse. In A. Carr (Ed.), *What Works with Children and Adolescents? A Critical Review of Psychological Interventions with Children, Adolescents and their Families* (pp. 155–177). London: Routledge.

Corrigan, P. (1991). Social skills training in adult psychiatric populations: a meta-analysis. *Journal of Behaviour Therapy and Experimental Psychiatry*, 22, 203–210.

Corsini, R. & Wedding, D. (2004). *Current Psychotherapies* (Seventh Edition). New York: Thompson-Wadsworth.

Cox, D. & Gonder-Frederick, L. (1992). Major developments in behavioural diabetes research. *Journal of Consulting and Clinical Psychology*, 60(4), 628–638.

Coyne, J., Stefanek, M. & Palmer, S. (2007). Psychotherapy and survival in cancer: the conflict between hope and evidence. *Psychological Bulletin*, 133(3), 367–394.

Craft, L. & Landers, D. (1998). The effect of exercise on clinical depression and depression resulting from mental illness: a meta-analysis. *Journal of Sport and Exercise Psychology*, 20, 339–357.

Craighead, W., Shets, E., Brosse, A. & Ilardi, S. (2007). Psychosocial treatments for major depressive disorder. In P. Nathan & J. Gorman (Ed.), *A Guide to Treatments that Work* (Third Edition, pp. 289–308). New York: Oxford University Press.

Craske, M. & Barlow, D. (2006). *Master your Anxiety and Panic: Therapist Guide* (Fourth Edition). Oxford: Oxford University Press.

Crawford, M., Thomas, O., Khan, N. & Kulinskaya, E. (2007). Psychosocial interventions following self-harm: systematic review of their efficacy in preventing suicide. *British Journal of Psychiatry*, 190, 11–17.

Creamer, M. & Carty, J. (2006). Post-traumatic stress disorder. In A. Carr & M. McNulty (Eds.), *Handbook of Adult Clinical Psychology: An Evidence Based Practice Approach* (pp. 423–557). London: Routledge.

Crits-Christoph, P. (1992). The efficacy of brief dynamic psychotherapy: a meta-analysis. *American Journal of Psychiatry*, 149, 151–8.

Crits-Christoph, P., Connolly, M., Azarian, K., Crits-Christoph, K. & Shappell, S. (1996). An open trial of brief supportive-expressive psychotherapy in the treatment of generalized anxiety disorder. *Psychotherapy*, 33, 418–430.

Crits-Christoph, P., Siqueland, L., Blaine, J., Frank, A., Luborsky, L., Onkey, L., Muenz, L., Thase, M., Weiss, R., Gastfrlend, D., Woody, G., Barber, J., Butler, S., Daley, D., Salloum, I., Bishop, S., Najavitis, L., Lis, J., Mercer, D., Griffin, M., Moras, K. & Beck, A. T. (1999). Psychosocial treatments for cocaine dependence: National Institute on Drug Abuse Collaborative Cocaine Treatment Study. *Archives of General Psychiatry*, 56, 493–502.

Crits-Christoph, P., Siqueland, L., McClamont, E., Weiss, R., Gastfriend, D., Frank, A., Moras, K., Barber, J., Blaine, J. & Thase, M. (2001). Impact of psychosocial treatments on associated problems of cocaine dependent patients. *Journal of Consulting and Clinical Psychology*, 69, 825–830.

Cruz, R. & Berrol, C. (2004). *Dance/Movement Therapists in Action: A Working Guide to Research Options*. Springfield, IL: Thomas.

Cuijpers, P. (1998). A psychoeducational approach to the treatment of depression: a meta-analysis of Lewinsohn's 'Coping with Depression' course. *Behaviour Therapy*, 29(3), 521–533.

Cuijpers, P., van Straten, A. & Smit, F. (2006). *Psychological Treatment of Late-Life Depression: A Meta-Analysis of Randomized Controlled Trials*. Chichester: Wiley.

Cuijpers, P., van Straten, A. & Warmerdam, L. (2007a). Behavioural activation treatments of depression: a meta-analysis. *Clinical Psychology Review*, 27(3), 318–326.

Cuijpers, P., van Straten, A. & Warmerdam, L. (2007b). Problem solving therapies for depression: a meta-analysis. *European Psychiatry*, 22(1), 9–15.

Culm, G. (1990) *Coping with Panic*. Pacific Grove, CA: Brooks Cole.

Curry, J., Rohde, P., Simons, A., Silva, S. & Vitello, B. (2006). Predictors and moderators of acute outcome in the treatment for adolescents with depression study (TADS). *Journal of the American Academy of Child and Adolescent Psychiatry*, 45(12), 1427–1439.

Curry, J., Wells, K., Lochman, J., Craighead, W. & Nagy, P. (2003). Cognitive-behavioural intervention for depressed, substance-abusing adolescents: development and pilot testing. *Journal of the American Academy of Child and Adolescent Psychiatry*, 42(6), 656–665.

Daley, D. & Marlatt, A. (2006). *Overcoming Your Alcohol or Drug Problem* (Second Edition). Oxford: Oxford University Press.

Dare, C. (1991). The place of psychotherapy in the management of anorexia nervosa. In J. Holmes (Ed.), *Psychotherapy in Psychiatric Practice* (pp. 395–418). Edinburgh: Churchill Livingstone.

Dare, C. (1995). Psychoanalytic psychotherapy (of eating disorders). In O. Gabbard (Ed.), *Treatment of Psychiatric Disorders* (pp. 2129–2151). Washington, DC: American Psychiatric Press.

Dare, C., Eisler, L., Russell, G., Treasure, J. & Dodge, L. (2001). Psychological therapies for adults with anorexia nervosa: randomized controlled trial of out-patient treatments. *British Journal of Psychiatry*, 178, 216–221.

Davenloo, H. (1978). *Basic Principles and Techniques in Short-term Dynamic Psychotherapy*. New York: Spectrum.

Davidson, K. (2000). *Cognitive Therapy for Personality Disorders: A Guide For Clinicians*. London: Arnold.

Davidson, K., Norrie, J., Turer, P., Gumley, A., Tata, P., Murray, H. & Palmer, S. (2006). The effectiveness of cognitive behaviour therapy for borderline personality disorder: results from the borderline personality disorder study of cognitive therapy (BOSCOT) trial. *Journal of Personality Disorders*, 20(5), 450–465.

Dawe, S., Rees, V., Mattick, R., Sitharthan, T. & Heather, N. (2002). Efficacy of moderation-oriented cue exposure for problem drinkers: a randomized controlled trial. *Journal of Consulting and Clinical Psychology*, 70, 1045–1050.

Dawson, G. & Watling, R. (2000). Interventions to facilitate auditory, visual, and motor integration in autism: a review of the evidence. *Journal of Autism and Developmental Disorders*, 30, 415–421.

Deacon, B. & Abramowitz, J. (2004). Cognitive behavioural treatments for anxiety disorders: a review of meta-analytic findings. *Journal of Clinical Psychology*, 60(4), 429–441.

De Backer, G., Ambrosioni, E., Borch-Johnsen, K., Brotons, C., Cifkova, R. & Dallongeville, J. (2004). European Society of Cardiology. American Heart Association. American College of Cardiology. European Guidelines on cardiovascular disease prevention in clinical practice. Third joint task force of European and other societies on cardiovascular disease prevention in clinical practice. *Atherosclerosis*, 173, 381–391.

Deblinger, A. & Heflinger, A. (1996). *Treating Sexually Abused Children and their Non-Offending Parents: A Cognitive Behavioural Approach*. Thousand Oaks, CA: Sage.

Deckersbach, T., Rauch, S., Buhlmann, U. & Wilhelm, S. (2006). Habit reversal versus supportive psychotherapy in Tourette's disorder: a randomized controlled trial and predictors of treatment response. *Behaviour Research and Therapy*, 44(8), 1079–1090.

de Jonghe, F., Kool, S., van Aalst, G., Dekker, J. & Peen, J. (2001). Combining psychotherapy and antidepressants in the treatment of depression. *Journal of Affective Disorders*, 64, 217–229.

De Leon, G. (2000). *The Therapeutic Community: Theory, Model, and Method*. New York: Springer.

De Leon, G. (2003). Therapeutic communities: research–practice reciprocity. In J. L. Sorensen, R. A. Rawson, J. Guydish & J. E. Zweben (Eds.), *Drug Abuse Treatment Through Collaboration: Practice and Research Partnerships that Work* (pp. 17–35). Washington, DC: American Psychological Association.

De Lima, M., Oliveira Soares, B., Reisser, A. & Farrell, M. (2002). Pharmacological treatment of cocaine dependence: a systematic review. *Addiction*, 97, 931–949.

Delprato, D. J. (2001). Comparisons of discrete-trial and normalized behavioural intervention for young children with autism. *Journal of Autism and Developmental Disorders*, 31, 315–325.

Del Vecchio, T. & O'Leary, K. (2004). Effectiveness of anger treatments for specific anger problems: a meta-analytic review. *Clinical Psychology Review*, 24, 15–34.

de Mello, M., Mari, J., Bacaltchuk, J., Verdeli, H. & Neugebauer, R. (2005). A systematic review of research findings on the efficacy of interpersonal therapy for depressive disorders. *European Archives of Psychiatry and Clinical Neuroscience*, 255(2), 75–82.

Den Boer, P., Van Den Bosch, R. & Wiersma, D. (2004). Why is self-help neglected in the treatment of emotional disorders? A meta-analysis. *Psychological Medicine*, 34(6), 959–971.

Department of Health (2001). *Treatment Choice in Psychological Therapies and Counselling*. London: Department of Health Publications.

des Portes, V., Hagerman, R. & Hendren, R. (2003). Pharmacotherapy. In S. Ozonoff, S. Rogers & R. Hendren (Eds.), *Autism Spectrum Disorders: A Research Review for Practitioners* (pp. 161–186). Washington, DC: American Psychiatric Press.

Dessaulles, A., Johnson, S. & Denton, W. (2003). Emotion-focused therapy for couples in the treatment of depression: a pilot study. *American Journal of Family Therapy*, 31, 345–353.

Devine, E. (1996). Meta-analysis of the effects of psychoeducational care in adults with asthma. *Research in Nursing and Health*, 19, 367–376.

Diamond, G. (2005). Attachment-based family therapy for depressed and anxious adolescents. In J. Lebow (Ed.), *Handbook of Clinical Family Therapy* (pp. 17–41). Hoboken, NJ: Wiley.

Diamond, G. & Josephson, A. (2005). Family-based treatment research: a 10-year update. *Journal of the American Academy of Child and Adolescent Psychiatry*, 44(9), 872–887.

Diamond, G., Reis, B., Diamond, G., Siqueland, L. & Isaacs, L. (2002). Attachment based family therapy for depressive adolescents: a treatment development study. *Journal of the American Academy of Child and Adolescent Psychiatry*, 41, 1190–1196.

Didden, R., Duker, P. C. & Corzilius, H. (1997). Meta-analytic study on treatment effectiveness for problem behaviours with individuals who have mental retardation. *American Journal on Mental Retardation*, 101, 387–399.

Didden, R., Korzilius, H., van Oorsouw, W. & Sturmey, P. (2006). Behavioural treatment of challenging behaviours in individuals with mild mental retardation: meta-analysis of single-subject research. *American Journal on Mental Retardation*, 111(4), 290–298.

DiGiuseppe, R. & Tafrate, R. (2003). Anger treatment for adults: a meta-analytic review. *Clinical Psychology. Science and Practice*, 10, 70–84.

Dinca, P. & Spencer, N. (2005) Systematic review of randomized controlled trials of atypical antipsychotics and selective serotonin reuptake inhibitors for behavioural problems associated with pervasive developmental disorders. *Journal of Psychopharmacology*, 19(5), 521–532.

Dishion, T. & Dodge, K. (2005). Peer contagion in interventions for children and adolescents: moving towards an understanding of the ecology and dynamics of change. *Journal of Abnormal Child Psychology*, 33(3), 395–400.

Dixon, K., Keefe, F., Scipio, C., Pent, L. & Abernetty, A. (2007). Psychological interventions for arthritis pain management in adults: a meta-analysis. *Health Psychology*, 26(3), 241–250.

Donaldson, D., Spirito, A., Arrigan, M. & Aspel, J. W. (1997). Structured disposition planning for adolescent suicide attempters in a general hospital: preliminary findings on short-term outcome. *Archives of Suicide Research*, 3, 271–282.

Donaldson, D., Spirito, A. & Esposito-Smythers, C. (2005). Treatment for adolescents following a suicide attempt: results of a pilot trial. *Journal of the American Academy of Child and Adolescent Psychiatry*, 44, 113–120.

Donaldson, D., Spirito, A. & Overholser, J. (2003). Treatment of adolescent suicide attempters. In A. Spirito & J. Overholser (Eds.), *Evaluating and Treating Adolescent Suicide Attempters: From Research to Practice* (pp. 295–321). San Diego, CA: Elsevier Academic Press.

Doody, R., Stevens, J. & Beck, C. (2001). Practice parameter: management of dementia (an evidence-based review). Report of the Quality Standards Subcommittee of the American Academy of Neurology. *Neurology*, 56, 1154–1166.

Dougherty, D., Rauch, S. & Jenike, M. (2007). Pharmacological treatments for obsessive compulsive disorder. In P. Nathan & J. Gorman (Eds.), *A Guide to Treatments that Work* (Third Edition, pp. 447–474). New York: Oxford University Press.

Driscoll, K., Cukrowicz, K., Reitzel, L., Hernandez, A., Petty, S. & Joiner, T. Jr. (2003). The effect of trainee experience in psychotherapy on client treatment outcome. *Behaviour Therapy*, 34, 165–177.

Dubicka, B., Hadley, S. & Roberts, C. (2006). Suicidal behaviour in youths with depression treated with new-generation antidepressants: meta-analysis. *British Journal of Psychiatry*, 189, 393–398.

Duncan, B., Miller, S., Reynolds, L., Sparks, J., Claud, D. & Brown, J. (2004b). The session rating scale: psychometric properties of a 'working' alliance scale. *Journal of Brief Therapy*, 3(1). Available at http://www.talkingcure.com/.

Duncan, B., Miller, S. & Sparks, J. A. (2004a). *The Heroic Clients: A Revolutionary Way to Improve Effectiveness Through Client-Directed, Outcome-Informed Therapy*. San Francisco: Jossey-Bass.

Durand, V. M. & Merges, E. (2001). Functional communication training: a contemporary behaviour analytic intervention for problem behaviours. *Focus on Autism and Other Developmental Disabilities*, 16, 110–119.

Durham, R., Chambers, J., MacDonald, R., Power, K. & Major, K. (2003). Does cognitive-behavioural therapy influence the long-term outcome of generalized anxiety disorder? An 8–14 year follow-up of two clinical trials. *Psychological Medicine*, 33, 499–509.

Durham, R., Fisher, P., Treliving, L., Hau, C., Richard, K. & Stewart, J. (1999). One year follow-up of cognitive therapy, analytic psychotherapy and anxiety management training for generalized anxiety disorder: symptom change, medication usage and attitudes to treatment. *Behavioural and Cognitive Psychotherapy*, 27, 19–35.

Dusseldorp, E., van Elderen, T., Maes, S., Meulman, J. & Kraaij, V. (1999). A meta-analysis of psychoeducational programs for coronary heart disease patients. *Health Psychology*, 18(5), 506–519.

Duterte, E., Segraves, T. & Althof, S. (2007). Psychotherapy and pharmacotherapy for sexual dysfunctions. In P. Nathan & J. Gorman (Eds.), *A Guide to Treatments that Work* (Third Edition, pp. 531–569). New York: Oxford University Press.

Dyregrov, A. & Yule, W. (2006). A review of PTSD in children. *Child and Adolescent Mental Health*, 11(4), 176–184.

D'Zurilla, T. & Nezu, A. (1999). *Problem Solving Therapy* (Second Edition). New York: Springer Verlag.

D'Zurilla, T. & Nezu, A. (2006). *Problem Solving Therapy* (Third Edition). New York: Springer Verlag.

Eccleston, C., Morley, S., Williams, A., Yorke, L. & Mastroyannopoulou, K. (2002). Systematic review of randomised controlled trials of psychological therapy for chronic pain in children and adolescents, with a subset meta-analysis of pain relief. *Pain*, 99(1–2), 157–165.

Eddy, K., Dutra, L., Bradley, R. & Westen, D. (2004). A multidimensional meta-analysis of psychotherapy and pharmacotherapy for obsessive-compulsive disorder. *Clinical Psychology Review*, 24(8), 1011–1030.

Edgeworth, J. & Carr, A. (2000). Child abuse. In A. Carr (Ed.), *What Works with Children and Adolescents? A Critical Review of Psychological Interventions with Children, Adolescents and their Families* (pp. 17–48). London: Routledge.

Edinger, J. & Means, M. (2005). Cognitive behavioural therapy for primary insomnia. *Clinical Psychology Review*, 25, 539–558.

Eisler, I. (2005). The empirical and theoretical base of family therapy and multiple family day therapy for adolescent anorexia nervosa. *Journal of Family Therapy*, 27, 104–113.

Eisler, I., Dare, C., Russell, G. F. M., Szumukler, G. I., le Grange, D. & Dodge, E. (1997). Family and individual therapy in anorexia nervosa: a 5-year follow-up. *Archives of General Psychiatry*, 54, 1025–1030.

Elliott, J. (1999). Practitioner review: school refusal: issues of conceptualisation, assessment, and treatment. *Journal of Child Psychology and Psychiatry*, 40(7), 1001–1012.

Elliott, R., Greenberg, L. & Lietaer, G. (2004). Research on experiential psychotherapies. In M. Lambert (Ed.), *Bergin and Garfield's Handbook of Psychotherapy and Behaviour Change* (Fifth Edition, pp. 493–539). New York: Wiley.

Ellis, A. & Greiger, R. (1986). *Handbook of Rational Emotive Therapy*. New York: Springer.

Emanuels-Zuurveen, L. & Emmelkamp, P. (1996). Individual behavioural-cognitive therapy vs. marital therapy for depression in maritally distressed couples. *British Journal of Psychiatry*, 169, 181–188.

Emanuels-Zuurveen, L. & Emmelkamp, P. M. (1997). Spouse-aided therapy with depressed patients. *Behaviour Modification*, 21, 62–77.

Emerson, E. (2001). *Challenging Behaviour: Analysis and Intervention in People with Severe Intellectual Disabilities* (Second Edition). Cambridge: Cambridge University Press.

Emmelkamp, P. (2004). Behaviour therapy with adults. In M. Lambert (Ed.), *Bergin and Garfield's Handbook of Psychotherapy and Behaviour Change* (Fifth Edition, pp. 393–446). New York: Wiley.

Emmelkamp, P., Benner, A., Kuipers, A., Feiertag, G., Koster, H. & van Apeldoorn, F. (2006). Comparison of brief dynamic and cognitive-behavioural therapies in avoidant personality disorder. *British Journal of Psychiatry*, 189, 60–64.

Emmelkamp, P., Bouman, T. & Scholing, A. (1992). *Anxiety Disorders*. Chichester: Wiley.

Emmelkamp, P., de Haan, E. & Hoogduin, C. (1990). Marital adjustment and obsessive compulsive disorder. *British Journal of Psychiatry*, 156, 55–60.

Emmelkamp, P. & DeLange, I. (1983). Spouse involvement in the treatment of obsessive-compulsive patients. *Behaviour Research and Therapy*, 21, 341–346.

Enright, S. & Carr, A. (2002). Prevention of post-traumatic adjustment problems in children and adolescents. In A. Carr (Ed.), *Prevention: What Works with Children and Adolescents? A Critical Review of Psychological Prevention Programmes for Children, Adolescents and their Families* (pp. 314–335). London: Routledge.

Epstein, L. (2003). Development of evidence-based treatments for paediatric obesity. In A. E. Kazdin & J. R. Weisz (Eds.), *Evidence-Based Psychotherapies for Children and Adolescents* (pp. 374–388). New York: Guilford Press.

Epstein, N. & Baucom, D. (2002). *Enhanced Cognitive-Behavioural Therapy for Couples: A Contextual Approach*. Washington, DC: American Psychological Association.

Esposito-Smythers, C., McClung, T. & Fairlie, A. (2006). Adolescent perceptions of a suicide prevention group on an inpatient unit. *Archives of Suicide Research*, 10(3), 265–275.

Evans, C., Connell, J., Barkham, M., Margison, F., McGrath, G., Mellor-Clark, J. & Audin, K. (2002). Towards a standardised brief outcome measure: psychometric properties and utility of the CORE-OM. *British Journal of Psychiatry*, 180, 51–60.

Evans, C., Mellor-Clark, J., Margison, F., Barkham, M., Audin, K., Connell, J. & McGrath, G. (2000). Core: clinical outcomes and routine evaluation. *Journal of Mental Health*, 9(3), 247–255.

Eysenck, H. (1952). The effects of psychotherapy: an evaluation. *Journal of Consulting Psychology*, 16, 319–324.

Fairburn, C. (1995). *Overcoming Binge Eating*. New York: Guilford Press.

Fairburn, C., Cooper, Z. & Shafran, R. (2003). Cognitive behaviour therapy for eating disorders: a transdiagnostic theory and treatment. *Behaviour Research and Therapy*, 41, 509–529.

Fairburn, C., Marcus, M. & Wilson, G. (1993). Cognitive behaviour therapy for binge eating and bulimia nervosa: a comprehensive treatment manual. In C. G. Fairburn & G. T. Wilson (Eds.), *Binge Eating: Nature, Assessment, and Treatment* (pp. 361–404). New York: Guilford Press.

Falloon, I., Boyd, J. & McGill, C. (1984). *Family Care of Schizophrenia*. New York: Guilford Press.

Falloon, I., Laporta, M., Fadden, G. & Graham-Hole, V. (1993). *Managing Stress in Families*. London: Routledge.

Farre, M., Mas, A., Torrens, M., Moreno, V. & Carni, J. (2002). Retention rate and illicit opioid use during methadone maintenance interventions: a meta-analysis. *Drug and Alcohol Dependence*, 65(3), 283–290.

Farrell, E., Cullen, R. & Carr, A. (2002). Prevention of adjustment problems in children with diabetes. In A. Carr (Ed.), *Prevention: What Works with Children and Adolescents? A Critical Review of Psychological Prevention Programmes for Children, Adolescents and their Families* (pp. 249–266). London: Routledge.

Farrington, D. & Welsh, B. (2003). Family-based prevention of offending: a meta-analysis. *Australian and New Zealand Journal of Criminology*, 36(2), 127–151.

Farthing, M. (2005). Treatment of irritable bowel syndrome. *British Medical Journal*, 330(7489), 429–430.

Fear Fighter. http://www.fearfighter.com/index.htm.

Feder, L. & Wilson, D. (2005). A meta-analytic review of court-mandated batterer intervention programs: can courts affect abusers' behaviour? *Journal of Experimental Criminology*, 1(2), 239–262.

Fernandez-Alderez, H., Clarkin, J., delCarmen Salgueiro, M. & Critchfield, K. (2006). Participant factors in treating personality disorders. In L. Castonguay & L. Beutler (Eds.), *Principles of Therapeutic Change that Work* (pp. 203–218). Oxford: Oxford University Press.

Findling, R., Feeny, N., Stansbrey, R., DelPorto-Bedoya, D. & Demeter, C. (2004). Somatic treatment for depressive illnesses in children and adolescents. *Psychiatric Clinics of North America*, 27, 113–137.

Finnegan, L. & Carr, A. (2002). Prevention of adjustment problems in children with autism. In A. Carr (Ed.), *Prevention: What Works with Children and Adolescents? A Critical Review of Psychological Prevention Programmes for Children, Adolescents and their Families* (pp. 107–128). London: Routledge.

Finney, J., Lemanek, K., Cataldo, M. & Katz, H. (1989). Paediatric psychology in primary health care: brief targeted therapy for recurrent abdominal pain. *Behaviour Therapy*, 20, 283–291.

Finney, J., Wilbourne, P. & Moos, R. (2007). Psychosocial treatments for substance use disorders. In P. Nathan & J. Gorman (Eds.), *A Guide to Treatments that Work* (Third Edition, pp. 179–202). New York: Oxford University Press.

Fiore, M., Bailey, W. & Cohen, S. (2000). *Treating Tobacco Use and Dependence: Quick Clinical Practice Guideline*. Rockville, MD: U.S. Department of Health and Human Services, Public Health Service.

Fisher, P. & Wells, A. (2005). How effective are cognitive and behavioural treatments for obsessive–compulsive disorder? A clinical significance analysis. *Behaviour Research and Therapy*, 43, 1543–1558.

Flammer, E. & Bongartz, W. (2003). On the efficacy of hypnosis: a meta-analytic study. *Contemporary Hypnosis*, 20, 179–197.

Foa, E. B., Keane, T. M. & Friedman, M. J. (2000). *Effective Treatments for PTSD: Practice Guidelines from the International Society for Traumatic Stress Studies*. New York: Guilford Press.

Foley, S. H., Rounsaville, B. J., Weissman, M. M., Sholomskas, D. & Chevron, E. (1989). Individual versus conjoint interpersonal psychotherapy for depressed patients with marital disputes. *International Journal of Family Psychiatry*, 10, 29–42.

Follette, W. & Greenberg, L. (2006). Technique factors in treating dysphoric disorders. In L. Castonguay & L. Beutler (Eds.), *Principles of Therapeutic Change that Work* (pp. 83–110). Oxford: Oxford University Press.

Fonagy, P., Clarkin, J., Gerber, A., Kächele, H., Krause, R. & Jones, E. (2002). *An Open Door Review of Outcome Studies in Psychoanalysis* (Second Edition). London: International Psychoanalytic Association (http://www.ipa.org.uk).

Fonagy, P. & Moran, G. (1990). Studies of the efficacy of child psychoanalysis. *Journal of Consulting and Clinical Psychology*, 58, 684–695.

Fonagy, P., Roth, A. & Higgitt, A. (2005). Psychodynamic psychotherapies: evidence-based practice and clinical wisdom. *Bulletin of the Menninger Clinic*, 69, 1–58.

Fonagy, P., Target, M., Cottrell, D., Phillips, J. & Kurtz, A. (2002). *What Works for Whom? A Critical Review of Treatments for Children and Adolescents*. New York: Guilford Press.

Fortner, B. (1999). *The Effectiveness of Grief Counselling and Therapy: A Quantitative Review*. Memphis, TN: University of Memphis.

Fortune, S. A. & Hawton, K. (2005). Deliberate self-harm in children and adolescents: a research update. *Current Opinion in Psychiatry*, 18, 401–406.

Fowler, D., Garety, P. & Kuipers, E. (1995). *Cognitive Behaviour Therapy for People with Psychosis*. Chichester: Wiley.

Fraiberg, S., Adelson, E. & Shapiro, V. (1975). Ghosts in the nursery: a psychoanalytic approach to impaired infant–mother relationships. *Journal of the American Academy of Child Psychiatry*, 14, 387–421.

Frank, E. (1999). Interpersonal and social rhythm therapy prevents depressive symptomatology in bipolar 1 patient. *Bipolar Disorder*, 1, 13.

Frank, E. (2005). *Treating Bipolar Disorder: A Clinician's Guide to Interpersonal and Social Rhythm Therapy*. New York: Guilford Press.

Frank, E., Kupfer, D., Thase, M., Mallinger, A., Swartz, H., Fagiolini, A., Grochocinski, V., Houck, P., Scott, J., Thompson, W. & Monk, T. (2005). Two-year outcomes for interpersonal and social rhythm therapy in individuals with bipolar I disorder. *Archives of General Psychiatry*, 62, 996–1004.

Frank, J. & Frank, J. (1991). *Persuasion and Healing: A Comparative Study of Psychotherapy* (Third Edition). Baltimore: Johns Hopkins University Press.

Franklin, M. & Foa, E. (2007). Cognitive behavioural treatment of obsessive compulsive disorder. In P. Nathan & J. Gorman (Eds.), *A Guide to Treatments that Work* (Third Edition, pp. 431–446). New York: Oxford University Press.

Freud, S. (1909). Notes upon a case of obsessional neurosis. In J. Strachey (Ed. & Trans.) *Standard Edition of the Complete Works of Sigmund Freud* (Volume 10, pp. 153–249). London: Hogarth Press.

Friedman, M., Detweiler-Bedell, J., Leventhal, H., Home, R., Keitner, G. & Miller, I. (2004). Combined psychotherapy and pharmacotherapy for the treatment of major depressive disorder. *Clinical Psychology Science and Practice*, 11, 47–68.

Friemoth, J. (2005). What is the most effective treatment for ADHD in children? *Journal of Family Practice*, 54(2), 166–168.

Fristad, M., Goldberg-Arnold, J. & Gavazzi, S. (2002). Multifamily psycho-education groups (MFPG) for families of children with bipolar disorder. *Bipolar Disorder*, 4, 254–262.

Fristad, M. A., Goldberg-Arnold, J. S. & Gavazzi, S. M. (2003). Multifamily psychoeducation groups in the treatment of children with mood disorders. *Journal of Marital and Family Therapy*, 29, 491–504.

Frost, L. & Bondy, A. (2002) *PECS: The Picture Exchange Communication System Training Manual* (Second Edition). Cherry Hill, NJ: Pyramid Educational Consultants.

Fuhriman, A. & Burlingame, G. (2001). *Handbook of Group Psychotherapy: An Empirical and Clinical Synthesis*. New York: Wiley.

Gabbard, F. (2004). *Long-Term Psychodynamic Psychotherapy: A Basic Text*. Washington, DC: American Psychiatric Press.

Gabbard, G. O., Lazar, S. G., Hornberger, J. & Spiegel, D. (1997). The economic impact of psychotherapy: a review. *American Journal of Psychiatry*, 154, 147–155.

Gaffan, E. A., Tsaousis, J. & Kemp-Wheeler, S. M. (1995). Researcher allegiance and meta-analysis: the case of cognitive therapy for depression. *Journal of Consulting and Clinical Psychology*, 63, 966–980.

Gallagher-Thompson, D. & Coon, D. W. (2007). Evidence-based psychological treatments for distress in family caregivers of older adults. *Psychology and Aging*, 22, 87–51.

Galloway, A., Gonzalez, J., Gutkin, T., Nelson, J., Saunders, A. & Shwery, C. (2004). Rational emotive therapy with children and adolescents: a meta-analysis. *Journal of Emotional and Behavioural Disorders*, 12(4), 222–235.

Garbutt, J., West, S., Carey, T., Lohr, K. & Crews, F. (1999). Pharmacological treatment of alcohol dependence: a review of the evidence. *Journal of the American Medical Association*, 281, 1318–1325.

Garland, E. (2002). Anxiety disorders. In S. Kutcher (Ed.), *Practical Child and Adolescent Psychopharmacology* (pp. 187–229). Cambridge: Cambridge University Press.

Garner, D., Vitousek, K. & Pike, K. (1997). Cognitive behavioural therapy for anorexia nervosa. In D. Garner & P. Garfinkel (Eds.), *Handbook of Treatment of Eating Disorders* (Second Edition, pp. 91–144). Chichester: Wiley.

Gatz, M., Fiske, A., Fox, L., Kaskie, B., Kasl-Godley, J., McCallum, T. & Loebach, J. (1998). Empirically validated psychological treatments for older adults. *Journal of Mental Health & Aging*, 4, 9–46.

Geddes, J. R., Burgess, S., Hawton, K., Jamison, K. & Goodwin, G. M. (2004). Long-term lithium therapy for bipolar disorder: systematic review and meta-analysis of randomized controlled trials. *American Journal of Psychiatry*, 161(2), 217–222.

Geddes, J., Carney, S., Davies, C., Furukawa, T., Kupfer, D., Frank, E. & Goodwin, G. (2003). Relapse prevention with antidepressant drug treatment in depressive disorders: a systematic review. *Lancet*, 361, 653–661.

Gibson, F. (2004). *The Past in the Present: Using Reminiscence in Health and Social Care*. Baltimore, MD: Health Professions Press.

Gilroy, A. (2006). *Art Therapy, Research and Evidence Based Practice*. London: Sage.

Glass, J., Lanctot, K., Herrmann, N., Sproule, B. & Busto, U. (2005). Sedative hypnotics in older people with insomnia: meta-analysis of risks and benefits. *British Medical Journal*, 331, 1169.

Glass, V. (1976). Primary, secondary and meta-analysis of research. *Educational Researcher*, 5, 3–8.

Glazener, C., Evans, J. & Pero, R. (2003). Alarm interventions for nocturnal enuresis in children. *Cochrane Database Systematic Reviews*, 2, CD002911.

Gold, C., Voracek, M. & Wigram, T. (2004). Effects of music therapy for children and adolescents with psychopathology: a meta-analysis. *Journal of Child Psychology and Psychiatry*, 45(6), 1054–1063.

Gold, J., Kant, A., Belmont, K. & Butler, L. (2007). Practitioner review: clinical applications of paediatric hypnosis. *Journal of Child Psychology and Psychiatry*, 48(8), 744–754.

Golden, T., Gaynes, B., Ekstrom, D., Hamer, R., Jacobsen, F., Suppes, T., Wisner, K. & Nemeroff, C. (2005). The efficacy of light therapy in the treatment of mood disorders: a review and meta-analysis of the evidence. *American Journal of Psychiatry*, 162(4), 656–662.

Goldstein, H. (2002). Communication intervention for children with autism: a review of treatment efficacy. *Journal of Autism and Developmental Disorders*, 32, 373–396.

Gollier, J., Legge, J. & Yehuda, R. (2007). Pharmacological treatment of post-traumatic stress disorder. In P. Nathan & J. Gorman (Eds.), *A Guide to Treatments that Work* (Third Edition, pp. 475–512). New York: Oxford University Press.

Gonder-Frederick, L. A., Cox, D. J. & Ritterband, L. M. (2002). Diabetes and behavioural medicine: the second decade. *Journal of Consulting and Clinical Psychology. Special Issue: Behavioural Medicine and Clinical Health Psychology*, 70(3), 611–625.

Goodheart, C., Kazdin, A. & Sternberg, R. (2006). *Evidence-Based Psychotherapy: Where Practice and Research Meet*. Washington, DC: American Psychological Association.

Goodwin, M. (2003). Evidence-based guidelines for treating bipolar disorder: recommendations from the British Association for Psychopharmacology. *Journal of Psychopharmacology*, 17, 149–173.

Goodyer, I., Dubicka, B., Wilkinson, P., Kelvin, R., Roberts, C., Byford, S., Breen, S., Ford, C., Barrett, B., Leech, A., Rothwell, J., White, L. & Harrington, R. (2007). Selective serotonin reuptake inhibitors (SSRIs) and routine specialist care with and without cognitive behaviour therapy in adolescents with major depression: randomised controlled trial. *British Medical Journal*, 335, 142–146.

Gossop, M., Mardsen, J. & Stewart, D. (2001). *NTORS after Five Years – The National Treatment Outcome Research Study – Changes in Substance Use, Health and Criminal Behaviour During the Five Years After Intake*. London: National Addiction Centre.

Gould, M. (2003). Youth suicide risk and preventive interventions: a review of the past 10 years. *Journal of the American Academy of Child and Adolescent Psychiatry*, 42, 386–405.

Gould, R., Mueser, K., Bolton, E., Mays, V. & Goff, D. (2001). Cognitive therapy for psychosis in schizophrenia: an effect size analysis. *Schizophrenia Research*, 48, 335–342.

Gowers, S. & Bryant-Waugh, R. (2004). Management of child and adolescent eating disorders: the current evidence base and future directions. *Journal of Child Psychology and Psychiatry*, 45(1), 63–83.

Gowing, L., Ali, R. & White, J. (2000). Buprenorphine for the management of opioid withdrawal. *Cochrane Database of Systematic Reviews*, Issue 3. Art. No.: CD002025. DOI: 10.1002/14651858.CD002025.pub3.

Gowing, L., Farrell, M., Ali, R. & White, J. (2001). Alpha2 adrenergic agonists for the management of opioid withdrawal. *Cochrane Database of Systematic Reviews*, Issue 1. Art. No.: CD002024. DOI: 10.1002/14651858.CD002024.pub2.

Gray, C. (2000). *The New Social Story Book*. Arlington, TX: Future Horizons.

Gregory, R., Canning, S. & Lee, T. (2004). Cognitive bibliotherapy for depression: a meta-analysis. *Professional Psychology: Research and Practice*, 35, 275–280.

Grey, I. & Hastings, R. (2005). Evidence-based practices in intellectual disability and behaviour disorders. *Current Opinion in Psychiatry*, 18, 469–475.

Griffith, J., Rowan-Szal, G., Roark, R. & Simpson, D. (2000). Contingency management in outpatient methadone treatment: a meta-analysis. *Drug and Alcohol Dependence*, 58(1–2), 55–66.

Grissom, R. (1996). The magical number.7 ±.2: meta-meta-analysis of the probability of superior outcome in comparisons involving therapy, placebo, and control. *Journal of Consulting and Clinical Psychology*, 64, 973–982.

Grosman, P., Niemann, L., Schmidt, S. & Walach, H. (2004). Mindfulness-based stress reduction and health benefits: a meta-analysis. *Journal of Psychosomatic Research*, 57(1), 35–43.

Groth-Marnat, G. & Edkins, G. (1996). Professional psychologists in general health care settings: a review of financial efficacy of direct treatment interventions. *Professional Psychology: Research and Practice*, 27, 161–174.

Grunes, M. S., Neziroglu, F. & McKay, D. (2001). Family involvement in the behavioural treatment of obsessive-compulsive disorder: a preliminary investigation. *Behaviour Therapy*, 32, 803–820.

Grunze, H., Kasper, S. & Goodwin, G. (2002). World Federation of Societies of Biological Psychiatry (WFSBP) guidelines for biological treatment of bipolar disorders. Part I: Treatment of bipolar depression. *World Journal of Biological Psychiatry*, 3, 115–124.

Grunze, H., Kasper, S. & Goodwin, G. (2003). The World Federation of Societies of Biological Psychiatry (WFSBP) Guidelines for the biological treatment of bipolar disorders. Part II: Treatment of mania. *World Journal of Biological Psychiatry*, 4, 5–13.

Guevara, J., Wolf, F., Grum, C. & Clark, N. (2003). Effects of educational interventions for self-management of asthma in children and adolescents: systematic review and meta-analysis. *British Medical Journal*, 326, 1308–1309.

Gupta, M., Coyne, J. & Beach, S. (2003). Couples treatment for major depression: critique of the literature and suggestions for some different directions. *Journal of Family Therapy*, 25, 317–346.

Gutierrez, M. & Scott, J. (2004). Psychological treatment for bipolar disorders: a review of randomised controlled trials. *European Archives of Psychiatry and Clinical Neuroscience*, 254, 92–98.

Haaga, D., Hall, S. & Haas, A. (2006). Participant factors in treating substance use disorders. In L. Castonguay & L. Beutler (Eds.), *Principles of Therapeutic Change that Work* (pp. 275–292). Oxford: Oxford University Press.

Haine, R., Sandler, I., Wolchik, S., Tein, J. & Dawson-McClure, S. (2003). Changing the legacy of divorce: evidence from prevention programs and future directions. *Family Relations*, 52(4), 397–405.

Hajek, P., Stead, L., West. R., Jarvis, M. & Lancaster, T. (2005). Relapse prevention interventions for smoking cessation. *Cochrane Database of Systematic Reviews*, Issue 1. Art. No.: CD003999. DOI: 10.1002/14651858.CD003999.pub2.

Hall, A. & Crisp, A. (1987). Brief psychotherapy in the treatment of anorexia nervosa: outcome at one year. *British Journal of Psychiatry*, 151, 185.

Hall, W. (2006). How have the SSRI antidepressants affected suicide risk? *Lancet*, 367, 1959–1962.

Halmi, K., Agras, W., Crow, S., Mitchell, J., Wilson, G., Bryson, S. & Kraemer, H. (2005). Predictors of treatment acceptance and completion in anorexia nervosa: implications for future study designs. *Archives of General Psychiatry*, 62, 776–781.

Hampson, S., Skinner, T., Hart, J., Storey, L., Gage, H., Foxcroft, D., Kimber, A., Craddock, S. & McEvilly, E. A. (2000). Behavioural interventions for adolescents with type 1 diabetes: how effective are they? *Diabetes Care*, 23, 1416–1422.

Handen, B. & Gilchrist, R. (2006). Practitioner review: psychopharmacology in children and adolescents with mental retardation. *Journal of Child Psychology and Psychiatry*, 47(9), 871–882.

Hansen, N. & Lambert, M. (2003). An evaluation of the dose–response relationship in naturalistic treatment settings using survival analysis. *Mental Health Services Research*, 5, 1–12.

Hansen, N., Lambert, M. & Forman, E. (2002). The psychotherapy dose–response effect and its implications for treatment delivery services. *Clinical Psychology Science and Practice*, 9, 329–343.

Harkins, L. & Beech, A. (2007). A review of the factors that can influence the effectiveness of sexual offender treatment: risk, need, responsively, and process issues. *Aggression and Violent Behaviour*, 12(6), 615–627.

Harrington, R., Kerfoot, M., Dyer, E., McNiven, F., Gill, J., Harrington, V., Woodham, A. & Byford, S. (1998). Randomized trial of a home based family intervention for children who have deliberately poisoned themselves. *Journal of the American Academy of Child and Adolescent Psychiatry*, 37, 512–518.

Harrington, R., Whittaker, J., Shoebridge, P. & Campbell, F. (1998). Systematic review of efficacy of cognitive behaviour therapies in childhood and adolescent depressive disorder. *British Medical Journal*, 316(7144), 1559–1563.

Harris, S., Handleman, J. & Jennett, H. (2005). Models of educational intervention for students with autism: home, centre and school-based programming. In F. Volkmar, R. Paul, A. Klin & D. Cohen (Eds.), *Handbook of Autism and Pervasive Developmental Disorders* (Third Edition, Volume 2, pp. 1043–1054). New York: Wiley.

Harvey, N. & Peet, M. (1991). Lithium maintenance: II. Effects of personality and attitude on health information acquisition and compliance. *British Journal of Psychiatry*, 158, 200–204.

Hastings, R. & Beck, A. (2004). Practitioner review: stress intervention for parents of children with intellectual disabilities. *Journal of Child Psychology and Psychiatry*, 45(8), 1338–1349.

Hawes, D. & Dadds, M. (2005). The treatment of conduct problems in children with callous-unemotional traits. *Journal of Consulting and Clinical Psychology*, 73(4), 737–741.

Hawton, K. (1995). Treatment of sexual dysfunctions by sex therapy and other approaches. *British Journal of Psychiatry*, 17, 307–314.

Hawton, K., Townsend, E., Arensman, E., Gunnell, D., Hazell, P., House, A. & van Heeringen, K. (1999). Psychosocial and pharmacological treatments for deliberate self harm. *Cochrane Database of Systematic Reviews*, Issue 4. Art. No.: CD001764. DOI: 10.1002/14651858.CD001764.

Hayes, S., Luoma, J., Bond, F., Masuda, A. & Lillis, J. (2006). Acceptance and commitment therapy: model, processes and outcomes. *Behaviour Research and Therapy*, 44, 1–26.

Hayes, S., Strosahl, K. & Wilson, K. (2003). *Acceptance and Commitment Therapy: An Experiential Approach to Behaviour Change*. New York: Guilford Press.

Hazell, P., O'Connell, D., Heathcote, D. & Henry, D. (2002). Tricyclic drugs for depression in children and adolescents. *Cochrane Database of Systematic Reviews*, Issue 2. Art. No.: CD002317. DOI: 10.1002/14651858.CD002317.

Healy, D. (2003). Lines of evidence on the risks of suicide with selective serotonin reuptake inhibitors. *Psychotherapy and Psychosomatics*, 72, 71–79.

Heather, N., Brodie, J., Wale, S., Wilkinson, G., Luce, A. & Webb, E. (2000). A randomized controlled trial of moderation-oriented cue exposure. *Journal of Studies on Alcohol*, 61, 561–570.

Hedges, L. & Olkin, I. (1985). *Statistical Methods for Meta-analysis*. Orlando, FL: Academic Press.

Heetema, J., Stteele, J. & Miller, W. (2005). Motivational interviewing. *Annual Review of Clinical Psychology*, 1, 91–111.

Hellstrom, K., Fellenius, J. & Ost, L. (1996). One versus five sessions of applied tension in the treatment of blood phobia. *Behaviour Research and Therapy*, 34, 101–112.

Hellstrom, W. (2006). Current and future pharmacotherapies of premature ejaculation. *Journal of Sexual Medicine*, 3, 332–341.

Hembree-Kigin, T. & McNeil, C. (1995). *Parent–Child Interaction Therapy*. New York: Plenum.

Henggeler, S. & Lee, S. (2003). Multisystemic treatment of serious clinical problems. In A. Kazdin & J. Weisz (Eds.), *Evidence Based Psychotherapies for Children and Adolescents* (pp. 301–324). New York: Guilford Press.

Henggeler, S., Schoenwald, S., Borduin, C., Rowland, M. & Cunningham, P. (1998). *Multisystemic Treatment of Antisocial Behaviour in Children and Adolescents*. New York: Guilford Press.

Henggeler, S. W., Schoenwald, S. K., Rowland, M. D. & Cunningham, P. B. (2002). *Multisystemic Treatment of Children and Adolescents with Serious Emotional Disturbance*. New York: Guilford Press.

Hepp, U., Wittmann, L., Schnyder, U. & Michel, K. (2004). Psychological and psychosocial interventions after attempted suicide: an overview of treatment studies. *Crisis*, 25, 108–117.

Herschell, A., McNeil, C. & McNeil, D. (2004). Clinical child psychology's progress in disseminating empirically supported treatments. *Clinical Psychology: Science and Practice*, 11, 267–288.

Hester, R., Squires, D. & Delaney, H. (2005). The drinker's check-up: 12-month outcomes of a controlled clinical trial of a stand-alone software program for problem drinkers. *Journal of Substance Abuse Treatment*, 28, 159–169.

Hettema, J., Steele, J. & Miller, W. (2005). Motivational interviewing. *Annual Review of Clinical Psychology*, 1, 91–111.

Heyne, D. & King, N. (2004). Treatment of school refusal. In P. Barrett & T. Ollendick

(Eds.), *Handbook of Interventions that Work with Children and Adolescents: Prevention and Treatment* (pp. 243–272). Chichester: Wiley.

Heyne, D., King N., Tonge, B., Rollings, S., Young, D., Pritchard, M. & Ollendick, T. (2002). Evaluation of child therapy and caregiver training in the treatment of school refusal. *Journal of the American Academy of Child and Adolescent Psychiatry*, 41, 687–695.

Hibbs, E. & Jensen, P. (2005). *Psychosocial Treatments for Child and Adolescent Disorders: Empirically Based Strategies for Clinical Practice* (Second Edition). Washington, DC: American Psychological Association.

Hicks, C. & Hickman, G. (1994). The impact of waiting-list times on client attendance for relationship counselling. *British Journal of Guidance & Counselling*, 22, 175–182.

Hinrichsen, G. & Clougherty, K. (2006). *Interpersonal Psychotherapy for Depressed Older Adults*. Washington, DC: American Psychological Association.

Hinshaw, S. (2005). Enhancing social competence in children with attention-deficit/hyperactivity disorder: challenges for the new millennium. In E. Hibbs & P. Jensen (Eds.), *Psychosocial Treatments for Child and Adolescent Disorders: Empirically Based Strategies for Clinical Practice* (Second Edition, pp. 351–376). Washington, DC: American Psychological Association.

Hinshaw, S., Klein, R. & Abikoff, H. (2007). Childhood attention-deficit hyperactivity disorder: nonpharmacological treatments and their combination with medication. In P. Nathan & J. Gorman (Eds.), *A Guide to Treatments that Work* (Third Edition, pp. 3–28). New York: Oxford University Press.

Hoag, M. & Burlingame, G. (1997). Evaluating the effectiveness of child and adolescent group treatment: a meta-analytic review. *Journal of Clinical Child Psychology*, 26, 234–246.

Hoek, L., Wyndaele, J. & Vermandel, A. (1998). The role of bladder biofeedback in the treatment of children with refractory nocturnal enuresis associated with idiopathic detrusor instability and small bladder capacity. *Journal of Urology*, 160, 858–860.

Hoffman, B., Papas, R., Chatkoff, D. & Kerns, R. (2007). Meta-analysis of psychological interventions for chronic low back pain. *Health Psychology*, 26(1), 1–9.

Holbrook, A. M., Crowther, R., Lotter, A., Cheng, C. & King, D. (1999). Meta-analysis of benzodiazepine use in the treatment of acute alcohol withdrawal. *Canadian Medical Association Journal*, 160, 649–655.

Holden, E. W., Deichmann, M. M. & Levy, J. D. (1999). Empirically supported treatments in paediatric psychology: recurrent paediatric headache. *Journal of Paediatric Psychology*, 24, 91–109.

Holden, U. & Woods, R. (1995). *Positive Approaches to Dementia Care* (Third Edition). Edinburgh: Churchill Livingstone.

Hollon, S. & Beck, A. (2004). Cognitive and cognitive-behavioural therapies. In M. Lambert (Ed.), *Bergin and Garfield's Handbook of Psychotherapy and Behaviour Change* (Fifth Edition, pp. 447–492). New York: Wiley.

Hollon, S., Stewart, M. & Strunk, D. (2006). Enduring effects for cognitive behaviour therapy in the treatment of depression and anxiety. *Annual Review of Psychology*, 57, 285–315.

Holroyd, K. A. (2002). Assessment and psychological management of recurrent headache disorders. *Journal of Consulting and Clinical Psychology. Special Issue: Behavioural Medicine and Clinical Health Psychology*, 70(3), 656–677.

Horner, R., Carr, E., Strain, P., Todd, A. & Reed, H. (2002). Problem behaviour interventions for young children with autism: a research synthesis. *Journal of Autism and Developmental Disorders*, 32, 423–446.

Houts, A. (2003). Behavioural treatment for enuresis. In A. Kazdin & J. Weisz (Eds.), *Evidence-Based Psychotherapies for Children and Adolescents* (pp. 389–406). New York: Guilford Press.

Houts, A. & Liebert, R. (1984). *Bedwetting: A Guide for Parents and Children*, Springfield, Il: Charles C Thomas.

Howard, K., Kopta, S., Krause, M. & Orlinsky, D. (1986). The dose–effect relationship in psychotherapy. *American Psychologist*, 41, 159–164.

Hubbard, R. L., Craddock, S. G. & Anderson, J. (2003). Overview of 5-year follow-up outcomes in the drug abuse treatment outcome studies (DATOS). *Journal of Substance Abuse Treatment*, 25(3), 125–134.

Hubble, M., Duncan, B. & Miller, S. (1999). *The Heart and Soul of Change: What Works in Therapy*. Washington, DC: American Psychological Association.

Huey, S. J., Henggeler, S. W., Rowland, M. D., Halliday-Boykins, C. A., Cunningham, P. B. & Pickrel, S. G. (2004). Multisystemic therapy effects on attempted suicide by youths presenting psychiatric emergencies. *Journal of the American Academy of Child and Adolescent Psychiatry*, 43, 183–190.

Hunsley, J. & DiGiulio, G. (2002). Dodo bird, phoenix or urban legend. *Scientific Review of Mental Health Practice*, 1(1), 11–22.

In-Albon, T. & Schneider, S. (2007). Psychotherapy of childhood anxiety disorders: a meta-analysis. *Psychotherapy and Psychosomatics*, 76(1), 15–24.

Irvin, J., Bowers, C., Dunn, M. & Wang, M. (1999). Efficacy of relapse prevention: a meta-analytic review. *Journal of Consulting and Clinical Psychology*, 67, 563–570.

Irvin Vidrine, J., Cofta-Woerpel, L., Daza, P., Wright, K. & Wetter, D. (2006). Smoking cessation 2: behavioural treatments. *Behavioural Medicine*, 32, 99–109.

Irwin, M., Cole, J. C. & Nicassio, P. M. (2006). Comparative meta-analysis of behavioural interventions for insomnia and their efficacy in middle-aged adults and in older adults 55+ years. *Health Psychology*, 25, 3–14.

Ishikawa, S., Okajima, I., Matsuoka, H. & Sakano Y. (2007) Cognitive behavioural therapy for anxiety disorders in children and adolescents: a meta-analysis. *Child and Adolescent Mental Health*, 12(4), 164–172.

Ismail, K., Winkley, K. & Rabe-Hesketh, S. (2004). Systematic review and meta-analysis of randomised controlled trials of psychological interventions to improve glycaemia control in patients with Type 2 diabetes. *Lancet*, 363, 1589–1597.

Iwaniec, D. (2004). *Children Who Fail to Thrive: A Practice Guide*. Chichester: Wiley.

Jaberghaderi, N., Greenwald, R., Rubin, A., Zand, S. O. & Dolatabadi, S. (2004). A comparison of CBT and EMDR for sexually-abused Iranian girls. *Clinical Psychology & Psychotherapy*, 11(5), 358–368.

Jacobson, J., Mulick, J. & Green, G. (1998). Cost-benefit estimates for early intensive behavioural intervention for young children with autism: general model and single state case. *Behavioural Interventions*, 13, 201–226.

Jacobson, M. & Schardt, D. (1999). *Diet, ADHD and behaviour: a quarter century review*. Washington, DC: Centre for Science in the Public Interest. http://www.fedupwithfoodadditives.info/information/CSPI%20Review%201999.pdf.

Jacobson, N. & Addis, M. (1993). Research on couples and couple therapy: what do we know? *Journal of Consulting and Clinical Psychology*, 61, 85–93.

Jacobson, N. & Christensen, A. (1998). *Acceptance and Change in Couple Therapy: A Therapist's Guide to Transforming Relationships*. New York: Norton.

Jacobson, N., Dobson, K., Fruzzetti, A., Schmaling, K. & Salusky, S. (1991). Marital therapy as a treatment for depression. *Journal of Consulting and Clinical Psychology*, 59, 547–557.

Jacobson, N., Follette, W. & Revenstorf, D. (1984). Psychotherapy outcome research: methods for reporting variability and evaluating clinical significance. *Behaviour Therapy*, 15(4), 336–352.

Jacobson, N., Roberts, L., Berns, S. & McGlinchey, B. (1999). Methods for defining and determining clinical significance of treatment effects: description, application, and alternatives. *Journal of Consulting and Clinical Psychology*, 67, 300–307.

Jadad, A., Booker, L., Gauld, M., Kakuma, R., Boyle, M. & Cunningham, C. (1999). The treatment of attention-deficit hyperactivity disorder: an annotated bibliography and critical appraisal of published systematic reviews and meta-analyses. *Canadian Journal of Psychiatry*, 44, 1025–1035.

Janicke, D. & Finney, J. (1999). Empirically supported treatments in paediatric psychology: recurrent abdominal pain. *Journal of Paediatric Psychology*, 24, 115–127.

Jelalian, E. & Saelens, B. (1999). Empirically supported treatments in paediatric psychology: paediatric obesity. *Journal of Paediatric Psychology*, 24, 223–248.

Jelalian, E., Wember, Y., Bungeroth, H. & Birmaher, V. (2007). Practitioner review: bridging the gap between empirically supported interventions and treatment of children and adolescents in paediatric obesity. *Journal of Child Psychology and Psychiatry*, 48(2), 115–127.

Jensen, P., Arnold, L., Swanson, J., Vitiello, B., Abikoff, H. & Greenhill, L. (2007). 3-year follow-up of the NIMH MTA study. *Journal of the American Academy of Child and Adolescent Psychiatry*, 46, 989–1002.

Johnson, S. (2003). The revolution in couple therapy: a practitioner–scientist perspective. *Journal of Marital and Family Therapy*, 29(3), 365–384.

Johnson, S. (2004). *The Practice of Emotionally Focused Couple Therapy: Creating Connection* (Second Edition). New York: Guilford Press.

Johnson, S., Hunsley, J., Greenberg, L. & Schindler, D. (1999). Emotionally focused couples therapy: status and challenges. *Clinical Psychology: Science and Practice*, 6(1), 67–79.

Johnston, M. & Vogele, C. (1993). Benefits of psychological preparation for surgery: a meta-analysis. *Annals of Behavioural Medicine*, 15, 245–256.

Jones, E. & Asen, E. (2002). *Systemic Couple Therapy and Depression*. London: Karnac.

Jones, K. & Vischi, T. (1979). The impact of alcohol, drug abuse, and mental health treatment on medical care utilization: a review of the research literature. *Medical Care*, 17, 43–131.

Jones, M. (1952). *A Study of Therapeutic Communities*. London: Tavistock.

Jones, S., Sellwood, W. & McGovern J. (2005). Psychological therapies for bipolar disorder: the role of model-driven approaches to therapy integration. *Bipolar Disorder*, 7, 22–32.

Jordan, R. & Jones, G. (1999). Review of research into educational interventions for children with autism in the UK. *Autism*, 3, 101–110.

Kadden, R., Carroll, K., Donovan, D., Cooney, N., Monti, P., Abrams, D., Litt, M. & Hester, R. (1994). *Cognitive-Behavioural Coping Skills Therapy Manual: A*

Clinical Research Guide for Therapists Treating Individuals with Alcohol Abuse and Dependence. Rockville, MD: NIAAA.

Kadera, S., Lambert, M. & Andrews, A. (1996). How much therapy is enough? A session-by-session analysis of the psychotherapy dose–effect relationship. *Journal of Psychotherapy Practice & Research*, 5, 132–151.

Kaltenthaler, E., Parry, G. & Beverley, C. (2004). Computerized cognitive behaviour therapy: a systematic review. *Behavioural and Cognitive Psychotherapy*, 32, 31–55.

Kaminer, Y. (2005). Challenges and opportunities of group therapy for adolescent substance abuse: a critical review. *Addictive Behaviours.*[Special Issue]*: Trends in the Treatment of Adolescent Substance Abuse*, 30(9), 1765–1774.

Kaminer, Y. & Waldron, H. (2006) Evidence-based cognitive-behavioural therapies for adolescent substance use disorders: applications and challenges. In H. Liddle & C. Rowe (Eds.), *Adolescent Substance Abuse: Research and Clinical Advances* (pp. 396–419). New York: Cambridge University Press.

Karasu, T. B. (1986). The specificity versus nonspecificity dilemma: toward identifying therapeutic change agents. *American Journal of Psychiatry*, 143, 687–695.

Kassinove, H. & Tafrate, R. (2002). *Anger Management: The Complete Treatment Guidebook for Practitioners*. Atascadero, CA: Impact.

Kato, P. M. & Mann, T. (1999). A synthesis of psychological interventions for the bereaved. *Clinical Psychology Review*, 19, 275–296.

Katz, L., Cox, B., Gunasekara, S. & Miller, A. (2004). Feasibility of dialectical behaviour therapy for suicidal adolescent inpatients. *Journal of the American Academy of Child and Adolescent Psychiatry*, 43, 276–282.

Kazantzis, N., Deane, F. & Ronan, K. (2000). Homework assignments in cognitive and behavioural therapy: a meta-analysis. *Clinical Psychology: Science & Practice*, 7, 189–202.

Kazdin, A. (1997). Parent management training: evidence, outcomes, and issues. *Journal of the American Academy of Child and Adolescent Psychiatry*, 36, 1349–1356.

Kazdin, A. (2003). Problem-solving skills training and parent management training for conduct problems. In A. Kazdin & J. Weisz (Eds.), *Evidence Based Psychotherapies for Children and Adolescents* (pp. 241–262). New York: Guilford Press.

Kazdin, A. (2004). Psychotherapy for children and adolescents. In M. Lambert (Ed.), *Bergin and Garfield's Handbook of Psychotherapy and Behaviour Change* (Fifth Edition, pp. 543–589). New York: Wiley.

Kazdin, A. (2007). Psychosocial treatments for conduct disorder in children and adolescents. In P. Nathan & J. Gorman (Eds.), *A Guide to Treatments that Work* (Third Edition, pp. 71–104). New York: Oxford University Press.

Kazdin, A., Bass, D., Ayers, W. & Rodgers, A. (1990). Empirical and clinical focus of child and adolescent psychotherapy research. *Journal of Consulting and Clinical Psychology*, 58, 729–740

Kazdin, A., Marciano, P. & Whitley, M. (2005). The therapeutic alliance in cognitive-behavioural treatment of children referred for oppositional, aggressive, and antisocial behaviour. *Journal of Consulting and Clinical Psychology*, 73(4), 726–730.

Kazdin, A. & Weisz, J. (2003). *Evidence-Based Psychotherapies for Children and Adolescents*. New York: Guilford Press.

Keck, P. & McElroy, S. (2007). Pharmacological treatments for bipolar disorder. In P. Nathan & J. Gorman (Eds.), *A Guide to Treatments that Work* (Third Edition, pp. 323–350). New York: Oxford University Press.

Keefe, F. J., Smith, S. J., Buffington, A. L. H., Gibson, J., Studts, J. L. & Caldwell, D. S. (2002). Recent advances and future directions in the biopsychosocial assessment and treatment of arthritis. *Journal of Consulting and Clinical Psychology*. [Special Issue]: *Behavioural Medicine and Clinical Health Psychology*, 70(3), 640–655.

Kelly, G. (1955). *The Psychology of Personal Constructs* (Vols 1 and 2). London: Routledge.

Kendall, P., Hudson, J., Choudhury, M., Webb, A. & Pimentel, S. (2005). Cognitive-behavioural treatment for childhood anxiety disorders. In E. Hibbs & P. Jensen (Eds.), *Psychosocial Treatments for Child and Adolescent Disorders: Empirically Based Strategies for Clinical Practice* (Second Edition, pp. 47–74). Washington, DC: American Psychological Association.

Kennedy, E. (2004). *Child and Adolescent Psychotherapy: A Systematic Review of Psychoanalytic Approaches.* London: NHS Strategic Health Authority (http://www.nclondon.nhs.uk/publications/workforce/child_and_adolescent_systematic_review.pdf).

Kerwin, M. W. (1999). Empirically supported treatments in paediatric psychology: severe feeding problems. *Journal of Paediatric Psychology*, 24, 193–214.

Kho, K., van Vreeswijk, M., Simpson, S. and Zwinderman, A. (2003). A meta-analysis of electroconvulsive therapy efficacy in depression. *Journal of ECT*, 19(3), 139–147.

Kibby, M., Tyc, V. & Mulhern, R. (1998). Effectiveness of psychological intervention for children and adolescents with chronic medical illness: a meta-analysis. *Clinical Psychology Review*, 18(1), 103–117.

King, C. A., Kramer, A. & Preuss, L. (2000). *Youth-Nominated Support Team Intervention Manual.* Ann Arbor, MI: University of Michigan, Department of Psychiatry.

King, C. A., Kramer, A., Preuss, L., Kerr, D. C., Weisse, L. & Venkataraman, S. (2006). Youth-nominated support team for suicidal adolescents (Version 1): a randomized controlled trial. *Journal of Consulting and Clinical Psychology*, 74, 199–206.

King, N. & Bernstein, G. (2001). School refusal in children and adolescents: a review of the past ten years. *Journal of the American Academy of Child and Adolescent Psychiatry*, 40(2), 197–205.

King, N., Tonge, B., Heyne, D. & Ollendick, T. (2000). Research on the cognitive-behavioural treatment of school refusal: a review and recommendations. *Clinical Psychology Review*, 20(4), 495–507.

King, N. J., Tonge, B. J., Heyne, B. J., Pritchard, M., Rollings, S., Young, D., Myerson, N. & Ollendick, T. H. (1998). Cognitive-behavioural treatment of school-refusing children: a controlled evaluation. *Journal of the American Academy of Child and Adolescent Psychiatry*, 37, 395–403.

Kingdon, D. & Turkington, D. (2005). *Cognitive Therapy of Schizophrenia: Guides to Evidence-Based Practice.* New York: Guilford Press.

Kipper, D. A. & Ritchie, T. (2003). The effectiveness of psychodramatic techniques: a meta-analysis. *Group Dynamics: Theory, Research and Practice*, 7(1), 13–25.

Kirsch, I., Deacon, B., Huedo-Medina, T., Scoboria, A., Moore, T. & Johnson, B. (2008). Initial severity and antidepressant benefits: a meta-analysis of data submitted to the Food and Drug Administration. *PLoS Med*, 5(2), e45. doi: 10.1371/journal.pmed.0050045.

Kirsch, I., Montgomery, G. & Sapirstein, G. (1995). Hypnosis as an adjunct to cognitive-behavioral psychotherapy: a meta-analysis. *Journal of Consulting and Clinical Psychology*, 63(2), 214–220.

Kissane, D. & Bloch, S. (2002). *Family Focused Grief Therapy: A Model of Family-Centred Care during Palliative Care and Bereavement*. Maidenhead: Open University Press.

Klassen, A., Miller, A., Raina, P., Lee, S. K. & Olsen, L. (1999). Attention-deficit hyperactivity disorder in children and youth: a quantitative systematic review of the efficacy of different management strategies. *Canadian Journal of Psychiatry*, 44, 1007–1016.

Klerman, G., Weissman, M. & Rounsaville, B. (1984). *Interpersonal Psychotherapy of Depression*. New York: Basic Books.

Klingberg, T., Fernell, E., Olesen, P. J., Johnson, M., Gustafsson, P., Dahlstrom, K., Gillberg, C., Forssberg, H. & Westerberg, H. (2005). Computerized training of working memory in children with ADHD – a randomized, controlled trial. *Journal of the American Academy of Child and Adolescent Psychiatry*, 44, 177–186.

Klomek, A. & Stanley, B. (2007). Psychosocial treatment of depression and suicidality in adolescents. *CNS Spectrums*, 12(2), 135–144.

Knapp, M., Thorgrimsen, L., Patel, A., Spector, A., Hallam, A., Woods, B. & Orrell, M. (2006). Cognitive stimulation therapy for people with dementia: cost-effectiveness analysis. *British Journal of Psychiatry*, 188, 574–580.

Koegel, R. & Koegel, L. (2006). *Pivotal Response Treatments for Autism: Communication, Social, & Academic Development*. Baltimore, MD: Paul H Brookes.

Koegel, R. L., Koegel, L. K. & Brookman, L. I. (2003). Empirically supported pivotal response interventions for children with autism. In A. Kazdin & J. Weisz (Eds.), *Evidence-Based Psychotherapies for Children and Adolescents* (pp. 341–357). New York: Guilford Press.

Koegel, R. L., Schreibman, L., Good, A., Cerniglia, L., Murphy, C. & Koegel, L. (1989). *How to Teach Pivotal Behaviours to Children with Autism: A Training Manual*. Santa Barbara, CA: University of California.

Koenigsberg, H. W., Woo-Ming, A. M. & Siever, L. J. (2007). Pharmacological treatments for personality disorders. In P. Nathan & J. Gorman (Eds.), *A Guide to Treatments that Work* (Third Edition, pp. 659–680). New York: Oxford University Press.

Koita, H., Sonoyama, S. & Takeuchi, K. (2003). Communication training with the Picture Exchange Communication System (PECS) for children with autistic disorder: the training program and current and future research. *Japanese Journal of Behaviour Analysis*, 18, 120–130.

Kolevzon, A., Mathewson, K. A. & Hollander, E. (2006). Selective serotonin reuptake inhibitors in autism: a review of efficacy and tolerability. *Journal of Clinical Psychiatry*, 67, 407–14.

Kolko, D. (1996). Individual cognitive behavioural treatment and family therapy for physically abused children and their offending parents: a comparison of clinical outcomes. *Child Maltreatment*, 1, 322–342.

Kolko, D. & Swenson, C. (2002), *Assessing and Treating Physically Abused Children and their Families: A Cognitive Behavioural Approach*. Thousand Oaks, CA: Sage.

Kopta, S., Howard, K., Lowry, J. & Beutler, L. (1994). Patterns of symptomatic recovery in psychotherapy. *Journal of Consulting & Clinical Psychology*, 62, 1009–1016.

Kosters, M., Burlingame, G., Nachtigall, C. & Strauss, B. (2006). A meta-analytic review of the effectiveness of inpatient group psychotherapy. *Group Dynamics: Theory, Research, and Practice*, 10(2), 146–163.

Kotses, H. & Harver, A. (1998). *Self-Management of Asthma*. New York: Informa Healthcare.

Kowatch, R., Fristad, M. & Birmaher, B. *et al.* (2005). Treatment guidelines for children and adolescents with bipolar disorder. *Journal of the American Academy of Child & Adolescent Psychiatry*, 44, 213–235.

Kownacki, R. & Shadish, W. (1999). Does Alcoholics Anonymous work?: the results from a meta-analysis of controlled experiments. *Substance Use & Misuse*, 34(13), 1897–1916.

Krabbendam, L. & Aleman, A. (2003). Cognitive rehabilitation in schizophrenia: a quantitative analysis of controlled studies. *Psychopharmacology*, 169, 376–382.

Kravits, T. R., Kamps, D. M., Kemmerer, K. & Potucek, J. (2002). Brief report: increasing communication skills for an elementary-aged student with autism using the Picture Exchange Communication System. *Journal of Autism and Developmental Disorders*, 32, 225–230.

Krijn, M., Emmelkamp, P., Olafsson, R. & Biemond, R. (2004). Virtual reality exposure therapy of anxiety disorders: a review. *Clinical Psychology Review*, 24, 259–281.

Kroenke, K. & Swindle, R. (2000). Cognitive behavioural therapy for somatization and symptom syndromes: a critical review of controlled clinical trials. *Psychotherapy and Psychosomatics*, 69, 205–215.

Kuipers, E. (2006). Family interventions in schizophrenia evidence for efficacy and proposed mechanisms of change. *Journal of Family Therapy*, 28, 73–80.

Kuipers, E., Garety, P., Fowler, D., Freeman, D., Dunn, G. & Bebbington, P. (2006). Cognitive, emotional, and social processes in psychosis: refining cognitive behavioural therapy for persistent positive symptoms. *Schizophrenia Bulletin*, 32(Supplement 1), S24–S31.

Kuipers, E., Leff, J. & Lam, D. (2002). *Family Work for Schizophrenia* (Second Edition). London: Gaskell.

Kuppenheimer, W. & Brown, R. (2002). Painful procedures in paediatric cancer: a comparison of interventions. *Clinical Psychology Review*, 22, 753–786.

Kurtz, M., Moberg, P., Gur, R. & Gur, R. (2001). Approaches to cognitive remediation of neuropsychological deficits in schizophrenia: a review and meta-analysis. *Neuropsychology Review*, 11, 197–210.

Kurtz, M. & Nichols, M. (2007). Cognitive rehabilitation for schizophrenia: a review of recent advances. *Current Psychiatry Reviews*, 3(3), 213–221.

Kutcher, S., Aman, M. & Brooks, S. (2004). International consensus statement on attention-deficit/hyperactivity disorder (ADHD) and disruptive behaviour disorders (DBDs): clinical implications and treatment practice suggestions. *European Neuropsychopharmacology*, 14(1), 11–28.

Lackner, J., Morley, S., Dowzer, C., Mesmer, C. & Hamilton, S., (2004). Psychological treatments for irritable bowel syndrome: a systematic review and meta-analysis. *Journal of Consulting and Clinical Psychology*, 72(6), 1100–1113.

Ladouceur, R. & Lachance, S. (2006). *Overcoming Pathological Gambling: Therapist Guide*. Oxford: Oxford University Press.

Laidlaw, K., Thompson, L., Dicksiskin, L. & Gallagher-Thompson, D. (2003). *Cognitive Behaviour Therapy with Older People*. Chichester: Wiley.

Lam, D., Bright, J., Jones, S., Hayward, P., Schuck, N. & Chisholm, D. (2000). Cognitive therapy for bipolar disorder – a pilot study of relapse prevention. *Cognitive Therapy and Research*, 24, 503–520.

Lam, D., Hayward, P., Bright, J. & Jones, S. (1999). *Cognitive Therapy for Bipolar Disorder*. Chichester: Wiley.

Lam, D., Hayward, P., Watkins, E., Wright, K. & Sham, P. (2005). Relapse prevention in patients with bipolar disorder: cognitive therapy outcome after two years. *American Journal of Psychiatry*, 162, 324–329.

Lam, D. & Jones, S. (2006). Bipolar disorder. In A. Carr & M. McNulty (Eds.), *Handbook of Adult Clinical Psychology* (pp. 346–382). London: Routledge.

Lam, D., Watkins, E., Hayward, P., Bright, J., Wright, K., Kerr, N., Parr-Davis, G. & Sham, P. (2003). A randomized controlled study of cognitive therapy for relapse prevention for bipolar affective disorder: outcome of the first year. *Archives of General Psychiatry*, 60(2), 145–152.

Lam, D. & Wong, G. (2005). Prodromes, coping strategies and psychological interventions in bipolar disorders. *Clinical Psychology Review*, 25, 1028–1042.

LaMalfa, G., Lassi, S., Bertelli, M. & Castellani, A. (2006). Reviewing the use of antipsychotic drugs in people with intellectual disability. *Human Psychopharmacology: Clinical and Experimental*, 21(2), 73–89.

Lambert, M. (1992). Psychotherapy outcome research: implications for integrative and eclectic therapists. In J. Norcross & M. Goldfried (Eds.), *Handbook of Psychotherapy Integration* (pp. 94–129). New York: Basic Books.

Lambert, M. (2004). *Bergin and Garfield's Handbook of Psychotherapy and Behaviour Change* (Fifth Edition). New York: Wiley.

Lambert, M. (2005). Early response in psychotherapy: further evidence for the importance of common factors rather than 'placebo effects'. *Journal of Clinical Psychology*, 61, 855–869.

Lambert, M. (2007). Presidential address: what we have learned from a decade of research aimed at improving psychotherapy outcome in routine care. *Psychotherapy Research*, 17, 1–14.

Lambert, M. & Barley, D. (2002). Research summary on the therapeutic relationship and psychotherapy outcome. In J. Norcross (Ed.), *Relationships that Work* (pp. 17–36). Oxford: Oxford University Press.

Lambert, M., Hansen, N. & Finch, A. (2001). Patient-focused research: using patient outcome data to enhance treatment effects. *Journal of Consulting and Clinical Psychology*, 69, 159–172.

Lambert, M., Morton, J., Hatfield, D., Harmon, C., Hamilton, S., Reid, R., Shimokawa, K., Christopherson, C. & Burlingame, G. B. (2004). *Administration and Scoring Manual for the OQ-45*. Orem, UT: American Professional Credentialing Services.

Lambert, M. & Ogles, B. (1997). The effectiveness of psychotherapy supervision. In C. E. Watkins Jr. (Ed.), *Handbook of Psychotherapy Supervision* (pp. 421–446). New York: Wiley.

Lambert, M. & Ogles, B. (2004). The efficacy and effectiveness of psychotherapy. In M. J. Lambert (Ed.), *Bergin and Garfield's Handbook of Psychotherapy and Behaviour Change* (Fifth Edition, pp. 139–193). New York: Wiley.

Lambert, M., Whipple, J. & Hawkins, E. (2003). Is it time for clinicians to routinely track patient outcome? A meta-analysis. *Clinical Psychology: Science and Practice*, 10, 288–301.

Lancaster, T. & Stead, L. (2005). Individual behavioural counselling for smoking cessation. *Cochrane Database of Systematic Reviews*, Issue 2. Art. No.: CD001292. DOI: 10.1002/14651858.CD001292.pub2.

Lancaster, T., Stead, L. & Silagy, C. (2000). Effectiveness of interventions to help people stop smoking: findings from the Cochrane Library. *British Medical Journal*, 321(7257), 355–358.

Landman, J. & Dawes, R. (1982). Psychotherapy outcome: Smith and Glass' conclusions stand up under scrutiny. *American Psychologist*, 37(5), 504–516.

Larson, D. & Hoyt, W. (2007). What has become of grief counselling? An evaluation of the empirical foundations of the new pessimism. *Professional Psychology: Research and Practice*, 38(4), 347–355.

Lask, B. & Bryant-Waugh, R. (2007). *Anorexia Nervosa and Related Eating Disorders in Childhood and Adolescence* (Third Edition). London: Routledge.

Last, C., Hansen, C. & Franco, N. (1998). Cognitive-behavioural treatment of school phobia. *Journal of the American Academy of Child & Adolescent Psychiatry*, 37, 404–411.

Leblanc, M. & Ritchie, M. (2001). A meta-analysis of play therapy outcomes. *Counselling Psychology Quarterly*, 14(2), 149–163.

Lebow, J., Kelly, J., Knobloch-Fedders, L. & Moos, R. (2006). Relationship factors in treating substance use disorders. In L. Castonguay & L. Beutler (Eds.), *Principles of Therapeutic Change that Work* (pp. 293–318). Oxford: Oxford University Press.

Lebowitz, B., Pearson, J. & Schneider, L. (1997). Diagnosis and treatment of depression in late life: consensus statement update. *Journal of the American Medical Association*, 278(14), 1186–1190.

Leckman, J., Hardin, M., Riddle, M., Stevenson, J., Ort, S. & Cohen, D. (1991). Clonidine treatment of Gilles de la Tourette's syndrome. *Archives of General Psychiatry*, 48, 324–328.

Lees, J., Manning, N. & Rawlings, B. (1999). *Therapeutic Community Effectiveness: A Systematic International Review of Therapeutic Community Treatment for People with Personality Disorders and Mentally Disordered Offenders*. York: University of York, NHS Centre for Reviews and Dissemination.

Leff, J., Verneals, S., Brewin, C. R., Wolff, G., Alexander, B., Asen, E., Dayson, D., Jones, E., Chisholm, D. & Everitt, B. (2000). The London depression intervention trial: randomized controlled trial of antidepressants v. couple therapy in the treatment and maintenance of people with depression living with a partner: clinical outcome and costs. *British Journal of Psychiatry*, 177, 95–100.

le Grange, D. & Lock, J. (2005). The dearth of psychological treatment studies for anorexia nervosa. *International Journal of Eating Disorders*, 37(2), 79–91.

le Grange, D. & Lock, J. (2007). *Treating Bulimia in Adolescents: A Family-Based Approach*. New York: Guilford Press.

le Grange, D., Crosby, R., Rathouz, P. & Leventhal, B. (2007). A randomized controlled comparison of family-based treatment and supportive psychotherapy for adolescent bulimia nervosa. *Archives of General Psychiatry*, 64, 1049–1056.

Lehman, A., Kreyenbuhl, J., Buchanan, R., Dickerson, F., Dixon, L., Goldberg, R., Green-Paden, L., Tenhula, W., Boerescu, D., Tek, C. & Sandson, N. (2004). The

Schizophrenia Patient Outcomes Research Team (PORT): updated treatment recommendations 2003. *Schizophrenia Bulletin*, 30(2), 193–217.

Lehrer, P., Feldman, J., Giardino, N., Song, H. & Schmaling, K. (2002). Psychological aspects of asthma. *Journal of Consulting and Clinical Psychology*, 70(3), 691–711.

Leiblum, S. (2006). *Principles and Practice of Sex Therapy* (Fourth Edition). New York: Guilford Press.

Leichsenring, F. (2001). Comparative effects of short-term psychodynamic psychotherapy and cognitive-behavioural therapy in depression: a meta-analytic approach. *Clinical Psychology Review*, 21, 401–419.

Leichsenring, F., Beutel, M. & Leibing, E. (2007). Psychodynamic psychotherapy for social phobia: a treatment manual based on supportive-expressive therapy. *Bulletin of the Menninger Clinic*, 71(1), 56–83.

Leichsenring, F. & Leibing, E. (2003). The effectiveness of psychodynamic therapy and cognitive behaviour therapy in the treatment of personality disorders: a meta-analysis. *American Journal of Psychiatry*, 160(7), 1223–1232.

Leichsenring, F., Rabung, S. & Leibing, E. (2004). The efficacy of short-term psychodynamic psychotherapy in specific psychiatric disorders: a meta-analysis. *Archives of General Psychiatry*, 61(12), 1208–1216.

Lemanek, K., Kamps, J. & Chung, N. (2001). Empirically supported treatments in paediatric psychology: regimen adherence. *Journal of Paediatric Psychology*, 26, 253–275.

Leon, A., Franklin, B., Costa, F., Balady, G., Berra, C., Stewart, K., Thompson, P., Williams, M. & Lauer, M. (2005). Cardiac rehabilitation and secondary prevention of coronary heart disease. *Circulation*, 111, 369–376.

Levitt, E. (1957). The results of psychotherapy with children: an evaluation. *Journal of Consulting and Clinical Psychology*, 21, 189–196.

Levy, S. E. & Hyman, S. L. (2005). Novel treatments for autistic spectrum disorders. *Mental Retardation and Developmental Disabilities Research Reviews*, 11, 131–142.

Lewinsohn, P., Antonuccio, D., Steinmetz, J. & Teri, L. (1984). *The Coping with Depression Course: A Psychoeducational Intervention for Unipolar Depression*. Eugene: Castalia Press.

Lewinsohn, P. & Clarke, G. (1999). Psychosocial treatments for adolescent depression. *Clinical Psychology Review*, 19(3), 329–342.

Lewinsohn, P., Munoz, R., Youngren, M. & Zeiss, A. (1986). *Control Your Depression*. Englewood Cliffs, NJ: Prentice-Hall.

Lewis, D. (1999). Computer-based approaches to patient education: a review of the literature. *Journal of the American Medical Informatics Association*, 6, 272–282.

Liabo, K., Newman, T., Stephens, J. & Lowe, K. (2001). *A Review of Key Worker Systems for Children with Disabilities and Development of Information Guides for Parents, Children, and Professionals*. Welsh Assembly Government, Cardiff: Welsh Office for Research and Development.

Liberman, R., DeRisi, W. & Mueser, K. (1989). *Social Skills Training for Psychiatric Patients*. New York: Pergamon.

Liddle, H. (2004). Family-based therapies for adolescent alcohol and drug use: research contributions and future research needs. *Addiction*, 99, 76–92.

Liddle, H. A. (2005). *Multidimensional Family Therapy for Adolescent Substance Abuse*. New York: Norton (www.chestnut.org/LI/cyt/products/MDFT_CYT_v5.pdf).

Liddle, H., Rodriguez, R., Dakof, G. & Kanzki, F. (2005). Multidimensional family therapy: a science-based treatment for adolescent drug abuse. In J. Lebow (Ed.), *Handbook of Clinical Family Therapy* (pp. 128–163). New York: Wiley.

Lieb, K., Zanarini, M. C., Schmahl, C., Linehan, M. M. & Bohus, M. (2004). Borderline personality disorder. *Lancet*, 364, 9432.

Lieberman, A. & Van Horn, P. (2005). *Don't Hit My Mommy: A Manual for Child–Parent Psychotherapy with Young Witnesses of Family Violence*. Washington, DC: Zero to Three Press.

Lieberman, A., Van Horn, P. & Ippen, C. (2005). Toward evidence-based treatment: child–parent psychotherapy with preschoolers exposed to marital violence. *Journal of the American Academy of Child and Adolescent Psychiatry*, 44(12), 1241–1248.

Lilienfeld, S. (2007). Psychological treatments that cause harm. *Perspectives on Psychological Science*, 2(1), 53–70.

Lincon, T., Wilhelm, K. & Nestoriuc, Y. (2007). Effectiveness of psychoeducation for relapse, symptoms, knowledge, adherence and functioning in psychotic disorders: a meta-analysis. *Schizophrenia Research*, 96(1–3), 232–245.

Linde, K., Berner, M., Egger, M. & Mulrow, C. (2005). St John's Wort for depression: meta-analysis of randomised controlled trials. *British Journal of Psychiatry*, 186, 99–107.

Linden, D. (2006). How psychotherapy changes the brain – the contribution of functional neuroimaging. *Molecular Psychiatry*, 11(6), 528–538.

Linden, W. & Chambers, L. (2004). Clinical effectiveness of non-drug treatment for hypertension: a meta-analysis. *Annals of Behavioural Medicine*, 16(1), 35–45.

Linden, W. & Moseley, J. (2006). The efficacy of behavioural treatments for hypertension. *Applied Psychophysiology and Biofeedback*, 31(1), 51–63.

Linehan, M. (1993a). *Cognitive-Behavioural Treatment of Borderline Personality Disorder*. New York: Guilford Press.

Linehan, M. (1993b). *Skills Training Manual for Treating Borderline Personality Disorder*. New York: Guilford Press.

Linehan, M., Comtois, K., Murray, A., Brown, M., Gallop, R., Heard, H., Korslund, K., Tutek, D., Reynolds, S. & Lindenboim, N. (2006). Two-year randomized controlled trial and follow-up of dialectical behaviour therapy vs therapy by experts for suicidal behaviours and borderline personality disorder. *Archives of General Psychiatry*, 63, 757–766.

Linehan, M., Davison, G., Lynch, T. & Sanderson, G. (2006). Technique factors in treating personality disorders. In L. Castonguay & L. Beutler (Eds.), *Principles of Therapeutic Change that Work* (pp. 239–252). Oxford: Oxford University Press.

Lingford-Hughes, A., Welch, S. & Nutt, D. (2004). Evidence-based guidelines for the pharmacological management of substance misuse, addiction and co-morbidity: recommendations from the British Association for Psychopharmacology. *Journal of Psychopharmacology*, 18(3), 293–335.

Lissau, I., Overpeck, M., Ruan, W., Due, P., Holstein, B. & Hediger, M. (2004). Body mass index and overweight in adolescent in 13 European countries, Israel and the United States. *Paediatric and Adolescent Medicine*, 158, 27–33.

Lochman, J., Barry, T. & Pardini, D. (2003). Anger control training for aggressive youth. In A. Kazdin & J. Weisz (Eds.), *Evidence-Based Psychotherapies for Children and Adolescents* (pp. 263–281). New York: Guilford Press.

Lock, J., le Grange, D., Agras, W. & Dare, C. (2001). *Treatment Manual for Anorexia Nervosa: A Family Based Approach*. New York: Guilford Press.

Loeber, R., Burke, J., Lahey, B., Winters, A. & Zera, M. (2000). Oppositional defiant and conduct disorder: a review of the past ten years, Part I. *Journal of the American Academy of Child and Adolescent Psychiatry*, 39(12), 1468–1484.

Loew, T., Richter, R., Calatzis, A. & Krause, S. (2002). Efficacy studies concerning psychodynamic psychotherapy – previously not included studies/Wirksamkeitsstudien zur Psychodynamischen Psychotherapie: Studien, die nicht berücksichtigt wurden. *PDP Psychodynamische Psychotherapie: Forum der tiefenpsychologisch fundierten Psychotherapie*, 1(2), 93–107.

Logsdon, R., McCurry, S. & Teri, L. (2007). Evidence-based psychological treatments for disruptive behaviours in individuals with dementia. *Psychology and Aging;* 22, 28–36.

Looper, K. J. & Kirmayer, L. J. (2002). Behavioural medicine approaches to somatoform disorders. *Journal of Consulting and Clinical Psychology* [Special Issue], 70(3), 810–827.

Losel, F. & Schmucker, M. (2005). Effectiveness of treatment for sexual offenders: a comprehensive meta-analysis. *Journal of Experimental Criminology*, 1(1), 117–146.

Lovaas, O. I. (1987). Behavioural treatment and normal educational and intellectual functioning in young autistic children. *Journal of Consulting and Clinical Psychology*, 55, 3–9.

Lovaas, O. (2002). *Teaching Children with Developmental Delays: Basic Intervention Techniques*. Austin, TX: Pro-Ed.

Lovaas, O. & Smith, T. (2003). Early and intensive behavioural intervention for autism. In A. Kazdin & J. Weisz (Eds.), *Evidence Based Psychotherapies for Children and Adolescents* (pp. 325–340). New York: Guilford Press.

Luborsky, L. (1984). *Principles of Psychoanalytic Psychotherapy: A Manual for Supportive-Expressive Treatment*. New York: Basic Books.

Luborsky, L., Diguer, L., Luborsky, E., Singer, B., Dickter, D. & Schmidt, K. A. (1993). The efficacy of dynamic psychotherapies: is it true that 'Everyone has won and all must have prizes'? In M. E. Miller, L. Luborsky, J. P. Barber & J. P. Docherty (Eds.), *Psychodynamic Treatment Research: A Handbook for Clinical Practice* (pp. 497–516). New York: Basic Books.

Luborsky, L., Diguer, L., Seligman, D. A., Rosenthal, R., Krause, E. D., Johnson, S., Halperin, G., Bishop, M., Berman, J. S. & Schweizer, E. (1999). The researcher's own therapy allegiance: a 'wild card' in comparisons of treatment efficacy. *Clinical Psychology: Science and Practice*, 6, 95–106.

Luborsky, L., Rosenthal, R., Diguer, L., Andrusyna, T. P., Levitt, J. T., Seligman, D. A., Berman, I. & Krause, E. D. (2002). The Dodo Bird verdict is alive and well – mostly. *Clinical Psychology: Science and Practice*, 9(1), 2–12.

Luborsky, L., Singer, B. & Luborsky, E. (1975). Comparative studies of psychotherapies: is it true that 'Everybody has won and all must have prizes'? *Archives of General Psychiatry*, 32, 995–1008.

Lue, T. F., Giuliano, F., Montorsi, F., Rosen, R. C., Andersson, K.-E., Althof, S., Christ, G., Hatzichristou, D., Hirsch, M., Kimoto, Y., Lewis, R., McKenna, K., Mac-Mahon, C., Morales, A., Mulcahy, J., Padma-Nathan, H., Pryor, J., Saenz de Tejada, I., Shabsigh, R. & Wagner, G. (2004). Summary of recommendations on sexual dysfunctions in men. *Journal of Sexual Medicine*, 1, 6–23.

Lussier, J., Heil, S., Mongeon, J., Badger, G. & Higgins, S. (2006). A meta-analysis of voucher-based reinforcement therapy for substance use disorders. *Addiction*, 101, 192–203.

Lyons, L. & Woods, P. (1991). The efficacy of rational-emotive therapy: a quantitative review of the outcome research. *Clinical Psychology Review*, 11(4), 357–369.

Macdonald, G. M., Higgins, J. P. T. & Ramchandani, P. (2006). Cognitive-behavioural interventions for children who have been sexually abused [Electronic Version]. *Cochrane Database of Systematic Reviews*, Issue 4. Art. No.: CD001930. DOI: 10.1002/14651858.CD001930.pub2.

MacKenzie, D., Wilson, D. & Kider, S. (2001). Effects of correctional boot camps on offending. *Annals of the American Academy of Political and Social Science*, 578, 126–143.

Mackin, R. & Areán, P. (2005). Evidence-based psychotherapeutic interventions for geriatric depression. *Psychiatric Clinics of North America*, 28, 805–820.

MacLeod, J. & Nelson, G. (2000). Programs for the promotion of family wellness and the prevention of child maltreatment: a meta-analytic review. *Child Abuse and Neglect*, 24, 1127–1149.

Madhusoodanan, S., Shah, P., Brenner, R. & Gupta, S. (2007). Pharmacological treatment of the psychosis of Alzheimer's disease: what is the best approach. *CNS Drugs*, 21(2), 101–115.

Magura, S., Staines, G. L., Blankertz, L. & Madison, E. M. (2004). The effectiveness of vocational services for substance users in treatment. *Substance Use & Misuse*, 39, 2165–2213.

Malan, D. (1995). *Individual Psychotherapy and the Science of Psychodynamics* (Second Edition). London: Butterworth- Heinemann.

Malan, D. & Osimo, F. (1992). *Psychodynamics, Training, and Outcome in Brief Psychotherapy*. London: Butterworth.

Maletzky, B. M. (2002). The paraphilias: research and treatment. In P. Nathan & J. Gorman (Eds.), *A Guide to Treatments that Work* (Second Edition, pp. 525–538). New York: Oxford University Press.

Maling, M., Gurtman, M. & Howard, K. (1995). The response of interpersonal problems to varying doses of psychotherapy. *Psychotherapy Research*, 5, 63–75.

Mancil, G. (2006). Functional communication training: a review of the literature related to children with autism. *Education and Training in Developmental Disabilities*, 41(3), 213–224.

Mann, K., Lehert, P. & Morgan, M. (2004). The efficacy of acamprosate in the maintenance of abstinence in alcohol-dependent individuals: results of a meta-analysis. *Alcohol Clinical and Experimental Research*, 28, 51–63.

Mansell, W., Colom, F. & Scott, J. (2005). The nature and treatment of depression in bipolar disorder: a review and implications for future psychological investigation. *Clinical Psychology Review*, 25, 1076–1100.

Manske, S., Miller, S., Moyer, C., Phaneuf, M. & Cameron, R. (2004). Best practice in group-based smoking cessation: results of a literature review applying effectiveness, plausibility and practicality criteria. *American Journal of Health Promotion*, 18, 409–423.

March, J., Frances, A. & Carpenter, D. (1997). The expert consensus guidelines series: treatment of obsessive compulsive disorder. *Journal of Clinical Psychiatry*, 4(suppl), 2–72.

March, J., Franklin, M. & Foa, E. (2005). Cognitive-behavioural psychotherapy for paediatric obsessive-compulsive disorder. In E. Hibbs & P. Jensen (Eds.), *Psychosocial Treatments for Child and Adolescent Disorders: Empirically Based Strategies for Clinical Practice* (Second Edition, pp. 121–142). Washington, DC: American Psychological Association.

Marks, I. (1980). *Living with Fear*. New York: McGraw-Hill.

Marks, I., Cavanagh, K. & Gega, L. (2007). *Hands-on Help: Computer Aided Psychotherapy*. London: Routledge.

Marshall, M., Crowther, R., Almaraz-Serrano, A., Creed, F., Sledge, W., Kluiter, H., Roberts, C., Hill, E., Wiersma, D., Bond, F., Huxley, P. & Tyrer, P. (2001). Systematic reviews of the effectiveness of day care for people with severe mental disorders: (1) acute day hospital versus admission; (2) vocational rehabilitation; (3) day hospital versus outpatient care. *Health Technology Assessment*, 5 (21).

Marshall, W. & McGuire, J. (2003). Effect sizes in the treatment of sexual offenders. *International Journal of Offender Therapy and Comparative Criminology*, 47, 653–663.

Marshall, W., Marshall, L., Serran, G. & Fernandez, Y. (2006). *Treating Sexual Offenders: An Integrated Approach*. New York: Routledge.

Martens, W. (2005). Efficacy of dialectical behaviour therapy for patients with borderline personality disorder. *Annals of the American Psychotherapy Association*, 8(4), 5–12.

Martin, D., Graske, J. & Davis, M. (2000). Relation of the therapeutic alliance with outcome and other variables: a meta-analytic review. *Journal of Consulting and Clinical Psychology*, 68, 438–450.

Mastergeorge, A., Rogers S., Corbett, B. & Solomon, M. (2003). Non-medical interventions for autism spectrum disorders. In S. Ozonoff, S. Rogers & R. Hendren (Eds.), *Autism Spectrum Disorders: A Research Review for Practitioners* (pp. 133–160). Washington, DC: American Psychiatric Press.

Masters, W. & Johnson, V. (1970). *Human Sexual Inadequacy*. Boston: Little-Brown.

Matson, J., Bamburg, J., Mayville, E., Pinkston, J., Bielecki, J. & Kuhn, D. (2000). Psychopharmacology and mental retardation: a 10 year review (1990–1999). *Research in Developmental Disabilities*, 21, 263–296.

Mayo-Smith, M. (1997). Pharmacological management of alcohol withdrawal: a meta-analysis and evidence-based practice guideline. *Journal of the American Medical Association*, 278, 144–151.

McCabe, M., McGillivray, J. & Newton, D. (2006). Effectiveness of treatment programmes for depression among adults with mild/moderate intellectual disability. *Journal of Intellectual Disability Research*, 50, 239–247.

McCart, M., Priester, P., Davies, W. & Azen, R. (2006) Differential effectiveness of cognitive-behavioural therapy and behavioural parent-training for antisocial youth: a meta-analysis. *Journal of Abnormal Child Psychology*, 34(4), 527–543.

McCarthy, B. & Fucito, L. (2005). Integrating medication, realistic expectations, and therapeutic interventions in the treatment of male sexual dysfunction. *Journal of Sex & Marital Therapy*, 31, 319–328.

McConnell, S. (2002). Interventions to facilitate social interaction for young children with autism: review of available research and recommendations for educational intervention and future research. *Journal of Autism and Developmental Disorders*, 32, 351–372.

McCrady, B., Haaga, D. & Lebow, J. (2006). Integration of therapeutic factors in treating substance use disorders. In L. Castonguay & L. Beutler (Eds.), *Principles of Therapeutic Change that Work* (pp. 341–352). Oxford: Oxford University Press.

McCrady, B. & Nathan, P. (2006). Technique factors in treating substance use disorders. In L. Castonguay & L. Beutler (Eds.), *Principles of Therapeutic Change that Work* (pp. 319–340). Oxford: Oxford University Press.

McCullough-Vaillant, L. (1997). *Changing Character: Short-Term Anxiety Regulating Psychotherapy for Restructuring Defences, Affects and Attachments.* New York: Basic Books.

McCurry, S. M., Logsdon, R. G., Teri, L. & Vitiello, M. V. (2007). Evidence-based psychological treatments for insomnia in older adults. *Psychology and Aging*, 22, 18–27.

McDermut, W., Miller, I. & Brown, R. (2001). The efficacy of group psychotherapy for depression: a meta-analysis. *Clinical Psychology: Science & Practice*, 8(1), 98–116.

McDougle, C., Posey, D. & Stigler, K. (2006). Pharmacological treatments. In S. Moldin & J. Rubenstein (Eds), *Understanding Autism: From Basic Neuroscience to Treatment* (pp. 417–443). Boca Raton, FL: CRC Press.

McEachin, J. J., Smith, T. & Lovaas, O. I. (1993). Long-term outcome for children with autism who received early intensive behavioral treatment. *American Journal on Mental Retardation*, 97(4), 359–372.

McEvoy, J., Scheifler, P. & Frances, A. (1999). The Expert Consensus Guidelines Series: treatment of schizophrenia. *Journal of Clinical Psychiatry*, 60(suppl 11), 1–80.

McFarlane, W. (2004). *Multifamily Groups in the Treatment of Severe Psychiatric Disorders.* New York: Guilford Press.

McGrath, M. L., Mellon, M. W. & Murphy, L. (2000). Empirically supported treatments in paediatric psychology: constipation and encopresis. *Journal of Paediatric Psychology*, 25, 225–254.

Mcintosh, V., Jordan, J. & Luty, S. (2005). Three psychotherapies for anorexia nervosa: a randomized controlled trial. *American Journal of Psychiatry*, 162, 741–747.

McQuaid, E. & Nassau, J. (1999). Empirically supported treatments of disease-related symptoms in paediatric psychology: asthma, diabetes, and cancer. *Journal of Paediatric Psychology*, 24, 305–313.

McRoberts, C., Burlingame, G. & Hoag, M. (1998). Comparative efficacy of individual and group psychotherapy: a meta-analytic perspective. *Group Dynamics: Theory, Research, and Practice*, 2, 101–117.

Mehta, M. (1990). A comparative study of family-based and patient-based behavioural management in obsessive-compulsive disorder. *British Journal of Psychiatry*, 157, 133–135.

Mellon, M. & McGrath, M. (2000). Empirically supported treatments in paediatric psychology: nocturnal enuresis. *Journal of Paediatric Psychology*, 25, 193–214.

Mellor-Clark, J. & Barkham, M. (2006). The CORE system: quality evaluation to develop practice-based evidence base, enhanced service delivery and best practice management. In C. Feltham & I. Horton (Eds.), *The Handbook of Counselling and Psychotherapy.* London: Sage.

Melvin, G., Tonge, B., King, N., Heyne, D., Gordon, M. & Ester, K. (2006). A comparison of cognitive-behavioural therapy, sertraline, and their combination for adolescent depression. *Journal of the American Academy of Child and Adolescent Psychiatry*, 45(10), 1151–1161.

Mendlowitz, S., Manassis, K., Bradley, S., Scapillato, D., Miezitis, S. & Shaw, B. F. (1999). Cognitive-behavioural group treatments in childhood and anxiety disorders: the role of parental involvement. *Journal of the American Academy of Child and Adolescent Psychiatry*, 38, 1223–1229.

Mercer, D. & Woody, G. (1999). *Individual Drug Counselling*. National Institute for Drug Abuse (http://www.nida.nih.gov/PDF/Manual3.pdf).

Mesibov, G., Shea, V. & Schopler, E. (2005). *The TEACCH Approach to Autism Spectrum Disorders*. New York: Springer.

Messer, S. & Warren, S. (1998). *Models of Brief Psychodynamic Psychotherapy: A Comparative Approach*. New York: Guilford Press.

Meston, C. (2006). Female orgasmic disorder: treatment strategies and outcome results. In I. Goldstein, C. Meston, S. Davis & A. Traish (Eds.), *Women's Sexual Function and Dysfunction: Study, Diagnosis, and Treatment* (pp. 449–461). London: Taylor & Francis.

Meston, C. & Bradford, A. (2007). Sexual dysfunctions in women. *Annual Review of Clinical Psychology*, 3, 233–256.

Metcalfe, C., Winter, D. & Viney, D. (2007). The effectiveness of personal construct psychotherapy in clinical practice: a systematic review and meta-analysis. *Psychotherapy Research*, 17(4), 431–442.

Meyers, R. & Smith, J. (1995). *Clinical Guide to Alcohol Treatment: The Community Reinforcement Approach*. New York: Guilford Press.

Michael, K. & Crowley, S. (2002). How effective are treatments for child and adolescent depression? A meta-analytic review. *Clinical Psychology Review*, 22, 247–269.

Mikkelsen, E. (2001). Enuresis and encopresis: ten years of progress. *Journal of the American Academy of Child and Adolescent Psychiatry*, 40(10), 1146–1158.

Miklowitz, D. & Craighead, W. (2007). Psychosocial treatments for bipolar disorder. In P. Nathan & J. Gorman (Eds.), *A Guide to Treatments that Work* (Third Edition, pp. 309–323). New York: Oxford University Press.

Miklowitz, D., George, E., Axelson, D., Kim, E., Birmaher, B., Schneck, C., Beresford, C., Craighead, W. & Brent, D. (2004). Family-focused treatment for adolescents with bipolar disorder. *Journal of Affective Disorders*, 82, 113–128.

Miklowitz, D., George, E. & Richards, J. (2003a). A randomized study of family-focused psychoeducation and pharmacotherapy in the outpatient management of bipolar disorder. *Archives of General Psychiatry*, 60(9), 904–912.

Miklowitz, D. & Goldstein, M. (1990). Behavioural family treatment for patients with bipolar affective disorder. *Behaviour Modification*, 14, 457–489.

Miklowitz, D. & Goldstein, M. (1997). *Bipolar Disorder: A Family-Focused Treatment Approach*. New York: Guilford Press.

Miklowitz, D., Otto, M., Frank, E., Reily Harrington, N., Wisniewski, S., Kogan, J., Nierenberg, A., Calabrese, R., Marangell, L., Gyulai, L., Araga, M., Gonzalez, J., Shirley, E., Thase, M. & Sachs, G. (2007). Psychosocial treatments for bipolar depression: a 1-year randomized trial from the Systematic Treatment Enhancement Program. *Archives of General Psychiatry*, 64(4), 419–427.

Miklowitz, D., Richards, J., George, E., Frank, E., Suddath, R. & Powell, K. (2003b). Integrated family and individual therapy for bipolar disorder: results of a treatment development study. *Journal of Clinical Psychiatry*, 64, 182–191.

Miller, A., Rathus, J. & Linehan, M. (2007). *Dialectical Behaviour Therapy with Suicidal Adolescents*. New York: Guilford Press.

Miller, A., Wyman, S., Glassman, S., Huppert, J. & Rathus, J. (2000). Analysis of behavioural skills utilized by adolescents receiving dialectical behaviour therapy. *Cognitive and Behavioural Practice*, 7, 183–187.

Miller, I., Solomon, D., Ryan, C. & Keitner, G. (2004). Does adjunctive family therapy enhance recovery from bipolar I mood episodes. *Journal of Affective Disorders*, 82, 431–436.

Miller, S., Duncan, B., Brown, J., Sparks, J. & Claud, D. (2003). The Outcome Rating Scale: a preliminary study of reliability, validity, and feasibility of a brief visual analogue measure. *Journal of Brief Therapy*, 2, 91–100 (http://www.talkingcure.com/).

Miller, S., Duncan, B., Sorrell, R. & Brown, G. (2005). The partners for change outcome management system. *Journal of Clinical Psychology*, 61(2), 199–208.

Miller, W. & Rollnick, S. (2002). *Motivational Interviewing: Preparing People for Change* (Second Edition). New York: Guilford Press.

Miller, W., Walters, S. & Bennett, M. (2001). How effective is alcoholism treatment in the United States? *Journal of Studies on Alcohol*, 62, 211–220.

Miller, W., Wilbourne, P. & Hettema, J. (2003). What works? A summary of alcohol treatment outcome research. In R. K. Hester & W. R. Miller (Eds.), *Handbook of Alcoholism Treatment Approaches: Effective Alternatives* (Third Edition, pp. 13–63). Boston, MA: Allyn & Bacon.

Miller, W., Zweben, A., DiClemente, C. & Rychtarik, R. (1994). *Motivational Enhancement Therapy Manual: A Clinical Research Guide for Therapists Treating Individuals with Alcohol Abuse and Dependence*. Rockville MD: NIAAA.

Millward, C., Ferriter, M., Calver, S. & Connell-Jones, G. (2004). Gluten- and casein-free diets for autistic spectrum disorder. *The Cochrane Database of Systematic Reviews*, 3.

Milne, D. & James, I. (2000). A systematic review of effective cognitive-behavioural supervision. *British Journal of Clinical Psychology*, 39, 111–127.

Milrod, B., Busch, F., Cooper, A. & Shapiro, T. (1997). *Manual of Panic-Focused Psychodynamic Psychotherapy*. Washington, DC: American Psychiatric Association.

Milrod, B., Busch, P., Leon, A., Aaronson, A. Rolphe, J., Rudden, M., Singer, M., Goldman, H., Richter, D. & Shear, M. (2000). Open trial of psychodynamic psychotherapy for panic disorder: a pilot study. *American Journal of Psychiatry*, 157(11), 1878–1880.

Mindell, J. (1999). Empirically supported treatments in paediatric psychology: bedtime refusal and night wakings in young children. *Journal of Paediatric Psychology*, 24(6), 465–481.

Miner, M., Borduin, C., Prescott, D., Bovensmann, H., Schepker, H., Du Bois, R., Schladale, J., Eher, R., Schmeck, K., Langfedt, T., Smit, A. & Pfäfflin, F. (2006). Standards of care for juvenile sexual offenders of the International Association for the Treatment of Sexual Offenders. *Sexual Offender Treatment*, 1(3), 1–6.

Minuchin, S., Rosman, B. & Baker, L. (1978). *Psychosomatic Families: Anorexia Nervosa in Context*. Cambridge, MA: Harvard University Press.

Mitchell, J. (2001). Psychopharmacology of eating disorders: current knowledge and future directions. In R. Striegel-Moore & L. Smolak (Eds.), *Eating Disorders: Innovative Directions in Research and Practice* (pp. 197–214). Washington, DC: American Psychological Association.

Mitchell, K. & Carr, A. (2000). Anorexia and bulimia. In A. Carr (Ed.), *What*

Works with Children and Adolescents? A Critical Review of Psychological Interventions with Children, Adolescents and their Families (pp. 233–257). London: Routledge.

Mitte, K. (2005a). Meta-analysis of cognitive behaviour treatments for generalized anxiety disorder: a comparison with pharmacotherapy. *Psychological Bulletin*, 151(5), 785–682.

Mitte, K. (2005b). A meta-analysis of the efficacy of psycho- and pharmacotherapy in panic disorder with and without agoraphobia. *Journal of Affective Disorders*, 88, 27–45.

Mitte, K., Noack, P., Steil, R. & Hautzinger, M. (2005). A meta-analytic review of the efficacy of drug treatment in generalized anxiety disorder. *Journal of Clinical Psychopharmacology*, 25, 141–150.

Moher, D., Schulz, K. & Atman, D. (2001). The CONSORT statement: revised recommendations for improving the quality of reports of parallel-group randomized trials. *Lancet*, 357, 1191–1194.

Mohr, D. (1995). Negative outcome in psychotherapy: a critical review. *Clinical Psychology: Science and Practice*, 2, 1–27.

Mojica, W., Suttorp, M., Sherman, S., Morton, S., Roth, E. & Maglione, M. (2004). Smoking-cessation interventions by type of provider: a meta-analysis. *American Journal of Preventive Medicine*, 26, 391–401.

Mojtabai, R., Nicholson, R. & Carpenter, B. (1998). Role of psychosocial treatments in management of schizophrenia: a meta-analysis review of controlled outcome studies. *Schizophrenia Bulletin*, 24, 569–587.

Montgomery, P. & Dennis, J. (2004). A systematic review of non-pharmacological therapies for sleep problems in later life. *Sleep Medicine Reviews*, 8(1), 47–62.

Monti, D., Peterson, C., Kunkel, E., Hauck, W., Peqignot, E., Rhodes, L. & Brainard, G. (2006). A randomized, controlled trial of mindfulness-based art therapy (MBAT) for women with cancer. *Psycho-Oncology*, 15(5), 363–373.

Moos, R., Moos, B. & Andrassy, J. (1999). Outcomes of four treatment approaches in community residential programs for patients with substance use disorders. *Psychiatric Services*, 50, 1577–1583.

Morgenthaler, T., Kramer, M., Alessi, C., Friedman, L., Boehlecke, B., Brown, T., Coleman, J., Kapur, V., Lee-Chiong, T., Owens, J., Pancer, J. & Swick, T. (2006). Practice parameters for the psychological and behavioural treatment of insomnia: an update. *Sleep*, 29(11), 1415–1419.

Morin, C., Bootzin, R., Buysse, D., Edinger, J., Espie, C. & Lichstein, K. (2006). Psychological and behavioural treatment of insomnia. *Sleep*, 29(11), 1398–1414.

Morin, C. & Espie, C. (2003). *Insomnia: Psychological Assessment and Management*. New York: Plenum.

Morley, S., Eccleston, C. & Williams, A. (1999). Systematic review and meta-analysis of randomized controlled trials of cognitive behaviour therapy and behaviour therapy for chronic pain in adults, excluding headache. *Pain*, 80, 1–13.

Morris, T. & March, J. (2004). *Anxiety Disorders in Children and Adolescents* (Second Edition). New York: Guilford Press.

Mostert, M. (2001). Facilitated communication since 1995: a review of published studies. *Journal of Autism and Developmental Disorders*, 31, 287–313.

Moyer, C. A., Rounds, J. & Hannum, J. W. (2004). A meta-analysis of massage therapy research. *Psychological Bulletin*, 130, 3–18.

MTA Cooperative Group (2004). National Institute of Mental Health multimodal treatment study of ADHD follow-up: 24-month outcomes of treatment strategies for attention-deficit /hyperactivity disorder. *Paediatrics*, 113, 754–761.

Muck, R., Zempolich, K. & Titus, J. (2001). An overview of the effectiveness of adolescent substance abuse treatment models. *Youth & Society*, 33, 143–168.

Mufson, L. & Dorta, K. (2003). Interpersonal psychotherapy for depressed adolescents. In A. Kazdin & J. Weisz (Eds.), *Evidence-Based Psychotherapies for Children and Adolescents* (pp. 148–164). New York: Guilford Press.

Mufson, L., Dorta, K., Moreau, D. & Weissman, M. (2005). Efficacy to effectiveness: adaptations of interpersonal psychotherapy for adolescent depression. In E. Hibbs & P. Jensen (Eds.), *Psychosocial Treatments for Child and Adolescent Disorders: Empirically Based Strategies for Clinical Practice* (Second Edition, pp. 165–186). Washington, DC: American Psychological Association.

Mumford, E., Schlesinger, H. J., Glass, G., Patrick, C. & Cuerdon, T. (1984). A new look at evidence about reduced cost of medical utilization following mental health treatment. *American Journal of Psychiatry*, 141, 1145–1158.

Muratori, F., Picchi, L., Bruni, G., Patarnello, M. & Romagnoli, G. (2003). A two-year follow-up of psychodynamic psychotherapy for internalizing disorders in children. *Journal of the American Academy of Child and Adolescent Psychiatry*, 42, 331–339.

Murphy, E. & Carr, A. (2000). Paediatric pain problems. In A. Carr (Ed.), *What Works with Children and Adolescents? A Critical Review of Psychological Interventions with Children, Adolescents and their Families* (pp. 258–279). London: Routledge.

Myers, J., Berliner, L., Briere, J. N., Hendrix, C., Jenny, C. & Reid, T. (2002). *APSAC Handbook on Child Maltreatment* (Second Edition). Thousand Oaks, CA: Sage.

Najavitis. L. (2007). Psychosocial treatments for posttraumatic stress disorder. In P. Nathan & J. Gorman (Ed.), *A Guide to Treatments that Work* (Third Edition, pp. 513–530). New York: Oxford University Press.

Nakash-Eisikovits, O., Dierberger, A. & Westen, D. (2002). A multidimensional meta-analysis of pharmacotherapy for bulimia nervosa: summarizing the range of outcomes in controlled clinical trials. *Harvard Review of Psychiatry*, 10(4), 193–211.

Nathan, P. & Gorman, J. (2007). *A Guide to Treatments that Work* (Third Edition). New York: Oxford University Press.

National Breast Cancer Centre and National Cancer Control Initiative. (2003). *Clinical Practice Guidelines for the Psychosocial Care of Adults with Cancer*. Camperdown: National Breast Cancer Centre and National Cancer Control Initiative.

National Comprehensive Cancer Network. (1999). NCCN practice guidelines for the management of psychosocial distress. *Oncology*, 13, 113–147.

National Institute of Mental Health in England (2003). *Personality Disorder: No Longer a Diagnosis of Exclusion*. Leeds: National Institute of Mental Health in England (http://www.dh.gov.uk/prod_consum_dh/groups/dh_digitalassets/@dh/@en/documents/digitalasset/dh_4054230.pdf).

National Organization for the Treatment of Abusers. http://www.nota.co.uk/.

National Research Council (2001). *Educating Children with Autism*. Washington, DC: National Academy Press.

Nau, S., McCrae, C., Cook, K. & Lichstein, K. (2005). Treatment of insomnia in older adults. *Clinical Psychology Review*, 25, 645–672.

Neal, M. & Barton-Wright, P. (2003). Validation therapy for dementia. *Cochrane Database of Systematic Reviews*, Issue 1. Art. No.: CD001394. DOI: 10.1002/14651858.CD001394.

Neill, J. (2003). Reviewing and benchmarking adventure therapy outcomes: applications of meta-analysis. *Journal of Experiential Education*, 25(3), 316–321.

Nemeroff, C. B. & Schatzberg, A. F. (2007). Pharmacological treatments for unipolar depression. In P. Nathan & J. Gorman (Eds.), *A Guide to Treatments that Work* (Third Edition, pp. 271–288). New York: Oxford University Press.

Nestoriuc, Y. & Martin, A. (2007). Efficacy of biofeedback for migraine: a meta-analysis. *Pain*, 128(1–2), 111–127.

Newman, M., Crits-Christoph, P., Connoly Gibbons, M. & Erickson, T. (2006a). Participant factors in treating anxiety disorders. In L. Castonguay & L. Beutler (Eds.), *Principles of Therapeutic Change that Work* (pp. 121–154). Oxford: Oxford University Press.

Newman, M., Stiles, W., Woody, S. & Janeck, A. (2006b). Integration of therapeutic factors in anxiety disorders. In L. Castonguay & L. Beutler (Eds.), *Principles of Therapeutic Change that Work* (pp. 187–202). Oxford: Oxford University Press.

New Zealand Guidelines Group (2002). *Cardiac Rehabilitation*. Wellington: NZGG (http://www.nzgg.org.nz/guidelines/0001/cardiac_rehabilitation.pdf).

Nezu, A. & Nezu, C. (2007). *Evidence-Based Outcome Research: A Practical Guide to Conducting Randomized Controlled Trials for Psychosocial Interventions*. New York: Oxford University Press.

NICE (2002a). *Nicotine Replacement Therapy (NRT) and Bupropion for Smoking Cessation*. London: National Institute of Clinical Excellence.

NICE (2002b). *Guidance on the Use of Computerized Cognitive Behavioural Therapy for Anxiety and Depression*. London: NICE.

NICE (2003). *Schizophrenia: Full National Clinical Guidelines on Core Interventions in Primary and Secondary Care*. London: Gaskell Press.

NICE (2004a). *Depression: Management of Depression in Primary and Secondary Care*. London: National Institute for Clinical Excellence.

NICE (2004b). *Self-Harm: The Short-Term Physical and Psychological Management and Secondary Prevention of Self-Harm in Primary and Secondary Care*. London: National Institute for Clinical Excellence.

NICE (2004c). *Guidance on Cancer Services: Improving Supportive and Palliative Care for Adults with Cancer. The Manual*. London: National Institute for Clinical Excellence.

NICE (2004d). *Eating Disorders: Core Interventions in the Treatment and Management of Anorexia Nervosa, Bulimia Nervosa and Related Eating Disorders. A National Clinical Practice Guideline*. London: National Institute for Clinical Excellence.

NICE (2004e). *Type 1 Diabetes: Diagnosis and Management of Type 1 Diabetes in Children and Young People*. London: National Institute for Clinical Excellence.

NICE (2005a). *Obsessive Compulsive Disorder: Core Interventions in the Treatment of Obsessive Compulsive Disorder and Body Dysmorphic Disorder*. London: National Institute for Clinical Excellence.

NICE (2005b). *Post-Traumatic Stress Disorder: The Management of PTSD in Adults and Children in Primary and Secondary Care*. London: Gaskell & The British Psychological Society.

NICE (2006). *Bipolar Disorder: The Management of Bipolar Disorder in Adults,*

Children and Adolescents, in Primary and Secondary Care. London: National Insitute for Clinical Excellence.

NICE (2007a). *Anxiety (Amended): Management of Anxiety (Panic Disorder, with and without Agoraphobia, and Generalized Anxiety Disorder) in Adults in Primary, Secondary and Community Care.* London: National Insitute for Clinical Excellence.

NICE (2007b). *Drug Misuse: Psychosocial Interventions.* London: National Insitute for Clinical Excellence.

NICE (2007c). *Dementia: The NICE-SCIE Guideline on Supporting People with Dementia and their Carers in Health and Social Care.* London: National Insitute for Clinical Excellence.

Nichols, S., Hupp, S., Jewell, J. & Zeigler, C. (2005). Review of social story interventions for children diagnosed with autism spectrum disorders. *Journal of Evidence-Based Practices for Schools*, 6 (1), 90–120.

Nixon, R. (2002). Treatment of behaviour problems in preschoolers: a review of parent training programs. *Clinical Psychology Review*, 22, 525–546.

Nock, M. (2003). Progress review of the psychosocial treatment of child conduct problems. *Clinical Psychology: Science and Practice*, 10, 1–28.

Norcross, J. (2002). *Psychotherapy Relationships that Work.* Oxford: Oxford University Press.

Norcross, J. (2005). The psychotherapist's own psychotherapy: educating and developing psychologists. *American Psychologist*, 60(8), 840–850.

Norcross, J., Beutler, L. & Levant, R. (2006). *Evidence-Based Practices in Mental Health: Debate and Dialogue on the Fundamental Questions.* Washington, DC: American Psychological Association.

Norcross, J. & Goldfried, M. (Eds.) (2003). *Handbook of Psychotherapy Integration* (Second Edition). New York: Basic Books.

Norcross, J., Santrock, J., Campbell, L., Smith, T., Sommer, R. & Zuckerman, E. (2003). *Authoritative Guide to Self-Help Resources in Mental Health.* New York: Guilford Press.

Nordhus, I. & Pallesen, S. (2003). Psychological treatment of late-life anxiety: an empirical review. *Journal of Consulting and Clinical Psychology*, 71(4), 643–651.

Norris, A. (1986). *Reminiscence with Elderly People.* London: Winslow.

Norton, P. & Price, E. (2007). A meta-analytic review of adult cognitive-behavioural treatment outcome across the anxiety disorders. *Journal of Nervous and Mental Disease*, 195(6), 521–531.

Nowinski, J., Baker, S. & Carroll, K. (1994). *Twelve Step Facilitation Therapy Manual: A Clinical Research Guide for Therapists Treating Individuals with Alcohol Abuse and Dependence.* Rockville, MD: NIAAA.

Ntais, C., Pakos, E., Kyzas, P. & Ioannidis, J. (2005). Benzodiazepines for alcohol withdrawal. *Cochrane Database of Systematic Reviews*, Issue 3. Art. No.: CD005063. DOI: 10.1002/14651858.CD005063.pub2.

O'Brien, C. & McKay, J. (2007). Psychopharmacological treatments for substance use disorders. In P. Nathan & J. Gorman (Eds.), *A Guide to Treatments that Work* (Third Edition, pp. 145–178). New York: Oxford University Press.

O'Connor, J., Brault, K., Robillard, S., Loiselle, J., Borgeat, F. & Stip, E. (2001). Evaluation of a cognitive-behavioural program for the management of chronic tic and habit disorders. *Behaviour Research and Therapy*, 39, 667–681.

Odom, S. L., Brown, W. H., Frey, T., Karasu, N., Smith-Canter, L. L. & Strain, P. S. (2003). Evidence-based practices for young children with autism: contributions from single-subject design research. *Focus on Autism and Other Developmental Disabilities*, 18, 166–175.

O'Farrell, T. & Fals-Stewart, W. (2003). Alcohol abuse. *Journal of Marital and Family Therapy*, 29 (1), 121–146.

O'Farrell, T. & Fals-Stewart, W. (2006). *Behavioural Couples Therapy for Alcoholism and Substance Abuse*. New York: Guilford Press.

O'Halloran, M. & Carr, A. (2000). Adjustment to parental separation and divorce. In A. Carr (Ed.), *What Works with Children and Adolescents? A Critical Review of Psychological Interventions with Children, Adolescents and their Families* (pp. 280–299). London: Routledge.

Olfson, M., Shaffer, D., Marcus, S. C. & Greenberg, T. (2003). Relationship between antidepressant medication treatment and suicide in adolescents. *Archives of General Psychiatry*, 60, 978–982.

Onder, G., Zanetti, O., Giacobini, E., Frisoni, G., Bartorelli, L. & Carbone, G. (2005). Reality orientation therapy combined with cholinesterase inhibitors in Alzheimer's disease: randomised controlled trial. *British Journal of Psychiatry*, 187, 450–455.

O'Reilly, G., Marshall, W., Carr, A. & Beckett, R. (2005). *Handbook of Clinical Intervention with Young People who Sexually Abuse*. London: Routledge.

Orlinsky, D., Tonnestad, M. & Willutzki, U. (2004). Fifty years of psychotherapy process–outcome research: continuity and change. In M. Lambert (Ed.), *Bergin and Garfield's Handbook of Psychotherapy and Behaviour Change* (Fifth Edition, pp. 307–389). New York: Wiley.

Orrell, M., Spector, A., Thorgrimsen, L. & Woods, B. (2005). A pilot study examining the effectiveness of maintenance Cognitive Stimulation Therapy (MCST) for people with dementia. *International Journal of Geriatric Psychiatry*, 20, 446–451.

Osborn, R., Demoncada, A. & Feuerstein, M. (2006). Psychosocial interventions for depression, anxiety, and quality of life in cancer survivors: meta-analyses. *International Journal of Psychiatry in Medicine*, 36(1), 13–34.

Oster, I., Svensk, A., Magnusson, E., Thyme, K., Sjodin, M., Astron, S. & Lindh, J. (2006). Art therapy improves coping resources: a randomized, controlled study among women with breast cancer. *Palliative and Supportive Care*, 4, 57–64.

Otto, M. W., Smits, J. A. & Reese, H. E. (2005). Combined psychotherapy and pharmacotherapy for mood and anxiety disorders in adults: review and analysis. *Clinical Psychology: Science and Practice*, 12, 72–86.

Overcoming Depression. http://www.calipso.co.uk/mainframe.htm.

Ozechowski, T. J. & Liddle, H. A. (2000). Family-based therapy for adolescent drug abuse: knowns and unknowns. *Clinical Child & Family Psychology Review*, 3, 269–298.

Ozonoff, S. & Cathcart, K. (1998). Effectiveness of a home program intervention for young children with autism. *Journal of Autism & Developmental Disorders*, 28, 25–32.

Padwal, R., Li, S. K. & Lau, D. C. W. (2003). Long-term pharmacotherapy for overweight and obesity: a systematic review and meta-analysis of randomised control trials. *International Journal of Obesity*, 27, 1437–1446.

Pallesen, S., Mitsem, M., Kvale, G., Johnsen, B. & Moide, H. (2005). Outcome of psychological treatments of pathological gambling: a review and meta-analysis. *Addiction*, 100, 1412–1422.

Pallesen, S., Moide, H., Arnestad, H., Laberg, J., Skutle, A., Iversen, E., Stoylen, I., Kvale, G. & Holsten, F. (2007). Outcome of pharmacological treatments of pathological gambling: a review and meta-analysis. *Journal of Clinical Psychopharmacology*, 27(4), 357–364.

Pallesen, S., Nordhus, I. & Kvale, G. (1998). Nonpharmacological interventions for insomnia in older adults: a meta-analysis of treatment efficacy. *Psychotherapy: Theory, Research, Practice, Training*, 35(4), 472–482.

Panerai, S., Ferrante, L., Caputo, V. & Impellizzeri, C. (1998). Use of structured teaching for treatment of children with autism and severe and profound mental retardation. *Education and Training in Mental Retardation and Developmental Disabilities*, 33, 367–374.

Panerai, S., Ferrante, L. & Zingale, M. (2002). Benefits of the Treatment and Education of Autistic and Communication Handicapped Children (TEACCH) programme as compared with a non-specific approach. *Journal of Intellectual Disability Research*, 46, 318–327.

Park, E., Tudiver, F., Schultz, J. & Campbell, T. (2004). Does enhancing partner support and interaction improve smoking cessation: a meta analysis. *Annals of Family Medicine*, 2, 170–174.

Patterson, G. (1976). *Living with Children*. Champaign, Il: Research Press.

Paul, G. (1967). Strategy of outcome research in psychotherapy. *Journal of Consulting Psychology*, 31, 109–118.

Paul, R. & Sutherland, D. (2005). Enhancing early language in children with autism spectrum disorders. In F. Volkmar, R. Paul, A. Klin & D. Cohen (Eds.), *Handbook of Autism and Pervasive Developmental Disorders* (Third Edition, Vol. 2, pp. 946–976). New York: Wiley.

Pavuluri, M., Birmaher, B. & Naylor, M. (2005). Pediatric bipolar disorder: 10-year review. *Journal of the American Academy of Child and Adolescent Psychiatry*, 44, 846–871.

Pavuluri, M., Grazyk, P., Henry, D., Carbray, J., Heidenreich, J. & Miklowitz, D. (2004). Child- and family-focused cognitive behavioural therapy for paediatric bipolar disorder: development and preliminary results. *Journal of the American Academy of Child and Adolescent Psychiatry*, 43(5), 528–537.

Paykina, N., Greenhill, L. & Gorman, J. (2007). Pharmacological treatments for attention-deficit hyperactivity disorder. In P. Nathan & J. Gorman (Eds.), *A Guide to Treatments that Work* (Third Edition, pp. 29–70). New York: Oxford University Press.

Pedersen, M. & Hesse, M. (2007). Residential treatment in Denmark: client characteristics and retention. *Therapeutic Communities: International Journal for Therapeutic and Supportive Organizations*, 28(2), 206–217.

Pedro-Carroll, J. & Jones, S. (2005). A preventive play intervention to foster children's resilience in the aftermath of divorce. In L. Reddy, T. Files-Hall & C. Schaefer (Eds.), *Empirically Based Play Interventions for Children* (pp. 51–75). Washington, DC: American Psychological Association.

Peet, M. & Harvey, N. (1991). Lithium maintenance: 1. A standard education programme for patients. *British Journal of Psychiatry*, 158, 197–200.

Pelchat, D., Bisson, J., Ricard, N., Perreault, M. & Bouchard, J. M. (1999). Longitudinal effects of an early family intervention programme on the adaptation of parents of children with a disability. *International Journal of Nursing Studies*, 36, 465–477.

Peleikis, D. & Dahl, A. (2005). A systematic review of empirical studies of psychotherapy with women who were sexually abused as children. *Psychotherapy Research*, 15(3), 304–315.

Pelham, W., Fabiano, G., Gnagy, E., Greiner, A. & Hoza, B. (2005). The role of summer treatment programs in the context of comprehensive treatment for attention deficit hyperactivity disorder. In E. Hibbs & P Jensen (Eds.), *Psychosocial Treatments for Child and Adolescent Disorders: Empirically Based Strategies for Clinical Practice* (Second Edition, pp. 377–409). Washington, DC: American Psychological Association (http://www.smbs.buffalo.edu/CENTERS/adhd/default.php).

Perez, R., Debord, K. & Bieschke, K. (1999). *Handbook of Counselling and Psychotherapy with Lesbian, Gay, and Bisexual Clients*. Washington, DC; American Psychological Association.

Perkins, K., Conklin, C. & Levine, M. (2007). *Cognitive Behaviour Therapy for Smoking Cessation: A Practical Guidebook to the Most Effective Treatments*. London: Routledge.

Perry, A., Tarrier, N., Morriss, R., McCarthy, E. & Limb, K. (1999). Randomised controlled trial of efficacy of teaching patients with bipolar disorder to identify early symptoms of relapse and obtain treatment. *British Medical Journal*, 16, 149–153.

Perry, C., Banon, E. & Ianni, F. (1999). Effectiveness of psychotherapy for personality disorders. *American Journal of Psychiatry*, 156, 1312–1321.

Persons, J., Davidson, J. & Tomkins, M. (2001). *Essential Components of Cognitive Behaviour Therapy for Depression*. Washington, DC: American Psychological Association.

Petrosino, A., Turpin-Petrosino, C. & Buehler, J. (2003). 'Scared Straight' and other juvenile awareness programs for preventing juvenile delinquency. *Annals of the American Academy of Political and Social Science*, 589, 41–62.

Pfammatter, M., Junghan, U. & Brenner, H. (2006). Efficacy of psychological therapy in schizophrenia: conclusions from meta-analyses. *Schizophrenia Bulletin*, 32(Suppl1), S64–S80.

Pharoah, F., Mari, J., Rathbone, J. & Wong, W. (2006) Family intervention for schizophrenia. *Cochrane Database of Systematic Reviews*, Issue 2. Art. No.: CD000088. DOI: 10.1002/14651858.CD000088.pub2.

Phillips, K. (2005). *The Broken Mirror: Understanding and Treating Body Dysmorphic Disorder*. New York: Oxford University Press.

Pike, K., Walsh, B., Vitousek, K., Wilson, G. & Bauer, J. (2003). Cognitive behaviour therapy in the posthospitalization treatment of anorexia nervosa. *American Journal of Psychiatry*, 160, 2046–2049.

Pilkington, K., Kirkwood, G. & Rampes, H. (2005). Yoga for depression: the research evidence. *Journal of Affective Disorders*, 89, 13–24.

Pilling, S., Bebbington, P., Kuipers, E., Garety, P., Geddes, J., Orbach, G. & Morgan, C. (2002a). Psychological treatments in schizophrenia: I. Meta-analysis of family intervention and cognitive behaviour therapy. *Psychological Medicine*, 32(5), 763–782.

Pilling, S., Bebbington, P., Kuipers, E., Garety, P., Geddes, J., Martidale, B., Orbach, G.

& Morgan, C. (2002b). Psychological treatments in schizophrenia: II. Meta-analyses of randomized controlled trials of social skills training and cognitive remediation. *Psychological Medicine*, 32, 783–791.

Pinquart, M. & Duberstein, P. (2007). Treatment of anxiety disorders in older adults: a meta-analytic comparison of behavioural and pharmacological interventions. *American Journal of Geriatric Psychiatry*, 15, 639–651.

Pinquart, M., Duberstein, P. & Lyness, J. (2006). Treatments for later-life depressive conditions: a meta-analytic comparison of pharmacotherapy and psychotherapy. *American Journal of Psychiatry*, 163, 1493–1501.

Pinquart, M. & Sorensen, S. (2006). Helping caregivers of persons with dementia: which interventions work and how large are their effects? *International Psychogeriatrics*, 18(4), 577–595.

Pitschel-Walz, G., Leucht, S., Bäuml, J., Kissling, W. & Engel, R. (2001). The effect of family interventions on relapse and rehospitalization in schizophrenia – a meta-analysis. *Schizophrenia Bulletin*, 27(1), 73–92.

Platt, J. (1995). Vocational rehabilitation of drug abusers. *Psychological Bulletin*, 117, 416–433.

Powers, S. (1999). Empirically-supported treatments in paediatric psychology: procedure-related pain. *Journal of Paediatric Psychology*, 24, 131–145.

Prendergast, M., Podus, D., Chang, E. & Urada, D. (2002). The effectiveness of drug abuse treatment: a meta-analysis of comparison group studies. *Drug and Alcohol Dependence*, 67, 53–72.

Prendergast, M., Podus, D., Finney, J., Greenwell, L. & Roll, J. (2006). Contingency management for treatment of substance use disorders: a meta-analysis. *Addiction*, 101, 1546–1560.

Pretlow, R. (1999). Treatment of nocturnal enuresis with an ultrasound bladder volume controlled alarm device. *Journal of Urology*, 162, 1224–1228.

Prizant, B. & Wetherby, A. (2005). Critical issues in enhancing communication abilities for persons with autism spectrum disorders. In F. Volkmar, R. Paul, A. Klin & D. Cohen (Eds.), *Handbook of Autism and Pervasive Developmental Disorders* (Third Edition, Vol. 2, pp. 925–945). New York: Wiley.

Prochaska, J. & DiClemente, C. (2003). The transtheoretical approach. In J. Norcross & M. Goldfried (Eds.), *Handbook of Psychotherapy Integration* (Second Edition, pp. 147–171). New York: Basic Books.

Prochaska, J. & Norcross, J. (2002). Stages of change. In J. Norcross (Ed.), *Psychotherapy Relationships that Work* (pp. 303–313). Oxford: Oxford University Press.

Project MATCH Research Group. (1998). Matching alcoholism treatments to client heterogeneity: Project MATCH three year drinking outcomes. *Alcoholism: Clinical and Experimental Research*, 22(6), 1300–1311.

Prout, H. & Nowak-Drabik, K. (2003). Psychotherapy with persons who have mental retardation: an evaluation of effectiveness. *American Journal on Mental Retardation*, 108(2), 82–93.

Puetz, T., O'Connor, P. & Dishman, R. (2006). Effects of chronic exercise on feelings of energy and fatigue: a quantitative synthesis. *Psychological Bulletin*, 132(6), 866–876.

Purdie, N., Hattie, J. & Carroll, A. (2002). A review of the research on interventions for attention deficit hyperactivity disorder: which treatment works best. *Review of Educational Research*, 72, 61–100.

Pusey, H. & Richards, D. (2001). A systematic review of the effectiveness of psycho-social interventions for carers of people with dementia. *Aging & Mental Health*, 5(2), 107–119.

Putnam, F. (2003). Ten-year research update review: child sexual abuse. *Journal of the American Academy of Child and Adolescent Psychiatry*, 42(3), 269–278.

Quinn, M., Carr, A., Carroll, L. & O'Sullivan, D. (2007). Parents Plus Programme 1. Evaluation of its effectiveness for preschool children with developmental dis-abilities and behavioural problems. *Journal of Applied Research in Intellectual Disabilities*, 20, 345–359.

Rains, J. C., Penzien, D. B., McCrory, D. C. & Gray, R. N. (2005). Behavioural headache treatment: history, review of the empirical literature, and methodological critique. *Headache*, 45, 92–109.

Ramchandani, P. & Jones, D. (2003). Treating psychological symptoms in sexually abused children: from research findings to service provision. *British Journal of Psychiatry*, 183, 484–490.

Ramchandani, P., Wiggs, L., Webb, V. & Stores, G. (2000). A systematic review of treat-ments for settling problems and night waking in young children. *British Medical Journal*, 320, 209–213.

RANZCP Clinical Practice Guidelines Team for Anorexia Nervosa (2004). Australian and New Zealand clinical practice guidelines for the treatment of anorexia ner-vosa. *Australian and New Zealand Journal of Psychiatry*, 38, 659–670.

Rapoport, J. & Inoff-Germain, G. (2000). Practitioner review: treatment of obsessive compulsive disorder in children and adolescents. *Journal of Child Psychology and Psychiatry*, 41, 419–431.

Rapport, M. & Moffitt, C. (2002). Attention deficit /hyperactivity disorder and meth-ylphenidate: a review of height/weight, cardiovascular, and somatic complaint side effects. *Clinical Psychology Review*, 22, 1107–1131.

Rathus, J. & Miller, A. (2002). Dialectical behaviour therapy adapted for suicidal adolescents. *Suicide and Life Threatening Behaviour*, 32, 146–157.

Rawson, R., Marinelli-Casey, P., Anglin, M., Dickow, A., Frazier, Y., Gallagher, C., Galloway, G., Herrell, J., Huber, A., McCann, M., Obert, J., Pennell, S., Reiber, C., Vandersloot, D. & Zweben, J. (2004). A multi-site comparison of psychosocial approaches for the treatment of methamphetamine dependence. *Addiction*, 99, 708–717.

Rawson, R., Obert, J. & McCann, M. (1995). *The Matrix Intensive Outpatient Program Therapist Manual*. Los Angeles, CA: Matrix Center (http://www.matrixinstitute.org/).

Ray, D., Bratton, S., Rhine, T. & Jones, L. (2001). The effectiveness of play ther-apy: responding to the critics. *International Journal of Play Therapy*, 10(1), 85–108.

Rea, M. M., Tompson, M. C., Miklowitz, D. J., Goldstein, M. J., Hwang, S. & Mintz, J. (2003). Family-focused treatment versus individual treatment for bipolar disorders and suicide disorder: results of a randomized clinical trial. *Journal of Consulting & Clinical Psychology*, 71(3), 482–492.

Rector, N. & Beck, A. (2001). Cognitive behavioural therapy for schizophrenia: an empirical review. *Journal of Nervous and Mental Disorders*, 189, 278–287.

Reddy, L., Files-Hall, T. & Svhaefer, C. (2005). *Empirically-Based Play Interventions for Children*. Washington, DC: American Psychological Association.

Reed, J. & Ones, D. (2006). The effect of acute aerobic exercise on positive activated affect: a meta-analysis. *Psychology of Sport and Exercise*, 7(5), 477–514.

Reeker, J., Ensing, D. & Elliott, R. (1997). A meta-analytic investigation of group treatment outcomes for sexually abused children. *Child Abuse & Neglect*, 21(7), 669–680.

Rees, K., Bennett, P., West, R., Davey Smith, G. & Ebrahim, S. (2004). Psychological interventions for coronary heart disease. *Cochrane Database of Systematic Reviews* 2004, Issue 2. Art. No.: CD002902.pub2. DOI: 10.1002/14651858.CD002902.pub2.

Regehr, C. & Sussman, T. (2004). Intersections between grief and trauma: towards an empirically based model for treating traumatic grief. *Brief Treatment and Crisis Intervention*, 4, 289–309.

Reid, W. J. (1997). Evaluating the Dodo's verdict: do all interventions have equivalent outcomes? *Social Work Research*, 21, 5–16.

Reinecke, M., Ryan, N. & Dubois, D. (1998). Cognitive-behavioural therapy of depression and depressive symptoms during adolescence: a review and meta-analysis. *Journal of the American Academy of Child and Adolescent Psychiatry*, 37(1), 26–34.

Reitzel, L. & Carbonell, J. (2006). The effectiveness of sexual offender treatment for juveniles as measured by recidivism: a meta-analysis. *Sexual Abuse: A Journal of Research and Treatment*, 18(4), 401–421.

Reitzel, L., Stellrecht, N., Gordon, K., Lima, E., Wingate, L., Brown, J., Wolfe, A., Zenoz, L. & Joiner, T. (2006). Does time between application and case assignment predict therapy attendance or premature termination? *Psychological Services*, 3(1), 51–60.

Renshaw, K. D., Steketee, G. & Chambless, D. L. (2005). Involving family members in the treatment of OCD. *Cognitive Behaviour Therapy*, 34, 164–175.

Research Units on Paediatric Psychopharmacology Autism Network (2005). Randomized, controlled, crossover trial of methylphenidate in pervasive developmental disorders with hyperactivity. *Archives of General Psychiatry*, 62, 1266–1274.

Reyno, S. & McGrath, P. (2006). Predictors of parent training efficacy for child externalizing behaviour problem – a meta-analytic review. *Journal of Child Psychology and Psychiatry*, 47(1), 9–111.

Reynolds, C., Frank, E. & Perel, J. (1999). Nortriptyline and interpersonal psychotherapy as maintenance therapies for recurrent major depression: a randomized controlled trial in patients older than 59 years. *Journal of the American Medical Association*, 281(1), 39–45.

Reynolds, M., Nabors, L. & Quinlan, A. (2000). The effectiveness of art therapy: does it work? *Art Therapy*, 17, 207–213.

Richter, R., Loew, T., Calatzis, A. & Krause, S. (2002). Depth-psychological orientated psychotherapy: controlled efficacy trials in psychodynamic psychotherapy/ Kontrollierte Wirksamkeitsstudien zur Psychodynamischen Psychotherapie: Tiefenpsychologisch fundierte Psychotherapie. *PDP Psychodynamische Psychotherapie: Forum der tiefenpsychologisch fundierten Psychotherapie*, 1(1), 19–36.

Ritter, M. & Graff-Low, K. (1996). Effects of dance/movement therapy: a meta-analysis. *The Arts in Psychotherapy*, 23(3), 249–260.

Ritterband, L. M., Cox, D. J., Walker, L. S., Kovatchev, B., McKnight, L. & Patel, K. (2003). An internet intervention as adjunctive therapy for paediatric encopresis. *Journal of Consulting & Clinical Psychology*, 71, 910–917.

Ritz, T. (2001). Relaxation therapy in adult asthma: is there new evidence for its effectiveness? *Behaviour Modification*, 25, 640–666.

Ritz, T., Datane, B. & Roth, W. T. (2004). Behavioural interventions in asthma: biofeedback techniques. *Journal of Psychosomatic Research*, 56, 711–720.

Roberts, A. R. & Everly, G. S. (2006). A meta-analysis of 36 crisis intervention studies. *Brief Treatment and Crisis Intervention: A Journal of Evidence-Based Practice*, 6, 10–21.

Robin, A. & Foster, S. (1989). *Negotiating Parent–Adolescent Conflict*. New York: Guilford Press.

Robins, C. & Chapman, A. (2004). Dialectical behaviour therapy: current status, recent developments, and future directions. *Journal of Personality Disorders*, 18, 73–89.

Robins, P., Smith, S., Glutting, J. & Bishop, C. (2005). A randomized controlled trial of a cognitive-behavioural family intervention for paediatric recurrent abdominal pain. *Journal of Paediatric Psychology*, 30, 397–408.

Rodebaugh, T., Holaway, T. & Heimberg, R. (2004). The treatment of social anxiety disorder. *Clinical Psychology Review*, 24, 883–908.

Roder, V., Muelle, D., Mueser, K. & Brenner, H. (2006). Integrated psychological therapy (IPT) for schizophrenia: is it effective? *Schizophrenia Bulletin*, 32(Suppl1), S81–S93.

Rodgers, M., Fayter, D., Richardson, G., Ritchie, G., Lewin, R. & Sowden, A. (2005). *The Effects of Psychosocial Interventions in Cancer and Heart Disease: A Review of Systematic Reviews*. York: Centre for Reviews and Dissemination.

Rogers, C. (1954). The case of Mrs Oak: a research analysis. In C. Rogers & R. Dymond (Eds.), *Psychotherapy and Personality Change* (pp. 259–348). Chicago: Chicago University Press.

Rogers, S. (2000). Interventions that facilitate socialization in children with autism. *Journal of Autism and Developmental Disorders*, 30(5), 399–409.

Rogers, S. (2006). Evidence-based interventions for language development in young children with autism. In T. Charman & W. Stone (Eds.), *Social & Communication Development in Autism Spectrum Disorders: Early Identification, Diagnosis, and Intervention* (pp. 143–179). New York: Guilford Press.

Rohde, P., Lewinsohn, P., Clarke, G., Hops, H. & Seeley, J. (2005). The adolescent coping with depression course: a cognitive behaviour approach to the treatment of adolescent depression. In E. Hibbs & P. Jensen (Eds.), *Psychosocial Treatments for Child and Adolescent Disorders: Empirically Based Strategies for Clinical Practice* (Second Edition, pp. 219–237). Washington, DC: American Psychological Association.

Roozen, H., Boulogne, J., Tulder, M., van den Brink, W., De Jong, C. & Kerkhof, A. (2004). A systematic review of the effectiveness of the community reinforcement approach in alcohol, cocaine and opioid addiction. *Drug and Alcohol Dependence*, 74, 1–13.

Rosen, G. & Davison, G. (2003). Psychology should list empirically supported principles of change (ESPs) and not credential trademarked therapies or other treatment packages. *Behaviour Modification*. [Special Issue]: *Empirically Supported Treatments*, 27(3), 300–312.

Rosenthal, R. (1994). Parametric measures of effect size. In H. Cooper & L. Hedges (Eds.), *The Handbook of Research Synthesis* (pp. 231–260). New York: Sage.

Rosenthal, R. & Rubin, D. (1982). A simple, general purpose display of magnitude of experimental effect. *Journal of Educational Psychology*, 74, 166–196.

Rosenzweig, S. (1936). Some implicit common factors in diverse methods of psychotherapy: 'At last the Dodo bird said, "Everybody has won and all must have prizes." ' *American Journal of Orthopsychiatry*, 6, 412–415.

Rossello, J. & Bernal, G. (2005). New developments in cognitive behavioural and interpersonal treatments for depressed Puerto Rican adolescents. In E. Hibbs & P. Jensen (Eds.), *Psychosocial Treatments for Child and Adolescent Disorders: Empirically Based Strategies for Clinical Practice* (Second Edition, pp. 187–218). Washington, DC: American Psychological Association.

Rossy, L., Buckelew, S., Dorr, N., Hagglund, K., Thayer, J., McIntosh, M., Hewett, J. & Johnson, J. (1999). A meta-analysis of fibromyalgia treatment interventions. *Annals of Behavioural Medicine*, 21(2), 180–191.

Roth, T. & Fonagy, P. (2005). *What Works for Whom? A Critical Review of Psychotherapy Research* (Second Edition). New York: Guilford Press.

Rotheram-Borus, M. (1998). *Intervention Manuals for Project TALC (Teens and Adults Learning to Communicate) Parents Living with AIDS*. Los Angeles: UCLA Semel Institute Centre for Community Health (http://chipts.ucla.edu/interventions/manuals/intervhra1.html).

Rotheram-Borus, M., Lee, M., Gwadz, M. & Draimin, B. (2001). An intervention for parents with AIDS and their adolescent children. *American Journal of Public Health*, 91, 1294–1302.

Rotheram-Borus, M., Lee, M., Leonard, N., Lin, Y., Franzke, L. & Turner, E. (2003). Four-year behavioural outcomes of an intervention for parents living with HIV and their adolescent children. *AIDS*, 17(8), 1217–1225.

Rotheram-Borus, M., Lee, M., Leonard, N., Lin, Y., Franzke, L. & Turner, E. (2006a). Intergenerational benefits of family-based HIV interventions. *Journal of Consulting and Clinical Psychology*, 74(3), 622–627.

Rotheram-Borus, M., Lee, M., Lin, Y. & Lester, P. (2004). Six-year intervention outcomes for adolescent children of parents with the human immunodeficiency virus. *Archives of Paediatrics & Adolescent Medicine*, 158(8), 742–748.

Rotheram-Borus, M., Piacentini, J., Cantwell, C., Belin, T. & Juwon, S. (2000). The 18-month impact of an emergency room intervention for adolescent female suicide attempters. *Journal of Consulting & Clinical Psychology*, 68, 1081–1093.

Rotheram-Borus, M., Stein, J. & Lester, P. (2006b). Adolescent adjustment over six years in HIV-affected families. *Journal of Adolescent Health*, 39(2), 174–182.

Rowe, C., Gómez, L. & Liddle, H. (2005). Family therapy research: empirical foundations and practice implications. In M. Nichols & R. Schwartz (Eds.), *Family Therapy: Concepts and Methods* (Seventh Edition). Boston, MA: Allyn & Bacon.

Rowe, C. & Liddle, H. (2003) Substance abuse. *Journal of Marital and Family Therapy*, 29, 86–120.

Roy-Byrne, P. & Cowley, D. (2007). Pharmacological treatments for panic disorder, generalized anxiety disorder, specific phobia, and social anxiety disorder. In P. Nathan & J. Gorman (Eds.), *A Guide to Treatments that Work* (Third Edition, pp. 395–430). New York: Oxford University Press.

Rush, J. & Frances, A. (2000). Expert consensus guidelines for treatment of psychiatric and behavioural problems in mental retardation. *American Journal on Mental Retardation*, 105(3), 159–228.

Ryle, A. (1990). *Cognitive-Analytic Therapy: Active Participation in Change.* Chichester: Wiley.

Ryle, A. (2003). Cognitive analytic therapy. In J. Norcross & M. Goldfried (Eds.), *Handbook of Psychotherapy Integration* (Second Edition, pp. 196–220). New York: Basic Books.

Sackett, D., Rosenberg, W., Gray, J., Haynes, R. & Richardson, W. (1996). Evidence based medicine: what it is and what it isn't. *British Medical Journal*, 312, 71–72.

Sackett, D., Straus, S., Richardson, W., Rosenberg, W. & Haynes, R. (2000). *Evidence Based Medicine: How to Practice and Teach EBM* (Second Edition). London: Churchill Livingstone.

Saigh, P., Brasssard, M. & Peverly, S. (2004). Cognitive-behavioural interventions for children and adolescents with PTSD. In S. Taylor (Ed.), *Advances in the Treatment of Posttraumatic Stress Disorder: Cognitive-Behavioural Perspectives* (pp. 243–263). New York: Springer.

Sajatovic, M., Davies, M. & Hrouda, D. (2004). Enhancement of treatment adherence among patients with bipolar disorder. *Psychiatric Services*, 55, 264–269.

Sallee, F., Nesbitt, L., Jackson, C., Sine, L. & Sethuraman, G. (1997). Relative efficacy of haloperidol and pimozide in children and adolescents with Tourette's disorder. *American Journal of Psychiatry*, 154, 1057–1062.

Sallows, G. & Graupner, T. (2005). Intensive behavioural treatment for children with autism: four-year outcome and predictors. *American Journal on Mental Retardation*, 110(6), 417–438.

Salmon, P. (2001). Effects of physical exercise on anxiety, depression, and sensitivity to stress: a unifying theory. *Clinical Psychology Review*, 21, 33–61.

Sandell, R., Blomberg, J. & Lazar, A. (1999). Reported long-term follow-up of long-term psychotherapies and psychoanalyses: first results of the Stockholm Outcome of Psychotherapy (STOP) project. *Zeitschrift für Psychosomatische Medizin und Psychoanalyse*, 45, 43–56.

Sanders, M., Markie-Dadds, C. & Turner, K. (1998a). *Facilitator's Kit for Enhanced Triple P.* Brisbane: Families International (http://www.pfsc.uq.edu.au/02_ppp/ppp.html).

Sanders, M., Markie-Dadds, C. & Turner, K. (1998b). *Practitioner's Kit for Standard Triple P.* Brisbane: Families International (http://www.pfsc.uq.edu.au/02_ppp/ppp.html).

Sanders, M., Markie-Dadds, C. & Turner, K. (2003). Theoretical, scientific and clinical foundations of the Triple P – Positive Parenting Program: a population approach to the promotion of parenting competence. *Parenting Research and Practice Monograph*, 1, 1–21 (http://www.triplep.net/files/pdf/Parenting_Research_and_Practice_Monograph_No.1.pdf).

Sanders, M., Rebgetz, M., Morrison, M., Bor, W., Gordon, A. & Dadds, M. (1989). Cognitive-behavioural treatment of recurrent non-specific abdominal pain in children: an analysis of generalization, maintenance, and side effects. *Journal of Consulting and Clinical Psychology*, 57, 294–300.

Sanders, M., Shepherd, R., Cleghorn, G. & Woolford, H. (1994). The treatment of recurrent abdominal pain in children: a controlled comparison of cognitive-behavioural family intervention and standard paediatric care. *Journal of Consulting and Clinical Psychology*, 62, 306–314.

Sandler, I., Ayers, T., Wolchik, S., Tein, J., Kwok, O. & Lin, K. (2003). Family bereavement program: efficacy of a theory-based preventive intervention for parentally-bereaved children and adolescents. *Journal of Consulting and Clinical Psychology*, 71, 587–600.

Sandler, I., West, S., Baca, L., Pillow, D., Gersten, J., Rogosch, F., Virdin, L., Beals, J., Reynolds, K., Kallgren, C., Tein, J., Kriege, G., Cole, E. & Ramirez, R. (1992). Linking empirically based theory and evaluation: the family bereavement programme. *American Journal of Community Psychology*, 20, 491–521.

Sanford, M., Boyle, M., McCleary, L., Miller, J., Steele, M., Duku, E. & Offord, D. (2006). A pilot study of adjunctive family psychoeducation in adolescent major depression: feasibility and treatment effect. *Journal of the American Academy of Child and Adolescent Psychiatry*, 45(4), 386–395.

Sansosti, F., Powell-Smith, K. & Kincaid, D. (2004) A research synthesis of social story interventions for children with autism spectrum disorders. *Focus on Autism and Other Developmental Disabilities*, 19(4), 194–204.

Santelli, B., Poyadue, F. S. & Young, J. L. (2001). *The Parent to Parent Handbook: Connecting Families of Children with Special Needs*. Baltimore: Paul H. Brookes.

Santiseban, S., Suarez-Morales, L., Robbins, M. & Szapocznik, J. (2006). Brief strategic family therapy: lessons learned in efficacy research and challenges to blending research and practice. *Family Process*, 45(2), 259–271.

Scahill, L. & Martin, A. (2005). Psychopharmacology. In F. Volkmar, R. Paul, A. Klin & D. Cohen (Eds.), *Handbook of Autism and Pervasive Developmental Disorders* (Third Edition, Vol. 2, pp. 1102–1122). New York: Wiley.

Scahill, L., Leckman, J., Schultz, R., Katsovich, L. & Peterson, B. (2003). A placebo-controlled trial of risperidone in Tourette syndrome. *Neurology*, 60, 1130–1135.

Schachar, R., Jadad, A., Gauld, M., Boyle, M., Booker, L., Snider, A., Kim, M. & Cunningham, C. (2002). Attention deficit-hyperactivity disorder: critical appraisal of extended treatment studies. *Canadian Journal of Psychiatry*, 47, 337–348.

Schmidt, U., Lee, S., Beecham, J., Perkins, S., Treasure, J., Yi, I., Winn, S., Robinson, P., Murphy, R., Keville, S., Johnson-Sabine, E., Jenkins, M., Frost, S., Dodge, L., Berelowitz, M. & Eisler, I. (2007). A randomized controlled trial of family therapy and cognitive behaviour therapy guided self-care for adolescents with bulimia nervosa and related disorders. *American Journal of Psychiatry*, 164, 591–598.

Schneider, L. S., Dagerman, K. & Insel, P. S. (2006). Efficacy and adverse effects of atypical antipsychotics for dementia: meta-analysis of randomized, placebo controlled trials. *American Journal of Geriatric Psychiatry*, 14(3), 191–210.

Schulberg, H., Katon, W., Simon, G. & Rush, A. (1998). Treating major depression in primary care practice: an update of the Agency for Health Care Policy and Research Practice Guidelines. *Archives of General Psychiatry*, 55(12), 1121–1127.

Schulberg, H., Raue, P. & Rollman, B. (2002). The effectiveness of psychotherapy in treating depressive disorders in primary care practice: clinical and cost perspectives. *General Hospital Psychiatry*, 24, 203–212.

Schulz, R., Martire, L. & Klinger, J. (2005). Evidence-based caregiver interventions in geriatric psychiatry. *Psychiatric Clinics of North America*, 28, 1007–1038.

Schulz, R., O'Brien, A., Czaja, S., Ory, M., Norris, R., Martire, L., Belle, S., Burgio, L., Gitlin, L., Coon, D., Burns, R., Gallagher-Thompson, D. & Stevens, A. (2002). Dementia care-giver intervention research: in search of clinical signficance. *Gerontologist*, 42, 589–602.

Schut, H., Stroebe, M., van den Bout, J. & Terheggen, M. (2001). The efficacy of bereavement interventions: determining who benefits. In M. Stroebe, W. Stroebe & R. Hansson (Eds.), *Handbook of Bereavement: Theory, Research, and Intervention* (pp. 705–737). New York: Cambridge University Press.

Scogin, F., Welsh, D., Hanson, A., Stump, J. & Coates, A. (2005). Evidence-based psychotherapies for depression in older adults. *Clinical Psychology: Science and Practice*, 12, 222–237.

Scott, J. & Baldwin, W. (2005). The challenge of early intervention. In D. Zager (Ed.), *Autism Spectrum Disorders: Identification, Education and Treatment* (Third Edition, pp. 173–228). Mahwah, NJ: Lawrence Erlbaum Associates, Inc.

Scott, J., Colom, F. & Vieta, E. (2007). A meta-analysis of adjunctive psychological therapies compared to usual psychiatric treatment for bipolar disorders. *International Journal of Neuropsychopharmacology*, 10(1), 123–129.

Scott, J., Garland, A. & Moorhead, S. (2001). A pilot study of cognitive therapy in bipolar disorders. *Psychological Medicine*, 31, 459–467.

Scott, J., Paykel, E. & Morriss, R. (2006). Cognitive-behavioural therapy for severe and recurrent bipolar disorders: randomised controlled trial. *British Journal of Psychiatry*, 188, 313–320.

Scottish Intercollegiate Guidelines Network (2002). *Cardiac Rehabilitation. A National Guideline*. Edinburgh: Scottish Intercollegiate Guidelines Network (http://www.sign.ac.uk/pdf/sign57.pdf).

Segal, Z., Kennedy, S., Cohen, N. & CANMAT Depression Work Group (2001). Clinical guidelines for the treatment of depressive disorders: V. Combining psychotherapy and pharmacotherapy. *Canadian Journal of Psychiatry*, 46, 59S–62S.

Segal, Z., Williams. M. & Teasdale, J. (2002). *Mindfulness-Based Cognitive Therapy for Depression*. New York: Guilford Press.

Seligman, M. (1995). The effectiveness of psychotherapy: the Consumer Reports Study. *American Psychologist*, 50, 965–974.

Seltzer, A., Roncari, I. & Garfinkel, P. (1980). Effect of patient education on medication compliance. *Canadian Journal of Psychiatry*, 25, 638–645.

Serfaty, M., Turkington, D., Heap, M., Ledsham, L. & Jolley, E. (1999). Cognitive therapy versus dietary counselling in the outpatient treatment of anorexia nervosa: effects of the treatment phase. *European Eating Disorders Review*, 7, 334–350.

Serketich, W. & Dumas, J. (1996). The effectiveness of behavioural parent training to modify antisocial behaviour in children: a meta-analysis. *Behaviour Therapy*, 27, 171–186.

Sexton, T. & Alexander, J. (2003). Functional family therapy: a mature clinical model for working with at-risk adolescents and their families. In T. Sexton, G. Weeks & M. Robbins (Eds.), *Handbook of Family Therapy* (pp. 323–350). New York: Routledge.

Shadish, W. & Baldwin, S. (2003). Meta-analysis of MFT interventions. *Journal of Marital and Family Therapy*, 29(4), 547–570.

Shadish, W. & Baldwin, S. (2005). Effects of behavioural martial therapy: a meta-analysis of randomized controlled trials. *Journal of Consulting and Clinical Psychology*, 73(1), 6–14.

Shadish, W., Matt, G., Navarro, A. & Phillips, G. (2000). The effects of psychological therapies under clinically representative conditions: a meta-analysis. *Psychological Bulletin*, 126(4), 512–529.

Shadish, W., Matt, G., Navarro, A., Siegle, G., Crits-Cristoph, P., Hazelrigg, H., Jorm,

A., Lyons, L., Nietzel, M., Prout, H., Robinson, L., Smith, M., Svartberg, M. & Weiss, B. (1997). Evidence that therapy works in clinically representative conditions. *Journal of Consulting Psychology*, 65(3), 355–365.

Shaffer, D. & Pfeffer, C. (2001). Practice parameter for the assessment and treatment of children and adolescents with suicidal behaviour. *Journal of the American Academy of Child and Adolescent Psychiatry*, 40, 495–499.

Shapiro, D. A. & Shapiro, D. (1982). Meta-analysis of comparative therapy outcome studies: a replication and refinement. *Psychological Bulletin*, 92, 581–604.

Shapiro, E., Shapiro, A., Fulop, G., Hubbard, M., Mandeli, J., Nordlie, J. & Phillips, R. (1989). Controlled study of haloperidol, pimozide and placebo for the treatment of Gilles de la Tourette's syndrome. *Archives of General Psychiatry*, 46, 722–730.

Shapiro, F. (1995). *Eye Movement Desensitization and Reprocessing: Basic Principles, Protocols, and Procedures*. New York: Guilford Press.

Shapiro, F. (2001). *Eye Movement Desensitization and Reprocessing: Basic Principles, Protocols and Procedures* (Second Edition). New York: Guilford Press.

Shapiro, J., Brownley, K., Berkman, N., Sedway, J., Lohr, K. & Bulik, C. (2007). Bulimia nervosa treatment: a systematic review of randomized controlled trials. *International Journal of Eating Disorders*, 40, 321–336.

Sharif, Z., Bradford, D., Stroup, S. & Lieberman, J. (2007). Pharmacological treatments for schizophrenia. In P. Nathan & J. Gorman (Ed.), *A Guide to Treatments that Work* (Third Edition, pp. 203–242). New York: Oxford University Press.

Shearer, J. (2006). Psychosocial approaches to psychostimulant dependence: a systematic review. *Journal of Substance Abuse Treatment*, 32(1), 41–52.

Shekelle, P., Woolf, S., Eccles, M. & Grimshaw, J. (2000). Developing guidelines. In M. Eccles & J. Grimshaw (Eds.), *Clinical Guidelines: From Conception to Use*. Abingdon: Radcliffe Medical.

Shirk, S. & Karver, M. (2003). Prediction of treatment outcome from relationship variables in child and adolescent therapy: a meta-analytic review. *Journal of Consulting and Clinical Psychology*, 71, 452–464.

Sholomskas, D., Syracuse-Siewert, G., Rounsaville, B., Ball, S., Nuro, K. & Carroll, K. (2005). We don't train in vain: a dissemination trial of three strategies of training clinicians in cognitive-behavioural therapy. *Journal of Consulting and Clinical Psychology*, 73(1), 106–115

Siev, J. & Chambless, D. (2007). Specificity of treatment effects: cognitive therapy and relaxation for generalized anxiety and panic disorders. *Journal of Consulting and Clinical Psychology*, 75(4), 513–522.

Silberstein, S. & Rosenberg, J. (2000). Multispecialty consensus on diagnosis and treatment of headache. *Neurology*, 54, 1553–1554.

Silverman, W., Kurtines, W., Ginsburg, G., Weems, C., Lumpkin, P. & Carmichael, D. (1999). Treating anxiety disorders in children with group cognitive behaviour therapy: a randomized clinical trial. *Journal of Consulting and Clinical Psychology*, 76, 995–1003.

Sim, J. & Adams, N. (2002). Systematic review of randomized controlled trials of nonpharmacological interventions for fibromyalgia. *Clinical Journal of Pain*, 18, 324–336.

Simon, G. (2002). Management of somatoform and factitious disorders. In P. Nathan & J. Gorman (Eds.), *A Guide to Treatments that Work* (Second Edition, pp. 447–463). New York: Oxford University Press.

Simon, G., Ludman, E., Bauer, M., Unutzer, J. & Operskalski B. (2006). Long-term effectiveness and cost of a systematic care program for bipolar disorder. *Archives of General Psychiatry*, 63, 500–508.

Simon, G., Ludman, E., Unutzer, J., Bauer, M., Operskalski, B. & Rutter, C. (2005) Randomized trial of a population-based care program for people with bipolar disorder. *Psychological Medicine*, 35, 13–24.

Simpson, E. & House, A. (2002). Involving users in the delivery and evaluation of mental health services: systematic review. *British Medical Journal*, 324(7375), 1265–1268.

Simpson, R., deBoer-Ott, S., Griswold, D., Myles, B., Byrd, S., & Ganz, J. (2005). *Autism Spectrum Disorders: Interventions and Treatments for Children and Youth.* Thousand Oaks, CA: Corwin Press.

Singer, G., Marquis, J., Powers, L., Blanchard, L., Divenere, N., Santelli, B., Ainbinder, J. & Sharp, M. (1999). A multi-site evaluation of parent to parent programs for parents of children with disabilities. *Journal of Early Intervention*, 22, 217–229.

Singh, A., Maison, J. & Cooper, C. (2005). The use of risperidone among individuals with mental retardation: clinically supported or not. *Research on Developmental Disabilities*, 26, 203–218.

Sinha, Y., Silove, N., Wheeler, D. & Williams, K. (2006). Auditory integration training and other sound therapies for autism spectrum disorders: a systematic review. *Archives of Disease in Childhood*, 91, 1018–1022.

Siqueland, L., Rynn, M. & Diamond, G. S. (2005). Cognitive behavioural and attachment based family therapy for anxious adolescents: Phase I and II studies. *Journal of Anxiety Disorders*, 19, 361–381.

Sitharthan, T., Sitharthan, G., Hough, M. & Kavanagh, D. (1997). Cue exposure in moderation drinking: a comparison with cognitive-behaviour therapy. *Journal of Consulting and Clinical Psychology*, 65, 878–882.

Skowron, E. & Reinemann, D. (2005). Effectiveness of psychological interventions for child maltreatment: a meta-analysis. *Psychotherapy: Theory, Research, Practice, Training*, 42(1), 52–71.

Smith, J. & Meyers, R. (2004). *Motivating Substance Abusers to Enter Treatment: Working with Family Members.* New York: Guilford Press.

Smith, L., Gates, S. & Foxcroft, D. (2006). Therapeutic communities for substance related disorder. *Cochrane Database of Systematic Reviews*, Issue 1. Art. No.: CD005338. DOI: 10.1002/14651858.CD005338.pub2.

Smith, M., Gerdner, L., Hall, J. & Buckwalter, K. (2004) History, development, and future of the progressively lowered stress threshold: a conceptual model for dementia care. *Journal of the American Geriatrics Society*, 52(10), 1755–1760.

Smith, M. & Glass, G. (1977). Meta-analysis of psychotherapy outcome studies. *American Psychologist*, 32(9), 752–760.

Smith, M., Glass, G. & Miller, T. (1980). *The Benefits of Psychotherapy.* Baltimore, MD: Johns Hopkins University Press.

Smith, M., Huang, M. & Manber, R. (2005). Cognitive behaviour therapy for chronic insomnia occurring within the context of medical and psychiatric disorders. *Clinical Psychology Review*, 25, 559–592.

Smith, M., Perlis, M., Park, A., Smith, M., Pennington, J. & Giles, D. (2002). Comparative meta-analysis of pharmacotherapy and behaviour therapy for persistent insomnia. *American Journal of Psychiatry*, 159(1), 5–11.

Smith, T. (1999). Outcome of early intervention for children with autism. *Clinical Psychology: Science and Practice*, 6, 33–49.

Smith, T., Barrett, M., Benjamin, L. & Barber, J. (2006). Relationship factors in treating personality disorders. In L. Castonguay & L. Beutler (Eds.), *Principles of Therapeutic Change that Work* (pp. 219–238). Oxford: Oxford University Press.

Smyth, J. (1998). Written emotional expression: effect sizes, outcome types, and moderating variables. *Journal of Consulting and Clinical Psychology*, 66, 174–184.

Snoek, F. & Skinner, T. (2005). *Psychology in Diabetes Care* (Second Edition). Chichester: Wiley.

Snyder, D. & Schneider, W. (2002). Affective reconstruction: a pluralistic, developmental approach. In A. Gurman & N. Jacobson (Eds.), *Clinical Handbook of Couples Therapy* (Third Edition, pp. 151–179). New York: Guilford Press.

Snyder, D., Wills, R. & Grady-Fletcher, F. (1991). Long-term effectiveness of behavioural versus insight-oriented marital therapy: a 4-year follow-up study. *Journal of Consulting and Clinical Psychology*, 59, 138–141.

Sorensen, S., Pinquart, M. & Duberstein, P. (2002). How effective are interventions with caregivers? An updated meta-analysis. *Gerontologist*, 42(3), 356–372.

Spector, A., Davies, S., Woods, B. & Orrell, M. (2000). Reality orientation for dementia: a systematic review of the evidence of effectiveness from randomized controlled trials. *Gerontologist*, 40(2), 206–212.

Spector, A., Thorgrimsen, L. & Woods, B. (2003). Efficacy of an evidence-based cognitive stimulation therapy programme for people with dementia: randomised controlled trial. *British Journal of Psychiatry*, 183, 248–254.

Spek, V., Cuijpers, P., Nyklicek, I., Riper, H., Keyzer, J. & Pop, V. (2007). Internet-based cognitive behaviour therapy for symptoms of depression and anxiety: a meta-analysis. *Psychological Medicine*, 37(3), 319–328.

Spence, S., Donovan, C. & Brechman-Toussaint, M. (2000). The treatment of childhood social phobia: the effectiveness of social skills training-based, cognitive behavioural intervention with and without parent involvement. *Journal of Child Psychology and Psychiatry*, 41(6), 713–726.

Spencer, T., Biederman, J. & Wilens, T. (2002). Attention deficit hyperactivity disorder. In S. Kutcher (Ed.), *Practical Child and Adolescent Psychopharmacology* (pp. 230–264). Cambridge: Cambridge University Press.

Spielmans, G., Pasek, L. & Mcfall, J. (2007). What are the active ingredients in cognitive and behavioural psychotherapy for anxious and depressed children? A meta-analytic review. *Clinical Psychology Review*, 27(5), 642–654.

Spirito, A. (1999). Empirically supported treatments in paediatric psychology. *Journal of Paediatric Psychology*, 24, 87–174.

Spirito, A., Boergers, J., Donaldson, D., Bishop, D. & Lewander, W. (2002). An intervention trial to improve adherence to community treatment of adolescents following a suicide attempt. *Journal of the American Academy of Child and Adolescent Psychiatry*, 41, 435–442.

Spirito, A. & Kazak, A. (2006). *Effective and Emerging Treatments in Paediatric Psychology*. Oxford: Oxford University Press.

Sprenkle, D. & Blow, A. (2004). Common factors and our sacred models. *Journal of Marital and Family Therapy*, 30, 113–130.

Srisurapanont, M. & Jarusuraisin, N. (2005). Naltrexone for the treatment of alcoholism: a meta-analysis of randomized controlled trials. *International Journal of Neuropsychopharmacology*, 8, 267–280.

Stanton, M. & Shadish, W. (1997). Outcome, attrition, and family-couples treatment for drug abuse: a meta-analysis and review of the controlled, comparative studies. *Psychological Bulletin*, 122(2), 170–191.

Stead, L. & Lancaster, T. (2005). Group behaviour therapy programmes for smoking cessation. *Cochrane Database of Systematic Reviews*, Issue 3. Art. No.: CD001007. DOI: 10.1002/14651858.CD001007.pub2.

Stead, L., Perera, R. & Lancaster, T. (2006). Telephone counselling for smoking cessation. *Cochrane Database of Systematic Reviews*, Issue 2. Art. No.: CD002850. DOI: 10.1002/14651858.CD002850.pub2.

Stefanek, M., Jacobsen, P. & Christensen, A. (2006). The Society of Behavioural Medicine's 'Great Debate': an introduction. *Annals of Behavioural Medicine*, 32(2), 83–84.

Stein, D. & Lambert, M. (1995). Graduate training in psychotherapy: are therapy outcomes enhanced? *Journal of Consulting and Clinical Psychology*, 63, 182–196.

Stein, M. & Seedat, M. (2004). Pharmacotherapy. In T. Morris & J. March (Eds.), *Anxiety Disorders in Children and Adolescents* (pp. 329–354). New York: Guilford Press.

Stevenson, J. (1999). The treatment of the long-term sequelae of child abuse. *Journal of Child Psychology and Psychiatry*, 40, 89–111.

Stewart, K. (2004). Pharmacological and behavioural treatments for migraine headaches: a meta-analytic review. *Dissertation Abstracts International: Section B: The Sciences and Engineering*, 65(3-B), 1535.

Stiles, W. & Wolfe, B. (2006). Relationship factors in treating anxiety disorders. In L. Castonguay & L. Beutler (Eds.), *Principles of Therapeutic Change that Work* (pp. 155–166). Oxford: Oxford University Press.

Stith, S. & Rosen, K. (2003). Effectiveness of couples treatment for spouse abuse. *Journal of Marital and Family Therapy*, 29, 407–426.

Stith, S., Rosen, K., McCollum, E. & Thomsen, C. (2004). Treating intimate partner violence within intact couple relationships: outcomes of multi-couple versus individual couple therapy. *Journal of Marital and Family Therapy*, 30, 305–318.

Storch, E., Geffken, G., Merio, L., Mann, G., Duke, D., Munson, M., Adkins, J., Grabill, K., Murphy, T. & Goodman, W. (2007). Family-based cognitive-behavioural therapy for paediatric obsessive-compulsive disorder: comparison of intensive and weekly approaches. *Journal of the American Academy of Child and Adolescent Psychiatry*, 46(4), 469–478.

Strang, J., Best, D., Ridge, G., Gossop, M. & Farrell, M. (2005). Randomised clinical trial of the effects of time on a waiting list on clinical outcomes in opiate addicts awaiting outpatient treatment. *Drugs: Education, Prevention & Policy*, 12(Suppl1), 115–118.

Stroebe, M., Schut, H. & Stroebe, M. (2005). Grief work disclosure and counselling. Do they help the bereaved? *Clinical Psychology Review*, 25, 395–414.

Stuart, R. (2005). Treatment for partner abuse: time for a paradigm shift. *Professional Psychology: Research and Practice*, 36, 254–263.

Stuart, S. & Bowers, W. (1995). Cognitive therapy with inpatients: review and meta-analysis. *Journal of Cognitive Psychotherapy*, 9(2), 85–92.

Sturmey, P. (2005). Secretin is an ineffective treatment for pervasive developmental disabilities: a review of 15 double-blind randomized controlled trials. *Research in Developmental Disabilities: A Multidisciplinary Journal*, 26(1), 87–97.

Sue, S. (2003). In defence of cultural competency in psychotherapy and treatment. *American Psychologist*, 58(11), 964–970.

Suh, J., Pettinati, H. & Kampman, K. (2006). The status of disulfiram: a half of a century later. *Journal of Clinical Psychopharmacology*, 26, 290–302.

Svartberg, M., Stiles, T. C. & Seltzer, M. H. (2004). Randomized, controlled trial of the effectiveness of short-term dynamic psychotherapy and cognitive therapy for cluster C personality disorders. *American Journal of Psychiatry*, 161, 810–817.

Swanson, J., Sergeant, J., Taylor, E., Sonuga–Barke, E., Jensen, P. & Cantwell, D. (1998). Attention deficit hyperactivity disorder and hyperkinetic disorder. *Lancet*, 351, 429–433.

Swinson, R. P. (2006). Working group on management of anxiety disorders. Clinical practice guidelines: management of anxiety disorders. *Canadian Journal of Psychiatry*, 51(8), 1S–90S.

Szapocznik, J., Hervis, O. & Schwartz, S. (2002). *Brief Strategic Family Therapy for Adolescent Drug Abuse*. Rockville, MD: National Institute for Drug Abuse.

Szapocznik, J. & Williams, R. A. (2000). Brief strategic family therapy: twenty-five years of interplay among theory, research and practice in adolescent behaviour problems and drug abuse. *Clinical Child and Family Psychology Review*, 3(2), 117–134.

Szymanski, L. & King, B. (1999). Practice parameters for the assessment and treatment of children, adolescents, and adults with mental retardation and comorbid mental disorders. *Journal of the American Academy of Child and Adolescent Psychiatry*, 38(12, Suppl), 5S–31S.

TADS team (2004). Fluoxetine, cognitive-behavioural therapy, and their combination for adolescents with depression: Treatment for Adolescents with Depression Study (TADS) randomized controlled trial. *JAMA: Journal of the American Medical Association*, 292(7), 807–820.

Tarrier, N. (2005). Cognitive behaviour therapy for schizophrenia – a review of development, evidence and implementation. *Psychotherapy and Psychosomatics*, 74, 136–144.

Tarrier, N. & Wykes, T. (2004). Is there evidence that cognitive behaviour therapy is an effective treatment for schizophrenia? A cautious or cautionary tale? *Behaviour Research and Therapy*, 42, 1377–1519.

Tatrow, K. & Montgomery, G. (2006). Cognitive behavioural therapy techniques for distress and pain in breast cancer patients: a meta-analysis. *Journal of Behavioural Medicine*, 29(1), 17–27.

Taylor, J. & Novaco, R. (2005). *Anger Treatment for People with Developmental Disabilities: A Theory, Evidence and Manual Based Approach*. Chichester: Wiley.

Taylor, R., Brown, A., Ebrahim, J., Noorani, H., Rees, K., Skidmore, B., Stone, J., Thompson, D. & Oldridge, N. (2004). Exercise-based rehabilitation for patients with coronary heart disease: systematic review and meta-analysis of randomized controlled trials. *American Journal of Medicine*, 116(10), 682–692.

Taylor, S. (2006). *Clinician's Guide to PTSD: A Cognitive Behavioural Approach*. New York: Guilford Press.

Taylor, S. & Asmundson, G. (2004). *Treating Health Anxiety: A Cognitive Behavioural Approach*. New York: Guilford Press.

Taylor, S. & Asmundson, G. (2006). Panic disorder. In A. Carr & M. McNulty (Eds.), *Handbook of Adult Clinical Psychology: An Evidence Based Practice Approach* (pp. 458–486). London: Routledge.

Taylor, S., Asmundson, G. J. & Coons, M. J. (2005). Current directions in the treatment of hypochondriasis. *Journal of Cognitive Psychotherapy*, 19, 285–304.

Taylor, T. & Chemtob, C. (2004). Efficacy of treatment for child and adolescent traumatic stress. *Archives of Paediatric Adolescent Medicine*, 158, 786–791.

Teesson, M., Ross, J., Darke, S., Lynskey, M., Ali, R., Ritter, A. & Cooke, R. (2006). One year outcomes for heroin dependence: findings from the Australian Treatment Outcome Study (ATOS). *Drug and Alcohol Dependence*, 83(2), 174–180.

Teichman, Y., Bar-El, Z., Shor, H., Sirota, P. & Elizur, A. (1995). A comparison of two modalities of cognitive therapy (individual and marital) in treating depression. *Psychiatry: Interpersonal & Biological Processes*, 58, 136–148.

Telch, C., Agras, W. & Linehan, M. (2001). Dialectical behaviour therapy for binge eating disorder. *Journal of Consulting and Clinical Psychology*, 69, 1061–1065.

Teri, L. (1990). *Managing and Understanding Behaviour Problems in Alzheimer's Disease and Related Disorders*. Training program with video and written manual. Washington, DC: University of Washington Alzheimer's Disease Research Center (http://depts.washington.edu/adrcweb/).

Teri, L., Logsdon, R. & McCurry, S. (2005). The Seattle Protocols: advances in behavioural treatment of Alzheimer's disease. In B. Vellas, L. Fitten, B. Winblad, H. Feldman, M. Grundman & E. Giacobini (Eds.), *Research and Practice in Alzheimer's Disease and Cognitive Decline* (Vol. 10, pp. 153–158). Paris: SERDI.

Teri, L., McKenzie, G. & LaFazia, D. (2005). Psychosocial treatment of depression in older adults with dementia. *Clinical Psychology Science and Practice*, 12, 303–316.

Tevyaw, T. & Monti, P. (2004). Motivational enhancement and other brief interventions for adolescent substance abuse: foundations, applications and evaluations. *Addiction*, 99, 63–75.

Thase, M. & Jindal, R. (2004). Combining psychotherapy and pharmacotherapy for treatment of mental disorders. In M. Lambert (Ed.), *Bergin and Garfield's Handbook of Psychotherapy and Behaviour Change* (Fifth Edition, pp. 743–766). New York: Wiley.

Thomas, R. & Zimmer-Gembeck, M. (2007). Behavioural outcomes of parent–child interaction therapy and Triple P – Positive Parenting Program: a review and meta-analysis. *Journal of Abnormal Child Psychology*, 35(3), 475–495.

Thompson, L., Coon, D. & Gallagher-Thompson, D. (2001). Comparison of desipramine and cognitive-behavioural therapy in the treatment of elderly outpatients with mild-to-moderate depression. *American Journal of Geriatric Psychiatry*, 9(3), 225–240.

Thompson-Brenner, H., Glass, S. & Western, D. (2003). A multidimensional meta-analysis of psychotherapy for bulimia nervosa. *Clinical Psychology: Science & Practice*, 10(3), 269–287.

Timmer, S., Urquiza, A., Zebell, N. & McGrath, J. (2005). Parent–child interaction therapy: application to physically abusive parent–child dyads. *Child Abuse & Neglect*, 29, 825–842.

Tincani, M. (2004). Comparing the Picture Exchange Communication System and sign language training for children with autism. *Focus on Autism and Other Developmental Disabilities*, 19, 152–163.

Tolan, P., Gorman-Smith, D. & Henry, D. (2005). Family violence. *Annual Review of Psychology*, 57, 557–583.

Toneatto, T. & Ladouceur, R. (2003). The treatment of pathological gambling: a critical review of the literature. *Psychology of Addictive Behaviours*, 17, 284–292.

Tonigan, J. S., Toscova, R. & Miller, W. R. (1996). Meta-analysis of the literature on Alcoholics Anonymous: sample and study characteristics moderate findings. *Journal of Studies on Alcohol*, 57, 65–72.

Toth, S., Rogosch, F., Manly, J. & Cicchetti, D. (2006). The efficacy of toddler–parent psychotherapy to reorganize attachment in the young offspring of mothers with major depressive disorder: a randomized preventive trial. *Journal of Consulting and Clinical Psychology*, 74(6), 1006–1016.

Townsend, E., Hawton, K., Altman, D. G., Arensman, E., Gunnell, D., Hazell, P., House, A. & Van Heeringen, K. (2001). The efficacy of problem-solving treatments after deliberate self-harm: meta-analysis of randomised controlled trials with respect to depression, hopelessness and improvement in problems. *Psychological Medicine*, 31, 979–988.

Treasure, J., Todd, G., Brolly, M., Nehmed, A. & Denman, F. (1995). A pilot study of a randomised trial of cognitive analytical therapy vs educational behavioural therapy for adult anorexia nervosa. *Behaviour Research & Therapy*, 33, 363–367.

Trowell, J., Kolvin, I., Weermanthri, T., Sadowski, H., Berelowitz, M., Glaser, D. & Leitch, I. (2002). Psychotherapy for sexually abused girls: psychopathological outcome findings and patterns of change. *British Journal of Psychiatry*, 180, 234–247.

Trowell, R., Joffe, I., Campbell, J., Clemente, C., Almqvist, F., Soininen, M., Koskenranta-Aalto, U., Weintraub, S., Kolaitis, G., Tomaras, G., Anastasopolous, D., Grayson, K., Barnes, J. & Tsiantis, J. (2007). Childhood depression: a place for psychotherapy: an outcome study comparing individual psychodynamic psycho-therapy and family therapy. *European Child and Adolescent Psychiatry*, 16, 157–167.

Tsai, A., Wadden, T., Womble, L. & Byrne, K. (2005). Commercial and self-help pro-grammes for weight control. *Psychiatric Clinics of North America*, 28(1), 171–192.

Tseng, W. & Streltzer, J. (2001). *Culture and Psychotherapy: A Guide to Clinical Practice*. Washington, DC; American Psychiatric Association.

Tune, L. (2007). Treaments for dementia. In P. Nathan & J. Gorman (Eds.), *A Guide to Treatments that Work* (Third Edition, pp. 105–143). New York: Oxford University Press.

Turk, D. (2002). Clinical effectiveness and cost-effectiveness of treatments for patients with chronic pain. *Clinical Journal of Pain*, 18(6), 355–365.

Turk, D. & Burwinkle, T. (2005). Clinical outcomes, cost-effectiveness, and the role of psychology in treatments for chronic pain sufferers. *Professional Psychology: Research and Practice*, 36, 602–610.

Turner, E., Matthews, A., Linardatos, E., Tell, R. & Rosenthal, R. (2008). Selective publication of antidepressant trials and its influence on apparent efficacy. *New England Journal of Medicine*, 358, 252–260.

Twamley, E., Jeste, D. & Bellack, A. (2003). A review of cognitive training in schizo-phrenia. *Schizophrenia Buletin*, 29, 359–382.

Twamley, E., Jeste, D. & Lehman, A. (2003). Vocational rehabilitation in schizo-phrenia and other psychotic disorders: a literature review and meta-analysis of RCTs. *Journal of Nervous and Mental Disease*, 191, 515–523.

UKATT Research Team (2005). Effectiveness of treatment for alcohol problems: findings of the randomized UK alcohol treatment trial (UKATT). *British Medical Journal*, 331(7516), 541–544.

Van der Wurff, F., Stek, M., Hoogendijk, W. & Beekman, A. (2003). Electroconvulsive therapy for the depressed elderly. *Cochrane Database of Systematic Reviews*, Issue 2. Art. No.: CD003593. DOI: 10.1002/14651858.CD003593.

Vanfleet, R., Ryan, S. & Smith, S. (2005). Filial therapy: a critical review. In L. Reddy, T. Files-Hall & Schaefer (Eds.), *Empirically Based Play Interventions* (pp. 241–264). Washington, DC: APA.

van Gent, E. & Zwart, F. (1991). Psychoeducation of partners of bipolar-manic patients. *Journal of Affective Disorders*, 21, 15–18.

Van Noppen, B., Steketee, G., McCorkle, B. & Pato, M. (1997). Group and multifamily behavioural treatment for obsessive compulsive disorder: a pilot study. *Journal of Anxiety Disorders*, 11, 431–446.

Vargas, S. & Camilli, G. (1999). A meta-analysis of research on sensory integration treatment. *American Journal of Occupational Therapy*, 53(2), 189–198.

Vasa, R., Carlino, A. & Pine, D. (2006). Pharmacotherapy of depressed children and adolescents: current issues and potential directions. *Biological Psychiatry*, 59(11), 1021–1028.

Verdellen, C., Keijsers, G., Cath, D. & Hoogduin, C. (2004). Exposure with response prevention versus habit reversal in Tourettes's syndrome: a controlled study. *Behaviour Research and Therapy*, 42, 501–511.

Viney, L., Metcalfe, C. & Winter, D. (2005). The effectiveness of personal construct psychotherapy: a systematic review and meta-analysis. In D. Winter & L. Viney (Eds.), *Personal Construct Psychotherapy: Advances in Theory, Practice and Research*. London: Whurr.

Vittengl, J., Clark, L., Dunn, T. & Jarrett, R. (2007). Reducing relapse and recurrence in unipolar depression: a comparative meta-analysis of cognitive-behavioural therapy. *Journal of Consulting and Clinical Psychology*, 75(3), 475–488.

Vogele, K. (2004). Hospitalization and stressful medical procedures. In A. Kaptein & J. Weinman (Eds.), *Health Psychology* (pp. 288–304). Malden, MA: Blackwell.

Wadden, T., Crerand, C. & Brock, J. (2005). Behavioural treatment of obesity. *Psychiatric Clinics of North America*, 28(1), 151–170.

Waldron, H. B. & Kaminer, Y. (2004). On the learning curve: cognitive-behavioural therapies for adolescent substance abuse. *Addiction*, 99, 93–105.

Walker, D., McGovern, S., Poey, E. & Otis, K. (2004). Treatment effectiveness for male adolescent sexual offenders: a meta-analysis and review. *Journal of Child Sexual Abuse*, 13, 281–293.

Walker, E., Kestler, L. & Bollini, A. (2004). Schizophrenia: etiology and course. *Annual Review of Psychology*, 55, 401–430.

Walker, J. & Furer, P. (2006). Hypochondriasis and somatization. In A. Carr & M. McNulty (Eds.), *Handbook of Adult Clinical Psychology: An Evidence Based Practice Approach* (pp. 593–426). London: Routledge.

Walsh, B., Kaplan, A. & Attia, E. (2006). Fluoxetine after weight restoration in anorexia nervosa: a randomized controlled trial. *Journal of the American Medical Association*, 295, 2605–2612.

Walter, G., Rey, J. & Mitchell, P. (1999). Electroconvulsive therapy in adolescents. *Journal of Child Psychology and Psychiatry*, 40(3), 325–334.

Walters, G. (2000). Behavioural self-control training for problem drinkers: a meta-analysis of randomised control studies. *Behaviour Therapy*, 31, 135–149.

Wampold, B. (2001). *The Great Psychotherapy Debate: Models, Methods, and Findings*. Mahwah, NJ: Lawrence Erlbaum Associates, Inc.

Wang, M., Wang, S. & Tsai, P. (2005). Cognitive behavioural therapy for primary insomnia: a systematic review. *Journal of Advances in Nursing*, 50(5), 553–564.

Warner, L., Mariathasan, J., Lawton-Smith, E. & Samele, C. (2006). *A Review of the Literature and Consultation on Choice and Decision Making for Users and Carers of Mental Health and Social Health Services*. London: Sainsbury Centre for Mental Health & King's Fund.

Webster-Stratton, C. & Reid, M. (2003). The Incredible Years parents, teachers and children training series: a multifaceted treatment approach for young children with conduct problems. In A. Kazdin & J. Weisz (Eds.), *Evidence Based Psychotherapies for Children and Adolescents* (pp. 224–262). New York: Guilford Press.

Wedding, D. & Corsini, R. (2005). *Case Studies in Psychotherapy* (Fourth Edition). New York: Thompson-Wadsworth.

Weersing, V. & Brent, D. (2003). Cognitive behavioural therapy for adolescent depression. In A. Kazdin & J. Weisz (Eds.), *Evidence-Based Psychotherapies for Children and Adolescents* (pp. 135–147). New York: Guilford Press.

Weissman, M., Markowitz, J. & Klerman, G. (2000). *Comprehensive Guide to Interpersonal Psychotherapy*. New York: Basic Books.

Weisz, J. (2004). *Psychotherapy for Children and Adolescents: Evidence-Based Treatments and Case Examples*. Cambridge: Cambridge University Press.

Weisz, J., Jensen-Doss, A. & Hawley, K. (2006). Evidence-based youth psychotherapies versus usual clinical care: a meta-analysis of direct comparisons. *American Psychologist*, 61(7), 671–689.

Weisz, J., McCarty, C. & Valeri, S. (2006). Effects of psychotherapy for depression in children and adolescents: a meta-analysis. *Psychological Bulletin*, 132, 132–149.

Weisz, J., Southmam-Gerow, M., Gordis, E. & Connor-Smith, J. (2003). Primary and secondary control enhancement training for youth depression: applying the deployment-focused model of treatment development and testing. In A. Kazdin & J. Weisz (Eds.), *Evidence-Based Psychotherapies for Children and Adolescents* (pp. 165–186). New York: Guilford Press.

Weisz, J., Weiss, B., Alicke, M. & Klotz, M. (1987). Effectiveness of psychotherapy with children and adolescents: a meta-analysis for clinicians. *Journal of Consulting and Clinical Psychology*, 55, 542–549.

Weisz, J., Weiss, B., Han, S. & Granger, D. (1995). Effects of psychotherapy with children and adolescents revisited: a meta-analysis of treatment outcome studies. *Psychological Bulletin*, 117(3), 450–468.

Wells, A. & Carter, K. (2006). Generalized anxiety disorder. In A. Carr & M. McNulty (Eds.), *Handbook of Adult Clinical Psychology: An Evidence Based Practice Approach* (pp. 423–457). London: Routledge.

Westen, D. & Morrison, K. (2001). A multidimensional meta-analysis of treatments for depression, panic, and generalized anxiety disorder: an empirical examination of the status of empirically supported therapies. *Journal of Consulting and Clinical Psychology*, 69(6), 875–899.

Westen, D., Novotny, C. & Thompson-Brenner, H. (2004). The empirical status of empirically supported psychotherapies: assumptions, findings, and reporting in controlled clinical trials. *Psychological Bulletin*, 130, 631–663.

Weydert, J., Ball, T. & Davis, M. (2003). Systematic review of treatments for recurrent abdominal pain. *Paediatrics*, 111, 1–11.

White, A., Rampes, H. & Campbell, J. (1997). Acupuncture and related interventions for smoking cessation. *Cochrane Database of Systematic Reviews*, Issue 1. Art. No.: CD000009. DOI: 10.1002/14651858.CD000009.pub2.

White, J. (1997). *Stresspac*. Oxford: Harcourt.

Whitehead, W. (2006). Hypnosis for irritable bowel syndrome: the empirical evidence of therapeutics effects. *International Journal of Clinical and Experimental Hypnosis*, 54, 7–20.

Whiting, P., Bagnall, A., Sowden, A., Cornell, J., Mulorw, D. & Ramirez, F. (2001). Interventions for the treatment and management of chronic fatigue syndrome: a systematic review. *Journal of the American Medical Association*, 286, 1360–1368.

Wiborg, I. & Dahl, A. (1996). Does brief dynamic psychotherapy reduce the relapse rate of panic disorder? *Archives of General Psychiatry*, 53, 689–694.

Wierzbicki, M. & Pekarik, G. (1993). A meta-analysis of psychotherapy dropout. *Professional Psychology: Research & Practice*, 24(2), 190–195.

Wilhelm, S., Deckersbach, T., Coffey, B., Bohne, A., Peterson, A. & Baer, L. (2003). Habit reversal versus supportive psychotherapy for Tourette's disorder: a randomized controlled trial, *American Journal of Psychiatry*, 160, 1175–1177.

Will, D. & Wrate, R. (1985). *Integrated Family Therapy*. London: Tavistock.

Williams, J., Hadjistavropoulos, T. & Sharpe, D. (2006). A meta-analysis of psychological and pharmacological treatments for body dysmorphic disorder. *Behaviour Research and Therapy*, 44(1), 99–111.

Williams, J., Mulrow, C., Chiquette, E., Hitchcock-Noel, P., Aguilar, C. & Cornell, J. (2000). A systematic review of newer pharmacotherapies for depression in adults: evidence report summary: clinical guideline, Part 2. *Annals of Internal Medicine*, 132(9), 743–756.

Williams, R. & Chang, S. (2000). A comprehensive and comparative review of adolescent substance abuse treatment outcome. *Clinical Psychology: Science and Practice*, 7, 138–166.

Willner, P. (2005). The effectiveness of psychotherapeutic interventions for people with learning disabilities: a critical review. *Journal of Intellectual Disability Research*, 49, 73–85.

Wilson, G. (2005). Psychological treatment of eating disorders. *Annual Review of Clinical Psychology*, 1, 439–465.

Wilson, G. & Fairburn, C. (2007). Treatments for eating disorders. In P. Nathan & J. Gorman (Eds.), *A Guide to Treatments that Work* (Third Edition, pp. 579–609). New York: Oxford University Press.

Wilson, G., Grilo, C. & Vitousek, K. (2007). Psychological treatment of eating disorders. *American Psychologist*, 62(3), 199–216.

Wilson, G., Vitousek, K. & Loeb, K. (2000). Stepped care treatment for eating disorders. *Journal of Consulting and Clinical Psychology*, 68, 564–572.

Wilson, J. & Gil, K. (1996). The efficacy of psychological and pharmacological interventions for the treatment of chronic disease-related and non-disease-related pain. *Clinical Psychology Review*, 16, 573–597.

Wilson, S. & Nutt, D. (2007). Management of insomnia: treatments and mechanisms. *British Journal of Psychiatry*, 191, 195–197.

Wincze, J. & Carey, M. (2001). *Sexual Dysfunction: A Guide for Assessment and Treatment* (Second Edition). New York: Guilford Press.

Winkley, K., Landau. S., Eisler, I. & Ismail, K. (2006). Psychological interventions to improve glycaemic control in patients with type 1 diabetes: systematic review and meta-analysis of randomized controlled trials. *British Medical Journal*, 333, 65–68.

Winter, D. (2003). The evidence base for personal construct psychotherapy. In F. Fransella (Ed.), *International Handbook of Personal Construct Psychology*. Chichester: Wiley.

Winter, D. & Viney, L. (2005). *Personal Construct Psychotherapy: Advances in Theory, Practice and Research*. London: Whurr.

Witkiewitz, K. & Marlatt, G. (2004). Relapse prevention for alcohol and drug problems: that was Zen, this is Tao. *American Psychologist*, 59, 224–235.

Wolpe, J. (1958). *Psychotherapy by Reciprocal Inhibition*. Stanford, CA: Stanford University Press.

Wolpert, M., Fuggle, P., Cottrell, D., Fonagy, P., Phillips, J., Pilling, S., Stein, S. & Target, M. (2006). *Drawing on the Evidence: Advice for Mental Health Professionals Working with Children and Adolescents*. London: CAMHS.

Wood, A., Trainor, G., Rothwell, J., Moore, A. & Harrington, R. (2001). Randomized trial of group therapy for repeated deliberate self-harm in adolescents. *Journal of the American Academy of Child and Adolescent Psychiatry*, 40, 1246–1253.

Wood, N., Crane, D., Schaalje, B. & Law, D. (2005). What works for whom: a meta-analytic review of marital and couples therapy in reference to marital distress. *American Journal of Family Therapy*, 33, 273–287.

woods, B., Spector, A., Jones, C., Orrell, M. & Davies, S. (2005). Reminiscence therapy for dementia. *Cochrane Database of Systematic Reviews*, Issue 2. Art. No.: CD001120. DOI: 10.1002/14651858.CD001120.pub2.

Woody, S. & Ollendick, T. (2006). Technique factors in treating anxiety disorders. In L. Castonguay & L. Beutler (Eds.), *Principles of Therapeutic Change that Work* (pp.167–186). Oxford: Oxford University Press.

Woolfenden, S., Williams, K. & Peat, J. (2002). Family and parenting interventions for conduct disorder and delinquency: a meta-analysis of randomised controlled trials. *Archives of Diseases in Childhood*, 86, 251–256.

Woolfolk, R. & Allen, L. (2007). *Treating Somatization: A Cognitive-Behavioural Approach*. New York: Guilford Press.

Worden, J. (2001). *Grief Counselling and Grief Therapy: A Handbook for the Mental Health Professional* (Third Edition). New York: Spinger.

World Health Organization (1992). *The ICD-10 Classification of Mental and Behavioural Disorders*. Geneva: WHO.

World Health Organization (1998). *Obesity: Preventing and Managing the Global Epidemic*. Geneva: WHO.

World Health Organization. http://www.who.int/mental_health/en/index.html.

Wright, J., Sabourin, S., Mondor, K., McDuff, P. & Mamodhoussen, S. (2007). The clinical representativeness of couple therapy outcome research. *Family Process*, 46(3), 301–316.

Wu, P., Wilson, K., Dimoulas, P. & Mills, E. (2006). Effectiveness of smoking cessation therapies: a systematic review and meta-analysis. *BMC Public Health*, 6, 300–316.

Wykes, T. & Reeder, C. (2005). *Cognitive Remediation Therapy for Schizophrenia: Theory and Practice*. London: Routledge.

Yin, T., Zhou, Q. & Bashford, C. (2002). Burden on family members. Caring for frail elderly: a meta-analysis of interventions. *Nursing Research*, 51(3), 199–208.

Yoder, P. & Stone, W. (2006). Randomized comparison of two communication interventions for preschoolers with autism spectrum disorders. *Journal of Consulting and Clinical Psychology*, 74(3), 426–435.

Young, K., Northern, J., Lister, K., Drummond, J. & O'Brien, W. (2007). A meta-analysis of family-behavioural weight-loss treatments for children. *Clinical Psychology Review*, 27(2), 240–249.

Zager, D. (2005). *Autism Spectrum Disorders: Identification, Education and Treatment* (Third Edition). Mahwah, NJ: Lawrence Erlbaum Associates, Inc.

Zametkin, A., Zoon, C., Klein, H. & Munson, S. (2004). Psychiatric aspects of child and adolescent obesity: a review of the past 10 years. *Journal of the American Academy of Child and Adolescent Psychiatry*, 43, 134–150.

Ziguras, S. & Stuart, G. (2000). A meta-analysis of the effectiveness of mental health case management over 20 years. *Psychiatric Services*, 51, 1410–1421.

Zimmermann, G., Favrod, J., Trieu, V. & Pomini, V. (2005). The effect of cognitive behavioural treatment on positive symptoms of schizophrenia spectrum disorders: a meta-analysis. *Schizophrenia Research*, 77, 1–9.

Zygmunt, A., Olfson, M. & Boyer, C. A. (2002). Interventions to improve medication adherence in schizophrenia. *American Journal of Psychiatry*, 159, 1653–1664.

Index

NTORS 202

obesity in adults 186–8; cognitive
behavioural programmes 186;
guidelines for practice 188; orlistat
187; pharmacotherapy 187; self-help
and commercial programmes 187;
sibutramine 187; surgery 187
obesity in childhood and adolescence 109
obsessive-compulsive disorder in adults
172–3; cognitive behaviour therapy
172; guidelines for practice 173;
multimodal programmes 173;
pharmacotherapy 173; systemic
therapy 173
obsessive-compulsive disorder in
children and adolescents 104–5
older adulthood problems 233–42;
anxiety 240–1; dementia 233–8;
depression 238–40; insomnia 241–2
opiate abuse 205
oppositional defiant disorder 76–80;
callous unemotional traits 79–80;
child-focused skills training 77–9
Incredible Years Programme 78, 138;
Parent Child Interaction Therapy
78–9, 138; Parent Management
Training 78, 138; parent training
77–80; parental stress 79; parental
support 79; practice guidelines 80;
therapeutic alliance 80; Triple P
programme 78–9, 138
orgasmic disorder 228
orlistat for obesity 187
Outcome Questionnaire-45 (OQ-45) 19,
64
Outcome Rating Scale (ORS) 19, 64
oversimplification 134, 242

pain in adults 182–6; massage 279–80;
sexual pain disorders 228–9
pain in children and adolescents
110–112; headaches 110–11; hypnosis
277–8; painful medical procedures
111–12; recurrent abdominal pain 111
panic disorder in adults 167–70;
cognitive behaviour therapy 168;
couples therapy 168–9; guidelines for
practice 170; pharmacotherapy 169;
psychoanalytic psychotherapy 169;
psychodynamic psychotherapy 169;
selective serotonin reuptake inhibitors

169; self-help for panic disorder in
adult 169; systemic couples therapy
168–9; tricyclic antidepressants 169
parent training, ADHD 74–5; feedback
78; Incredible Years Programme 78,
138; intellectual disability 121–2;
oppositional defiant disorder 77–80;
Parent Child Interaction Therapy
78–9, 138; Parent Management
Training 78, 138; parental stress 79;
parental support 79; therapeutic
alliance 80; Triple P programme 78–9,
138
Partner for Change Outcome
Management System (PCOMS) 65
partnerships for research, service–
university 296
Paul, G. 29
Perls, F. 3
personal construct psychotherapy,
effectiveness 37
personal therapy 62
personality disorders 216–22; borderline
personality disorder 217–8; client and
therapist characteristics 220; cluster C
personality disorders 218–9; cognitive
behaviour therapy 216–17, 219;
dialectical behaviour therapy 217;
guidelines for practice 221–2;
pharmacotherapy 221; psychoanalytic
therapy 216–18; psychodynamic
therapy 216–18; therapeutic alliance
220; therapeutic communities 219;
therapeutic techniques 220–1
pervasive developmental disabilities and
autism spectrum disorders 125–35,
146–7; applied behaviour analysis
(ABA) 126; auditory integration
training 132; behavioural interventions
for challenging behaviour 131; dietary
interventions 133; early intervention
125–6; facilitated communication 132;
guidelines for practice 134;
hyperactivity and inattention 131;
ineffective interventions 132–3;
pharmacotherapy for challenging
behaviour in autism 131; Picture
Exchange Communication System
(PECS) 129; pivotal response training
127–8; risperidone for challenging
behaviour 131; secretin 133; selective
serotonin reuptake inhibitors for